CHOOSE FROM 8,000 COMPANIES AND MULTIPLY YOUR JOB PROSPECTS

If you want to add to your list of possible employers even more companies than we have provided in this book and software set, here's your opportunity. We've compiled an extensive database of 8,000 major public and private US companies and, for your convenience, divided them by region to help you pinpoint your job search to the areas that interest you the most.

More information — company listings contain more information, including annual sales, change in sales from prior year, status as a public or private company, ticker symbols and stock exchanges for public companies, and the name of the CFO.

More companies — 3 times as many companies in each region and state!

More current — the database is updated quarterly, providing you with the most up-to-date information.

Windows or Macintosh disk available for the following regions for only $49.95 each:

- **NORTHEAST** (CT, ME, MA, NH, NY, RI, VT)
  over 1,500 companies • Item #HEMNE

- **MID-ATLANTIC** (DE, DC, MD, NJ, PA, VA, WV)
  over 1,100 companies • Item #HEMMA

- **SOUTHEAST** (AL, FL, GA, KY, MS, NC, SC, TN)
  over 900 companies • Item #HEMSE

- **GREAT LAKES** (IL, IN, MI, OH, WI)
  over 1,100 companies • Item #HEMGL

- **NORTHWEST AND GREAT PLAINS**
  (ID, IA, MN, MT, NE, ND, OR, SD, WA, WY)
  over 500 companies • Item #HEMNW

- **SOUTHWEST AND SOUTH CENTRAL**
  (AR, CO, KS, LA, MO, NM, OK, TX)
  over 1,200 companies • Item #HEMSW

- **WEST** (AK, AZ, CA, HI, NV, UT)
  over 1,400 companies • Item #HEMW

ORDER ALL SEVEN REGIONS AND SAVE OVER 40%!
Only $199.95 for the entire contents of Hoover's MasterList Database
Windows or Macintosh Diskette • $199.95 • ITEM #EP9

Please specify Windows or Macintosh version when ordering. License permits extraction of data for creating letters and labels for single user only. Technical support is not available for this software program.

TO ORDER OR FOR A FREE CATALOG, CALL 800-486-8666
TO SEE OUR CATALOG ON THE INTERNET, GO TO
http://www.hoovers.com or gopher://gopher.hoovers.com

The Reference Press, Inc., 6448 Highway 290 E., Suite E–104, Austin, Texas 78723
512-454-7778 • Fax 512-454-9401

Hoover's Masterlist of America's Top 2,500 Employers

A DIGITAL GUIDE TO THE LARGEST & FASTEST-GROWING U.S. COMPANIES THAT ARE HIRING NOW

Hoover's MasterList of America's Top 2,500 Employers is intended to provide its readers with accurate and authoritative information about the enterprises profiled in it. The Reference Press asked all profiled companies and organizations to provide information for its books. Many did so; a number did not. The information contained herein is as accurate as we could reasonably make it. In many cases we have relied on third-party material that we believe to be trustworthy but were unable to verify independently. We do not warrant that the book is absolutely accurate or without any errors. Readers should not rely on any information contained here in instances where such reliance might cause loss or damage. The editors, publisher, and their data suppliers specifically disclaim all warranties, including the implied warranties of merchantability and fitness for a specific purpose. This book is sold with the understanding that neither the editors nor the publisher is engaged in providing investment, financial, accounting, legal, or other professional advice.

Many of the names of products and services mentioned in this book are the trademarks or service marks of the companies manufacturing or selling them and are subject to protection under US law. Space has not permitted us to indicate which names are subject to such protection, and readers are advised to consult with the owners of such marks regarding their use. *Hoover's MasterList*® is a registered trademark of The Reference Press, Inc.

The Reference Press, Inc.

Copyright © 1995 by The Reference Press, Inc. All rights reserved. No part of this book may be reproduced or transmitted in any form or by any means, electronic or mechanical, including by photocopying, facsimile transmission, recording, or using any information storage and retrieval system, without permission in writing from The Reference Press, Inc., except that brief passages may be quoted by a reviewer in a magazine, newspaper, on-line, or broadcast review.

10 9 8 7 6 5 4 3 2 1

Publisher Cataloging-In-Publication Data

Hoover's MasterList of America's Top 2,500 Employers.
Edited by Thomas Trotter

    Includes indexes.
    1. Business enterprises — Directories. 2. Corporations — Directories.
HF3010 338.7

The information in *Hoover's MasterList of America's Top 2,500 Employers* is also available on America Online, eWorld, Compuserve, NlightN, and on the Internet and as part of the Farcast news service (e-mail: info@farcast.com). A catalog of The Reference Press products is available on the Web at World Wide Web (http://www.hoovers.com) and Gopher (gopher.hoovers.com).

ISBN 1-878753-82-7 trade paper

This book was produced by The Reference Press using Claris Corporation's FileMaker Pro 2.1, Adobe Systems Inc.'s PageMaker 4.2, Quark Inc.'s Quark XPress software, and Adobe fonts from the Clearface and Futura families. Cover design is by Kristin M. Jackson of Austin, Texas. Electronic prepress and printing was done by Port City Press, Inc. in Baltimore, Maryland. Text paper is 60# Postmark White (manufactured by Union Camp). Cover stock is 10 pt., coated one side, text weight.

US AND WORLD DIRECT SALES	**US WHOLESALE ORDERS**
The Reference Press, Inc.	Warner Publisher Services Book Division
6448 Highway 290 E., Suite E-104	9210 King Palm Drive
Austin, Texas 78723	Tampa, Florida 33619
Phone: 512-454-7778	Phone: 800-873-BOOK
Fax: 512-454-9401	Fax: 813-664-8193
e-mail: refpress6@aol.com	
US BOOKSELLERS AND JOBBERS	**CANADIAN BOOKSELLERS AND WHOLESALER ORDERS**
Little, Brown and Co.	H. B. Fenn and Company Ltd.
200 West Street	1090 Lorimar Drive
Waltham, Massachusetts 02154	Mississauga, Ontario L5S 1R7, Canada
Phone: 800-759-0190	Phone: 905-670-FENN
Fax: 617-890-0875	Fax: 905-670-3422

THE REFERENCE PRESS

Founder: Gary Hoover
Chairman, President, CEO, and Senior Editor: Patrick J. Spain
Vice-President of Sales and Marketing: Dana L. Smith
Senior Managing Editor: James R. Talbot
Director of Sales and Marketing for Electronic Products: Tom Linehan
Senior Editor of Online Publishing: Matt Manning
Controller: Deborah L. Dunlap
Desktop Publishing Manager: Holly Hans Jackson
Advertising and Publicity Manager: Angela J. Schoolar
Senior Researcher: Laraine Johnston
Office Manager: Tammy Fisher
Fulfillment Manager: Beth DeVore
Customer Service Manager: Rhonda T. Mitchell

Editor, *Hoover's MasterList of America's Top 2,500 Employers*
Thomas Trotter

Editors
Peter Hines, Jeanne Minnich, Pamela Penick, Dixie Peterson, Jennifer A. Sherman, Patrick J. Spain, James R. Talbot, Tracy Wilson

Writers
Joy Aiken, Stuart Hampton, Paul Mitchell, Lisa C. Norman, Barbara M. Spain, Alice Wightman

Desktop Publishers
Estella Chaparro, Michelle de Ybarrondo, JoAnn Estrada, Brenda Forsythe, Corey R. Isbell, Holly Hans Jackson, Kristin M. Jackson

Fact Checkers/Proofreaders
Megan Brown, Melanie Hall, Jenny Hill, Kate Howard, Diane Lee, Elizabeth Gagne Morgan, John Willis

Researchers
Tweed Chouinard, Patricia DeNike, Chuck Green, J. Kirkland Greer III, Sarah Hallman, Jim Harris, Jill Holsinger, Laraine Johnston, Mark Lambert, Tracey Rogers

On-line Production
Wendy Franz, Nancy Gravley, Kyna Horton, Anita Joe, Debbie Torrez

The Reference Press Mission Statement

1. To produce business information products and services of the highest quality, accuracy, and readability.
2. To make that information available whenever, wherever, and however our customers want it through mass distribution at affordable prices.
3. To continually expand our range of products and services and our markets for those products and services.
4. To reward our employees, suppliers, and shareholders based on their contributions to the success of our enterprise.
5. To hold to the highest ethical business standards, erring on the side of generosity when in doubt.

ABBREVIATIONS

Acctg – Accounting
Admin – Administration
Administrator – Administrator
Asst – Assistant
Assoc – Associate
Ben – Benefits
Bldg – Building
Bus – Business
CAD/CAM – Computer-Aided Design/Computer-Aided Manufacturing
Chm – Chairman
Chief Acctg Off – Chief Accounting Officer
Chief Admin Off – Chief Administrative Officer
CEO – Chief Executive Officer
CFO – Chief Financial Officer
COO – Chief Operating Officer
Comm – Communications
Controller – Controller
Corp – Corporate
Dev – Development
Dir – Director
Div – Division
Emp – Employee
Exec – Executive
EVP – Executive Vice-President
Fin – Finance
Gen – General
Gen Counsel – General Counsel
Gen Mgr – General Manager
Govt – Government
HMO – Health Maintenance Organization

HR – Human Resources
Info – Information
LAN – Local-Area Network
LCD – Liquid Crystal Display
LED – Light-Emitting Diode
LNG – Liquified Natural Gas
LP – Limited Partnership
Ltd. – Limited
Mgmt – Management
Mgr – Manager
Mng – Managing
Mfg – Manufacturing
Mktg – Marketing
Natl – National
Off – Officer
Ops – Operations
Personnel – Personnel
Pres – President
R&D – Research & Development
Rel – Relations
Sec – Secretary
SEVP – Senior Executive Vice-President
SVP – Senior Vice-President
Svcs – Services
Sys – Systems
Tech – Technology
Treas – Treasurer
VC – Vice-Chairman
VP – Vice-President
WAN – Wide-Area Network

Contents

List of Lists 8
About *Hoover's MasterList of America's Top 2,500 Employers* 9
Job-Hunting Resources 13
Temporary Employment Agencies 23
A List-Lover's Compendium 33
America's Top 2,500 Employers 71
Index of Companies by Name 340
Index of Companies by Industry 364
Index of Companies by Metropolitan Area 390

List of Lists

Top 500 Companies by Employees in *Hoover's MasterList of America's Top 2,500 Employers* 34–38

Top 500 Companies by One-Year Absolute Employee Growth in *Hoover's MasterList of America's Top 2,500 Employers* 39–43

Top 500 Companies by One-Year Percentage Employee Growth in *Hoover's MasterList of America's Top 2,500 Employers* 44–48

FORTUNE's 100 Fastest-Growing Companies 49–52

Inc.'s 100 Fastest-Growing Small Public Companies 53–56

The 25 Largest Companies on *Inc.*'s 500 Fastest-Growing Private Companies List 57

Business Week's 100 Best Small Companies 58–61

100 Best Companies to Work For 62

America's 100 Most-Admired Corporations 63

85 Best Companies for Minorities 64

100 Best Companies for Gay Men and Lesbians 65

100 Companies Providing the Most Opportunities for Hispanics 66

Top 20 Woman-Owned Businesses 67

Top 20 Black-Owned Businesses 67

Top 20 Hispanic-Owned Businesses 67

100 Companies That Will Change the Face of Tomorrow's Business 68

18 Visionary Companies 69

50 Leading Retained Search Firms in North America 69

ABOUT HOOVER'S MASTERLIST OF AMERICA'S TOP 2,500 EMPLOYERS

With the possible exception of what to wear to the interview, the most vexing question facing job hunters is: Who's hiring? If you read the press, the current trends in the corporate world seem to be downsizing and moving offshore. However, companies both large and small are still hiring people every day.

So where do you look to find out who's hiring? You could start with this book. If you added up the employees of the companies in this book, starting with the software programmers at Autodesk in Sausalito, California, and ending with the magazine reporters at Ziff-Davis Publishing in New York, you'd find that the companies in *Hoover's MasterList of America's Top 2,500 Employers* employ over 32 million people. In the last year alone, these companies added nearly 1 million more workers to their payrolls.

CHOOSING THE COMPANIES

To compile the information in this book, we began by researching nearly 10,000 companies, both public and private. We studied annual reports and other company documents, faxed requests for information, and made countless telephone calls. We consulted lists in publications such as *Forbes, FORTUNE*, and *Inc*. As the data began to take shape, we developed a sliding scale of which employers we wanted to include in this book, that is, which ones were "large" and which ones were "fast-growing." In order to qualify for inclusion, a company's work force had to have a)

grown by at least 15% over the past year; b) grown by at least 10% and totaled more than 500; c) grown by 5% and totaled more than 1,000; or d) totaled more than 2,500.

At first glance, it might seem surprising to find companies with shrinking work forces in a book of leading employers. Numerous companies in *Hoover's MasterList of America's Top 2,500 Employers* dropped *thousands* of employees over the past year. Why did we include them? Because no matter how many jobs large corporations like GTE and DuPont drop, they are still leaders in hiring new workers. General Electric, for example, saw overall employment dip from 231,000 to 222,000 last year, but they made 5,500 new hires over the same period. And Ford lost a little more than 3,000 total jobs last year while hiring roughly 15,000 new employees.

We also believed it was important to include these large corporations because the percentage change in their total number of employees is not always directly related to hiring and firing. Often the change in size of a major corporation's work force is due to its selling off a subsidiary or merging with another company. For example, The Travelers Co. added 35,000 jobs last year. The reason? It merged with Primerica. Over the same period, American Express had dropped 49,698 jobs. A disastrous year? Hardly. American Express had simply spun off a major segment of its business, its Lehman Brothers investment bank.

We've also included a group of large privately held companies for which we could not determine the number of employees added or dropped in the last year.

Private companies tend to be more, well, private about such information. But whether they want to keep it a secret or not, these are large corporations that you would be wise to consider as future employers. We also included a number of large universities. Often overlooked by job seekers, universities are among the largest and most active employers in the nation.

ORGANIZATION OF THE BOOK

The Top 2,500 Employers

To help you find a job close to home (or as far away as possible, depending on your state of mind), we have organized the companies by state and have indexed them by metropolitan area. We've also included an index of companies by industry. And if your future employer is revealed to you — but not its location — through a vision or by a telepsychic, don't fret: we've added an alphabetical list of companies as well. We have listed each company's headquarters location, although many of the larger companies have offices across the nation (IBM, for instance, has an office or two outside of its Armonk, New York, home). We did not bend our rules to ensure an equal sampling for each state — California, as would be expected, has many more entries than Hawaii. But in every state except Wyoming and North Dakota, we were able to uncover at least a handful of companies that met our standards. We hope that in the next edition we will be able to cover all 50 states.

We have also included phone and fax numbers, brief industry descriptions, and the names of chief executives and senior human resources officers. Some companies reported to us that they did not have one person in charge of personnel, that hiring was done at a departmental level; their entries have been marked accordingly. In these cases, you should call or fax the company to find out to whom you should send a resume.

Job Hunting Resources

This section provides some further tools for your job search. First, we've excerpted a selection from *Net Money* that covers on-line tools for conducting a job search. Next, we included a list of corporate web sites. The information contained at these sites can be useful in selecting companies to contact and in preparing for your interview. Finally, knowing that we can't provide you with all the information you might need (however hard we might try), we've included a list of other useful books on job hunting that will help you with a variety of job-search skills, such as crafting a perfect resume and preparing yourself for an interview.

Temporary Personnel Agencies

The temporary-employment industry has grown fat off other industries' attempts to stay lean and mean. Many now offer health plans and paid vacations and specialize in servicing particular industries. We included in-depth profiles of five of the leading firms and capsule information on ten others to familiarize you with these businesses. These 15 temp agencies presently employ over 2 million contract workers. Many provide training for their employees and should be given serious consideration, especially if you are entering the job market for the first time.

Lists

This section begins with lists of the top 500 companies in this book by total employees, one-year absolute employee growth, and one-year percentage employee growth. The employee information in the book is taken from the most current available sources and usually reflects data for the companies' 1994 or 1993 fiscal years. The other lists in this section have been excerpted from a variety of sources to provide you with additional viewpoints on the American employment scene.

A DIGITAL GUIDE TO JOB HUNTING

The Internet

The Internet is a fantastic resource for job seekers. Why wait for the Sunday paper to check the want ads? Career Mosaic on the Internet has lists of jobs that are immediately available at large and small companies alike: Adaptec, Chemical Bank, Oracle, and Symantec, to name just a few.

Thousands of corporations, including The Reference Press, have established web sites on the Net where you can learn more about them. We've included a list of the addresses for some of the more interesting companies, ones that also happen to be included in Hoover's MasterList of

▼ The Reference Press   http://www.hoovers.com

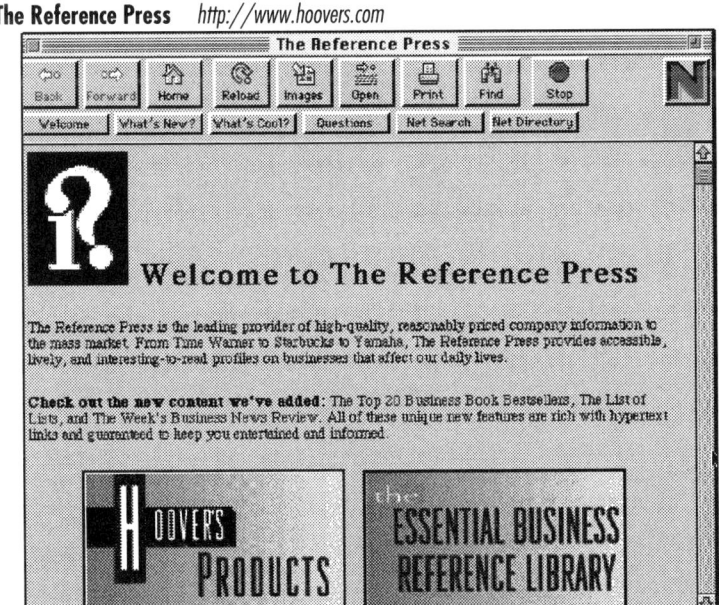

America's Top 2,500 Employers. And throughout the book, we've interspersed home pages and addresses of other on-line employment information you might find helpful. The Reference Press web site can be found at "http://www.hoovers.com", and a portion of our home page is reproduced above. Other Reference Press information can be found on America Online (keyword: hoovers), CompuServe (go: hoovers), eWorld (shortcut: hoovers), and other on-line and Internet-based services.

The Fax Icons

The Reference Press has written detailed profiles (similar to the profiles of the temp agencies in this book) of nearly a third of the companies listed in *Hoover's MasterList of America's Top 2,500 Employers*. If a company has a fax machine icon next to it, you can receive a profile on it by fax for only $2.95. Call 1-800-510-4452, 24 hours a day, 7 days a week, and have your credit card number (American Express, MasterCard, or VISA), fax number, and the five-digit company code number (located on the fax icon) ready. A voice-automated system will guide you through your order, and you'll receive your company profile within minutes. Or you can call 1-800-486-8666 to order a free catalog of the entire library of business reference books offered by The Reference Press.

The Software

To make sending out resumes a snap, we've included free software that contains all 2,500 companies in an easy-to-use database. Developed in Claris's FileMaker Pro for Windows (a run-time copy of which is part of our software package), the program combines a simple intuitive interface (no user manual required) with a powerful yet flexible search engine. You can also use our software to export the data into other applications, such as word processors, spreadsheets, or other databases. Printing cover letters and mailing labels for your prospective employers will be a snap.

Happy Hunting!

The Editors
The Reference Press, Inc.
March 1995

HOOVER'S MASTERLIST OF AMERICA'S TOP 2,500 EMPLOYERS

JOB-HUNTING RESOURCES

Excerpted from Net Money

Careers Starting The Job Search
Starting the job search

Don't sit around waiting for the help-wanted section of the Sunday newspaper. The Net has it all: electronic want ads, resume banks, and even career counseling services to help you on your way to job satisfaction (or at least job possession). Start off in one of the megaservices, such as **E-Span** or **Employment Opportunities and Resume Postings**. **Career Direction** and **Mind Garden**, both on eWorld, probe your psyche and then help you use that new-found self-awareness to land a job (be it in public service or cutthroat high finance).

On the Net

Across the board

BBS Job Listings Good Net-Samaritan Harold Lemon has assembled a list of BBSs that proved useful to him in his own job search; he's noted which BBSs charge fees and which are mainly of local interest. ✓**INTERNET**→*www* http://www.review.com/

Career Center Quite a trip. You probably won't use all the resources here, but the center has that do-everything-in-the-comfort-of-your-own-home feeling that takes the edge off the anxiety-filled process of job searching. From job listings to resume advice to one-on-one private counseling, the center is packed with services, each of which is described in greater detail throughout this sec-

Depression-era unemployment—downloaded from CompuServe's Archive Forum

tion of the book. First-timers should start their investigation in the Career Guidance section. ✓**AMERICA ONLINE**→*keyword* career

Careers BB Some members are just seeking advice about life in the office; others are eagerly seeking work in every field imaginable (broadcasting, court reporting, farming). There's lots of electronic interviewing going on here, with prospective employees far outnumbering prospective employers (most of whom run computer-related businesses). And finally, there's plenty of professional networking. ✓**PRODIGY**→*jump* careers bb

E-Span One of the most complete and omnipresent job-search services in Cyberspace, E-Span features career advice, resume-building assistance, interviewing suggestions, and job listings. The heart of E-Span is its database of job listings, which can be searched by occupation or location. Employers range from Sony to the state of Wisconsin; while job postings are voluminous, they favor the computer and financial industries. Listings remain on E-Span for up to four weeks and are updated weekly. Responses should be sent directly to the potential employer, although E-Span is happy to accept resumes for its online file bank. Note to AOL users: at present, the counseling portion of the service is not available. ✓**AMERICA ONLINE**→*keyword* jobs ✓**COMPUSERVE**→*go* espan ✓**GENIE**→*keyword* job ✓**INTERNET**→*www* http://www.espan.com/js/js.html **Register:** ✓**INTERNET**→resumes@espan3.espan.com ⌨ Email resume for inclusion in database

Employment Opportunities and Resume Postings This mega-index of job services provides links to several government job centers, the bionet Usenet groups (which are filled with help-

Reprinted by permission from *Net Money* (Random House Electronic Publishing, 1995). Copyright © 1995 by Michael Wolff & Company, Inc.

Starting The Job Search Careers

wanted postings for the sciences), and personnel listings for many academic institutions. The *Occupations Outlook Handbook*, a very good source for career planning, can also be reached from this site. Overall, a good place to begin a job search. ✓**INTERNET**→*gopher* cwis.usc.edu→Other Gophers and Information Resources→Gopher Jewels→Personal Development and Recreation→Employment Opportunities and Resume Postings→Employment Opportunities and Resume Postings

Online Career Center This well-designed site is a not-for-profit cooperative that provides career counseling and a growing database with about 8,000 jobs and resumes. Job listings range from openings for trading-room support on Wall Street to emergency-room nurses in Ohio to marketing executives in Zurich. In addition to the large number of entry-level positions directed toward the Net-savvy college crowd, the OCC lists opportunities for experienced professionals. Participating employers include giants like AT&T, Bank of America, Eastman Kodak, Kraft, Unisys, and the CIA. Both job and resume files are searchable. The service also lists local employment job fairs. While the OCC charges nothing for resume listings, companies advertising jobs pay a one-time fee of $3,900 and subscription dues of $50 a year. ✓**INTERNET**→*gopher* garnet.msen.com→Online Career Center→Online Career Center

The Princeton Review WWW server Though it's known primarily as a college counseling service, the Princeton Review also offers career advice for recent grads. Called "How to Survive Without Your Parent's Money," this online document leads former students through the initial motivational process, the inevitable procrastination that ensues, resumes, interviews, and even the alternating exhilaration and disappointment of the first job. Princeton's advice on internships and career changes is well presented. ✓**INTERNET**→*www* http://www.review.com/career/8000.html

Rice University Job Information So, you want to search for a job online, and you don't want to miss anything. Suggestion: don't miss Rice, which links to all the major online career databases, U.S. government job listings, relevant Usenet newsgroups, and many college and university job listings. ✓**INTERNET**→*gopher* riceinfo.rice.edu→Information by Subject Area→Jobs and Employment

Finding yourself

Career Analysis Service Just download the service's questionnaire, complete it, and email it back to the online career counselor, who will consider your answers in the context of 13,500 different jobs. Doctor? Lawyer? Indian chief? Butcher? Baker? Candlestick maker? Dishwasher? Freelance writer? Pharmaceutical representative? There is an additional charge of $39.95 for this service. ✓**AMERICA ONLINE**→*keyword* career→Career Guidance Services→Career Analysis Service $

Career Direction Just lost your job and need to regroup? Concerned that your career options aren't what they could be? The Lee Hecht Harrison career-consulting firm has prepared a series of self-awareness tests and a strategy guide to help you find a job by finding yourself. In the Personal Values and Mission survey, you'll be asked to do a little soul-searching—What are the things you are passionate about? Do you believe that family is more important than work? The Career Options section helps you assess your skills and abilities; if you're in between jobs and financially insecure, the Transition Preparation guide proposes strategies for coping with the psychological and fiscal strain. ✓**EWORLD**→*go* lhh→Career Direction

Career Focus 2000 If you don't know what you want to do, this is the place to zero in on your options. This series of four downloadable workbooks helps you analyze your career leanings by matching your test results to the interests and skill requirements of 1,000 jobs, then helps guide you in your job search. ✓**AMERICA ONLINE**→*keyword* career→Career Guidance Services→Career Focus 2000

Job Hunting Get a job! And get one with this guide, which helps you plan your assault on companies and recruiters. From cover letters to follow-up calls, Lee Hecht Harrison explains it all, demystifying the career search. ✓**EWORLD**→*go* lhh→Job Hunting

Mind Garden: Personal & Career Understanding "Who am I? Why am I? Which am I? How am I?" Heady questions, certainly, but never fear: the answers are growing in the Mind Garden. Through a series of interactive online workbooks, various occupational professionals help you know yourself. Who are you? Well, you're someone of uniquely imbalanced aptitudes, and you need to "learn to change unwanted attitudes and behavior" by embarking on "a journey of self-discovery." Why are you? Clarify your values

Careers Starting The Job Search

to steel yourself for tough life decisions. Career or family? More money or better hours? (Those without values of their own will be happy to learn that the Mind Garden furnishes "historical values.") Which are you? Decide by learning about popular personality classification systems such as the Meyers-Briggs type indicator, psychological temperament indicators, the Enneagram, and five factor codes. And finally, how are you? Anxious and fretful, and desperately in need of the Mind Garden's stress-beating strategies. ✓EWORLD →*go* mindgarden

Online Counseling Free consultation with a professional career counselor: just leave a message on the Appointment Book board to schedule your meeting. Another message board, Ask the Counselor, creates a public discussion area where both counselors and members offer advice on jobs and job hunting. And who are these counselors? Their profiles are available online. ✓AMERICA ONLINE→*keyword* career→Career Counseling Services

Advice columns

Dr. Job This weekly question-and-answer session with *Crain's* business journalist Sandra Pesman addresses everything from succeeding at a second career to keeping a job during the difficult process of sex-reassignment surgery. Past issues, archived online, contain a plethora of useful tips for job hunters. Do you know how to tailor your resume for computer keywords or how to dress for success on an interview? Ask Dr. Job. ✓GENIE→*keyword* dr.job

Counselors

JobPlace (ml) They write in from the career guidance offices of Smith, Skidmore, Syracuse, and other colleges and universities asking the list a host of questions: How to advise their students who are job searching, develop better career resources for their school, or get further training as a counselor? Even if you're not a guidance counselor, this list is still an interesting place to lurk and learn about job market do's and don'ts. Listen as one counselor asks if a student with a foreign sounding name should note his citizenship on a resume, as another questions how a full-time student and former homemaker who's been out of the workforce for 12 years should explain her hiatus on her resume, and as yet another wonders if resumes in Germany are handwritten? ✓INTERNET→*email* listserv@ukcc.uky.edu ✏ *Type in message body:* subscribe jobplace <your full name>

Employment agencies

The Employment Agency Databases Information on thousands of employment agencies and headhunters, primarily executive-search firms. The Custom Databanks Database offers descriptions of thousands of search firms, while the Recruiters Plus Database lets the search firms create their own profiles. Search either database by locale, field, or job title. ✓AMERICA ONLINE→*keyword* career→Employment Agency Database

State Employment Offices (All States) A list of all 50 state employment offices, complete with mailing addresses and phone numbers. ✓INTERNET→*gopher* gopher.uoregon.edu→UO Colleges and Schools→School of Law→Law Career Services→Career Services Notices→State employment offices for all states (Large File!)

Networking contacts

Job Seeking (echo) In this conference, members involved or interested in particular professions post brief notes and queries which can be (and most often are) answered by others in the field. ✓JOBNET

Talent Bank You've probably heard it a hundred times: to find a job, you need to network. Believe it or not, that word hasn't always carried online connotations. In the Talent Bank, the fine art of meeting and greeting flourishes—each participant fills out a personal profile which is then filed in a searchable database. Want to find someone else interested in a career in desktop publishing? Curious how electrical engineers slightly older than yourself are faring in the job market? Just tinker with your search terms, make a match, and discuss your occupational hopes and fears. ✓AMERICA ONLINE→*keyword* career→Talent Bank

Products

Career Resource Library Tunnel into the stacks of the library for information about job resources not currently available on America Online. Intended to be a clearinghouse of catalogs and product announcements by those in the career-guidance business, the library is dominated by the products and services of JIST Works, Inc. ✓AMERICA ONLINE→*keyword* career→Career Resource Library

JobHunt v5 Complete job-search tool. Provides contact info, prints personalized letters, labels, and envelopes. Search companies by different criteria. ✓PC OHIO→d→*Download a file:* JOBHUNT5.ZIP (DOS)

CYBERPOWER!™

Finding A Job

I worked as a radio engineer in northern Illinois until late last winter, when I was fired. At first, I thought I would bounce right back, but I've had a hard time finding work. I feel like my interview skills are rusty, and I have nightmares about rumpled suits and ink-stained resumes. How do I get my confidence back, and how do I get a job? I'll go anywhere.

Most career counseling and placement services recognize that unemployment wreaks psychological havoc in addition to its economic effects, and the best online services take pains to address various aspects of joblessness. Take E-SPAN's Interactive Employment Network, and particularly the Career Manager service (http://www.espan.com/js/js.html), which contains dozens of resources for the occupationally gun-shy.

You mention that you're afraid of ruining your chances by submitting a sloppy resume. Well, don't let that happen. Visit Joyce Lain Kennedy's Electronic Resume Writing Tips, and learn how to write the best resume you possibly can. Then enter E-SPAN's job library and see what might be waiting for you in the world of occupational opportunity. E-SPAN has sorted its jobs by both keyword and region, so if you get an endless list of available positions, you should narrow your search until the results are specific enough to digest. For radio engineers in the Midwest, the forecast is bright—we took the liberty of conducting a search for you, and turned up nearly a dozen jobs, from electronic packaging engineers in Nebraska to cellular telecommunications engineers in Ohio. If you want to develop radio test equipment and optimization techniques, you might want to think about the Ohio job, which includes extensive travel in the domestic United States. But the best bet is right in your backyard—Maxwell-Marcus is looking for a Senior RF systems engineer in the Chicago suburb of Hoffman

Estates, Illinois. "Work in the advanced cellular technology department. Applicants need MSEE and should be very experienced in theoretical modeling of radio systems and radio hardware architecture. Candidates are invited to send a resume." Senior RF systems engineer, Maxwell-Marcus…it has a nice ring to it, no?

If one of your brilliant resumes actually nets you an interview with the company, you'll almost certainly want to use E-SPAN's interview resources to prepare for your meeting. Study the practice questions and answers in the online version of "You're Hired!— The Ultimate Job Search Simulator," or order the entire simulator for $26.95. (This may be $26.95 more than you can afford so long as you are out of work, but it is probably a good investment.) Tell me about yourself. What are your major strengths? What are some of your biases or hang-ups? What is your idea of success? What have you learned from your failures? And are you continually invigorated by the world of radio engineering?

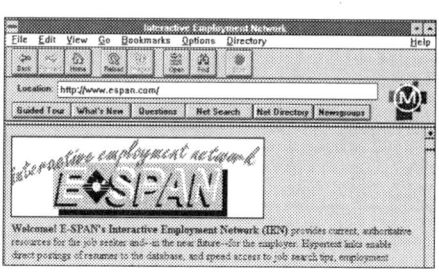

E-SPAN Home page

Finally, if your job hunt doesn't go as smoothly as you had hoped—say the man at Maxwell-Marcus didn't like your rumpled suit—spend some time with E-SPAN's support group, which addresses the difficulties of financial management, the tricky business of motivation, and even emergency "CPR for a Lifeless Job Search."

Subject **Careers**

The job market

What do almost all workers have in common? A desperate need to understand the changing job market. A good place to start is the Department of Labor Occupational Outlook Handbook which offers detailed profiles of thousands of careers. A wealth of statistics has been compiled and analyzed to project the hottest careers in the handbook's "Tomorrow's Jobs." The **US News College Fair Forum** on CompuServe and **Career Articles** on AOL also provide estimates on everything from salary to future job security. Bulletin boards and newsgroups like **Job Discuss, Careers Online,** and misc. jobs.misc offer dispatches from the working world: find out how others cope with discrimination, job loss, or an especially nasty boss.

Career Mosaic screen shot—from http://www.careermosaic.com/cm

On the Net

Across the board

Career Articles An archive of articles, with new additions each month, about assorted career topics. "Changing Careers: Why and When," "Jobs of the Future," and "Evaluating a Job Offer" are just a few of the titles on file. ✓AMERICA ONLINE→*keyword* career→Career Articles

Mercury News Employment Articles Part of AOL's extensive Mercury Center, this substantial database collects articles on occupational and employment-related issues from the *San Jose Mercury News.* ✓AMERICA ONLINE→*keyword* mercury→Employment→Browse Mercury News Employment Articles

US News College Fair Forum Now that you're finishing school, what are you going to do with your life? No, no—beyond the graduation night parties and summer-after-college romances. Stuck for an answer? Well, *U.S. News* has prepared a series of 1995 Career Guides for selected professions—medicine, law, manufacturing, finance, etc.—which provide education, salary, and employment stats, as well as prospects for growth. These files contain excerpts from the Department of Labor's *Occupational Outlook Handbook* (OOH), which detail the duties, earnings potential, and future of selected professions. Other useful portions of the *OOH*—especially resume-writing tips and job-search contacts—are also available. CompuServants may also download the Federal Jobs database. ✓**COMPUSERVE**→*go* usncollege→Libraries→Career

Job profiles

Department of Labor Occupational Outlook Handbook A huge, searchable repository of career information including job descriptions, job projections, and career advice. Do you want to be an economist? Actor? Professional fisherman? The *OOH* details education requirements, job conditions, day-to-day responsibilities, labor organizations, and earning potential for each job, along with employment projections that extend well into the next century.

Each job comes complete with a list of relevant professional organizations, unions, publications, etc., which are themselves often sources of job listings and career advice. A feature entitled "Tomorrow's Jobs"

Careers Starting The Job Search

collects the Labor Department's educated guesses about work in the upcoming decades. (Health care? Up. Farming? Down. Big surprise.) In addition, the *OOH* includes a wealth of practical job-search information—tips on how to find job leads, craft a powerful resume, and turn an interview into a victory.

And finally, those seeking help in retraining or going back to school will find information on fellowships and public assistance programs. On AOL, the handbook is divided into a searchable database and a set of informative articles called the Occupational Profiles Database. ✓**INTERNET**→ *gopher* umslvma.umsl.edu→The Library→Government Information (US Federal & State Info & Docs)→ Occupational Outlook Handbooks ✓**AMERICA ONLINE**→*keyword* career →Occupational Profiles Database

Job talk

Careers (echo) Get your views on affirmative action off your chest. Exchange tips on career building. Find out the comparative benefits of an electrical engineering or computer science degree. Discussion swings from passionate to downright pragmatic. Most of the positions announced are computer-industry related. Watch out for get-rich-quick-through-your-PC schemes. ✓**ILINK**

Job Discuss (echo) Discussion is a little frantic, and job seekers and employers can't resist posting their ads, but the people here seem willing to help one another. In fact, they can barely restrain themselves—at the drop of a hat, they'll share tips for job-search strategies, offer advice about references, and plan out strategies for dodging the dreaded salary-requirement question. Just yell. ✓**FIDONET**

> "As for mandatory drug testing. Domino's Pizza? Tests. Barnes & Noble? Doesn't test."

misc.jobs.misc (ng) Don't post job offers or resumes here, unless they are well disguised as queries about the working world. This group is all talk and no action: speculating, analyzing, anguishing, along with a little networking. Discussions cover topics such as whether casual clothing is appropriate in the workplace, what personality types are best suited for specific jobs, and how the work ethic is faring inside Generation X. There's also some practical interchange—advice on legally relocating to Canada or finding the best headhunter. ✓**USENET**

Labor statistics

Bureau of Labor Statistics Database The massive public database of the Bureau of Labor Statistics—LABSTAT to cognoscenti—furnishes current and historical data from more than 20 statistical surveys that pertain to consumer health and employment. Employment projections by industry? Geographical profiles? Department store inventory price index? All available. ✓**INTERNET**→*gopher* stats.bls.gov

Lifestyle profiles

Career Mosaic "Who's doing the cool work these days?" asks this site's home page. The answer? Computer science majors. Sponsored by an advertising agency, the service is geared toward college students and provides information about hot companies and lifestyles around the world. To date, Career Mosaic has only a dozen sponsor companies, and although no jobs are posted here, the service allows searches of the ba.jobs.offered newsgroup and contains a library full of useful information, including a sample interactive resume and information on the top 50 job markets in the U.S. ✓**INTERNET**→ *www* http://www.careermosaic.com/cm

Rights & assistance

Careers On-Line A service for disabled workers. Find out about your rights and your employer's obligations. Job listings are also available here. ✓**INTERNET**→ *www* http://disserv.stu.umn.edu:80/cl

Catalogue of Federal Domestic Assistance Find out what government assistance you are entitled to for a job search or retraining. This is not a listing of jobs available in the federal government (see FEDJOBS), but it is a listing of federal job programs. Displaced homemakers, senior citizens, victims of industrial migration—you may be eligible! ✓**INTERNET**→*gopher* gopher.rtd.utk.edu→ Federal Government Information→ Catalogue of Federal Domestic Assistance→Jobs

Piss List A list of companies with mandatory drug testing—often referred to by the euphemism "human quality test programs"—as well as those that have policies against testing. Domino's Pizza? Tests. Barnes & Noble. Doesn't test. ✓**INTERNET**→*www* http://rafferty.com/~piss/

Reprinted by permission from *Net Money* (Random House Electronic Publishing, 1995). Copyright © 1995 by Michael Wolff & Company, Inc.

Corporate Web Sites for Companies Listed in This Book

3COM Corporation http://www.3com.com
Adaptec, Inc. http://www.adaptec.com
Adobe Systems Incorporated
http://www.adobe.com
Advanced Micro Devices, Inc.
http://www.amd.com
Advantis http://www.ibm.net/adv
America Online, Inc. http://www.blue.aol.com
Ameritech Corporation
http://www.ameritech.com
AMP Incorporated http://www.amp.com
Apple Computer, Inc. http://www.apple.com
AT&T Corporation http://www.att.com
BankAmerica Corporation
http://www.bankamerica.com
Bell Atlantic Corporation
http://www.bell-atl.com
Bell Communications Research Inc.
http://www.bellcore.com
CBS Inc. http://www.cbs.com
Cheyenne Software, Inc. http://www.chey.com
Cisco Systems, Inc. http://www.cisco.com
Club Med, Inc.
http://www.hotwired.com/Coin/Spnsrs/
Clubmed
Compaq Computer Corporation
http://www.compaq.com
Cray Research, Inc. http://www.cray.com
Data General Corporation http://www.dg.com
Dataware Technologies Inc.
http://www.dataware.com
Del Monte Foods Company
http://sjmercury.com/advert/delmonte/
delhome.html
Dell Computer Corporation
http://www.dell.com
Dial-A-Mattress Franchise Corporation
http://www.info@mattress.com
Digital Equipment Corporation
http://www.digital.com
Dow Jones & Company, Inc.
http://dowvision.wais.net
The Dun & Bradstreet Corporation
http://www.dnb.com
Edward D. Jones & Co.
http://www.vpm.com/edj/edj.html
Electronic Data Systems Corporation
http://www.eds.com
Federal Express Corporation
http://www.fedex.com
First Interstate Bancorp
http://www.hexadecimal.com/fi
FMR Corporation http://www.fid-inv.com
General Electric Company http://www.ge.com
Gupta Corporation http://www.gupta.com
Hewlett-Packard Company http://www.hp.com
Hyatt Corporation
http://www.travelweb.com/thisco/common/
search.html

Informix Corporation http://www.informix.com
Intel Corporation http://www.intel.com
International Business Machines Corporation
http://www.ibm.com
J. C. Penney Company, Inc.
http://www.jcpenney.com/
J.P. Morgan & Co. Incorporated
http://www.jpmorgan.com
Levi Strauss Associates Inc.
http://www.levi.com
Mecklermedia Corporation
http://www.mecklerweb.com
Microsoft Corporation
http://www.microsoft.com
NetManage, Inc. http://www.netmanage.com
NeXT, Inc. http://www.next.com
Northwest Airlines Corporation
http://www.winternet.com/~tela/nwa-info.html
Oracle Systems Corporation
http://www.oracle.com
The Promus Companies Incorporated
http://www.promus.com
QUALCOMM Incorporated
http://www.qualcomm.com
Reebok International Ltd.
http://www.planetreebok.com
Rockwell International Corporation
http://www.rockwell.com
Silicon Graphics, Inc. http://www.sgi.com
Southwest Airlines Co.
http://xmission.com~aoi/f0wn.html
Sprint Corporation http://www.sprintlink.net/
Sun Microsystems, Inc. http://www.sun.com
Sybase, Inc. http://www.sybase.com
Synopsys, Inc. http://www.synopsys.com
Tandem Computers Incorporated
http://www.tandem.com
Telebit Corporation http://www.telebit.com
Time Warner Inc. http://www.timeinc.com
TRW Inc. http://www.trw.com
U.S. Robotics, Inc.
http://www.primenet.com/usr
United Parcel Service of America, Inc.
http://www.ups.com
Wall Data, Inc. http://www.walldata.com
The Walt Disney Company
http://www.disney.com
Wells Fargo & Company
http://www.wellsfargo.com
West Publishing Co. http://www.westpub.com
Xerox Corporation http://www.xerox.com
Ziff-Davis Publishing Company
http://www.interactive-week.com

Useful Books on Job-Hunting

The 100 Best Companies to Work for in America, Robert Levering and Milton Moskowitz, 2nd ed., Doubleday, 1993.

The 100 Best Jobs for the 1990s & Beyond, Carol Kleiman, Dearborn Financial Publishing, Inc., 1992.

175 High-Impact Cover Letters, Richard H. Beatty, John Wiley & Sons, 1992.

200 Letters for Job Hunters, William S. Frank, Ten Speed Press, 1993.

1995 National Job Hotline Directory, Marcia P. Williams and Sue A. Cubbage, McGraw-Hill, Inc., 1994.

The Adams Jobs Almanac 1995, Bob Adams, Inc., 1995.

The Almanac of American Employers 1994–1995, Jack W. Plunkett, Corporate Job Outlook, 1994.

Alternative Careers, John Wiley & Sons, Inc., 1995.

Beatty's Job Search Networking, Richard H. Beatty, Bob Adams, Inc., 1994.

The Career Coach, Carol Kleiman, Dearborn Financial Publishing, Inc., 1994.

The Complete Job-Search Handbook, Howard Figler, Henry Holt & Co., 1988.

The Complete Q & A Job Interview Book, Jeffrey G. Allen, John Wiley & Sons, 1988.

Cover Letters, John Wiley & Sons, Inc., 1995.

Designing Creative Resumes, Gregg Berryman, William Kaufman, Inc., 1985.

Electronic Job Search Revolution, Joyce Lain Kennedy and Thomas J. Morrow, John Wiley & Sons, Inc., 1994.

Electronic Resume Revolution, Joyce Lain Kennedy and Thomas J. Morrow, John Wiley & Sons, Inc., 1994.

Electronic Resumes for the New Job Market, Peter Weddle, Impact Publications, 1995.

Every Woman's Essential Job Hunting & Resume Book, Laura Morin, Bob Adams, Inc., 1994.

Help! My Job Interview is Tomorrow!, Mary Ellen Templeton, Neal-Schuman Publishers, 1991.

How to Get a Job in 90 Days or Less, Matthew J. DeLuca, McGraw-Hill, Inc., 1995.

Interviewing, Arlene S. Hirsch, John Wiley & Sons, Inc., 1995.

Jobs Rated Almanac, Les Krantz, 3rd ed., John Wiley & Sons, Inc., 1995.

Make Your Job Interview a Success, J. I. Biegeleisen, Macmillan, 1994.

Net Money, Kelly Maloni, Ben Greenman and Kristin Miller, Michael Wolff & Company, Inc., 1995.

Networking, Douglass B. Richardson, John Wiley & Sons, Inc., 1995.

The New Rules of the Job Search Game, Jackie Larson, Bob Adams, Inc., 1994.

The On-Line Job Search Companion, James Gonyea, McGraw-Hill, Inc., 1995.

The Resume Catalog: 200 Damn Good Examples, Yana Parker, Ten Speed Press, 1988.

Resumes, Taunee Besson, John Wiley & Sons, Inc., 1994.

Resumes That Get Jobs, Jean Reed, Prentice-Hall, 1994.

Resumes That Knock 'Em Dead, Martin John Yate, Bob Adams, Inc., 1988.

What Color Is Your Parachute? 1995, Richard Nelson Bolles, Ten Speed Press, 1995.

Winning Resumes for the Nineties, Matthew Green, Penguin Group, 1994.

 **HOOVER'S MASTERLIST OF AMERICA'S TOP 2,500 EMPLOYERS**

LEADING TEMPORARY PERSONNEL AGENCIES

KELLY SERVICES, INC.

OVERVIEW

Kelly celebrates its 50th birthday in 1996, so it seems ironic to call this a "temporary service." The Troy, Michigan–based company provides more than 600,000 employees to some 185,000 customers and is one of the US's largest temporary-employment agencies, along with Manpower, Olsten, and Adia. Founder William Kelly, now nearly 90, is still chairman of the board, although his adopted son, Terence Adderley, serves as president and CEO. Together they control a majority of the company's outstanding shares.

Temporary Services, a subsidiary, offers office clerical, technical, marketing, and semiskilled light industrial personnel. The company provides computer-based training, skills testing, and managed services on a temporary basis to companies in the US, Canada, Europe, Australia, and New Zealand. Another subsidiary, Kelly Assisted Living Services, provides personal care and daily living assistance to people who need care at home.

Gains in the economies of the US, the UK, Canada, Australia, and New Zealand have helped Kelly. The company also anticipates that the passage of the Family Leave Act, which could affect 60% of the US work force, could boost business.

WHEN

William Russell Kelly, a college dropout and former car salesman, returned from WWII with a knowledge of what business machines could do. In 1946 he set up Russell Kelly Office Services in his Detroit, Michigan, office to provide copying and typing services and to calculate inventory for other businesses. As companies began to acquire their own machines, Kelly learned that they still needed people to work at their offices.

Kelly reincorporated his rapidly expanding business as Personnel Service in 1952. In 1955 the company opened its first branch office in Louisville, Kentucky, and by the end of that year had 35 offices throughout the US. In 1957 the company became Kelly Girl Service, a change motivated by the all-female composition of the company's work force. Kelly Girl went public in 1962, boasting 148 branches. In 1966 the company adopted its present name, Kelly Services. By 1979 there was a Kelly office in every state.

Having offered only office services during the 1960s, Kelly pursued opportunities in other areas needing temporary workers. The company began providing everything from convention hostesses, blue-collar workers, and data processors to door-to-door marketers and drafters. The company's first foreign office was opened in Toronto in 1968, with a Paris office following in 1972 and a London office in 1973.

Employers saw the benefits of hiring "Kelly Girls" to meet seasonal needs and special projects. A tough US economy in the 1970s saw a surge in corporate interest in temporary employees. Because the cost of hiring and training a permanent employee can run up to 150% of a new recruit's salary, employers began avoiding the risk and expense of hiring, opting for well-trained temps instead.

In 1976 Kelly Services acquired a modest health care services company and used it to form Kelly Home Care (later Kelly Health Care). In the 1980s this division abandoned the Medicaid and Medicare markets and shifted to private-sector care. Renamed Kelly Assisted Living Services in 1984, the unit offered aides to perform various household duties and nurses to conduct home visits for the elderly and disabled. Also in the 1980s Kelly Services began hiring retired people as part of its ENCORE Program to use their experience in temporary positions.

International expansion has been a central focus for Kelly. From 1988 through 1993, 13 international acquisitions expanded the company in Europe, North America, and Australia/New Zealand. In 1994 Kelly acquired Your Staff, a 5,000-employee company in the US that leases entire human resources departments, including benefits and payroll services. Other acquisitions included the Swiss temporary and permanent employment agency OK Personnel (which has 30 branches) and the 51% of ComTrain, a California software firm, that it did not already own. Kelly also introduced its KellySelect service, which allows a company to try out prospective permanent employees on a temporary basis.

The company has reorganized and reshuffled its executive suite to accommodate expansion. These efforts paid off in 1994 as earnings rose 37% to $61.1 million on sales of almost $2.4 billion.

Nasdaq symbol: KELYA
Fiscal year ends: Sunday nearest December 31

WHO

Chairman: William R. Kelly, age 88
President and CEO: Terence E. Adderley, age 60, $730,000 pay
EVP Administration: Robert E. Thompson, age 51, $348,000 pay (prior to promotion)
EVP Operations: Robert G. Barranco, age 53, $365,000 pay (prior to promotion)
SVP, General Counsel, and Secretary: Eugene L. Hartwig, age 60, $266,000 pay
SVP and General Manager, Major Markets Division: Donald A. Bobo, age 52
SVP and General Manager, Metro Markets Division: Carolyn R. Fryar, age 51
SVP and CFO: Paul K. Geiger
SVP Human Resources: Joanne E. Start, age 49
Auditors: Price Waterhouse

WHERE

HQ: 999 W. Big Beaver Rd., Troy, MI 48084
Phone: 810-362-4444
Fax: 810-244-4924 (Investor Relations)

Kelly Services operates over 1,000 offices in the US, Australia, Canada, Denmark, France, Ireland, Mexico, the Netherlands, New Zealand, Norway, Puerto Rico, and the UK.

	1993 Sales	
	$ mil.	% of total
US	1,719	88
Other countries	235	12
Total	**1,954**	**100**

WHAT

Selected Operations

US
Kelly Assisted Living Services
Kelly Professional Services
Kelly Properties
Kelly Services
Kelly Temporary Services
Your Staff

North America (except US)
Kelly Temporary Services (Canada)
Kelly Temporary Services (Mexico)
Lenore Simpson Personnel (Canada)
Les Services Kelly (Canada)

Pacific Rim
Kelly Temporary Services (Australia)
Kelly Temporary Services (New Zealand)

Europe
Karin Lanng Kelly (Denmark)
Kelly Personal Byrået (Norway)
Kelly Services (UK)
Kelly Uitzendburo (the Netherlands)
Kelly Vikarer (Denmark)
OK Personnel (Switzerland)
Société Services Kelly (France)

KEY COMPETITORS

Adia	MacTemps
Administaff	Manpower
Amserv Healthcare	Norrell
Barrett Business Services	Olsten
Career Horizons	Staff Builders
HealthInfusion	TAD Technical
Hospital Staffing Services	Volt Information
In Home Health	Western Temporary Services
Interim Services	

HOW MUCH

	9-Year Growth	1984	1985	1986	1987	1988	1989	1990	1991	1992	1993
Sales ($ mil.)	11.4%	741	876	1,034	1,161	1,269	1,378	1,471	1,438	1,723	1,954
Net income ($ mil.)	5.9%	27	33	36	51	60	71	71	39	39	45
Income as % of sales	—	3.6%	3.7%	3.5%	4.3%	4.8%	5.1%	4.8%	2.7%	2.3%	2.3%
Earnings per share ($)	6.0%	0.70	0.86	0.97	1.34	1.61	1.89	1.90	1.02	1.04	1.18
Stock price – high ($)	—	9.23	19.85	26.05	30.95	30.08	33.60	32.20	33.40	35.00	36.50
Stock price – low ($)	—	6.48	9.05	19.20	18.55	21.45	21.45	21.80	21.60	22.20	22.00
Stock price – close ($)	13.0%	9.23	19.85	20.93	24.95	23.68	31.40	26.20	25.20	35.00	27.75
P/E – high	—	13	23	27	23	19	18	17	33	34	31
P/E – low	—	9	11	20	14	13	11	12	21	21	19
Dividends per share ($)	13.6%	0.20	0.24	0.27	0.45	0.38	0.46	0.53	0.58	0.58	0.63
Book value per share ($)	15.2%	2.87	3.41	3.94	4.91	6.13	7.55	8.98	9.44	9.74	10.23
Employees	4.3%	432,850	478,075	529,600	553,600	558,750	583,900	578,800	553,900	584,000	634,300

1993 Year-end:
Debt ratio: 0.0%
Return on equity: 11.8%
Cash (mil.): $181
Current ratio: 2.87
Long-term debt (mil.): $0
No. of shares (mil.): 38
Dividends
 Yield: 2.3%
 Payout: 53.4%
Market value (mil.): $1,048

Stock Price History
High/Low 1984–93

MANPOWER INC.

OVERVIEW

Manpower, based in Milwaukee, is the world's largest temporary-employment company, with operations spanning the globe and employing more than one million people. In addition to temporary services, the company also provides permanent-employment services, including employee testing and training. One of Manpower's advantages is that it can fulfill the worldwide staffing needs of multinational companies on a contract basis. Such contracts constitute about 50% of business.

The company has been significantly restructured since 1989, when it was the object of a vicious struggle between the head of its former UK parent, Blue Arrow, and Mitchell Fromstein, its US chief. Fromstein won, bringing Manpower back to the US in 1991.

Although Manpower has suffered in the recessions that hammered the US, Japan, and Europe, much of its wretched-looking results have been the result of amortized write-offs of goodwill (the difference between the actual value of the company and its purchase price) related to the Blue Arrow purchase. The company was expected to be profitable in 1994.

WHEN

Manpower was founded by 2 Milwaukee lawyers, Elmer Winter and Aaron Scheinfeld, in 1948. In the beginning Manpower concentrated on supplying temporary help to industry during the first flush of the postwar boom. In the next few years the company expanded, and in 1956 it began growing through franchising. During the 1960s the company began opening franchises in Europe, Asia, and South America. It continued to emphasize blue-collar placements, however, unlike many of its competitors.

But Manpower's true growth into a powerhouse was orchestrated by Mitchell Fromstein, whose connection with the company began when he was Manpower's advertising account executive in the 1960s. Fromstein joined Manpower's board in 1971 and became president and CEO in 1976. In the 1970s Manpower embarked on a series of acquisitions and began to shift its emphasis from industrial to clerical placements. In the mid-1970s, with Scheinfeld deceased and Winter eager to sell out, Parker Pen came along. Parker, also based in Wisconsin, was trying to re-energize its fading fortunes after the arrival of the disposable pen. In 1976 Parker bought Manpower, sold the pen business 10 years later, and became Manpower Inc. Fromstein continued as president and CEO, with a 20% interest in the company.

In the late 1970s Manpower entered the computer age with a will, instituting a computer training program for its temporary employees. The company grew in the character of employment in the US evolved from the norm of career-long employment with one company to a series of shorter-term jobs with many employers. In addition to providing short-term workers, Manpower also began offering hiring and training services for "permanent" employees, thus saving companies in-house recruitment and training costs.

In 1987 Manpower was acquired by Blue Arrow, a temporary-employment agency based in the UK, and the combined companies became known as Manpower. Almost immediately tensions arose between Fromstein and his new boss, Antony Berry, who accused Fromstein of obstructing efforts to unite the 2 companies. Fromstein was fired in 1988. But he did not go away quietly. Manpower's worldwide franchisees revolted against Berry, and the UK began an investigation of the means used to finance the acquisition of Manpower (a $1.5 billion stock sale by NatWest). Berry was ousted in 1989 and Fromstein regained control. A big push by American interests (particularly Southeastern Asset Management, of Memphis) changed the composition of Manpower's ownership during that year, from just 9% American in January to over 60% by the end of the year. This gave Fromstein the support he needed to move Manpower back to Wisconsin in 1991.

Since then Fromstein has worked to disentangle the 2 companies by selling off Blue Arrow's nonemployment-related holdings.

With its management trauma behind it, Manpower has reset its sights on growth. Its bottom line has been aided by the shift from permanent to temporary employment patterns. And more important, the goodwill write-offs have ended. In 1994 Manpower opened new offices in the US and abroad.

NYSE symbol: MAN
Fiscal year ends: December 31

WHO

Chairman, President, and CEO: Mitchell S. Fromstein, age 66, $1,260,463 pay
EVP, Principal Financial Officer, and Secretary: Jon F. Chait, age 43, $450,116 pay
Controller, Treasurer, and Principal Accounting Officer: David E. Zblewski, age 55, $185,000 pay
SVP and General Counsel: Walt Koslowski
VP North American Administration (HR): David Wescoe
Auditors: Arthur Andersen & Co.

WHERE

HQ: 5301 North Ironwood Rd., Milwaukee, WI 53217
Phone: 414-961-1000
Fax: 414-961-7081

	1993 Manpower Worldwide Offices	
	Owned	Franchise or other
Europe outside UK	727	—
US	502	418
UK	154	5
Israel	35	—
South America	33	—
Japan	26	—
Mexico	13	—
Canada	7	50
Australia	—	5
Other countries	94	—
Total	**1,591**	**478**

	1993 Sales		1993 Pretax Income	
	$ mil.	% of total	$ mil.	% of total
Europe	1,859	58	33	—
US	1,068	34	55	—
Other countries	253	8	7	—
Adjustments	—	—	(122)	—
Total	3,180	100	(27)	—

WHAT

Services
Employee testing and training
Industrial trades temporary staffing
Medical staffing services
Office and clerical temporary staffing
Permanent employment agency services

KEY COMPETITORS

Adia Services	Hooper Holmes
Alternate Resources Group	Interim Services
	Kelly Services
BIS	Mac Temps
Butler International	NRI
CDI	Olsten
Diversified Human Resources	Randstad
	Right Management Consultants
Eastridge Group	
ECCO	Source Services
Harcourt General	Vendex
Heidrick & Struggles	Watsco

HOW MUCH

	Annual Growth	1984	1985	1986	1987	1988	1989	1990	1991	1992	1993
Sales ($ mil.)	30.8%	—	—	—	635	2,457	2,729	3,054	2,800	3,187	3,180
Net income ($ mil.)	—	—	—	—	12	2	(1,208)	(82)	(53)	(47)	(49)
Income as % of sales	—	—	—	—	1.9%	0.1%	—	—	—	—	—
Earnings per share ($)	—	—	—	—	0.46	0.03	(16.75)	(1.13)	(0.73)	(0.54)	(0.66)
Stock price – high ($)	—	—	—	—	—	—	—	—	15.13	17.13	17.88
Stock price – low ($)	—	—	—	—	—	—	—	—	11.13	13.25	13.50
Stock price – close ($)	9.3%	—	—	—	—	—	—	—	14.75	14.50	17.63
P/E – high	—	—	—	—	—	—	—	—	—	—	—
P/E – low	—	—	—	—	—	—	—	—	—	—	—
Dividends per share ($)	—	—	—	—	—	—	—	—	0.00	0.00	0.00
Book value per share ($)	—	—	—	—	—	4.58	4.56	3.77	3.05	2.17	1.39
Employees	(7.2%)	—	—	—	—	—	—	1,507,600	1,506,500	1,206,600	1,206,700

1993 Year-end:
Debt ratio: 62.6%
Return on equity: —
Cash (mil.): $63
Current ratio: 1.38
Long-term debt (mil.): $130
No. of shares (mil.): 74
Dividends
 Yield: —
 Payout: —
Market value (mil.): $1,299

Stock Price History
High/Low 1991–93

THE OLSTEN CORPORATION

OVERVIEW

What's the worst that could befall Olsten, the US's 2nd largest (behind Manpower) temporary-employment agency? A return to traditional employment patterns. Luckily, there's no danger of that now that companies use temps during high-demand periods while keeping their own staffs lean and mean.

In 1994 Olsten's 1,200 offices provided over 435,000 temporary employees to more than 90,000 North American businesses and health care companies, supplying office and clerical workers, accountants and other professionals, and health care workers for hospitals and in-home care. Olsten also operates a clinical pharmacy network and conducts pre-employment and insurance medical exams through its ASB Meditest unit. As the company has grown, it has taken on the traditional role of a primary permanent employer, offering training programs and benefits.

Although most of Olsten's offices are company-owned, a number of operations in smaller, less-competitive markets are franchised or licensed.

Although Olsten is public, Stuart Olsten, son of founder William Olsten, remains active in company management, and family members own 23% of the company.

WHEN

In 1950, 31-year-old William Olsten found his niche in the postwar boom by recognizing that businesses needed office workers to fill in for absent permanent workers (or to work in vacant positions until they were filled).

In a time when clerical work had been ceded to women, who left the work force in droves after the war, clerical workers were hard to get. Olsten, in partnership with his brother-in-law, combed the streets of suburban New York, recruiting women in their neighborhoods for temp work, which may have been more palatable to husbands who did not want their wives "really" working. At the same time, Olsten applied his unorthodox marketing methods (circulating cars and trucks with signs or loudspeaker announcements) to finding business clients.

"Temping" was a fixture by the beginning of the 1960s, when Olsten's Temporary Office Personnel began to expand through franchising, with an office in Chicago. By 1965 the company had 20 offices in 9 states. In the 1960s, Olsten began to expand the services its temps offered, from clerical and secretarial work into the professions, such as engineering. The company's name was changed in 1967 to The Olsten Corporation.

In the late 1960s Olsten caught the diversification bug, buying two medical laboratories, Rush Laboratories (1969) and Path-Tek Laboratories (1970).

Olsten expanded steadily in the 1970s, helped by the recessions, the flood of baby boomers into the labor force, and the ever-changing nature of employment in the US. Also during the 1970s, as medical technology (and expenses) surged, the company began its involvement with the medical staffing industry, particularly home health care, which is much less expensive than hospital or nursing home care. This segment began growing even more rapidly in the 1980s and now represents more than 50% of company sales. Medicare/Medicaid payments have thus become a significant source of revenue to the company.

The temp industry experienced explosive growth in the 1980s and began to consolidate, with a few giants swallowing up small local operations and penetrating the suburban and rural areas to which many businesses had begun moving.

Olsten expanded its health care services through a number of acquisitions in the late 1980s and early 1990s, including CarePlus (1989) and Upjohn HealthCare Services (1990).

William Olsten stepped down from management in 1990 and died in 1991. He was succeeded by Frank Liguori.

Olsten suffered in the recession of the late 1980s and early 1990s, and in 1990 the recession and the costs of the Upjohn acquisition reduced earnings. The company recovered with the economy in 1992 but was thrown for a loss by the expenses associated with its largest merger ever, with Lifetime Corporation. This acquisition made Olsten the largest home health care provider in North America and more than doubled its size. In 1994, Olsten bought part of a Mexican staffing company, now named Olsten STAFF S.A.

NYSE symbol: OLS
Fiscal year ends: Sunday nearest December 31

WHO

Chairman and CEO: Frank N. Liguori, age 47, $1,121,154 pay
VC and President: Stuart Olsten, age 42, $449,519 pay
EVP; President, Olsten Kimberly QualityCare: Robert A. Fusco, age 43, $452,390 pay
EVP; President, Olsten Staffing Services: Richard A. Piske III, age 45, $320,433 pay
EVP: Gerald J. Kapalko, age 47, $234,846 pay
SVP and General Counsel: William P. Costantini, age 46
SVP Finance and Treasurer: Anthony J. Puglisi, age 44
SVP Human Resources: Martin Gelerman, age 58
Auditors: Coopers & Lybrand

WHERE

HQ: 175 Broad Hollow Rd., Melville, NY 11747
Phone: 516-844-7800
Fax: 516-844-7022

Olsten operates company-owned, franchised, and licensed offices in the US, Canada, and the UK under the names Olsten Kimberly QualityCare, Olsten Staffing Services, and Office Angels.

WHAT

	1993 Sales		1993 Pretax Income	
	$ mil.	% of total	$ mil.	% of total
Health care	1,278	59	48	—
Staffing services	883	41	28	—
Corporate & other	(3)	—	(74)	—
Total	**2,158**	**100**	**2**	**—**

Operating Units
ASB Meditest
Office Angels
Olsten Kimberly QualityCare
Olsten Professional Accounting Services
Olsten Staffing Services

KEY COMPETITORS

Adia
Administaff
BankTemps
Barrett Business Services
Career Horizons
Hospital Staffing Services
Interim Services
Kelly Services
MacTemps
Manpower
Norrell
Payroll Transfers
Robert Half International
Staff Builders
Staff Leasing
Vincam

HOW MUCH

	Annual Growth	1984	1985	1986	1987	1988	1989	1990	1991	1992	1993
Sales ($ mil.)	29.0%	219	263	314	410	516	580	623	844	987	2,158
Net income ($ mil.)	—	6	7	9	13	17	18	12	15	21	(12)
Income as % of sales	—	2.7%	2.8%	3.0%	3.2%	3.4%	3.1%	2.0%	1.7%	2.1%	—
Earnings per share ($)	—	0.26	0.32	0.40	0.57	0.75	0.78	0.53	0.62	0.87	(0.30)
Stock price – high ($)	—	3.25	7.38	11.17	16.13	16.28	15.59	11.76	16.68	26.85	32.00
Stock price – low ($)	—	2.17	2.90	6.92	7.27	10.07	10.67	5.17	7.17	15.67	22.00
Stock price – close ($)	29.3%	2.90	7.27	8.46	11.40	12.01	11.17	8.00	16.34	26.68	29.38
P/E – high	—	13	23	28	28	22	20	22	27	31	—
P/E – low	—	8	9	17	13	13	14	10	12	18	—
Dividends per share ($)	19.0%	0.05	0.06	0.07	0.09	0.11	0.15	0.16	0.16	0.19	0.24
Book value per share ($)	18.8%	1.59	1.85	2.19	2.66	3.32	3.98	4.34	4.82	6.86	7.52
Employees	10.1%	—	—	—	—	273,700	327,170	338,500	343,275	391,375	443,600

1993 Year-end:
Debt ratio: 36.9%
Return on equity: —
Cash (mil.): $25
Current ratio: 2.46
Long-term debt (mil.): $176
No. of shares (mil.): 40
Dividends
  Yield: 0.8%
  Payout: —
Market value (mil.): $1,189

Stock Price History High/Low 1984–93

ADIA S.A.

OVERVIEW

Adia is one of the largest temporary-employment agencies in the world and, along with the US's Manpower, one of the few that truly operates internationally. The Swiss company has operations on 5 continents and is thus capable of providing services to its clients on a worldwide contract basis.

Adia was founded by accountant Henri-Ferdinand Lavanchy in 1957 when a client asked him to find someone to fill a job. Adia began its international expansion with an office in Belgium in 1961. After opening several European offices in the 1960s, it entered the US in 1972. In 1979, when Adia went public in Switzerland, Lavanchy retired from active management. Martin Pestalozzi, his successor, stepped up the international expansion through acquisitions. In 1984 the US operation, Adia Services, went public and began its own series of purchases.

In 1989 Adia's managers sold about 50% of the company to Omni, a holding company controlled by Swiss financier Werner Ray. In 1991, his empire in trouble, Ray tried to sell his 53% interest in Adia but was thwarted by Adia management (who own a significant interest in the company). Ray then disappeared and in 1992 was tracked down in the Bahamas, where he remains. Omni's liquidators approved the sale of Ray's interest in Adia to Asko Deutsche Kaufhaus (a retailer) and Swiss investor Klaus Jacobs in 1991, and Pestalozzi's management group was ousted. In 1993 Jacobs bought out Asko's interest.

Since then Adia has reorganized, selling noncore operations, cutting costs, and improving its computer system. In 1995 Adia bought out its US investors, despite a shareholder suit, reprivatizing Adia Services. Although the parent company is based in Switzerland, Adia Services, which runs the worldwide employment business, operates from the US.

WHO

Chairman: Klaus J. Jacobs
CEO; CEO, Adia Services (US): John P. Bowmer
President, European Operations: Manfred K. Atzert
CFO; CFO, Adia Services (US): Jon H. Rowbery
VP Worldwide Quality and Human Resources: Barbara LaTour
Auditors: Revisuisse Price Waterhouse

WHERE

HQ: CH-1261 Chéserex, Switzerland
Phone: +41-2-269-1222   **Fax:** +41-21-323-9217
US HQ: Adia Services, Inc., 64 Willow Place, Menlo Park, CA 94025
Phone: 415-610-1000   **Fax:** 415-610-1076

	1993 Sales	
	$ mil.	% of total
Europe	943.7	45
North America	942.5	45
Other countries	210.8	10
Total	**2,097.0**	**100**

WHAT

Selected Operations
Accountants on Call (US)
Adia Financial Services Ltd. (Cayman Islands)
Adia Financial Services N.V. (Curaçao)
Aktie 68 (the Netherlands)
Alfred Marks Bureau Ltd. (Ireland)
Centacom Staff (Australia)
FirstWord (US)
Jon & Associates (Australia)
Lee Hecht Harrison Ltd. (UK)
Nursefinders (US)
Quick Medical Service (France)
Staffinders (US)
Task Force Group PLC (UK)
West Personnel (US)

KEY COMPETITORS

Alternative Resources
Bis
Career Horizons
Kelly Services
MacTemps
Manpower
Norrell
Olsten
Vendex

HOW MUCH

Principal exchange: Zurich FY ends: December 31	5-Year Growth	1988	1989	1990	1991	1992	1993
Sales ($ mil.)	(8.8%)	3,319.9	2,578.4	3,221.1	2,371.4	2,191.3	2,097.0
Net income ($ mil.)	—	135.9	130.4	90.6	18.4	(149.5)	(85.7)
Income as % of sales	—	4.1%	5.1%	2.8%	0.8%	—	—
Earnings per share ($)	—	9.76	57.32	39.57	7.26	(35.74)	(13.10)
Stock price – high ($)	—	1,350.77	1,336.60	1,385.72	642.62	282.54	133.33
Stock price – low ($)	—	726.45	1,060.70	498.31	239.23	104.47	56.90
Stock price – close ($)	(36.8%)	1,266.03	1,128.40	607.53	259.75	116.34	127.75
P/E – high	—	138	23	35	89	—	—
P/E – low	—	74	19	13	33	—	—
Dividends per share ($)	(100.0%)	10.58	14.07	17.02	0.00	0.00	0.00
Book value per share ($)	(2.79%)	38.28	118.88	144.12	66.52	2.53	33.75
Employees	102.2%	212,900	—	—	—	—	430,478

1993 Year-end:
Debt ratio: 64.8%
Return on equity: —
Cash (mil.): $103.1
Current ratio: 1.39
Long-term debt (mil.): $316.6
No. of shares (mil.): 6.5
Dividends
  Yield: —
  Payout: —
Market value (mil.): $836.8

Note: Financial data converted to US $ using year-end exchange rates.

MACTEMPS, INC.

OVERVIEW

According to John Chuang, if you're a technowhiz, you don't need a job, you need an agent. You need — MacTemps. Although by no means the largest temporary-help agency in the US, MacTemps is one of the fastest-growing companies in the field. This is because MacTemps uses people with highly specialized computer skills and offers a 110% guarantee of satisfaction to its customers.

MacTemps got its start in 1986 when Harvard undergraduates John Chuang, Steve Kapner, and Mia Wenjen pooled their meager resources to buy a printer for their own use, with the idea of charging other students to use it along with the computers that they each owned personally. Even combined, their resources were insufficient to buy the laser printer they desired, and they had to have 8 cosigners on their $5,000 loan. They set up the equipment in a Harvard Square storefront, provided desktop publishing services under the name Laser Designs, and began raking in the cash. That year sales were over $55,000.

With the business booming, the 3 began exploring methods of expansion and, rejecting the idea of opening more locations, decided to take advantage of their access to computer-literate people (some of their self-service clientele) and open a temporary-help agency in 1987. In 1988 the company opened an office in New York. Renamed MacTemps (because of its early specialization in Macintoshes) in 1992, the company continued expanding nationally and by 1994 had 22 offices in the US and one in London. MacTemps plans to open more offices in Europe and to increase its penetration in the US by opening new offices in cities where offices are already operating.

After graduation Kapner and Wenjen left the business (their combined interest in MacTemps is 18%). Chuang (who owns the other 82%) stayed on, running the business while attending Harvard Business School.

MacTemps is different from many of its competitors in the skills it requires of its employees. Unlike many agencies, it does not hire people and train them but rather uses testing to eliminate the unqualified. MacTemps, like other large temporary agencies, offers vacation and health benefits to its employees based on the number of hours worked annually.

WHO

Chairman, President, and CEO: John Chuang, age 29
VP Finance: Nunzio Domilici
VP Marketing: Jae Ho Synn
VP Operations (HR): Michael Smith

WHERE

HQ: 66 Church St., Cambridge, MA 02138
Phone: 617-868-6800   **Fax:** 617-868-6820

1993 Offices
Atlanta
Boston
Chicago
Cleveland
Dallas
Denver
Detroit
Houston
London
Los Angeles
Miami
Minneapolis
New York
Orange County (CA)
Philadelphia
Phoenix
Rochelle Park (NJ)
San Diego
San Francisco
Santa Clara (CA)
Seattle
Stamford (CT)
Washington, DC

WHAT

Selected Employment Categories

Design and Production
Desktop publishing
Graphic design
Illustration
Pre-press technology
Production management

Technical Support
Help desk
Installations
LAN administration
PC/MAC specialties
Upgrades

KEY COMPETITORS

Adia Services
Alternative Resources
Bis
Career Horizons
Interim Services
Kelly Services
Manpower
Norrell
Olsten
Registry
Source Services
Vendex

HOW MUCH

Private company FY ends: December 31	5-Year Growth	1989	1990	1991	1992	1993	1994
Sales ($ mil.)	54.3%	4.8	9.2	13.0	20.5	29.1	42.0
Employees	33.8%	1,381	2,282	3,267	4,491	5,221	5,927

HOOVER'S MASTERLIST OF AMERICA'S TOP 2,500 EMPLOYERS   31

OTHER TEMPORARY EMPLOYMENT AGENCIES

ACCUSTAFF INCORPORATED
6440 Atlantic Blvd.　　　　　　　Phone: 904-725-5574
Jacksonville, FL 32211　　　　　Fax: 904-725-8513
Pres & CEO: Derek E. Dewan
HR Mgr: Andrea Giggetts
For Branch Office Locations, call: 800-852-2281
General office personnel to businesses, professional & service organizations & government agencies

ROBERT HALF INTERNATIONAL INC.
2884 Sand Hill Rd., Ste. 200　　Phone: 415-854-9700
Menlo Park, CA 94025　　　　　Fax: 415-854-9735
Chm & CEO: Harold M. Messmer, Jr.
Dir HR: Susan Rhodes
For Branch Office Locations, call: 800-804-8367
Accounting & finance personnel

CAREER HORIZONS, INC.
177 Crossways Park Dr.　　　　Phone: 516-496-2300
Woodbury, NY 11797　　　　　Fax: 516-496-3167
Pres & CEO: Joel B. Miller
No Central Personnel Officer
For Branch Office Locations, call: 516-496-2300
General office personnel

STAFF BUILDERS INC.
1981 Marcus Ave.　　　　　　　Phone: 516-358-1000
Lake Success, NY 11042　　　　Fax: 516-358-1036
Chm & Pres: Stephen Savitsky
VP HR: Don Ramsey
For Branch Office Locations, call: 800-852-8273
General office personnel

INTERIM SERVICES INC.
2050 Spectrum Blvd.　　　　　Phone: 305-938-7600
Fort Lauderdale, FL 33309　　Fax: 305-938-7780
Pres & CEO: Raymond Marcy
VP Admin (HR): Thomas L. Mirgon
For Branch Office Locations, call: 305-938-7600
General office personnel

TAD RESOURCES INTERNATIONAL, INC.
639 Massachussetts Ave.　　　Phone: 617-868-1650
Cambridge, MA 02139　　　　Fax: 617-492-1432
Pres: David J. McGrath
No Central Personnel Officer
For Branch Office Locations, call: 800-767-5776
Technical & engineering personnel

NORRELL CORPORATION
3535 Piedmont Rd. NE　　　　Phone: 404-240-3000
Atlanta, GA 30305　　　　　　Fax: 404-240-3312
Pres & CEO: C. Douglas Miller
VP HR: Linda B. Arnold
For Branch Office Locations, call: 800-274-1431
General office personnel

VOLT INFORMATION SCIENCES, INC.
1133 Sixth Ave., 19th Fl.　　　Phone: 212-704-2400
New York, NY 10036　　　　　Fax: 212-704-2424
Chm, Pres & CEO: William Shaw
VP HR: Norma Kraus
For Branch Office Locations, call: 800-292-0120
Engineering, design, data processing, scientific & technical support personnel

PAYROLL TRANSFERS, INC.
3710 Corporex Dr., Ste. 300　　Phone: 813-664-0404
Tampa, FL 33619　　　　　　　Fax: 813-621-6816
Pres: Marc Moore
Dir HR: Cynthia Klinghoffer
For Branch Office Locations, call: 800-343-5099
General office personnel

WESTERN STAFF SERVICES, INC.
301 & 303 Lennon Ln.　　　　　Phone: 510-930-5300
Walnut Creek, CA 94598-2453　Fax: 510-952-2525
Chm & CEO: W. Robert Stover
Mgr HR: Randy Zierfuss
For Branch Office Locations, call: 510-930-5300
Clerical, light industrial & medical personnel

HOOVER'S MASTERLIST OF AMERICA'S TOP 2,500 EMPLOYERS

A LIST LOVER'S COMPENDIUM

Top 500 Companies by Employees in *Hoover's MasterList of America's Top 2,500 Employers*

Rank	Company	Number of Employees	Rank	Company	Number of Employees
1	General Motors Corporation	710,800	51	The Great Atlantic & Pacific Tea Company, Inc.	94,000
2	United States Postal Service	691,723	52	Little Caesar Enterprises, Inc.	92,000
3	Wal-Mart Stores, Inc.	528,000	53	The Goodyear Tire & Rubber Company	91,754
4	PepsiCo, Inc.	423,000	54	Exxon Corporation	91,000
5	Sears, Roebuck and Co.	359,000	55	Beverly Enterprises, Inc.	89,000
6	Kmart Corporation	344,000	56	Borg-Warner Security Corporation	87,000
7	Ford Motor Company	322,213	57	AlliedSignal Inc.	86,400
8	AT&T Corporation	308,700	58	Minnesota Mining and Manufacturing Company	86,016
9	United Parcel Service of America, Inc.	286,000	59	Kaiser Foundation Health Plan, Inc.	84,885
10	IBM	256,207	60	UAL Corporation	83,400
11	General Electric Company	222,000	61	ConAgra, Inc.	83,000
12	J. C. Penney Company, Inc.	193,000	62	H&R Block, Inc.	82,800
13	The Kroger Co.	190,000	63	Publix Super Markets, Inc.	82,000
14	Dayton Hudson Corporation	174,000	64	Johnson & Johnson	81,600
15	Philip Morris Companies Inc.	173,000	65	Citicorp	81,500
16	McDonald's Corporation	169,000	66	GM Hughes Electronics Corporation	78,000
17	United Technologies Corporation	168,600	67	NYNEX Corporation	76,200
18	Lockheed Martin Corporation	163,700	68	Albertson's, Inc.	75,000
19	Marriott International, Inc.	163,440	69	Tenneco Inc.	75,000
20	Sara Lee Corporation	146,000	70	Emerson Electric Co.	73,900
21	Blue Cross and Blue Shield Association	135,883	71	Bell Atlantic Corporation	73,600
22	University of California	131,661	72	Arthur Andersen & Co, S.C.	72,722
23	Columbia/HCA Healthcare Corporation	131,600	73	WMX Technologies, Inc.	72,600
24	ARAMARK Corporation	131,000	74	Army & Air Force Exchange Service	72,562
25	Chrysler Corporation	128,000	75	International Paper Company	72,500
26	American Stores Company	127,000	76	KPMG Peat Marwick L.L.P.	72,000
27	The Boeing Company	123,000	77	Rockwell International Corporation	71,891
28	Flagstar Companies, Inc.	123,000	78	Delta Air Lines, Inc.	71,412
29	General Mills, Inc.	121,290	79	The University of Texas System	71,109
30	Motorola, Inc.	120,000	80	Cargill, Incorporated	70,700
31	AMR Corporation	118,900	81	McDonnell Douglas Corporation	70,016
32	GTE Corporation	117,446	82	Electronic Data Systems Corporation	70,000
33	E.I. du Pont de Nemours and Company	114,000	83	Federated Department Stores, Inc.	67,300
34	The May Department Stores Company	113,000	84	Ameritech Corporation	67,192
35	Winn-Dixie Stores, Inc.	112,000	85	RJR Nabisco, Inc.	66,500
36	Melville Corporation	111,082	86	Humana Inc.	65,800
37	Woolworth Corporation	111,000	87	Coopers & Lybrand L.L.P.	65,500
38	Eastman Kodak Company	110,400	88	Food Lion, Inc.	65,494
39	Safeway Inc.	105,900	89	The Travelers Inc.	65,000
40	The Prudential Insurance Company of America	105,534	90	The Walt Disney Company	65,000
			91	Halliburton Company	64,700
			92	American Express Company	64,654
41	Westinghouse Electric Corporation	101,654	93	State Farm Mutual Automobile Insurance Company	64,520
42	Federal Express Corporation	101,000			
43	Hewlett-Packard Company	98,400	94	Raytheon Company	63,800
44	ITT Corporation	98,000	95	Ernst & Young LLP	63,500
45	The Limited, Inc.	97,500	96	Aluminum Company of America	63,400
46	Xerox Corporation	97,000	97	V. F. Corporation	62,000
47	The Procter & Gamble Company	96,500	98	Walgreen Co.	62,000
48	BankAmerica Corporation	96,428	99	Mobil Corporation	61,900
49	BellSouth Corporation	95,084	100	TRW Inc.	61,200
50	Digital Equipment Corporation	94,200			

Top 500 Companies by Employees in *Hoover's MasterList of America's Top 2,500 Employers* (continued)

Rank	Company	Number of Employees	Rank	Company	Number of Employees
101	U S WEST, Inc.	60,778	151	The Gap, Inc.	44,000
102	Baxter International Inc.	60,400	152	Northwest Airlines Corporation	43,358
103	American Financial Corporation	60,350	153	Anheuser-Busch Companies, Inc.	43,345
104	Pacific Telesis Group	60,050	154	Continental Airlines Holdings, Inc.	43,100
105	Meijer, Inc.	60,000	155	Eckerd Corporation	43,000
106	SBC Communications, Inc.	59,400	156	Hilton Hotels Corporation	43,000
107	Texas Instruments Incorporated	59,048	157	Wendy's International, Inc.	43,000
108	NationsBank Corporation	57,463	158	Aetna Life and Casualty Company	42,600
109	Textron Inc.	56,000	159	SUPERVALU Inc.	42,500
110	Tyson Foods, Inc.	55,800	160	Kimberly-Clark Corporation	42,131
111	The Dow Chemical Company	55,436	161	Tandy Corporation	42,000
112	Metropolitan Life Insurance Company	55,000	162	Borden, Inc.	41,900
113	Toys "R" Us, Inc.	55,000	163	Merrill Lynch & Co., Inc.	41,900
114	Johnson Controls, Inc.	54,800	164	Ogden Corporation	41,800
115	Seagate Technology, Inc.	53,000	165	Chemical Banking Corporation	41,567
116	Honeywell Inc.	52,300	166	Carlson Companies, Inc.	41,000
117	Hyatt Corporation	52,275	167	Pfizer Inc.	40,500
118	American Home Products Corporation	51,399	168	Price/Costco, Inc.	40,000
119	Montgomery Ward Holding Corp.	51,350	169	Fluor Corporation	39,807
120	CIGNA Corporation	50,600	170	Whirlpool Corporation	39,590
121	The Home Depot, Inc.	50,600	171	Consolidated Freightways, Inc.	39,100
122	Caterpillar Inc.	50,443	172	CPC International Inc.	39,000
123	National Medical Enterprises, Inc.	50,423	173	American Standard Companies, Inc.	38,500
124	The Dun & Bradstreet Corporation	50,400	174	Hillhaven Corporation	38,100
125	Price Waterhouse LLP	50,122	175	Eaton Corporation	38,000
126	Georgia-Pacific Corporation	50,000	176	The United States Shoe Corporation	38,000
127	Sprint Corporation	50,000	177	Ryder System, Inc.	37,949
128	Time Warner Inc.	50,000	178	The Black & Decker Corporation	37,300
129	Abbott Laboratories	49,659	179	The University of Michigan	37,013
130	Bristol-Myers Squibb Company	49,500	180	ABM Industries Incorporated	37,000
131	Cooper Industries, Inc.	49,500	181	Browning-Ferris Industries, Inc.	37,000
132	The Allstate Corporation	49,000	182	Weyerhaeuser Company	36,748
133	Unisys Corporation	49,000	183	American Greetings Corporation	36,600
134	USAir Group, Inc.	48,500	184	Gannett Co., Inc.	36,500
135	Schlumberger NV	48,000	185	Levi Strauss Associates Inc.	36,400
136	State University of New York	47,964	186	MCI Communications Corporation	36,235
137	Chevron Corporation	47,576	187	Dana Corporation	36,000
138	Union Pacific Corporation	47,126	188	The TJX Companies, Inc.	36,000
139	Merck & Co., Inc.	47,100	189	H. J. Heinz Company	35,700
140	CSX Corporation	47,063	190	Dillard Department Stores, Inc.	35,536
141	Pinkerton's Security & Investigation Services	47,000	191	Ingersoll-Rand Company	35,143
142	National Association of Securities Dealers, Inc.	46,900	192	Fruit of the Loom, Inc.	35,000
			193	James River Corporation of Virginia	35,000
143	American Brands, Inc.	46,660	194	Norwest Corporation	35,000
144	Roadway Services, Inc.	46,600	195	Tennessee Restaurant Co.	35,000
145	Amoco Corporation	46,317	196	Warner-Lambert Company	35,000
			197	Yellow Corporation	35,000
146	Banc One Corporation	45,300	198	Deere & Company	34,252
147	Dole Food Company, Inc.	45,300	199	The Chase Manhattan Corporation	34,000
148	Chiquita Brands International, Inc.	45,000	200	The Coca-Cola Company	34,000
149	Masco Corporation	45,000			
150	Campbell Soup Company	44,378			

Top 500 Companies by Employees in *Hoover's MasterList of America's Top 2,500 Employers* (continued)

Rank	Company	Number of Employees	Rank	Company	Number of Employees
201	Corning Incorporated	34,000	251	Harris Corporation	28,300
202	W. R. Grace & Co.	34,000	252	Colgate-Palmolive Company	28,000
203	The Gillette Company	33,400	253	Pathmark Stores, Inc.	28,000
204	American Automobile Association	33,000	254	The Marmon Group, Inc.	27,700
205	American International Group, Inc.	33,000	255	Rite Aid Corporation	27,364
206	HealthTrust, Inc., The Hospital Company	33,000	256	Loews Corporation	27,100
207	Morrison Restaurants, Inc.	33,000	257	Aon Corporation	27,000
208	Nordstrom, Inc.	33,000	258	Mars, Inc.	27,000
209	Wackenhut Corporation	33,000	259	The Times Mirror Company	26,936
210	First Union Corporation	32,861	260	AMP Incorporated	26,900
211	Eli Lilly and Company	32,700	261	Scott Paper Company	26,900
212	Loral Corporation	32,600	262	Parker Hannifin Corporation	26,730
213	Nationwide Insurance Enterprise	32,583	263	First Interstate Bancorp	26,589
214	Pitney Bowes Inc.	32,539	264	Dean Witter, Discover & Co.	26,564
215	Texaco Inc.	32,514	265	Coca-Cola Enterprises Inc.	26,500
216	The Southland Corporation	32,406	266	Bruno's, Inc.	26,486
217	R.R. Donnelley & Sons Company	32,100	267	Foodmaker, Inc.	26,170
218	EG&G, Inc.	32,000	268	Andrew Corporation	26,118
219	Ralston Purina Group	31,703	269	Trans World Airlines, Inc.	26,100
220	Ashland, Inc.	31,600	270	DHL Worldwide Express	26,000
221	PPG Industries, Inc.	31,400	271	Fleet Financial Group, Inc.	26,000
222	Cox Enterprises, Inc.	31,000	272	SYSCO Corporation	26,000
223	ServiceMaster L.P.	31,000	273	Dresser Industries, Inc.	25,926
224	Burlington Northern Inc.	30,502	274	The Penn Traffic Company	25,800
225	General Dynamics Corporation	30,500	275	Marsh & McLennan Companies, Inc.	25,600
226	Monsanto Company	30,019	276	Conrail, Inc.	25,406
227	Hy-Vee Food Stores, Inc.	30,000	277	Champion International Corporation	25,250
228	Mercantile Stores Company, Inc.	30,000	278	Atlantic Richfield Company	25,100
229	Northrop Grumman Corporation	30,000	279	The Dial Corp.	25,025
230	Shoney's, Inc.	30,000	280	American Red Cross	25,000
231	The Stop & Shop Companies, Inc.	30,000	281	Fred Meyer, Inc.	25,000
232	Thrifty PayLess Inc.	30,000	282	Universal Corporation	25,000
233	The Vons Companies, Inc.	30,000	283	Giant Food Inc.	24,500
234	KeyCorp	29,983	284	Mercy Health Services	24,362
235	Avon Products, Inc.	29,800	285	Edison Brothers Stores, Inc.	24,200
236	The Ohio State University	29,576	286	Shaw Industries, Inc.	24,200
237	Intel Corporation	29,500	287	Manor Care, Inc.	24,100
238	Bechtel Group, Inc.	29,400	288	Host Marriott Corporation	24,000
239	Norfolk Southern Corporation	29,304	289	National Railroad Passenger Corporation	24,000
240	IBP, Inc.	29,200	290	Premark International, Inc.	24,000
241	Brinker International, Inc.	29,000	291	Tele-Communications, Inc.	24,000
242	Litton Industries, Inc.	29,000	292	Tyco International Ltd.	24,000
243	Reynolds Metals Company	29,000	293	Bob Evans Farms, Inc.	23,800
244	Stone Container Corporation	29,000	294	Burlington Industries, Inc.	23,800
245	Owens-Illinois, Inc.	28,900	295	Circuit City Stores, Inc.	23,625
246	Lowe's Companies, Inc.	28,843	296	Cummins Engine Company, Inc.	23,600
247	The Southern Company	28,743	297	MacAndrews & Forbes Holdings Inc.	23,500
248	The University of Wisconsin System	28,606	298	National Semiconductor Corporation	23,400
249	Computer Sciences Corporation	28,600	299	Fleming Companies, Inc.	23,300
250	Alco Standard Corporation	28,500	300	The Promus Companies Incorporated	23,100

Top 500 Companies by Employees in *Hoover's MasterList of America's Top 2,500 Employers* (continued)

Rank	Company	Number of Employees	Rank	Company	Number of Employees
301	The Anschutz Corporation	23,000	351	Delaware North Companies Inc.	20,000
302	Broadway Stores Inc.	23,000	352	Domino's Pizza, Inc.	20,000
303	McDermott International, Inc.	23,000	353	Knight-Ridder, Inc.	20,000
304	Pacific Gas and Electric Company	23,000	354	Metromedia Company	20,000
305	Service Merchandise Company, Inc.	22,879	355	RGIS Inventory Specialists	20,000
306	Pittston Services Group	22,800	356	University of Illinois	20,000
307	The University of Iowa	22,410	357	The University of Maryland System	20,000
308	Shell Oil Company	22,212	358	National City Corporation	19,960
309	National Service Industries, Inc.	22,200	359	Occidental Petroleum Corporation	19,860
310	Zenith Electronics Corporation	22,100	360	H. E. Butt Grocery Company	19,772
311	Ames Department Stores, Inc.	22,000	361	The Mead Corporation	19,600
312	Automatic Data Processing, Inc.	22,000	362	SunTrust Banks, Inc.	19,532
313	Berkshire Hathaway Inc.	22,000	363	Family Restaurants Inc.	19,513
314	Brown Group, Inc.	22,000	364	Petrie Retail, Inc.	19,500
315	DynCorp	22,000	365	Phillips Petroleum Company	19,400
316	Integrated Health Services, Inc.	22,000	366	First Data Corporation	19,300
317	Liberty Mutual Insurance Group	22,000	367	The Unicom Corporation	19,265
318	Navy Exchange System	22,000	368	Capital Cities/ABC, Inc.	19,250
319	USX Corporation - Marathon Group	21,914	369	Bally Entertainment Corporation	19,200
320	Cracker Barrel Old Country Store, Inc.	21,796	370	Union Camp Corporation	19,126
321	Mayo Foundation	21,770	371	Ruddick Corporation	19,090
322	Schering-Plough Corporation	21,600	372	Advance Publications, Inc.	19,000
323	USX Corporation - Delhi Group	21,527	373	Illinois Tool Works Inc.	19,000
324	USX Corporation - U.S. Steel Group	21,527	374	ShopKo Stores, Inc.	19,000
325	Hills Department Stores, Inc.	21,500	375	Smith's Food & Drug Centers, Inc.	19,000
326	University of Florida	21,404	376	The Texas A&M University System	19,000
327	Mellon Bank Corporation	21,400	377	Waban, Inc.	19,000
328	Crown Cork & Seal Company, Inc.	21,254	378	The Stanley Works	18,988
329	PNC Bank Corporation	21,100	379	Southern Pacific Rail Corporation	18,982
330	Wegmans Food Markets Inc.	21,100	380	Tennessee Valley Authority	18,974
331	Armstrong World Industries, Inc.	21,000	381	Barnett Banks, Inc.	18,649
332	Caldor Corporation	21,000	382	Bank of Boston Corporation	18,644
333	Caterair International Corp.	21,000	383	Becton, Dickinson and Company	18,600
334	Genuine Parts Co.	21,000	384	The Upjohn Company	18,600
335	KinderCare Learning Centers, Inc.	21,000	385	The Grand Union Holdings Corporation	18,500
336	Mattel, Inc.	21,000	386	Read-Rite Corporation	18,472
337	Teledyne, Inc.	21,000	387	Lear Seating Corporation	18,470
338	Maytag Corporation	20,951	388	Circus Circus Enterprises, Inc.	18,400
339	Wells Fargo & Company	20,800	389	Holy Cross Health System	18,360
340	Harcourt General, Inc.	20,742	390	Duke Power Company	18,274
341	Bethlehem Steel Corporation	20,700	391	University of Minnesota	18,212
342	FMC Corporation	20,696	392	The Freeman Companies	18,205
343	Echlin Inc.	20,600	393	Long John Silver's Restaurants, Inc.	18,100
344	Dover Corporation	20,500	394	Payless Cashways Inc.	18,100
345	Office Depot, Inc.	20,400	395	Eastman Chemical Company	18,043
346	Springs Industries, Inc.	20,300	396	Belk Stores Services, Inc.	18,000
347	The Quaker Oats Company	20,200	397	Brunswick Corporation	18,000
348	INTERCO Incorporated	20,045	398	Consolidated Stores Corporation	18,000
349	American Electric Power Company, Inc.	20,007	399	Hechinger Company	18,000
350	The Circle K Corporation	20,000	400	Intermountain Health Care, Inc.	18,000

Top 500 Companies by Employees in *Hoover's MasterList of America's Top 2,500 Employers* (continued)

Rank	Company	Number of Employees	Rank	Company	Number of Employees
401	Lefrak Organization Inc.	18,000	451	Rust International Inc.	16,000
402	Life Care Centers of America	18,000	452	Sizzler International, Inc.	16,000
403	Revco D.S., Inc.	18,000	453	Venture Stores, Inc.	16,000
404	WestPoint Stevens, Inc.	18,000	454	Vishay Intertechnology, Inc.	16,000
405	NBD Bancorp, Inc.	17,836	455	Weis Markets, Inc.	16,000
406	Carson Pirie Scott & Co.	17,800	456	The Timken Company	15,985
407	Living Centers of America, Inc.	17,800	457	TRINOVA Corporation	15,923
408	Steelcase Inc.	17,800	458	USAA	15,905
409	Deluxe Corporation	17,748	459	Bausch & Lomb Incorporated	15,900
410	Interpublic Group of Companies, Inc.	17,600	460	Family Dollar Stores, Inc.	15,900
411	Consolidated Edison Company of New York, Inc.	17,586	461	OrNda HealthCorp	15,900
412	Viacom Inc.	17,500	462	Avery Dennison Corporation	15,750
413	Catholic Healthcare West Inc.	17,451	463	Mercy Health System	15,739
414	The Johns Hopkins University Inc.	17,397	464	AutoZone, Inc.	15,700
415	Boise Cascade Corporation	17,362	465	Horizon Healthcare Corporation	15,700
416	First Chicago Corporation	17,355	466	The LTV Corporation	15,700
417	CNA Financial Corporation	17,200	467	McGraw-Hill, Inc.	15,661
418	The Sherwin-Williams Company	17,200	468	Carnival Corporation	15,650
419	SCEcorp	17,193	469	The Bank of New York Company, Inc.	15,621
420	New York Life Insurance Company	17,169	470	Allina Health System	15,600
421	Mirage Resorts, Incorporated	17,100	471	Longs Drug Stores Corporation	15,600
422	The University of Missouri System	17,060	472	Science Applications International Corporation	15,600
423	Great Western Financial Corporation	17,029	473	Wachovia Corporation	15,531
424	American Retail Group, Inc.	17,000	474	Continental Grain Company	15,500
425	Hannaford Bros. Co. Inc.	17,000	475	Regis Corporation	15,500
426	JMB Realty Corporation	17,000	476	Kellwood Company	15,400
427	University of Southern California	17,000	477	Strawbridge & Clothier	15,298
428	Household International, Inc.	16,900	478	Microsoft Corporation	15,257
429	Case Corporation	16,892	479	Best Buy Co., Inc.	15,200
430	Airborne Freight Corporation	16,800	480	Charming Shoppes, Inc.	15,200
431	Wang Laboratories, Inc.	16,792	481	J.P. Morgan & Co. Incorporated	15,193
432	Praxair, Inc.	16,766	482	Southwest Airlines Co.	15,175
433	E-Systems, Inc.	16,700	483	Edward J. DeBartolo Corporation	15,000
434	Entergy Corporation	16,679	484	Emory University Inc.	15,000
435	Jefferson Smurfit Corporation	16,600	485	Gates Corporation	15,000
436	Russell Corporation	16,594	486	The Hearst Corporation	15,000
437	Health Care and Retirement Corporation	16,500	487	Newell Co.	15,000
438	John Hancock Mutual Life Insurance Company	16,500	488	Schottenstein Stores Corporation	15,000
			489	Temple-Inland Inc.	15,000
439	Sonoco Products Company	16,472	490	Trump Organization	15,000
440	Deloitte & Touche	16,310	491	The University of Alabama	15,000
			492	Western Atlas, Inc.	15,000
441	The Coastal Corporation	16,300	493	Merry-Go-Round Enterprises, Inc.	14,970
442	Heritage Media Corporation	16,300	494	The University of Tennessee	14,967
443	Federal-Mogul Corporation	16,200	495	Kohl's Corporation	14,900
444	Inland Steel Industries, Inc.	16,200	496	The Pep Boys - Manny, Moe & Jack	14,895
445	Owens-Corning Fiberglass Corporation	16,200	497	Whitman Corporation	14,868
446	Kellogg Company	16,151	498	ALLTEL Corporation	14,864
447	SSM Health Care System Inc.	16,051	499	Phelps Dodge Corporation	14,799
448	Arvin Industries, Inc.	16,000	500	Barnes & Noble, Inc.	14,700
449	Fleetwood Enterprises, Inc.	16,000		Cincinnati Bell Inc.	14,700
450	Manville Corporation	16,000		Trinity Industries, Inc.	14,700
				VICORP Restaurants, Inc.	14,700

Top 500 Companies by One-Year Absolute Employee Growth in Hoover's MasterList of America's Top 2,500 Employers

Rank	Company	Absolute Growth	Rank	Company	Absolute Growth
1	Wal-Mart Stores, Inc.	94,000	51	Tracor Inc.	5,500
2	PepsiCo, Inc.	51,000	52	Tyson Foods, Inc.	5,442
3	Lockheed Martin Corporation	35,300	53	Browning-Ferris Industries, Inc.	5,400
4	The Travelers Inc.	35,000	54	WMX Technologies, Inc.	5,400
5	United Parcel Service of America, Inc.	19,000	55	Discovery Zone, Inc.	5,333
6	Wegmans Food Markets Inc.	14,700	56	MCI Communications Corporation	5,271
7	Motorola, Inc.	13,000	57	American Greetings Corporation	5,200
8	Banc One Corporation	12,600	58	Ernst & Young LLP	5,123
9	Viacom Inc.	12,500	59	Alco Standard Corporation	5,000
10	Aon Corporation	12,000	60	The Gap, Inc.	5,000
11	Philip Morris Companies Inc.	12,000	61	Tandy Corporation	5,000
12	The Home Depot, Inc.	11,700	62	V. F. Corporation	5,000
13	Integrated Health Services, Inc.	11,100	63	Circus Circus Enterprises, Inc.	4,936
14	Meijer, Inc.	10,000	64	Mirage Resorts, Incorporated	4,900
15	Seagate Technology, Inc.	10,000	65	Outback Steakhouse, Inc.	4,850
16	ServiceMaster L.P.	9,900	66	Doubletree Corporation	4,809
17	General Mills, Inc.	9,789	67	GTI Corporation	4,806
18	First Union Corporation	9,402	68	Bob Evans Farms, Inc.	4,800
19	Rust International Inc.	9,200	69	Continental Airlines Holdings, Inc.	4,800
20	Office Depot, Inc.	9,100	70	Michaels Stores, Inc.	4,730
21	Publix Super Markets, Inc.	9,000	71	Florida Progress Corporation	4,723
22	Merck & Co., Inc.	8,700	72	Johnson Controls, Inc.	4,700
23	Yellow Corporation	8,200	73	Quorum Health Group, Inc.	4,700
24	Loral Corporation	8,100	74	The Prudential Insurance Company of America	4,534
25	Read-Rite Corporation	8,024	75	Stant Corporation	4,500
26	Sara Lee Corporation	8,000	76	Walgreen Co.	4,300
27	National Association of Securities Dealers, Inc.	7,800	77	Regency Health Services, Inc.	4,268
28	H. E. Butt Grocery Company	7,772	78	Entergy Corporation	4,222
29	Roadway Services, Inc.	7,600	79	Albertson's, Inc.	4,000
30	Lowe's Companies, Inc.	7,574	80	Cole National Corporation	4,000
31	HEALTHSOUTH Corporation	7,319	81	Dayton Hudson Corporation	4,000
32	ARAMARK Corporation	7,000	82	Insignia Financial Group Inc.	4,000
33	Flagstar Companies, Inc.	7,000	83	Pinkerton's Security & Investigation Services	4,000
34	Winn-Dixie Stores, Inc.	7,000	84	Foodmaker, Inc.	3,985
35	Circuit City Stores, Inc.	6,990	85	Lear Seating Corporation	3,970
36	Horizon Healthcare Corporation	6,700	86	Wang Laboratories, Inc.	3,942
37	NationsBank Corporation	6,635	87	FMR Corporation	3,900
38	Checkers Drive-In Restaurants, Inc.	6,575	88	Fruit of the Loom, Inc.	3,900
39	Genesis Health Ventures, Inc.	6,500	89	Carson Pirie Scott & Co.	3,800
40	Proffitt's, Inc.	6,400	90	Grand Casinos, Inc.	3,800
41	Arthur Andersen & Co, S.C.	6,244	91	Southwest Airlines Co.	3,778
42	Federal Express Corporation	6,000	92	NovaCare, Inc.	3,762
43	Little Caesar Enterprises, Inc.	6,000	93	Cracker Barrel Old Country Store, Inc.	3,761
44	Mattel, Inc.	6,000	94	State Farm Mutual Automobile Insurance Company	3,752
45	Norwest Corporation	6,000	95	Cyprus Amax Minerals Company	3,750
46	Time Warner Inc.	6,000	96	Service Corporation International	3,702
47	Food Lion, Inc.	5,773	97	Harsco Corporation	3,700
48	Best Buy Co., Inc.	5,600	98	Intel Corporation	3,700
49	OrNda HealthCorp	5,600	99	DAKA International, Inc.	3,653
50	Enterprise Rent-A-Car Co.	5,500	100	Pitney Bowes Inc.	3,581

Top 500 Companies by One-Year Absolute Employee Growth in Hoover's MasterList of America's Top 2,500 Employers (continued)

Rank	Company	Absolute Growth	Rank	Company	Absolute Growth
101	Novell, Inc.	3,579	151	Furr's Supermarkets, Inc.	2,400
102	Mariner Health Group, Inc.	3,530	152	Cardinal Health, Inc.	2,300
103	Household International, Inc.	3,503	153	Dollar General Corporation	2,300
104	Cincinnati Bell Inc.	3,500	154	Emerson Electric Co.	2,300
105	RJR Nabisco, Inc.	3,500	155	Gaylord Entertainment Co.	2,300
106	Dillard Department Stores, Inc.	3,404	156	Cincinnati Milacron Inc.	2,292
107	Boyd Gaming Corporation	3,400	157	Southwest Gas Corporation	2,291
108	Buffets, Inc.	3,400	158	Freeport-McMoRan Copper & Gold Inc.	2,287
109	Mellon Bank Corporation	3,400	159	Gates Corporation	2,270
110	Newell Co.	3,400	160	McGraw-Hill, Inc.	2,268
111	PETsMART, Inc.	3,400	161	ConAgra, Inc.	2,213
112	Jefferson-Pilot Corporation	3,350	162	"21" International Holdings, Inc.	2,200
113	Hooper Holmes, Inc.	3,311	163	Applebee's International, Inc.	2,200
114	PNC Bank Corporation	3,300	164	Bell Atlantic Corporation	2,200
115	Oracle Systems Corporation	3,253	165	DynCorp	2,200
116	Allegheny Power System, Inc.	3,200	166	Harnischfeger Industries Incorporated	2,200
117	Boomtown, Inc.	3,067	167	Hewlett-Packard Company	2,200
118	UNC Inc.	3,047	168	Levi Strauss Associates Inc.	2,200
119	Bruno's, Inc.	3,032	169	Main St. & Main, Inc.	2,200
120	Peter Kiewit Sons', Inc.	3,020	170	OfficeMax, Inc.	2,200
121	Sun Healthcare Group, Inc.	3,010	171	Titan Wheel International, Inc.	2,200
122	Charming Shoppes, Inc.	3,000	172	American Medical Response, Inc.	2,168
123	Liberty Mutual Insurance Group	3,000	173	Allmerica Property & Casualty Companies, Inc.	2,130
124	McDonald's Corporation	3,000	174	Medaphis Corporation	2,109
125	The Stop & Shop Companies, Inc.	3,000	175	Trinity Industries, Inc.	2,100
126	The TJX Companies, Inc.	3,000	176	Vencor, Inc.	2,045
127	The Walt Disney Company	3,000	177	Kaiser Foundation Health Plan, Inc.	2,027
128	Alberto-Culver Company	2,900	178	Value Health, Inc.	2,012
129	Corning Incorporated	2,900	179	The Charles Schwab Corporation	2,000
130	The New York Times Company	2,900	180	Community Health Systems, Inc.	2,000
131	Mohawk Industries, Inc.	2,886	181	Consolidated Stores Corporation	2,000
132	Command Security Corporation	2,800	182	Echlin Inc.	2,000
133	The Coca-Cola Company	2,700	183	Fleetwood Enterprises, Inc.	2,000
134	Eckerd Corporation	2,700	184	The Goldman Sachs Group, LP	2,000
135	FHP International Corporation	2,700	185	The Hearst Corporation	2,000
136	Heilig-Meyers Co.	2,686	186	Hilton Hotels Corporation	2,000
137	Charter Medical Corporation	2,600	187	The May Department Stores Company	2,000
138	Computer Sciences Corporation	2,600	188	Musicland Group Inc.	2,000
139	Genuine Parts Co.	2,600	189	Petrie Retail, Inc.	2,000
140	John Hancock Mutual Life Insurance Company	2,597	190	Tele-Communications, Inc.	2,000
141	CoreStates Financial Corporation	2,544	191	Textron Inc.	2,000
142	Nabors Industries, Inc.	2,532	192	Weis Markets, Inc.	2,000
143	American Standard Companies, Inc.	2,500	193	AST Research, Inc.	1,991
144	AutoZone, Inc.	2,500	194	ALLTEL Corporation	1,988
145	Burlington Coat Factory Warehouse Corporation	2,500	195	Diagnostek, Inc.	1,970
146	The Gillette Company	2,500	196	Schneider National Inc.	1,950
147	Hannaford Bros. Co. Inc.	2,500	197	Strawbridge & Clothier	1,945
148	PhyCor, Inc.	2,500	198	LDDS Communications, Inc.	1,939
149	Shaw Industries, Inc.	2,494	199	Arrow Electronics, Inc.	1,938
150	Megafoods Stores, Inc.	2,422	200	Keane, Inc.	1,937

Top 500 Companies by One-Year Absolute Employee Growth in Hoover's MasterList of America's Top 2,500 Employers (continued)

Rank	Company	Absolute Growth	Rank	Company	Absolute Growth
201	Centex Corporation	1,930	251	Abbott Laboratories	1,541
202	Masco Corporation	1,900	252	AnnTaylor Stores Corporation	1,540
203	Omnicom Group Inc.	1,900	253	Caremark International, Inc.	1,530
204	Casino America, Inc.	1,875	254	The Pep Boys - Manny, Moe & Jack	1,504
205	Chemical Banking Corporation	1,870	255	Avnet, Inc.	1,500
206	AMC Entertainment Inc.	1,847	256	Davco Restaurants Inc.	1,500
207	AMP Incorporated	1,800	257	Dixie Yarns, Inc.	1,500
208	Federal-Mogul Corporation	1,800	258	Duchossois Industries, Inc.	1,500
209	Flying J Inc.	1,800	259	Fay's, Incorporated	1,500
210	Greyhound Lines, Inc.	1,800	260	Hasbro, Inc.	1,500
211	Merrill Lynch & Co., Inc.	1,800	261	Louisiana-Pacific Corporation	1,500
212	NIKE, Inc.	1,800	262	Modine Manufacturing Company	1,500
213	Pittston Services Group	1,800	263	Pentair, Inc.	1,500
214	Randalls Food Markets	1,800	264	Sensormatic Electronics Corporation	1,500
215	SYSCO Corporation	1,800	265	ShowBiz Pizza Time, Inc.	1,500
216	Waban, Inc.	1,800	266	Mountasia Entertainment International, Inc.	1,477
217	Whole Foods Market, Inc.	1,800	267	Primark Corporation	1,468
218	Booz, Allen & Hamilton Inc.	1,781	268	Gateway 2000 Inc.	1,463
219	Pediatric Services of America, Inc.	1,770	269	First Tennessee National Corporation	1,444
220	Applied Materials, Inc.	1,758	270	UNUM Corporation	1,440
221	Detroit Diesel Corporation	1,755	271	Exide Corporation	1,435
222	MBNA	1,753	272	MTS Inc.	1,431
223	Conseco, Inc.	1,750	273	MAXXAM Inc.	1,416
224	Franklin Resources, Inc.	1,736	274	Sanderson Farms, Inc.	1,413
225	Tosco Corporation	1,735	275	Cintas Corporation	1,411
226	Starbucks Corporation	1,732	276	The Continuum Company, Inc.	1,410
227	United HealthCare Corporation	1,702	277	WPL Holdings, Inc.	1,409
228	First Bank System, Inc.	1,700	278	American Studios, Inc.	1,400
229	Hills Department Stores, Inc.	1,700	279	Bausch & Lomb Incorporated	1,400
230	IBP, Inc.	1,700	280	First Fidelity Bancorporation	1,400
231	ICF Kaiser International, Inc.	1,700	281	Home Holdings Inc.	1,400
232	Kennametal Inc.	1,700	282	International Data Group	1,400
233	R.R. Donnelley & Sons Company	1,700	283	Stewart Enterprises, Inc.	1,400
234	Dover Corporation	1,673	284	Tandycrafts, Inc.	1,400
235	Casino Magic Corporation	1,650	285	Kansas City Southern Industries, Inc.	1,399
236	CompUSA Inc.	1,635	286	Schwegmann Giant Super Markets	1,374
237	Countrywide Credit Industries, Inc.	1,632	287	Cygne Designs Inc.	1,370
238	Russell Corporation	1,632	288	Dart Group Corporation	1,370
239	Weatherford International Incorporated	1,628	289	North American Mortgage Co.	1,350
240	Robbins & Myers, Inc.	1,611	290	Price Waterhouse LLP	1,341
241	Dean Foods Company	1,600	291	Supercuts, Inc.	1,340
242	Leggett & Platt, Inc.	1,600	292	First Security Corporation	1,331
243	Stater Bros. Holdings Inc.	1,600	293	Dell Computer Corporation	1,330
244	Vishay Intertechnology, Inc.	1,600	294	Paging Network, Inc.	1,330
245	ITT Educational Services, Inc.	1,597	295	Coastal Healthcare Group, Inc.	1,321
246	Ruddick Corporation	1,590	296	The Standard Products Co.	1,313
247	The Sports Authority, Inc.	1,587	297	American Freightways Corporation	1,309
248	Oregon Steel Mills, Inc.	1,571	298	Arnold Industries Inc.	1,300
249	Solectron Corporation	1,566	299	The Bombay Company, Inc.	1,300
250	USG Corporation	1,550	300	Freedom Newspapers Inc.	1,300

Top 500 Companies by One-Year Absolute Employee Growth in Hoover's MasterList of America's Top 2,500 Employers (continued)

Rank	Company	Absolute Growth	Rank	Company	Absolute Growth
301	IMC Global, Inc.	1,300	351	Fabri-Centers of America, Inc.	1,100
302	National Service Industries, Inc.	1,300	352	GranCare, Inc.	1,100
303	Swift Transportation Co., Inc.	1,300	353	Huntsman Chemical Corporation	1,100
304	Thermo Electron Corporation	1,300	354	Manor Care, Inc.	1,100
305	Willcox & Gibbs, Inc.	1,300	355	Perkins Family Restaurants, L.P.	1,100
306	York International Corporation	1,300	356	Tultex Corporation	1,100
307	Fluor Corporation	1,275	357	Res-Care, Inc.	1,094
308	Showboat, Inc.	1,270	358	Information Resources, Inc.	1,093
309	Bay Networks Inc.	1,264	359	Yucaipa Companies	1,091
310	PacifiCare Health Systems, Inc.	1,253	360	Papa John's International, Inc.	1,087
311	Ingram Industries Inc.	1,251	361	Union Pacific Corporation	1,087
312	Hale Halsell Co.	1,241	362	Parker Hannifin Corporation	1,084
313	USAA	1,238	363	Whirlpool Corporation	1,070
314	Alleghany Corporation	1,237	364	Thermo Instrument Systems Inc.	1,067
315	Ingles Markets, Incorporated	1,237	365	Meridian Bancorp, Inc.	1,064
316	The Penn Traffic Company	1,233	366	Players International Inc.	1,064
317	AGCO Corporation	1,216	367	Dentsply International Inc.	1,060
318	SCI Systems, Inc.	1,216	368	Merry-Go-Round Enterprises, Inc.	1,059
319	Ohio Edison Co.	1,214	369	K-III Communications Corporation	1,055
320	Old Dominion Freight Line, Inc.	1,205	370	Canandaigua Wine Company, Inc.	1,050
321	Children's Discovery Centers of America, Inc.	1,200	371	Fresh Choice, Inc.	1,050
322	Consolidated Freightways, Inc.	1,200	372	Multicare Cos Inc.	1,050
323	Holiday Cos.	1,200	373	Healthcare Services Group, Inc.	1,040
324	Illinois Tool Works Inc.	1,200	374	Cabletron Systems, Inc.	1,038
325	Morton International, Inc.	1,200	375	Ladd Furniture, Inc.	1,030
326	Revco D.S., Inc.	1,200	376	Safeskin Corporation	1,026
327	Rock Bottom Restaurants, Inc.	1,200	377	CSS Industries, Inc.	1,021
328	Rural/Metro Corporation	1,200	378	Sonic Corp.	1,017
329	Sports & Recreation, Inc.	1,200	379	State Street Boston Corporation	1,017
330	National City Corporation	1,194	380	Great Western Financial Corporation	1,013
331	CML Group, Inc.	1,193	381	Automatic Data Processing, Inc	1,000
332	Deere & Company	1,182	382	Big B, Inc.	1,000
333	VT Inc.	1,182	383	Brinker International, Inc.	1,000
334	Goody's Family Clothing, Inc.	1,175	384	Brunswick Corporation	1,000
335	Automotive Industries Holding, Inc.	1,167	385	Champion Enterprises, Inc.	1,000
336	Southern National Corporation	1,163	386	Club Corporation International	1,000
337	COMSAT Corporation	1,155	387	CPC International Inc.	1,000
338	Mayo Foundation	1,155	388	Dana Corporation	1,000
339	United States Banknote Corporation	1,155	389	Edward J. DeBartolo Corporation	1,000
340	Foamex International Inc.	1,135	390	FIserv, Inc.	1,000
341	Ameristar Casinos Inc.	1,127	391	Fisher Scientific International, Inc.	1,000
342	Newmont Gold Company	1,124	392	Fred Meyer, Inc.	1,000
343	GEICO Corporation	1,122	393	Great Lakes Chemical Corporation	1,000
344	National Health Laboratories, Inc.	1,110	394	Haworth, Inc.	1,000
345	First American Financial Corporation	1,109	395	Hechinger Company	1,000
346	Airborne Freight Corporation	1,100	396	Hendrick Automotive Group	1,000
347	AMSTED Industries Incorporated	1,100	397	Heritage Media Corporation	1,000
348	Coca-Cola Bottling Co. Consolidated	1,100	398	Host Marriott Corporation	1,000
349	CPI Corporation	1,100	399	J. C. Penney Company, Inc.	1,000
350	Eagle Hardware & Garden, Inc.	1,100	400	Pathmark Stores, Inc.	1,000

Top 500 Companies by One-Year Absolute Employee Growth in Hoover's MasterList of America's Top 2,500 Employers (continued)

Rank	Company	Absolute Growth	Rank	Company	Absolute Growth
401	Regis Corporation	1,000	451	American Eagle Outfitters, Inc.	837
402	Renco Group Inc.	1,000	452	Cirrus Logic, Inc.	836
403	Safeway Inc.	1,000	453	Fifth Third Bancorp	828
404	Shorewood Packaging Corporation	1,000	454	Microsoft Corporation	827
405	J.R. Simplot Company	1,000	455	Arkansas Best Corporation	826
406	Smith's Food & Drug Centers, Inc.	1,000	456	Octel Communications Corporation	826
407	Smithfield Foods, Inc.	1,000	457	J.P. Morgan & Co. Incorporated	825
408	St. Paul Companies, Inc.	1,000	458	M.S. Carriers, Inc.	823
409	TCF Financial Corporation	1,000	459	PACCAR Inc.	823
410	Teleflex Inc.	1,000	460	The Cherry Corporation	812
411	Wackenhut Corporation	1,000	461	Sportmart Inc.	806
412	Warner-Lambert Company	1,000	462	Catherines Stores Corporation	805
413	Wendy's International, Inc.	1,000	463	Tranzonic Companies	805
414	AMRESCO, Inc.	998	464	Airgas, Inc.	800
415	Cisco Systems, Inc.	992	465	Arbor Drugs, Inc.	800
416	J. Crew Group Inc.	987	466	Bed Bath & Beyond, Inc.	800
417	Celex Group Inc.	976	467	Continental Grain Company	800
418	Federal Signal Corporation	975	468	Dress Barn, Inc.	800
419	Rollins, Inc.	968	469	Drug Emporium, Inc.	800
420	Boatmen's Bancshares, Inc.	961	470	The Equitable Companies, Incorporated	800
421	Kohl's Corporation	960	471	Giant Food Inc.	800
422	Brown & Sharpe Manufacturing Company	957	472	Grow Group, Inc.	800
			473	H&R Block, Inc.	800
423	EMC Corporation	952	474	Interpublic Group of Companies, Inc.	800
424	G&K Services, Inc.	952	475	Jacobs Engineering Group Inc.	800
425	Michael Baker Corporation	949	476	Marsh Supermarkets, Inc.	800
426	Adelphia Communications Corporation	940	477	Paine Webber Group Inc.	800
427	The Gymboree Corporation	919	478	Prime Hospitality Corporation	800
428	MicroAge Computer Centers, Inc.	908	479	Sbarro, Inc.	800
429	Authentic Fitness Corporation	907	480	ShopKo Stores, Inc.	800
430	Sybase, Inc.	901	481	SouthTrust Corporation	800
431	AdvantageHEALTH Corporation	900	482	Stein Mart, Inc.	800
432	Aztar Corporation	900	483	Breed Technologies, Inc.	790
433	Excel Industries, Inc.	900	484	The Good Guys, Inc.	788
434	General Instrument Corporation	900	485	Healthcare America, Inc.	782
435	GTECH Holdings Corporation	900	486	Bertucci's Inc.	780
436	Healthsource, Inc.	900	487	Carnival Corporation	780
437	Western Atlas, Inc.	900	488	The Men's Wearhouse, Inc.	779
438	One Price Clothing Stores, Inc.	894	489	TNT Freightways Corporation	779
439	U. S. Bancorp	883	490	Pennzoil Company	776
440	Crown Cork & Seal Company, Inc.	876	491	Micro Warehouse, Inc.	775
441	Rock-Tenn Co.	874	492	CACI International Inc.	769
442	Bailey Corporation	873	493	Amgen Inc.	765
443	Guilford Mills, Inc.	871	494	Principal Financial Group	758
444	Innodata Corporation	869	495	IHOP Corporation	755
445	KeyCorp	866	496	Compuware Corporation	754
446	W. W. Grainger, Inc.	865	497	Apple South, Inc.	750
447	A. L. Pharma Inc.	860	498	Bergen Brunswig Corporation	750
448	Alexander & Baldwin, Inc.	850	499	NACCO Industries, Inc.	749
449	TPI Enterprises, Inc.	850	500	Ross Stores, Inc.	749
450	Applied Extrusion Technologies, Inc.	838			

Top 500 Companies by One-Year Percentage Employee Growth in Hoover's MasterList of America's Top 2,500 Employers

Rank	Company	Percentage of Growth	Rank	Company	Percentage of Growth
1	The Maxim Group, Inc.	900.0	51	Imperial Credit Industries, Inc.	170.7
2	Investment Technology Group, Inc.	885.7	52	Cardinal Health, Inc.	164.3
3	Cinema Ride, Inc.	850.0	53	Professional Sports Care Management, Inc.	163.8
4	Pediatric Services of America, Inc.	769.6	54	Allegheny Power System, Inc.	163.5
5	Discovery Zone, Inc.	695.3	55	Physicians Clinical Laboratory, Inc.	162.5
6	Jefferson-Pilot Corporation	670.0	56	Tracor Inc.	161.8
7	F & E Resource Systems Technology, Inc.	547.1	57	Sevenson Environmental Services Inc.	161.6
8	Mountasia Entertainment International, Inc.	547.0	58	Conseco, Inc.	157.7
9	Celex Group Inc.	545.3	59	Physician Reliance Network, Inc.	156.2
10	Alpine Group, Inc.	538.2	60	Venturian Corporation	155.7
11	Cygne Designs Inc.	489.3	61	Bell Microproducts Inc.	153.2
12	D.I.Y. Home Warehouse, Inc.	471.4	62	Grand Casinos, Inc.	152.0
13	BancFirst Corporation	447.9	63	Healthsource, Inc.	150.0
14	Commerce Bancorp, Inc.	447.5	64	Kendall-Jackson Winery Ltd.	150.0
15	United Wisconsin Services, Inc.	397.3	65	PerSeptive Biosystems, Inc.	149.6
16	Diagnostek, Inc.	371.7	66	Checkers Drive-In Restaurants, Inc.	148.6
17	Southwest Gas Corporation	353.0	67	PETsMART, Inc.	147.8
18	American Recreation Company Holdings, Inc.	345.8	68	International Family Entertainment, Inc.	147.1
19	ACC Corp.	340.0	69	Rational Software Corporation	146.7
20	Applied Extrusion Technologies, Inc.	319.8	70	Schwegmann Giant Super Markets	146.0
21	Cedar Group, Inc.	304.2	71	American Vanguard Corporation	144.4
22	Florida Progress Corporation	300.4	72	Herley Industries, Inc.	142.1
23	Boomtown, Inc.	296.9	73	The Whitlock Group	141.4
24	Tranzonic Companies	284.5	74	CAI Wireless Systems, Inc.	140.9
25	Proffitt's, Inc.	278.3	75	Megafoods Stores, Inc.	136.2
26	Ultrak, Inc.	272.7	76	Rust International Inc.	135.3
27	Robbins & Myers, Inc.	262.0	77	United Waste Systems, Inc.	135.0
28	The 3DO Company	256.8	78	DeSoto, Inc.	134.1
29	Diversified Communications Industries, Ltd.	250.0	79	Selas Corporation of America	133.3
30	Viacom Inc.	250.0	80	Weatherford International Incorporated	131.0
31	Network Imaging Corporation	242.7	81	PMR Corporation	130.6
32	Omega Environmental, Inc.	242.1	82	Option Care, Inc.	129.7
33	Littlefield, Adams & Co.	241.7	83	Spartech Corporation	128.6
34	Autotote Corporation	241.1	84	Homecare Management, Inc.	128.2
35	Softkey International Inc.	235.8	85	The Continuum Company, Inc.	127.1
36	Northland Cranberries, Inc.	233.5	86	Ventritex, Inc.	126.1
37	AMRESCO, Inc.	231.0	87	Software Technical Services, Inc.	125.8
38	Wegmans Food Markets Inc.	229.7	88	Vencor, Inc.	125.1
39	Main St. & Main, Inc.	215.7	89	Softmart, Inc.	125.0
40	Synetic, Inc.	211.4	90	American White Cross, Inc.	124.0
41	Authentic Fitness Corporation	204.7	91	Quorum Health Group, Inc.	123.7
42	People's Choice TV Corporation	193.1	92	America Online, Inc.	123.3
43	BitWise Designs, Inc.	185.0	93	Olympic Financial Ltd.	122.4
44	Value Health, Inc.	184.9	94	Outback Steakhouse, Inc.	121.3
45	Staodyn, Inc.	183.1	95	Players International Inc.	119.4
46	Stant Corporation	180.0	96	Dataware Technologies Inc.	117.4
47	Mariner Health Group, Inc.	179.2	97	Herbalife International, Inc.	117.0
48	ITT Educational Services, Inc.	177.4	98	Canandaigua Wine Company, Inc.	116.7
49	Tosco Corporation	174.5	99	The Travelers Inc.	116.7
50	Kitty Hawk, Inc.	172.0	100	Input/Output, Inc.	113.8

Top 500 Companies by One-Year Percentage Employee Growth in Hoover's MasterList of America's Top 2,500 Employers (continued)

Rank	Company	Percentage of Growth	Rank	Company	Percentage of Growth
101	Command Security Corporation	112.0	151	Cabot Medical Corporation	91.8
102	Supercuts, Inc.	111.8	152	Applebee's International, Inc.	91.7
103	Roosevelt Financial Group, Inc.	111.5	153	MicroAge Computer Centers, Inc.	91.5
104	Insignia Financial Group Inc.	111.1	154	Tucker Drilling Company, Inc.	91.5
105	Ameristar Casinos Inc.	110.4	155	Celtrix Pharmaceuticals, Inc.	91.4
106	Casino Magic Corporation	110.0	156	Unitel Video, Inc.	91.0
107	Graff Pay-Per-View Inc.	110.0	157	UNC Inc.	90.1
108	Microchip Technology, Incorporated	109.7	158	Casino America, Inc.	89.3
109	MASSBANK Corporation	109.2	159	Michaels Stores, Inc.	89.1
110	Semitool, Inc.	109.2	160	NCI Building Systems, Inc.	88.6
111	Rock Bottom Restaurants, Inc.	109.1	161	Empi, Inc.	88.3
112	Plains Resources Inc.	109.0	162	Miles Homes, Inc.	88.1
113	Micro Warehouse, Inc.	107.5	163	Cheyenne Software, Inc.	87.8
114	Papa John's International, Inc.	107.1	164	American Studios, Inc.	87.5
115	Oxford Health Plans, Inc.	106.9	165	ABS Industries, Inc.	86.8
116	Gateway 2000 Inc.	106.9	166	Ultimate Electronics, Inc.	86.6
117	AMBAC Inc.	106.7	167	Cirrus Logic, Inc.	85.9
118	GTI Corporation	105.7	168	Cerplex Group, Inc.	85.3
119	Oregon Steel Mills, Inc.	105.5	169	Eagle Hardware & Garden, Inc.	84.6
120	Enzon, Inc.	105.0	170	Interplay Productions Inc.	84.6
121	Pollo Tropical Inc.	104.1	171	Media Vision Technology Inc.	84.4
122	FTP Software, Inc.	104.0	172	New Image Industries Inc.	83.3
123	Medaphis Corporation	103.4	173	PhyCor, Inc.	83.3
124	Mylan Laboratories Inc.	103.3	174	Shorewood Packaging Corporation	83.3
125	Thermo Voltek Corporation	102.9	175	WesBanco, Inc.	83.2
126	Express Scripts, Inc.	102.9	176	CDW Computer Centers, Inc.	83.0
127	Rimage Corporation	102.5	177	Allmerica Property & Casualty Companies, Inc.	82.9
128	Integrated Health Services, Inc.	101.8	178	Silverado Foods, Inc.	82.7
129	National TechTeam, Inc.	101.3	179	Novell, Inc.	82.6
130	AGCO Corporation	101.2	180	Keane, Inc.	82.0
131	Quantum Health Resources, Inc.	101.2	181	Genesis Health Ventures, Inc.	81.3
132	HEALTHSOUTH Corporation	101.0	182	Plaza Home Mortgage Corporation	80.9
133	Castle Energy Corporation	101.0	183	Funco Inc.	80.6
134	Sofamor Danek Group, Inc.	101.0	184	Horizon Bancorp Inc.	80.6
135	Arnold Industries Inc.	100.0	185	Office Depot, Inc.	80.5
136	Spelling Entertainment Group, Inc.	100.0	186	Equity Residential Properties Trust	80.3
137	Atchison Casting Corporation	99.7	187	Aon Corporation	80.0
138	DS Bancor, Inc.	98.8	188	Pyxis Corporation	80.0
139	United States Banknote Corporation	97.9	189	Conso Products Company	80.0
140	American Medical Response, Inc.	97.7	190	Nabors Industries, Inc.	79.9
141	Fresh Choice, Inc.	97.2	191	LDDS Communications, Inc.	79.5
142	Delrina Corporation	96.4	192	Titan Wheel International, Inc.	78.6
143	Boca Research Inc.	96.2	193	Primark Corporation	78.5
144	Integrated Waste Services, Inc.	95.9	194	StrataCom Inc.	78.1
145	Berkshire Realty Co.	94.4	195	Breed Technologies, Inc.	77.9
146	Corrpro Cos Inc.	93.6	196	PC Connection	77.8
147	Cole National Corporation	93.0	197	Walker Richer & Quinn Inc.	77.8
148	Bailey Corporation	92.9	198	Urban Outfitters Inc.	77.7
149	PeopleSoft, Inc.	92.6	199	Celebrity, Inc.	77.2
150	C-COR Electronics, Inc.	92.4	200	Read-Rite Corporation	76.8

Top 500 Companies by One-Year Percentage Employee Growth in Hoover's MasterList of America's Top 2,500 Employers (continued)

Rank	Company	Percentage of Growth	Rank	Company	Percentage of Growth
201	Whole Foods Market, Inc.	76.6	251	EMC Corporation	63.5
202	Alpha-Beta Technology, Inc.	76.1	252	Merit Medical Systems, Inc.	63.3
203	Wall Data, Inc.	75.6	253	USA Waste Services, Inc.	62.5
204	Insituform Mid-America, Inc.	75.1	254	Norwood Promotional Products Inc.	62.3
205	Kimco Development Corporation	74.6	255	Brown & Sharpe Manufacturing Company	62.0
206	X-Rite, Inc.	74.5	256	J & J Snack Foods Corp.	61.9
207	Regency Health Services, Inc.	74.5	257	Sullivan Dental Products, Inc.	61.5
208	Horizon Healthcare Corporation	74.4	258	North American Mortgage Co.	61.4
209	Comverse Technology Inc.	74.0	259	Mark VII, Inc.	61.1
210	Franklin Resources, Inc.	73.4	260	Adelphia Communications Corporation	60.8
211	A-Mark Financial Corporation	73.3	261	Starbucks Corporation	60.7
212	Synopsys, Inc.	73.2	262	Sun Healthcare Group, Inc.	60.3
213	United States Filter Corporation	73.0	263	The BISYS Group, Inc.	60.0
214	Bay Networks Inc.	72.8	264	Diamond Multimedia Systems, Inc.	60.0
215	Fourth Shift Corporation	72.7	265	Mastech Systems Corporation	60.0
216	Willcox & Gibbs, Inc.	72.2	266	TELACU Industries	60.0
217	Future Healthcare Inc.	72.2	267	Heart Technology, Inc.	59.8
218	RadiSys Corporation	72.1	268	Falcon Products, Inc.	59.7
219	Special Devices, Inc.	72.1	269	Gupta Corporation	59.3
220	Three-Five Systems, Inc.	72.0	270	Thermedics Inc.	59.2
221	Arizona Instrument Corporation	71.6	271	CompUSA Inc.	59.1
222	Parametric Technology Corporation	71.2	272	Sanderson Farms, Inc.	58.8
223	Evergreen Media Corporation	70.6	273	Celgene Corporation	58.7
224	CFI ProServices, Inc.	70.6	274	ERC Industries, Inc.	58.7
225	Children's Discovery Centers of America, Inc.	70.6	275	RoTech Medical Corporation	58.6
226	COMSAT Corporation	70.2	276	RF Monolithics, Inc.	58.4
227	STERIS Corporation	70.1	277	Park-Ohio Industries, Inc.	58.3
228	Cisco Systems, Inc.	68.4	278	Best Buy Co., Inc.	58.3
229	Mohawk Industries, Inc.	68.3	279	Fossil, Inc.	58.1
230	RailTex, Inc.	68.2	280	United Meridian Corporation	58.1
231	Marvel Entertainment Group, Inc.	68.0	281	Besicorp Group Inc.	58.0
232	Avid Technology, Inc.	67.9	282	U.S. Robotics, Inc.	57.6
233	Renal Treatment Centers Inc.	67.8	283	Kentek Information Systems, Inc.	57.5
234	Fair, Isaac and Company, Incorporated	67.1	284	Devon Energy Corporation	56.9
235	Argosy Gaming Company	66.7	285	Pacific Sunwear of California, Inc.	56.8
236	Community Health Systems, Inc.	66.7	286	GulfMark International, Inc.	56.7
237	Data Transmission Network Corporation	66.7	287	Micronics Computers, Inc.	56.7
238	Sports & Recreation, Inc.	66.7	288	Right Management Consultants, Inc.	56.6
239	Damark International, Inc.	66.6	289	Greenwich Air Services Inc.	56.5
240	Intelcom Group, Inc.	66.0	290	Lowrance Electronics, Inc.	56.1
241	Safeskin Corporation	66.0	291	PLATINUM technology, inc.	55.9
242	Catherines Stores Corporation	65.2	292	Doubletree Corporation	55.7
243	Synercom Technology, Inc.	65.1	293	Callaway Golf Company	55.7
244	Natural Wonders, Inc.	65.0	294	Del Webb Corporation	55.6
245	H. E. Butt Grocery Company	64.8	295	Merrill Corporation	55.4
246	Enterprise Rent-A-Car Co.	64.7	296	Sybase, Inc.	55.4
247	MFS Communications Company, Inc.	63.9	297	Iwerks Entertainment Inc.	55.2
248	Agouron Pharmaceuticals, Inc.	63.6	298	CIBER, Inc.	54.9
249	Hometown Buffet Inc.	63.6	299	Lawson Associates, Inc.	54.7
250	Cyrix Corporation	63.6	300	Great American Management & Investment, Inc.	54.5

Top 500 Companies by One-Year Percentage Employee Growth in Hoover's MasterList of America's Top 2,500 Employers (continued)

Rank	Company	Percentage of Growth
301	OrNda HealthCorp	54.4
302	Jan Bell Marketing, Inc.	54.2
303	HUBCO, Inc.	54.2
304	PAXAR Corporation	54.0
305	Physician Corporation of America	53.9
306	Mercury Finance Co.	53.8
307	Sanifill, Inc.	53.8
308	Tandycrafts, Inc.	53.8
309	Intelligent Electronics, Inc.	53.8
310	AutoFinance Group, Inc.	53.6
311	Cyprus Amax Minerals Company	53.6
312	Mid Atlantic Medical Services Inc.	53.5
313	Business Records Corporation Holding Co.	53.5
314	Arrow Electronics, Inc.	53.4
315	Healthcare America, Inc.	53.3
316	Abaxis, Inc.	53.1
317	United American Healthcare Corporation	53.0
318	Jean Philippe Fragrances, Inc.	52.9
319	EZCORP, Inc.	52.8
320	Octel Communications Corporation	52.7
321	Solectron Corporation	52.6
322	Chronimed, Inc.	52.1
323	Chico's FAS, Inc.	52.0
324	Innodata Corporation	51.7
325	Boyd Gaming Corporation	51.5
326	Lam Research Corporation	51.4
327	Pioneer Group, Inc.	51.4
328	Detroit Diesel Corporation	50.9
329	Sodak Gaming, Inc.	50.7
330	QUALCOMM Incorporated	50.6
331	Island Lincoln-Mercury Inc.	50.5
332	Sport Supply Group, Inc.	50.5
333	Countrywide Credit Industries, Inc.	50.4
334	National RV Holdings Inc.	50.4
335	Capital Bancorp	50.3
336	LaserMaster Technologies, Inc.	50.3
337	Hamilton Financial Services Corporation	50.2
338	Cellstar Corporation	50.1
339	Home Theater Products International	50.0
340	LSI Industries Inc.	50.0
341	Orbit Semiconductor, Inc.	50.0
342	PRI Automation, Inc.	50.0
343	CSS Industries, Inc.	49.9
344	Paging Network, Inc.	49.8
345	Nathan's Famous, Inc.	49.2
346	"21" International Holdings, Inc.	48.9
347	Clear Channel Communications, Inc.	48.8
348	Quick & Reilly Group, Inc.	48.8
349	NovaCare, Inc.	48.5
350	RWD Technologies, Inc.	48.2

Rank	Company	Percentage of Growth
351	PacifiCare Health Systems, Inc.	48.1
352	Booz, Allen & Hamilton Inc.	48.1
353	Patrick Industries, Inc.	48.0
354	Random Access, Inc.	47.8
355	Advanced Polymer Systems, Inc.	47.6
356	Bugaboo Creek Steak House, Inc.	47.6
357	National Vision Associates Ltd.	47.6
358	Pico Products, Inc.	47.6
359	International Game Technology	47.5
360	Shoe Carnival, Inc.	47.4
361	Newmont Gold Company	47.3
362	VT Inc.	47.3
363	Pet Food Warehouse, Inc.	47.0
364	The Dwyer Group, Inc.	47.0
365	ServiceMaster L.P.	46.9
366	Tetra Tech, Inc.	46.8
367	Cliffs Drilling Company	46.6
368	Patterson Dental Company	46.6
369	Hooper Holmes, Inc.	46.1
370	Old Dominion Freight Line, Inc.	46.0
371	Freeport-McMoRan Copper & Gold Inc.	45.9
372	Oakwood Homes Corporation	45.7
373	VMARK Software, Inc.	45.7
374	Service Corporation International	45.6
375	Holiday RV Superstores, Inc.	45.6
376	A. L. Pharma Inc.	45.3
377	DM Management Company	45.3
378	Fretter, Inc.	45.2
379	Acclaim Entertainment, Inc.	45.1
380	Aaron Rents, Inc.	44.8
381	The Bombay Company, Inc.	44.8
382	MapInfo Corporation	44.8
383	The Charles Schwab Corporation	44.4
384	Deckers Outdoor Corporation	44.4
385	Rural/Metro Corporation	44.4
386	KLLM Transport Services, Inc.	44.3
387	AST Research, Inc.	44.2
388	Southern National Corporation	44.2
389	The Men's Wearhouse, Inc.	44.1
390	Falcon Systems Inc.	44.0
391	InaCom, Inc.	43.9
392	XTRA Corporation	43.8
393	Genetics Institute, Inc.	43.8
394	Accolade Inc.	43.8
395	Webster Financial Corporation	43.6
396	Datastorm Technologies Inc.	43.5
397	RehabCare Corporation	43.5
398	WPL Holdings, Inc.	43.5
399	IVAX Corporation	43.4
400	DIGICON	43.4

Top 500 Companies by One-Year Percentage Employee Growth in Hoover's MasterList of America's Top 2,500 Employers (continued)

Rank	Company	Percentage of Growth	Rank	Company	Percentage of Growth
401	FMR Corporation	43.3	451	Cabletron Systems, Inc.	39.5
402	Bachman Information Systems, Inc.	43.3	452	California Microwave, Inc.	39.5
403	Novellus Systems, Inc.	42.9	453	Healthwise of America, Inc.	39.5
404	Coastal Healthcare Group, Inc.	42.9	454	Progress Software Corporation	39.2
405	Black Hawk Gaming and Development Co., Inc.	42.9	455	Proxima Corporation	39.0
406	Maxco, Inc.	42.9	456	Chipcom Corporation	39.0
407	Salick Health Care, Inc.	42.9	457	Arctco, Inc.	38.9
408	The Gymboree Corporation	42.6	458	Stewart Enterprises, Inc.	38.9
409	ICF Kaiser International, Inc.	42.5	459	GBC Technologies, Inc.	38.6
410	United Video Satellite Group Inc.	42.5	460	Banc One Corporation	38.5
411	OTR Express Inc.	42.4	461	Cooker Restaurant Corporation	38.5
412	United States Cellular Corporation	42.4	462	Hyperion Software Corporation	38.4
413	Southern Energy Homes, Inc.	42.2	463	Medicine Shoppe International, Inc.	38.3
414	Franklin Quest Co.	42.2	464	U.S. Long Distance Corporation	38.2
415	Alamo Group, Inc.	42.1	465	Westcott Communications, Inc.	38.1
416	Circuit City Stores, Inc.	42.0	466	AirTran Corporation	38.0
417	Northrim Bank	41.9	467	First Mortgage Corporation	37.9
418	Howtek, Inc.	41.9	468	Anchor Gaming	37.9
419	System Software Associates, Inc.	41.7	469	M.S. Carriers, Inc.	37.8
420	Health-Mor Inc.	41.5	470	Gilead Sciences, Inc.	37.8
421	CDP Technologies, Inc.	41.4	471	Brock Control Systems, Inc.	37.8
422	D. R. Horton, Inc.	41.4	472	ECCS Inc.	37.7
423	Integon Corporation	41.4	473	Oasis Residential, Inc.	37.6
424	Cooper Development Company	41.4	474	Sensormatic Electronics Corporation	37.5
425	Thermo Instrument Systems Inc.	41.3	475	Cincinnati Milacron Inc.	37.4
426	AnnTaylor Stores Corporation	41.0	476	Showboat, Inc.	37.4
427	Artisoft, Inc.	40.8	477	Applied Materials, Inc.	37.1
428	Washington Homes, Inc.	40.7	478	Dial-A-Mattress Franchise Corporation	36.9
429	Spectrum Control, Inc.	40.7	479	Furr's Supermarkets, Inc.	36.9
430	Tandy Brands, Inc.	40.7	480	FourGen Software Inc.	36.9
431	ABT Building Products Corporation	40.7	481	Genetic Therapy, Inc.	36.8
432	Charter Medical Corporation	40.6	482	Circus Circus Enterprises, Inc.	36.7
433	Swift Transportation Co., Inc.	40.6	483	Pulte Corporation	36.6
434	Nextel Communications, Inc.	40.5	484	Energy West, Incorporated	36.5
435	SCIMED Life Systems, Inc.	40.5	485	Marquette Electronics, Inc.	36.4
436	BHC Communications, Inc.	40.5	486	INFOMART	36.4
437	Contel Cellular Inc.	40.3	487	Supercom, Inc.	36.4
438	Mirage Resorts, Incorporated	40.2	488	Redwood Empire Bancorp	36.0
439	First Union Corporation	40.1	489	American Freightways Corporation	35.8
440	Cerprobe Corporation	40.0	490	Adesa Corporation	35.7
441	Flying J Inc.	40.0	491	Champion Enterprises, Inc.	35.7
442	Grow Group, Inc.	40.0	492	DAKA International, Inc.	35.6
443	Mattel, Inc.	40.0	493	Lowe's Companies, Inc.	35.6
444	NAI Technologies, Inc.	40.0	494	Outlet Communications, Inc.	35.6
445	RF Power Products, Inc.	40.0	495	Dyersburg Fabrics Inc.	35.5
446	Stac Electronics	40.0	496	Fastenal Company	35.5
447	Tarrant Distributors Inc.	40.0	497	Platinum Software Corporation	35.5
448	TCF Financial Corporation	40.0	498	United HealthCare Corporation	35.5
449	Automotive Industries Holding, Inc.	39.8	499	Syntellect Inc.	35.4
450	Peter Kiewit Sons', Inc.	39.7	500	CITATION Computer Systems, Inc.	35.4

FORTUNE's 100 Fastest-Growing Companies

Rank	Company	3–5 Year Annual Sales Growth (%)	Business Description
1	Grow Biz International	285	Business services - franchiser of sports, toy, computer & CD disc consignment stores
2	Eagle Hardware & Garden	258	Building products - home improvement centers
3	Columbia/HCA Healthcare	240	Hospitals - for-profit hospitals & outpatient surgery centers
4	Discovery Zone	229	Leisure & recreational services - children's recreational centers
5	Castle Energy	215	Oil & gas - US exploration & production
6	Lone Star Steakhouse & Saloon	210	Retail - food & restaurants
7	Electronics for Imaging	189	Computers - color desktop publishing system
8	Tricord Systems	188	Computers - network servers
9	Avid Technology	183	Video equipment - digital editing systems
10	Newfield Exploration	183	Oil & gas - US exploration & production
11	Funco	179	Retail - video game stores
12	Wellfleet Communications	173	Computers - internetworking equipment
13	Health Systems International	165	Health care - comprehensive health care services; health & life insurance
14	GranCare	149	Health care - outpatient & home
15	Pages	147	Publishing - children's books, cassettes, video tapes & computer software; incentive/recognition awards
16	Xircom	145	Computers - network hardware
17	Aquila Gas Pipeline	142	Oil & gas - production & pipeline
18	Outback Steakhouse	139	Retail - Outback Steakhouse & Carrabba's Italian Grill restaurants
19	Regal Cinemas	138	Motion pictures - theaters
20	Tide West Oil	137	Oil & gas - US exploration & production
21	Hauser Chemical Research	133	Chemicals - anticancer chemicals, bulk pharmaceuticals & natural flavor ingredients
22	BE Aerospace	131	Aerospace - aircraft equipment
23	Dentsply International	131	Medical equipment - x-ray products
24	Gateway 2000	128	Computers - mail order microcomputers
25	WCT Communications	127	Telecommunications services - long distance services

FORTUNE's 100 Fastest-Growing Companies (continued)

Rank	Company	3-5 Year Annual Sales Growth (%)	Business Description
26	PeopleSoft	126	Computers - human resource systems software
27	Boston Chicken	124	Retail - restaurant operators & franchisers
28	Callaway Golf	124	Leisure & recreational products - golf clubs (Big Bertha)
29	Asanté Technologies	123	Computers - networking products
30	Wholesale Cellular USA	122	Telecommunications equipment
31	USA Waste Services	121	Pollution control equipment & services - solid waste management
32	NetFRAME Systems	118	Computers - network servers
33	Checkers Drive-In Restaurants	118	Retail - fast-food restaurants
34	Cisco Systems	116	Computers - internetworking hardware
35	Wall Data	115	Computers - software to connect PCs & mainframes
36	Roberts Pharmaceuticals	114	Drugs
37	Ashworth	114	Apparel - men's casual wear
38	Medisys	112	Healthcare - outpatient & home
39	Deckers Outdoor	112	Shoes & related apparel - sandals (Teva)
40	Primark	109	Diversified operations - leasing services; ground transport; mortgage banking
41	Papa John's International	106	Retail - pizza restaurants
42	Mesa Airlines	104	Transportation - airline
43	PLATINUM technology	102	Computers - database management software for mainframes
44	EZCORP	101	Financial - pawn shops (EZ Pawn)
45	Safeskin	99	Medical & dental supplies - hypoallergenic disposable latex gloves
46	Alternative Resources	97	Personnel - employment services to information processing centers
47	Future Now	97	Computers - turnkey microcomputer systems services
48	Parametric Technology	97	Computers - computer-aided design software
49	Santa Fe Pacific Gold	95	Gold mining & processing
50	Fresh America	95	Food - wholesale fruit & vegetables to Sam's Wholesale Club

FORTUNE's 100 Fastest-Growing Companies (continued)

Rank	Company	3–5 Year Annual Sales Growth (%)	Business Description
51	Synopsys	93	Computers - integrated circuit design software
52	Advance Ross	92	Pollution control equipment & services - electrostatic precipitator systems
53	CrossComm	92	Computers - internetworking equipment
54	Rio Hotel & Casino	92	Leisure & recreational services - hotels & casinos
55	Purepac	92	Drugs - generic
56	RHI Entertainment	91	Motion pictures & services
57	Megahertz	89	Computers - data & fax modems for portable computers; computer servers
58	American United Global	89	Computers - retail & wholesale
59	Integrated Circuit Systems	89	Electrical components - integrated circuits
60	LDDS Communications	88	Telecommunications services - #4 US long distance carrier
61	Sofamor/Danek Group	88	Medical products - spinal implant devices
63	Amgen	87	Biomedical & genetic products
63	Amtech	86	Telecommunications equipment - wireless electronic identification systems
64	PictureTel	86	Telecommunications equipment - video conferencing
65	PETsMART	82	Retail - pet supply superstores
66	Quantum Health Resources	82	Medical services - long-term in-home health care services
67	Auspex Systems	82	Computers - file servers
68	Encore Wire	82	Wire & cable products - copper electrical building wire & cable
69	Decora Industries	80	Chemicals - specialty
70	FTP Software	79	Computers - internetworking software
71	Rehability	79	Health care - outpatient & home
72	Video Lottery Technologies	78	Leisure & recreational products - video lottery terminals & on-line lottery systems
73	Leasing Solutions	76	Leasing - computers
74	In Home Health	76	Health care - outpatient & home
75	Actel	76	Electrical components - field programmable gate arrays

FORTUNE's 100 Fastest-Growing Companies (continued)

Rank	Company	3–5 Year Annual Sales Growth (%)	Business Description
76	Jean Philippe Fragrances	76	Cosmetics & toiletries
77	PhyCor	76	Hospitals
78	NYCOR	75	Machinery - rotary compressors & thermoelectric modules
79	Quorum Health Group	75	Hospitals & hospital management
80	Sodak Gaming	75	Leisure & recreational products - slot & gaming machines
81	Chipcom	74	Computers - hubs for networks
82	HS Resources	73	Oil & gas - US exploration & production
83	Physician Corp. of America	73	Health maintenance organization
84	Gupta	72	Computers - database management systems software
85	Artisoft	72	Computers - local area network software & hardware
86	Fresh Choice	71	Retail - self-service salad bar restaurants
87	Adams Resources & Energy	71	Oil & gas - production & pipeline
88	SynOptics Communications	70	Computers - local area network hub products & management systems
89	Chiron	70	Biomedical & genetic products - anticancer treatments, vaccines & blood diagnostics
90	Starbucks	69	Retail - coffee & other beverages
91	Gymboree	69	Retail - children's apparel & toys
92	Sun Healthcare Group	68	Nursing homes - Alzheimer's disease patient facilities
93	Sybase	68	Computers - database management software
94	Office Depot	68	Retail - office equipment & supplies
95	Express Scripts	68	Medical services - pharmacy benefit management
96	NovaCare	68	Medical services - hospital, outpatient & home therapy & rehabilitation services
97	Zoom Telephonics	68	Computers - modems for data & fax
98	Wellcare Management Group	67	Health maintenance organization
99	MAXXIM Medical	67	Medical products - physical therapy & pain management products
100	Trident Microsystems	67	Computers - peripheral equipment

Source: *FORTUNE*; August 8, 1994

Inc.'s 100 Fastest-Growing Small Public Companies

Rank	Company	Sales Growth 1989–93 (% Increase)	1993 Sales ($ thou.)	Business Description
1	Grow Biz International	20,704	51,803	Business services - franchiser of sports, toy, computer & CD disc consignment stores
2	Lone Star Steakhouse & Saloon	20,495	95,767	Retail - food & restaurants
3	PairGain Technologies	19,521	35,907	Telecommunications equipment - high-speed digital line technology
4	Xircom	12,706	82,212	Computers - network hardware
5	Avid Technology	12,375	112,900	Video equipment - digital editing systems
6	Excel Technology	9,867	30,000	Lasers - systems & components
7	Parallan Computer	9,788	21,952	Computers - network servers
8	Heart Technology	9,562	21,159	Medical products - drill for clogged arteries (Rotablator)
9	BroadBand Technologies	9,073	15,136	Fiber optics - R&D
10	Cheyenne Software	8,384	50,735	Computers - local area network software
11	Tricord Systems	7,077	80,024	Computers - network servers
12	Cellular Inc.	6,775	33,689	Telecommunications equipment - cellular telephone systems
13	Universal Electronics	6,527	89,001	Audio & video home products - remote control devices for TVs, VCRs & stereos
14	Wonderware	6,524	21,328	Computers - software for industrial automation
15	International Gaming Management	6,374	20,912	Leisure & recreational services
16	Wellfleet Communications	6,010	180,126	Computers - internetworking equipment
17	Pages Inc.	5,778	77,000	Publishing - children's books, cassettes, video tapes & computer software; incentive/recognition awards
18	Sodak Gaming	5,640	69,000	Leisure & recreational products - slot & gaming machines
19	Electronics for Imaging	5,270	89,526	Computers - color desktop publishing system
20	Stac Electronics	4,799	36,984	Computers - peripheral equipment & software
21	Vermont Teddy Bear	4,743	17,000	Toys - teddy bears
22	Medco Research	4,350	9,345	Medical services - cardiovascular drug research
23	Dura Pharmaceuticals	4,175	15,816	Drugs & medical products for respiratory health care
24	Value-Added Communications	4,082	66,500	Telecommunications services - automated call processing systems for institutions
25	Quickturn	4,016	54,865	Electrical components

Inc.'s 100 Fastest-Growing Small Public Companies (continued)

Rank	Company	Sales Growth 1989–93 (% Increase)	1993 Sales ($ thou.)	Business Description
26	Boston Chicken	3,882	42,530	Retail - restaurant operators & franchisers
27	Steris	3,682	26,662	Medical products - sterilizers for surgical equipment
28	NetFRAME Systems	3,654	66,935	Computers - network servers
29	QuickResponse Services	3,453	22,457	Business services - database management
30	PeopleSoft	3,029	58,191	Computers - human resource systems software
31	Hauser Chemical Research	2,629	59,268	Chemicals - anticancer chemicals, bulk pharmaceuticals & natural flavor ingredients
32	Mitek Surgical Products	2,597	21,277	Medical products - surgical implants
33	Wall Data	2,560	64,641	Computers - software to connect PCs & mainframes
34	DNX	2,433	23,000	Medical products & testing services
35	Callaway Golf	2,353	254,645	Leisure & recreational products - golf clubs (Big Bertha)
36	Education Alternatives	2,320	30,055	Consulting - public school management
37	Hollywood Entertainment	2,184	17,339	Retail - video rentals
38	Premiere Page	2,165	20,927	Telecommunications services - paging products & services
39	First Team Sports	2,134	38,244	Leisure & recreational products - in-line roller skates & related accessories
40	Snapple Beverage	2,087	516,005	Beverages - iced tea & fruit drinks
41	Applied Innovation	2,085	16,100	Telecommunications equipment - network management systems for telephone companies
42	Outback Steakhouse	2,083	271,164	Retail - Outback Steakhouse & Carrabba's Italian Grill restaurants, located in Florida & Texas
43	Monterey Pasta	2,052	5,379	Food - gourmet pasta
44	Medi-Mail	2,050	25,000	Drugs & sundries - mail order pharmaceuticals
45	Charter Golf	2,039	45,823	Leisure & recreational products - golf apparel
46	Brothers Gourmet Coffee	1,994	128,040	Food - coffee
47	Checkers Drive-In Restaurants	1,971	189,544	Retail - fast-food restaurants
48	Just Toys	1,949	42,568	Toys - games & hobby products
49	Cardiovascular Imaging Systems	1,771	8,082	Medical instruments - ultrasound imaging catheters
50	EcoScience	1,764	5,872	Chemicals - pesticides

Inc.'s 100 Fastest-Growing Small Public Companies (continued)

Rank	Company	Sales Growth 1989–93 (% Increase)	1993 Sales ($ thou.)	Business Description
51	Papa John's International	1,721	89,234	Retail - food & restaurants
52	Deckers Outdoor	1,691	57,086	Shoes & related apparel - sandals (Teva)
53	Merit Medical Systems	1,668	25,431	Medical products - disposable proprietary products for cardiology & radiology
54	Pollo Tropical	1,651	19,300	Retail - food & restaurants
55	VTel	1,546	31,452	Telecommunications equipment - multi-media conferencing systems
56	Sunbelt	1,546	58,092	Building products - retail & wholesale
57	Roberts Pharmaceutical	1,510	89,000	Drugs
58	Wind River Systems	1,488	25,053	Computers - real-time embedded applications software (WindPower)
59	MRV Communications	1,477	7,426	Electrical components - semiconductor laser diodes & light-emitting diodes for use with fiber optic systems
60	U.S. Long Distance	1,448	134,126	Telecommunications services - long-distance telephone service
61	Sulcus Computer	1,390	52,000	Computers - software
62	Synopsys	1,387	108,000	Computers - integrated circuit design software
63	Parametric Technology	1,379	163,088	Computers - computer-aided design software
64	U.S. Alcohol Testing of America	1,377	4,166	Medical instruments - blood-alcohol concentration measuring instruments
65	Safeskin	1,332	57,264	Medical & dental supplies - hypoallergenic disposable latex gloves
66	Level One Communications	1,326	25,984	Electronic components - transmission networking semiconductors
67	Mycogen	1,227	120,513	Biomedical & genetic products -biopesticides
68	Megahertz	1,225	53,496	Computers - data & fax modems for portable computers; computer servers
69	Alliance Semiconductor	1,204	22,238	Electrical components - high-speed SRAM memory semiconductors
70	Artisoft	1,173	84,642	Computers - local area network software and hardware
71	Dataware Technologies	1,138	19,328	Computers - retrieval software for CD-ROM applications
72	CrossComm	1,134	49,790	Computers - internetworking equipment
73	Natural Wonders	1,126	119,591	Retail - educational & scientific products
74	VISX	1,122	22,074	Lasers - nearsightedness treatment systems
75	Digidesign International	1,101	20,865	Electrical products - digital audio recording systems

Inc.'s 100 Fastest-Growing Small Public Companies (continued)

Rank	Company	Sales Growth 1989-93 (% Increase)	1993 Sales ($ thou.)	Business Description
76	Score Board	1,084	75,362	Leisure & recreational products - sports picture cards
77	PETsMART	1,081	187,900	Retail - pet supply superstores
78	Med/Waste	1,081	1,901	Disposal of hazardous medical waste
79	Future Healthcare	1,055	9,932	Medical services - clinical testing of drugs for pharmaceutical companies
80	Molecular Dynamics	1,047	38,100	Instruments - scientific
81	HS Resources	1,041	47,346	Oil & gas - US exploration & production
82	PLATINUM technology	1,037	62,165	Computers - database management software for mainframes
83	Biosys	988	9,589	Chemicals - specialty
84	Homecare Management	973	26,393	Health care - outpatient & home; pharmaceutical supplies
85	FTP Software	968	58,726	Computers - internetworking software
86	Data Race	961	43,932	Computers - high-speed modems
87	Trident Microsystems	951	77,726	Computers - peripheral equipment
88	Vestar	950	36,428	Drugs
89	Premier Anesthesia	947	92,500	Medical services
90	CliniCom	939	20,146	Computers - software
91	Intermedia Communications of Florida	924	8,000	Telecommunications services - alternative access telephone services
92	Network Computing Devices	894	144,265	Computers - workstations & terminals
93	Ultra Pac	888	27,572	Containers - paper & plastic
94	Amtech	888	59,424	Telecommunications equipment - wireless electronic identification systems
95	Uncle B's Bakery	886	4,711	Food - bagels
96	BitWise Designs	876	5,068	Computers - workstations for imaging marketplace; portable computers
97	Video Lottery Technologies	861	174,600	Leisure & recreational products - video lottery terminals & on-line lottery systems
98	PictureTel	847	176,252	Telecommunications equipment - video conferencing
99	Alpha 1 Biomedicals	835	1,375	Drugs
100	Leasing Solutions	833	50,818	Leasing - computers

Source: *Inc.*, May 1994

The 25 Largest Companies on *Inc.*'s 500 Fastest-Growing Private Companies List

Company	1993 Sales ($ thou.)	Sales Growth 1989-1993 (% increase)	Business Description
Ma Laboratories	248,785	6,771	Mfrs. & distr. computers & computer components
Melaleuca	206,828	1,121	Markets pharmaceuticals & personal-care & cleaning prods.
Cedar Computer Center	198,915	2,057	Retails computer equip.
Payroll Transfers	174,665	8,950	Provides temporary-employment contracting & leasing svcs.
I-Net	147,982	681	Provides network-integration, imaging & outsourcing svcs.
Insight Direct	131,633	997	Markets computers & computer prods.
Diamond Multimedia Systems	130,271	8,499	Designs, mfrs. & markets computer boards
Winner International	118,565	1,082	Mfrs. & distr. home-, auto- & personal-security devices
Viking Components	110,061	1,813	Mfrs. & distr. computer-memory prods.
Village Homes of Colorado	87,037	567	Provides home-building & residential-development svcs.
America II Electronics	75,906	8,615	Stocks & distr. wholesale integrated circuits semiconductors
American Harvest	72,047	1,674	Develops, mfrs. & markets kitchen appliances
Concept Automation	69,500	561	Integrates computer systs.
CompuTrend Systems	67,881	1,088	Mfrs. & distr. computer prods.
Enrich International	67,621	2,318	Distr. & sells herbal products
Kitty Hawk Group	65,779	687	Provides air-charter-mgmt. & air-cargo airline svcs.
Pampered Chef	65,310	1,760	Sells kitchen tools
Florida Infusion Services	62,809	1,271	Distr. pharmaceuticals & medical supplies
Bock Pharmacal Co.	58,468	621	Distr. & markets pharmaceutical prods.
Mid-Com Communications	56,623	11,385	Resells inbound & outbound long-distance svcs.
Nest Entertainment	55,130	1,197	Develops educational prods. for children
Alternative Resources	53,061	1,715	Provides personnel to information-process. centers
HazWaste Industries	50,455	939	Provides environmental consulting svcs.
Covey Leadership Center	48,516	645	Provides leadership-development training
Teltrust	47,699	1,600	Provides operator svcs. & public pay phones

Source: *Inc.*, October 1994

Business Week's 100 Best Small Companies

Rank	Company	3-YEAR AVERAGE GROWTH Sales (%)	Profits (%)	Return on Capital (%)	Business Description
1	Papa John's International	108.0	117.2	55.7	Retail - pizza restaurants
2	Deckers Outdoor	119.7	150.5	40.7	Shoes & related apparel - sandals (Teva)
3	Applied Innovation	118.7	139.8	40.6	Telecommunications equipment - network management systems
4	Barrett Business Services	55.9	144.3	50.2	Personnel - employee leasing & temporary help
5	Integracare	138.5	42.1	63.0	Health care - outpatient & home physical therapy
6	Brock Control Systems	38.3	127.7	70.7	Computers - software for sales force automation
7	K-Tel International	11.4	532.1	87.5	Music & video packaged consumer entertainment & convenience products
8	Wall Data	141.9	202.1	32.1	Computers - software to connect PCs & mainframes
9	FTP Software	72.2	44.3	61.8	Computers - internetworking software
10	Leasing Solutions	73.4	104.5	39.3	Leasing - computers
11	Davidson & Associates	86.1	37.1	51.4	Computers - educational & entertainment software
12	Supreme International	33.4	141.2	47.4	Apparel - men's & boys' sportswear
13	Chico's FAS	42.1	73.0	62.6	Retail - apparel & shoes
14	Lone Star Steakhouse & Saloon	190.8	230.8	27.6	Retail - food & restaurants
15	Gotham Apparel	55.2	73.5	50.1	Apparel
16	Sodak Gaming	94.3	51.6	43.6	Leisure & recreational products - slot & gaming machines
17	Checkmate Electronics	91.5	232.9	28.4	Optical character recognition - bar code readers
18	Interlinq Software	64.8	135.5	33.5	Computers - software
19	Asanté Technologies	166.2	26.5	44.4	Computers - networking products
20	Fossil	45.9	36.0	69.5	Precious metals & jewelry - fashion watches
21	Royal Grip	90.4	28.8	48.6	Leisure & recreational products
22	Netmanage	597.9	750.6	23.6	Computers - software
23	Express Scripts	62.5	68.4	41.1	Medical services - pharmacy benefit management
24	River Oaks Furniture	58.1	67.7	42.7	Furniture
25	M-Wave	33.3	102.4	46.4	Electrical components

Business Week's 100 Best Small Companies (continued)

Rank	Company	3-YEAR AVERAGE GROWTH Sales (%)	Profits (%)	Return on Capital (%)	Business Description
26	Landry's Seafood Restaurants	28.8	112.2	46.7	Retail - seafood restaurants in Texas & Louisiana
27	Amrion	60.3	211.3	29.0	Retail - mail-order vitamins & nutritional products
28	Gymboree	70.6	173.0	28.8	Retail - children's apparel & toys
29	Swing-N-Slide	52.1	36.7	49.7	Leisure & recreational products - playground equipment
30	Wonderware	126.7	184.0	25.8	Computers - software for industrial automation
31	Network Six	94.6	155.5	26.9	Computers - consulting & system integration services
32	Bestop	23.8	81.5	52.9	Automotive & trucking - soft tops for automobiles
33	Monaco Coach	38.2	11.8	65.2	Automotive - high-end RVs and motor homes
34	Triconex	48.2	132.8	30.8	Instruments - control
35	Pollo Tropical	81.0	119.8	27.2	Retail - food & restaurants
36	Seda Speciality Packaging	48.6	97.8	32.7	Plastics - packages & closures
37	Medical Diagnostics	17.2	118.5	40.1	Medical services - magnetic resonance imaging services
38	GBC Technologies	48.0	74.4	33.2	Computers - wholesale
39	Hollywood Entertainment	110.6	167.2	22.1	Retail - video rentals
40	Integrated Circuit Systems	113.8	204.1	20.6	Electrical components - integrated circuits
41	Daig	39.9	135.4	29.2	Medical products - minimally invasive surgical instruments
42	Champion Industries	3.8	65.7	51.1	Printing - business cards, multi-colored brochures & forms
43	Pinnacle Micro	52.6	32.2	38.1	Computers - optical storage drives
44	Healthdyne Technologies	25.8	32.0	52.8	Medical products
45	Bio-Dental Technologies	77.3	192.6	22.4	Dental equipment & services provided through catalogs & telemarketing
46	Cobra Golf	25.0	44.5	49.0	Leisure & recreational products - oversized golf clubs
47	National Techteam	41.0	352.2	24.4	Computers - services
48	Ultimate Electronics	29.7	100.5	34.3	Retail - consumer electronics in Colorado & Utah
49	Bollinger Industries	51.0	60.9	32.0	Leisure & recreational products - weight lifting equipment
50	Transmedia Network	71.5	102.5	25.8	Business services - restaurant discount membership cards

Business Week's 100 Best Small Companies (continued)

Rank	Company	3-YEAR AVERAGE GROWTH Sales (%)	Profits (%)	Return on Capital (%)	Business Description
51	Cyrix	66.3	18.0	33.8	Electrical components - math coprocessor & 486-clone microprocessors
52	Jean Philippe Fragrances	88.9	100.5	23.9	Cosmetics & toiletries
53	USA Waste Services	176.8	235.6	9.1	Pollution control equipment & services - solid waste management
54	Pomeroy Computer Resources	43.6	23.6	37.2	Computers - retail & wholesale
55	Digidesign	39.3	36.4	35.9	Electrical products - digital audio recording systems
56	Xircom	102.7	105.1	21.7	Computers - network hardware
57	PeopleSoft	109.0	169.8	16.7	Computers - human resource systems software
58	CFI ProServices	36.6	234.6	23.5	Computers - software
59	Dorchester Hugoton	29.5	49.4	36.4	Oil & gas - US exploration
60	Best Power Technology	21.3	67.3	38.5	Computers - battery backup systems
61	Taco Cabana	47.1	36.3	32.5	Retail - Taco Cabana restaurants
62	Safeskin	83.8	214.6	15.0	Medical & dental supplies - hypoallergenic disposable latex gloves
63	Starcraft Automotive	18.8	54.7	38.7	Automotive & trucking - parts
64	Speizman Industries	23.7	86.2	32.5	Machinery - general industrial
65	Homecare Management	72.1	86.1	23.6	Health care - outpatient & home; pharmaceutical supplies
66	Catalina Marketing	40.2	103.6	26.0	Business services - market research & point-of-sale grocery store coupon issuer
67	Wholesome & Hearty Foods	99.8	103.1	20.4	Food - meat products
68	American United Global	68.9	349.3	13.4	Computers - retail & wholesale
69	Cheesecake Factory	21.7	49.9	36.6	Retail - restaurants in Southern California, Atlanta & Washington, DC; cheesecake
70	Coastcast	25.0	82.0	30.7	Leisure & recreational products - golf club heads
71	Cornerstone Imaging	59.6	329.2	10.7	Computers - high-resolution graphics monitors & add-in cards
72	Active Voice	31.4	27.5	35.8	Telecommunications equipment - voice processing systems
73	Ashworth	81.2	138.7	14.4	Apparel - golf apparel & shoes
74	Canterbury Corporate Services	40.3	162.3	19.8	Schools
75	Duracraft	27.4	80.8	28.7	Appliances - fans, portable heaters, humidifiers & vaporizers
76	DIY Home Warehouse	31.2	40.5	29.6	Building products - retail & wholesale
77	Mikohn Gaming	42.6	158.9	17.4	Leisure & recreational products - slot machine systems & keno displays

Business Week's 100 Best Small Companies (continued)

Rank	Company	3-YEAR AVERAGE GROWTH Sales (%)	Profits (%)	Return on Capital (%)	Business Description
78	Jack Henry & Associates	27.4	77.9	27.8	Computers - software
79	Medicus Systems	22.9	28.4	35.4	Computers - decision-support software
80	Recovery Engineering	*58.2	113.3	17.2	Pollution control equipment & services - small-scale water purification products
81	Zebra Technologies	31.7	19.1	30.9	Optical character recognition - bar code printing
82	National Health Enhancement Sys.	38.8	105.4	21.2	Computers - software for healthcare providers
83	SSE Telecom	45.8	38.7	25.8	Telecommunications equipment - satellite earth stations & modems
84	EIS International	57.2	88.8	18.2	Telecommunications equipment - outbound telemarketing/call processing system
85	Eateries	33.1	201.2	16.1	Retail - family-style restaurants (Garfield's) & sports bars
86	Day Runner	28.9	28.3	29.5	Business services - paper-based personal organizers
87	Ballard Medical Products	31.9	45.4	26.3	Medical & dental supplies
88	St. John Knits	20.2	81.7	26.8	Apparel
89	National Home Centers	25.9	135.2	21.2	Building products - retail
90	Urban Outfitters	31.5	65.7	25.7	Retail - apparel & shoes
91	Res-Care	18.9	47.9	29.1	Training centers - physically & mentally disabled; Job Corps training centers
92	Brooktrout Technology	47.0	91.0	17.6	Telecommunications equipment - PC-based facsimile & voice processing systems
93	Three-Five Systems	28.8	103.1	22.3	Electrical components - liquid crystal & light-emitting diode displays
94	West Marine	23.7	51.5	26.8	Retail - boating supplies & apparel
95	Cerner	32.8	110.9	17.4	Computers - software for health care providers
96	Craftmade International	29.3	72.2	22.5	Housewares - ceiling fans & lights
97	IQ Software	39.3	31.8	22.6	Computers - software
98	Roper Industries	34.7	72.5	19.5	Instruments - fluid handling & industrial control
99	CCA Industries	24.3	97.2	20.2	Wholesale distribution - consumer products
100	American Business Information	23.1	55.6	23.4	Business services - mailing lists & directories

Source: *Business Week*; May 23, 1994

100 Best Companies to Work For

Company	City	Company	City
Acipco	Birmingham, AL	Lowe's	North Wilkesboro, NC
Advanced Micro Devices	Sunnyvale, CA	Lyondell Petrochemical	Houston
Alagasco	Birmingham, AL	Marquette Electronics	Milwaukee
Anheuser-Busch	St. Louis	Mary Kay Cosmetics	Dallas
Apogee Enterprises	Minneapolis	McCormick	Hunt Valley, MD
Armstrong	Lancaster, PA	Merck	Whitehouse Station, NJ
Avis	Garden City, NY	Methodist Hospital	Houston
Baptist Hospital of Miami	Miami	Microsoft	Redmond, WA
BE&K	Birmingham, AL	Herman Miller	Zeeland, MI
Ben & Jerry's Homemade	Waterbury, VT	3M	St. Paul
Beth Israel Hospital Boston*	Boston	Moog	East Aurora, NY
Leo Burnett	Chicago	J.P. Morgan	New York
Chaparral Steel	Midlothian, TX	Morrison & Foerster	San Francisco
Compaq Computer	Houston	Motorola	Schaumburg, IL
Cooper Tire	Findlay, OH	Nissan Motor Manufacturing	Smyrna, TN
Corning	Corning, NY	Nordstrom	Seattle
Cray Research	Eagan, MN	Northwestern Mutual Life	Milwaukee
Cummins Engine	Columbus, IN	Odetics	Anaheim
Dayton Hudson	Minneapolis	Patagonia	Ventura, CA
John Deere	Moline, IL	J. C. Penney	Plano, TX
Delta Air Lines*	Atlanta	Physio-Control	Redmond, WA
Donnelly*	Holland, MI	Pitney Bowes	Stamford, CT
Du Pont	Wilmington, DE	Polaroid	Cambridge, MA
A. G. Edwards	St. Louis	Preston Trucking	Preston, MD
Erie Insurance	Erie, PA	Procter & Gamble	Cincinnati
Federal Express*	Memphis	Publix Super Markets*	Lakeland, FL
Fel-Pro*	Skokie, IL	Quad/Graphics	Pewaukee, WI
First Federal Bank of California	Santa Monica	Reader's Digest	Pleasantville, NY
H. B. Fuller	St. Paul, MN	REI	Seattle
General Mills	Minneapolis	Rosenbluth International*	Philadelphia
Goldman Sachs	New York	SAS Institute	Cary, NC
W. L. Gore & Associates	Newark, DE	J. M. Smucker	Orrville, OH
Great Plains Software	Fargo, ND	Southwest Airlines*	Dallas
Hallmark Cards*	Kansas City, MO	Springfield ReManufacturing	Springfield, MO
Haworth	Holland, MI	Springs	Fort Mill, SC
Hershey Foods	Hershey, PA	Steelcase	Grand Rapids
Hewitt Associates	Lincolnshire, IL	Syntex	Palo Alto, CA
Hewlett-Packard	Palo Alto, CA	Tandem	Cupertino, CA
Honda of America Manufacturing	Marysville, OH	TDIndustries	Dallas
IBM	Armonk, NY	Tennant	Minneapolis
Inland Steel	Chicago	UNUM	Portland, ME
Intel	Santa Clara, CA	USAA*	San Antonio
Johnson & Johnson	New Brunswick, NJ	U S West	Englewood, CO
SC Johnson Wax	Racine, WI	Valassis Communications	Livonia, MI
Kellogg	Battle Creek, MI	Viking Freight System	San Jose
Knight-Ridder	Miami	Wal-Mart	Bentonville, AR
Lands' End	Dodgeville, WI	Wegmans	Rochester, NY
Lincoln Electric	Cleveland	Weyerhaeuser	Tacoma, WA
Los Angeles Dodgers	Los Angeles	Worthington Industries	Columbus, OH
Lotus Development	Cambridge, MA	Xerox	Stamford, CT

Source: Levering, Robert and Moskowitz, Milton. *The 100 Best Companies to Work For in America*. New York: Doubleday, 1993.

*Indicates one of Top Ten

America's 100 Most-Admired Corporations

Rank	Company
1	Rubbermaid
2	Microsoft
3	Coca-Cola
4	Motorola
5	Home Depot
6	Intel
7	Procter & Gamble
8	3M
9	United Parcel Service
10	Hewlett-Packard
11	United HealthCare
12	Gillette
13	Boeing
14	General Electric
15	Albertson's
16	Levi Strauss Associates
17	Johnson & Johnson
18	Corning
19	AT&T
20	Fluor
20	Pfizer
22	J.P. Morgan
23	Oracle Systems
24	Merck
25	Herman Miller
25	Nike
25	Walt Disney
28	U.S. Healthcare
29	Du Pont
29	Publix Super Markets
31	Kimberly-Clark
32	Toys "R" Us
33	General Mills
34	Electronic Data Systems
35	Leggett & Platt
35	Union Pacific
37	Enron
38	Dow Chemical
38	Shell Oil
40	Goodyear Tire & Rubber
41	Shaw Industries
42	Norfolk Southern
42	Southwest Airlines
44	Columbia/HCA Healthcare
44	Ford Motor
46	Berkshire Hathaway
47	Amoco
47	Nucor
49	Unifi
50	Emerson Electric

Rank	Company
50	Sysco
52	Wal-Mart Stores
53	Capital Cities/ABC
53	Mobil
55	Sara Lee
56	Northwestern Mutual Life
56	Walgreen
58	Deere
59	PacifiCare Health Sys.
59	Roadway Services
61	Compaq Computer
62	American Intl. Group
62	Armstrong World Ind.
62	Federal Express
62	Golden West Financial
66	Abbott Laboratories
66	Banc One
66	Illinois Tool Works
66	Morgan Stanley Group
70	Exxon
71	Wash. Mutual Sav. Bank
72	PepsiCo
72	SBC Communications
74	AlliedSignal
75	Centex
75	Martin Marietta
77	McKesson
78	Intl. Flavors & Frag.
79	Chevron
79	Schering-Plough
81	Chrysler
82	Xerox
83	Colgate-Palmolive
83	Viacom
85	CSX
85	UST
85	VF
88	Auto Data Processing
88	Bankers Trust New York
88	Merrill Lynch
91	Caterpillar
92	Dow Jones
92	Reader's Digest Assn.
92	Time Warner
95	Anheuser-Busch
96	ConAgra
96	HON Industries
98	MCI Communications
99	Burlington Resources
100	Springs Industries

Source: *FORTUNE*; March 6, 1995

85 Best Companies for Minorities

Company	Headquarters
Allstate Insurance Company	Northbrook, IL
American Airlines	Dallas/Ft. Worth, TX
American Express Company	New York, NY
American Telephone & Telegraph Company	New York, NY
Ameritech	Chicago, IL
Amtrak	Washington, DC
Anheuser-Busch Cos., Inc.	St. Louis, MO
Atlantic Richfield Company	Los Angeles, CA
Avis Rent-A-Car System, Inc.	Garden City, NY
Avon Products, Inc.	New York, NY
Bell Atlantic Corporation	Philadelphia, PA
Borden, Inc.	Columbus, OH
Bristol-Myers Squibb Co.	New York, NY
Burger King Corporation	Miami, FL
Leo Burnett Advertising Co.	Chicago, IL
Campbell Soup Company	Camden, NJ
Champion International Corporation	Stamford, CT
Chevron Corporation	San Fransico, CA
Chrysler Corporation	Highland Park, MI
Clorox Company	Oakland, CA
Coca-Cola Company	Atlanta, GA
Colgate-Palmolive Company	New York, NY
Adolph Coors Company	Golden, CO
Corning Incorporated	Corning, NY
Dayton Hudson Corporation	Minneapolis, MN
The Detroit Free Press	Detroit, MI
Dow Chemical Company	Midland, MI
Du Pont	Wilmington, DE
Eastman Kodak Company	Rochester, NY
The Equitable Companies Incorporated	New York, NY
Ernst & Young	New York, NY
Exxon Corporation	Irving, TX
Federal Express Corporation	Memphis, TN
Gannett Co., Inc.	Arlington, VA
General Electric Company	Fairfield, CT
General Foods USA	White Plains, NY
General Mills, Inc.	Minneapolis, MN
General Motors Corporation	Detroit, MI
Hallmark Cards, Inc.	Kansas City, MO
Hewlett-Packard Company	Palo Alto, CA
Hoechst Celanese Corporation	Somerville, NJ
Hogan & Hartson	Washington, DC
Honeywell Inc.	Minneapolis, MN
International Business Machines Corporation	Armonk, NY
Johnson & Johnson	New Brunswick, NJ
Kellogg Company	Battle Creek, MI
Levi Strauss & Co.	San Francisco, CA
McDonald's Corporation	Oak Brook, IL
Marriott Corporation	Washington, DC
MCI Communications Corp.	Washington, DC
Merck & Co., Inc.	Rahway, NJ
Merrill Lynch & Co., Inc.	New York, NY
Metropolitan Life Insurance Company	New York, NY
Morrison & Foerster	San Francisco, CA
Motorola, Inc.	Schaumburg, IL
The New York Times Company	New York, NY
NYNEX Corporation	New York, NY
O'Melveny & Myers	Los Angeles, CA
Pacific Gas and Electric Co.	San Francisco, CA
J. C. Penney Company, Inc.	Dallas, TX
PepsiCo, Inc.	Purchase, NY
Pfizer Inc.	New York, NY
Philip Morris Companies, Inc.	New York, NY
Polaroid Corporation	Cambridge, MA
PPG Industries, Inc.	Pittsburgh, PA
The Procter & Gamble Co.	Cincinnati, OH
The Prudential Insurance Company of America	Newark, NJ
The Quaker Oats Company	Chicago, IL
Ryder System, Inc.	Miami, FL
Sara Lee Corporation	Chicago, IL
Sidley & Austin	Chicago, IL
Simpson Thacher & Bartlett	New York, NY
Sony Music Entertainment Inc.	New York, NY
Sprint Corporation	Westwood, KS
3M	St. Paul, MN
Time Warner Inc.	New York, NY
TRW Inc.	Cleveland, OH
Turner Broadcasting System, Inc.	Atlanta, GA
United Parcel Service, Inc.	Atlanta, GA
The Upjohn Company	Kalamazoo, MI
US West, Inc.	Englewood, CO
Warner-Lambert Company	Morris Plains, NJ
The Washington Post Company	Washington, DC
Weil, Gotshal & Manges	New York, NY
Xerox Corporation	Stamford, CT

Source: Graham, Lawrence Otis. *The Best Companies for Minorities*. New York: Plume, 1993.

100 Best Companies for Gay Men and Lesbians

Company	City
American Friends Service Committee	Philadelphia, PA
American Psychological Association	Washington, DC
American Telephone & Telegraph Co.	Basking Ridge, NJ
Andersen Consulting/Arthur Andersen & Co.	Chicago, IL
Apple Computer Inc.	Cupertino, CA
Arizona Public Service	Phoenix, AZ
The ASK Group	Santa Clara, CA
Bank of America	San Francisco, CA
Ben & Jerry's Homemade Inc.	Waterbury, VT
Blue Cross and Blue Shield of Massachusetts	Boston, MA
The Body Shop Inc.	Wake Forest, NC
Borland International Inc.	Scotts Valley, CA
The Boston Globe	Boston, MA
Bureau of National Affairs Inc.	Washington, DC
Celestial Seasonings Inc.	Boulder, CO
Children's Hospital of Boston	Boston, MA
Children's Television Workshop	New York, NY
CMP Publications Inc.	Manhasset, NY
Colgate Palmolive Co.	New York, NY
Columbia University	New York, NY
Commonwealth Edison Co.	Chicago, IL
CoreStates Bank N.A.	Philadelphia, PA
CUNA Mutual Insurance Group	Madison, WI
Dayton Hudson Corp.	Minneapolis, MN
Digital Equipment Corp. (DEC)	Maynard, MA
The Walt Disney Company	Burbank, CA
Dow Chemical Corp.	Midland, MI
E. I. DuPont de Nemours	Wilmington, DE
Eastern Mountain Sports	Peterborough, NH
Episcopal Diocese of Newark	Newark, NJ
Federal National Mortgage Association (Fannie Mae)	Washington, DC
Frame Technology Corp.	San Jose, CA
Gannett Co., Inc.	Arlington, VA
Gardener's Supply Co.	Burlington, VT
Genentech Inc.	South San Francisco, CA
General Motors Corp.	Detroit, MI
Greenpeace International	Washington, DC
Harley Davidson Inc.	Milwaukee, WI
Harvard University	Cambridge, MA
Herman Miller	Zeeland, MI
Hewlett-Packard Co.	Palo Alto, CA
HBO/Time Warner Inc.	New York, NY
IDS Financial Services Inc.	Minneapolis, MN
International Business Machines Corp. (IBM)	Armonk, NY
Kaiser-Permanente	Oakland, CA
Kiwi Airlines	Newark, NJ
Eastman Kodak Co.	Rochester, NY
Labor Unions	
Levi Strauss & Co.	San Francisco, CA
Los Angeles Times	Los Angeles, CA
Lotus Development Corp.	Cambridge, MA
Massachusetts Institute of Technology (MIT)	Cambridge, MA
MCA, Inc.	Universal City, CA
Methodist Hospital of Indianapolis	Indianapolis, IN
Microsoft Corp.	Redmond, WA
Milbank, Tweed, Hadley & McCloy	New York, NY
Minnesota Comunications Group	St. Paul, MN
Minnesota Mining & Manufacturing Co. (3M Corp.)	St. Paul, MN
Montefiore Medical Center	Bronx, NY
Morrison & Foerster	San Francisco, CA
Municipal Government	
Nabisco Foods Group/RJR Nabisco	East Hanover, NJ
National Organization for Women (NOW)	Washington, DC
National Public Radio (NPR)	Washington, DC
New York University	New York, NY
NeXT Computer Inc.	Redwood City, CA
Oracle Corp.	Redwood Shores, CA
Orrick, Herrington & Sutcliffe	San Francisco, CA
Pacific Gas & Electric Co.	San Francisco, CA
Pitney Bowes	Stamford, CT
Planned Parenthood	New York, NY
Portland Cable Access	Portland, OR
Principal Financial Group Inc.	Des Moines, IA
Procter & Gamble	Cincinnati, OH
Public Broadcasting System (PBS)	Washington, DC
Recreational Equipment Inc. (REI)	Kent, WA
Schiff, Hardin & Waite	Chicago, IL
Scholastic Inc.	New York, NY
Charles Schwab and Co., Inc.	San Francisco, CA
Joseph E. Seagram & Sons, Inc.	New York, NY
Seattle City Light Co.	Seattle, WA
Seattle Times	Seattle, WA
Showtime Networks Inc.	New York, NY
Silicon Graphics	Mountain View, CA
Stanford University	Palo Alto, CA
Starbucks Coffee Co.	Seattle, WA
Sun Microsystems Inc.	Mountain View, CA
United States Government (Civil Service)	Washington, DC
University of Chicago	Chicago, IL
University of Minnesota	St. Paul, MN
U.S. West	Englewood, CO
Viacom International Inc.	New York, NY
The Village Voice	New York, NY
Wells Fargo & Co.	San Francisco, CA
WGBH	Boston, MA
Working Assets Funding Service	San Francisco, CA
WQED	Pittsburgh, PA
Xerox Corp.	Stamford, CT
YWCA of Greater Milwaukee	Milwaukee, WI
Ziff-Davis Publishing Co.	New York, NY

Source: Mickens, Ed. *The 100 Best Companies for Gay Men and Lesbians*. New York: Pocket Books, 1994.

100 Companies Providing the Most Opportunities for Hispanics

Company	Company
Aetna	Lockheed
AFLAC	McDonald's
Allstate	MCI
American Airlines	MetLife
American Express	Miller Brewing
Ameritech	Mobil
Anheuser-Busch	Motorola
Apple Computer	NationsBank
Arco	Nestlé USA
AT&T	Nissan
Avon	Nordstrom
Bank of America	Northern Telecom
Bell South	Northrop
Boeing	Nu Skin
Bristol-Myers Squibb	Nynex
Burger King	Pacific Bell
Chase Manhattan	Pacific Gas & Electric
Chevron	Pentax
Chrysler	Pepsico
Chubb	Pepsi-Cola
Citibank	Philip Morris
Coca-Cola	Pitney Bowes
Colgate-Palmolive	Procter & Gamble
Compaq Computer	Prudential
Coors	Quaker Oats
Delta Airlines	Reebok
Diamond Shamrock	R.J. Reynolds
Dupont	Rockwell
Eastman Kodak	Ryder
EDS	Sathers
Eli Lilly	SBC Communications
Federal Express	Schieffelin & Somerset
Fiesta Food Mart	Seagram
Ford	Sears, Roebuck
Frito-Lay	Shell
General Electric	Smithkline Beecham
General Motors	Southland
Goya Foods	State Farm
HEB	Sun Microsystems
Hewlett-Packard	Texaco
Hoechst Celanese	Texas Instruments
Home Savings	Time Warner
Honda	Toyota
IBM	Toys "R" Us
ITT	Union Bank
J. C. Penney	United Airlines
Johnson & Johnson	US West
Kaiser Permanente	Walgreens
Kraft General Foods	WMX Technologies
Levi Strauss	Xerox

Source: *HISPANIC*, January/February 1995

Top 20 Woman-Owned Businesses

Rank	Company	Owner	1993 Sales ($ mil.)
1	Little Caesar Enterprises	Marian Ilitch	2,300
2	Raley's	Joyce Raley Teel	1,700
3	Roll International	Lynda Resnick	1,300
4	Axel Johnson	Antonia Axson Johnson	800
5	Minyard Food Stores	Liz Minyard & Gretchen Minyard Williams	760
6	Warnaco Group	Linda Wachner	704
7	Jenny Craig	Jenny Craig	465
8	Jockey International	Donna Wolf Steigerwaldt	450
9	Donna Karan	Donna Karan	408
10	Copley Press	Helen Copley	363
11	Chas. Levy	Barbara Levy Kipper	335
12	Gear Holdings	Bettye Martin-Musham	300
13	Esprit de Corp.	Susie Tompkins	300
14	Lundy Packing	Annabelle Lundy Fetterman	294
15	Owen Healthcare	Dian Graves Owen	291
16	Carole Little	Carole Little	283
17	Tootsie Roll Industries	Ellen Gordon	260
18	Bernard Chaus	Josephine Chaus	230
19	Resort Condominiums International	Christel DeHaan	230
20	Thomas Cook Travel	Linda Paresky	220

Source: *Working Woman*, May 1994

Top 20 Black-Owned Businesses

Rank	Company	1993 Sales ($ mil.)
1	TLC Beatrice International Holdings Inc.	1,700.0
2	Johnson Publishing Co. Inc.	293.8
3	Philadelphia Coca-Cola Bottling Co. Inc.	290.0
4	H.J. Russell & Co.	152.4
5	RMS Technologies Inc.	115.2
6	The Anderson-Dubose Co.	115.0
7	Gold Line Refining Ltd.	108.1
8	Threads 4 Life (D.B.A. Cross Colours)	97.0
9	Soft Sheen Products Inc.	96.6
10	Garden State Cable TV	96.0
11	Envirotest Systems Corp.	90.0
12	The Bing Group	83.3
13	Barden Communications Inc.	82.4
14	Pulsar Data Systems Inc.	79.1
15	Drew Pearson Companies	77.5
16	Uniworld Group Inc.	77.1
17	Burrell Communications Group	74.7
18	Black Entertainment Television Holdings	74.2
19	Essence Communications Inc.	71.1
20	Mays Chemical Company Inc.	65.0

Source: *Black Enterprise*, June 1994

Top 20 Hispanic-Owned Businesses

Rank	Company	1993 Sales ($ mil.)
1	Burt on Broadway/Arapahoe	529.1
2	Goya Foods Inc.	480.0
3	Troy Ford	260.4
4	Sedano's Supermarkets	236.5
5	Galeana's Van Dyke Dodge	188.9
6	Ancira Enterprises Inc.	181.1
7	Cal-State Lumber Sales Inc.	168.4
8	International Bancshares Corp.	160.5
9	Normac Foods Inc.	160.4
10	CareFlorida Inc.	151.6
11	Infotec Development Inc.	135.0
12	Vincam Group Inc. (The)	134.5
13	CTA Incorporated	133.0
14	Capital Bancorp	117.5
15	Lloyd A. Wise Inc.	116.9
16	COLSA Corp.	112.0
17	Gaseteria Oil Corp.	106.0
18	Avanti Press	105.0
19	Eagle Brands Inc.	102.2
20	Private Jet Expeditions Inc.	100.0

Source: *Hispanic Business*, June 1994

100 Companies That Will Change the Face of Tomorrow's Business

Company	Location	Company	Location
3Com Corp.	Santa Clara, CA	Mitek Surgical Products, Inc.	Norwood, MA
Acxiom Corporation	Conway, AR	Molten Metal Technology	Waltham, MA
American Medical Response, Inc.	Boston, MA	Mothers Work, Inc.	Philadelphia, PA
Asanté Technologies, Inc.	San Jose, CA	National Health Corp.	Grand Prairie, TX
Ascend Communications, Inc.	Alameda, CA	NetFRAME Systems, Inc.	Milpitas, CA
Atmel Corporation	San Jose, CA	Neurogen Corp.	Branford, CT
Bay Networks, Inc.	Santa Clara, CA	Newbridge Networks Corp.	Kanata, Ontario
Better Education, Inc.	Yorktown, VA	Nextel Communications, Inc.	Rutherford, NJ
The Body Shop International PLC	Littlehampton, UK	On Assignment, Inc.	Calabasas, CA
C-Cube Microsystems, Inc.	Milpitas, CA	Orbital Sciences Corp.	Dulles, VA
Cambridge NeuroScience, Inc.	Cambridge, MA	Orthogene, Inc.	Sausalito, CA
Cambridge Technology Partners	Cambridge, MA	Parametric Technology Corp.	Waltham, MA
Catalina Marketing Corp.	St. Petersburg, FL	PARCPlace Systems, Inc.	Sunnyvale, CA
CERNER Corporation	Kansas City, MO	Phenix Biocomposites, Inc.	St. Peter, MN
Chipcom Corporation	Southborough, MA	Pleasant Company	Middleton, WI
Cirrus Logic, Inc.	Fremont, CA	The Progressive Corp.	Mayfield Heights, OH
Computer Network Technology Corp.	Maple Grove, MN	Qualcomm, Inc.	San Diego, CA
Corel Corporation	Ottawa, Ontario	Quantum Health Resources, Inc.	Orange, CA
Corrections Corporation of America	Nashville, TN	Quorum Health Group, Inc.	Brentwood, TN
Davidson & Associates, Inc.	Torrance, CA	Res-Care, Inc.	Louisville, KY
Decision Quest	Torrance, CA	Research Management Consultants, Inc.	Camarillo, CA
Digital Link Corp.	Sunnyvale, CA	Roper Industries, Inc.	Commerce, GA
Dionex Corporation	Sunnyvale, CA	Ryka, Inc.	Norwood, MA
DNX Corporation	Princeton, NJ	Sentinel Systems, Inc.	Hampton, VA
EcoScience Corp.	Worcester, MA	Shaman Pharmaceuticals, Inc.	San Francisco, CA
Education Alternatives, Inc.	Minneapolis, MN	SRX, Inc.	Plano, TX
Ensys Environmental Products	Morrisville, NC	Stores Automated Systems, Inc.	Bristol, PA
Envirotest Systems Corp.	Tucson, AZ	Sunrise Medical, Inc.	Torrance, CA
Fore Systems, Inc.	Warrendale, PA	Swift Transportation Co., Inc.	Sparks, NV
Frontier Insurance Group, Inc.	Rock Hill, NY	Sybase, Inc.	Emeryville, CA
GTI Corporation	San Diego, CA	Synaptic Pharmaceutical Corp.	Paramus, NJ
Harmony Brook, Inc.	Eagan, MN	Synopsys, Inc.	Mountain View, CA
Hauser Chemical Research, Inc.	Boulder, CO	SyStemix, Inc.	Palo Alto, CA
Health Management Associates	Naples, FL	Tecnol Medical Products, Inc.	Fort Worth, TX
Healthdyne Technologies, Inc.	Marietta, GA	Tetra Tech, Inc.	Pasadena, CA
Heart Technology, Inc.	Redmond, WA	Thermo Electron Corp.	Waltham, MA
Hemosol, Inc.	Etobicoke, Ontario	Three-Five Systems, Inc.	Phoenix, AZ
Homecare Management, Inc.	Ronkonkoma, NY	Transmedia Network, Inc.	Miami, FL
Information America, Inc.	Atlanta, GA	TRESP Associates, Inc.	Alexandria, VA
Informix Corporation	Menlo Park, CA	Vivra, Inc.	Burlingame, CA
Integrated Health Services, Inc.	Owings Mills, MD	Vivus	Menlo Park, CA
International High Tech Marketing Inc.	Miami, FL	Wall Data Inc.	Kirkland, WA
InVision Systems Corporation	Vienna, VA	Whole Foods Market, Inc.	Austin, TX
Just for Feet, Inc.	Birmingham, AL	Wholesome & Hearty Foods, Inc.	Portland, OR
Landstar Systems, Inc.	Shelton, CT	Work/Family Directions	Boston, MA
Life Resuscitation Technologies, Inc.	Chicago, IL	Workstation Technologies, Inc.	Irvine, CA
MediCenter, Inc.	Lawton, OK	Xilinx, Inc.	San Jose, CA
Medicus Systems Corp.	Evanston, IL	Xircom, Inc.	Calabasas, CA
Medrad, Inc.	Pittsburgh, PA	Zebra Technologies Corp.	Vernon Hills, IL
Megahertz Holding Corp.	Salt Lake City, UT	Zia Metallurgical Processes, Inc.	Dallas, TX

Source: Silver, A. David. *Quantum Companies: 100 Companies That Will Change the Face of Tomorrow's Business*. Princeton, New Jersey: Peterson's/Pacesetter Books, 1995.

18 Visionary Companies

Company
3M
American Express
Boeing
Citicorp
Ford
General Electric
Hewlett-Packard
IBM
Johnson & Johnson
Marriott
Merck
Motorola
Nordstrom
Philip Morris
Proctor & Gamble
Sony
Wal-Mart
Walt Disney

Source: Collins, James C. and Porras, Jerry I. *Built to Last: Successful Habits of Visionary Companies*. New York: Harper Business, 1994.

50 Leading Retained Search Firms in North America

Company	Location
Allerton Heneghan & O'Neill	Chicago, IL
Martin H. Bauman Associates	New York, NY
Bishop Partners	New York, NY
Boyden	New York, NY
The Caldwell Partners Amrop International	Toronto, Ontario
Callan & Associates	Oak Brook, IL
Cejka & Co.	St. Louis, MO
Clarey & Andrews	Northbrook, IL
Coleman Lew & Associates	Charlotte, NC
Conrey Paul Ray Int'l	Mexico City, Mexico
Thorndike Deland Associates	New York, NY
Dieckmann & Associates	Chicago, IL
Robert W. Dingman Co.	Westlake Village, CA
Diversified Search Cos.	Philadelphia, PA
Bert H. Early Associates	Chicago, IL
Fenwick Partners	Lexington, MA
Francis & Associates	West Des Moines, IA
Jay Gaines & Co.	New York, NY
Gould & McCoy	New York, NY
Hayden Group	Boston, MA
The Heidrick Partners	Chicago, IL
Heidrick & Struggles	Chicago, IL
The Hetzel Group	Inverness, IL
Hockett Associates	Los Altos, CA
William C. Houze & Co.	La Quinta, CA
Houze, Shourds & Montgomery	Long Beach, CA
Isaacson, Miller	Boston, MA
Pendleton James & Associates	New York, NY
A.T. Kearney Executive Search	Chicago, IL
Kenny, Kindler, Hunt & Howe	New York, NY
Korn/Ferry International	New York, NY
Lamalie Amrop International	New York, NY
Herbert Mines Associates	New York, NY
Mirtz Morice	Stamford, CT
Nadzam, Lusk & Associates	Santa Clara, CA
Norman Broadbent International	New York, NY
Preng & Associates	Houston, TX
Paul Ray Berndtson Int'l	Fort Worth, TX
Russell Reynolds Associates	New York, NY
Norman Roberts & Associates	Los Angeles, CA
Seitchik Corwin & Seitchik	San Francisco, CA
Smith, Goerss & Ferneborg	San Francisco, CA
Spencerstuart	New York, NY
Tanton/Mitchell Paul Ray Berndtson	Vancouver, B.C.
Travis & Company	Sudbury, MA
Ward Howell International	New York, NY
Daniel Wier & Associates	Los Angeles, CA
Wilkinson & Ives	San Francisco, CA
Witt/Kieffer Ford Hadelman & Lloyd	Oak Brook, IL
Egon Zehnder International	New York, NY

Source: *Executive Recruiter News*, December 1992

HOOVER'S MASTERLIST OF AMERICA'S TOP 2,500 EMPLOYERS

AMERICA'S TOP 2,500 EMPLOYERS

ALABAMA

AMERICAN BUILDINGS COMPANY
State Docks Rd.
Eufaula, AL 36072-0800
Pres & CEO: Robert T. Ammerman
Dir HR: Bill O'Neill
Employees: 1,275
Jobs Added Last Year: 125 (+10.9%)
Building products - prefabricated metal buildings

Phone: 334-687-2032
Fax: 334-687-7156

BOOKS-A-MILLION, INC.
402 Industrial Ln.
Birmingham, AL 35211
Pres, CEO & COO: Clyde B. Anderson
Dir HR: Christine Sanders
Employees: 1,596
Jobs Added Last Year: 146 (+10.1%)
Retail - book superstores in southeast US

Phone: 205-942-3737
Fax: 205-945-1772

AMSOUTH BANCORPORATION
1400 AmSouth-Sonat Tower
Birmingham, AL 35203
Chm & CEO: John W. Woods
EVP & HR Dir: David B. Edmonds
Employees: 5,597
Jobs Cut Last Year: 435 (-7.2%)
Banks - Southeast

Phone: 205-320-7151
Fax: 205-326-4072

BOYD BROS. TRANSPORTATION INC.
Rte. 1, PO Box 40
Clayton, AL 36016
Pres & CEO: Donald G. Johnston
Dir HR: Harry Murdaugh
Employees: 700
Jobs Added Last Year: 67 (+10.6%)
Transportation - flatbed trucks

Phone: 205-775-3261
Fax: 205-775-9271

BE&K INC.
2000 International Park Dr.
Birmingham, AL 35243
Chm & CEO: Theodore C. Kennedy
Dir HR: Marshall Johnson
Employees: 3,300
Jobs Added Last Year: —
Construction - engineering & maintenance

Phone: 205-969-3600
Fax: 205-972-6300

BRUNO'S, INC.
800 Lakeshore Pkwy.
Birmingham, AL 35211
Chm & CEO: Ronald G. Bruno
VP HR: Richard H. Marty
Employees: 26,486
Jobs Added Last Year: 3,032 (+12.9%)
Retail - supermarkets (Food World, Piggly Wiggly, Food Fair, Foodmax & Bruno's)

Phone: 205-940-9400
Fax: 205-940-9534

BIG B, INC.
2600 Morgan Rd.
Bessemer, AL 35023
Chm & CEO: Anthony J. Bruno
VP HR: Eugene Beckman
Employees: 5,000
Jobs Added Last Year: 1,000 (+25%)
Retail - drug stores

Phone: 205-424-3421
Fax: 205-426-8748

CAVALIER HOMES OF ALABAMA, INC.
Hwy. 41 N. and Cavalier Rd.
Addison, AL 35540
Pres: Jerry F. Wilson
Dir Personnel: Becky Richardson
Employees: 2,000
Jobs Added Last Year: 513 (+34.5%)
Building - mobile homes

Phone: 205-747-1575
Fax: 205-747-2107

BLOUNT, INC.
4520 Executive Park Dr.
Montgomery, AL 36116-1602
Pres & CEO: John Panettiere
SVP Admin & Corp Sec (HR): D. Joseph McInnes
Employees: 4,700
Jobs Cut Last Year: 100 (-2.1%)
Machinery - timber harvesting & log loading machinery, industrial tractors & loaders; chain saw components

Phone: 205-244-4000
Fax: 205-244-4313

CITATION CORPORATION
2 Office Park Circle, Ste. 204
Birmingham, AL 35223
CEO: T. Morris Hackney
Dir HR: Tom Surtees
Employees: 2,441
Jobs Added Last Year: 447 (+22.4%)
Automotive & trucking - iron & steel castings used in brackets, brake systems, universal joints & suspension systems

Phone: 205-871-5731
Fax: 205-870-8211

ALABAMA

COMPASS BANCSHARES, INC.
15 S. 20th St. Phone: 205-933-3000
Birmingham, AL 35233 Fax: 205-933-3266
Chm & CEO: D. Paul Jones, Jr.
SVP & Dir HR: E. Lee Harris, Jr.
Employees: 4,000
Jobs Added Last Year: 100 (+2.6%)
Banks - Southeast

DELCHAMPS, INC.
305 Delchamps Dr. Phone: 205-433-0431
Mobile, AL 36602 Fax: 205-433-0437
Chm, Pres & CEO: Randy Delchamps
VP Personnel: Thomas R. Trebesh
Employees: 8,500
Jobs Added Last Year: 613 (+7.8%)
Retail - supermarkets

FIRST ALABAMA BANCSHARES, INC.
417 N. 20th St., PO Box 10247 Phone: 205-326-7100
Birmingham, AL 35202-0247 Fax: 205-326-7571
Chm & CEO: J. Stanley Mackin
SVP HR & Regional Personnel Dir: David Herring
Employees: 4,696
Jobs Added Last Year: 231 (+5.2%)
Banks - Southeast

HEALTHSOUTH CORPORATION
2 Perimeter Park South Phone: 205-967-7116
Birmingham, AL 35243 Fax: 205-969-4719
Chm, Pres & CEO: Richard M. Scrushy
Group VP HR: Brad Hale
Employees: 14,562
Jobs Added Last Year: 7,319 (+101%)
Hospitals - hospitals, health care centers & clinics throughout the U.S.

INTERGRAPH CORPORATION
Huntsville, AL 35894-0001 Phone: 205-730-2000
Chm & CEO: James W. Meadlock Fax: 205-730-2164
VP Corp HR: Milford B. French
Employees: 9,500
Jobs Cut Last Year: 800 (-7.8%)
Computers - graphics, CAD/CAM systems, micro stations

KINDERCARE LEARNING CENTERS, INC.
2400 Presidents Dr. Phone: 205-277-5090
Montgomery, AL 36116 Fax: 205-270-0080
Pres & CEO: Tull N. Gearreald, Jr.
VP HR: Kay G. Channell
Employees: 21,000
Jobs Added Last Year: –
Schools - center-based child care & pre-school educational services

MORRISON RESTAURANTS, INC.
4721 Morrison Dr. Phone: 205-344-3000
Mobile, AL 36625 Fax: 205-344-3066
Chm, Pres & CEO: Samuel E Beall III
SVP HR: Ronald Vilord
Employees: 33,000
Jobs Cut Last Year: 4,000 (-10.8%)
Retail - restaurants (Ruby Tuesday, Mozzarella's, Tia's & Morrison's) & contract food services

NICHOLS RESEARCH CORPORATION
4040 S. Memorial Pkwy. Phone: 205-883-1140
Huntsville, AL 35815-1502 Fax: 205-880-0367
CEO: Chris H. Horgen
Dir HR: Scott Parker
Employees: 1,022
Jobs Added Last Year: 120 (+13.3%)
Engineering - R&D services

PRECISION STANDARD, INC.
1943 50th St. North Phone: 205-591-3009
Birmingham, AL 35212 Fax: 205-595-6631
Pres & CEO: Matthew L. Gold
VP HR: Ray Pike
Employees: 2,520
Jobs Added Last Year: 296 (+13.3%)
Aerospace - aircraft equipment

PROTECTIVE LIFE CORPORATION
2801 Hwy. 280 South Phone: 205-879-9230
Birmingham, AL 35223 Fax: 205-868-3270
Chm, Pres & CEO: Drayton Nabers, Jr.
VP HR: William J. Hamer, Jr.
Employees: 1,150
Jobs Added Last Year: 57 (+5.2%)
Insurance - life

ALABAMA

RUSSELL CORPORATION
PO Box 272 Phone: 205-329-4000
Alexander City, AL 35010 Fax: 205-329-4474
CEO: John C. Adams
VP HR: Dick Dickson
Employees: 16,594
Jobs Added Last Year: 1,632 (+10.9%)
Apparel

RUST INTERNATIONAL INC.
100 Corporate Pkwy. Phone: 205-995-7878
Birmingham, AL 35242 Fax: 205-995-7150
Pres & CEO: Rodney C. Gilbert
VP Admin (HR): Edward Maryniak
Employees: 16,000
Jobs Added Last Year: 9,200 (+135.3%)
Pollution control - hazardous waste remediation

SCI SYSTEMS, INC.
2101 W. Clinton Ave. Phone: 205-882-4601
Huntsville, AL 35805 Fax: 205-882-4804
Chm, CEO & Acting CFO: Olin B. King
VP Personnel: Francis X. Henry
Employees: 12,027
Jobs Added Last Year: 1,216 (+11.2%)
Electrical components - contract manufacturing of printed circuit boards; aerospace & defense computers

SOUTHERN ENERGY HOMES, INC.
Hwy. 41 North, PO Box 269 Phone: 205-747-1544
Addison, AL 35540 Fax: 205-747-2963
Pres & CEO: Wendell L. Batchelor
Personnel Dir: Jim Cain
Employees: 1,650
Jobs Added Last Year: 490 (+42.2%)
Building - residential & commercial

SOUTHTRUST CORPORATION
420 N. 20th St. Phone: 205-254-5009
Birmingham, AL 35203 Fax: 205-254-6688
Chm & CEO: Wallace D. Malone, Jr.
SVP HR: Charles D. Whitfield, Jr.
Employees: 7,300
Jobs Added Last Year: 800 (+12.3%)
Banks - Southeast

TORCHMARK CORPORATION
2001 Third Ave. South Phone: 205-325-4200
Birmingham, AL 35233 Fax: 205-325-4198
Chm & CEO: Ronald K. Richey
Dir Personnel: George Thompson
Employees: 6,052
Jobs Cut Last Year: 190 (-3%)
Insurance - life

THE UNIVERSITY OF ALABAMA
701 20th St. South, Ste. 1070 Phone: 205-934-4636
Birmingham, AL 35294 Fax: 205-975-8505
Chancellor: Philip E. Austin
VP Admin & HR: John H. Walker
Employees: 15,000
Jobs Added Last Year: —
University

VULCAN MATERIALS COMPANY
One Metroplex Dr. Phone: 205-877-3000
Birmingham, AL 35209 Fax: 205-877-3094
Chm & CEO: Herbert A. Sklenar
SVP HR: R. Morrieson Lord
Employees: 6,320
Jobs Added Last Year: 47 (+.7%)
Building products - asphalt, concrete & gravel; chemicals

ALASKA

CARR-GOTTSTEIN FOODS CO.
6411 A St. Phone: 907-561-1944
Anchorage, AK 99518 Fax: 907-564-2580
Pres & CEO: Mark Williams
Dir HR: Eric Tollessen
Employees: 3,700
Jobs Added Last Year: 400 (+12.1%)
Retail - supermarkets in Alaska (largest private employer in the state)

NATIONAL BANCORP OF ALASKA, INC.
310 W. Northern Lights Blvd. Phone: 907-276-1132
Anchorage, AK 99503 Fax: 907-267-5595
Chm: Edward B. Rasmuson
HR Off: Fran Webber
Employees: 1,202
Jobs Added Last Year: 65 (+5.7%)
Banks - West

GENERAL COMMUNICATION, INC.
2550 Denali St., Ste. 1000 Phone: 907-265-5600
Anchorage, AK 99503 Fax: 907-265-5676
Pres & CEO: Ronald A. Duncan
VP MIS & Admin (HR): Ed Spradling
Employees: 410
Jobs Added Last Year: 60 (+17.1%)
Telecommunications services - long distance services

NORTHRIM BANK
3111 C St. Phone: 907-562-0062
Anchorage, AK 99503 Fax: 907-562-1758
Chm & CEO: Arnold G. Espe
Dir HR: Charlie Cash
Employees: 105
Jobs Added Last Year: 31 (+41.9%)
Banks - West

▼ **Get Net International** http://www.getnet.com/employment

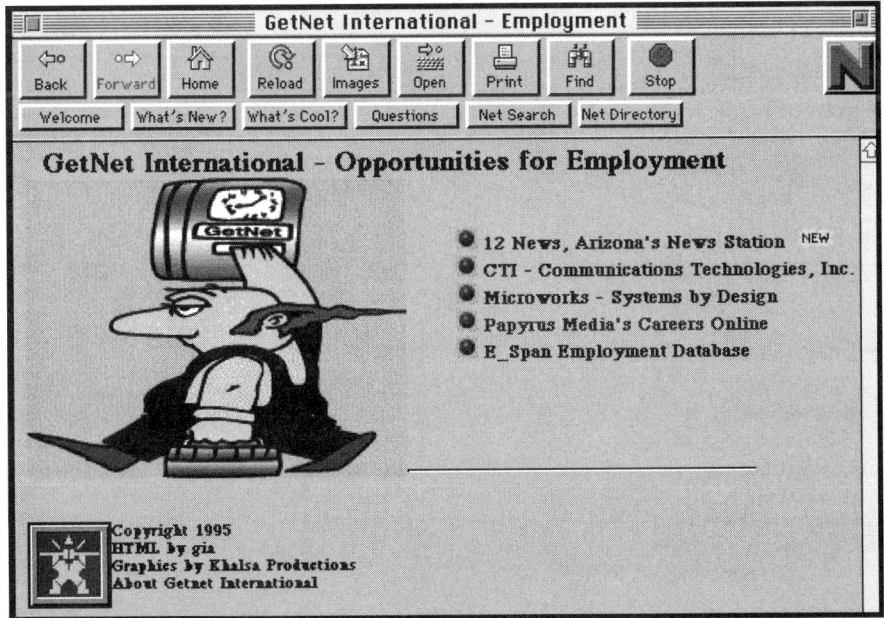

An in-depth profile of this company is available by fax. Call 800-510-4452 and use your touch-tone phone to put in the 5-digit code at the prompt. Only $2.95 each with your credit card. See page 12 for more details.

ARIZONA

ABCO MARKETS INC.
3001 W. Indian School Phone: 602-222-1600
Phoenix, AZ 85017 Fax: 602-222-1473
Pres & CEO: Edward G. Hill, Jr.
Dir HR: Dennis Williams
Employees: 4,800
Jobs Added Last Year: —
Retail - supermarkets in Phoenix & Tucson

ADFLEX SOLUTIONS, INC.
2001 W. Chandler Blvd. Phone: 602-963-4584
Chandler, AZ 85224 Fax: 602-786-8280
Pres & CEO: Rolando C. Esteverena
VP HR: R. Charles Furviss
Employees: 2,465
Jobs Added Last Year: 287 (+13.2%)
Electrical components - circuits used to connect electronic components in PCs, disk drives & other consumer products

AMERICA WEST AIRLINES, INC.
4000 Sky Harbor Blvd. Phone: 602-693-0800
Phoenix, AZ 85034 Fax: 602-693-5546
Chm & CEO: William A. Franke
Senior Dir HR: Ted Szaniawski
Employees: 10,544
Jobs Cut Last Year: 385 (-3.5%)
Transportation - airline

APOLLO GROUP, INC.
4615 E. Elwood St. Phone: 602-966-5394
Phoenix, AZ 85040 Fax: 602-968-1159
Chm, Pres & CEO: John G. Sperling
Dir HR: Kathryn Zuber
Employees: 3,442
Jobs Added Last Year: 158 (+4.8%)
Schools - higher education programs for working adults

ARIZONA INSTRUMENT CORPORATION
4114 E. Wood St. Phone: 602-470-1414
Phoenix, AZ 85040-1941 Fax: 602-731-3434
Pres & CEO: John P. Hudnall
Dir HR: Susan D. Berry
Employees: 115
Jobs Added Last Year: 48 (+71.6%)
Instruments - measurement & control

ARTISOFT, INC.
2202 N. Forbes Blvd. Phone: 602-670-7100
Tucson, AZ 85745 Fax: 602-670-7101
Interim Chm, Pres & CEO: William C. Keiper
VP HR: Paul G. Dombroski
Employees: 600
Jobs Added Last Year: 174 (+40.8%)
Computers - LAN software & hardware

AZTAR CORPORATION
2390 E. Camelback Rd. Phone: 602-381-4100
Phoenix, AZ 85016 Fax: 602-381-4107
Chm, Pres & CEO: Paul E. Rubeli
VP Admin & Sec (HR): Nelson W. Armstrong, Jr.
Employees: 8,200
Jobs Added Last Year: 900 (+12.3%)
Leisure & recreational services - casinos

BASHAS' INC.
22402 S. Alma School Rd. Phone: 602-895-9350
Chandler, AZ 85248 Fax: 602-895-1206
Chm & CEO: Edward N. Basha, Jr.
VP HR: Fred Felix
Employees: 5,000
Jobs Added Last Year: 200 (+4.2%)
Retail - supermarkets in Arizona

CARLISLE PLASTICS, INC.
1314 N. 3rd St., Ste 300 Phone: 602-407-2100
Phoenix, AZ 85004 Fax: 617-523-5428
CEO: William H. Binnie
HR Mgr: Judy Guilbeaux
Employees: 2,700
Jobs Added Last Year: 0
Rubber & plastic products - plastic containers, bags & household items

CERPROBE CORPORATION
600 S. Rockford Dr Phone: 602-967-7885
Tempe, AZ 85281 Fax: 602-967-7758
Pres & CEO: C. Zane Close
HR Mgr: Yvonne Krueger
Employees: 161
Jobs Added Last Year: 46 (+40%)
Semiconductor test equipment

ARIZONA

THE CIRCLE K CORPORATION
3003 N. Central Ave. Phone: 602-437-0600
Phoenix, AZ 85012 Fax: 602-530-5278
CEO: John F. Antioco, Jr.
Dir HR: Terry S. Broekemeier
Employees: 20,000
Jobs Cut Last Year: 1,487 (-6.9%)
Retail - convenience stores

DEL WEBB CORPORATION
6001 N. 24th St. Phone: 602-808-8000
Phoenix, AZ 85016 Fax: 602-808-8097
CEO: Philip J. Dion
VP HR: M. Lynn Schuttenberg
Employees: 1,400
Jobs Added Last Year: 500 (+55.6%)
Real estate operations

THE DIAL CORP.
Dial Tower Phone: 602-207-4000
Phoenix, AZ 85077 Fax: 602-207-5473
Chm, Pres & CEO: John W. Teets
VP HR: Joan F. Ingalls
Employees: 25,025
Jobs Cut Last Year: 5,087 (-16.9%)
Diversified operations - consumer, personal care & cleaning products; in-flight catering; exhibition management

DOUBLETREE CORPORATION
410 N. 44th St., Ste. 700 Phone: 602-220-6666
Phoenix, AZ 85008 Fax: 602-220-6602
Pres & CEO: Richard M. Kelleher
VP HR: William C. Barnett
Employees: 13,438
Jobs Added Last Year: 4,809 (+55.7%)
Hotels (DoubleTree & Guest Quarters Suites)

ENVIROTEST SYSTEMS CORPORATION
2525 E. Camelback Rd., Ste. 720 Phone: 602-912-1100
Phoenix, AZ 85016 Fax: 602-912-1105
Pres & CEO: Ralph E. Reins
VP HR: Lucy Nelson
Employees: 2,576
Jobs Added Last Year: 385 (+17.6%)
Pollution control services - auto emissions testing

INTER-TEL, INC.
7300 W. Boston St. Phone: 602-961-9000
Chandler, AZ 85226 Fax: 602-961-1370
Chm & CEO: Steven G. Mihaylo
HR Coordinator: Ellen Munoz
Employees: 725
Jobs Added Last Year: 124 (+20.6%)
Telecommunications equipment

MAGMA COPPER CO.
7400 N. Oracle Rd., Ste. 200 Phone: 602-575-5600
Tucson, AZ 85704 Fax: 602-575-5647
Pres & CEO: J. Burgess Winter
VP HR: Marshall H. Campbell
Employees: 4,286
Jobs Cut Last Year: 197 (-4.4%)
Metals - copper, gold & silver

MAIN ST. & MAIN, INC.
8700 E. Via de Ventura Phone: 602-852-9000
Scottsdale, AZ 85258 Fax: 602-852-0001
Chm & CEO: Steven A. Sherman
Dir HR: Allison Hayhurst
Employees: 3,220
Jobs Added Last Year: 2,200 (+215.7%)
Retail - restaurants

MEGAFOODS STORES, INC.
1455 S. Stapley Dr., Ste. 15 Phone: 602-926-1087
Mesa, AZ 85204 Fax: 602-926-1237
Chm, Pres & CEO: Dean G. Miller
Dir HR: Eden C. Higgins
Employees: 4,200
Jobs Added Last Year: 2,422 (+136.2%)
Retail - supermarkets in Arizona, San Diego, Las Vegas & San Antonio

MICROAGE COMPUTER CENTERS, INC.
2308 S. 55th St. Phone: 602-968-3168
Tempe, AZ 85282-1896 Fax: 602-966-7339
Chm & CEO: Jeffrey D. McKeever
VP HR: Craig J. Cantoni
Employees: 1,900
Jobs Added Last Year: 908 (+91.5%)
Wholesale - master resale of computer hardware & software; direct sales of computer equipment & services

ARIZONA

MICROCHIP TECHNOLOGY, INCORPORATED
2355 W. Chandler Blvd.
Chandler, AZ 85224
Pres & CEO: Steve Sanghi
VP HR: Mike Jones
Employees: 1,258
Jobs Added Last Year: 658 (+109.7%)
Electronic components - embedded controller semiconductors
Phone: 602-786-7200
Fax: 602-899-9210

RURAL/METRO CORPORATION
8401 E. Indian School Rd.
Scottsdale, AZ 85251
Pres & CEO: Robert H. Manschot
VP HR: Tracy Bannon
Employees: 3,900
Jobs Added Last Year: 1,200 (+44.4%)
Medical services - emergency & general transport services, fire protection & other safety-related services
Phone: 602-994-3886
Fax: 602-481-3260

PETSMART, INC.
10000 N. 31st Ave.
Phoenix, AZ 85051
Chm & CEO: Samuel J. Parker
VP HR: Peter Kanton
Employees: 5,700
Jobs Added Last Year: 3,400 (+147.8%)
Retail - pet supply superstores
Phone: 602-944-7070
Fax: 602-395-6502

SALT RIVER PROJECT AGRICULTURAL IMPROVEMENT & POWER DISTRICT
1521 N. Project Dr.
Tempe, AZ 85281
Pres: William P. Schrader
Mgr HR: Kathy Haake
Employees: 4,600
Jobs Added Last Year: —
Utility - electric power
Phone: 602-236-5900
Fax: 602-236-4350

PHARMACEUTICAL MARKETING SERVICES INC.
2394 E. Camelback Rd.
Phoenix, AZ 85016
CEO: Dennis M. J. Turner
Dir HR: Carolyn Berry
Employees: 675
Jobs Added Last Year: 115 (+20.5%)
Business services - marketing products & services for the pharmaceutical industry
Phone: 602-381-9800
Fax: 602-381-9650

SHAMROCK FOODS COMPANY INC.
2228 North Black Canyon Hwy.
Phoenix, AZ 85009
CEO: Norman P. McClelland
Dir HR: Bonnie Taylor
Employees: 1,500
Jobs Added Last Year: 300 (+25%)
Food - distribution, dairy products
Phone: 602-272-6721
Fax: 602-233-2791

PHELPS DODGE CORPORATION
2600 N. Central Ave.
Phoenix, AZ 85004-3089
Chm, Pres & CEO: Douglas C. Yearley
VP HR: John C. Replogle
Employees: 14,799
Jobs Added Last Year: 49 (+.3%)
Metals - copper
Phone: 602-234-8100
Fax: 602-234-8337

SYNTELLECT INC.
15810 N. 28th Ave.
Phoenix, AZ 85023
CEO: Thomas R. Mayer
Dir HR: Evon Theis
Employees: 256
Jobs Added Last Year: 67 (+35.4%)
Telecommunications equipment - interactive voice response systems
Phone: 602-789-2800
Fax: 602-789-2899

PINNACLE WEST CAPITAL CORP.
400 E. Van Buren St., Ste. 700
Phoenix, AZ 85004
Chm, Pres & CEO: Richard Snell
VP HR: Armando B. Flores
Employees: 7,915
Jobs Cut Last Year: 5 (-.1%)
Utility - electric power
Phone: 602-379-2500
Fax: 602-379-2640

THREE-FIVE SYSTEMS, INC.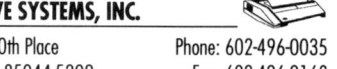
10230 S. 50th Place
Phoenix, AZ 85044-5209
Chm, Pres & CEO: David R. Buchanan
VP HR: Elizabeth Sharp
Employees: 141
Jobs Added Last Year: 59 (+72%)
Electrical components - liquid crystal & light-emitting diode displays
Phone: 602-496-0035
Fax: 602-496-0168

ARKANSAS

ACXIOM CORPORATION
301 Industrial Blvd. Phone: 501-336-1000
Conway, AR 72032-7103 Fax: 501-336-3913
Chm & CEO: Charles D. Morgan, Jr.
SVP People Svcs & Mktg: Phil Bartos
Employees: 2,000
Jobs Added Last Year: 460 (+29.9%)
Computers - data processing services for direct marketing industry

ALLTEL CORPORATION
One Allied Dr. Phone: 501-661-8000
Little Rock, AR 72202 Fax: 501-664-3469
Chm, Pres & CEO: Joe T. Ford
VP HR: John L. Comparin
Employees: 14,864
Jobs Added Last Year: 1,988 (+15.4%)
Utility - local & long distance telephone service; data processing management; cellular phone service

AMERICAN FREIGHTWAYS CORP. — 12657
2200 Forward Dr. Phone: 501-741-9000
Harrison, AR 72601 Fax: 501-741-3003
Chm, Pres & CEO: F. Sheridan Garrison
VP HR: Steve McMath
Employees: 4,964
Jobs Added Last Year: 1,309 (+35.8%)
Transportation - less-than-truckload freight in central & southern US

ARKANSAS BEST CORPORATION
1000 S. 21st St. Phone: 501-785-6000
Fort Smith, AR 72901 Fax: 501-785-6009
Pres, CFO & COO: Robert A. Young III
Dir HR: Joe Davis
Employees: 11,371
Jobs Added Last Year: 826 (+7.8%)
Transportation - truck

BALDOR ELECTRIC CO.
5711 R. S. Boreham, Jr. St. Phone: 501-646-4711
Fort Smith, AR 72902 Fax: 501-648-5792
CEO: R. L. Qualls
Dir HR: Charles H. Cramer
Employees: 2,953
Jobs Cut Last Year: 23 (-.8%)
Machinery - electrical

BEVERLY ENTERPRISES, INC. — 10211
1200 S. Waldron Rd., Ste. 155 Phone: 501-452-6712
Fort Smith, AR 72903 Fax: 501-452-5131
Chm, Pres & CEO: David R. Banks
VP HR: Carol Johansen
Employees: 89,000
Jobs Cut Last Year: 4,000 (-4.3%)
Nursing homes - #1 US for-profit nursing home chain

DILLARD DEPARTMENT STORES, INC. — 10463
1600 Cantrell Rd. Phone: 501-376-5200
Little Rock, AR 72201 Fax: 501-376-5917
Chm & CEO: William Dillard
Personnel Dir: Joyce Wisner
Employees: 35,536
Jobs Added Last Year: 3,404 (+10.6%)
Retail - department stores in the South & Midwest

HUDSON FOODS, INC.
1225 Hudson Rd. Phone: 501-636-1100
Rogers, AR 72756 Fax: 501-631-5192
Chm & CEO: James T. Hudson
Dir HR: Larry Landrith
Employees: 8,554
Jobs Added Last Year: 325 (+3.9%)
Food - processed poultry & meat products

J.B. HUNT TRANSPORT SERVICES, INC.
615 J.B. Hunt Corporate Dr. Phone: 501-820-0000
Lowell, AR 72745 Fax: 501-820-8395
Pres & CEO: Kirk Thompson
EVP HR & Risk Mgmt: Stephen L. Palmer
Employees: 10,476
Jobs Cut Last Year: 725 (-6.5%)
Transportation - truck

NATIONAL HOME CENTERS, INC.
Hwy. 265 North Phone: 501-756-1700
Springdale, AR 72765 Fax: 501-756-9122
CEO: Dwain A. Newman
No central personnel officer
Employees: 933
Jobs Added Last Year: 203 (+27.8%)
Building products - retail

An in-depth profile of this company is available by fax. Call 800-510-4452 and use your touch-tone phone to put in the 5-digit code at the prompt. Only $2.95 each with your credit card. See page 12 for more details.

ARKANSAS

PAM TRANSPORTATION SERVICES, INC.
Hwy. 412 West Phone: 501-361-9111
Tontitown, AR 72770 Fax: 501-361-5335
Pres & CEO: Robert W. Weaver
Dir Off Personnel: Linda Scott
Employees: 1,000
Jobs Added Last Year: 73 (+7.9%)
Transportation - truck

USA TRUCK, INC.
3108 Industrial Park Rd. Phone: 501-471-2500
Van Buren, AR 72956 Fax: 501-471-2577
Pres & CEO: Robert M. Powell
Dir HR: Bud Pierce
Employees: 935
Jobs Added Last Year: 174 (+22.9%)
Transportation - truck

TYSON FOODS, INC. 14965
2210 W. Oaklawn Phone: 501-756-4000
Springdale, AR 72762-6999 Fax: 501-756-4061
VC, Pres & CEO: Leland E. Tollett
Group VP HR: William P. Jaycox
Employees: 55,800
Jobs Added Last Year: 5,442 (+10.8%)
Food - poultry, beef & pork products

WAL-MART STORES, INC. 11600
Bentonville, AR 72716 Phone: 501-273-4000
Pres & CEO: David D. Glass Fax: 501-273-8650
SVP Personnel: Cole Petersen
Employees: 528,000
Jobs Added Last Year: 94,000 (+21.7%)
Retail - discount & variety, warehouse (Sam's); book & music distribution (Western Merchandising)

▼ **Career Taxi** http://www.iquest.net/Career_Taxi/taxi.html

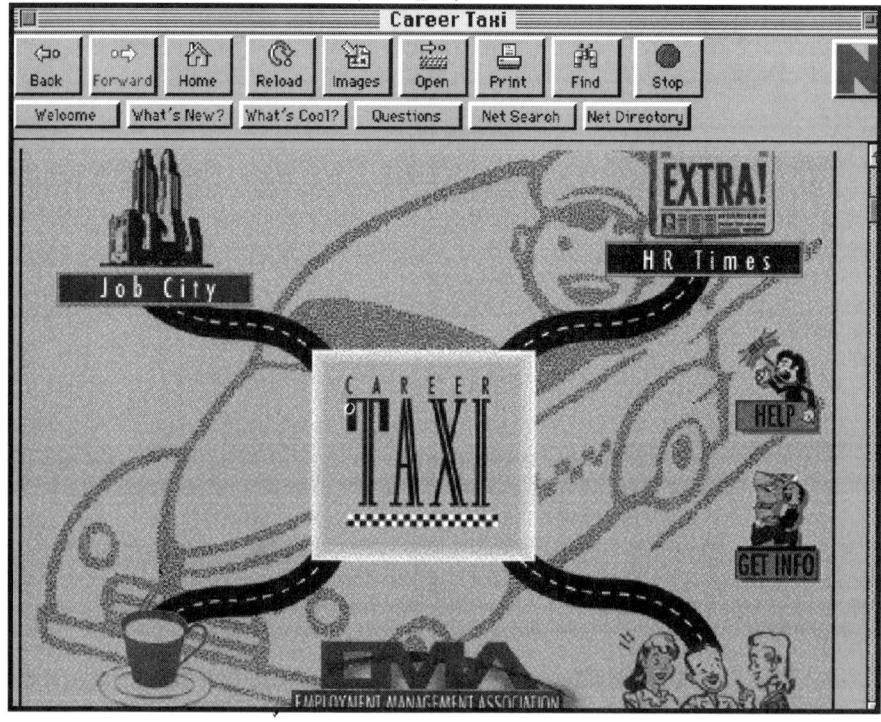

80 HOOVER'S MASTERLIST OF AMERICA'S TOP 2,500 EMPLOYERS

CALIFORNIA

3COM CORPORATION
5400 Bayfront Plaza
Santa Clara, CA 95052-8145
Chm, Pres & CEO: Eric A. Benhamou
Dir HR: Susan Gellen
Employees: 2,306
Jobs Added Last Year: 335 (+17%)
Computers - LAN routers, hubs, remote access servers, switches & adapters

Phone: 408-764-5000
Fax: 408-764-5001

3D SYSTEMS CORPORATION
26081 Avenue Hall
Valencia, CA 91355
Chm & CEO: Arthur B. Sims
VP, CFO & Sec (HR): Gordon L. Almquist
Employees: 185
Jobs Added Last Year: 30 (+19.4%)
Instruments - stereolithographic devices that create 3D models from computer CAD/CAM generated specifications

Phone: 805-295-5600
Fax: 805-295-0249

THE 3DO COMPANY
600 Galveston Dr.
Redwood City, CA 94063-1140
Chm, Pres & CEO: M. William "Trip" Hawkins III
Mgr HR: Shelli Meneghetti
Employees: 339
Jobs Added Last Year: 244 (+256.8%)
Video home products - CD-ROM-based entertainment systems

Phone: 415-261-3000
Fax: 415-261-3231

AAMES FINANCIAL CORPORATION
3731 Wilshire Blvd., 10th Fl.
Los Angeles, CA 90010
CEO: Gary K. Judis
HR Mgr: Nanette Duff Sullivan
Employees: 303
Jobs Added Last Year: 75 (+32.9%)
Financial - mortgages & related services

Phone: 213-351-6100
Fax: 213-380-9365

ABAXIS, INC.
1320 Chesapeake Terrace
Sunnyvale, CA 94089
Pres: Gary H. Stroy
Administrative Asst to Pres (HR): Gina Czerwinski
Employees: 75
Jobs Added Last Year: 26 (+53.1%)
Medical instruments - portable blood analyzer

Phone: 408-734-0200
Fax: 408-734-2874

ABM INDUSTRIES INCORPORATED
50 Fremont St., Ste. 2600
San Francisco, CA 94105-2230
CEO: William W. Steele
Dir HR: Donna Dell
Employees: 37,000
Jobs Cut Last Year: 3,000 (-7.5%)
Building - janitorial services & equipment

Phone: 415-597-4500
Fax: 415-597-7160

ACCOLADE INC.
5300 Stevens Creek Blvd.
San Jose, CA 95129
CEO: Peter Harris
HR Mgr: Suzanne Garcia
Employees: 138
Jobs Added Last Year: 42 (+43.8%)
Computers - interactive game software (Jack Nicklaus Golf, Charles Barkley Basketball)

Phone: 408-985-1700
Fax: 408-246-0885

ADAPTEC, INC.
691 S. Milpitas Blvd.
Milpitas, CA 95035
Chm & CEO: John G. Adler
VP Admin (HR): Daniel W. Bowman
Employees: 1,582
Jobs Added Last Year: 266 (+20.2%)
Computers - small computer system interface (SCSI) hardware & software

Phone: 408-945-8600
Fax: 408-262-2533

ADOBE SYSTEMS INCORPORATED
1585 Charleston Rd.
Mountain View, CA 94039-1225
Chm & CEO: John E. Warnock
HR Dir: Rebecca Guerra
Employees: 1,000
Jobs Added Last Year: 113 (+12.7%)
Computers - font (Postscript) & desktop publishing (Pagemaker) software

Phone: 415-961-4400
Fax: 415-961-3769

ADVANCED MARKETING SERVICES
5880 Oberlin Dr., Ste. 400
San Diego, CA 92121-9653
Pres: Charles C. Tillinghast III
Dir HR: Alisa Judge
Employees: 312
Jobs Added Last Year: 49 (+18.6%)
Wholesale distribution - books, audiocassettes & video cassettes, primarily to warehouse clubs

Phone: 619-457-2500
Fax: 619-452-2237

 An in-depth profile of this company is available by fax. Call 800-510-4452 and use your touch-tone phone to put in the 5-digit code at the prompt. Only $2.95 each with your credit card. See page 12 for more details.

81

CALIFORNIA

ADVANCED MEDICAL, INC.
9775 Businesspark Ave. Phone: 619-566-0426
San Diego, CA 92131 Fax: 619-693-9434
CEO: Jeffrey Picower
HR Dir: Elinor Colby
Employees: 1,124
Jobs Added Last Year: 232 (+26%)
Drugs

AGOURON PHARMACEUTICALS, INC.
10350 N. Torrey Pines Rd., Ste. 100 Phone: 619-622-3000
La Jolla, CA 92037-1020 Fax: 619-622-3298
Pres & CEO: Peter Johnson
Dir HR: Pat Moses
Employees: 180
Jobs Added Last Year: 70 (+63.6%)
Drugs

ADVANCED MICRO DEVICES, INC.
One AMD Place Phone: 408-732-2400
Sunnyvale, CA 94088-3453 Fax: 408-982-6164
Chm & CEO: W. Jeremiah Sanders III
SVP HR: Stanley Winvick
Employees: 12,065
Jobs Added Last Year: 511 (+4.4%)
Electrical components - semiconductors (CPUs, EPROMs & others)

AIRTOUCH COMMUNICATIONS
425 Market St. Phone: 415-658-2000
San Francisco, CA 94105 Fax: 415-989-7606
Chm & CEO: Sam Ginn
VP HR: Dwight Jasmann
Employees: 4,500
Jobs Cut Last Year: 130 (-2.8%)
Telecommunications services - cellular telephone services

ADVANCED POLYMER SYSTEMS, INC.
3696 Haven Ave. Phone: 415-366-2626
Redwood City, CA 94063 Fax: 415-365-6490
Pres & CEO: John J. Meakem, Jr.
Dir HR: Shelly Howell
Employees: 93
Jobs Added Last Year: 30 (+47.6%)
Medical products

ALLERGAN, INC.
2525 Dupont Dr., PO Box 19534 Phone: 714-752-4500
Irvine, CA 92713-9534 Fax: 714-253-5596
Pres & CEO: Wiliam C. Shepard
Corp VP HR: Richard J. Hilles
Employees: 4,749
Jobs Cut Last Year: 409 (-7.9%)
Medical products - eye care

ADVANCED TISSUE SCIENCES, INC.
10933 N. Torrey Pines Rd. Phone: 619-450-5730
La Jolla, CA 92037-9553 Fax: 619-450-5703
CEO & Pres: Arthur J. Benvenuto
Dir HR: Julie DeMeules
Employees: 145
Jobs Added Last Year: 27 (+22.9%)
Biomedical & genetic products

ALTERA CORPORATION
2610 Orchard Pkwy. Phone: 408-894-7000
San Jose, CA 95134-2020 Fax: 408-296-3140
Chm, Pres & CEO: Rodney Smith
VP HR: Sandra J. Scarsella
Employees: 527
Jobs Added Last Year: 50 (+10.5%)
Electrical components - programmable logic devices

ADVENTIST HEALTH SYSTEM/WEST
2100 Douglas Blvd. Phone: 916-781-2000
Roseville, CA 95661-9002 Fax: 916-783-9146
Chm: Thomas J. Mostert
Dir HR: Roger Ashley
Employees: 13,000
Jobs Added Last Year: —
Hospitals

ALZA CORPORATION
950 Page Mill Rd. Phone: 415-494-5000
Palo Alto, CA 94303-0802 Fax: 415-494-5129
Chm, Pres & CEO: Ernest Mario
VP HR: Harold Fethe
Employees: 1,075
Jobs Added Last Year: 237 (+28.3%)
Medical products - rate-controlled delivery systems

CALIFORNIA

A-MARK FINANCIAL CORPORATION
100 Wilshire Blvd., 3rd Fl.   Phone: 310-319-0200
Santa Monica, CA 90401   Fax: 310-319-0279
Chm & Pres: Steven C. Markoff
SVP (HR): John Ferm
Employees: 104
Jobs Added Last Year: 44 (+73.3%)
Precious metals & jewelry - wholesale

AMERICAN PRESIDENT COMPANIES
1111 Broadway   Phone: 510-272-8000
Oakland, CA 94607   Fax: 510-272-7941
Chm, Pres & CEO: John M. Lillie
VP HR: Nancy Williams
Employees: 5,437
Jobs Added Last Year: 228 (+4.4%)
Transportation - container shipping

AMERICAN PROTECTIVE SERVICES, INC.
7770 Pardee Ln.   Phone: 510-568-0276
Oakland, CA 94621-1454   Fax: 510-430-1130
Pres: Dwight S. Pedersen
Dir HR: Marisa Englund
Employees: 13,758
Jobs Added Last Year: –
Protection - security guard services

AMERICAN UNITED GLOBAL, INC.
11634 Patton Rd.   Phone: 310-862-8163
Downey, CA 90241-5295   Fax: 310-861-4955
Pres & CEO: John M. Shahid
Mgr HR : Jack Saatjiin
Employees: 740
Jobs Added Last Year: 73 (+10.9%)
Pumps & seals - O-rings & bonded sealing devices for the automotive, aerospace & communications industries

AMERICAN VANGUARD CORPORATION
4100 E. Washington Blvd.   Phone: 213-264-3910
Los Angeles, CA 90023   Fax: 213-264-3910
Pres & CEO: Eric G. Wintemute
No central personnel officer
Employees: 132
Jobs Added Last Year: 78 (+144.4%)
Chemicals - specialty

AMGEN INC.
1840 De Havilland Dr.   Phone: 805-447-1000
Thousand Oaks, CA 91320-1789   Fax: 805-499-9315
Chm & CEO: Gordon M. Binder
VP HR: William F. Puchlevic
Employees: 3,100
Jobs Added Last Year: 765 (+32.8%)
Biomedical & genetic products - therapeutics based on advanced cellular & molecular biology

ANTHONY INDUSTRIES, INC.
4900 S. Eastern Ave.   Phone: 213-724-2800
Los Angeles, CA 90040   Fax: 213-724-0470
Pres & CEO: Bernard I. Forester
Dir Emp Ben: Michelle Lee
Employees: 3,700
Jobs Added Last Year: 500 (+15.6%)
Leisure & recreational products - skis (K2, Olin), fishing tackle, life vests, wet suits, outdoor apparel & bicycles

APPLE COMPUTER, INC.
One Infinite Loop   Phone: 408-996-1010
Cupertino, CA 95014   Fax: 408-996-0275
Pres & Chm: Michael H. Spindler
SVP HR: Kevin J. Sullivan
Employees: 14,592
Jobs Cut Last Year: 346 (-2.3%)
Computers - microcomputers & peripherals; software (Claris); on-line service (eWorld); PDAs (Newton)

APPLIED MATERIALS, INC.
3050 Bowers Ave., PO Box 58039   Phone: 408-727-5555
Santa Clara, CA 95054-3299   Fax: 408-748-9943
Chm & CEO: James C. Morgan
Group VP & Global HR: Glen O. Toney
Employees: 6,497
Jobs Added Last Year: 1,758 (+37.1%)
Machinery - semiconductor manufacturing equipment

ASPECT TELECOMMUNICATIONS CORPORATION
1730 Fox Dr.   Phone: 408-441-2200
San Jose, CA 95131-2312   Fax: 408-441-2260
Pres & CEO: James R. Carreker
VP HR & Admin: Shelley C. Brown
Employees: 625
Jobs Added Last Year: 125 (+25%)
Telecommunications equipment - automated call distribution equipment

CALIFORNIA

AST RESEARCH, INC.
16215 Alton Pkwy., PO Box 19658 Phone: 714-727-4141
Irvine, CA 92713-9658 Fax: 714-727-8584
Chm, Pres & CEO: Safi U. Qureshey
SVP Admin (HR): Richard P. Ottaviano
Employees: 6,500
Jobs Added Last Year: 1,991 (+44.2%)
Computers - servers, desktop & laptop

AVERY DENNISON CORPORATION
150 N. Orange Grove Blvd. Phone: 818-304-2000
Pasadena, CA 91103 Fax: 818-792-7312
Chm & CEO: Charles D. Miller
VP HR: Susan B. Garelli
Employees: 15,750
Jobs Cut Last Year: 750 (-4.5%)
Office & art materials - pressure-sensitive adhesives & materials; identification & retail systems; specialty chemicals

ATLANTIC RICHFIELD COMPANY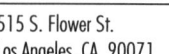
515 S. Flower St. Phone: 213-486-3511
Los Angeles, CA 90071 Fax: 213-486-2063
Pres & CEO: Mike R. Bowlin
VP HR: John H. Kelly
Employees: 25,100
Jobs Cut Last Year: 1,700 (-6.3%)
Oil & gas - integrated

BANKAMERICA CORPORATION
Bank of America Center Phone: 415-622-3530
San Francisco, CA 94104 Fax: 415-622-7915
Chm, Pres & CEO: Richard M. Rosenberg
Group EVP & Corp HR: Kathleen J. Burke
Employees: 96,428
Jobs Cut Last Year: 2,756 (-2.8%)
Banks - money center

ATMEL CORPORATION
2125 O'Nel Dr. Phone: 408-441-0311
San Jose, CA 95131 Fax: 408-436-4200
Chm, Pres & CEO: George Perlegos
Dir HR: Valerie Menager
Employees: 1,282
Jobs Added Last Year: 291 (+29.4%)
Electrical components - high-performance semiconductors using CMOS technology

BAY NETWORKS INC.
4401 Great America Pkwy. Phone: 408-988-2400
Santa Clara, CA 95054 Fax: 508-436-3436
Pres & CEO: Andrew K. Ludwick
VP HR: David M. Lietzke
Employees: 3,000
Jobs Added Last Year: 1,264 (+72.8%)
Computers - internetworking equipment, LAN hub products & management systems

AUTHENTIC FITNESS CORPORATION
6040 Bandini Blvd. Phone: 213-726-1262
Commerce, CA 90040 Fax: 213-721-3613
Chm & CEO: Linda J. Wachner
VP HR & Admin: David Grundman
Employees: 1,350
Jobs Added Last Year: 907 (+204.7%)
Apparel - swimwear, swim accessories & fitness apparel (Speedo, Catalina & Oscar de la Renta)

BECHTEL GROUP, INC.
50 Beale St. Phone: 415-768-1234
San Francisco, CA 94105 Fax: 415-768-0263
Pres & CEO: Riley P. Bechtel, Jr.
VP & Mgr HR: Shirley Gaufin
Employees: 29,400
Jobs Cut Last Year: 1,500 (-4.9%)
Construction - engineering & environmental services

AUTODESK, INC.
2320 Marinship Way Phone: 415-332-2344
Sausalito, CA 94965 Fax: 415-331-8093
Chm, Pres & CEO: Carol A. Bartz
VP HR: Steven McMahon
Employees: 1,788
Jobs Added Last Year: 223 (+14.2%)
Computers - computer automated design software

BECKMAN INSTRUMENTS, INC.
2500 Harbor Blvd. Phone: 714-871-4848
Fullerton, CA 92634-3100 Fax: 714-773-8283
Chm & CEO: Louis T. Rosso
VP HR: Richard K. Sears
Employees: 6,600
Jobs Cut Last Year: 300 (-4.3%)
Medical instruments - sample preparation

CALIFORNIA

BELL INDUSTRIES, INC.
11812 San Vicente Blvd.
Los Angeles, CA 90049-5069
Chm & CEO: Theodore Williams
Dir HR: Stephen Antonoff
Employees: 1,400
Jobs Added Last Year: 100 (+7.7%)
Electronics - semiconductor parts distribution; electronic imaging equipment distribution

Phone: 310-826-2355
Fax: 310-447-3265

BELL MICROPRODUCTS INC.
1941 Ringwood Ave.
San Jose, CA 95131-1721
Chm, Pres & CEO: W. Donald Bell
VP HR: Anne M. Lynch
Employees: 238
Jobs Added Last Year: 144 (+153.2%)
Electronics - parts distribution to computer industry

Phone: 408-451-9400
Fax: 408-451-1694

BERGEN BRUNSWIG CORPORATION
4000 Metropolitan Dr.
Orange, CA 92668-3510
Chm & CEO: Robert E. Martini
VP HR: Carol Scherman
Employees: 4,250
Jobs Added Last Year: 750 (+21.4%)
Drugs & sundries - wholesale

Phone: 714-385-4000
Fax: 714-385-1442

BOOLE & BABBAGE, INC.
3131 Zanker Rd.
San Jose, CA 95134-1933
Pres & CEO: Paul E. Newton
VP Ops (HR): Dick Ali
Employees: 725
Jobs Added Last Year: 72 (+11%)
Computers - mainframe automation (AutoOPERATOR) & client/server (AutoCOMMAND) software

Phone: 408-526-3000
Fax: 408-526-3055

BROADWAY STORES INC.
3880 N. Mission Rd.
Los Angeles, CA 90031-3179
Pres & CEO: David L. Dworkin
EVP HR: Robert J. Lambert
Employees: 23,000
Jobs Added Last Year: 0
Retail - major department stores (Broadway, Emporium, Weinstocks)

Phone: 213-227-2000
Fax: 213-227-2774

BUGLE BOY INDUSTRIES
2900 Madera Rd.
Simi Valley, CA 93065
CEO: William Mow
SVP HR: Ken Sekella
Employees: 2,267
Jobs Added Last Year: 437 (+23.9%)
Apparel

Phone: 805-582-1010
Fax: 805-522-1278

CALIFORNIA MICROWAVE, INC.
985 Almanor Ave.
Sunnyvale, CA 94086
Chm, Pres & CEO: Philip F. Otto
Dir HR Employment: Ginger Washburn
Employees: 1,887
Jobs Added Last Year: 534 (+39.5%)
Telecommunications equipment - satellite earth stations & microwave radios for wireless communications

Phone: 408-732-4000
Fax: 408-732-4244

CALLAWAY GOLF COMPANY
2285 Rutherford Rd.
Carlsbad, CA 92008-8815
Chm & CEO: Ely Callaway
VP HR: Elizabeth O'Mea
Employees: 1,071
Jobs Added Last Year: 383 (+55.7%)
Leisure & recreational products - golf clubs, notably the Big Bertha metal wood club

Phone: 619-931-1771
Fax: 619-931-9539

CATHOLIC HEALTHCARE WEST INC.
1700 Montgomery St., Ste. 300
San Francisco, CA 94111
Pres & CEO: Richard J. Kramer
Dir HR: Lawrence Kren
Employees: 17,451
Jobs Cut Last Year: 1,355 (-7.2%)
Hospitals

Phone: 415-397-9000
Fax: 415-397-1823

CELTRIX PHARMACEUTICALS, INC.
2500 Faber Place
Palo Alto, CA 94303
Pres & CEO (HR): Dale A. Stringfellow
Employees: 134
Jobs Added Last Year: 64 (+91.4%)
Drugs

Phone: 415-494-2500
Fax: 415-856-0533

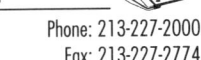

An in-depth profile of this company is available by fax. Call 800-510-4452 and use your touch-tone phone to put in the 5-digit code at the prompt. Only $2.95 each with your credit card. See page 12 for more details.

85

CALIFORNIA

CENTRAL GARDEN & PET CO.
3697 Mt. Diablo Blvd., Ste. 310   Phone: 510-283-4573
Lafayette, CA 94549   Fax: 510-283-6165
Chm & CEO: William E. Brown
VP Mktg & HR: Al Manseau
Employees: 1,246
Jobs Added Last Year: 270 (+27.7%)
Wholesale distribution - garden, pool & pet supplies

CERPLEX GROUP, INC.
3332 E. LaPalma Ave.   Phone: 714-632-2600
Anaheim, CA 92806   Fax: 714-632-2619
Chm & CEO: William A. Klein
Personnel Dir: Robert P. Bunce
Employees: 1,575
Jobs Added Last Year: 725 (+85.3%)
Computers - repair services for computers, peripherals & circuit boards

CERTIFIED GROCERS OF CALIFORNIA, LTD
2601 S. Eastern Ave.   Phone: 213-723-7476
Los Angeles, CA 90040   Fax: 213-724-7667
Pres & CEO: Alfred A. Plamann
VP HR: Donald G. Grose
Employees: 2,500
Jobs Added Last Year: —
Retail - supermarkets

THE CHARLES SCHWAB CORP.
101 Montgomery St.   Phone: 415-627-7000
San Francisco, CA 94104   Fax: 415-627-8538
Chm & CEO: Charles R. Schwab
EVP HR: Luis E. Valencia
Employees: 6,500
Jobs Added Last Year: 2,000 (+44.4%)
Financial - securities brokerage

CHART HOUSE ENTERPRISES, INC.
115 S. Acacia Ave.   Phone: 619-755-8281
Solana Beach, CA 92075-1803   Fax: 619-481-0693
Chm, Pres & CEO: John M. Creed
Dir HR: Rob Wieana
Employees: 6,100
Jobs Added Last Year: 700 (+13%)
Retail - restaurants

THE CHEESECAKE FACTORY INCORPORATED
26635 Agoura Rd., Ste. 101   Phone: 818-880-9323
Calabasas, CA 91302-2978   Fax: 818-880-6501
Pres & CEO: David Overton
SVP (HR): Linda Candioty
Employees: 2,250
Jobs Added Last Year: 350 (+18.4%)
Retail - restaurants in Southern California, Atlanta & Washington, DC; cheesecake

CHEVRON CORPORATION
225 Bush St.   Phone: 415-894-7700
San Francisco, CA 94104   Fax: 415-894-0593
Chm & CEO: Kenneth T. Derr
VP HR: Ronald Kiskis
Employees: 47,576
Jobs Cut Last Year: 1,669 (-3.4%)
Oil & gas - integrated

CHILDREN'S DISCOVERY CENTERS OF AMERICA
851 Irwin St., Ste. 200   Phone: 415-257-4200
San Raphael, CA 94901-3343   Fax: 415-459-1374
Pres & CEO: Richard A. Niglio
VP HR: Paulette Barry
Employees: 2,900
Jobs Added Last Year: 1,200 (+70.6%)
Schools - preschool & child care

CHIRON CORPORATION
4560 Horton St.   Phone: 510-655-8730
Emeryville, CA 94608-2916   Fax: 510-655-9910
Pres & CEO: Edward E. Penhoet
Dir HR: Barbara Kerr
Employees: 2,179
Jobs Added Last Year: 312 (+16.7%)
Biomedical & genetic products - anticancer treatments, vaccines & blood diagnostics

THE CHRONICLE PUBLISHING COMPANY, INC.
901 Mission St.   Phone: 415-777-1111
San Francisco, CA 94103   Fax: 415-777-7131
CEO: John B. Sias
No central personnel officer
Employees: 3,100
Jobs Added Last Year: 100 (+3.3%)
Publishing - newspapers; TV stations; cable systems

CALIFORNIA

CINEMA RIDE, INC.
12001 Ventura Place, Ste. 600 Phone: 818-761-1002
Studio City, CA 91604 Fax: 818-761-1072
Chm, Pres & CEO: Mitch Francis
CFO, COO, EVP, Sec & Treas (HR): Gary H. Packman
Employees: 57
Jobs Added Last Year: 51 (+850%)
Leisure & recreational products - motion simulator rides (Galactic Flight, Atlantis Submarine Race & Coaster Crazy)

CIRCON CORPORATION
460 Ward Dr. Phone: 805-967-0404
Santa Barbara, CA 93111-2310 Fax: 805-967-5035
Chm, Pres & CEO: Richard A. Auhll
VP HR: Jon St. Clair
Employees: 792
Jobs Added Last Year: 98 (+14.1%)
Medical instruments - endoscopes

CIRRUS LOGIC, INC.
3100 W. Warren Ave. Phone: 510-623-8300
Fremont, CA 94538 Fax: 510-226-2240
Pres & CEO: Michael L. Hackworth
VP HR: William H. Bennett
Employees: 1,809
Jobs Added Last Year: 836 (+85.9%)
Electrical components - semiconductors for hard drive & graphics controllers, accelerators & modems

CISCO SYSTEMS, INC.
1525 O'Brien Dr. Phone: 415-326-1941
Menlo Park, CA 94025 Fax: 415-326-1989
Pres & CEO: John T. Chambers
Dir HR: Barbara Beck
Employees: 2,443
Jobs Added Last Year: 992 (+68.4%)
Computers - internetworking systems

CKE RESTAURANTS, INC.
1200 N. Harbor Blvd. Phone: 714-774-5796
Anaheim, CA 92801 Fax: 714-778-7183
Chm: William P. Foley
Dir HR: Victoria Straschil
Employees: 11,500
Jobs Added Last Year: 0
Retail - restaurants (Carl's Jr. & Boston Chicken franchisee)

THE CLOROX COMPANY
1221 Broadway Phone: 510-271-7000
Oakland, CA 94612-1888 Fax: 510-465-8875
Chm & CEO: G. Craig Sullivan
VP HR: Janet M. Brady
Employees: 4,850
Jobs Added Last Year: 150 (+3.2%)
Soap & cleaning preparations (Clorox, Formula 409, Soft Scrub, Tilex) & consumer products (Brita, Kingsford)

THE CLOTHESTIME, INC.
5325 E. Hunter Ave. Phone: 714-779-5881
Anaheim, CA 92807 Fax: 714-779-2032
Chm & CEO: John Ortega
Dir HR: Michele Bentley
Employees: 3,825
Jobs Added Last Year: 625 (+19.5%)
Retail - apparel & shoes

COMPRESSION LABS, INCORPORATED
2860 Junction Ave. Phone: 408-435-3000
San Jose, CA 95134 Fax: 408-922-5574
Chm, Pres & CEO: John E. Tyson
VP HR: Bonnie L. Nunke
Employees: 434
Jobs Added Last Year: 80 (+22.6%)
Telecommunications equipment - video conferencing

COMPUTER SCIENCES CORPORATION
2100 E. Grand Ave. Phone: 310-615-0311
El Segundo, CA 90245 Fax: 310-640-2648
Chm & CEO: William R. Hoover
VP HR: L. Scott Sharpe
Employees: 28,600
Jobs Added Last Year: 2,600 (+10%)
Consulting - business reengineering & information systems consulting, integration & outsourcing

CONNER PERIPHERALS, INC.
3081 Zanker Rd. Phone: 408-456-4500
San Jose, CA 95134-2128 Fax: 408-456-4501
Chm & CEO: Finis F. Conner
VP HR: Greg Goodere
Employees: 9,097
Jobs Cut Last Year: 3,205 (-26.1%)
Computers - disk drives

An in-depth profile of this company is available by fax. Call 800-510-4452 and use your touch-tone phone to put in the 5-digit code at the prompt. Only $2.95 each with your credit card. See page 12 for more details.

CALIFORNIA

CONSOLIDATED FREIGHTWAYS, INC.
3240 Hillview Ave.   Phone: 415-494-2900
Palo Alto, CA 94304   Fax: 415-813-0158
Pres & CEO: Donald E. Moffitt
VP, Corp Counsel & HR: Arthur A. Hackworth
Employees: 39,100
Jobs Added Last Year: 1,200 (+3.2%)
Transportation - truck (CF, Con-Way); air freight (Emery)

CROWLEY MARITIME CORPORATION
155 Grand Ave.   Phone: 510-251-7500
Oakland, CA 94612   Fax: 510-251-7625
Chm & CEO: Thomas B. Crowley, Sr.
SVP HR: William A. Pennella
Employees: 5,000
Jobs Added Last Year: 0
Transportation - marine towing, cargo handling

COOPER DEVELOPMENT COMPANY
455 E. Middlefield Rd.   Phone: 415-969-9030
Mountain View, CA 94043   Fax: 415-961-5486
Chm & Pres: Parker G. Montgomery
Chief Admin Off & VP (HR): Carol Kaufman
Employees: 205
Jobs Added Last Year: 60 (+41.4%)
Diversified operations - skin care products; sunglasses

DAMES & MOORE, INC.
911 Wilshire Blvd., Ste. 700   Phone: 213-683-1560
Los Angeles, CA 90017   Fax: 213-628-0015
Chm & CEO: George D. Leal
VP HR: Cynthia Hartley
Employees: 3,100
Jobs Added Last Year: 100 (+3.3%)
Engineering - R&D services

CORNERSTONE IMAGING INC.
1990 Concourse Dr.   Phone: 408-435-8900
San Jose, CA 95131   Fax: 408-435-8998
Pres & CEO: Thomas T. van Overbeek
HR Generalist: Denise Wescott
Employees: 101
Jobs Added Last Year: 19 (+23.2%)
Computers - high-resolution graphics monitors & add-in cards

DAVIDSON & ASSOCIATES, INC.
19840 Pioneer Ave.   Phone: 310-793-0600
Torrance, CA 90503   Fax: 310-793-0601
CEO: Robert M. Davidson
HR Mgr: Lonna Lynn
Employees: 327
Jobs Added Last Year: 76 (+30.3%)
Computers - educational & entertainment software (Math Blaster, Kid CAD, The Multimedia Workshop)

COUNTRYWIDE CREDIT INDUSTRIES
155 N. Lake Ave.   Phone: 818-304-8400
Pasadena, CA 91101-1857   Fax: 818-584-2268
Chm & Pres: David S. Loeb
Mng Dir HR: Gail Thakarar
Employees: 4,867
Jobs Added Last Year: 1,632 (+50.4%)
Financial - mortgages & related services

DAY RUNNER, INC.
2750 W. Moore Ave.   Phone: 714-680-3500
Fullerton, CA 92633   Fax: 714-680-0540
Chm & CEO: Mark A. Vidovich
VP HR: Lee R. Coffey
Employees: 598
Jobs Added Last Year: 67 (+12.6%)
Business services - paper-based personal organizers

CRAIG CORPORATION
116 N. Robertson Blvd.   Phone: 213-239-0555
Los Angeles, CA 90048   Fax: 213-239-0548
Chm & CEO: James J. Cotter
No central personnel officer
Employees: 8,000
Jobs Cut Last Year: 200 (-2.4%)
Retail - supermarkets

DECKERS OUTDOOR CORPORATION
1140 Mark Ave.   Phone: 805-684-7722
Carpinteria, CA 93013   Fax: 805-684-1252
Chm, Pres & CEO: Douglas Otto
Dir HR: Janice Howell
Employees: 325
Jobs Added Last Year: 100 (+44.4%)
Shoes & related apparel - sandals (Teva)

CALIFORNIA

DEL MONTE FOODS COMPANY — 40118
One Market Plaza
San Francisco, CA 94119
Pres & CEO: Robert W. D'Ornellas
VP Corp Personnel: Mark J. Buxton
Employees: 14,000
Jobs Cut Last Year: 500 (-3.4%)
Food - canned
Phone: 415-247-3000
Fax: 415-247-3565

DOLE FOOD COMPANY, INC. — 10303
31355 Oak Crest Dr.
Westlake Village, CA 91361
Chm & CEO: David H. Murdock
VP HR: George R. Horne
Employees: 45,300
Jobs Cut Last Year: 4,700 (-9.4%)
Food - canned fruits & juices
Phone: 818-879-6600
Fax: 818-879-6618

DELRINA CORPORATION
6830 Via Del Oro, Ste. 200
San Jose, CA 95119-1353
Chm & CEO: Dennis Bennie
Dir HR: Teresa Coraggio
Employees: 438
Jobs Added Last Year: 215 (+96.4%)
Computers - PC fax (WinFax) & forms (FormFlow) software
Phone: 408-363-2345
Fax: 408-363-2340

DREYER'S GRAND ICE CREAM, INC.
5929 College Ave.
Oakland, CA 94618
Chm & CEO: T. Gary Rogers
No central personnel officer
Employees: 1,829
Jobs Added Last Year: 382 (+26.4%)
Food - dairy products
Phone: 510-652-8187
Fax: 510-601-4405

DHL WORLDWIDE EXPRESS — 40126
333 Twin Dolphin Dr.
Redwood City, CA 94065
Chm, Pres & CEO: Patrick Foley
SVP HR: Gary Sellers
Employees: 26,000
Jobs Added Last Year: 0
Transportation - air express
Phone: 415-593-7474
Fax: 415-593-1689

E. & J. GALLO WINERY — 40140
PO Box 1130, 600 Yosemite Blvd.
Modesto, CA 95353
Chm: Ernest Gallo
VP HR: Robert Deitrich
Employees: 4,000
Jobs Added Last Year: 0
Beverages - wine (Bartles & James, Carlo Rossi, Gallo, Thunderbird)
Phone: 209-579-3111
Fax: 209-579-3249

DIAMOND MULTIMEDIA SYSTEMS, INC.
1130 E. Arques Ave.
Sunnyvale, CA 94086
Pres & CEO: William J. Schroeder
Controller (HR): Song Kim
Employees: 200
Jobs Added Last Year: 75 (+60%)
Computers - system boards for audio, video & communications bundled with software
Phone: 408-325-7000
Fax: 408-325-7070

EARLE M. JORGENSEN HOLDING COMPANY, INC.
3050 E. Birch St.
Brea, CA 92621
Pres & CEO: Neven C. Hulsey
VP Admin & HR: Steven Wild
Employees: 2,561
Jobs Cut Last Year: 39 (-1.5%)
Steel - production; aluminum product distribution
Phone: 714-579-8823
Fax: 714-524-1072

DIONEX CORPORATION
1228 Titan Way, PO Box 3603
Sunnyvale, CA 94088
Pres & CEO: A. Blaine Bowman
Dir HR: Brian Webb
Employees: 633
Jobs Added Last Year: 64 (+11.2%)
Instruments - chemical analysis
Phone: 408-737-0700
Fax: 408-730-9403

ELECTRONIC ARTS INC. — 14059
1450 Fashion Island Blvd.
San Mateo, CA 94404-2064
Chm, Pres & CEO: Lawrence F. Probst III
SVP, CFO & Chief Admin Off (HR): E. Stanton McKee, Jr.
Employees: 1,077
Jobs Added Last Year: 167 (+18.4%)
Computers - interactive entertainment & education software for personal computers & video-game players
Phone: 415-571-7171
Fax: 415-571-6375

 An in-depth profile of this company is available by fax. Call 800-510-4452 and use your touch-tone phone to put in the 5-digit code at the prompt. Only $2.95 each with your credit card. See page 12 for more details.

CALIFORNIA

ELECTRONICS FOR IMAGING, INC.
2855 Campus Dr. Phone: 415-286-8600
San Mateo, CA 94403-5702 Fax: 415-286-8544
Chm, Pres & CEO: Efraim Arazi
Dir HR: Janice Smith
Employees: 173
Jobs Added Last Year: 44 (+34.1%)
Computers - color desktop publishing systems (Fiery)

FALCON SYSTEMS INC.
1417 N. Market Blvd. Phone: 916-928-9255
Sacramento, CA 95834-1936 Fax: 916-928-9355
Pres: Craig Caudill
HR Mgr: Jack Bacagalupi
Employees: 72
Jobs Added Last Year: 22 (+44%)
Computers - peripherals & mass storage devices for UNIX systems

ENVIRONMENTAL SYSTEMS RESEARCH INSTITUTE
380 New York Street Phone: 909-793-2853
Redlands, CA 92373 Fax: 909-793-5953
Pres: Jack Dangermond
Dir Personnel: Chuck Becker
Employees: 760
Jobs Added Last Year: 130 (+20.6%)
Computers - information systems software; consulting & database construction

FAMILY RESTAURANTS INC.
18831 Von Karman Ave. Phone: 714-757-7900
Irvine, CA 92715 Fax: 714-757-7984
Chm & CEO: Jack Goodall
Chief Admin Off (HR): Patti Johnson
Employees: 19,513
Jobs Cut Last Year: 1,855 (-8.7%)
Retail - restaurants (Chi Chi's, Coco's, El Torito & JoJos)

EPIC DESIGN TECHNOLOGY, INC.
2901 Tasman Dr., Ste. 212 Phone: 408-988-2997
Santa Clara, CA 95054 Fax: 408-988-8424
CEO: Sang S. Wang
Dir HR: Angela Wanninger
Employees: 79
Jobs Added Last Year: 16 (+25.4%)
Computers - simulation & analysis software for integrated circuit design (TimeMill)

FHP INTERNATIONAL CORPORATION
9900 Talbert Ave. Phone: 714-963-7233
Fountain Valley, CA 92708 Fax: 714-964-5922
VC, Pres & CEO: Westcott W. Price III
Corp Dir Emp: Peter Chart
Employees: 14,000
Jobs Added Last Year: 2,700 (+23.9%)
Health maintenance organization

ESPRIT DE CORP.
900 Minnesota St. Phone: 415-648-6900
San Francisco, CA 94107 Fax: 415-550-3960
CEO: David Folkman
Dir HR: Debra J. Sisson
Employees: 4,150
Jobs Added Last Year: –
Apparel - men's, women's & children's clothing

FIBREBOARD CORPORATION
2121 N. California Blvd. Phone: 510-274-0700
Walnut Creek, CA 94596 Fax: 510-274-0715
Pres & CEO: John D. Roach
Dir HR: Terry Kontonickas
Employees: 2,500
Jobs Added Last Year: 300 (+13.6%)
Building products - wood; ski resorts

FAIR, ISAAC AND COMPANY, INCORPORATED
120 N. Redwood Dr. Phone: 415-472-2211
San Rafael, CA 94903 Fax: 415-492-9381
Pres & CEO: Larry E. Rosenberger
VP HR: John Waller
Employees: 580
Jobs Added Last Year: 233 (+67.1%)
Business services - development of statistical tools used by credit grantors

FIDELITY NATIONAL FINANCIAL, INC.
2100 SE Main St., Ste. 400 Phone: 714-852-9770
Irvine, CA 92714 Fax: 714-476-0845
Chm & CEO: William P. Foley II
HR Mgr: Kristi Ecker
Employees: 4,700
Jobs Added Last Year: 700 (+17.5%)
Insurance - multiline & misc.

CALIFORNIA

FIRST AMERICAN FINANCIAL CORPORATION
114 E. Fifth St. Phone: 714-558-3211
Santa Ana, CA 92701-4699 Fax: 714-541-6372
Chm: D. P. Kennedy
Pres (HR): Parker S. Kennedy
Employees: 8,694
Jobs Added Last Year: 1,109 (+14.6%)
Financial - mortgages & related services

FOODMAKER, INC.
9330 Balboa Ave. Phone: 619-571-2121
San Diego, CA 92123 Fax: 619-571-2101
Chm, Pres & CEO: Jack W. Goodall
VP HR: Robert L. Jones
Employees: 26,170
Jobs Added Last Year: 3,985 (+18%)
Retail - restaurants (Jack-in-the-Box & Chi-Chi's)

FIRST INTERSTATE BANCORP
633 W. Fifth St. Phone: 213-614-3001
Los Angeles, CA 90071 Fax: 213-614-3741
CEO: William E. B. Siart
EVP HR: Lillian R. Gorman
Employees: 26,589
Jobs Cut Last Year: 401 (-1.5%)
Banks - money center

FOSTER POULTRY FARMS INC.
1000 Davis St. Phone: 204-394-7901
Livingston, CA 95334 Fax: 209-394-6342
Pres & CEO: Robert A. Fox
Dir Personnel: Tim Walsh
Employees: 6,200
Jobs Added Last Year: –
Food - poultry processing

FIRST MORTGAGE CORPORATION
3230 Fallowfield Dr. Phone: 909-595-1996
Diamond Bar, CA 91765 Fax: 909-595-7430
Pres & CEO: Clement Ziroli
VP HR: Chris Cooper
Employees: 269
Jobs Added Last Year: 74 (+37.9%)
Financial - mortgages & related services

FOUNDATION HEALTH CORP.
3400 Data Dr. Phone: 916-631-5000
Rancho Cordova, CA 95670 Fax: 916-631-5149
Chm, Pres & CEO: Daniel D. Crowley
SVP HR: Dan Smithson
Employees: 4,978
Jobs Added Last Year: 578 (+13.1%)
Health care - outpatient & home

FLEETWOOD ENTERPRISES, INC.
3125 Myers St., PO Box 7638 Phone: 909-351-3500
Riverside, CA 92503-5527 Fax: 909-351-3690
Chm & CEO: John C. Crean
VP Admin & HR: Robert W. Graham
Employees: 16,000
Jobs Added Last Year: 2,000 (+14.3%)
Automotive - RVs & travel trailers

FRANKLIN RESOURCES, INC.
777 Mariners Island Blvd. Phone: 415-312-2000
San Mateo, CA 94404 Fax: 415-378-5755
Pres & CEO: Charles B. Johnson
VP HR: Donna S Ikeda
Employees: 4,100
Jobs Added Last Year: 1,736 (+73.4%)
Financial - real estate investment trust management

FLUOR CORPORATION
3333 Michelson Dr. Phone: 714-975-2000
Irvine, CA 92730 Fax: 714-975-5271
Chm & CEO: Leslie G. McCraw
VP HR & Admin: Charles J. Bradley, Jr.
Employees: 39,807
Jobs Added Last Year: 1,275 (+3.3%)
Construction - engineering & related services

FREEDOM NEWSPAPERS INC.
PO Box 19549 Phone: 714-553-9292
Irvine, CA 92713 Fax: 714-474-4943
CEO: James N. Rosse
No central personnel officer
Employees: 6,800
Jobs Added Last Year: 1,300 (+23.6%)
Publishing - newspapers; TV

CALIFORNIA

FRESENIUS USA INC.
2637 Shadelands Dr. Phone: 510-295-0200
Walnut Creek, CA 94598 Fax: 510-988-1900
CEO: Ben J. Lipps
Dir HR: Dick Grobin
Employees: 845
Jobs Added Last Year: 195 (+30%)
Medical instruments - dialysis systems & related products

GF INDUSTRIES INC.
930 98th Ave. Phone: 415-312-8600
Oakland, CA 94603 Fax: 415-312-8077
CEO: Wilfred Uytengsu
No central personnel officer
Employees: 5,200
Jobs Added Last Year: 200 (+4%)
Food - snacks & biscuits

FRESH CHOICE, INC.
2901 Tasman Dr., Ste. 109 Phone: 408-986-8661
Santa Clara, CA 95054 Fax: 408-986-8334
Chm, Pres & CEO: Martin T. Culver
Dir HR: Lori Stewart
Employees: 2,130
Jobs Added Last Year: 1,050 (+97.2%)
Retail - self-service, salad bar restaurants

GILEAD SCIENCES, INC.
346 Lakeside Dr. Phone: 415-574-3000
Foster City, CA 94404 Fax: 415-578-9264
CEO: Michael L. Riordan
Dir HR: Linda A. Fitzpatrick
Employees: 175
Jobs Added Last Year: 48 (+37.8%)
Biomedical & genetic products - human therapeutics for viral infections, vascular disease, inflammatory disease & cancer

FRITZ COMPANIES, INC.
706 Mission St. Phone: 415-904-8360
San Francisco, CA 94103 Fax: 415-541-7813
Chm, Pres & CEO: Lynn C. Fritz
Dir HR: Bob Davidson
Employees: 3,140
Jobs Added Last Year: 640 (+25.6%)
Transportation - customs brokerage & freight forwarding

GM HUGHES ELECTRONICS CORP.
7200 Hughes Terrace, PO Box 80028 Phone: 310-568-7200
Los Angeles, CA 90080-0028 Fax: 310-568-6390
Chm & CEO: C. Michael Armstrong
SVP HR: Ted G. Westerman
Employees: 78,000
Jobs Cut Last Year: 12,000 (-13.3%)
Electronics - defense, automotive & telecommunications systems

THE GAP, INC.
One Harrison Phone: 415-952-4400
San Francisco, CA 94105 Fax: 415-896-0322
Chm & CEO: Donald G. Fisher
SVP HR: G. Brent Stanley
Employees: 44,000
Jobs Added Last Year: 5,000 (+12.8%)
Retail - apparel & shoes

GOLDEN WEST FINANCIAL CORP.
1901 Harrison St. Phone: 510-446-3420
Oakland, CA 94612 Fax: 510-446-4259
Chm & CEO: Herbert M. Sandler
SVP HR: Susan Lennox
Employees: 4,376
Jobs Added Last Year: 357 (+8.9%)
Financial - savings & loans

GENENTECH, INC.
460 Point San Bruno Blvd. Phone: 415-225-1000
South San Francisco, CA 94080-4990 Fax: 415-225-2021
Pres & CEO: G. Kirk Raab
VP HR: Larry Setren
Employees: 2,510
Jobs Added Last Year: 179 (+7.7%)
Biomedical & genetic products

THE GOOD GUYS, INC.
7000 Marina Blvd. Phone: 415-615-5000
Brisbane, CA 94005-1840 Fax: 415-615-6287
Pres & CEO: Robert A. Gunst
VP HR: Geradette M. Vaz
Employees: 3,642
Jobs Added Last Year: 788 (+27.6%)
Retail - consumer electronics

CALIFORNIA

GOTTSCHALKS INC.
7 River Park Place East Phone: 209-434-8000
Fresno, CA 93720 Fax: 209-434-4804
Chm & CEO: Joe Levy
Dir HR: Marci Woolsen
Employees: 5,000
Jobs Added Last Year: 416 (+9.1%)
Retail - apparel & shoes

GTI CORPORATION
9171 Towne Centre Dr. Phone: 619-546-0531
San Diego, CA 92122 Fax: 619-546-0568
Pres & CEO: Gary L. Luick
No central personnel officer
Employees: 9,354
Jobs Added Last Year: 4,806 (+105.7%)
Electrical components - circuit boards, electronic processing equipment

GRANCARE, INC. [13710]
One Ravinia Dr., Ste. 1240 Phone: 404-393-0199
Culver City, CA 30146 Fax: 404-393-8054
Chm, Pres & CEO: Gene E. Burleson
VP & Dir HR: Mark H. Rubenstein
Employees: 11,000
Jobs Added Last Year: 1,100 (+11.1%)
Medical services - institutional pharmacies

GUPTA CORPORATION [14102]
1060 Marsh Rd. Phone: 415-321-9500
Menlo Park, CA 94025 Fax: 415-321-5471
Chm, Pres & CEO: Umang P. Gupta
Dir HR: Joanne Webster
Employees: 325
Jobs Added Last Year: 121 (+59.3%)
Computers - database management systems software

GRANITE CONSTRUCTION INC.
585 W. Beach St. Phone: 408-724-1011
Watsonville, CA 95076-5125 Fax: 408-722-9657
Pres & CEO: David H. Watts
VP & Dir HR: Michael L. Thomas
Employees: 3,087
Jobs Added Last Year: 686 (+28.6%)
Construction - highways, dams, tunnels, mass transit systems

THE GYMBOREE CORPORATION [16057]
700 Airport Blvd., Ste. 200 Phone: 415-579-0600
Burlingame, CA 94010-1912 Fax: 415-579-1733
Pres & CEO: Nancy J. Pedot
VP HR: Nancy Hauge
Employees: 3,076
Jobs Added Last Year: 919 (+42.6%)
Retail - children's apparel & toys

GREAT WESTERN FINANCIAL CORP. [10677]
9200 Oakdale Ave. Phone: 818-775-3411
Chatsworth, CA 91311-6519 Fax: 818-775-3434
Chm & CEO: James F. Montgomery
SVP HR: Patricia A. Benninger
Employees: 17,029
Jobs Added Last Year: 1,013 (+6.3%)
Financial - savings & loans

H. F. AHMANSON & COMPANY [10691]
4900 Rivergrade Rd. Phone: 818-960-6311
Irwindale, CA 91706 Fax: 818-814-3675
Chm, Pres & CEO: Charles R. Rinehart
First VP HR: Merrill S. Wall
Employees: 10,479
Jobs Added Last Year: 161 (+1.6%)
Financial - savings & loans

GRUBB & ELLIS CO.
One Montgomery St. Phone: 415-956-1990
San Francisco, CA 94104 Fax: 415-274-9700
Chm: Joseph F. Hanauer
Dir HR: Laura Ferracane
Employees: 4,600
Jobs Cut Last Year: 300 (-6.1%)
Real estate operations

HAMILTON FINANCIAL SERVICES CORPORATION
525 Market St., Ninth Fl. Phone: 415-597-5600
San Francisco, CA 94105 Fax: 415-597-7240
Pres: William Kirschenbaum
VP HR: Evelyn Boetes
Employees: 383
Jobs Added Last Year: 128 (+50.2%)
Financial - mortgages & related services

CALIFORNIA

HARPER GROUP, INC.
260 Townsend St. Phone: 415-978-0600
San Francisco, CA 94107-0933 Fax: 415-978-1773
Pres & CEO: Peter Gilbert
VP HR: Dennis Cullen
Employees: 3,025
Jobs Cut Last Year: 150 (-4.7%)
Transportation - air freight

HOMETOWN BUFFET INC.
9171 Town Centre Dr., Ste. 575 Phone: 619-546-9096
San Diego, CA 92122 Fax: 619-546-0179
Pres: C. Dennis Scott
Mgr HR: Cindy Leven
Employees: 1,800
Jobs Added Last Year: 700 (+63.6%)
Retail - food & restaurants

HERBALIFE INTERNATIONAL, INC. [15594]
9800 La Cienega Blvd. Phone: 310-410-9600
Inglewood, CA 90301 Fax: 310-216-7255
Chm, Pres & CEO: Mark Hughes
Dir HR: Pam Kogan
Employees: 638
Jobs Added Last Year: 344 (+117%)
Retail - multitier sales of vitamins, diet personal care, health & fitness products

HUGHES MARKETS, INC.
14005 Live Oak Ave. Phone: 818-856-6580
Irwindale, CA 91706 Fax: 818-856-6020
Pres & CEO: Fred B. McLaren
Dir HR: David McMahon
Employees: 4,900
Jobs Cut Last Year: 200 (-3.9%)
Retail - supermarkets

HEWLETT-PACKARD COMPANY [10723]
3000 Hanover St. Phone: 415-857-1501
Palo Alto, CA 94304 Fax: 415-857-7299
Chm, Pres & CEO: Lewis E. Platt
VP Personnel: F. E. Peterson
Employees: 98,400
Jobs Added Last Year: 2,200 (+2.3%)
Computers - mini & micro, peripheral & network equipment; electronic test & medical equipment

IHOP CORPORATION
525 N. Brand Blvd. Phone: 818-240-6055
Glendale, CA 91203-1903 Fax: 818-240-0270
Chm, Pres & CEO: Richard K. Herzer
VP HR: Naomi K. Shively
Employees: 2,945
Jobs Added Last Year: 755 (+34.5%)
Retail - restaurants (International House of Pancakes)

HILTON HOTELS CORPORATION [10733]
9336 Civic Center Dr. Phone: 310-278-4321
Beverly Hills, CA 90210 Fax: 310-205-4599
Chm & CEO: Barron Hilton
SVP Labor Rel & Personnel Admin: James M. Anderson
Employees: 43,000
Jobs Added Last Year: 2,000 (+4.9%)
Hotels (Conrad, Hilton, Waldorf-Astoria) & casinos (Flamingo)

ILC TECHNOLOGY, INC.
399 Java Dr. Phone: 408-745-7900
Sunnyvale, CA 94089 Fax: 408-744-0829
Pres & CEO: Henry C. Baumgartner
Mgr HR: Gerda White
Employees: 498
Jobs Added Last Year: 76 (+18%)
Instruments - control

HOME THEATER PRODUCTS INTERNATIONAL
1620 S. Lewis St. Phone: 714-937-9300
Anaheim, CA 92805 Fax: 714-937-9309
CEO: Paul Safronchik
Dir HR: Doug Roy
Employees: 150
Jobs Added Last Year: 50 (+50%)
Audio & video home products

IMPERIAL CREDIT INDUSTRIES, INC.
20371 Irvine Ave. Phone: 714-556-0122
Santa Ana Heights, CA 92707 Fax: 714-252-2881
CEO: H. Wayne Snavely
VP & Mgr HR: Veronica F. Villani
Employees: 1,080
Jobs Added Last Year: 681 (+170.7%)
Financial - mortgages & related services

CALIFORNIA

INFORMIX CORPORATION
4100 Bohannon Dr. Phone: 415-926-6300
Menlo Park, CA 94025 Fax: 415-926-6593
Chm, Pres & CEO: Phillip E. White
VP HR: Ira H. Dorf
Employees: 1,718
Jobs Added Last Year: 273 (+18.9%)
Computers - data management software

INTEGRATED DEVICE TECHNOLOGY, INC.
2975 Stender Way Phone: 408-727-6116
Santa Clara, CA 95054 Fax: 408-492-8674
CEO: Leonard C. Perham
Dir HR: Thomas B. Wroblewski
Employees: 2,615
Jobs Added Last Year: 201 (+8.3%)
Electrical components - semiconductors

INTEL CORPORATION
2200 Mission College Blvd. Phone: 408-765-8080
Santa Clara, CA 95052-8119 Fax: 408-765-1402
Pres & CEO: Andrew S. Grove
VP & Dir HR: Kirby A. Dyess
Employees: 29,500
Jobs Added Last Year: 3,700 (+14.3%)
Electrical components - semiconductors; peripheral equipment, supercomputers

INTERNATIONAL RECTIFIER CORPORATION
233 Kansas St. Phone: 310-322-3331
El Segundo, CA 90245 Fax: 310-322-3332
Pres & CEO: Eric Lidow
Dir HR: Dennis Marchand
Employees: 3,000
Jobs Added Last Year: 30 (+1%)
Electrical components - power regulating semiconductors

INTERNATIONAL TECHNOLOGY CORPORATION
23456 Hawthorne Blvd. Phone: 310-378-9933
Torrance, CA 90505 Fax: 310-791-2587
Pres & CEO: Robert B. Sheh
VP HR: Gail M. Fulwider
Employees: 3,164
Jobs Cut Last Year: 257 (-7.3%)
Pollution control - environmental management services, hazardous waste disposal

INTERPLAY PRODUCTIONS INC.
17922 Fitch Ave Phone: 714-553-6655
Irvine, CA 92714 Fax: 714-252-2820
Pres & CEO: Brian Fargo
HR Dir: Lisa Fisher
Employees: 240
Jobs Added Last Year: 110 (+84.6%)
Computers - interactive videogame software

IWERKS ENTERTAINMENT INC.
4540 W. Valerio St. Phone: 818-841-7766
Burbank, CA 91505 Fax: 818-841-7847
Chm & CEO: Stanley B. Kinsey
Dir HR: Catherine Giffen
Employees: 253
Jobs Added Last Year: 90 (+55.2%)
Motion pictures - speciality theaters with high-end visual & audio systems

JACOBS ENGINEERING GROUP INC.
251 S. Lake Ave. Phone: 818-449-2171
Pasadena, CA 91101 Fax: 818-578-6893
Pres & CEO: Noel G. Watson
Dir Corp HR: William Gebhardt
Employees: 13,100
Jobs Added Last Year: 800 (+6.5%)
Construction - heavy

KAISER FOUNDATION HEALTH PLAN
One Kaiser Plaza Phone: 510-271-5910
Oakland, CA 94612 Fax: 510-271-5917
Chm & CEO: David M. Lawrence
VP HR: Alfred Bolden
Employees: 84,885
Jobs Added Last Year: 2,027 (+2.4%)
Health maintenance organization

KAUFMAN AND BROAD HOME CORPORATION
10877 Wilshire Blvd. Phone: 310-443-8000
Los Angeles, CA 90024 Fax: 310-443-8089
Pres & CEO: Bruce E. Karatz
VP HR: Alan Kaye
Employees: 1,372
Jobs Added Last Year: 153 (+12.6%)
Building - residential & commercial

CALIFORNIA

KENDALL-JACKSON WINERY LTD.
421 Aviation Blvd.　　　　　Phone: 707-544-4000
Santa Rosa, CA 95403　　　Fax: 707-544-4013
CEO: Jess S. Jackson
Personnel Mgr: Carol Felch
Employees: 300
Jobs Added Last Year: 180 (+150%)
Beverages - wine

LINEAR TECHNOLOGY CORPORATION
1630 McCarthy Blvd.　　　Phone: 408-432-1900
Milpitas, CA 95035-7487　Fax: 408-434-0507
Pres & CEO: Robert H. Swanson, Jr.
VP Fin & CFO (HR): Paul Coghlan
Employees: 1,000
Jobs Added Last Year: 130 (+14.9%)
Electrical components - electronic sensing and measuring devices

KINGSTON TECHNOLOGY CORPORATION
17600 Newhope St.　　　　Phone: 714-435-2600
Fountain Valley, CA 92708　Fax: 714-434-2699
Pres: John Tu
HR Dir: Daniel Hsu
Employees: 310
Jobs Added Last Year: 55 (+21.6%)
Computers - memory, processor & storage add-in peripherals for PCs

LITTON INDUSTRIES, INC.
2140 Burbank Blvd.　　　　Phone: 818-598-5000
Woodland Hills, CA 91367-6675　Fax: 818-598-5940
Pres & CEO: John M. Leonis
VP HR: Mathias J. Diederich
Employees: 29,000
Jobs Cut Last Year: 3,300 (-10.2%)
Diversified operations - defense electronics; military shipbuilding

KOMAG, INCORPORATED
275 S. Hillview Dr.　　　　Phone: 408-946-2300
Milpitas, CA 95035　　　　Fax: 408-946-1126
Pres & CEO: Stephen C. Johnson
VP HR: Kathryn A. McGann
Employees: 3,497
Jobs Added Last Year: 407 (+13.2%)
Computers - thin-film heads for hard disk drives

LONGS DRUG STORES CORPORATION
141 N. Civic Dr., PO Box 5222　Phone: 510-937-1170
Walnut Creek, CA 94596　　Fax: 510-210-6886
Chm & CEO: Robert M. Long
VP Personnel: Les C. Anderson
Employees: 15,600
Jobs Added Last Year: 600 (+4%)
Retail - drug stores in the western US (primarily California) & Hawaii

LAM RESEARCH CORPORATION
4650 Cushing Pkwy.　　　　Phone: 510-659-0200
Fremont, CA 94538　　　　Fax: 510-659-1560
Chm & CEO: Roger D. Emerick
VP HR: Tina Sankoff
Employees: 1,640
Jobs Added Last Year: 557 (+51.4%)
Machinery - etching equipment for semiconductor manufacturing

LR HOLDINGS, INC.
1165 Triton Dr.　　　　　　Phone: 415-349-5966
Foster City, CA 94404-1213　Fax: 415-573-7743
Pres & CEO: Hazem Ouf
VP HR: Arden Howell
Employees: 4,300
Jobs Added Last Year: —
Retail - restaurants (Lyons)

LEVI STRAUSS ASSOCIATES INC.
1155 Battery St.　　　　　　Phone: 415-544-6000
San Francisco, CA 94111　　Fax: 415-544-3939
Chm & CEO: Robert D. Haas, Sr.
SVP HR: Donna J. Goya
Employees: 36,400
Jobs Added Last Year: 2,200 (+6.4%)
Apparel (Brittania, Dockers, Levi's)

MAC FRUGAL'S BARGAINS - CLOSE-OUTS, INC.
2430 E. Del Amo Blvd.　　　Phone: 310-537-9220
Dominguez, CA 90220-6306　Fax: 310-632-4477
Pres & CEO: Leonard S. Williams
VP HR: Frank Bianchi
Employees: 6,500
Jobs Cut Last Year: 368 (-5.4%)
Retail - discount & variety

CALIFORNIA

MAIL BOXES ETC.
6060 Cornerstone Ct. West Phone: 619-455-8800
San Diego, CA 92121-3795 Fax: 619-546-7488
VC, Pres & CEO: Anthony W. DeSio
Mgr HR & Admin: Sheryl Hradecky
Employees: 165
Jobs Added Last Year: 25 (+17.9%)
Business services - postal operations & communications

MCKESSON CORPORATION
McKesson Plaza, One Post St. Phone: 415-983-8300
San Francisco, CA 94104 Fax: 415-983-7160
Chm & CEO: Alan J. Seelenfreund
VP HR & Admin: William A. Armstrong
Employees: 14,500
Jobs Added Last Year: 500 (+3.6%)
Drugs & sundries - wholesale; service merchandising; bottled water

MATTEL, INC.
333 Continental Blvd. Phone: 310-524-2000
El Segundo, CA 90245-5012 Fax: 310-524-3861
Chm & CEO: John W. Amerman
SVP HR & Admin: E. Joseph McKay
Employees: 21,000
Jobs Added Last Year: 6,000 (+40%)
Toys - dolls (Barbie, Lion King, Sally Secrets), games, action & activity toys (Corgi)

MEDIA ARTS GROUP, INC.
10 Almaden Blvd., Ste. 900 Phone: 408-947-4680
San Jose, CA 95113 Fax: 408-947-4642
Chm & CEO: Kenneth E. Raasch
Corp Sec (HR): Sue Edstrom
Employees: 750
Jobs Added Last Year: 170 (+29.3%)
Housewares - collectible lithographs (Elvis, JFK), miniature cottages & other figurines

MAXIM INTEGRATED PRODUCTS, INC.
120 San Gabriel Dr. Phone: 408-737-7600
Sunnyvale, CA 94086 Fax: 408-737-7194
Chm, Pres & CEO: John F. "Jack" Gifford
CFO & VP Acctg, Fin & Personnel: Michael J. Byrd
Employees: 1,016
Jobs Added Last Year: 212 (+26.4%)
Electrical components - linear & mixed signal integrated circuits

MEDIA VISION TECHNOLOGY INC.
47300 Bayside Pkwy Phone: 510-770-8600
Fremont, CA 94538 Fax: 510-770-8648
Pres, CEO & COO: G. Robert Brownell
Mgr HR: Roberta Riga
Employees: 332
Jobs Added Last Year: 152 (+84.4%)
Computers - multimedia peripheral equipment, including sound & video boards

MAXTOR CORPORATION
211 River Oaks Pkwy. Phone: 408-432-1700
San Jose, CA 95134 Fax: 408-432-4510
Pres & CEO: C. S. Park
VP HR: Patricia M Roboostoff
Employees: 6,400
Jobs Cut Last Year: 2,500 (-28.1%)
Computers - hard disk drives

MERCURY GENERAL CORPORATION
4484 Wilshire Blvd. Phone: 213-937-1060
Los Angeles, CA 90010 Fax: 213-857-7116
Pres & CEO: George Joseph
Dir HR: Michael Turney
Employees: 1,300
Jobs Added Last Year: 145 (+12.6%)
Insurance - property & casualty

MCCLATCHY NEWSPAPERS, INC.
2100 Q St. Phone: 916-321-1846
Sacramento, CA 95816 Fax: 916-321-1996
Pres & CEO: Erwin Potts
VP HR: Peter M. CaJacob
Employees: 6,304
Jobs Added Last Year: 39 (+.6%)
Publishing - newspapers *(The Sacramento* (CA) *Bee)*

MERCURY INTERACTIVE CORPORATION
3333 Octavius Dr. Phone: 408-987-0100
Santa Clara, CA 95054 Fax: 408-982-0149
CEO: Aryeh Finegold
Dir HR: Betty Hardonag
Employees: 147
Jobs Added Last Year: 32 (+27.8%)
Computers - automated testing for software development

CALIFORNIA

MERISEL, INC.
200 Continental Blvd. Phone: 310-615-3080
El Segundo, CA 90245-0948 Fax: 310-615-1238
Co-Chm & CEO: Michael D. Pickett
VP HR: Ed Johnson
Employees: 2,502
Jobs Added Last Year: 563 (+29%)
Computers - wholesale software

NATIONAL HEALTH LABORATORIES, INC.
4225 Executive Sq., Ste. 800 Phone: 619-550-0600
La Jolla, CA 92037-1485 Fax: 619-658-6693
Pres & CEO: James Maher
Mgr HR: Merle Cochrane
Employees: 8,500
Jobs Added Last Year: 1,110 (+15%)
Medical & dental supplies

MICRONICS COMPUTERS, INC.
232 E. Warren Ave. Phone: 510-651-2300
Fremont, CA 94539 Fax: 510-651-5666
Chm & CEO: Steven P. Kitrosser
Dir HR: Thomas Zippiroli
Employees: 412
Jobs Added Last Year: 149 (+56.7%)
Computers - system boards for PCs

NATIONAL MEDICAL ENTERPRISES
2700 Colorado Ave. Phone: 310-998-8000
Santa Monica, CA 90404-4070 Fax: 310-998-6293
Chm & CEO: Jeffrey C. Barbakow
SVP HR: Alan R. Ewalt
Employees: 50,423
Jobs Cut Last Year: 1,483 (-2.9%)
Hospitals - general & specialty

MICROSEMI CORPORATION
2830 S. Fairview St. Phone: 714-979-8220
Santa Ana, CA 92704 Fax: 714-557-5989
Chm, Pres & CEO: Philip Frey, Jr.
VP HR: James Thomas
Employees: 2,021
Jobs Added Last Year: 447 (+28.4%)
Electrical components - semiconductors

NATIONAL RV HOLDINGS INC.
3411 N. Perris Blvd. Phone: 909-943-6007
Perris, CA 92571 Fax: 909-943-5204
Pres & CEO: Wayne M. Mertes
Dir HR: Mike Hannah
Employees: 403
Jobs Added Last Year: 135 (+50.4%)
Automotive - RVs & motorhomes (Dolphin, Sea Breeze & Tropi-Cal)

MMI MEDICAL, INC.
1611 Pomona Rd. Phone: 909-736-4570
Corona, CA 91720 Fax: 909-466-8303
Pres & CEO: Alan D. Margulis
Mgr HR: Terri L. Olson
Employees: 325
Jobs Added Last Year: 70 (+27.5%)
Medical services - diagnostic imaging services

NATIONAL SEMICONDUCTOR CORP.
2900 Semiconductor Dr. Phone: 408-721-5000
Santa Clara, CA 95052-8090 Fax: 408-739-9803
Pres & CEO: Gilbert F. Amelio
VP HR: Robert G. MacLean
Employees: 23,400
Jobs Cut Last Year: 3,800 (-14%)
Electrical components - semiconductors

MTS INC.
2500 Del Monte St., Bldg. C Phone: 916-373-2500
West Sacramento, CA 95691 Fax: 916-373-2535
Pres & CEO: Russell M. Solomon
Personnel Mgr: Genny Danielson
Employees: 6,700
Jobs Added Last Year: 1,431 (+27.2%)
Retail - records, books & videos (Tower Records)

NATURAL WONDERS, INC.
4209 Technology Dr. Phone: 510-252-9600
Fremont, CA 94538 Fax: 510-252-6791
Chm, Pres & CEO: Robert S. Rubinstein
Dir Personnel: Karen Daley
Employees: 1,870
Jobs Added Last Year: 737 (+65%)
Retail - educational & scientific products

CALIFORNIA

NETMANAGE, INC.
10725 N. de Anza Blvd. Phone: 408-973-7171
Cupertino, CA 95014-2030 Fax: 408-257-6405
Chm, Pres & CEO: Zvi Alon
Dir HR: Pat Roboostaff
Employees: 105
Jobs Added Last Year: 20 (+23.5%)
Computers - communications software (Internet Chameleon)

NORTH AMERICAN MORTGAGE CO.
3883 Airway Dr. Phone: 707-523-5000
Santa Rosa, CA 95403 Fax: 707-546-4030
CEO: John F. Farrell, Jr.
Dir HR: Stacey Schrock
Employees: 3,550
Jobs Added Last Year: 1,350 (+61.4%)
Financial - mortgages & related services

NETWORK GENERAL CORPORATION
4200 Bohannon Dr. Phone: 415-473-2000
Menlo Park, CA 94025 Fax: 415-321-0855
CEO: Leslie G. Denend
Dir HR: Sally Takemoto
Employees: 493
Jobs Added Last Year: 86 (+21.1%)
Computers - LAN analysis software

NORTHROP GRUMMAN CORP. 11093
1840 Century Park East Phone: 310-553-6262
Los Angeles, CA 90067 Fax: 310-553-2076
Chm, Pres & CEO: Kent Kresa
Corp VP & Chief HR: Arthur F. Dauer
Employees: 30,000
Jobs Cut Last Year: 3,600 (-10.7%)
Aerospace - aircraft equipment & electronic systems

NEW IMAGE INDUSTRIES INC.
21218 Vanowen St. Phone: 818-702-0285
Canoga Park, CA 91303 Fax: 818-702-8868
Pres: Roger A. Leddington
HR: Tracy Chandler
Employees: 66
Jobs Added Last Year: 30 (+83.3%)
Computers - graphics

NOVELLUS SYSTEMS, INC.
81 Vista Montana Phone: 408-943-9700
San Jose, CA 95134 Fax: 408-943-3422
Pres & CEO: Richard S. Hill
HR Mgr: Karen Gaffmann
Employees: 530
Jobs Added Last Year: 159 (+42.9%)
Machinery - semiconductor manufacturing equipment

NEW UNITED MOTOR MFG. 40345
45500 Fremont Blvd. Phone: 510-498-5500
Fremont, CA 94538 Fax: 510-498-1037
Pres & CEO: Iwao Itoh
VP HR: D. William Childs
Employees: 4,300
Jobs Added Last Year: 331 (+8.3%)
Automotive manufacturing (GM-Toyota joint venture)

OCCIDENTAL PETROLEUM CORP. 11110
10889 Wilshire Blvd. Phone: 310-208-8800
Los Angeles, CA 90024-4201 Fax: 310-824-2372
Chm, Pres & CEO: Ray R. Irani
EVP HR: Ronald H. Asquith
Employees: 19,860
Jobs Cut Last Year: 3,740 (-15.8%)
Oil & gas - integrated; chemicals; pipelines

NEXT COMPUTER, INC. 41290
900 Chesapeake Dr. Phone: 415-366-0900
Redwood City, CA 94063-4727 Fax: 415-780-3714
Chm & CEO: Steven Paul Jobs
Mgr HR: Paul Bianchi
Employees: 250
Jobs Added Last Year: 50 (+25%)
Computers - object-oriented operating systems

OCTEL COMMUNICATIONS CORP. 14306
1001 Murphy Ranch Rd. Phone: 408-321-2000
Milpitas, CA 95035-7912 Fax: 408-321-6978
Chm, Pres & CEO: Robert Cohn
VP HR: John Viera
Employees: 2,393
Jobs Added Last Year: 826 (+52.7%)
Telecommunications equipment - voice & information processing systems

 An in-depth profile of this company is available by fax. Call 800-510-4452 and use your touch-tone phone to put in the 5-digit code at the prompt. Only $2.95 each with your credit card. See page 12 for more details.

99

CALIFORNIA

OPTICAL COATING LABORATORY, INC.
2789 Northpoint Pkwy. Phone: 707-545-6440
Santa Rosa, CA 95407-7397 Fax: 707-525-7410
Chm, Pres & CEO: Herbert M. Dwight, Jr.
VP HR: William E. Burgess
Employees: 1,162
Jobs Added Last Year: 55 (+5%)
Instruments - optical thin film-coated products

PACIFIC HOLDING CO.
10900 Wilshire Blvd., 16th Fl. Phone: 310-208-6055
Los Angeles, CA 90024 Fax: 310-824-2159
Chm: David H. Murdock
VP HR: Eileen Miles
Employees: 3,900
Jobs Added Last Year: 210 (+5.7%)
Diversified operations - real estate; building materials

ORACLE SYSTEMS CORPORATION
500 Oracle Pkwy. Phone: 415-506-7000
Redwood Shores, CA 94065 Fax: 415-506-7200
Pres & CEO: Lawrence J. Ellison
SVP HR: Phillip E. Wilson
Employees: 12,500
Jobs Added Last Year: 3,253 (+35.2%)
Computers - database management systems & software (#1 in industry); video servers

PACIFIC SCIENTIFIC CO.
620 Newport Center Dr., Ste. 700 Phone: 714-720-1714
Newport Beach, CA 92660 Fax: 714-720-1083
Chm, Pres & CEO: Edgar S. Brower
Corp Dir HR: Thomas I. Griffith
Employees: 1,836
Jobs Added Last Year: 474 (+34.8%)
Electronics - meters, controls & safety devices; dimmable fluorescent lighting system that fits regular incandescent lamps

ORBIT SEMICONDUCTOR, INC.
1215 Bordeaux Dr. Phone: 408-744-1800
Sunnyvale, CA 94089 Fax: 408-747-1263
Pres & CEO: Gary P. Kennedy
HR Mgr: Dana Myers
Employees: 180
Jobs Added Last Year: 60 (+50%)
Electrical components - semiconductors & related services for integrated circuit development

PACIFIC SUNWEAR OF CALIFORNIA, INC.
5037 E. Hunter Ave. Phone: 714-693-8066
Anaheim, CA 92807-6001 Fax: 714-693-8165
Pres, CEO & Chm: Michael W. Rayden
Dir HR: Ryanne Heffernan
Employees: 701
Jobs Added Last Year: 254 (+56.8%)
Retail - casual apparel & accessories

PACIFIC ENTERPRISES
633 W. Fifth St. Phone: 213-895-5000
Los Angeles, CA 90071-2006 Fax: 213-629-1225
Chm & CEO: Willis B. Wood, Jr.
VP HR: Debra L. Reed
Employees: 9,300
Jobs Cut Last Year: 584 (-5.9%)
Utility - gas distribution (Southern California Gas)

PACIFIC TELESIS GROUP
130 Kearny St. Phone: 415-394-3000
San Francisco, CA 94108 Fax: 415-362-2913
Chm, Pres & CEO: Philip J. Quigley
EVP HR: Jim R. Moberg
Employees: 60,050
Jobs Cut Last Year: 1,296 (-2.1%)
Utility - telephone (Pac Bell & PacTel) services in California & Nevada

PACIFIC GAS AND ELECTRIC CO.
77 Beale St., PO Box 770000 Phone: 415-973-7000
San Francisco, CA 94177 Fax: 415-543-7813
Pres & CEO: Stanley T. Skinner
VP HR: Barbara Coull Willliams
Employees: 23,000
Jobs Cut Last Year: 3,600 (-13.5%)
Utility - electric & gas power

PACIFICARE HEALTH SYSTEMS, INC.
5995 Plaza Dr. Phone: 714-952-1121
Cypress, CA 90630-5028 Fax: 714-220-3725
Pres & CEO: Alan R. Hoops
VP HR: Wanda Lee
Employees: 3,856
Jobs Added Last Year: 1,253 (+48.1%)
Health maintenance organization - operations in California, Oklahoma, Texas, Florida, Washington & Oregon

CALIFORNIA

PARCPLACE SYSTEMS, INC.
999 E. Arques Ave.　　　　Phone: 408-481-9090
Sunnyvale, CA 94086　　　Fax: 408-481-0219
Pres & CEO: William P. Lyons
Mgr HR: Nancy Miller
Employees: 177
Jobs Added Last Year: 24 (+15.7%)
Computers - object-oriented software development tools

PLANTRONICS, INC.
337 Encinal St., PO Box 1802　　Phone: 408-426-6060
Santa Cruz, CA 95061-1802　　　Fax: 408-426-6098
Pres & CEO: Robert S. Cecil
VP HR: Thomas A. Suchevits
Employees: 1,350
Jobs Added Last Year: 161 (+13.5%)
Telecommunications equipment - telephone headsets & related accessories

PEOPLESOFT, INC.
1331 N. California Blvd.　　Phone: 510-946-9460
Walnut Creek, CA 94596-4537　　Fax: 510-946-9461
Chm, Pres & CEO: David A. Duffield
VP HR: Steve Zarate
Employees: 362
Jobs Added Last Year: 174 (+92.6%)
Computers - human resource systems software

PLATINUM SOFTWARE CORPORATION
15615 Alton Pkwy., Ste. 300　　Phone: 714-727-1250
Irvine, CA 92718-3308　　　　　Fax: 714-727-1255
CEO: Carmelo J. Santoro
Dir HR: Ernie Bloch
Employees: 657
Jobs Added Last Year: 172 (+35.5%)
Computers - financial & management information software

PHYSICIANS CLINICAL LABORATORY
2495 Natomas Park Dr.　　Phone: 916-444-3500
Sacramento, CA 95833　　　Fax: 916-444-7930
Pres & CEO: Nathan L. Headley
VP HR: Timothy H. McGeachy
Employees: 1,050
Jobs Added Last Year: 650 (+162.5%)
Medical services - clinical laboratory services in California

PLAZA HOME MORTGAGE CORPORATION
1820 E. First St., 3rd Fl.　　Phone: 714-564-3000
Santa Ana, CA 92705　　　Fax: 714-564-8181
Chm & CEO: John T. French
SVP HR: John Barbadian
Employees: 1,395
Jobs Added Last Year: 624 (+80.9%)
Financial - mortgages & related services

PICO PRODUCTS, INC.
12500 Foothill Blvd.　　Phone: 818-897-0028
Lakeview Terrace, CA 91342　　Fax: 818-899-1381
Pres: Everett T. Keech
HR: Molly Couler
Employees: 310
Jobs Added Last Year: 100 (+47.6%)
Telecommunications equipment - satellite systems for commercial applications

PMC INC.
12243 Branford St.　　Phone: 818-896-1101
Sun Valley, CA 91352　　Fax: 818-897-0180
Pres & CEO: Philip E. Kamins
Dir HR: Karen Ferguson
Employees: 3,756
Jobs Added Last Year: 56 (+1.5%)
Chemicals - specialty, plastic & foam; bird repellent

PINKERTON'S SECURITY & INVESTIGATION SVCS.
15910 Ventura Blvd., Ste. 900　　Phone: 818-380-8800
Encino, CA 91436-3095　　　　　Fax: 818-380-8997
Pres & CEO: Denis R. Brown
VP HR: Gary H. Hasenbank
Employees: 47,000
Jobs Added Last Year: 4,000 (+9.3%)
Protection - security & investigative services

PMR CORPORATION
3990 Old Town Ave., Ste. 206A　　Phone: 619-295-2227
San Diego, CA 92110　　　　　　Fax: 619-260-1151
CEO: Allen Tepper
Dir HR: Janell Williams
Employees: 565
Jobs Added Last Year: 320 (+130.6%)
Medical services - psychiatric partial-hospitalization program management

CALIFORNIA

POTLATCH CORPORATION
One Maritime Plaza   Phone: 415-576-8800
San Francisco, CA 94111   Fax: 415-576-8840
Chm & CEO: John M. Richards
VP Emp Rel: Barbara M. Failing
Employees: 6,900
Jobs Cut Last Year: 100 (-1.4%)
Paper & paper products

PROXIMA CORPORATION
9440 Carroll Park Dr.   Phone: 619-457-5500
San Diego, CA 92121-2256   Fax: 619-457-9647
Chm & CEO: Kenneth E. Olson
VP HR: Frank J. Drdek
Employees: 449
Jobs Added Last Year: 126 (+39%)
Video equipment - projection equipment for use with PCs, including LCD panels & projectors

PSICOR, INC.
16818 Via del Campo Ct.   Phone: 619-485-5599
San Diego, CA 92127   Fax: 619-485-5107
Chm, Pres & CEO: Michael W. Dunaway
VP HR: Cynthia Bekdache
Employees: 608
Jobs Added Last Year: 79 (+14.9%)
Medical services - personnel & equipment for open-heart surgery & related procedures

PYXIS CORPORATION
9380 Carroll Park Dr.   Phone: 619-625-3300
San Diego, CA 92121   Fax: 619-625-3310
Pres & CEO: Gerald Forth
HR Mgr: Debby Weaver
Employees: 324
Jobs Added Last Year: 144 (+80%)
Medical products - medication & supply management & control system

QUALCOMM INCORPORATED
6455 Lusk Blvd.   Phone: 619-587-1121
San Diego, CA 92121-2779   Fax: 619-452-9096
Chm & CEO: Irwin M. Jacobs
VP HR: Daniel L. Sullivan
Employees: 1,900
Jobs Added Last Year: 638 (+50.6%)
Telecommunications equipment - digital wireless communications systems

QUANTUM CORPORATION
500 McCarthy Blvd.   Phone: 408-894-4000
Milpitas, CA 95035-7909   Fax: 408-894-3207
Chm & CEO: William J. Miller
VP HR: Deborah E. Barber
Employees: 2,984
Jobs Added Last Year: 529 (+21.5%)
Computers - hard disk drives, tape drives & solid state disks

QUANTUM HEALTH RESOURCES, INC.
790 The City Dr. South   Phone: 714-750-1610
Orange, CA 92668   Fax: 714-750-3235
Chm & CEO: Douglas H. Stickney
Emp Rel: Jan Brodowski
Employees: 1,006
Jobs Added Last Year: 506 (+101.2%)
Medical services - long term in-home health care services to patients with chronic conditions

RADIUS, INC.
1710 Fortune Dr.   Phone: 408-434-1010
San Jose, CA 95131   Fax: 408-434-0770
Chm, Pres & CEO: Michael D. Boich
VP HR: Dawn Thompson
Employees: 363
Jobs Added Last Year: 50 (+16%)
Computers - Macintosh graphics boards & high-resolution color monitors

RALEY'S INC.
500 W. Capitol Ave.   Phone: 916-373-3333
West Sacramento, CA 95605   Fax: 916-444-3733
Pres & CEO: Charles L. Collings
VP HR: Sam McPherson
Employees: 7,150
Jobs Added Last Year: —
Retail - supermarkets & drug stores

RATIONAL SOFTWARE CORPORATION
2800 San Tomas Expwy.   Phone: 408-496-3600
Santa Clara, CA 95051   Fax: 408-496-3973
Pres: Paul D. Levy
Dir HR: Burr Gibboni
Employees: 375
Jobs Added Last Year: 223 (+146.7%)
Computers - software development products, troubleshooting services

CALIFORNIA

RAYCHEM CORPORATION
300 Constitution Dr.   Phone: 415-361-4180
Menlo Park, CA 94025   Fax: 415-361-2108
Pres & CEO: Robert J. Saldich
VP HR: Stephen A. Balogh
Employees: 10,769
Jobs Cut Last Year: 3 (0%)
Electrical products - insulation products, telephone & cable accessories

READ-RITE CORPORATION
345 Los Coches St.   Phone: 408-262-6700
Milpitas, CA 95035   Fax: 408-956-3205
Chm & CEO: Cyril J. Yansouri
VP HR: Sherry F. McVicar
Employees: 18,472
Jobs Added Last Year: 8,024 (+76.8%)
Computers - magnetic recording heads

REDWOOD EMPIRE BANCORP
111 Santa Rosa Ave.   Phone: 707-545-9611
Santa Rosa, CA 95404-4905   Fax: 707-526-2109
Pres: Barry S. Slatt
EVP & HR Dir: Kelly Hinde
Employees: 253
Jobs Added Last Year: 67 (+36%)
Banks - West

REGENCY HEALTH SERVICES, INC.
2742 Dow Ave.   Phone: 714-544-4443
Tustin, CA 92680-7245   Fax: 714-544-8803
Pres & COO: Rickard K. Matros
VP HR: Steve Ronilo
Employees: 10,000
Jobs Added Last Year: 4,268 (+74.5%)
Nursing homes - health care facility operations

ROCKWELL INTERNATIONAL CORP.
2201 Seal Beach Blvd.   Phone: 310-797-3311
Seal Beach, CA 90740-8250   Fax: 310-797-5690
Chm & CEO: Donald R. Beall
SVP Organization & HR: Robert H. Murphy
Employees: 71,891
Jobs Cut Last Year: 5,137 (-6.7%)
Aerospace - aircraft equipment, electronics; automotive; graphics

ROLL INTERNATIONAL
12233 W. Olympic Blvd., Ste. 380   Phone: 310-442-5700
Los Angeles, CA 90064   Fax: 310-207-1557
Co-Chm & Pres: Stewart A. Resnick
Dir HR: Dennis G. Rhyne
Employees: 6,000
Jobs Added Last Year: 0
Retail - mail order & direct flowers (Teleflora) & collectibles (Franklin Mint)

ROPAK CORPORATION
600 S. State College Blvd.   Phone: 714-870-9757
Fullerton, CA 92631   Fax: 714-447-3871
Chm & CEO: William H. Roper
Dir HR: Gary Montgomery
Employees: 761
Jobs Added Last Year: 85 (+12.6%)
Containers - paper & plastic

ROSS STORES, INC.
8333 Central Ave.   Phone: 510-505-4400
Newark, CA 94560-3433   Fax: 510-505-4181
Chm & CEO: Norman A. Ferber
SVP HR: Stephen F. Joyce
Employees: 8,949
Jobs Added Last Year: 749 (+9.1%)
Retail - apparel & shoes

ROTONICS MANUFACTURING INC.
17022 S. Figueroa St.   Phone: 310-538-4932
Gardena, CA 90248   Fax: 310-516-6838
CEO: Sherman McKinniss
Admin Asst (HR): Dawn Whitney
Employees: 378
Jobs Added Last Year: 58 (+18.1%)
Rubber & plastic products - molded products for agricultural & industrial use

RYKOFF-SEXTON, INC.
761 Terminal St.   Phone: 213-622-4131
Los Angeles, CA 90021   Fax: 213-486-9161
Pres & CEO: Mark Van Stekelenburg
SVP HR & Gen Counsel: Robert J. Harter, Jr.
Employees: 5,330
Jobs Cut Last Year: 100 (-1.8%)
Food - wholesale to restaurants, health care facilities, schools & colleges, hotels & airlines

CALIFORNIA

SAFETY COMPONENTS INTERNATIONAL, INC.
3190 Pullman St. Phone: 714-662-7756
Costa Mesa, CA 92626 Fax: 714-662-2163
CEO: Robert A. Zummo
Dir HR: Eva Rodriguez
Employees: 541
Jobs Added Last Year: 70 (+14.9%)
Automotive & trucking - air bags; projectiles & components for tactical ammunition

SAFEWAY INC.
Fourth & Jackson Sts. Phone: 510-891-3000
Oakland, CA 94660 Fax: 510-891-3603
Pres & CEO: Steven A. Burd
EVP Labor Relations, HR, Law & Public Affairs: Kenneth W. Oder
Employees: 105,900
Jobs Added Last Year: 1,000 (+1%)
Retail - supermarkets in the US (#3 in the nation) & Canada

ST. IVES LABORATORIES, INC.
9201 Oakdale Ave, Phone: 818-709-5500
Chatsworth, CA 91311-6521 Fax: 818-341-8569
CEO: Gary H. Worth
VP HR: Rich Harvey
Employees: 508
Jobs Added Last Year: 85 (+20.1%)
Cosmetics & toiletries

SALICK HEALTH CARE, INC.
407 N. Maple Dr. Phone: 213-966-3400
Beverly Hills, CA 90210 Fax: 213-966-3688
CEO: Bernard Salick
VP HR: Janele Waterman
Employees: 1,200
Jobs Added Last Year: 360 (+42.9%)
Health care - outpatient care for cancer patients; cancer care coverage

SAN DIEGO GAS & ELECTRIC COMPANY
101 Ash St. Phone: 619-696-2000
San Diego, CA 92101 Fax: 619-233-6875
Chm, Pres & CEO: Thomas A. Page
VP HR: Margot A. Kyd
Employees: 4,229
Jobs Cut Last Year: 81 (-1.9%)
Utility - electric power

SAVE MART SUPERMARKETS
1800 Standiford Ave. Phone: 209-577-1600
Modesto, CA 95350 Fax: 209-577-3857
Chm & CEO: Robert M. Piccinini
Dir HR & Law: Mike Silveira
Employees: 6,265
Jobs Cut Last Year: 735 (-10.5%)
Retail - supermarkets

SCECORP
2244 Walnut Grove Ave. Phone: 818-302-2222
Rosemead, CA 91770 Fax: 818-302-4815
Chm & CEO: John E. Bryson
VP Health Care & Emp Svcs: Margaret H. Jordan
Employees: 17,193
Jobs Cut Last Year: 66 (-.4%)
Utility - electric power (Southern California Edison)

SCIENCE APPLICATIONS INTERNATIONAL
10260 Campus Point Dr. Phone: 619-546-6000
San Diego, CA 92121 Fax: 619-535-7992
Chm & CEO: J. Robert Beyster
VP HR: Bernard Theule
Employees: 15,600
Jobs Cut Last Year: 600 (-3.7%)
Engineering - R&D services, systems integration

SEAGATE TECHNOLOGY, INC.
920 Disc Dr. Phone: 408-438-6550
Scotts Valley, CA 95066 Fax: 408-438-6172
Chm, Pres, CEO & COO: Alan F. Shugart
SVP Admin (HR): Robert A. Kundtz
Employees: 53,000
Jobs Added Last Year: 10,000 (+23.3%)
Computers - Winchester disk drives

SIERRA PACIFIC INDUSTRIES
3735 El Cajon Ave. Phone: 916-275-8812
Shasta Lake, CA 96019 Fax: 916-365-9475
Pres & CEO: A. A. "Red" Emmerson
Dir HR: Ed Bond
Employees: 2,800
Jobs Added Last Year: 300 (+12%)
Building products - lumber

CALIFORNIA

SIERRA SEMICONDUCTOR CORPORATION
2075 N. Capitol Ave. Phone: 408-263-9300
San Jose, CA 95132 Fax: 408-263-3337
Chm & CEO: James V. Diller
VP HR: George Antennuci
Employees: 460
Jobs Added Last Year: 89 (+24%)
Electrical components - semiconductors

SMART & FINAL INC.
4700 S. Boyle Ave. Phone: 213-589-1054
Los Angeles, CA 90058 Fax: 805-564-6729
Pres & CEO: Roger M. Laverty III
VP HR: Daniel A. Zaich
Employees: 2,903
Jobs Added Last Year: 257 (+9.7%)
Retail - supermarkets

SILICON GRAPHICS, INC.
2011 N. Shoreline Blvd. Phone: 415-960-1980
Mountain View, CA 94043-1389 Fax: 415-390-6220
Chm & CEO: Edward R. McCracken
VP Emp Rel: Leilani Gayles
Employees: 4,400
Jobs Added Last Year: 650 (+17.3%)
Computers - workstations with graphics hardware & software & video servers

SOLECTRON CORPORATION
777 Gibraltar Dr. Phone: 408-957-8500
Milpitas, CA 95035 Fax: 408-956-6075
Chm & CEO: Winston H. Chen
Mgr HR: John Tiffany
Employees: 4,545
Jobs Added Last Year: 1,566 (+52.6%)
Electrical components - contract manufacture of printed circuit boards & other electrical products

SILICON VALLEY GROUP, INC.
2240 Ringwood Ave. Phone: 408-434-0500
San Jose, CA 95131 Fax: 408-432-8629
Chm & CEO: Papken S. Der Torossian
VP HR: Barbara Hale
Employees: 1,907
Jobs Added Last Year: 193 (+11.3%)
Machinery - semiconductor manufacturing equipment

SOMATIX THERAPY CORPORATION
1301 Marina Village Pkwy. Phone: 510-748-3000
Alameda, CA 94501-1034 Fax: 510-814-8002
Pres & CEO: David W. Carter
VP HR: Arlene Jordan-Levy
Employees: 111
Jobs Added Last Year: 26 (+30.6%)
Biomedical & genetic products - gene therapy

SIZZLER INTERNATIONAL, INC.
12655 W. Jefferson Blvd. Phone: 310-827-2300
Los Angeles, CA 90066 Fax: 310-822-5786
CEO: Kevin W. Perkins
VP HR: Leon E. Clancy, Jr.
Employees: 16,000
Jobs Cut Last Year: 600 (-3.6%)
Retail - restaurants (Sizzler, KFC & Buffalo Ranch)

SOUTHERN PACIFIC RAIL CORP.
One Market Plaza Phone: 415-541-1000
San Francisco, CA 94105-1806 Fax: 415-541-1256
CEO: Edward L. Moyers
VP HR: Judy Holm
Employees: 18,982
Jobs Cut Last Year: 3,811 (-16.7%)
Transportation - rail

SJW CORPORATION
374 W. Santa Clara St. Phone: 408-279-7810
San Jose, CA 95196 Fax: 408-279-7934
CEO: J. W. Weinhardt
Emp Supervisor: Nancy O'Conner
Employees: 310
Jobs Added Last Year: 43 (+16.1%)
Utility - water supply

SPECIAL DEVICES, INC.
16830 W. Placerita Canyon Rd. Phone: 805-259-0753
Newhall, CA 91321 Fax: 805-254-4721
Chm & Pres: Thomas F. Treinen
Mgr HR: Tracy Koll
Employees: 950
Jobs Added Last Year: 398 (+72.1%)
Electrical components - initiators for airbags & explosives

CALIFORNIA

SPELLING ENTERTAINMENT GROUP, INC.
5700 Wilshire Blvd.　　Phone: 213-965-5700
Los Angeles, CA 90036　　Fax: 213-965-5895
Pres & CEO: Steve Berrard
VP (HR): Cheryl Wingard
Employees: 1,000
Jobs Added Last Year: 500 (+100%)
Broadcasting - TV programs & feature films

STRATACOM INC.
1400 Parkmoor Ave.　　Phone: 408-294-7600
San Jose, CA 95126-3723　　Fax: 408-294-7600
Pres & CEO: Richard M. Moley
Dir HR: Tom Schaeffer
Employees: 650
Jobs Added Last Year: 285 (+78.1%)
Computers - asynchronous transfer mode networking systems (FastPacket)

THE SPORTS CLUB COMPANY, INC.
2425 Olympic Blvd., Ste. 4060W　　Phone: 310-453-1400
Santa Monica, CA 90404　　Fax: 310-829-4884
Pres & CEO: D. Michael Talla
HR: Rashmi Patel
Employees: 1,100
Jobs Added Last Year: 64 (+6.2%)
Leisure & recreational services - fitness clubs

SUMMIT CARE CORPORATION
2600 W. Magnolia Blvd.　　Phone: 818-841-8750
Burbank, CA 91505-3031　　Fax: 818-841-4044
CEO: William C. Scott
Dir HR: David Milovich
Employees: 2,300
Jobs Added Last Year: 400 (+21.1%)
Health maintenance organization

STAC ELECTRONICS
12636 High Bluff Dr., 4th Fl.　　Phone: 619-794-4300
San Diego, CA 92130-2093　　Fax: 619-794-4572
Chm, Pres & CEO: Gary W. Clow
HR Mgr: Sharon Worden
Employees: 210
Jobs Added Last Year: 60 (+40%)
Computers - peripheral equipment & software for compression of data on hard disk storage devices for PCs

SUN MICROSYSTEMS, INC.
2550 Garcia Ave.　　Phone: 415-960-1300
Mountain View, CA 94043-1100　　Fax: 415-969-9131
Chm, Pres & CEO: Scott G. McNealy
VP HR: Kenneth M. Alvares
Employees: 13,000
Jobs Cut Last Year: 253 (-1.9%)
Computers - workstations (#1 in the world)

STANFORD UNIVERSITY HOSPITAL
300 Pasteur Dr.　　Phone: 415-723-4000
Palo Alto, CA 94305-5250　　Fax: 415-723-8163
CEO: Kenneth D. Bloem
Dir HR: Felix R. Barthelemy
Employees: 4,400
Jobs Added Last Year: —
Hospital

SUNRISE MEDICAL INC.
2355 Crenshaw Blvd., Ste. 150　　Phone: 310-328-8018
Torrance, CA 90501　　Fax: 310-328-8184
Chm & CEO: Richard H. Chandler
Dir Corp HR: Deborah Beasley
Employees: 2,625
Jobs Added Last Year: 387 (+17.3%)
Medical supplies - wheelchairs, walkers, crutches & special beds for nursing homes; in-home treatment aids

STATER BROS. HOLDINGS INC.
21700 Barton Rd.　　Phone: 909-783-5000
Colton, CA 92324　　Fax: 909-783-5035
Chm, Pres & CEO: Jack H. Brown
Group SVP HR: Donald Baker
Employees: 9,800
Jobs Added Last Year: 1,600 (+19.5%)
Retail - supermarkets in San Bernadino & Riverside counties

SUPERCOM, INC.
410 S. Abbott Ave.　　Phone: 408-456-8888
Milpitas, CA 95035-5257　　Fax: 408-263-3003
CEO: James Fang
Dir HR: B. B. Sato
Employees: 300
Jobs Added Last Year: 80 (+36.4%)
Computers - retail personal computers, accessories & home entertainment

CALIFORNIA

SUPERCUTS, INC.
550 California St.
San Francisco, CA 94104
Chm & CEO: David E. Lipson
VP HR: Suzan Pepper
Employees: 2,539
Jobs Added Last Year: 1,340 (+111.8%)
Retail - hair salons
Phone: 415-693-4700
Fax: 415-693-4940

SYNOPSYS, INC.
700 E. Middlefield Rd.
Mountain View, CA 94043-4033
Pres & CEO: Aart J. de Geus
No central personnel officer
Employees: 1,022
Jobs Added Last Year: 432 (+73.2%)
Computers - integrated circuit design software
Phone: 415-962-5000
Fax: 415-965-8637

SUPERIOR INDUSTRIES INTERNATIONAL, INC.
7800 Woodley Ave.
Van Nuys, CA 91406
CEO: Louis L. Borick
Dir Industrial Rel (HR): George Musson
Employees: 3,200
Jobs Added Last Year: 200 (+6.7%)
Automotive & trucking - original equipment
Phone: 818-781-4973
Fax: 818-780-5631

TANDEM COMPUTERS INC.
19333 Vallco Pkwy.
Cupertino, CA 95014-2599
Pres & CEO: James G. Treybig
SVP & COO (HR): Robert C. Marshall
Employees: 8,466
Jobs Cut Last Year: 1,497 (-15%)
Computers - fault-tolerant minicomputers
Phone: 408-725-6000
Fax: 408-285-4545

SWINERTON & WALBERG CO.
580 California St.
San Francisco, CA 94104
Pres: David H. Grubb
Personnel Mgr: Linda Carlson
Employees: 1,200
Jobs Added Last Year: 100 (+9.1%)
Building - commercial contracting
Phone: 415-421-2980
Fax: 415-984-1384

TELACU INDUSTRIES
5400 E. Olympic Blvd.
Los Angeles, CA 90022-5147
Pres & CEO: David C. Lizarraga
Dir HR: Gabriella Barbarena
Employees: 960
Jobs Added Last Year: 360 (+60%)
Financial - mortgage banking; real estate development
Phone: 213-721-1655
Fax: 213-724-3372

SYBASE, INC.
6475 Christie Ave.
Emeryville, CA 94608
Chm, Pres & CEO: Mark B. Hoffman
VP HR: Sally A. DeStefano
Employees: 2,528
Jobs Added Last Year: 901 (+55.4%)
Computers - database management software
Phone: 510-596-3500
Fax: 510-658-9441

TELEDYNE, INC.
1901 Avenue of the Stars
Los Angeles, CA 90067-6046
Chm & CEO: William P. Rutledge
Dir HR: Dan Lucasik
Employees: 21,000
Jobs Cut Last Year: 2,800 (-11.8%)
Diversified operations - aviation; electronics; specialty metals; industrial products; consumer products (Water Pik)
Phone: 310-277-3311
Fax: 310-551-4365

SYMANTEC CORPORATION
10201 Torre Ave.
Cupertino, CA 95014-2132
Pres & CEO: Gordon E. Eubanks, Jr.
Dir HR: David Sornson
Employees: 1,204
Jobs Added Last Year: 192 (+19%)
Computers - information management, productivity & development software (Norton Utilities)
Phone: 408-253-9600
Fax: 408-253-4092

TETRA TECH, INC.
670 N. Rosemead Blvd.
Pasadena, CA 91107
Chm, Pres & CEO: Li-San Hwang
Dir HR: Richard Lemmon
Employees: 891
Jobs Added Last Year: 284 (+46.8%)
Pollution control services - environmental consulting
Phone: 818-449-6400
Fax: 818-351-1188

CALIFORNIA

THRIFTY OIL CO.
10000 Lakewood Blvd. Phone: 310-923-9876
Downey, CA 90240 Fax: 310-869-9739
Pres: Ted Orden
Dir HR: Beverly Brooks
Employees: 1,000
Jobs Added Last Year: 200 (+25%)
Oil refining & marketing; convenience stores

UNION BANK
350 California St. Phone: 415-705-7350
San Francisco, CA 94104-1476 Fax: 415-445-0425
Pres & CEO: Kanetaka Yoshida
SVP (HR): Roger Crawford
Employees: 7,000
Jobs Cut Last Year: 121 (-1.7%)
Banks - West

THE TIMES MIRROR COMPANY
Times Mirror Sq. Phone: 213-237-3700
Los Angeles, CA 90053 Fax: 213-237-3800
Chm, Pres & CEO: Robert F. Erburu
VP HR: James R. Simpson
Employees: 26,936
Jobs Cut Last Year: 1,377 (-4.9%)
Publishing - newspapers (*Los Angeles Times*), magazines & books (Abrams & Irwin)

UNITED STATES FILTER CORPORATION
73-710 Fred Waring Dr., Ste. 222 Phone: 619-340-0098
Palm Desert, CA 92260 Fax: 619-341-9368
Chm Pres & CEO: Richard J. Heckmann
SVP Admin (HR): Jerry Rogers
Employees: 1,180
Jobs Added Last Year: 498 (+73%)
Filtration products - engineered systems for water purification, wastewater treatment, filtration & special separations

TRANSAMERICA CORPORATION
600 Montgomery St., 23rd Fl. Phone: 415-983-4000
San Francisco, CA 94111-2770 Fax: 415-983-4234
Pres & CEO: Frank C. Herringer
VP HR: Rona I. King
Employees: 10,700
Jobs Added Last Year: 0
Insurance - life; consumer & commercial lending

UNIVERSITY OF CALIFORNIA
300 Lakeside Dr., 22nd Fl. Phone: 510-987-0700
Oakland, CA 94612 Fax: 510-987-0894
Pres: Jack W. Peltason
Dir Personnel: Alice Gregory
Employees: 131,661
Jobs Cut Last Year: 618 (-.5%)
University

TRIMARK HOLDINGS, INC.
2644 30th St. Phone: 310-314-2000
Santa Monica, CA 90405-3009 Fax: 310-399-4238
CEO: Roger A. Burlage
HR Coordinator: Jennifer Sullivan
Employees: 62
Jobs Added Last Year: 13 (+26.5%)
Motion pictures & services - international distribution (Vidmark)

UNIVERSITY OF SOUTHERN CALIFORNIA
3620 S. Vermont Ave. Phone: 213-743-2111
Los Angeles, CA 90089 Fax: 213-740-7750
Pres: Steven B. Sample
Exec Dir Personnel Svcs: Janis Romero
Employees: 17,000
Jobs Added Last Year: —
University

UNIHEALTH AMERICA
4100 W. Alameda Ave. Phone: 818-566-6300
Burbank, CA 91505 Fax: 818-566-7070
Pres & CEO: Terry R. Hartshorn
SVP HR: Stanley M. Croonquist, Jr.
Employees: 11,367
Jobs Added Last Year: 389 (+3.5%)
Hospitals - nonprofit health care system

UNOCAL CORPORATION
1201 W. Fifth St. Phone: 213-977-7600
Los Angeles, CA 90017 Fax: 213-977-5362
CEO: Roger C. Beach
VP Corp HR: Charles O. Strathmman
Employees: 13,613
Jobs Cut Last Year: 1,074 (-7.3%)
Oil & gas - integrated; chemicals

CALIFORNIA

URS CORPORATION
100 California St., Ste. 500   Phone: 415-774-2700
San Francisco, CA 94111   Fax: 415-398-1904
CEO: Martin M. Koffel
Dir HR: Barbara Gay
Employees: 1,100
Jobs Added Last Year: 100 (+10%)
Engineering - R&D services

VACU DRY CO.
7765 Healdsburg Ave.   Phone: 707-829-4600
Sebastopol, CA 95472-3309   Fax: 707-829-4610
Pres & CEO: Donal Sugrue
Dir HR: Esther K. Castain
Employees: 250
Jobs Added Last Year: 50 (+25%)
Food - low-moisture fruits, bulk & concentrated apple juice & drink mixes

VALLEY FORGE CORPORATION
100 Smith Ranch Rd., Ste. 326   Phone: 415-492-1500
San Rafael, CA 94903-1994   Fax: 415-492-0128
Pres (HR): David R. Brining
Employees: 445
Jobs Added Last Year: 75 (+20.3%)
Marine teak accessories, lights, horns & windshield wipers

VANS, INC.
2095 N. Batavia St.   Phone: 714-974-7414
Orange, CA 92665-3101   Fax: 714-998-6564
Pres & CEO: Christopher G. Staff
Dir HR: Jacquelyn Cleary
Employees: 2,621
Jobs Added Last Year: 357 (+15.8%)
Shoes & related apparel - casual footwear

VARIAN ASSOCIATES, INC.
3050 Hansen Way   Phone: 415-493-4000
Palo Alto, CA 94304-1000   Fax: 415-493-0307
Chm & CEO: J. Tracy O'Rourke
VP HR: Ernest Felago
Employees: 8,100
Jobs Added Last Year: 300 (+3.8%)
Instruments - scientific; communications equipment

VENTRITEX, INC.   14920
701 E. Evelyn Ave.   Phone: 408-738-4883
Sunnyvale, CA 94086   Fax: 408-735-8750
Pres & CEO: Frank M. Fischer
Mgr HR: Jean Munson
Employees: 355
Jobs Added Last Year: 198 (+126.1%)
Medical products - implanted defibrillators

VIKING OFFICE PRODUCTS, INC.   12076
13809 S. Figueroa St.   Phone: 213-321-1493
Los Angeles, CA 90061-1000   Fax: 310-329-5017
Chm, Pres & CEO: Irwin Helford
VP Admin & Sec (HR): Stephen R. Kroll
Employees: 1,221
Jobs Added Last Year: 154 (+14.4%)
Retail - mail order & direct office products

VIVRA INC.
400 Primrose, Ste. 200   Phone: 415-348-8200
Burlingame, CA 94010   Fax: 415-397-0136
Pres & CEO: Kent J. Thiry
Dir HR: Pat Pettus
Employees: 3,300
Jobs Added Last Year: 530 (+19.1%)
Health care - kidney dialysis & health care services

THE VONS COMPANIES, INC.   11589
618 Michillinda Ave.   Phone: 818-821-7000
Arcadia, CA 91007   Fax: 818-821-7933
VC & CEO: Lawrence A. Del Santo
VP HR: Dick W. Gonzales
Employees: 30,000
Jobs Cut Last Year: 2,300 (-7.1%)
Retail - supermarkets (Vons, Pavilions, EXPO, Williams Bros. & Tianguis) in Southern California & Las Vegas

THE WALT DISNEY COMPANY   11603
500 S. Buena Vista St.   Phone: 818-560-1000
Burbank, CA 91521   Fax: 818-560-1930
Chm, Pres & CEO: Michael D. Eisner
EVP Law & HR: Sanford M. Litvack
Employees: 65,000
Jobs Added Last Year: 3,000 (+4.8%)
Motion pictures & services; theme parks & resorts, book publishing (Hyperion)

CALIFORNIA

WATSON PHARMACEUTICALS INC.
132-A Business Center Dr. Phone: 909-270-1400
Corona, CA 91720-1724 Fax: 909-270-1096
CEO: Allen Y. Chao
Mgr HR: Mary Evertsen
Employees: 362
Jobs Added Last Year: 63 (+21.1%)
Drugs - generic

WESTERN DIGITAL CORPORATION
8105 Irvine Center Dr. Phone: 714-932-5000
Irvine, CA 92718 Fax: 714-863-1656
Chm, Pres & CEO: Charles A. Haggerty
VP HR: Scott T. Hughes
Employees: 6,593
Jobs Cut Last Year: 729 (-10%)
Computers - disk drives & semiconductors

WELLPOINT HEALTH NETWORKS INC.
21555 Oxnard St. Phone: 818-703-4000
Woodland Hills, CA 91367 Fax: 818-703-2083
Chm & CEO: Leonard D. Schaeffer
VP HR: Claire Ellinger
Employees: 2,760
Jobs Added Last Year: 60 (+2.2%)
Health maintenance organization - operations in California

WILBUR-ELLIS COMPANY
320 California St., Ste. 200 Phone: 415-772-4000
San Francisco, CA 94104 Fax: 415-772-4011
Pres & CEO: Brayton Wilbur, Jr.
Dir Personnel: Ofelia Uriarte
Employees: 1,800
Jobs Added Last Year: 171 (+10.5%)
Chemicals - wholesale herbicides, pesticides & general farm supplies

WELLS FARGO & COMPANY
420 Montgomery St. Phone: 415-477-1000
San Francisco, CA 94163 Fax: 415-362-6958
Chm & CEO: Carl E. Reichardt
EVP & Personnel Dir: Patricia Callahan
Employees: 20,800
Jobs Cut Last Year: 300 (-1.4%)
Banks - money center

WILLIAMS-SONOMA, INC.
100 N. Point St. Phone: 415-421-7900
San Francisco, CA 94133 Fax: 415-983-9887
CEO: W. Howard Lester
VP HR: Claudia Abrams
Employees: 4,200
Jobs Cut Last Year: 200 (-4.5%)
Retail - cookware & related housewares through stores & direct mail; home furnishings, gardening equipment

WEST MARINE, INC.
500 Westridge Dr. Phone: 408-728-2700
Watsonville, CA 95076-3502 Fax: 408-728-2736
Chm & CEO: Randolph K. Repass
Asst VP HR: Linda Kennedy
Employees: 1,095
Jobs Added Last Year: 254 (+30.2%)
Retail - boating supplies & apparel

XILINX, INC.
2100 Logic Dr. Phone: 408-559-7778
San Jose, CA 95124-3400 Fax: 408-559-7114
Pres: Bernard V. Vonderschmitt
VP HR: Ray F. Madorin
Employees: 689
Jobs Added Last Year: 145 (+26.7%)
Electrical components - field-programmable gate array semiconductors

WESTERN ATLAS, INC.
360 N. Crescent Dr. Phone: 310-888-2500
Beverly Hills, CA 90210 Fax: 310-888-2848
Chm & CEO: Alton Brann
Dir HR: Jim Robertson
Employees: 15,000
Jobs Added Last Year: 900 (+6.4%)
Oil & gas - field services

XIRCOM, INC.
26025 Mureau Rd. Phone: 818-878-7600
Calabasas, CA 91302 Fax: 818-878-7630
Pres & CEO: Dirk I. Gates
Dir HR: Dennis Hamby
Employees: 193
Jobs Added Last Year: 39 (+25.3%)
Computers - network hardware

CALIFORNIA

YOUNG'S MARKET CO.
2164 N. Batavia St.   Phone: 714-283-4933
Orange, CA 92665   Fax: 714-283-6176
Pres & CEO: Vernon O. Underwood, Jr.
VP HR: Naomi Buenaslor
Employees: 1,600
Jobs Added Last Year: 100 (+6.7%)
Food, spirits & wine - wholesale

YUCAIPA COMPANIES
777 S. Harbor Blvd.   Phone: 714-738-2000
La Habra, CA 90631   Fax: 714-738-2134
Chm: Ronald W. Burkle
VP HR: Don Ropele
Employees: 14,687
Jobs Added Last Year: 1,091 (+8%)
Retail - supermarkets (Food 4 Less, Alpha Beta, Boys Viva, Cala, Bell, Ralphs, Bell, Falley & Dominick's)

▼ **Help Wanted** *http://www.webcom.com:80/~career*

An in-depth profile of this company is available by fax. Call 800-510-4452 and use your touch-tone phone to put in the 5-digit code at the prompt. Only $2.95 each with your credit card. See page 12 for more details.

COLORADO

ACCESS GRAPHICS INC.
1426 Pearl St. Phone: 303-938-9333
Boulder, CO 80302 Fax: 303-938-8210
Pres & CEO: John B. Ramsey
HR Mgr: Billie J. Stremel
Employees: 265
Jobs Added Last Year: 60 (+29.3%)
Computers - workstations & graphics products distribution

THE ANSCHUTZ CORPORATION
555 17th St., Ste. 2400 Phone: 303-298-1000
Denver, CO 80202 Fax: 303-298-8881
CEO: Philip F. Anschutz
Dir HR: Phyllis Murphy
Employees: 23,000
Jobs Added Last Year: —
Diversified operations - oil; railroads; real estate; mining

BARRETT RESOURCES CORPORATION
1125 17th St., Ste. 2400 Phone: 303-297-3900
Denver, CO 80202 Fax: 303-297-0807
Chm & CEO: William J. Barrett
Asst Treas (HR): Frona Henson
Employees: 78
Jobs Added Last Year: 15 (+23.8%)
Oil & gas - US exploration & production

BESTOP, INC.
2100 W. Midway Blvd. Phone: 303-465-1755
Bloomfield, CO 80020 Fax: 303-466-3436
Pres & CEO: Richard E. Sabourin
Dir HR: Jenny Donaldson
Employees: 650
Jobs Added Last Year: 136 (+26.5%)
Automotive & trucking - soft tops for automobiles

BLACK HAWK GAMING AND DEVELOPMENT CO.
2060 Broadway, Ste. 400 Phone: 303-444-0240
Boulder, CO 80302 Fax: 303-444-7968
CEO: Robert D. Greenlee
Dir HR: Kim Smith
Employees: 300
Jobs Added Last Year: 90 (+42.9%)
Leisure & recreational products - coin-operated amusement devices

CH2M HILL COS.
6060 S. Willow Dr. Phone: 303-771-0900
Denver, CO 80111 Fax: 303-220-5106
CEO: Ralph R. Peterson
VP HR: Fred Berry
Employees: 5,874
Jobs Added Last Year: 538 (+10.1%)
Engineering design & consulting

CIBER, INC.
5251 DTC Pkwy. Phone: 303-220-0100
Englewood, CO 80011 Fax: 303-220-7100
Chm, Pres & CEO: Bobby G. Stevenson
Office Mgr (HR): Dana Harr
Employees: 1,007
Jobs Added Last Year: 357 (+54.9%)
Computers - contract software programming

COMMNET CELLULAR INC.
5990 Greenwood Plaza Blvd. Phone: 303-694-3234
Englewood, CO 80111 Fax: 303-694-3293
Chm, Pres & CEO: Arnold C. Pohs
VP HR: Tom Calandra
Employees: 404
Jobs Added Last Year: 74 (+22.4%)
Telecommunications equipment - cellular telephone systems

CORPORATE EXPRESS, INC.
325 Interlocken Pkwy. Phone: 303-373-2800
Broomfield, CO 80021 Fax: 303-438-5181
Chm & CEO: Jirka Rysavy
Dir HR: Richard W. Hediger
Employees: 3,300
Jobs Added Last Year: 191 (+6.1%)
Retail catalog office equipment & supplies

CYPRUS AMAX MINERALS COMPANY
9100 E. Mineral Circle Phone: 303-643-5000
Englewood, CO 80112 Fax: 303-643-5049
Co-Chm, Pres & CEO: Milton H. Ward
VP HR: Gerald H. Peppard
Employees: 10,750
Jobs Added Last Year: 3,750 (+53.6%)
Metal ores - copper, zinc, gold, lithium, talc

COLORADO

DATA STORAGE MARKETING, INC.
5718 Central Ave. Phone: 303-442-4747
Boulder, CO 80301 Fax: 303-442-7985
Pres: Thomas Ward
Mgr HR: Julie Ekberg
Employees: 200
Jobs Added Last Year: 50 (+33.3%)
Computers - wholesale components & peripheral equipment; microcomputer manufacturing

GATES CORPORATION
900 S. Broadway Phone: 303-744-1911
Denver, CO 80217 Fax: 303-744-4000
Chm & CEO: Charles C. Gates, Jr.
VP Administrative Svcs (HR): D. R. Ahlman
Employees: 15,000
Jobs Added Last Year: 2,270 (+17.8%)
Rubber products - belts & hoses; auto components; oil & gas exploration

INTELCOM GROUP, INC.
1050 17th St., Ste. 1610 Phone: 303-572-5960
Denver, CO 80265 Fax: 303-592-7014
Pres: William J. Maxwell
VP HR: Valerie Randall
Employees: 714
Jobs Added Last Year: 284 (+66%)
Utility - local telecom access

JONES INTERCABLE, INC.
9697 E. Mineral Ave. Phone: 303-792-3111
Englewood, CO 80112 Fax: 303-790-0533
Chm & CEO: Glenn R. Jones
Group VP HR: Raymond L. Vigil
Employees: 2,850
Jobs Added Last Year: 70 (+2.5%)
Cable TV

KENTEK INFORMATION SYSTEMS, INC.
2945 Wilderness Place Phone: 303-440-5500
Boulder, CO 80301 Fax: 303-440-9600
Pres & CEO: Philip Shires
HR Mgr: Deborah Cason
Employees: 315
Jobs Added Last Year: 115 (+57.5%)
Computers - LED-based page printers

M.D.C. HOLDINGS, INC.
3600 S. Yosemite St., Ste. 900 Phone: 303-773-1100
Denver, CO 80237 Fax: 303-741-4134
CEO: Larry A. Mizel
VP & COO (HR): Gary Reece
Employees: 773
Jobs Added Last Year: 143 (+22.7%)
Financial - investment management

MANVILLE CORPORATION
717 17th St. Phone: 303-978-2000
Denver, CO 80202 Fax: 303-978-2363
Chm, Pres & CEO: W. Thomas Stephens
Dir Ben: Ann Henley
Employees: 16,000
Jobs Added Last Year: 200 (+1.3%)
Building products, paperboard & packaging products, engineered products

NEWMONT GOLD COMPANY
1700 Lincoln St. Phone: 303-863-7414
Denver, CO 80203 Fax: 303-837-5837
VC, Pres & CEO: Ronald C. Cambre
Dir HR: Lou Lazo
Employees: 3,500
Jobs Added Last Year: 1,124 (+47.3%)
Gold mining & processing

PRIMA ENERGY CORPORATION
1801 Broadway, Ste. 500 Phone: 303-297-2100
Denver, CO 80202 Fax: 303-297-7708
Pres, CEO & CFO: Richard H. Lewis
Off Mgr (HR): Nancy Hewit
Employees: 52
Jobs Added Last Year: 8 (+18.2%)
Oil & gas - US exploration & production

PUBLIC SERVICE COMPANY OF COLORADO
1225 17th St. Phone: 303-571-7511
Denver, CO 80202 Fax: 303-834-6551
Chm, Pres & CEO: Delwin D. Hock
VP Administrative Svcs (HR): Marilyn E. Taylor
Employees: 6,507
Jobs Cut Last Year: 61 (-.9%)
Utility - electric power

COLORADO

RANDOM ACCESS, INC.
8000 E. Iliff
Denver, CO 80231
Phone: 303-745-9600
Fax: 303-745-0242
Pres, CEO & COO: Richard A. Crawford
Dir HR: Brenda Cutaia
Employees: 300
Jobs Added Last Year: 97 (+47.8%)
Computers - direct sales to companies

ROCK BOTTOM RESTAURANTS, INC.
1215 Spruce St., Ste. 102
Boulder, CO 80302
Phone: 303-443-8422
Fax: 303-443-1280
Chm & CEO: Frank B. Day
Dir HR: Emily Rusnak
Employees: 2,300
Jobs Added Last Year: 1,200 (+109.1%)
Retail - restaurants featuring microbreweries (Rock Bottom) & specialty beers (Old Chicago)

STAODYN, INC.
1225 Florida Ave.
Longmont, CO 80501
Phone: 303-772-3631
Fax: 303-651-0266
CEO: W. Bayne Gibson
HR Mgr: Joanne Roth
Employees: 167
Jobs Added Last Year: 108 (+183.1%)
Medical products - physical therapy equipment

STORAGE TECHNOLOGY CORP.
2270 S. 88th St.
Louisville, CO 80028-4309
Phone: 303-673-5151
Fax: 303-673-5019
Chm, Pres & CEO: Ryal R. Poppa
Corp VP HR: Sewell I. Sleek
Employees: 10,100
Jobs Added Last Year: 0
Computers - disk & tape storage & retrieval systems

TELE-COMMUNICATIONS, INC.
5619 DTC Pkwy.
Englewood, CO 80111
Phone: 303-267-5500
Fax: 303-779-1228
Pres & CEO: John C. Malone
No central personnel officer
Employees: 24,000
Jobs Added Last Year: 2,000 (+9.1%)
Cable TV (#1 in the US)

U S WEST, INC.
7800 E. Orchard Rd.
Englewood, CO 80111
Phone: 303-793-6500
Fax: 303-793-6654
Chm, Pres & CEO: Richard D. McCormick
SVP & Chief HR Off: J. Thomas Bouchard
Employees: 60,778
Jobs Cut Last Year: 2,929 (-4.6%)
Utility - telephone, long distance services, cable, cellular communications, multimedia

ULTIMATE ELECTRONICS, INC.
9901 W. 50th Ave.
Wheat Ridge, CO 80033
Phone: 303-420-1366
Fax: 303-420-5630
Chm & CEO: William J. Pearse
Recruiting Mgr (HR): Mary Tiffin
Employees: 1,000
Jobs Added Last Year: 464 (+86.6%)
Retail - consumer electronics in Colorado & Utah

UNITED ARTISTS THEATRE CIRCUIT, INC.
9110 E. Nichols Ave., Ste. 200
Englewood, CO 80112
Phone: 303-792-3600
Fax: 303-790-8907
Chm & CEO: Stewart Blair
Dir HR: Elizabeth Moravak
Employees: 12,000
Jobs Added Last Year: –
Motion pictures - theaters (#1 in the US)

VICORP RESTAURANTS, INC.
400 W. 48th Ave., PO Box 16601
Denver, CO 80216
Phone: 303-296-2121
Fax: 303-297-8637
Chm: Charles R. Frederickson
VP Training & HR: Sylvia J. Ferry
Employees: 14,700
Jobs Added Last Year: 300 (+2.1%)
Retail - Bakers Square & Village Inn restaurants

WESTERN GAS RESOURCES, INC.
12200 N. Pecos St.
Denver, CO 80234-3439
Phone: 303-452-5603
Fax: 303-452-0186
Chm & CEO: Brion G. Wise
Dir HR: Dave DeBell
Employees: 931
Jobs Added Last Year: 190 (+25.6%)
Oil & gas - production & pipeline

CONNECTICUT

ADVO, INC. [12490]
One Univac Ln., PO Box 755   Phone: 203-285-6100
Windsor, CT 06095-0755   Fax: 203-285-6393
Chm & CEO: Robert Kamerschen
SVP HR: J. Thomas Van Berkem
Employees: 5,300
Jobs Cut Last Year: 400 (-7%)
Business services - direct marketing

AETNA LIFE AND CASUALTY CO. [10039]
151 Farmington Ave.   Phone: 203-273-0123
Hartford, CT 06156   Fax: 203-275-2677
Chm, Pres & CEO: Ronald E. Compton
SVP HR: Mary Ann Champlin
Employees: 42,600
Jobs Cut Last Year: 400 (-.9%)
Insurance - multiline

AIR EXPRESS INTERNATIONAL CORPORATION
120 Tokeneke Rd.   Phone: 203-655-7900
Darien, CT 06820   Fax: 203-655-5779
Pres & CEO: Guenter Rohrmann
Dir Personnel: Billie Raisides
Employees: 3,688
Jobs Added Last Year: 118 (+3.3%)
Transportation - air & sea freight forwarding

AMDURA CORPORATION
900 Main St. South, PO Box 870   Phone: 203-262-0570
Southbury, CT 06488-8870   Fax: 203-262-1270
Chm & CEO: Frederick Whitridge, Jr.
No central personnel officer
Employees: 1,520
Jobs Added Last Year: 280 (+22.6%)
Metal products - lifting equipment, hardware & accessories; recycling & waste management equipment

AMERICAN BRANDS, INC. [10075]
1700 E. Putnam Ave., PO Box 811   Phone: 203-698-5000
Old Greenwich, CT 06870-0811   Fax: 203-637-2580
Chm & CEO: Thomas C. Hays
VP & Chief Admin Off (HR): Steven C. Mendenhall
Employees: 46,160
Jobs Added Last Year: 440 (+1%)
Diversified operations - liquor (Gilbey's, Jim Beam); office products (Swingline); golfing equipment (Titleist)

AMERICAN WHITE CROSS, INC.
349 Lake Rd.   Phone: 203-774-8541
Dayville, CT 06241   Fax: 203-774-1507
Pres & CEO: Howard Koenig
Dir Personnel: Roxanne Peckham
Employees: 1,075
Jobs Added Last Year: 595 (+124%)
Medical supplies - private-label disposable health & personal-care products including bandages, swabs & cotton rolls

AMES DEPARTMENT STORES, INC. [42031]
2418 Main St.   Phone: 203-257-2000
Rocky Hill, CT 06067   Fax: 203-257-7806
CEO: Joseph Ettore
Dir HR: Richard L. Carter
Employees: 22,000
Jobs Cut Last Year: 1,000 (-4.3%)
Retail - discount & variety stores

AMPHENOL CORPORATION
358 Hall Ave.   Phone: 203-265-8900
Wallingford, CT 06492   Fax: 203-265-8793
Chm & CEO: Lawrence J. DeGeorge
Dir HR: Wayne Simms
Employees: 5,408
Jobs Cut Last Year: 305 (-5.3%)
Electrical, electronic & fiber optic connectors

BLYTH INDUSTRIES, INC.
2 Greenwich Plaza   Phone: 203-661-1926
Greenwich, CT 06830   Fax: 203-661-1969
CEO: Robert B. Goergen
VP HR: Erik Sprotte
Employees: 1,350
Jobs Added Last Year: 150 (+12.5%)
Housewares - scented candles, outdoor citronella candles & fragrance products

CALDOR CORPORATION
20 Glover Ave.   Phone: 203-849-2000
Norwalk, CT 06856-5620   Fax: 203-849-2019
Chm & CEO: Don R. Clarke
SVP HR: Dennis M. Lee
Employees: 21,000
Jobs Cut Last Year: 3,000 (-12.5%)
Retail - discount & variety

An in-depth profile of this company is available by fax. Call 800-510-4452 and use your touch-tone phone to put in the 5-digit code at the prompt. Only $2.95 each with your credit card. See page 12 for more details.

CONNECTICUT

CENTURY COMMUNICATIONS CORPORATION
50 Locust Ave. Phone: 203-972-2000
New Canaan, CT 06840 Fax: 203-966-9228
Chm & CEO: Leonard Tow
SVP (HR): Claire L. Tow
Employees: 2,500
Jobs Added Last Year: 200 (+8.7%)
Cable TV; cellular telephone network

CROMPTON & KNOWLES CORPORATION
One Station Place Phone: 203-353-5400
Stamford, CT 06902 Fax: 203-353-5424
Chm, Pres & CEO: Vincent A. Calarco
Dir HR: Ester Mattson
Employees: 2,309
Jobs Added Last Year: 266 (+13%)
Chemicals - specialty

CHAMPION INTERNATIONAL CORP.
One Champion Plaza Phone: 203-358-7000
Stamford, CT 06921 Fax: 203-358-2975
Chm & CEO: Andrew C. Sigler
SVP Organizational Dev & HR: Mark V. Childers
Employees: 25,250
Jobs Cut Last Year: 2,050 (-7.5%)
Paper & paper products

CUC INTERNATIONAL INC.
707 Summer St. Phone: 203-324-9261
Stamford, CT 06901 Fax: 203-348-3468
Chm & CEO: Walter A. Forbes
VP HR: Fran Johnson
Employees: 6,500
Jobs Added Last Year: 500 (+8.3%)
Retail - mail order & direct via computer

COLONIAL DATA TECHNOLOGIES CORPORATION
80 Pickett District Rd. Phone: 203-355-3178
New Milford, CT 06776 Fax: 203-354-2392
CEO: Robert J. Schock
Mgr HR: Kimberly Schock
Employees: 76
Jobs Added Last Year: 16 (+26.7%)
Telecommunications equipment - calling number identification displays

DAIRY MART CONVENIENCE STORES, INC.
One Vision Dr. Phone: 203-741-4444
Enfield, CT 06082 Fax: 203-741-3072
Pres & COO: Robert B. Stein, Jr.
EVP HR: Mitchell J. Kupperman
Employees: 5,500
Jobs Added Last Year: 228 (+4.3%)
Retail - convenience stores

CONNECTICUT MUTUAL LIFE INSURANCE CO.
140 Garden St. Phone: 203-987-6500
Hartford, CT 06154 Fax: 203-987-6532
Pres & CEO: David E. Sams, Jr.
SVP HR: David J. Beed
Employees: 5,000
Jobs Added Last Year: —
Insurance - life

DELOITTE & TOUCHE
10 Westport Rd. Phone: 203-761-3000
Wilton, CT 06897 Fax: 203-834-2200
Chm & CEO: J. Michael Cook
Natl Dir HR: James H. Wall
Employees: 16,310
Jobs Added Last Year: 510 (+3.2%)
Business services - accounting & consulting

CRANE CO.
100 First Stamford Place Phone: 203-363-7300
Stamford, CT 06902 Fax: 203-363-7295
Chm, Pres & CEO: Robert S. Evans
Dir HR: Richard Phillips
Employees: 8,700
Jobs Added Last Year: 200 (+2.4%)
Diversified operations - aerospace; defense products; millwork

DEVON GROUP, INC.
6 Stamford Forum, Ste. 501 Phone: 203-964-1444
Stamford, CT 06901-3227 Fax: 203-964-1036
Chm & CEO: Marne Obernauer, Jr.
No central personnel officer
Employees: 1,800
Jobs Added Last Year: 100 (+5.9%)
Printing - advertising & editorial production, computerized typesetting, composition, printing, binding & related services

CONNECTICUT

DRESS BARN, INC.
88 Hamilton Ave. Phone: 203-327-4242
Stamford, CT 06902 Fax: 203-359-4458
Chm & CEO: Elliot S. Jaffe
VP HR: David Montieth
Employees: 5,600
Jobs Added Last Year: 800 (+16.7%)
Retail - apparel & shoes

DS BANCOR, INC.
33 Elizabeth St. Phone: 203-736-9921
Derby, CT 06418 Fax: 203-736-6060
Pres & CEO: Harry P. DiAdamo, Jr.
VP & Dir HR: Bonnie Smith
Employees: 332
Jobs Added Last Year: 165 (+98.8%)
Financial - savings & loans

THE DUN & BRADSTREET CORP.   [10483]
200 Nyala Farms Phone: 203-222-4200
Westport, CT 06880 Fax: 203-222-4201
Pres & CEO: Robert E. Weissman
SVP HR: John J. Fitzpatrick
Employees: 50,400
Jobs Cut Last Year: 2,000 (-3.8%)
Business services - marketing (A.C. Nielson) & credit information, software & financial services (Moody's)

DURACELL INTERNATIONAL, INC.
Berkshire Corporate Park Phone: 203-796-4000
Bethel, CT 06801 Fax: 203-796-4187
Chm & CEO: Charles R. Perrin
SVP HR: Nancy A. Reardon
Employees: 7,700
Jobs Cut Last Year: 300 (-3.8%)
Electrical products - batteries

EAGLE FINANCIAL CORP.
222 Main St. Phone: 203-584-6300
Bristol, CT 06010 Fax: 203-585-2939
Pres & CEO: Robert J. Britton
VP HR: Adele L. Reale
Employees: 376
Jobs Added Last Year: 62 (+19.7%)
Financial - savings & loans

ECHLIN INC.
100 Double Beach Rd. Phone: 203-481-5751
Branford, CT 06405 Fax: 203-488-0370
Chm & CEO: Frederick J. Mancheski
VP HR: Milton J. Makoski
Employees: 20,600
Jobs Added Last Year: 2,000 (+10.8%)
Automotive & trucking - brake, engine, power transmission & steering & suspension parts

EIS INTERNATIONAL, INC.   [15796]
1351 Washington Blvd. Phone: 203-351-4800
Stamford, CT 06902 Fax: 203-961-8632
Chm, Pres & CEO: Joseph J. Porfeli
Dir HR: Jo Lovell
Employees: 300
Jobs Added Last Year: 42 (+16.3%)
Telecommunications equipment - inbound & outbound telemarketing/call processing systems

ELXSI CORPORATION   [13258]
115 E. Putnam Ave. Phone: 203-661-9645
Greenwich, CT 06830-5643 Fax: 203-661-1119
Chm, Pres & CEO: Alexander M. Milley
VP, Bickford's (HR): Kenneth Allen
Employees: 1,719
Jobs Added Last Year: 115 (+7.2%)
Retail - restaurants (Howard Johnson's & Bickford's); video inspection equipment for wastewater systems

ESSTAR INC.
555 Long Wharf Dr., Ste. 12 Phone: 203-777-2274
New Haven, CT 06511 Fax: 203-785-8851
CEO: Robert A. Haversat, Sr.
No central personnel officer
Employees: 3,900
Jobs Cut Last Year: 100 (-2.5%)
Metal products - hardware

EXECUTONE INFORMATION SYSTEMS, INC.
478 Wheelers Farms Rd. Phone: 203-876-7600
Milford, CT 06460 Fax: 203-882-0503
Pres & CEO: Alan Kessman
Corp HR Mgr: Bruce Olin
Employees: 2,400
Jobs Added Last Year: 200 (+9.1%)
Telecommunications equipment - hospital, voice & data communications equipment

An in-depth profile of this company is available by fax. Call 800-510-4452 and use your touch-tone phone to put in the 5-digit code at the prompt. Only $2.95 each with your credit card. See page 12 for more details.

117

CONNECTICUT

FIRST BRANDS CORPORATION
83 Wooster Heights Rd., Bldg. 301   Phone: 203-731-2300
Danbury, CT 06813-1911   Fax: 203-731-2518
CEO: Alfred E. Dudley
Dir HR: Ronald F. Dainton
Employees: 3,700
Jobs Cut Last Year: 50 (-1.3%)
Soap & cleaning preparations, plastic wrap (Glad), engine additive products (STP) & car polish (Simoniz)

FORSCHNER GROUP, INC.
151 Long Hill Cross Rds.   Phone: 203-929-6391
Shelton, CT 06484   Fax: 203-929-3786
Co-Chm & CEO: James W. Kennedy
Dir Personnel: Lesley Olsen
Employees: 160
Jobs Added Last Year: 34 (+27%)
Housewares - Swiss Army Knife importing & cutlery

GARTNER GROUP INC.
56 Top Gallant Rd., PO Box 10212   Phone: 203-964-0096
Stamford, CT 06904-2212   Fax: 203-324-7901
Pres & CEO: Manuel A. Fernandez
SVP HR: Lindon Smith
Employees: 912
Jobs Added Last Year: 237 (+35.1%)
Business services - subscription research services to users of advanced technology

GENERAL ELECTRIC COMPANY
3135 Easton Tpke.   Phone: 203-373-2459
Fairfield, CT 06431   Fax: 203-373-3131
Chm & CEO: John F. Welch, Jr.
SVP HR: William Conaty
Employees: 222,000
Jobs Cut Last Year: 9,000 (-3.9%)
Diversified operations - financing; aircraft engines; industrial products; appliances; broadcasting (NBC); power systems

GENERAL HOST CORPORATION
One Station Place   Phone: 203-357-9900
Stamford, CT 06902   Fax: 203-357-0148
Chm, Pres & CEO: Harris J. Ashton
VP (HR): Carol Cox
Employees: 7,400
Jobs Added Last Year: 10 (+.1%)
Retail - gardening, crafts, Christmas merchandise

GENERAL SIGNAL CORPORATION
High Ridge Park   Phone: 203-329-4100
Stamford, CT 06904-2351 Fax: 203-329-4159
Chm & CEO: Edmund M. Carpenter
VP HR: George Falconer
Employees: 12,900
Jobs Cut Last Year: 800 (-5.8%)
Instruments - control

GTE CORPORATION
One Stamford Forum   Phone: 203-965-2000
Stamford, CT 06904   Fax: 203-965-2277
Chm & CEO: Charles R. Lee
SVP HR & Admin: J. Randall MacDonald
Employees: 117,446
Jobs Cut Last Year: 13,554 (-10.3%)
Utility - telephone service, cellular communications, information services, in-flight telephone service (Airfone)

HARTFORD BOILER INSPECTION AND INS. CO.
One State St., PO Box 5024   Phone: 203-722-1866
Hartford, CT 06102-5024   Fax: 203-722-5106
Pres & CEO: Gordon W. Kreh
Asst VP (HR): Susan W. Ahrens
Employees: 4,200
Jobs Added Last Year: 164 (+4.1%)
Insurance - property & casualty; engineering services; investments

HUBBELL INC.
584 Derby Milford Rd.   Phone: 203-799-4100
Orange, CT 06477-4024   Fax: 203-799-4223
Chm, Pres & CEO: G. J. Ratcliffe
Dir HR: George Zurman
Employees: 5,885
Jobs Added Last Year: 353 (+6.4%)
Electrical products - electrical wiring devices, industrial controls

HYPERION SOFTWARE CORPORATION
777 Long Ridge Rd.   Phone: 203-321-3500
Stamford, CT 06902-1247   Fax: 203-322-3904
Chm, Pres & CEO: James A. Perakis
HR Dir: Paul Avalone
Employees: 580
Jobs Added Last Year: 161 (+38.4%)
Computers - executive information systems software

CONNECTICUT

INTERLAKEN CAPITAL INC.
165 Mason St. Phone: 203-629-8750
Greenwich, CT 06830 Fax: 203-629-8554
CEO: William R. Berkley
Personnel Mgr: Margaret Crawford
Employees: 11,000
Jobs Added Last Year: —
Financial - investment bankers

KAMAN CORPORATION
Blue Hills Ave. Phone: 203-243-7100
Bloomfield, CT 06002 Fax: 203-243-6365
Chm & CEO: Charles H. Kaman
VP (HR): Candace A. Clark
Employees: 5,400
Jobs Added Last Year: 37 (+.7%)
Aerospace - aircraft equipment

LEXMARK INTERNATIONAL INC.
55 Railroad Ave. Phone: 203-629-6700
Greenwich, CT 06836 Fax: 203-629-6725
Chm, Pres & CEO: Marvin L. Mann
VP HR & Info Programs: A. Richard Murphy
Employees: 4,000
Jobs Added Last Year: 0
Computers - printers & keyboards

LOCTITE CORPORATION
1001 Trout Brook Crossing Phone: 203-520-5000
Rocky Hill, CT 06067 Fax: 203-520-5073
Pres, CEO & COO: David Freeman
VP HR & Training: Don Atencio
Employees: 3,700
Jobs Added Last Year: 11 (+.3%)
Paints & allied products

LYNCH CORPORATION
8 Sound Shore Dr., Ste. 290 Phone: 203-629-3333
Greenwich, CT 06830 Fax: 203-629-3718
Chm & CEO: Mario J. Gabelli
VP Admin, Sec & Gen Counsel (HR): Robert Hurwich
Employees: 609
Jobs Added Last Year: 75 (+14%)
Diversified operations - telecommunications; transportation; investments

MARINER HEALTH GROUP, INC.
47 Water St. Phone: 203-445-4000
Mystic, CT 06355 Fax: 203-572-8546
CEO: Arthur W. Stratton, Jr.
Acting Dir HR: Joan Wiegers
Employees: 5,500
Jobs Added Last Year: 3,530 (+179.2%)
Subacute health care services

MASHANTUCKET PEQUOT GAMING ENTERPRISE
R.R. 2 Phone: 203-885-3000
Ledyard, CT 06339 Fax: 203-536-3412
Pres & CEO: G. Michael Brown
VP HR: Al Piudente
Employees: 9,100
Jobs Added Last Year: —
Leisure & recreational services - casino (Foxwood High Stakes Bingo and Casino) in Connecticut

MECKLERMEDIA CORPORATION
20 Ketchum St. Phone: 203-226-6967
Westport, CT 06880 Fax: 203-454-5840
Chm, Pres & CEO (HR): Alan M. Meckler
Employees: 53
Jobs Added Last Year: 11 (+26.2%)
Publishing - magazines *(Internet World* & *Virtual Reality World)*; trade shows

MICRO WAREHOUSE, INC.
47 S. Water St. Phone: 203-854-1700
South Norwalk, CT 06854 Fax: 203-854-0203
Chm, Pres & CEO: Peter Godfrey
Dir HR: Angela Mizak
Employees: 1,496
Jobs Added Last Year: 775 (+107.5%)
Retail - mail order computers & software *(MacWAREHOUSE* & *MicroWAREHOUSE)*

NINE WEST GROUP INC.
9 W. Broad St. Phone: 203-328-4383
Stamford, CT 06902 Fax: 314-434-0409
Co-Chm & Pres: Vincent Camuto
HR Mgr: Debra Trautman
Employees: 4,021
Jobs Added Last Year: 521 (+14.9%)
Shoes & related apparel

CONNECTICUT

NOISE CANCELLATION TECHNOLOGIES, INC.
800 Summer St. Phone: 203-961-0500
Stamford, CT 06901 Fax: 203-348-4100
CEO: John McCloy
Dir HR: Fronnie Redd
Employees: 172
Jobs Added Last Year: 32 (+22.9%)
Engineering - noise & vibration reduction technology

PITNEY BOWES INC.
World Headquarters Phone: 203-356-5000
Stamford, CT 06926-0700 Fax: 203-351-6303
Chm, Pres & CEO: George B. Harvey
VP Personnel: Johnna G. Torsone
Employees: 32,539
Jobs Added Last Year: 3,581 (+12.4%)
Office equipment & supplies - mailing & copier systems, facsimile machines

OLIN CORPORATION
120 Long Ridge Rd. Phone: 203-356-2000
Stamford, CT 06904-1355 Fax: 203-356-2052
Chm & CEO: John W. Johnstone, Jr.
VP HR: Peter C. Kosche
Employees: 13,967
Jobs Added Last Year: 467 (+3.5%)
Diversified operations - chemicals; defense products & ammunition; metals

PITTSTON SERVICES GROUP
PO Box 120070 Phone: 203-978-5200
Stamford, CT 06912-0070 Fax: 203-978-5210
Chm, Pres & CEO: Joseph C. Farrell
VP Admin & HR: Frank Lennon
Employees: 22,800
Jobs Added Last Year: 1,800 (+8.6%)
Diversified operations - air freight (Burlington); logistics; security services (Brink's)

OXFORD HEALTH PLANS, INC.
800 Connecticut Ave. Phone: 203-852-1442
Norwalk, CT 06854 Fax: 203-851-2464
Chm & CEO: Stephen F. Wiggins
VP HR: Jeanne D. Wisniewski
Employees: 720
Jobs Added Last Year: 372 (+106.9%)
Health maintenance organization in New York City metropolitan area

PRAXAIR, INC.
39 Old Ridgebury Rd. Phone: 203-794-3000
Danbury, CT 06810-5113 Fax: 203-867-2555
Chm & CEO: H. William Lichtenberger
VP HR & Quality: Lawrence F. Doyle
Employees: 16,766
Jobs Cut Last Year: 1,826 (-9.8%)
Chemicals - industrial gases

PEOPLE'S CHOICE TV CORPORATION
2 Corporate Dr. Phone: 203-929-2800
Shelton, CT 06484 Fax: 203-929-1454
CEO: Matthew Oristano
Dir Admin (HR): Pamela Yager
Employees: 170
Jobs Added Last Year: 112 (+193.1%)
Broadcasting - radio & TV

RAYONIER, INC.
1177 Summer St. Phone: 203-348-7000
Stamford, CT 06905 Fax: 203-964-4528
Chm, Pres & CEO: Ronald M. Gross
SVP Admin (HR): John P. O'Grady
Employees: 2,600
Jobs Added Last Year: 0
Paper & paper products

PERKIN-ELMER CORPORATION
761 Main Ave. Phone: 203-762-1000
Norwalk, CT 06859-0001 Fax: 203-762-6000
Pres & CEO: Gaynor N. Kelley
VP HR: Michael McPartland
Employees: 6,563
Jobs Added Last Year: 208 (+3.3%)
Instruments - scientific

RAYTECH CORPORATION
One Corporate Dr. Phone: 203-925-8023
Shelton, CT 06484 Fax: 203-925-8088
CEO & Pres: Craig R. Smith
CFO & Corp VP Admin (HR): Albert A. Canosa
Employees: 1,187
Jobs Added Last Year: 225 (+23.4%)
Automotive & trucking - original equipment

CONNECTICUT

SMITH CORONA CORPORATION
65 Locust Ave.   Phone: 203-972-1471
New Canaan, CT 06840   Fax: 203-972-4220
Chm & CEO: G. Lee Thompson
VP HR: David Vorostko
Employees: 3,400
Jobs Added Last Year: 100 (+3%)
Office equipment & supplies

SOUTHERN NEW ENGLAND TELECOMM.
227 Church St.   Phone: 203-771-5200
New Haven, CT 06510   Fax: 203-772-4855
Chm & CEO: Daniel J. Miglio
VP HR: E. William Kobernusz
Employees: 10,476
Jobs Cut Last Year: 740 (-6.6%)
Utility - telephone

THE STANLEY WORKS
1000 Stanley Dr.   Phone: 203-225-5111
New Britain, CT 06053   Fax: 203-827-3895
Chm & CEO: Richard H. Ayers
VP HR: Barbara W. Bennett
Employees: 18,988
Jobs Added Last Year: 338 (+1.8%)
Tools - hand-held, power & industrial; hardware; locks; door systems

STURM, RUGER & COMPANY, INC.
Lacey Place   Phone: 203-259-7843
Southport, CT 06490   Fax: 203-254-2195
Chm, CEO & Treas: William B. Ruger
Personnel Mgr: Carol Markland
Employees: 1,719
Jobs Added Last Year: 170 (+11%)
Guns

TOSCO CORPORATION
72 Cummings Point Rd.   Phone: 203-977-1000
Stamford, CT 06902   Fax: 203-964-3187
Chm, Pres & CEO: Thomas D. O'Malley
VP HR, Tosco Refining: Timothy J. McGarvey
Employees: 2,729
Jobs Added Last Year: 1,735 (+174.5%)
Oil refining & marketing

TRC COMPANIES, INC.
5 Waterside Crossing   Phone: 203-289-8631
Windsor, CT 06095   Fax: 203-282-4018
Chm & CEO: Vincent A. Rocco
VP HR: Charles Anderson
Employees: 830
Jobs Added Last Year: 95 (+12.9%)
Pollution control - environmental consulting

ULTRAMAR CORPORATION
2 Pickwick Plaza, Ste. 300   Phone: 203-622-7000
Greenwich, CT 06830   Fax: 203-622-7007
Chm & CEO: Jean Gaulin
VP, Gen Counsel & Sec (HR): Patrick Guarino
Employees: 3,000
Jobs Cut Last Year: 100 (-3.2%)
Oil & gas - refining & marketing

UNION CARBIDE CORPORATION
39 Old Ridgebury Rd.   Phone: 203-794-2000
Danbury, CT 06817-0001   Fax: 203-794-4336
Chm & CEO: Robert D. Kennedy
VP HR: Malcolm A. Kessinger
Employees: 13,051
Jobs Cut Last Year: 2,024 (-13.4%)
Chemicals - diversified

UNIROYAL CHEMICAL COMPANY, INC.
World Headquarters   Phone: 203-573-2000
Middlebury, CT 06749   Fax: 203-573-3077
Chm, Pres & CEO: Robert J. Mazaika
VP HR: Neil A. Melore
Employees: 2,700
Jobs Added Last Year: —
Chemicals - diversified

UNITED STATES SURGICAL CORP.
150 Glover Ave.   Phone: 203-845-1000
Norwalk, CT 06856   Fax: 203-845-4478
Chm, Pres & CEO: Leon C. Hirsch
Senior Dir HR: David A. Renker
Employees: 7,610
Jobs Cut Last Year: 490 (-6%)
Medical products - surgical staplers, sutures & clamps

CONNECTICUT

UNITED TECHNOLOGIES CORP.
United Technologies Bldg. Phone: 203-728-7000
Hartford, CT 06101 Fax: 203-728-7979
Pres & CEO: George David
SVP HR & Organization: William L. Bucknall, Jr.
Employees: 168,600
Jobs Cut Last Year: 9,400 (-5.3%)
Diversified operations - building systems (Carrier & Otis); jet engines; flight systems

UNITED WASTE SYSTEMS, INC.
4 Greenwich Office Park Phone: 203-622-3131
Greenwich, CT 06830 Fax: 203-622-6080
Chm & CEO: Bradley S. Jacobs
Dir HR: Richard Upton
Employees: 825
Jobs Added Last Year: 474 (+135%)
Pollution control - trash disposal

UST INC.
100 W. Putnam Ave. Phone: 203-661-1100
Greenwich, CT 06830-5316 Fax: 203-622-3626
CEO: Vincent A. Gierer, Jr.
SVP HR: Richard Kohlberger
Employees: 3,651
Jobs Added Last Year: 82 (+2.3%)
Tobacco

VALUE HEALTH, INC.
22 Waterville Rd. Phone: 203-678-3400
Avon, CT 06001 Fax: 203-677-1752
Chm & CEO: Robert E. Patricelli
Office Mgr (HR): Myra Davis
Employees: 3,100
Jobs Added Last Year: 2,012 (+184.9%)
Medical services - pharmacy & mental health benefit programs

WARRANTECH CORPORATION
300 Atlantic St. Phone: 203-975-1100
Stamford, CT 06901 Fax: 203-357-0449
Chm & CEO: Joel San Antonio
Ofc Mgr, Asst to Chm & HR Dir: Kim Caban
Employees: 200
Jobs Added Last Year: 42 (+26.6%)
Financial - extended warranty services

WEBSTER FINANCIAL CORPORATION
First Federal Plaza Phone: 203-755-1422
Waterbury, CT 06720 Fax: 203-755-5539
Pres & CEO: James C. Smith
SVP (HR): Renee P. Seefried
Employees: 827
Jobs Added Last Year: 251 (+43.6%)
Financial - savings & loans

XEROX CORPORATION
800 Long Ridge Rd. Phone: 203-968-3000
Stamford, CT 06904 Fax: 203-968-4312
Chm & CEO: Paul A. Allaire
VP HR: Anne M. Mulcahy
Employees: 97,000
Jobs Cut Last Year: 2,300 (-2.3%)
Office equipment & supplies - document & imaging systems; insurance

YALE UNIVERSITY
451 College St. Phone: 203-432-2321
New Haven, CT 06520 Fax: 203-432-7891
Pres: Richard C. Levin
VP HR: Peter Vallone
Employees: 8,500
Jobs Added Last Year: —
University

DELAWARE

AMERICA SERVICE GROUP, INC.
Two Penn's Way, Ste. 200　　Phone: 302-322-8200
New Castle, DE 19720　　Fax: 302-322-0960
Pres & CEO: Jeffrey A. Reasons
Dir HR: Steve Zalik
Employees: 1,330
Jobs Added Last Year: 311 (+30.5%)
Health care - outpatient & home

E.I. DU PONT DE NEMOURS AND CO.
1007 Market St.　　Phone: 302-774-1000
Wilmington, DE 19898　　Fax: 302-774-7322
Chm & CEO: Edgar S. Woolard, Jr.
SVP HR: D. John Ogren
Employees: 114,000
Jobs Cut Last Year: 10,916 (-8.7%)
Diversified operations - oil production (Conoco); chemicals & consumer products (Corian, Teflon, Stainmaster, Lycra)

AUTOTOTE CORPORATION
100 Bellevue Rd., PO Box 6009　　Phone: 302-737-4300
Newark, DE 19714-6009　　Fax: 302-453-8128
Chm & CEO: A. Lorne Weil
Mgr HR: Cathy Angle
Employees: 996
Jobs Added Last Year: 704 (+241.1%)
Leisure & recreational products - betting machines for racetracks

THE E.W. SCRIPPS COMPANY
1105 N. Market St.　　Phone: 302-478-4141
Wilmington, DE 19801　　Fax: 302-427-7663
Chm & CEO: Lawrence A. Leser
VP HR: Gregory L. Ebel
Employees: 7,600
Jobs Cut Last Year: 600 (-7.3%)
Publishing - newspapers; TV & radio stations & cable TV systems

BENEFICIAL CORPORATION
301 N. Walnut St.　　Phone: 302-425-2500
Wilmington, DE 19801　　Fax: 302-425-2518
Chm & CEO: Finn M. W. Caspersen
Dir HR: Calvin Christopher
Employees: 7,900
Jobs Cut Last Year: 200 (-2.5%)
Financial - consumer loans

HERCULES INCORPORATED
Hercules Plaza, 1313 N. Market St.　　Phone: 302-594-5000
Wilmington, DE 19894-0001　　Fax: 302-594-5400
Chm, Pres & CEO: Thomas L. Gossage
VP HR: Edward V. Carrington
Employees: 14,083
Jobs Cut Last Year: 1,336 (-8.7%)
Chemicals - polymers; food

THE COLUMBIA GAS SYSTEM, INC.
20 Montchanin Rd.　　Phone: 302-429-5000
Wilmington, DE 19807-0020　　Fax: 302-429-5730
Chm, Pres & CEO: John H. Croom
VP HR: Dennis P. Geran
Employees: 10,114
Jobs Cut Last Year: 58 (-.6%)
Oil & gas - production & pipeline

MBNA
400 Christiana Rd.　　Phone: 302-453-9930
Newark, DE 19713　　Fax: 302-456-8150
Chm & CEO: Alfred Lerner
Dir Personnel: Steve Chambers
Employees: 7,500
Jobs Added Last Year: 1,753 (+30.5%)
Financial - credit card issuance

DELMARVA POWER & LIGHT COMPANY
800 King St., PO Box 231　　Phone: 302-429-3011
Wilmington, DE 19899　　Fax: 302-429-3665
Chm, Pres & CEO: Howard E. Cosgrove
VP HR: Donald E. Cain
Employees: 2,810
Jobs Cut Last Year: 26 (-.9%)
Utility - electric power

ROLLINS LEASING CORPORATION
One Rollins Plaza, PO Box 1791　　Phone: 302-426-2700
Wilmington, DE 19899　　Fax: 302-426-3599
Chm & CEO: John W. Rollins
Pres & COO (HR): John W. Rollins, Jr.
Employees: 2,924
Jobs Added Last Year: 248 (+9.3%)
Leasing - trucks

DELAWARE

W. L. GORE & ASSOCIATES INC.
555 Papermill Rd. Phone: 302-738-4880
Newark, DE 19711 Fax: 302-738-7710
Pres & CEO: Robert W. Gore
Mgr Personnel: Barbara Debnam
Employees: 5,700
Jobs Added Last Year: 530 (+10.3%)
Diversified operations - fabrics; electronics; industrial & medical products

WSFS FINANCIAL CORPORATION
838 Market St. Phone: 302-792-6000
Wilmington, DE 19899 Fax: 302-571-7215
Chm, Pres & CEO: Marvin N. Schoenhals
VP HR: Vicki Myoda
Employees: 470
Jobs Added Last Year: 92 (+24.3%)
Banks - Northeast

▼ Contract Employment Weekly http://www.ceweekly.wa.com

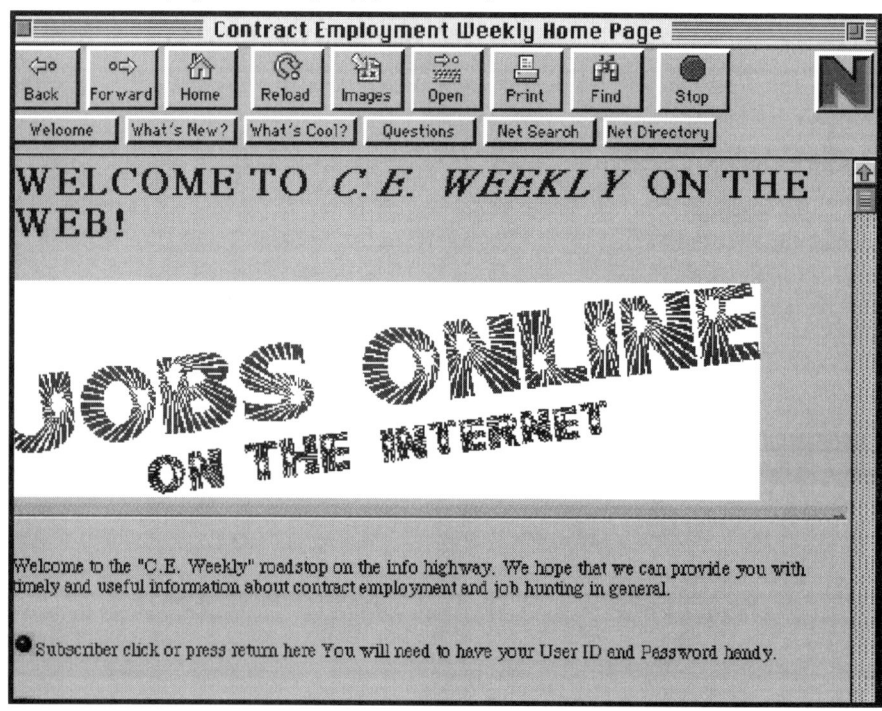

DISTRICT OF COLUMBIA

AMERICAN RED CROSS
431 18th St. NW
Washington, DC 20006
Pres: Elizabeth Dole
VP HR: James E. Thomas III
Employees: 25,000
Jobs Added Last Year: 0
Nonprofit organization
Phone: 202-737-8300
Fax: 202-639-3711

HARMAN INTERNATIONAL INDUSTRIES, INC.
1101 Pennsylvania Ave. NW
Washington, DC 20004
Chm & CEO: Sidney Harman
VP HR: Frederick R. Philpott
Employees: 4,710
Jobs Added Last Year: 272 (+6.1%)
Audio & video home products
Phone: 202-393-1101
Fax: 202-393-3064

DANAHER CORPORATION
1250 24th St. NW, Ste. 800
Washington, DC 20037
Pres & CEO: George M. Sherman
VP HR: Dennis Longo
Employees: 7,300
Jobs Added Last Year: 200 (+2.8%)
Tools - hand held & fasteners; process & environmental controls; parts for auto & diesel truck engines
Phone: 202-828-0850
Fax: 202-828-0860

MCI COMMUNICATIONS CORP.
1801 Pennsylvania Ave. NW
Washington, DC 20006
Chm & CEO: Bert C. Roberts, Jr.
Chief HR Off: John Zimmerman
Employees: 36,235
Jobs Added Last Year: 5,271 (+17%)
Telecommunications services - #2 US long distance carrier & messaging services
Phone: 202-872-1600
Fax: 202-887-3140

FEDERAL NATL. MORTGAGE ASSOC.
3900 Wisconsin Ave. NW
Washington, DC 20016
Chm & CEO: James A. Johnson
VP HR: Leon Z. Hollins
Employees: 3,200
Jobs Added Last Year: 200 (+6.7%)
Financial - mortgages & related services
Phone: 202-752-7000
Fax: 202-752-6099

NASD, INC.
1735 K St. NW
Washington, DC 20006-1506
Pres & CEO: Joseph R. Hardiman
SVP HR & Service Quality: James F. Peck
Employees: 46,900
Jobs Added Last Year: 7,800 (+19.9%)
Stock exchange (Nasdaq)
Phone: 202-728-8000
Fax: 202-728-8882

GEICO CORPORATION
One GEICO Plaza
Washington, DC 20076-0001
Pres & CEO: Olza M. Nicely
SVP HR: Marion Byrd
Employees: 8,125
Jobs Added Last Year: 1,122 (+16%)
Insurance - property & casualty
Phone: 301-986-3000
Fax: 301-986-2113

NATL. RAILROAD PASSENGER CORP.
60 Massachusetts Ave. NE
Washington, DC 20002
Chm, Pres & CEO: Thomas M. Downs
Asst VP Personnel: Neil D. Mann
Employees: 24,000
Jobs Added Last Year: 0
Transportation - rail (Amtrak)
Phone: 202-906-3860
Fax: 202-906-3865

THE GEORGE WASHINGTON UNIVERSITY
2121 I St. NW, 8th Fl.
Washington, DC 20037
Pres: Stephen J. Trachtenberg
Dir HR: Jim Clifford
Employees: 10,000
Jobs Added Last Year: --
University
Phone: 202-994-1000
Fax: 202-994-0654

POTOMAC ELECTRIC POWER COMPANY
1900 Pennsylvania Ave. NW
Washington, DC 20068
Chm & CEO: Edward F. Mitchell
VP HR: Anthony S. Macerollo
Employees: 4,863
Jobs Cut Last Year: 30 (-.6%)
Utility - electric power
Phone: 202-872-2456
Fax: 202-331-6874

An in-depth profile of this company is available by fax. Call 800-510-4452 and use your touch-tone phone to put in the 5-digit code at the prompt. Only $2.95 each with your credit card. See page 12 for more details.

DISTRICT OF COLUMBIA

SMITHSONIAN INSTITUTION
1000 Jefferson Dr. SW   Phone: 202-357-2700
Washington, DC 20560   Fax: 202-786-2515
CEO: I. Michael Heyman
Dir HR: Marilyn Marton
Employees: 6,800
Jobs Added Last Year: 0
Leisure & recreational services - museum

STUDENT LOAN MARKETING ASSOC.
1050 Thomas Jefferson St. NW   Phone: 202-333-8000
Washington, DC 20007   Fax: 202-298-3160
Pres & CEO: Lawrence A. Hough
SVP Personnel & Admin: Gerald Cohen
Employees: 4,510
Jobs Added Last Year: 160 (+3.7%)
Financial - student loans

UNITED STATES POSTAL SERVICE
475 L'Enfant Plaza SW   Phone: 202-268-2000
Washington, DC 20260   Fax: 202-268-2175
Chm: Marvin H. Runyon
VP Emp Rel: Suzanne J. Henry
Employees: 691,723
Jobs Cut Last Year: 33,567 (-4.6%)
Transportation - mail delivery

WASHINGTON GAS LIGHT COMPANY
1100 H St. NW   Phone: 703-750-4440
Washington, DC 20080   Fax: 703-750-7593
Chm & CEO: Patrick J. Maher
VP HR: Robert Sykes
Employees: 2,647
Jobs Cut Last Year: 23 (-.9%)
Utility - natural gas distribution

THE WASHINGTON POST COMPANY
1150 15th St. NW   Phone: 202-334-6000
Washington, DC 20071   Fax: 202-334-1031
Chm & CEO: Donald E. Graham
VP HR: Beverly R. Keil
Employees: 6,600
Jobs Added Last Year: 200 (+3.1%)
Publishing - newspapers & magazines (Newsweek); TV broadcasting; training centers (Stanley H. Kaplan)

WOODWARD & LOTHROP, INCORPORATED
1025 F St. NW   Phone: 202-347-5300
Washington, DC 20002   Fax: 202-879-8397
Chm & CEO: Robert B. Mang
SVP Personnel: Joseph Culver
Employees: 12,702
Jobs Added Last Year: —
Retail - regional department stores (Woodward & Lothrop, John Wanamaker)

THE WYATT COMPANY
601 13th St. NW, Ste. 1000   Phone: 202-508-4600
Washington, DC 20005   Fax: 202-508-4688
CEO: A. W. Smith, Jr.
Dir HR: Ralph Christensen
Employees: 3,500
Jobs Added Last Year: 100 (+2.9%)
Consulting

FLORIDA

ABR INFORMATION SERVICES, INC.
34125 US Hwy. 19 North   Phone: 813-785-2819
Palm Harbor, FL 34684-2116   Fax: 813-785-4306
CEO: James E. MacDougald
VP HR: Suzanne MacDougald
Employees: 236
Jobs Added Last Year: 38 (+19.2%)
Business services - health care benefits administration, information & compliance services

ALAMO RENT A CAR, INC.
110 SE Sixth St.   Phone: 305-522-0000
Ft. Lauderdale, FL 33301   Fax: 305-468-2162
Chm & CEO: Michael S. Egan
Exec Dir HR Dev: Connie Hoffmann
Employees: 7,000
Jobs Added Last Year: 500 (+7.7%)
Leasing - auto rental

AMERICAN AUTOMOBILE ASSOCIATION
1000 AAA Dr.   Phone: 407-444-7000
Heathrow, FL 32746-5063   Fax: 407-444-7380
CEO: Paul R. Verkuil
Dir HR: Karen Wall
Employees: 33,000
Jobs Added Last Year: —
Leisure & recreational services - auto club

AMERICAN BANKERS INSURANCE GROUP, INC.
11222 Quail Roost Dr.   Phone: 305-253-2244
Miami, FL 33157   Fax: 305-252-6987
Chm & CEO: R. Kirk Landon
SVP, ABLAC Subsidiary (HR): Phil Sharkey
Employees: 2,100
Jobs Added Last Year: 339 (+19.3%)
Insurance - life

AMERICAN MEDIA, INC.
600 S. East Coast Ave.   Phone: 407-586-1111
Lantana, FL 33462   Fax: 407-540-1018
Chm, Pres & CEO: Peter J. Callahan
VP HR: Susan Napolitano
Employees: 1,650
Jobs Added Last Year: 320 (+24.1%)
Publishing - periodicals (*National Enquirer, The Star*)

ATLANTIS GROUP, INC.
2665 S. Bayshore Dr., 8th Fl.   Phone: 305-858-2200
Miami, FL 33133   Fax: 305-285-0102
Chm, Pres & CEO: Earl W. Powell
VP HR: David Velmosky
Employees: 1,500
Jobs Added Last Year: 200 (+15.4%)
Diversified operations - plastic film; furniture

AVATAR HOLDINGS, INC.
255 Alhambra Circle   Phone: 305-442-7000
Coral Gables, FL 33134   Fax: 305-443-3844
Pres & CEO: Edwin Jacobson
VP HR: Rick Franks
Employees: 1,124
Jobs Added Last Year: 68 (+6.4%)
Real estate development

BARNETT BANKS, INC.
50 N. Laura St.   Phone: 904-791-7720
Jacksonville, FL 32202-3638   Fax: 904-791-7166
Chm & CEO: Charles E. Rice
Chief HR Exec: Paul T. Kerins
Employees: 18,649
Jobs Cut Last Year: 3,530 (-15.9%)
Banks - Southeast

BE AEROSPACE, INC.
1300 Corporate Center Way   Phone: 407-791-5000
Wellington, FL 33414   Fax: 407-791-7900
Chm & CEO: Amin J. Khoury
Dir HR: Larry Spence
Employees: 1,700
Jobs Added Last Year: 202 (+13.5%)
Aerospace - aircraft equipment

BENIHANA NATIONAL CORP.
8685 NW 53rd Terrace   Phone: 305-593-0770
Miami, FL 33166   Fax: 305-592-6371
CEO & Chm: Rocky H. Aoki
Dir HR: Maria Gutierrez
Employees: 1,031
Jobs Added Last Year: 63 (+6.5%)
Retail - Japanese food restaurants

FLORIDA

BOCA RESEARCH INC.
6413 Congress Ave. Phone: 407-997-6227
Boca Raton, FL 33487 Fax: 407-997-0918
CEO & Pres: Tony Zalenski
Dir HR: Marty Richardson
Employees: 257
Jobs Added Last Year: 126 (+96.2%)
Computers - memory, communications & video add-in boards for PCs

BREED TECHNOLOGIES, INC.
5300 Old Tampa Hwy. Phone: 813-284-6000
Lakeland, FL 33811 Fax: 813-688-6714
Chm, Pres, CEO & COO: Allen K. Breed
HR Mgr: Deborah Ludwikowsky
Employees: 1,804
Jobs Added Last Year: 790 (+77.9%)
Automotive & trucking - original equipment, air bags

C. H. HEIST CORPORATION
810 N. Belcher Rd. Phone: 813-461-5656
Clearwater, FL 34625 Fax: 813-447-1146
Pres: Charles H. Heist
Dir HR: Gail Orffeo
Employees: 3,500
Jobs Added Last Year: 600 (+20.7%)
Industrial maintenance

CAPITAL BANCORP
1221 Brickell Ave. Phone: 305-536-1500
Miami, FL 33131 Fax: 305-536-1604
Chm & CEO: Daniel Holtz
VP HR: James Stanton
Employees: 950
Jobs Added Last Year: 318 (+50.3%)
Banks - Southeast

CARNIVAL CORPORATION
Carnival Place, 3655 NW 87th Ave. Phone: 305-599-2600
Miami, FL 33178-2248 Fax: 305-471-4700
Chm & CEO: M. Micky Arison
Dir Emp Policies & Ben: Susan Herrmann
Employees: 15,650
Jobs Added Last Year: 780 (+5.2%)
Leisure & recreational services - cruise lines (Carnival Cruise, Holland America, Windstar Cruises)

CARNIVAL HOTELS AND CASINOS
3250 Mary St. Phone: 305-445-2493
Miami, FL 33133 Fax: 305-858-6239
Chm & CEO: Sherwood M. Weiser
HR: Harry Spicer
Employees: 12,000
Jobs Added Last Year: —
Hotels & motels

CATALINA LIGHTING, INC.
6073 NW 167th St., Ste. 16 Phone: 305-558-4777
Miami, FL 33015 Fax: 305-584-4927
CEO: Robert Hersh
HR Dir: Carmen Pulido
Employees: 270
Jobs Added Last Year: 60 (+28.6%)
Building products - lighting fixtures

CATALINA MARKETING CORPORATION
11300 Ninth St. North Phone: 813-579-5000
St. Petersburg, FL 33716-2329 Fax: 813-570-8507
Pres & CEO: George Off
VP Admin (HR): William F. Losasso
Employees: 350
Jobs Added Last Year: 52 (+17.4%)
Business services - market research & point-of-sale grocery store coupon issuer

CHECKERS DRIVE-IN RESTAURANTS
600 Cleveland St., Ste. 1050 Phone: 813-441-3500
Clearwater, FL 34617-1079 Fax: 813-443-7047
VC & CEO: James F. White, Jr.
VP HR: Anthony L. Austin
Employees: 11,000
Jobs Added Last Year: 6,575 (+148.6%)
Retail - fast-food restaurants

CHICO'S FAS, INC.
15550 McGregor Blvd. Phone: 813-277-6200
Fort Myers, FL 33908 Fax: 813-277-5237
Interim CEO: Marvin Gralnick
Personnel & Payroll Supervisor: Sandra McMenamy
Employees: 745
Jobs Added Last Year: 255 (+52%)
Retail - apparel & shoes

FLORIDA

CLAIRE'S STORES, INC.
3 SW 129th Ave. Phone: 305-433-3900
Pembroke Pines, FL 33027 Fax: 305-433-3999
Pres & CEO: Rowland Schaefer
Exec Dir HR: Tina Perkins
Employees: 5,200
Jobs Added Last Year: 0
Retail - jewelry stores

CORDIS CORPORATION
14201 NW 60th Ave. Phone: 305-824-2000
Miami Lakes, FL 33014 Fax: 305-824-2080
Chm & CEO: Robert C. Strauss
Dir HR: Carolyn Donaldson
Employees: 3,370
Jobs Added Last Year: 720 (+27.2%)
Medical instruments - diagnostic coronary angiographic equipment

COULTER CORPORATION
11800 SW 147th Ave. Phone: 305-380-3800
Miami, FL 33196 Fax: 305-380-8312
Chm: Wallace Coulter
Dir HR: James Ring
Employees: 5,000
Jobs Added Last Year: 0
Medical products - medical equipment & electronic equipment

DIGITAL COMMUNICATIONS TECHNOLOGY
3941 SW 47th Ave. Phone: 305-791-6711
Fort Lauderdale, FL 33314-2808 Fax: 305-791-6788
CEO: Jack D. Brown, Jr.
Controller (HR): Bill Bein
Employees: 201
Jobs Added Last Year: 48 (+31.4%)
Machinery - magnetic controlled industrial heaters

DISCOUNT AUTO PARTS, INC.
4900 Frontage Rd. South Phone: 813-687-9226
Lakeland, FL 33801 Fax: 813-284-2063
Pres & CEO: Peter J. Fontaine
Dir HR: Bobbie Bricker
Employees: 2,172
Jobs Added Last Year: 372 (+20.7%)
Auto parts - retail

DIVERSIFIED COMMUNICATIONS INDUSTRIES
777 S. Flagler Dr., Ste. 700 Phone: 407-655-9101
West Palm Beach, FL 33401 Fax: 407-659-7877
Chm & CEO: Joseph F. Bradway, Jr.
No central personnel officer
Employees: 70
Jobs Added Last Year: 50 (+250%)
Electrical components - power supplies

ECKERD CORPORATION
8333 Bryan Dairy Rd. Phone: 813-399-6000
Largo, FL 34647 Fax: 813-399-6409
Chm & CEO: Stewart Turley
Dir HR: Wayne A. Saunders
Employees: 43,000
Jobs Added Last Year: 2,700 (+6.7%)
Retail - drug stores & photofinishing stores

FLAIR CORPORATION
4647 SW 40th Ave. Phone: 904-237-1220
Ocala, FL 34474-5799 Fax: 904-854-1402
Chm & CEO: Richard A. Bearse
Mgr HR: Paula Peterson
Employees: 900
Jobs Added Last Year: 200 (+28.6%)
Specialized air filtration equipment

FLORIDA PROGRESS CORPORATION
One Progress Plaza Phone: 813-824-6400
St. Petersburg, FL 33701 Fax: 813-824-6751
CEO: Jack B. Critchfield
Principal HR Representative: Elaine Heffner
Employees: 6,295
Jobs Added Last Year: 4,723 (+300.4%)
Utility - electric power

FPL GROUP, INC.
700 Universe Blvd. Phone: 407-694-3509
Juno Beach, FL 33408 Fax: 407-694-6385
Chm, Pres & CEO: James L. Broadhead
SVP HR: Lawrence J. Kelleher
Employees: 12,400
Jobs Cut Last Year: 2,130 (-14.7%)
Utility - electric power (Florida Power & Light)

FLORIDA

GREENWICH AIR SERVICES INC.
4590 NW 36th St.   Phone: 305-526-7000
Miami, FL 33152   Fax: 305-526-7005
Chm & CEO: Eugene P. Conese, Sr.
VP HR & Admin: William Skelley
Employees: 884
Jobs Added Last Year: 319 (+56.5%)
Transportation - repair & rebuilding of airplane engines

HARRIS CORPORATION
1025 W. NASA Blvd.   Phone: 407-727-9100
Melbourne, FL 32919   Fax: 407-727-5118
Chm & CEO: John T. Hartley
VP HR: Nick E. Heldreth
Employees: 28,300
Jobs Added Last Year: 0
Diversified - telecommunications; semiconductors; electronic systems; office equipment (Lanier)

HEALTH MANAGEMENT ASSOCIATES, INC.
5811 Pelican Bay Blvd.   Phone: 813-598-3131
Naples, FL 33963-2710   Fax: 813-597-5794
Chm, Pres & CEO: William J. Schoen
Dir HR: Fred Prow
Employees: 6,000
Jobs Added Last Year: 700 (+13.2%)
Hospitals

HOLIDAY RV SUPERSTORES, INC.
7851 Greenbriar Pkwy.   Phone: 407-363-9211
Orlando, FL 32819   Fax: 407-351-5140
Pres, Chm & CEO: Newton C. Kindlund
Personnel Mgr: Paula Ouellette
Employees: 198
Jobs Added Last Year: 62 (+45.6%)
Retail - RVs & boats

HOME SHOPPING NETWORK, INC.
2501 118th Ave. North   Phone: 813-572-8585
St. Petersburg, FL 33716   Fax: 813-539-6505
Pres & CEO: Gerald Hogan
SVP HR: Edward Vaughn, Jr.
Employees: 5,000
Jobs Cut Last Year: 18 (-.4%)
Retail - cable TV shopping channel

INPHYNET MEDICAL MANAGEMENT INC.
1200 S. Pine Island Rd., Ste. 600   Phone: 305-475-1300
Fort Lauderdale, FL 33324   Fax: 305-424-2939
Pres & CEO: Clifford Findeiss
SVP Admin (HR): Maria Prado
Employees: 3,300
Jobs Added Last Year: 470 (+16.6%)
Medical services - physician management for hospitals, HMOs & government organizations

INTEGRACARE INC.
551 SE Eighth St.   Phone: 407-274-0204
Delray Beach, FL 33483   Fax: 407-274-0109
CEO: Dana J. Pusateri
HR Mgr: Lee Ann Christy
Employees: 330
Jobs Added Last Year: 71 (+27.4%)
Health care - outpatient & home physical therapy

ISLAND LINCOLN-MERCURY INC.
1850 E. Merritt Island Causeway   Phone: 407-452-9220
Merritt Island, FL 32952   Fax: 407-453-3498
Pres: R. Bruce Deardoff
HR: Fran Parnell
Employees: 152
Jobs Added Last Year: 51 (+50.5%)
Retail - new & used cars

IVAX CORPORATION
8800 NW 36th St.   Phone: 305-590-2200
Miami, FL 33178-2404   Fax: 305-590-2252
Chm & CEO: Phillip Frost
Dir HR: Marsha Buckner
Employees: 2,110
Jobs Added Last Year: 639 (+43.4%)
Medical products - pharmaceuticals & test kits; specialty chemicals

JAN BELL MARKETING, INC.
13801 NW 14th St.   Phone: 305-846-8000
Sunrise, FL 33323   Fax: 305-846-2887
CEO: Alan H. Lipton
Dir HR: Bill Laney
Employees: 1,252
Jobs Added Last Year: 440 (+54.2%)
Retail - jewelry

FLORIDA

KNIGHT-RIDDER, INC.
One Herald Plaza
Miami, FL 33132-1693
Chm & CEO: James K. Batten
VP HR: Mary Jean Connors
Employees: 20,000
Jobs Added Last Year: 0
Phone: 305-376-3800
Fax: 305-376-3828
Publishing - newspapers (*Miami Herald*); electronic publishing; financial information database

MEDICAL TECHNOLOGY SYSTEMS, INC.
12920 Automobile Blvd.
Clearwater, FL 34622
Pres & CEO: Todd E. Siegel
Dir HR: Peter Benjamin
Employees: 271
Jobs Added Last Year: 50 (+22.6%)
Phone: 813-576-6311
Fax: 813-579-8067
Medical products - punch-card medication dispensing systems

LENNAR CORPORATION
700 NW 107th Ave.
Miami, FL 33172
CEO: Leonard Miller
Dir HR: Pauletta Roberts
Employees: 1,326
Jobs Added Last Year: 309 (+30.4%)
Phone: 305-559-4000
Fax: 305-226-4158
Real estate development - Florida's largest home builder

MORSE OPERATIONS
6363 NW 6 Way, Ste. 400
Ft. Lauderdale, FL 33309
Chm: Edward J. Morse
HR: Betty Anne Beaver
Employees: 1,563
Jobs Added Last Year: 141 (+9.9%)
Phone: 305-351-0055
Fax: 305-771-6493
Retail - new & used cars

LEVITZ FURNITURE INC.
6111 Broken Sound Pkwy. NW
Boca Raton, FL 33487-2799
Chm & CEO: Robert M. Elliott
VP HR: Nicholas S. Massulo
Employees: 6,276
Jobs Added Last Year: 165 (+2.7%)
Phone: 407-994-6006
Fax: 407-998-5615
Retail - home furnishings

OFFICE DEPOT, INC.
2200 Old Germantown Rd.
Delray Beach, FL 33445
Chm & CEO: David I. Fuente
EVP HR: F. Terry Bean
Employees: 20,400
Jobs Added Last Year: 9,100 (+80.5%)
Phone: 407-278-4800
Fax: 407-265-4403
Retail - office equipment & supplies

LINCARE HOLDINGS, INC.
19337 US 19 North, Ste. 500
Clearwater, FL 34624
Pres & CEO: James T. Kelly
Dir Emp Rel: Byron R. Krogen
Employees: 1,400
Jobs Added Last Year: 200 (+16.7%)
Phone: 813-530-7700
Fax: 813-532-9692
Medical services - home respiratory care

OUTBACK STEAKHOUSE, INC.
550 N. Reo St., Ste. 204
Tampa, FL 33609
Chm & CEO: Chris T. Sullivan
VP Training & Dev (HR): Trudy I. Cooper
Employees: 8,850
Jobs Added Last Year: 4,850 (+121.3%)
Phone: 813-282-1225
Fax: 813-282-1209
Retail - restaurants (Outback Steakhouse & Carrabba's Italian Grill) located in Florida & Texas

LYKES BROS. INC.
111 E. Madison St.
Tampa, FL 33602
Chm, Pres & CEO: Thompson L. Rankin
Dir HR: Ron Cox
Employees: 3,500
Jobs Added Last Year: 300 (+9.4%)
Phone: 813-223-3981
Fax: 813-273-5493
Diversified operations - food processing; insurance

OXBOW CORPORATION
1601 Forum Place
West Palm Beach, FL 33402
Pres: William I. Koch
Dir Personnel: Karen Brannon
Employees: 1,600
Jobs Added Last Year: 100 (+6.7%)
Phone: 407-697-4300
Fax: 407-640-8747
Diversified operations - energy; fossil fuel; real estate

An in-depth profile of this company is available by fax. Call 800-510-4452 and use your touch-tone phone to put in the 5-digit code at the prompt. Only $2.95 each with your credit card. See page 12 for more details.

FLORIDA

PAGES, INC.
801 94th Ave. North Phone: 813-578-3300
St. Petersburg, FL 33702 Fax: 813-578-3100
CEO & Chm: S. Robert Davis
Dir HR: Stella Farr
Employees: 590
Jobs Added Last Year: 100 (+20.4%)
Publishing - children's books, cassettes, videotapes & computer software; incentive/recognition awards

PHYSICIAN CORP. OF AMERICA
5835 Blue Lagoon Dr., Ste. 300 Phone: 305-267-6633
Miami, FL 33126-2050 Fax: 305-265-2590
Chm & CEO: E. Stanley Kardatzke
VP HR: Shannon L. Lob
Employees: 1,917
Jobs Added Last Year: 671 (+53.9%)
Health maintenance organization

POLLO TROPICAL INC.
7901 SW 67th Ave. Phone: 305-662-3938
Miami, FL 33143 Fax: 305-670-6403
CEO: Larry J. Harris
HR Dir: Bill Walton
Employees: 602
Jobs Added Last Year: 307 (+104.1%)
Retail - restaurants

PUBLIX SUPER MARKETS, INC.
1936 George Jenkins Blvd. Phone: 813-688-1188
Lakeland, FL 33801 Fax: 813-680-5257
Chm & CEO: Howard M. Jenkins
VP Personnel: Edward H. Ruth
Employees: 82,000
Jobs Added Last Year: 9,000 (+12.3%)
Retail - supermarkets (#1 in Florida)

PUEBLO XTRA INTERNATIONAL, INC.
1300 NW 22nd Ave. Phone: 305-977-2500
Pompano Beach, FL 33069 Fax: 305-979-5770
Chm: Gustavo A. Cisneros
Dir HR: Manny Chacon
Employees: 10,600
Jobs Cut Last Year: 600 (-5.4%)
Retail - supermarkets in Florida, Puerto Rico & US Virgin Islands

QUALITY PRODUCTS, INC.
3820 Northdale Blvd. Phone: 813-963-1300
Tampa, FL 33624 Fax: 813-963-7995
CEO: James S. Renaldo
VP & Dir HR: Jill Shirley
Employees: 178
Jobs Added Last Year: 34 (+23.6%)
Diversified operations - toys; hunting equipment; bench presses

QUICK & REILLY GROUP, INC.
230 S. County Rd. Phone: 407-655-8000
Palm Beach, FL 33480 Fax: 407-655-9010
Chm: Leslie C. Quick, Jr.
VP HR: Elizabeth O'Hearn
Employees: 848
Jobs Added Last Year: 278 (+48.8%)
Financial - discount securities brokerage

RAYMOND JAMES FINANCIAL, INC.
880 Carillon Pkwy. Phone: 813-573-3800
St. Petersburg, FL 33716 Fax: 813-573-8244
Chm & CEO: Thomas A. James
VP HR: Chris Whittman
Employees: 2,527
Jobs Added Last Year: 354 (+16.3%)
Financial - securities brokerage

REPTRON ELECTRONICS, INC.
14401 McCormick Dr. Phone: 813-854-2351
Tampa, FL 33626 Fax: 813-855-1697
Pres & CEO: Michael L. Musto
Corp Dir HR: Tom Ginnetti
Employees: 750
Jobs Added Last Year: 147 (+24.4%)
Electronics - wholesale components, primarily semiconductors

REXALL SUNDOWN, INC.
851 Broken Sound Pkwy. NW Phone: 407-241-9400
Boca Raton, FL 33487 Fax: 407-995-0197
CEO: Carl DeSantis
Dir HR: Roy Lantz
Employees: 725
Jobs Added Last Year: 165 (+29.5%)
Vitamins & nutritional products

FLORIDA

ROTECH MEDICAL CORPORATION
4506 L.B. McLeod Rd., Ste. F   Phone: 407-841-2115
Orlando, FL 32811   Fax: 407-841-9318
Chm & Pres: William P. Kennedy
Payroll Personnel Dir: Rosa Johnson
Employees: 652
Jobs Added Last Year: 241 (+58.6%)
Health care - respiratory & convalescent therapy services & equipment

RYDER SYSTEM, INC.
3600 NW 82nd Ave.   Phone: 305-593-3726
Miami, FL 33166   Fax: 305-593-3336
Chm, Pres & CEO: M. Anthony Burns
EVP HR & Admin: C. Robert Campbell
Employees: 37,949
Jobs Added Last Year: 613 (+1.6%)
Leasing - trucks

SAFESKIN CORPORATION
5100 Town Center Circle, Ste. 560   Phone: 407-395-9988
Boca Raton, FL 33486   Fax: 407-394-7981
Pres & Co-CEO: Neil K. Braverman
Controller (HR): Seth Goldman
Employees: 2,581
Jobs Added Last Year: 1,026 (+66%)
Medical & dental supplies - hypoallergenic disposable latex gloves

SENSORMATIC ELECTRONICS CORP.
500 NW 12th Ave.   Phone: 305-420-2000
Deerfield Beach, FL 33442-1795   Fax: 305-420-2017
Chm, Pres & CEO: Ronald G. Assaf
Dir HR: Larry Smith
Employees: 5,500
Jobs Added Last Year: 1,500 (+37.5%)
Protection - electronic article surveillance products & systems for retail and industrial applications

SOUND ADVICE, INC.
1901 Tigertail Blvd.   Phone: 305-922-4434
Dania, FL 33004   Fax: 305-926-4389
Chm, Pres & CEO: Peter Beshouri
Mgr HR: Bonnie Shaw
Employees: 900
Jobs Added Last Year: 100 (+12.5%)
Retail - consumer electronics

THE SPORTS AUTHORITY, INC.
3383 N. State Rd. 7   Phone: 305-735-1701
Fort Lauderdale, FL 33319   Fax: 305-484-0837
Chm, Pres & CEO: Jack A. Smith
VP HR: Paul D. Lockard
Employees: 7,758
Jobs Added Last Year: 1,587 (+25.7%)
Retail - sporting goods (#1 in US)

SPORTS & RECREATION, INC.
4701 W. Hillsborough Ave.   Phone: 813-886-9688
Tampa, FL 33614-5419   Fax: 813-884-5291
Chm & CEO: Jim W. Bradke
Dir HR: Dana Cook
Employees: 3,000
Jobs Added Last Year: 1,200 (+66.7%)
Retail - brand-name sports equipment & apparel

ST. JOE PAPER COMPANY
1650 Prudential Dr., Ste. 400   Phone: 904-396-6600
Jacksonville, FL 32207   Fax: 904-396-4042
Chm & CEO: Winfred L. Thornton
No central personnel officer
Employees: 4,900
Jobs Cut Last Year: 140 (-2.8%)
Paper & paper products; Florida's largest private property owner

STEIN MART, INC.
1200 Gulf Life Dr.   Phone: 904-346-1500
Jacksonville, FL 32207   Fax: 904-398-4341
Chm & CEO: Jay Stein
SVP HR: Hunt Hawkins
Employees: 4,500
Jobs Added Last Year: 800 (+21.6%)
Retail - apparel & shoes

SUNBEAM-OSTER COMPANY, INC.
200 E. Las Olas Blvd., Ste. 2100   Phone: 305-767-2100
Fort Lauderdale, FL 33301-2248   Fax: 305-767-2107
Chm & CEO: Roger Schipke
EVP HR: Jim Wilson
Employees: 10,500
Jobs Added Last Year: 0
Appliances - household; outdoor furniture

An in-depth profile of this company is available by fax. Call 800-510-4452 and use your touch-tone phone to put in the 5-digit code at the prompt. Only $2.95 each with your credit card. See page 12 for more details.

FLORIDA

SUNGLASS HUT INTERNATIONAL, INC.
255 Alhambra Circle
Coral Gables, FL 33134-7403
CEO, Chm & Pres: Jack B. Chadsey
VP HR: Leslie Berkovitz
Employees: 3,300
Jobs Added Last Year: 600 (+22.2%)
Retail - sunglasses
Phone: 305-461-6100
Fax: 305-461-6280

UNIVERSITY OF FLORIDA
226 Tigert Hall
Gainesville, FL 32611
Chancellor: Charles B. Reed
Dir HR: Jack Hidler
Employees: 21,404
Jobs Added Last Year: —
University
Phone: 904-392-3261
Fax: 904-392-6278

TECH DATA CORPORATION
5350 Tech Data Dr.
Clearwater, FL 34620-3134
Chm & CEO: Steven A. Raymund
VP HR: Lawrence W. Hamilton
Employees: 1,350
Jobs Added Last Year: 325 (+31.7%)
Computers - wholesale hardware & software
Phone: 813-539-7429
Fax: 813-538-7050

VIROGROUP, INC.
428 Pine Island Rd. SW
Cape Coral, FL 33991
Pres & CEO: Sylvester "Bud" Ogden
Dir HR: Lee A. Glotzback III
Employees: 304
Jobs Added Last Year: 39 (+14.7%)
Pollution control equipment & services
Phone: 813-574-1919
Fax: 813-574-8106

TECO ENERGY CORPORATION
Teco Plaza, 702 N. Franklin St.
Tampa, FL 33602
Chm, Pres & CEO: Timothy L. Guzzle
VP HR: Keith S. Surgenor
Employees: 6,391
Jobs Added Last Year: 118 (+1.9%)
Utility - electric power
Phone: 813-228-4111
Fax: 813-228-1219

W. R. GRACE & CO.
One Town Center Rd.
Boca Raton, FL 33486-1010
Pres & CEO: J. P. Bolduc
SVP HR: Pamela J. Hamilton
Employees: 34,000
Jobs Cut Last Year: 10,100 (-22.9%)
Chemicals - diversified; health care
Phone: 407-362-2000
Fax: 407-362-2193

TODHUNTER INTERNATIONAL, INC.
222 Lakeview Ave., Ste. 1500
West Palm Beach, FL 33401
Chm & CEO: A. Kenneth Pincourt, Jr.
No central personnel officer
Employees: 400
Jobs Added Last Year: 100 (+33.3%)
Beverages - citrus-based alcoholic spirits
Phone: 407-655-8977
Fax: 407-655-9718

WACKENHUT CORPORATION
1500 San Remo Ave.
Coral Gables, FL 33146
Chm & CEO: George R. Wackenhut
VP HR: Sandra Nusbaum
Employees: 33,000
Jobs Added Last Year: 1,000 (+3.1%)
Protection - safety equipment & services
Phone: 305-666-5656
Fax: 305-662-7336

TPI ENTERPRISES, INC.
777 S. Flagler Dr.
West Palm Beach, FL 33401-6105
Pres & CEO: J. Gary Sharp
Dir HR: Julie Collins
Employees: 11,100
Jobs Added Last Year: 850 (+8.3%)
Retail - restaurants
Phone: 407-835-8888
Fax: 407-835-4982

WACKENHUT CORRECTIONS CORPORATION
1500 San Remo Ave.
Coral Gables, FL 33146
Pres & CEO: George C. Zoley
VP HR: Sandra Nusbaum
Employees: 2,360
Jobs Added Last Year: 471 (+24.9%)
Protection - correctional & detention facilities
Phone: 305-662-7396
Fax: 305-662-7406

FLORIDA

WALTER INDUSTRIES, INC.
1500 N. Dale Mabry Hwy.   Phone: 813-871-4811
Tampa, FL 33607   Fax: 813-871-4430
Pres & CEO: G. Robert Durham
VP HR: Gerald W. Hermann
Employees: 7,700
Jobs Added Last Year: 178 (+2.4%)
Diversified operations - home building & financing; natural resources; industrial manufacturing

WATSCO, INC.
2665 S. Bayshore Dr.   Phone: 305-858-0828
Coconut Grove, FL 33133   Fax: 305-858-4492
Chm, Pres & CEO: Albert H. Nahmad
VP HR: Raymond Koniecke
Employees: 903
Jobs Added Last Year: 167 (+22.7%)
Diversified operations - climate control manufacture & sale (as Rheem distributor); temporary personnel services

WILLCOX & GIBBS, INC.
150 Alhambra Circle, Ste. 900   Phone: 305-446-8000
Coral Gables, FL 33134   Fax: 305-446-8128
Pres & CEO: Alain C. Viry
No central personnel officer
Employees: 3,100
Jobs Added Last Year: 1,300 (+72.2%)
Electronics - wholesale electrical parts & supplies

WINDMERE CORPORATION
5980 Miami Lakes Dr.   Phone: 305-362-2611
Miami Lakes, FL 33014   Fax: 305-364-0635
CEO: David M. Friedson
Dir HR: David Warren
Employees: 8,200
Jobs Added Last Year: 575 (+7.5%)
Appliances - personal & health care, fans, hair dryers

WINN-DIXIE STORES, INC.
5050 Edgewood Ct.   Phone: 904-783-5000
Jacksonville, FL 32254-3699   Fax: 904-783-5294
Chm & Principal Exec Off: A. Dano Davis
VP & Dir Assoc Rel & HR: L. H. May
Employees: 112,000
Jobs Added Last Year: 7,000 (+6.7%)
Retail - supermarkets

GEORGIA

AARON RENTS, INC.
309 E. Paces Ferry Rd. NE Phone: 404-231-0011
Atlanta, GA 30305-2377 Fax: 404-240-6584
Chm, Pres & CEO: R. C. Loudermilk, Sr.
No central personnel officer
Employees: 2,100
Jobs Added Last Year: 650 (+44.8%)
Leasing - rent-to-own home furnishings, household appliances & consumer electronics

AFLAC INCORPORATED
1932 Wynnton Rd. Phone: 706-323-3431
Columbus, GA 31999 Fax: 706-324-6330
VC, Pres & CEO: Daniel P. Amos
VP HR: Ann B. Henderson
Employees: 3,902
Jobs Added Last Year: 284 (+7.8%)
Insurance - health, life & medical

AGCO CORPORATION
4830 River Green Pkwy. Phone: 404-813-9200
Duluth, GA 30136 Fax: 404-813-6118
Chm & CEO: Robert J. Ratliff
Dir HR: John Broadwell
Employees: 2,417
Jobs Added Last Year: 1,216 (+101.2%)
Machinery - farm, including tractors (Massey Ferguson) & implements

ALLIED HOLDINGS INC.
160 Clairmont Ave., Ste. 510 Phone: 404-370-1100
Decatur, GA 30030 Fax: 404-370-4206
Chm & CEO: Robert J. Rutland
Dir Payroll & Personnel: Paul Books
Employees: 2,389
Jobs Added Last Year: 289 (+13.8%)
Business services - transportation of cars & trucks

AMERICAN BUSINESS PRODUCTS, INC.
2100 RiverEdge Pkwy. Phone: 404-953-8300
Atlanta, GA 30328 Fax: 404-952-2343
CEO: Thomas R. Carmody
No central personnel officer
Employees: 4,320
Jobs Added Last Year: 420 (+10.8%)
Paper - business forms

AMERICAN CANCER SOCIETY
1599 Clifton Rd. Northeast Phone: 404-320-3333
Atlanta, GA 30329 Fax: 404-325-0230
Natl Pres: Irvin D. Fleming
VP HR: Aurelia C. Stanley
Employees: 4,500
Jobs Cut Last Year: 150 (-3.2%)
Charitable organization

APPLE SOUTH, INC.
Hancock at Washington Phone: 706-342-4552
Madison, GA 30650 Fax: 706-342-4057
Chm & CEO: Tom E. DuPree, Jr.
SVP HR & Sec: John G. McLeod, Jr.
Employees: 6,000
Jobs Added Last Year: 750 (+14.3%)
Retail - restaurants (#1 Applebees franchisee)

ATLANTA GAS LIGHT COMPANY
303 Peachtree St. NE Phone: 404-584-4000
Atlanta, GA 30302 Fax: 404-584-3709
Pres & CEO: David R. Jones
Dir HR: James W. Connally
Employees: 3,764
Jobs Added Last Year: 0
Utility - gas distribution

AVONDALE MILLS, INC.
PO Box 1109 Phone: 404-267-2226
Monroe, GA 30655 Fax: 404-267-2543
Pres & CEO: G. Stephen Felker
Dir Benefits (HR): Bob Crowe
Employees: 4,000
Jobs Added Last Year: 0
Textiles - mill products

BEAZER HOMES USA, INC.
1927 Lakeside Pkwy., Ste. 602 Phone: 404-250-3420
Tucker, GA 30084 Fax: 404-250-3428
Pres & CEO: Ian J. McCarthy
Ben Mgr (HR): Jennifer Jones
Employees: 710
Jobs Added Last Year: 159 (+28.9%)
Building - single-family homes

GEORGIA

BELLSOUTH CORPORATION [10200]
1155 Peachtree St. NE Phone: 404-249-2000
Atlanta, GA 30309-3610 Fax: 404-249-5599
Chm, Pres & CEO: John L. Clendenin
Dir HR: Laura Walker
Employees: 95,084
Jobs Cut Last Year: 2,028 (-2.1%)
Utility - telephone; cellular paging; directories

BROCK CONTROL SYSTEMS, INC.
2859 Paces Ferry Rd. Phone: 404-431-1200
Atlanta, GA 30339 Fax: 404-431-1201
CEO & Chm: Richard T. Brock
Mgr Hr: Alex Richards
Employees: 197
Jobs Added Last Year: 54 (+37.8%)
Computers - software for sales force automation

CAGLE'S, INC. [11794]
2000 Hills Ave. NW Phone: 404-355-2820
Atlanta, GA 30318 Fax: 404-355-9326
Chm & CEO: J. Douglas Cagle
SVP Fin, Treas & CFO (HR): Kenneth R. Barkley
Employees: 3,200
Jobs Added Last Year: 0
Food - fresh & frozen chicken products processing & distribution to supermarkets, distributors & restaurants

CARMIKE CINEMAS, INC. [12900]
1301 First Ave. Phone: 706-576-3400
Columbus, GA 31901-2109 Fax: 706-576-3471
Pres & CEO: Michael W. Patrick
Dir HR: Dorothy Moore
Employees: 6,600
Jobs Added Last Year: 145 (+2.2%)
Motion pictures - movie theaters, primarily in small towns

CHARTER MEDICAL CORPORATION
3414 Peachtree Rd. NE, Ste. 1400 Phone: 404-841-9200
Atlanta, GA 30326 Fax: 404-841-5793
Chm & CEO: Mac Crawford
VP Administrative Svcs (HR): C. Clark Wingfield, Jr.
Employees: 9,000
Jobs Added Last Year: 2,600 (+40.6%)
Hospitals - nation's largest psychiatric hospital & mental health-care company

THE COCA-COLA COMPANY [10359]
One Coca-Cola Plaza NW Phone: 404-676-2121
Atlanta, GA 30313 Fax: 404-676-6792
Chm & CEO: Roberto C. Goizueta
VP HR: Michael W. Walters
Employees: 34,000
Jobs Added Last Year: 2,700 (+8.6%)
Beverages - soft drinks

COCA-COLA ENTERPRISES INC.
Coca-Cola Plaza NW Phone: 404-676-2100
Atlanta, GA 30313 Fax: 404-676-6792
VC & CEO: Summerfield K. Johnston, Jr.
VP HR: Jarrett H. Jones
Employees: 26,500
Jobs Added Last Year: 500 (+1.9%)
Beverages - soft drink bottling

CONTEL CELLULAR INC. [13092]
245 Perimeter Center Pkwy. Phone: 404-804-3400
Atlanta, GA 30346-2304 Fax: 404-391-1876
Pres & CEO: Dennis L. Whipple
Dir HR: Jim Jimenez
Employees: 1,605
Jobs Added Last Year: 461 (+40.3%)
Telecommunications services - cellular telephone service

COOPERSMITH INC.
3500 One Peachtree Center Phone: 404-581-8354
Atlanta, GA 30308 Fax: 404-581-8330
Chm: Frederick E. Cooper
Dir Admin: George Curtis
Employees: 12,250
Jobs Added Last Year: —
Food - bread, cake, rolls & other baked goods (Smith's)

COX ENTERPRISES, INC. [40110]
1400 Lake Hearn Dr. Phone: 404-843-5000
Atlanta, GA 30319 Fax: 404-843-5142
Chm & CEO: James Cox Kennedy
VP HR: Timothy W. Hughes
Employees: 31,000
Jobs Added Last Year: 135 (+.4%)
Publishing - newspapers (*Atlanta Constitution, Atlanta Journal*); TV & radio broadcasting; cable TV

An in-depth profile of this company is available by fax. Call 800-510-4452 and use your touch-tone phone to put in the 5-digit code at the prompt. Only $2.95 each with your credit card. See page 12 for more details.

GEORGIA

CRAWFORD & CO. RISK MANAGEMENT SVCS.
5620 Glenridge Dr., NE   Phone: 404-256-0830
Atlanta, GA 30342   Fax: 404-847-4028
Chm, Pres & CEO: F. L. Minix
SVP HR: G. N. Cox
Employees: 7,390
Jobs Cut Last Year: 464 (-5.9%)
Insurance - property & casualty

EMORY UNIVERSITY INC.
1380 Oxford Rd. NE   Phone: 404-727-6123
Atlanta, GA 30322   Fax: 404-727-3750
Pres: William M. Chace
Assoc VP HR: Alice Miller
Employees: 15,000
Jobs Added Last Year: —
University

CROWN CRAFTS, INC.
1600 RiverEdge Pkwy., Ste 200   Phone: 404-644-6400
Atlanta, GA 30328   Fax: 404-644-6410
Pres & CEO: Michael H. Bernstein
Dir HR: Bonnie Wasdin
Employees: 1,923
Jobs Added Last Year: 173 (+9.9%)
Textiles - comforters & accessories; cotton throw rugs, bedspreads & blankets

EQUIFAX INC.
1600 Peachtree St. NW   Phone: 404-885-8000
Atlanta, GA 30302   Fax: 404-888-5043
Chm & CEO: C. B. Rogers, Jr.
VP Emp Rel: Becky Padgett
Employees: 12,800
Jobs Added Last Year: 400 (+3.2%)
Business services - credit reporting & insurance support services

DELTA AIR LINES, INC.
Hartsfield Atlanta International Airport   Phone: 404-715-2600
Atlanta, GA 30320   Fax: 404-765-2233
Chm, Pres & CEO: Ronald W. Allen
SVP Personnel: Maurice W. Worth
Employees: 71,412
Jobs Cut Last Year: 2,121 (-2.9%)
Transportation - airline (#3 in US)

FIRST FINANCIAL MANAGEMENT
3 Corporate Sq., Ste. 700   Phone: 404-321-0120
Atlanta, GA 30329   Fax: 404-633-2412
Chm, Pres & CEO: Patrick H. Thomas
SVP HR: Frank M. Malone
Employees: 11,500
Jobs Cut Last Year: 1,100 (-8.7%)
Financial - credit card processing & worldwide money-transfer services (Western Union)

DORSEY TRAILERS, INC.
2727 Paces Ferry Rd.   Phone: 404-438-9595
Atlanta, GA 30339   Fax: 404-438-8190
Pres & CEO: Marilyn R. Marks
VP HR: Kenny Sawyer
Employees: 1,325
Jobs Added Last Year: 220 (+19.9%)
Automotive & trucking - customized truck trailers

FLOWERS INDUSTRIES, INC.
PO Box 1338   Phone: 912-226-9110
Thomasville, GA 31799   Fax: 912-226-9231
Chm & CEO: Amos R. McMullian
Dir HR: Scott Rich
Employees: 8,400
Jobs Cut Last Year: 500 (-5.6%)
Food - breads, snacks, vegetable & convenience food products

ELECTROMAGNETIC SCIENCES, INC.
660 Engineering Dr.   Phone: 404-263-9200
Norcross, GA 30091-7700   Fax: 404-263-8130
CEO: Thomas E. Sharon
HR Mgr: Michael R. Robertson
Employees: 700
Jobs Added Last Year: 100 (+16.7%)
Telecommunications services - wireless communications

GENUINE PARTS CO.
2999 Circle 75 Pkwy.   Phone: 404-953-1700
Atlanta, GA 30339   Fax: 404-956-2211
Chm: Larry L. Prince
SVP Personnel: Louis W. Rice, Jr.
Employees: 21,000
Jobs Added Last Year: 2,600 (+14.1%)
Auto parts - wholesale

GEORGIA

GEORGIA-PACIFIC CORPORATION
133 Peachtree St. NE Phone: 404-652-4000
Atlanta, GA 30303 Fax: 404-521-4422
Chm & CEO: Alston D. Correll
SVP HR & Admin: David W. Reynolds
Employees: 50,000
Jobs Cut Last Year: 2,000 (-3.8%)
Building products - wood; paper & paper products

THE HOME DEPOT, INC.
2727 Paces Ferry Rd. Phone: 404-433-8211
Atlanta, GA 30339 Fax: 404-431-2707
Chm, CEO & Sec: Bernard Marcus
SVP HR: Stephen R. Massona
Employees: 50,600
Jobs Added Last Year: 11,700 (+30.1%)
Building products - retail

GOLD KIST INC.
244 Perimeter Center Pkwy. Phone: 404-393-5000
Atlanta, GA 30346 Fax: 404-393-5061
Chm & CEO: Harold O. Chitwood
VP HR: W. Andy Epperson
Employees: 14,000
Jobs Added Last Year: —
Food - poultry & pork products

INTERFACE, INC.
Orchard Hill Rd., PO Box 1503 Phone: 706-882-1891
LaGrange, GA 30241 Fax: 706-882-0500
Chm & CEO: Ray C. Anderson
VP HR: Rodney Fuller
Employees: 4,425
Jobs Added Last Year: 690 (+18.5%)
Textiles - home furnishings

GOLDEN POULTRY CO., INC.
244 Perimeter Ctr. Pkwy. NE Phone: 404-393-5000
Atlanta, GA 30346 Fax: 404-393-5421
CEO: Kenneth N. Whitmire
VP HR: W.A. Anderson
Employees: 4,565
Jobs Added Last Year: 436 (+10.6%)
Food - chicken processing

INTERMET CORPORATION
2859 Paces Ferry Rd. Phone: 404-431-6000
Atlanta, GA 30339 Fax: 404-431-6001
Chm & CEO: John Doddridge
VP HR: James W. Rydel
Employees: 4,498
Jobs Added Last Year: 251 (+5.9%)
Automotive & trucking - iron castings

GULFSTREAM AEROSPACE CORPORATION
500 Gulfstream Rd. Phone: 912-964-3000
Savannah, GA 31402 Fax: 912-965-3775
Pres, CEO & COO: Fred Breidenbach
VP HR: Don Laidlaw
Employees: 3,800
Jobs Added Last Year: 0
Aerospace - corporate jets

IQ SOFTWARE CORPORATION
3295 River Exchange Dr., Ste. 550 Phone: 404-446-8880
Norcross, GA 30092-9909 Fax: 404-448-4088
Pres & CEO: Charles R. Chitty
VP Admin & CFO (HR): Michael Casey
Employees: 161
Jobs Added Last Year: 37 (+29.8%)
Computers - client-server query & reporting tools software (Intelligent Query, IQ Access)

HBO & COMPANY
301 Perimeter Center North Phone: 404-393-6000
Atlanta, GA 30346 Fax: 404-393-6092
Pres & CEO: Charles W. McCall
VP HR: Chris Ramsey
Employees: 1,884
Jobs Added Last Year: 168 (+9.8%)
Computers - health care information systems services

ISOLYSER COMPANY, INC.
4320 International Blvd. Phone: 404-381-7566
Norcross, GA 30093 Fax: 404-381-7581
CEO: Robert L. Taylor
Dir HR: Mickey Alan
Employees: 245
Jobs Added Last Year: 35 (+16.7%)
Medical products - disposable

GEORGIA

JOHN H. HARLAND COMPANY
2939 Miller Rd. Phone: 404-981-9460
Decatur, GA 30035 Fax: 404-593-5200
Chm, Pres & CEO: Robert R. Woodson
VP & Dir HR: Arlene Bates
Employees: 7,300
Jobs Added Last Year: 600 (+9%)
Paper - business forms

L A T SPORTSWEAR INC.
1200 Airport Dr. Phone: 404-521-0142
Ball Ground, GA 30107-5010 Fax: 404-479-4078
CEO: Isadore E. Mitzner
Personnel Mgr: Jill Daniels
Employees: 536
Jobs Added Last Year: 122 (+29.5%)
Apparel - knitted sportswear

LONGHORN STEAKS, INC.
8215 Roswell Rd., Bldg. 200 Phone: 404-399-9595
Atlanta, GA 30350 Fax: 404-399-7796
Pres & CEO: Richard E. Rivera
Emp Mgr & Dir HR: Nancy Winship
Employees: 2,220
Jobs Added Last Year: 338 (+18%)
Retail - restaurants

LXE INC.
303 Research Dr. Phone: 404-447-4224
Norcross, GA 30092-9200 Fax: 404-447-4397
Chm & CEO: Thomas E. Sharon
Mgr HR: Michael Robertson
Employees: 407
Jobs Added Last Year: 57 (+16.3%)
Telecommunications equipment - radio-linked data communications systems

THE MAXIM GROUP, INC.
1035 Cobb Industrial Dr., N.E. Phone: 404-590-9369
Marietta, GA 30066 Fax: 404-590-8141
Pres, CEO & Treas: A. J. Nassar
Dir HR: Larry Van Etten
Employees: 300
Jobs Added Last Year: 270 (+900%)
Retail - floor covering products

MEDAPHIS CORPORATION
2700 Cumberland Pkwy., Ste. 300 Phone: 404-319-3300
Atlanta, GA 30339 Fax: 404-957-0670
Chm, Pres & CEO: Randolph G. Brown
VP Corp Svcs (HR): Denis Cortese
Employees: 4,148
Jobs Added Last Year: 2,109 (+103.4%)
Business services - medical accounts-receivable management services

MOHAWK INDUSTRIES, INC.
1755 The Exchange Phone: 404-951-6000
Atlanta, GA 30339 Fax: 404-951-6152
Chm & CEO: David L. Kolb
Dir HR: Jerry Melton
Employees: 7,114
Jobs Added Last Year: 2,886 (+68.3%)
Textiles - carpet

MOUNTASIA ENTERTAINMENT INTERNATIONAL
5895 Windward Pkwy., Ste. 220 Phone: 404-442-6640
Alpharetta, GA 30202-3656 Fax: 404-442-6644
Chm, Pres & CEO: L. Scott Demerau
HR Dir: Jalayne Markey
Employees: 1,747
Jobs Added Last Year: 1,477 (+547%)
Multiattraction amusement facilities which include miniature golf, go-karts, game rooms, batting cages, etc.

NATIONAL SERVICE INDUSTRIES, INC.
1420 Peachtree St., NE Phone: 404-853-1000
Atlanta, GA 30309 Fax: 404-853-1015
Chm & CEO: D. Raymond Riddle
Staff VP HR: F. Andrew Logue
Employees: 22,200
Jobs Added Last Year: 1,300 (+6.2%)
Diversified operations - textile rental; chemicals; lighting equipment

NATIONAL VISION ASSOCIATES LTD.
296 S. Clayton St. Phone: 404-822-3600
Lawrenceville, GA 30245-5737 Fax: 404-822-3601
Pres & CEO: James W. Krause
VP HR: Robert W. Stein
Employees: 1,550
Jobs Added Last Year: 500 (+47.6%)
Retail - optical goods stores

GEORGIA

OXFORD INDUSTRIES, INC.
222 Piedmont Ave., NE Phone: 404-659-2424
Atlanta, GA 30308 Fax: 404-525-3650
Chm & Pres: J. Hicks Lanier
VP Corp HR: Herb Kraft
Employees: 9,331
Jobs Added Last Year: 48 (+.5%)
Apparel - shirts, slacks & sportswear for men, women & children

PEDIATRIC SERVICES OF AMERICA, INC.
5834-C Peachtree Corners East Phone: 404-441-1580
Norcross, GA 30092 Fax: 404-729-0316
CEO: Joseph D. Sansone
Dir HR: Paula Holcomb
Employees: 2,000
Jobs Added Last Year: 1,770 (+769.6%)
Health care - pediatric home health care services

POST PROPERTIES, INC.
3350 Cumberland Circle Phone: 404-850-4400
Atlanta, GA 30339 Fax: 404-859-0100
Chm: John A. Williams
HR Mgr: Kelly O'Brien
Employees: 1,000
Jobs Added Last Year: 100 (+11.1%)
Real estate operations

THE RITZ-CARLTON HOTEL COMPANY, INC.
3414 Peachtree Rd. NE, Ste. 300 Phone: 404-237-5500
Atlanta, GA 30326 Fax: 404-261-0119
Chm & CEO: William B. Johnson
VP HR: Leonardo Inghilleri
Employees: 14,000
Jobs Added Last Year: —
Hotels (30 luxury hotels worldwide)

RIVERWOOD INTERNATIONAL CORPORATION
3350 Cumberland Circle Phone: 404-644-3000
Atlanta, GA 30339 Fax: 404-644-2921
Pres & CEO: Thomas H. Johnson
SVP HR: Robert Bing
Employees: 8,500
Jobs Added Last Year: —
Building products - wood

ROCK-TENN CO.
504 Thrasher St. Phone: 404-448-2193
Norcross, GA 30071 Fax: 404-263-4483
Chm, Pres & CEO: Bradley Currey, Jr.
VP Risk Mgmt & Admin (HR): Brad Newman
Employees: 5,928
Jobs Added Last Year: 874 (+17.3%)
Paper & paper products - recycled paperboard & packaging products

ROLLINS, INC.
2170 Piedmont Rd. NE Phone: 404-888-2000
Atlanta, GA 30324 Fax: 404-888-2730
Pres & CEO: R. Randall Rollins
Asst VP HR: Kathleen Mayton
Employees: 8,878
Jobs Added Last Year: 968 (+12.2%)
Diversified - pest control, plant rental & lawn care (Orkin); electronic security systems (Rollins)

RPC ENERGY SERVICES, INC.
2170 Piedmont Rd. NE Phone: 404-888-2950
Atlanta, GA 30324 Fax: 404-888-2722
Chm & CEO: R. Randall Rollins
No central personnel officer
Employees: 1,171
Jobs Added Last Year: 148 (+14.5%)
Oil & gas - field services

SAVANNAH FOODS & INDUSTRIES, INC.
PO Box 339 Phone: 912-234-1261
Savannah, GA 31402 Fax: 912-651-5159
Chm & CEO: William W. Sprague III
VP HR: Preston M. Blackwelder
Employees: 2,244
Jobs Added Last Year: 225 (+11.1%)
Food - sugar & refining

SCIENTIFIC-ATLANTA, INC.
One Technology Pkwy. South Phone: 404-903-5000
Atlanta, GA 30092-2967 Fax: 404-903-4617
Pres & CEO: James F. McDonald
SVP HR: Brian Koenig
Employees: 4,000
Jobs Added Last Year: 400 (+11.1%)
Telecommunications equipment - cable TV & satellite networks

GEORGIA

SHAW INDUSTRIES, INC.
616 East Walnut Ave.
Dalton, GA 30720
Pres & CEO: Robert E. Shaw
Dir Corp HR: Jim Lord
Employees: 24,200
Jobs Added Last Year: 2,494 (+11.5%)
Textiles - tufted carpet
Phone: 706-278-3812
Fax: 706-275-1040

SYNOVUS FINANCIAL CORPORATION
901 Front Ave., Ste. 301
Columbus, GA 31901
CEO: James H. Blanchard
SVP Dir Career Svcs: Steve Evans
Employees: 4,540
Jobs Added Last Year: 455 (+11.1%)
Banks - Southeast
Phone: 706-649-2387
Fax: 706-649-2479

SOFTWARE TECHNICAL SERVICES, INC.
3020 Holcomb Bridge Rd.
Norcross, GA 30071
CEO: Rita Narasimham
Dir HR: Nancy Ozment
Employees: 280
Jobs Added Last Year: 156 (+125.8%)
Computers - software consulting & contract programming services
Phone: 404-449-8966
Fax: 404-449-5407

TOTAL SYSTEM SERVICES, INC. 11494
1200 Sixth Ave.
Columbus, GA 31902
Chm & CEO: Richard W. Ussery
VP HR: Elizabeth R. James
Employees: 1,411
Jobs Added Last Year: 185 (+15.1%)
Financial - credit card processing
Phone: 706-649-2204
Fax: 706-649-4499

THE SOUTHERN COMPANY 11372
64 Perimeter Center East
Atlanta, GA 30346
Chm & CEO: Edward L. Addison
VP HR: William C. Archer III
Employees: 28,743
Jobs Cut Last Year: 342 (-1.2%)
Utility - electric power in Alabama, Florida, Georgia & Mississippi
Phone: 404-393-0650
Fax: 404-668-3559

TURNER BROADCASTING SYSTEM 12404
One CNN Center, 100 Intl. Blvd.
Atlanta, GA 30303
Chm & Pres: Robert E. "Ted" Turner III
VP Admin (HR): Willaim M. Shaw
Employees: 5,317
Jobs Added Last Year: 78 (+1.5%)
Cable TV (CNN); sports teams (Braves & Hawks); movie production (Castle Rock & New Line)
Phone: 404-827-1700
Fax: 404-827-2437

SOUTHWIRE COMPANY, INC.
One Southwire Dr.
Carrollton, GA 30119
Chm & CEO: Roy Richards, Jr.
VP HR: William Hearnburg
Employees: 5,000
Jobs Added Last Year: 0
Wire & cable products, metal fabricating, rods
Phone: 404-832-4242
Fax: 404-832-4929

UNITED PARCEL SERVICE OF AMERICA 40483
55 Glenlake Pkwy.
Atlanta, GA 30328
Chm & CEO: Kent C. Nelson
SVP HR: John J. Kelley
Employees: 286,000
Jobs Added Last Year: 19,000 (+7.1%)
Transportation - air & ground package delivery (#1 in the world)
Phone: 404-828-6000
Fax: 404-828-6593

SUNTRUST BANKS, INC. 11416
25 Park Place NE
Atlanta, GA 30303
Chm & CEO: James B. Williams
SVP HR: Robert H. Bowen
Employees: 19,232
Jobs Added Last Year: 576 (+3%)
Banks - Southeast
Phone: 404-588-7711
Fax: 404-827-6001

WESTPOINT STEVENS, INC.
400 W. Tenth St.
West Point, GA 31833
Chm & CEO: Holcombe T. Green., Jr.
VP HR: Foy F. Fisher
Employees: 18,000
Jobs Added Last Year: 0
Textiles - home furnishings
Phone: 706-645-4000
Fax: 706-645-4068

HAWAII

ALEXANDER & BALDWIN, INC.
822 Bishop St., PO Box 3440   Phone: 808-525-6611
Honolulu, HI 96801-3440   Fax: 808-525-6652
Pres & CEO: John C. Couch
VP & Chief Admin Off (HR): Miles B. King
Employees: 3,709
Jobs Added Last Year: 850 (+29.7%)
Transportation - shipping

FIRST HAWAIIAN, INC.
1132 Bishop St.   Phone: 808-525-7000
Honolulu, HI 96813   Fax: 808-525-8753
Chm & CEO: Walter A. Dods, Jr.
No central personnel officer
Employees: 3,035
Jobs Cut Last Year: 81 (-2.6%)
Banks - West

BANCORP HAWAII, INC.
130 Merchant St.   Phone: 808-537-8111
Honolulu, HI 96813   Fax: 808-533-0175
Chm & CEO: Lawrence Johnson
EVP & Mgr (HR): Duane Seekin
Employees: 4,424
Jobs Added Last Year: 149 (+3.5%)
Banks - West

HAWAIIAN ELECTRIC INDUSTRIES, INC.
900 Richards St.   Phone: 808-543-5662
Honolulu, HI 96813   Fax: 808-543-7966
Pres & CEO: Robert F. Clarke
VP HR: Joan Diamond
Employees: 3,399
Jobs Added Last Year: 108 (+3.3%)
Utility - electric power

▼ **Job Junction** http://www.iquest.net/iq/jobjunction.html

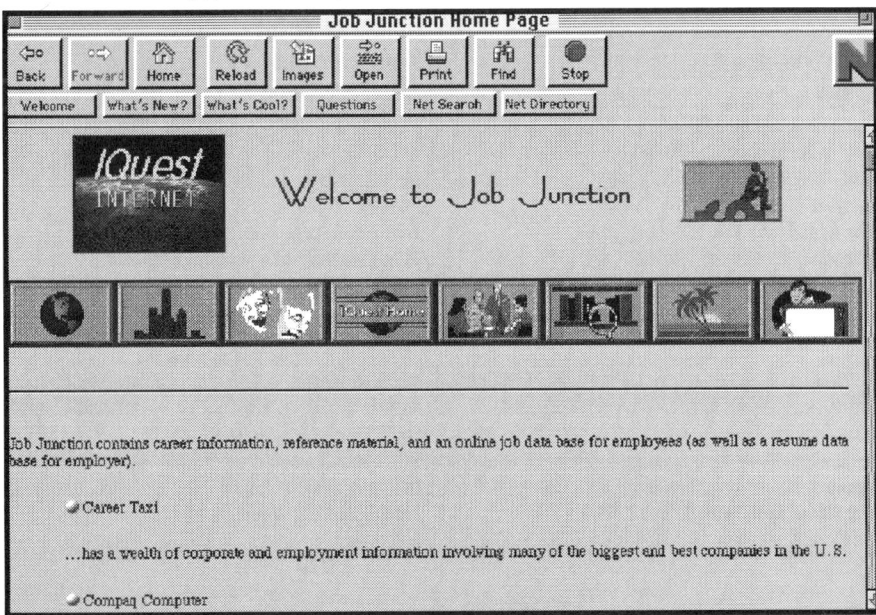

IDAHO

ALBERTSON'S, INC.
PO Box 20, 250 Parkcenter Blvd.   Phone: 208-385-6200
Boise, ID 83726   Fax: 208-385-6349
Chm & CEO: Gary G. Michael
SVP HR: Stephen D. Young
Employees: 75,000
Jobs Added Last Year: 4,000 (+5.6%)
Retail - supermarkets

MICRON TECHNOLOGY, INC.
2805 E. Columbia Rd.   Phone: 208-368-4000
Boise, ID 83706-9698   Fax: 208-368-4435
Chm & CEO: Steven R. Appleton
Dir HR: Susan Metzger
Employees: 5,450
Jobs Added Last Year: 550 (+11.2%)
Electrical components - memory chips (RAM, SRAM, VRAM)

BMC WEST CORPORATION
1475 Tyrell Ln.   Phone: 208-338-1700
Boise, ID 83706   Fax: 208-338-4367
Pres & CEO: Donald S. Hendrickson
No central personnel officer
Employees: 1,308
Jobs Added Last Year: 183 (+16.3%)
Building products - retail & wholesale

MORRISON KNUDSEN CORPORATION
Morrison Knudsen Plaza   Phone: 208-386-5000
Boise, ID 83729   Fax: 208-386-7186
EVP Fin & Admin & Sec (Acting CEO): Stephen G. Hanks
VP HR: Alvia L. Henderson
Employees: 11,910
Jobs Cut Last Year: 490 (-4%)
Construction - heavy

BOISE CASCADE CORPORATION
One Jefferson Sq.   Phone: 208-384-6161
Boise, ID 83728-0001   Fax: 208-384-7298
Pres, CEO & COO: George J. Harad
SVP HR: Alice E. Hennessey
Employees: 17,362
Jobs Added Last Year: 140 (+.8%)
Paper & paper products

J.R. SIMPLOT COMPANY
999 Main St., Ste. 1300   Phone: 208-336-2110
Boise, ID 83702   Fax: 208-389-7515
Pres & CEO: Stephen A. Beebe
VP HR: Ted Roper
Employees: 10,000
Jobs Added Last Year: 1,000 (+11.1%)
Diversified operations - food processing (french fried potatoes for McDonald's); fertilizer & livestock

COEUR D'ALENE MINES CORPORATION
505 Front Ave., PO Box I   Phone: 208-667-3511
Coeur d'Alene, ID 83816-0316   Fax: 208-765-0324
Chm, Pres & CEO: Dennis E. Wheeler
HR Mgr: Gary R. Banbury
Employees: 575
Jobs Added Last Year: 150 (+35.3%)
Silver mining & processing

TJ INTERNATIONAL, INC.
380 E. ParkCenter Blvd., Ste. 300 Phone: 208-345-8500
Boise, ID 83706   Fax: 208-345-3431
Pres & CEO: Tom Denig
Dir Hr: Rob Adams
Employees: 3,600
Jobs Added Last Year: 200 (+5.9%)
Building products - wood windows & patio doors

HECLA MINING COMPANY
6500 Mineral Dr.   Phone: 208-769-4100
Coeur d'Alene, ID 83814-1931   Fax: 208-769-4107
CEO: Arthur Brown
Dir HR: John Langstaff
Employees: 919
Jobs Added Last Year: 93 (+11.3%)
Gold mining & processing

WEST ONE BANCORP
101 S. Capitol Blvd.   Phone: 208-383-7000
Boise, ID 83702   Fax: 208-383-3858
Chm & CEO: Daniel R. Nelson
SVP & Dir (HR): Gary Peters
Employees: 5,000
Jobs Added Last Year: 707 (+16.5%)
Banks - West

ILLINOIS

ABBOTT LABORATORIES
One Abbott Park Rd. Phone: 708-937-6100
Abbott Park, IL 60064-3500 Fax: 708-937-1511
Chm & CEO: Duane L. Burnham
SVP HR: Robert N. Beck
Employees: 49,659
Jobs Added Last Year: 1,541 (+3.2%)
Drugs, hospital equipment, pesticides, health care products (Murine, Selsun Blue) & nutritional supplements (Similac)

ABC RAIL PRODUCTS CORPORATION
200 S. Michigan Ave., 13th Fl. Phone: 312-322-0360
Chicago, IL 60604-2402 Fax: 312-322-0377
Chm & CEO: Donald W. Grinter
VP HR: Joseph A. Parsons
Employees: 1,402
Jobs Added Last Year: 126 (+9.9%)
Transportation equipment - freight rail equipment

ACE HARDWARE CORPORATION
2200 Kensington Ct. Phone: 708-990-6600
Oak Brook, IL 60521 Fax: 708-573-4894
Pres & CEO: Roger E. Peterson
VP HR: Fred J. Neer
Employees: 3,883
Jobs Added Last Year: 478 (+14%)
Building products - retail & wholesale

ACME METALS INCORPORATED
13500 S. Perry Ave. Phone: 708-849-2500
Riverdale, IL 60627 Fax: 708-841-6010
Chm & CEO: Brian W. H. Marsden
VP Emp Rel: Richard J. Stefan
Employees: 2,750
Jobs Cut Last Year: 24 (-.9%)
Metal processing & fabrication

ADVANCE ROSS CORPORATION
233 S. Wacker Dr., Ste. 9700 Phone: 312-382-1100
Chicago, IL 60606-6502 Fax: 312-382-1109
Chm & CEO: Harve A. Ferrill
No central personnel officer
Employees: 253
Jobs Added Last Year: 57 (+29.1%)
Pollution control - electrostatic precipitator systems

ADVANTIS
231 N. Martingale Rd. Phone: 708-240-3000
Schaumburg, IL 60173 Fax: 708-240-3857
Chm & CEO: Syd N. Heaton
VP HR & Admin: Jim P. Doyle
Employees: 3,200
Jobs Added Last Year: –
Telecommunications services - data network for corporate use (IBM-Sears joint venture)

ALBERTO-CULVER COMPANY
2525 Armitage Ave. Phone: 708-450-3000
Melrose Park, IL 60160-1163 Fax: 708-450-3354
Pres & CEO: Howard B. Bernick
VP HR: Douglas Menealy
Employees: 11,500
Jobs Added Last Year: 2,900 (+33.7%)
Cosmetics & toiletries

THE ALLSTATE CORPORATION
Allstate Plaza Phone: 708-402-5000
Northbrook, IL 60062 Fax: 708-402-0045
Chm & CEO: Jerry D. Choate
SVP Corp HR: Edward J. Dixon
Employees: 49,000
Jobs Cut Last Year: 2,515 (-4.9%)
Insurance - property & casualty

AMERIHOST PROPERTIES, INC.
2400 E. Devon Ave., Ste. 280 Phone: 708-298-4500
Des Plaines, IL 60018-4617 Fax: 708-298-4505
Pres & CEO: Michael P. Holtz
Dir HR: Bill Roclaw
Employees: 1,915
Jobs Added Last Year: 114 (+6.3%)
Hotels & motels

AMERITECH CORPORATION
30 S. Wacker Dr. Phone: 312-750-5000
Chicago, IL 60606 Fax: 312-207-1601
Chm, Pres & CEO: Richard C. Notebaert
SVP HR: W.M. Oliver
Employees: 67,192
Jobs Cut Last Year: 4,108 (-5.8%)
Utility - telephone; cellular; directories; library information systems

An in-depth profile of this company is available by fax. Call 800-510-4452 and use your touch-tone phone to put in the 5-digit code at the prompt. Only $2.95 each with your credit card. See page 12 for more details.

ILLINOIS

AMOCO CORPORATION
200 E. Randolph Dr. Phone: 312-856-6111
Chicago, IL 60601 Fax: 312-856-2460
Chm, Pres & CEO: H. Laurance Fuller
SVP HR, Public & Govt Affairs: R. Wayne Anderson
Employees: 46,317
Jobs Cut Last Year: 677 (-1.4%)
Oil & gas - integrated

AMSTED INDUSTRIES INCORPORATED
205 N. Michigan Ave., 44th Fl. Phone: 312-645-1700
Chicago, IL 60601 Fax: 312-819-8425
Pres & CEO: Gordon R. Lohman
Dir Personnel: Arthur M. Meske
Employees: 9,000
Jobs Added Last Year: 1,100 (+13.9%)
Machinery - railroad & industrial equipment; building products

ANDREW CORPORATION
10500 W. 153rd St. Phone: 708-349-3300
Orland Park, IL 60462 Fax: 708-349-5943
Chm, Pres & CEO: Floyd L. English
VP HR: Joan P. Bowman
Employees: 26,118
Jobs Added Last Year: 496 (+1.9%)
Telecommunications equipment - antennas & radar systems

AON CORPORATION
123 N. Wacker Dr. Phone: 312-701-3000
Chicago, IL 60606 Fax: 312-701-3100
Chm, Pres & CEO: Patrick G. Ryan
VP Professional Dev (HR): Stephen C. Taylor
Employees: 27,000
Jobs Added Last Year: 12,000 (+80%)
Insurance - accident & health

ARCHER-DANIELS-MIDLAND CO.
4666 Faries Pkwy., PO Box 1470 Phone: 217-424-5200
Decatur, IL 62525 Fax: 217-424-5839
Chm & CEO: Dwayne O. Andreas
VP Emp Rel: Dale F. Benson
Employees: 14,168
Jobs Added Last Year: 644 (+4.8%)
Food - flour & grain; ethanol; soybeans; cotton

ARGOSY GAMING COMPANY
219 Piasa St. Phone: 618-474-7500
Alton, IL 62002-6232 Fax: 618-474-7762
VC, CEO & Gen Counsel: J. Thomas Long
HR Dir: Dan Bolin
Employees: 1,000
Jobs Added Last Year: 400 (+66.7%)
Leisure & recreational services - riverboat casinos (Alton Belle)

ARTHUR ANDERSEN & CO, S.C.
69 W. Washington St. Phone: 312-580-0069
Chicago, IL 60602-3094 Fax: 312-507-2548
Chm, CEO & Mng Partner: Lawrence A. Weinbach
HR: Peter Pesce
Employees: 72,722
Jobs Added Last Year: 6,244 (+9.4%)
Business services - accounting & technical consulting

ARTHUR J. GALLAGHER & CO.
2 Pierce Place Phone: 708-773-3800
Itasca, IL 60143-3141 Fax: 708-285-4000
Pres & CEO: J. Patrick Gallagher, Jr.
VP HR: Bette Brinkerhoff
Employees: 2,700
Jobs Added Last Year: 400 (+17.4%)
Insurance - brokerage

AUTOFINANCE GROUP, INC.
601 Oakmont Ln. Phone: 708-655-7100
Westmont, IL 60559-5549 Fax: 708-655-2376
CEO: A. E. Steinhaus
No central personnel officer
Employees: 106
Jobs Added Last Year: 37 (+53.6%)
Financial - cars

BAKER & MCKENZIE
130 E. Randolph Dr. Phone: 312-861-8800
Chicago, IL 60601 Fax: 312-861-8823
Chm Exec Committee: John V. McGuigan
Dir HR: Mary Weis
Employees: 5,098
Jobs Added Last Year: 44 (+.9%)
Law firm (world's largest)

ILLINOIS

BALLY ENTERTAINMENT CORP.
8700 W. Bryn Mawr Ave. Phone: 312-399-1300
Chicago, IL 60631 Fax: 312-693-2982
Chm, Pres & CEO: Arthur M. Goldberg
VP HR: Harold Morgan
Employees: 19,200
Jobs Cut Last Year: 11,800 (-38.1%)
Leisure & recreational services - casinos

BAXTER INTERNATIONAL INC.
One Baxter Pkwy. Phone: 708-948-2000
Deerfield, IL 60015 Fax: 708-948-2887
Chm & CEO: Vernon R. Loucks, Jr.
SVP HR: Herbert F. Walker
Employees: 60,400
Jobs Cut Last Year: 900 (-1.5%)
Medical products & health services

BELL & HOWELL CO.
5215 Old Orchard Rd. Phone: 708-470-7100
Skokie, IL 60077 Fax: 708-470-9425
Chm, Pres & CEO: William J. White
VP HR: Maria T. Rubly
Employees: 5,718
Jobs Cut Last Year: 52 (-.9%)
Diversified operations - publishing; information systems; mail handling equipment

BLUE CROSS & BLUE SHIELD ASSOC.
676 N. St. Clair St. Phone: 312-440-6000
Chicago, IL 60611 Fax: 312-440-6409
Pres & CEO: Patrick G. Hayes
VP & Chief Admin Off (HR): Kris Kurschner
Employees: 135,883
Jobs Cut Last Year: 7,117 (-5%)
Insurance - prepaid health care plans

BORG-WARNER SECURITY CORP.
200 S. Michigan Ave. Phone: 312-322-8500
Chicago, IL 60604 Fax: 312-322-8849
Chm & CEO: Donald C. Trauscht
SVP HR: John O'Brien
Employees: 87,000
Jobs Added Last Year: —
Protection - guard, alarm, armored transportation & courier services

BRUNSWICK CORPORATION
One N. Field Ct. Phone: 708-735-4700
Lake Forest, IL 60045-4811 Fax: 708-735-4765
Chm, Pres & CEO: Jack F. Reichert
Dir HR: Patrick J. Gannon
Employees: 18,000
Jobs Added Last Year: 1,000 (+5.9%)
Leisure & recreational products - boats, sporting goods & bowling center

BUDGET RENT A CAR CORPORATION
4225 Naperville Rd. Phone: 708-955-1900
Lisle, IL 60532 Fax: 708-955-7799
Pres & CEO: William N. Plamondon
SVP HR: Gene Williams
Employees: 10,400
Jobs Added Last Year: 0
Leasing - car & truck rental

CAREMARK INTERNATIONAL, INC.
2215 Sanders Rd., Ste. 400 Phone: 708-559-4700
Northbrook, IL 60062 Fax: 708-559-4792
Chm & CEO: C. A. Lance Piccolo
VP HR: Kent J. DeLucenay
Employees: 7,800
Jobs Added Last Year: 1,530 (+24.4%)
Health care - outpatient & home

CATERPILLAR INC.
100 NE Adams St. Phone: 309-675-1000
Peoria, IL 61629-7310 Fax: 309-675-5948
Chm & CEO: Donald V. Fites
VP HR: Wayne M. Zimmerman
Employees: 50,443
Jobs Cut Last Year: 1,897 (-3.6%)
Machinery - construction & mining; engines & power generation systems

CBI INDUSTRIES, INC.
800 Jorie Blvd. Phone: 708-572-7000
Oak Brook, IL 60521-2268 Fax: 708-572-7405
Chm, Pres & CEO: John E. Jones
VP HR: Stephen M. Duffy
Employees: 13,920
Jobs Cut Last Year: 180 (-1.3%)
Construction - heavy

 An in-depth profile of this company is available by fax. Call 800-510-4452 and use your touch-tone phone to put in the 5-digit code at the prompt. Only $2.95 each with your credit card. See page 12 for more details.

ILLINOIS

CDW COMPUTER CENTERS, INC.
1020 E. Lake Cook Rd. Phone: 708-465-6000
Buffalo Grove, IL 60089 Fax: 708-465-7700
Chm, CEO, Sec & Treas: Michael P. Krasny
VP HR: Mary C. Gerltis
Employees: 247
Jobs Added Last Year: 112 (+83%)
Computers - direct marketing of computers, peripherals & software

CELEX GROUP INC.
919 Springer Dr. Phone: 708-953-1222
Lombard, IL 60148 Fax: 708-953-2110
CEO & Chm: Mac Anderson
HR Mgr: Tracy Temple
Employees: 1,155
Jobs Added Last Year: 976 (+545.3%)
Retail - motivational & gift products (Successories)

THE CHERRY CORPORATION
3600 Sunset Ave. Phone: 708-662-9200
Waukegan, IL 60087-3298 Fax: 708-360-3508
Chm & Pres: Peter B. Cherry
Dir HR: Nancy Guarascio
Employees: 3,659
Jobs Added Last Year: 812 (+28.5%)
Electrical components - automotive switching devices; keyboards, switches & semiconductors

CHICAGO AND NORTH WESTERN
One North Western Center Phone: 312-559-7000
Chicago, IL 60606 Fax: 312-559-7072
Chm, Pres & CEO: Robert Schmiege
VP HR: Robert F. Ard
Employees: 6,158
Jobs Cut Last Year: 111 (-1.8%)
Transportation - rail

CIRCUIT SYSTEMS, INC.
2350 E. Lunt Ave. Phone: 708-439-1999
Elk Grove Village, IL 60007 Fax: 708-437-5910
Pres & CEO: D. S. Patel
HR: William Blair
Employees: 520
Jobs Added Last Year: 90 (+20.9%)
Electrical components - printed circuit boards

CNA FINANCIAL CORPORATION
CNA Plaza Phone: 312-822-5000
Chicago, IL 60685 Fax: 312-822-6419
CEO: Laurence A. Tisch
VP Home Off HR: Lynn Dragisic
Employees: 17,200
Jobs Cut Last Year: 600 (-3.4%)
Insurance - property & casualty

COCA-COLA BOTTLING CO. OF CHICAGO
7400 N. Oak Park Ave. Phone: 312-775-0900
Niles, IL 60714 Fax: 312-647-7104
CEO: Marvin J. Herb
Dir HR: Robert T. Palo
Employees: 4,200
Jobs Added Last Year: —
Beverages - soft drink bottling

COTTER & COMPANY
2740 N. Clybourn Ave. Phone: 312-975-2700
Chicago, IL 60614 Fax: 312-975-1712
Pres & CEO: Daniel A. Cotter
Mgr HR: Pat Kelley
Employees: 4,400
Jobs Added Last Year: —
Building products - retail

DEAN FOODS COMPANY
3600 N. River Rd. Phone: 708-678-1680
Franklin Park, IL 60131 Fax: 708-678-2779
Chm & CEO: Howard M. Dean
Dir HR: Jerry Berger
Employees: 12,100
Jobs Added Last Year: 1,600 (+15.2%)
Food - dairy products

DEERE & COMPANY
John Deere Rd. Phone: 309-765-8000
Moline, IL 61265-8098 Fax: 309-765-5772
Chm & CEO: Hans W. Becherer
SVP Engineering, Tech & HR: Michael S. Plunkett
Employees: 34,252
Jobs Added Last Year: 1,182 (+3.6%)
Machinery - farm & construction

ILLINOIS

DESOTO, INC.
16750 S. Vincennes Rd. Phone: 708-331-8800
South Holland, IL 60473 Fax: 708-210-0345
CEO: William Spier
Dir HR: Cheryl Davis
Employees: 618
Jobs Added Last Year: 354 (+134.1%)
Paints & allied products

DISCOVERY ZONE, INC.
205 N. Michigan Ave. Phone: 312-616-3800
Chicago, IL 60601 Fax: 312-616-3830
Chm & CEO: Donald F. Flynn
VP Admin (HR): James K. Dublin
Employees: 6,100
Jobs Added Last Year: 5,333 (+695.3%)
Leisure & recreational services - children's recreational centers

DUCHOSSOIS INDUSTRIES, INC.
845 N. Larch Ave. Phone: 708-279-3600
Elmhurst, IL 60126 Fax: 708-530-6091
Chm: Richard L. Duchossois
Dir HR: Lyn Fleichhacker
Employees: 8,000
Jobs Added Last Year: 1,500 (+23.1%)
Diversified operations - transportation; entertainment; defense; consumer products

EAGLE FOOD CENTERS, INC.
Rte. 67 & Knoxville Rd. Phone: 309-787-7730
Milan, IL 61264 Fax: 309-787-7895
Pres & CEO: Gerald E. Barber
VP Labor Relations: Randy Smith
Employees: 9,007
Jobs Added Last Year: 448 (+5.2%)
Retail - supermarkets

ELCO INDUSTRIES, INC.
1111 Samuelson Rd. Phone: 815-397-5151
Rockford, IL 61125 Fax: 815-398-4569
CEO & Pres: John Lutz
Personnel Mgr: Mike Muskievicz
Employees: 1,833
Jobs Added Last Year: 233 (+14.6%)
Metal products - fasteners

ELEK-TEK INC.
7350 N. Linder Ave. Phone: 708-677-7660
Skokie, IL 60077 Fax: 708-677-1081
Pres & CEO: Cameron B. Estes, Jr.
Dir HR: Rory Zaks
Employees: 788
Jobs Added Last Year: 185 (+30.7%)
Computers - superstores

ENCYCLOPAEDIA BRITANNICA INC.
310 S. Michigan Ave. Phone: 312-347-7000
Chicago, IL 60604 Fax: 312-347-7135
Pres & CEO: Peter B. Norton
VP HR: Karl Steinberg
Employees: 2,350
Jobs Added Last Year: 350 (+17.5%)
Publishing - reference books (Britannica & Merriam-Webster); educational services (Evelyn Wood speed reading)

EQUITY RESIDENTIAL PROPERTIES TRUST
2 North Riverside Plaza, Ste. 600 Phone: 312-474-1300
Chicago, IL 60606 Fax: 312-454-0434
Pres & CEO: Douglas Crocker II
VP HR & Admin: Beverley Petrunich
Employees: 1,635
Jobs Added Last Year: 728 (+80.3%)
Real estate investment trust

FEDERAL SIGNAL CORPORATION
1415 W. 22nd St. Phone: 708-954-2000
Oak Brook, IL 60521-9945 Fax: 708-954-2030
Chm, Pres & CEO: Joseph J. Ross
No central personnel officer
Employees: 5,243
Jobs Added Last Year: 975 (+22.8%)
Diversified operations - emergency vehicles; cutting tools; communications equipment

FIRST CHICAGO CORPORATION
One First National Plaza Phone: 312-732-4000
Chicago, IL 60670 Fax: 312-732-5976
Chm & CEO: Richard L. Thomas
EVP HR: Marvin James Alef, Jr.
Employees: 17,355
Jobs Added Last Year: 357 (+2.1%)
Banks - money center

ILLINOIS

THE FLORSHEIM SHOE COMPANY
130 S. Canal St. Phone: 312-559-2500
Chicago, IL 60606 Fax: 312-559-7408
Pres & CEO: Ronald J. Mueller
Dir HR: John Diebold
Employees: 3,300
Jobs Added Last Year: 100 (+3.1%)
Men's shoes

FMC CORPORATION
200 E. Randolph Dr. Phone: 312-861-6000
Chicago, IL 60601 Fax: 312-861-6176
Chm & CEO: Robert N. Burt
VP HR: Lawrence P. Holleran
Employees: 20,696
Jobs Cut Last Year: 1,401 (-6.3%)
Diversified operations - chemicals; defense systems; machinery & equipment

FOLLETT CORPORATION
2233 West St. Phone: 708-583-2000
River Grove, IL 60171 Fax: 708-452-9347
Pres & CEO: P.R. M. Litzsinger
HR: Carl Dickes
Employees: 6,342
Jobs Cut Last Year: 158 (-2.4%)
Diversified operations - college bookstores; software; publishing

FRUIT OF THE LOOM, INC.
233 S. Wacker Dr. Phone: 312-876-1724
Chicago, IL 60606 Fax: 312-993-1749
Chm & CEO: William Farley
VP Admin (HR): Burgess D. Ridge
Employees: 35,000
Jobs Added Last Year: 3,900 (+12.5%)
Apparel - underwear, T-shirts, infant & toddler clothing, sweatshirts

GATX CORPORATION
500 W. Monroe St. Phone: 312-621-6200
Chicago, IL 60661-3676 Fax: 312-621-6646
Chm & CEO: James J. Glasser
VP HR: William Chambers
Employees: 5,500
Jobs Added Last Year: 400 (+7.8%)
Transportation - equipment & leasing

GAYLORD CONTAINER CORPORATION
500 Lake Cook Rd., Ste. 400 Phone: 708-405-5500
Deerfield, IL 60015-4921 Fax: 708-405-5585
CEO: Marvin A. Pomerantz
Dir HR: Mike McDermott
Employees: 4,300
Jobs Added Last Year: 150 (+3.6%)
Containers - brown corrugated containers & paper bags

GENERAL BINDING CORPORATION
One GBC Plaza Phone: 708-272-3700
Northbrook, IL 60062-4195 Fax: 708-272-1389
Pres & CEO: Rudolph Grua
Dir Personnel: Gary Smith
Employees: 3,199
Jobs Cut Last Year: 164 (-4.9%)
Office equipment & supplies - binding, laminating & paper-shredding systems

GENERAL INSTRUMENT CORPORATION
181 W. Madison St. Phone: 312-541-5000
Chicago, IL 60602 Fax: 312-541-8038
CEO: Daniel F. Akerson
VP HR: Lee Keenan
Employees: 10,100
Jobs Added Last Year: 900 (+9.8%)
Telecommunications equipment - digital set-top TV converters; semiconductors

W. W. GRAINGER, INC.
5500 W. Howard St. Phone: 708-982-9000
Skokie, IL 60077-2699 Fax: 708-982-3489
Chm: David W. Grainger
VP HR: Neil Ormond
Employees: 9,643
Jobs Added Last Year: 865 (+9.9%)
Machinery - electrical

GREAT AMERICAN MGMNT. & INVESTMENT
2 N. Riverside Plaza Phone: 312-466-4010
Chicago, IL 60606 Fax: 312-454-0614
CEO: Rod F. Dammeyer
Dir HR: Gerald A. Spector
Employees: 618
Jobs Added Last Year: 218 (+54.5%)
Diversified operations - building, electrical, industrial, automotive & specialty products; investments

ILLINOIS

HARTMARX CORPORATION
101 N. Wacker Dr. Phone: 312-372-6300
Chicago, IL 60606 Fax: 312-444-2710
Chm & CEO: Elbert O. Hand
Mgr Emp Rel: Lorraine Dickson
Employees: 11,200
Jobs Cut Last Year: 1,800 (-13.8%)
Apparel - menswear (#1 in the US) & womenswear

IDEX CORPORATION
630 Dundee Rd. Phone: 708-498-7070
Northbrook, IL 60062 Fax: 708-498-3940
Chm, Pres & CEO: Donald N. Boyce
VP HR: Jerry Derck
Employees: 2,400
Jobs Added Last Year: 400 (+20%)
Machinery - general industrial

HELENE CURTIS INDUSTRIES, INC.
325 N. Wells St. Phone: 312-661-0222
Chicago, IL 60610 Fax: 312-836-0125
Pres & CEO: Ronald J. Gidwitz
VP HR: Robert Niles
Employees: 3,500
Jobs Added Last Year: 0
Cosmetics & toiletries

ILLINOIS CENTRAL CORPORATION
455 N. Cityfront Plaza Dr. Phone: 312-755-7500
Chicago, IL 60611-5504 Fax: 312-755-7839
Pres & CEO: E. Hunter Harrison
VP HR: Jim Harrell
Employees: 2,825
Jobs Cut Last Year: 92 (-3.2%)
Transportation - rail

HENRY CROWN AND CO.
222 N. LaSalle St. Phone: 312-236-6300
Chicago, IL 60601 Fax: 312-899-5039
CEO: Lester Crown
Dir HR: Patricia Slizewski
Employees: 7,000
Jobs Added Last Year: —
Diversified operations - real estate; securities; envelopes; furniture

ILLINOIS POWER COMPANY
500 S. 27th St. Phone: 217-424-6600
Decatur, IL 62525-1805 Fax: 217-424-6978
Chm, Pres & CEO: Larry D. Haab
Dir HR: Robert Krupp
Employees: 4,540
Jobs Cut Last Year: 84 (-1.8%)
Utility - electric power

HOUSEHOLD INTERNATIONAL, INC.
2700 Sanders Rd. Phone: 708-564-5000
Prospect Heights, IL 60070 Fax: 708-205-7452
Chm: Donald C. Clark
VP HR: Colin P. Kelly
Employees: 16,900
Jobs Added Last Year: 3,503 (+26.1%)
Financial - consumer loans, life insurance

ILLINOIS TOOL WORKS INC.
3600 W. Lake Ave. Phone: 708-724-7500
Glenview, IL 60025-5811 Fax: 708-657-4261
Chm & CEO: John D. Nichols
SVP HR: John Karpan
Employees: 19,000
Jobs Added Last Year: 1,200 (+6.7%)
Metal products - fasteners; industrial fluids & adhesives

HYATT CORPORATION

200 W. Madison St. Phone: 312-750-1234
Chicago, IL 60606 Fax: 312-750-8550
Chm & CEO: Jay A. Pritzker
SVP Planning & HR: Timothy Wolf
Employees: 52,275
Jobs Added Last Year: 0
Luxury hotels; arena management; cruises (Royal Caribbean); credit reporting (Trans Union)

IMC GLOBAL, INC.
2100 Sanders Rd. Phone: 708-272-9200
Northbrook, IL 60062-6146 Fax: 708-205-4805
Chm & CEO: Wendell F. Bueche
SVP HR: Allen C. Miller
Employees: 6,500
Jobs Added Last Year: 1,300 (+25%)
Fertilizers

ILLINOIS

INFORMATION RESOURCES, INC. 13766
150 N. Clinton St. Phone: 312-726-1221
Chicago, IL 60661 Fax: 312-726-0360
Chm & CEO: Gian M. Fulgoni
VP HR: Julie Chandler
Employees: 5,800
Jobs Added Last Year: 1,093 (+23.2%)
Business services - market research

INLAND STEEL INDUSTRIES, INC. 10786
30 W. Monroe St. Phone: 312-346-0300
Chicago, IL 60603 Fax: 312-899-3672
Chm, Pres & CEO: Robert J. Darnall
VP HR: Judd R. Cool
Employees: 16,200
Jobs Cut Last Year: 980 (-5.7%)
Steel - production & distribution

INTERLAKE CONVEYORS INC.
550 Warrenville Rd. Phone: 708-852-8800
Lisle, IL 60532-4387 Fax: 708-719-7152
Chm & CEO: W. Robert Reum
Dir HR: Lorene Flewellen
Employees: 4,778
Jobs Cut Last Year: 124 (-2.5%)
Machinery - material handling

JMB REALTY CORPORATION
900 N. Michigan Ave. Phone: 312-440-4800
Chicago, IL 60611 Fax: 312-915-2310
Pres & CEO: Neil Bluhm
Dir HR: Gail Silvers
Employees: 17,000
Jobs Added Last Year: —
Real estate operations

JOHNSON PUBLISHING COMPANY 40251
820 S. Michigan Ave. Phone: 312-322-9200
Chicago, IL 60605 Fax: 312-322-0918
Chm & CEO: John H. Johnson
Personnel Dir: La Doris Foster
Employees: 2,600
Jobs Cut Last Year: 185 (-6.6%)
Diversified - periodical publishing (*Ebony* & *Jet*), radio broadcasting, cosmetics & hair care

JUNO LIGHTING, INC.
2001 S. Mt. Prospect Rd. Phone: 708-827-9880
Des Plaines, IL 60017-5065 Fax: 708-827-2925
CEO: Robert S. Fremont
HR Mgr: Patricia Perez
Employees: 770
Jobs Added Last Year: 70 (+10%)
Building products - recessed & trac lighting fixtures

JUPITER INDUSTRIES, INC.
919 North Michigan Ave. Phone: 312-642-6000
Chicago, IL 60611 Fax: 312-642-2316
Chm & CEO: Edward W. Ross
Dir HR: Karen Brown
Employees: 7,000
Jobs Added Last Year: —
Diversified operations - real estate; transport services; natural gas; insurance

KEMPER CORPORATION 10843
One Kemper Dr. Phone: 708-320-3435
Long Grove, IL 60049 Fax: 708-320-4535
Chm & CEO: David B. Mathis
VP HR: David M. Cervone
Employees: 6,335
Jobs Cut Last Year: 711 (-10.1%)
Financial - securities brokerage, asset management; life insurance

THE KEMPER NATIONAL INSURANCE COMPANIES
One Kemper Dr. Phone: 708-320-2000
Long Grove, IL 60049 Fax: 708-320-2494
Acting CEO: Alfred K. Kenyon
VP HR: Fred McCullough
Employees: 9,000
Jobs Added Last Year: —
Insurance - property & casualty

LEO BURNETT COMPANY, INC.
35 W. Wacker Dr., Ste. 2200 Phone: 312-220-5959
Chicago, IL 60601 Fax: 312-220-6533
Pres & CEO: William T. Lynch
EVP HR: Jerry L. Strimbu
Employees: 6,581
Jobs Added Last Year: —
Advertising

ILLINOIS

THE MARMON GROUP, INC.
225 W. Washington St. Phone: 312-372-9500
Chicago, IL 60606 Fax: 312-845-5305
Pres & CEO: Robert A. Pritzker
Personnel Dir: George Frese
Employees: 27,700
Jobs Added Last Year: 700 (+2.6%)
Diversified operations - industrial materials, automobile & medical products

MCDONALD'S CORPORATION
McDonald's Plaza Phone: 708-575-3000
Oak Brook, IL 60521 Fax: 708-575-3392
Chm & CEO: Michael R. Quinlan
SVP Personnel: Stanley R. Stein
Employees: 169,000
Jobs Added Last Year: 3,000 (+1.8%)
Retail - fast-food restaurants (#1 in the world)

MEDICUS SYSTEMS CORPORATION
One Rotary Center, Ste. 400 Phone: 708-570-7500
Evanston, IL 60201 Fax: 708-570-7518
Pres & CEO: Richard C. Jelinek
Dir HR: Mary Stewart
Employees: 285
Jobs Added Last Year: 70 (+32.6%)
Computers - decision-support software for the health care industry

MERCURY FINANCE CO.
40 Skokie Blvd., Ste. 200 Phone: 708-564-3720
Northbrook, IL 60062 Fax: 708-564-3758
Pres & CEO: John N. Brincat
Dir HR: Robert Lutgen
Employees: 1,200
Jobs Added Last Year: 420 (+53.8%)
Financial - auto & consumer loans & credit insurance

MOLEX INC.
2222 Wellington Ct. Phone: 708-969-4550
Lisle, IL 60532 Fax: 708-969-1352
CEO: Frederick A. Krehbiel
Dir HR: Neil Lefort
Employees: 8,100
Jobs Added Last Year: 500 (+6.6%)
Electrical connectors

MONTGOMERY WARD
One Montgomery Ward Plaza Phone: 312-467-2000
Chicago, IL 60671 Fax: 312-467-3975
Chm & CEO: Bernard F. Brennan
EVP HR: Robert A. Kasenter
Employees: 51,350
Jobs Cut Last Year: 10,950 (-17.6%)
Retail - major department stores (Montgomery Ward & Lechmere)

MOORMAN MANUFACTURING COMPANY
1000 N. 30th St. Phone: 217-222-7100
Quincy, IL 62301 Fax: 217-222-4069
Chm, Pres & CEO: Tom M. McKenna
VP HR: Terry Lunt
Employees: 2,900
Jobs Cut Last Year: 100 (-3.3%)
Veterinary products & services - livestock feed & equipment

MORNINGSTAR INC.
225 W. Wacker Dr. Phone: 312-696-6000
Chicago, IL 60606-1224 Fax: 312-696-6001
Pres & CEO: Joseph Mansueto
Dir HR: Julia Katz
Employees: 375
Jobs Added Last Year: 95 (+33.9%)
Publishing - information on mutual funds & stocks

MORTON INTERNATIONAL, INC.
100 N. Riverside Place Phone: 312-807-2000
Chicago, IL 60606-1596 Fax: 312-807-2241
Chm, Pres & CEO: S. Jay Stewart
VP HR: John C. Hedley
Employees: 11,900
Jobs Added Last Year: 1,200 (+11.2%)
Chemicals - adhesives, coatings & specialty products; salt; automobile airbags

MOTOROLA, INC.
1303 E. Algonquin Rd. Phone: 708-576-5000
Schaumburg, IL 60196 Fax: 708-576-8003
VC & CEO: Gary Tooker
EVP & Dir HR: James Donnelly
Employees: 120,000
Jobs Added Last Year: 13,000 (+12.1%)
Diversified operations - cellular telephones & switches; networking equipment; semiconductors

ILLINOIS

NALCO CHEMICAL COMPANY
One Nalco Center Phone: 708-305-1000
Naperville, IL 60563-1198 Fax: 708-305-2900
Chm & CEO: E. J. Mooney
SVP HR: James F. Lambe
Employees: 6,800
Jobs Added Last Year: 86 (+1.3%)
Chemicals - specialty

NAVISTAR INTERNATIONAL CORP.
455 N. Cityfront Plaza Dr. Phone: 312-836-2000
Chicago, IL 60611 Fax: 312-836-2192
Chm & CEO: James C. Cotting
SVP Emp Rel & Admin: John M. Sheahin
Employees: 13,612
Jobs Cut Last Year: 333 (-2.4%)
Trucks - medium & heavy

NEWELL CO.
29 E. Stephenson St. Phone: 815-235-4171
Freeport, IL 61032-0943 Fax: 815-233-8060
VC & CEO: William P. Sovey
VP Personnel Rel: William K. Doppstadt
Employees: 15,000
Jobs Added Last Year: 3,400 (+29.3%)
Diversified operations - hardware; housewares; office & industrial products

NICOR INC.
1844 Ferry Rd., PO Box 3014 Phone: 708-305-9500
Naperville, IL 60566-3014 Fax: 708-983-4566
Chm & CEO: Richard G. Cline
VP HR: John C. Flowers
Employees: 3,500
Jobs Added Last Year: 0
Utility - gas distribution

NORTHERN TRUST CORPORATION
50 S. La Salle St. Phone: 312-630-6000
Chicago, IL 60675 Fax: 312-630-1512
Pres & COO: William A. Osborne
SVP HR: William Setterstrom
Employees: 6,249
Jobs Added Last Year: 451 (+7.8%)
Banks - Midwest

NORTHWESTERN STEEL & WIRE COMPANY
121 Wallace St. Phone: 815-625-2500
Sterling, IL 61081 Fax: 815-625-0440
Chm, Pres & CEO: Robert N. Gurnitz
VP HR: John C. Meyer
Employees: 2,517
Jobs Added Last Year: 17 (+.7%)
Steel - wide flange beams, angles, channels & flat bars; hot rolled rod & wire products

OLD REPUBLIC INTERNATIONAL CORPORATION
307 N. Michigan Ave. Phone: 312-346-8100
Chicago, IL 60601 Fax: 312-726-0309
Pres & CEO: A. C. Zucaro
Dir Personnel: Charles Strizak
Employees: 5,600
Jobs Added Last Year: 700 (+14.3%)
Insurance - property & casualty

OPTION CARE, INC.
100 Corporate North, Ste. 212 Phone: 708-615-1690
Bannockburn, IL 60015 Fax: 708-615-1794
CEO: John N. Kapoor
No central personnel officer
Employees: 379
Jobs Added Last Year: 214 (+129.7%)
Health care - outpatient & home

OUTBOARD MARINE CORPORATION
100 Sea-Horse Dr. Phone: 708-689-6200
Waukegan, IL 60085 Fax: 708-689-5555
Chm, Pres & CEO: James C. Chapman
VP HR: Richard H. Medland
Employees: 8,472
Jobs Added Last Year: 398 (+4.9%)
Leisure & recreational products - powerboats (Chris-Craft) & marine motors (Johnson, Evinrude)

PEOPLES ENERGY CORPORATION
122 S. Michigan Ave. Phone: 312-431-4000
Chicago, IL 60603 Fax: 312-431-0112
Chm & CEO: Richard E. Terry
Dir HR: John Ibach
Employees: 3,419
Jobs Added Last Year: 239 (+7.5%)
Utility - gas distribution

ILLINOIS

PEPPER COS. INC.
643 N. Orleans St. Phone: 312-266-4703
Chicago, IL 60610 Fax: 312-266-2792
Chm: Richard S. Pepper
SVP HR: John Beasley
Employees: 921
Jobs Added Last Year: 121 (+15.1%)
Building - general contracting

PITTWAY CORPORATION
200 S. Wacker Dr., Ste. 700 Phone: 312-831-1070
Chicago, IL 60606-5802 Fax: 312-831-0808
Pres & CEO: King Harris
No central personnel officer
Employees: 4,800
Jobs Added Last Year: 300 (+6.7%)
Diversified operations - burglar & fire alarms (Ademco Security); trade magazine publishing (Penton); real estate

PLATINUM TECHNOLOGY, INC.
1815 S. Meyers Rd. Phone: 708-620-5000
Oakbrook Terrace, IL 60181 Fax: 708-691-0710
Chm, Pres & CEO: Andrew J. Filipowski
Dir HR: Jennifer Werneke
Employees: 382
Jobs Added Last Year: 137 (+55.9%)
Computers - database management software for mainframes

PREMARK INTERNATIONAL, INC.
1717 Deerfield Rd. Phone: 708-405-6000
Deerfield, IL 60015 Fax: 708-405-6013
Chm & CEO: Warren L. Batts
SVP HR: James C. Coleman
Employees: 24,000
Jobs Added Last Year: 0
Diversified operations - plastic containers (Tupperware); food & fitness equipment; appliances (West Bend)

THE QUAKER OATS COMPANY
Quaker Tower, 321 N. Clark St. Phone: 312-222-7111
Chicago, IL 60610-4714 Fax: 312-222-8304
Chm & CEO: William D. Smithburg
SVP HR: Douglas J. Ralston
Employees: 20,200
Jobs Cut Last Year: 900 (-4.3%)
Food - cereals, beverages (Gatorade, Snapple), food (Aunt Jemima, Rice-A-Roni, Van Camp's)

QUIXOTE CORPORATION
One E. Wacker Dr. Phone: 312-467-6755
Chicago, IL 60601 Fax: 312-467-1356
Chm, Pres & CEO: Philip E. Rollhaus, Jr.
Office Mgr (HR): Dorothy French
Employees: 1,156
Jobs Added Last Year: 170 (+17.2%)
Diversified operations - highway safety devices; stenographic equipment; compact discs

R.R. DONNELLEY & SONS COMPANY
77 W. Wacker Dr. Phone: 312-326-8000
Chicago, IL 60601 Fax: 312-326-8543
Chm & CEO: John R. Walter
SVP HR, Compensation & Ben: Steven J. Baumgartner
Employees: 32,100
Jobs Added Last Year: 1,700 (+5.6%)
Printing - commercial (world's largest); direct marketing services

ROTARY INTERNATIONAL
One Rotary Ctr., 1560 Sherman Ave. Phone: 708-866-3243
Evanston, IL 60201 Fax: 708-328-8554
Gen Sec: Herbert A. Pigman
HR Div Mgr: Fred Hall
Employees: 617
Jobs Added Last Year: 63 (+11.4%)
Membership organization - business & charitable activities

SAFETY-KLEEN CORPORATION
1000 N. Randall Rd. Phone: 708-697-8460
Elgin, IL 60123 Fax: 708-468-8560
Pres & COO: John G. Johnson, Jr.
SVP HR: Robert J. Burian
Employees: 6,600
Jobs Cut Last Year: 200 (-2.9%)
Pollution control - contaminated fluid recycling

SARA LEE CORPORATION
3 First National Plaza Phone: 312-726-2600
Chicago, IL 60602-4260 Fax: 312-726-3712
Chm & CEO: John H. Bryan
SVP HR: Gary C. Grom
Employees: 146,000
Jobs Added Last Year: 8,000 (+5.8%)
Diversified operations - foods & coffee; hosiery (Hanes & L'eggs); shoecare (Kiwi); leather goods (Coach)

An in-depth profile of this company is available by fax. Call 800-510-4452 and use your touch-tone phone to put in the 5-digit code at the prompt. Only $2.95 each with your credit card. See page 12 for more details.

ILLINOIS

SEARS, ROEBUCK AND CO.
Sears Tower
Chicago, IL 60684
Chm, Pres & CEO: Edward A. Brennan
VP HR: Warren F. Cooper
Employees: 359,000
Jobs Cut Last Year: 44,000 (-10.9%)
Retailer - major department stores; auto repair & parts (Western Auto)
Phone: 312-875-2500
Fax: 312-875-8351

SPS TRANSACTION SERVICES, INC.
2500 Lake Cook Rd.
Riverwoods, IL 60015
Pres: Robert L. Wieseneck
VP HR: Stu Holman
Employees: 1,970
Jobs Added Last Year: 180 (+10.1%)
Business services - point-of-sale transaction processing
Phone: 708-405-3700
Fax: 708-405-3854

SERVICEMASTER L.P.
One ServiceMaster Way
Downers Grove, IL 60515-9969
Pres & CEO: Carlos H. Cantu
VP HR: Teri Welch
Employees: 31,000
Jobs Added Last Year: 9,900 (+46.9%)
Building - maintenance & services
Phone: 708-964-1300
Fax: 708-719-6878

STATE FARM
One State Farm Plaza
Bloomington, IL 61710
Chm, Pres & CEO: Edward B. Rust, Jr.
VP Personnel: John Coffey
Employees: 64,520
Jobs Added Last Year: 3,752 (+6.2%)
Insurance - property & casualty
Phone: 309-766-2311
Fax: 309-766-6169

SPECIALTY FOODS CORP.
520 Lake Cook Rd., Ste. 520
Deerfield, IL 60015
Pres & CEO: Thomas B. Herskovits
VP HR: John D. Reisenberg
Employees: 13,100
Jobs Added Last Year: —
Food - cheese, baked goods, prepared meats, pickles & chips
Phone: 708-267-3000
Fax: 708-267-0015

STONE CONTAINER CORPORATION
150 N. Michigan Ave.
Chicago, IL 60601-7568
Chm, Pres & CEO: Roger W. Stone
VP HR: Gayle M Sparapani
Employees: 29,000
Jobs Cut Last Year: 2,200 (-7.1%)
Paper & paper products - paperboard & paper packaging, white paper & pulp
Phone: 312-346-6600
Fax: 312-580-4919

SPIEGEL, INC.
3500 Lacey Rd.
Downers Grove, IL 60515-5432
VC, Pres & CEO: John J. Shea
VP HR: Harold S. Dahlstrand
Employees: 11,104
Jobs Cut Last Year: 2,396 (-17.7%)
Retail - mail order & Eddie Bauer outdoorwear stores
Phone: 708-986-8800
Fax: 708-769-3101

SWEETHEART HOLDINGS, INC.
7575 S. Kostner Ave.
Chicago, IL 60652
Pres & CEO: William F. McLaughlin
VP HR: James Mullen
Employees: 8,500
Jobs Added Last Year: —
Paper & paper products
Phone: 312-767-3300
Fax: 312-767-9454

SPORTMART INC.
7233 W. Dempster St.
Niles, IL 60714
Chm, Pres & CEO: Larry J. Hochberg
VP HR: Joe DeFalco
Employees: 3,804
Jobs Added Last Year: 806 (+26.9%)
Retail - sporting goods
Phone: 708-966-1700
Fax: 708-966-6892

SYSTEM SOFTWARE ASSOCIATES
500 W. Madison St., 32nd Fl.
Chicago, IL 60661
Chm, Pres & CEO: Larry J. Ford
Dir HR: Rick Steel
Employees: 1,700
Jobs Added Last Year: 500 (+41.7%)
Computers - business application software
Phone: 312-641-2900
Fax: 312-641-3737

ILLINOIS

TELEPHONE AND DATA SYSTEMS, INC. [12376]
30 N. LaSalle St., Ste. 4000   Phone: 312-630-1900
Chicago, IL 60602-2587   Fax: 312-630-1908
Pres & CEO: Leroy T. Carlson, Jr.
VP HR: C. Theodore Herbert
Employees: 4,343
Jobs Added Last Year: 540 (+14.2%)
Utility - telephone; cellular telephones; radio paging

TOOTSIE ROLL INDUSTRIES, INC. [11490]
7401 S. Cicero Ave.   Phone: 312-838-3400
Chicago, IL 60629   Fax: 312-838-3564
Chm & CEO: Melvin J. Gordon
Personnel Dir: Maurice Buddemeier
Employees: 1,700
Jobs Added Last Year: 200 (+13.3%)
Food - confectionery (Tootsie Roll, Charms, Mason Dots)

TELLABS, INC.
4951 Indiana Ave.   Phone: 708-969-8800
Lisle, IL 60532   Fax: 708-852-7346
Pres & CEO: Michael J. Birck
Dir Compensation, Ben & HR: Dave Southard
Employees: 2,216
Jobs Added Last Year: 122 (+5.8%)
Telecommunications equipment - advanced equipment for voice & data transport & access systems

TRUCK COMPONENTS INC.
302 Peoples Ave.   Phone: 815-964-8725
Rockford, IL 61104   Fax: 815-964-5961
Pres & CEO: Thomas W. Cook
Dir Personnel: Steve Smith
Employees: 1,925
Jobs Added Last Year: 140 (+7.8%)
Automotive & trucking - wheel-end components & iron castings

TENNESSEE RESTAURANT CO.
One Pierce Place, Ste. 100E   Phone: 708-250-0471
Itasca, IL 60143   Fax: 708-250-0382
Chm & CEO: Donald N. Smith
VP HR: Jane Scott
Employees: 35,000
Jobs Added Last Year: —
Retail - restaurants (Perkins & Friendly Ice Cream)

TRUE NORTH COMMUNICATIONS INC. [10595]
101 E. Erie St.   Phone: 312-751-7000
Chicago, IL 60611   Fax: 312-751-3501
Chm & CEO: Bruce Mason
VP & Mgr HR: Doris Radcliffe
Employees: 3,709
Jobs Added Last Year: 78 (+2.1%)
Advertising - direct marketing, PR & sales promotions

TITAN WHEEL INTERNATIONAL, INC.
2701 Spruce St.   Phone: 217-228-6011
Quincy, IL 62301   Fax: 217-228-3166
Pres & CEO: Maurice M. Taylor, Jr.
Corp Dir HR: Henry Washington
Employees: 5,000
Jobs Added Last Year: 2,200 (+78.6%)
Metal products - fabrication

U.S. ROBOTICS, INC. [15388]
8100 N. McCormick Blvd.   Phone: 708-982-5010
Skokie, IL 60076   Fax: 708-982-5235
Chm, Pres & CEO: Casey G. Cowell
VP HR: Elizabeth S. Ryan
Employees: 755
Jobs Added Last Year: 276 (+57.6%)
Computers - modems (Courier, Sportster, WorldPort & Megahertz)

TNT FREIGHTWAYS CORPORATION
9700 Higgins Rd., Ste. 570   Phone: 708-696-0200
Rosemont, IL 60018   Fax: 708-696-2080
Pres & CEO: John C. Carruth
Office Mgr (HR): Rosemary Maziarka
Employees: 11,000
Jobs Added Last Year: 779 (+7.6%)
Transportation - truck

UAL CORPORATION [11520]
1200 E. Algonquin Rd.   Phone: 708-952-4000
Elk Grove Township, IL 60007   Fax: 708-952-7578
Chm & CEO: Gerald Greenwald
SVP HR: Paul G. George
Employees: 83,400
Jobs Cut Last Year: 600 (-.7%)
Transportation - United Airlines

ILLINOIS

THE UNICOM CORPORATION
One First National Plaza, 37th Fl. Phone: 312-394-4321
Chicago, IL 60690-0767 Fax: 312-394-3110
Chm & CEO: James J. O'Connor
Dir HR: Ted Horwath
Employees: 19,265
Jobs Cut Last Year: 605 (-3%)
Utility - electric power (Commonwealth Edison)

USG CORPORATION
125 S. Franklin St. Phone: 312-606-4000
Chicago, IL 60606-4678 Fax: 312-606-4093
Chm & CEO: Eugene B. Connolly
VP HR Ops: S. Gary Snodgrass
Employees: 13,400
Jobs Added Last Year: 1,550 (+13.1%)
Building products - gypsum wallboard & ceiling tiles

UNITED STATES CELLULAR CORPORATION
8410 W. Bryn Mawr, Ste. 700 Phone: 312-399-8900
Chicago, IL 60631 Fax: 312-399-8936
CEO: H. Donald Nelson
VP HR: Doug Arnold
Employees: 1,246
Jobs Added Last Year: 371 (+42.4%)
Telecommunications services

THE VIGORO CORPORATION
225 N. Michigan Ave. Phone: 312-819-2020
Chicago, IL 60601 Fax: 312-819-2027
Pres & CEO: Robert E. Fowler, Jr.
Office Mgr (HR): John Overbeck
Employees: 1,700
Jobs Added Last Year: 300 (+21.4%)
Fertilizers - potash & nitrogen

THE UNIVERSITY OF CHICAGO
5801 S. Ellis Ave. Phone: 312-702-1234
Chicago, IL 60637 Fax: 312-702-8324
Pres: Hugo F. Sonnenschein
Assoc VP HR: Henry Webber
Employees: 11,800
Jobs Added Last Year: –
University

VITALINK PHARMACY SERVICES, INC.
1250 E. Diehl Rd., Ste. 208 Phone: 708-505-1320
Naperville, IL 60563 Fax: 708-505-1319
CEO: Don Tomasso
Dir HR: Tom Lauderback
Employees: 700
Jobs Added Last Year: 170 (+32.1%)
Medical services - institutional pharmacy services to nursing facilities

UNIVERSITY OF ILLINOIS
346 Henry Admin. Bldg. Phone: 217-333-2464
Urbana, IL 61801 Fax: 217-244-5821
Pres: Stanley O. Ikenberry
Vice Chancellor HR & Admin: Charles Colbert
Employees: 20,000
Jobs Added Last Year: –
University

WALGREEN CO.
200 Wilmot Rd. Phone: 708-940-2500
Deerfield, IL 60015 Fax: 708-940-2804
Chm & CEO: Charles R. Walgreen III
SVP HR: John A. Rubino
Employees: 62,000
Jobs Added Last Year: 4,300 (+7.5%)
Retail - drug stores (#1 in the US)

UOP
25 E. Algonquin Rd. Phone: 708-391-2000
Des Plaines, IL 60017 Fax: 708-391-2253
Pres & CEO: Michael D. Winfield
VP HR: Aaron R. Phillips
Employees: 4,000
Jobs Added Last Year: –
Chemicals - catalysts for the petroleum industry

WALLACE COMPUTER SERVICES, INC.
4600 W. Roosevelt Rd. Phone: 312-626-2000
Hillside, IL 60162 Fax: 708-449-1161
Pres & CEO: Robert J. Cronin
Dir HR: Barry L. White
Employees: 3,530
Jobs Added Last Year: 180 (+5.4%)
Paper - business forms, industrial & consumer catalogs, pressure-sensitive labels & other office supplies

ILLINOIS

WHITMAN CORPORATION
3501 Algonquin Rd. Phone: 708-818-5000
Rolling Meadows, IL 60008 Fax: 708-818-5045
Chm & CEO: Bruce S. Chelberg
SVP HR: Lawrence J. Pilon
Employees: 14,868
Jobs Added Last Year: 494 (+3.4%)
Diversified operations - soft drink bottling (Pepsi General); auto service (Midas); refrigeration equipment

WICKES LUMBER COMPANY
706 N. Deer Path Dr. Phone: 708-367-3400
Vernon Hills, IL 60061 Fax: 708-367-3750
Chm & CEO: J. Steven Wilson
Dir HR: Bob Adams
Employees: 4,800
Jobs Added Last Year: 708 (+17.3%)
Building products - retail & wholesale lumber

WISCONSIN CENTRAL TRANSPORTATION
6250 N. River Rd., Ste. 9000 Phone: 708-318-4600
Rosemont, IL 60018 Fax: 708-318-4618
Pres & CEO: Edward A. Burkhardt
Asst VP HR: David French
Employees: 1,053
Jobs Added Last Year: 124 (+13.3%)
Transportation - #1 US regional railroad holding company

WM. WRIGLEY JR. COMPANY
410 N. Michigan Ave. Phone: 312-644-2121
Chicago, IL 60611 Fax: 312-644-2135
Pres & CEO: William Wrigley
VP Personnel: David E. Boxell
Employees: 6,700
Jobs Added Last Year: 300 (+4.7%)
Food - gum (Big Red, Doublemint, Juicy Fruit, Spearmint)

WMX TECHNOLOGIES, INC.
3003 Butterfield Rd. Phone: 708-572-8800
Oak Brook, IL 60521 Fax: 708-572-3094
Chm & CEO: Dean L. Buntrock
VP HR: John Machota
Employees: 72,600
Jobs Added Last Year: 5,400 (+8%)
Pollution control - waste collection, disposal & recycling, air pollution control, industrial remediation

WOODHEAD INDUSTRIES, INC.
2150 E. Lake Cook Rd. Phone: 708-465-8300
Buffalo Grove, IL 60089 Fax: 708-272-8133
CEO: C. Mark DeWinter
VP HR: Robert A. Moultan
Employees: 947
Jobs Added Last Year: 131 (+16.1%)
Electrical products - control & power distribution devices

YOUNG MEN'S CHRISTIAN ASSOCIATION
101 N. Wacker Dr., Ste. 1400 Phone: 312-977-0031
Chicago, IL 60606 Fax: 312-977-9063
CEO: David Mercer
HR: Wyley Moore
Employees: 10,299
Jobs Added Last Year: –
Leisure & recreational services - athletic facilities

ZEBRA TECHNOLOGIES CORP.
333 Corporate Woods Pkwy. Phone: 708-634-6700
Vernon Hills, IL 60061 Fax: 708-913-8766
Chm & CEO: Edward L. Kaplan
Dir HR: Ellen Barnes
Employees: 380
Jobs Added Last Year: 86 (+29.3%)
Optical character recognition - bar code printing

ZEIGLER COAL HOLDING COMPANY
50 Jerome Ln. Phone: 618-394-2400
Fairview Heights, IL 62208 Fax: 618-394-2473
Chm & CEO: Michael K. Reilly
VP HR: William Kuzma, Jr.
Employees: 3,965
Jobs Added Last Year: –
Coal

ZENITH ELECTRONICS CORPORATION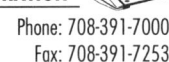
1000 Milwaukee Ave. Phone: 708-391-7000
Glenview, IL 60025 Fax: 708-391-7253
Chm & CEO: Jerry K. Pearlman
VP HR: Michael J. Kaplan
Employees: 22,100
Jobs Cut Last Year: 2,900 (-11.6%)
Audio & video home products

INDIANA

ADESA CORPORATION
1919 S. Post Rd. Phone: 317-862-7220
Indianapolis, IN 46239 Fax: 317-862-7231
Pres & CEO: D. Michael Hockett
Dir HR: Steve Kotz
Employees: 1,900
Jobs Added Last Year: 500 (+35.7%)
Business services - auto auctions; auto repair/reconditioning

ANACOMP, INC.
11550 N. Meridian St. Phone: 317-844-9666
Indianapolis, IN 46240 Fax: 317-848-1360
Chm & CEO: Louis P. Ferrero
VP HR: Patricia J. Wilkins
Employees: 4,400
Jobs Added Last Year: 200 (+4.8%)
Computers - microfilming & data storage services

ARVIN INDUSTRIES, INC.
One Noblitt Plaza, PO Box 3000 Phone: 812-379-3000
Columbus, IN 47202-3000 Fax: 812-379-3688
Chm & CEO: Bryon O. Pond
VP HR: Ray Mack
Employees: 16,000
Jobs Cut Last Year: 200 (-1.2%)
Automotive & trucking - original equipment

BALL CORPORATION
345 S. High St., PO Box 2407 Phone: 317-747-6100
Muncie, IN 47307-0407 Fax: 317-747-6203
Acting Pres & CEO: George A. Sissel
VP HR: David A. Westerlund
Employees: 13,807
Jobs Cut Last Year: 147 (-1.1%)
Glass & metal packaging products, primarily for food & beverages; aerospace & communications products

CENTRAL NEWSPAPERS, INC.
135 N. Pennsylvania St. Phone: 317-231-9200
Indianapolis, IN 46204-2480 Fax: 317-231-9208
Pres & CEO: Frank E. Russell
No central personnel officer
Employees: 5,000
Jobs Added Last Year: 140 (+2.9%)
Publishing - newspapers

CLARK EQUIPMENT COMPANY
100 N. Michigan St. Phone: 219-239-0100
South Bend, IN 46634 Fax: 219-239-0236
Chm, Pres & CEO: Leo J. McKernan
Dir HR: Richard Rosenthal
Employees: 5,948
Jobs Cut Last Year: 368 (-5.8%)
Machinery - material handling

COACHMEN INDUSTRIES, INC.
601 E. Beardsley Ave. Phone: 219-262-0123
Elkhart, IN 46514 Fax: 219-262-8823
Chm & CEO: Thomas H. Corson
VP HR: James R. Frahm
Employees: 2,750
Jobs Added Last Year: 135 (+5.2%)
Building - mobile homes & RVs

CONSECO, INC.
11825 N. Pennsylvania St. Phone: 317-573-6100
Carmel, IN 46032 Fax: 317-573-2847
Chm, Pres & CEO: Stephen C. Hilbert
VP HR: Dennis J. Dunlap
Employees: 2,860
Jobs Added Last Year: 1,750 (+157.7%)
Insurance - life

CONSOLIDATED PRODUCTS, INC.
36 S. Pennsylvania St. Phone: 317-633-4100
Indianapolis, IN 46204 Fax: 317-633-4105
Pres & CEO: Alan B. Gilman
VP HR: John P. Hawes
Employees: 6,471
Jobs Added Last Year: 323 (+5.3%)
Retail - restaurants (Steak n Shake)

CTS CORPORATION
905 West Blvd. North Phone: 219-293-7511
Elkhart, IN 46514 Fax: 219-293-6146
Chm, Pres & CEO: Joseph P. Walker
VP HR: James L. Cummins
Employees: 4,202
Jobs Added Last Year: 227 (+5.7%)
Electrical components for the automotive, data processing, communications equipment & defense industries

INDIANA

CUMMINS ENGINE COMPANY, INC.
500 Jackson St., PO Box 3005   Phone: 812-377-5000
Columbus, IN 47202-3005   Fax: 812-377-3334
Chm & CEO: James A. Henderson
VP HR: Brenda S. Pitts
Employees: 23,600
Jobs Added Last Year: 200 (+.9%)
Diesel engines for commercial vehicles, marine & industrial uses

ELI LILLY AND COMPANY
Lilly Corporate Center   Phone: 317-276-2000
Indianapolis, IN 46285   Fax: 317-276-2095
Chm & CEO: Randall L. Tobias
VP HR: Pedro P. Granadillo
Employees: 32,700
Jobs Added Last Year: 500 (+1.6%)
Drugs, medical devices, diagnostic products & animal health products

ESSEX GROUP INC.
1601 Wall St.   Phone: 219-461-4000
Ft. Wayne, IN 46802   Fax: 219-461-4150
Pres & CEO: Stanley C. Craft
VP HR: Dominick Lucenta
Employees: 4,000
Jobs Added Last Year: 460 (+13%)
Wire & cable products & electrical insulation

EXCEL INDUSTRIES, INC.
1120 N. Main St.   Phone: 219-264-2131
Elkhart, IN 46514   Fax: 219-264-2136
Chm & CEO: James J. Lohman
Dir HR: Richard R. Rumfelt
Employees: 4,000
Jobs Added Last Year: 900 (+29%)
Automotive & trucking - window systems

FINISH LINE, INC.
3308 N. Mitthoeffer Rd.   Phone: 317-899-1022
Indianapolis, IN 46236   Fax: 317-899-0237
Chm, Pres & CEO: Alan H. Cohen
VP Fin & CFO (HR): Steven J. Schneider
Employees: 2,285
Jobs Added Last Year: 460 (+25.2%)
Retail - apparel & shoes

FORUM GROUP, INC.
8900 Keystone Crossing   Phone: 317-846-0700
Indianapolis, IN 46240   Fax: 317-575-1246
CEO: Mark Pacala
Dir HR: Nancy Connolly
Employees: 4,200
Jobs Added Last Year: 200 (+5%)
Real estate operations

GREAT LAKES CHEMICAL CORPORATION
PO Box 2200   Phone: 317-497-6100
West Lafayette, IN 47906-0200   Fax: 317-497-6234
Pres & CEO: Robert B. McDonald
Dir HR: J. Michael Roberts
Employees: 8,000
Jobs Added Last Year: 1,000 (+14.3%)
Chemicals - specialty

GUIDANT CORPORATION
307 E. McCarty St.   Phone: 317-276-8734
Indianapolis, IN 46225   Fax: 317-276-7488
Pres & CEO: Ronald W. Dollens
VP HR & Bus Dev: James A. Baumgardt
Employees: 4,644
Jobs Added Last Year: 91 (+2%)
Medical products - cardiac rhythm management & coronary artery disease intervention

HILLENBRAND INDUSTRIES, INC.
700 State Rte. 46 East   Phone: 812-934-7000
Batesville, IN 47006-9166   Fax: 812-934-7364
Pres & CEO: W. August Hillenbrand
VP HR: David L. Robertson
Employees: 9,800
Jobs Cut Last Year: 900 (-8.4%)
Diversified operations - hospital beds; caskets (Batesville); security locks (Medeco)

HOLY CROSS HEALTH SYSTEM
3606 E. Jefferson Blvd.   Phone: 219-233-8558
South Bend, IN 46615   Fax: 219-233-8891
Chm: Edward Osborn
VP HR: Dave Dickerson
Employees: 18,360
Jobs Added Last Year: —
Hospitals

An in-depth profile of this company is available by fax. Call 800-510-4452 and use your touch-tone phone to put in the 5-digit code at the prompt. Only $2.95 each with your credit card. See page 12 for more details.

161

INDIANA

INDIANA FEDERAL CORPORATION
56 S. Washington St. Phone: 219-462-4131
Valparaiso, IN 46383 Fax: 219-464-2041
Pres & CEO: Peter R. Candela
VP & Dir HR: Mark Zimmerman
Employees: 311
Jobs Added Last Year: 58 (+22.9%)
Banks - Midwest

LIBERTY HOMES, INC.
1101 Eisenhower Dr. North Phone: 219-533-0431
Goshen, IN 46526 Fax: 219-533-0438
CEO: Edward J. Hussey
No central personnel officer
Employees: 775
Jobs Added Last Year: 125 (+19.2%)
Building - mobile homes & RVs

IRWIN FINANCIAL CORPORATION
500 Washington St. Phone: 812-376-1020
Columbus, IN 47201 Fax: 812-376-1709
Pres & CEO: John A. Nash
VP & HR Dir: Carrie Houston
Employees: 1,180
Jobs Added Last Year: 308 (+35.3%)
Banks - Midwest

LINCOLN NATIONAL CORPORATION
200 E. Berry St. Phone: 219-455-2000
Fort Wayne, IN 46802-2706 Fax: 219-455-5064
Chm & CEO: Ian M. Rolland
SVP & Dir HR: George E. Davis
Employees: 10,286
Jobs Cut Last Year: 1,604 (-13.5%)
Insurance - property & casualty

ITT EDUCATIONAL SERVICES, INC.
5975 Castle Creek Pkwy. N Dr. Phone: 317-594-9499
Indianapolis, IN 46250 Fax: 317-594-4289
Chm, Pres & CEO: Rene R. Champagne
Dir Personnel: Brad Rainier
Employees: 2,497
Jobs Added Last Year: 1,597 (+177.4%)
Schools - technical institutes

MARSH SUPERMARKETS, INC.
9800 Crosspoint Blvd. Phone: 317-594-2100
Indianapolis, IN 46256-3350 Fax: 317-594-2704
Pres & CEO: Don E. Marsh
VP HR: Bruce A. Bain
Employees: 11,300
Jobs Added Last Year: 800 (+7.6%)
Retail - supermarkets (Marsh, LoBill Foods) & convenience stores (Village Pantry)

IWC RESOURCES CORPORATION
1220 Waterway Blvd. Phone: 317-631-3224
Indianapolis, IN 46202 Fax: 317-263-6414
Pres: James T. Morris
VP (HR): Les Williams
Employees: 1,089
Jobs Added Last Year: 185 (+20.5%)
Utility - water supply

MAYFLOWER GROUP, INC.
9998 N. Michigan Rd. Phone: 317-875-1000
Carmel, IN 46032 Fax: 317-875-2214
Chm, Pres & CEO: Michael L. Smith
SVP HR: Simon Morse
Employees: 11,000
Jobs Cut Last Year: 100 (-.9%)
Transportation - home moving services & school transportation services

KIMBALL INTERNATIONAL, INC.
1600 Royal St. Phone: 812-482-1600
Jasper, IN 47549-1001 Fax: 812-482-8012
Pres & CEO: Douglas A. Habig
VP HR: Randy Catt
Employees: 8,140
Jobs Added Last Year: 519 (+6.8%)
Furniture

NATIONAL STEEL CORPORATION
4100 Edison Lakes Pkwy. Phone: 219-273-7000
Mishawaka, IN 46545-3440 Fax: 219-273-7869
Pres & COO: V. John Goodwin
VP HR: Richard P. Coffee
Employees: 9,490
Jobs Cut Last Year: 809 (-7.9%)
Steel - production

INDIANA

NIPSCO INDUSTRIES, INC.
5265 Hohman Ave. Phone: 219-853-5200
Hammond, IN 46320-1775 Fax: 219-647-6073
Chm, Pres & CEO: Gary L. Neale
VP HR: Owen C. Johnson
Employees: 4,286
Jobs Cut Last Year: 161 (-3.6%)
Utility - electric power

PATRICK INDUSTRIES, INC.
1800 S. 14th St., PO Box 638 Phone: 219-294-7511
Elkhart, IN 46515 Fax: 219-522-5213
Chm & Principal Exec Off: Mervin D. Lung
VP (HR): Tom Behr
Employees: 1,203
Jobs Added Last Year: 390 (+48%)
Building products - components for manufactured housing & RVs

PAUL HARRIS STORES, INC.
6003 Guion Rd. Phone: 317-293-3900
Indianapolis, IN 46254 Fax: 317-298-6940
Chm, Pres & CEO (HR): Charlotte G. Fischer
Employees: 2,650
Jobs Added Last Year: 1 (+0%)
Retail - apparel & shoes

ROBINSON NUGENT, INC.
800 E. Eighth St., PO Box 1208 Phone: 812-945-0211
New Albany, IN 47151 Fax: 812-945-0804
Pres & CEO: Larry W. Burke
Dir HR: Michael Schreiweis
Employees: 551
Jobs Added Last Year: 71 (+14.8%)
Electrical connectors

SCHULT HOMES CORPORATION
221 US 20 West, PO Box 151 Phone: 219-825-5881
Middlebury, IN 46540 Fax: 800-955-2355
Chm, Pres & CEO: Walter E. Wells
Dir HR: Mike Worrell
Employees: 2,149
Jobs Added Last Year: 324 (+17.8%)
Building - residential & commercial

SHOE CARNIVAL, INC.
8233 Baumgart Rd. Phone: 812-867-6471
Evansville, IN 47711 Fax: 812-867-3625
Pres & CEO: David H. Russell
VP HR: Susan Hirsch
Employees: 2,300
Jobs Added Last Year: 740 (+47.4%)
Retail - apparel & shoes

SKYLINE CORPORATION
2520 By-Pass Rd., PO Box 743 Phone: 219-294-6521
Elkhart, IN 46515 Fax: 219-293-0693
Chm & CEO: Arthur J. Decio
VP HR: Tom McGillicuddy
Employees: 3,280
Jobs Added Last Year: 560 (+20.6%)
Automotive - mobile homes & RVs

STANT CORPORATION
425 Commerce Dr. Phone: 317-962-6655
Richmond, IN 47374 Fax: 317-962-6866
Pres & CEO: David R. Paridy
SVP (HR): W. Thomas Margetts
Employees: 7,000
Jobs Added Last Year: 4,500 (+180%)
Automotive - gas caps, radiator caps, thermostats & other parts for auto manufacturers & the replacement market

WABASH NATIONAL CORPORATION
1000 Sagamore Pkwy. South Phone: 317-448-1591
Lafayette, IN 47905 Fax: 317-447-9405
Pres & CEO: Donald J. Ehrlich
VP HR: E. Charles Fish
Employees: 2,066
Jobs Added Last Year: 288 (+16.2%)
Automotive & trucking - intermodal truck trailers

IOWA

CASEY'S GENERAL STORES, INC.
One Convenience Blvd. Phone: 515-965-6100
Ankeny, IA 50021-8045 Fax: 515-965-6160
Chm & CEO: Donald F. Lamberti
Dir HR: Bill Walljaster
Employees: 7,273
Jobs Added Last Year: 608 (+9.1%)
Retail - convenience stores

HON INDUSTRIES INC.
414 E. Third St., PO Box 1109 Phone: 319-264-7400
Muscatine, IA 52761-7109 Fax: 319-264-7217
Pres & CEO: Jack D. Michaels
VP HR: Daniel G. DePuydt
Employees: 6,257
Jobs Added Last Year: 331 (+5.6%)
Furniture - office

EMC INSURANCE GROUP INC.
717 Mulberry St. Phone: 515-280-2581
Des Moines, IA 50309 Fax: 515-280-2975
Pres & CEO: Bruce G. Kelley
HR Dir: Doug Zmolek
Employees: 1,558
Jobs Added Last Year: 403 (+34.9%)
Insurance - property & casualty

HY-VEE FOOD STORES, INC.
1801 Osceola Ave. Phone: 515-774-2121
Chariton, IA 50049 Fax: 515-774-7211
Chm & CEO: Ronald D. Pearson
Mgr HR: Jerry Willis
Employees: 30,000
Jobs Added Last Year: —
Retail - supermarkets, drug & convenience stores

FLEXSTEEL INDUSTRIES, INC.
PO Box 877 Phone: 319-556-7730
Dubuque, IA 52004 Fax: 319-556-8345
Pres & CEO: K. Bruce Lauritsen
Assoc Rel Mgr (HR): James Schiltz
Employees: 2,340
Jobs Added Last Year: 240 (+11.4%)
Furniture

IES INDUSTRIES INC.
200 First St. SE Phone: 319-398-4411
Cedar Rapids, IA 52401 Fax: 319-398-4623
Chm, Pres & CEO: Lee Liu
VP HR: Thomas R. Seldon
Employees: 2,792
Jobs Added Last Year: 90 (+3.3%)
Utility - electric power

GREAT LAKES AVIATION LTD.
1965 330th St. Phone: 712-262-1000
Spencer, IA 51301-9211 Fax: 712-262-7215
CEO: Douglas G. Voss
HR Mgr: Juli A. Durda
Employees: 853
Jobs Added Last Year: 216 (+33.9%)
Transportation - airline

LEE ENTERPRISES, INCORPORATED
400 Putnam Bldg., 215 N. Main St. Phone: 319-383-2100
Davenport, IA 52801-1924 Fax: 319-323-9609
Pres & CEO: Richard D. Gottleib
Dir HR: Vito Kurattis
Employees: 4,700
Jobs Added Last Year: 0
Publishing - newspapers; network-affiliated TV stations; graphic arts products for the newspaper industry

HEARTLAND EXPRESS, INC.
2777 Heartland Dr. Phone: 319-645-2728
Coralville, IA 52241 Fax: 319-645-2338
Chm, Pres & Sec: Russell A. Gerdin
VP Mktg (HR): Richard L. Meehan
Employees: 628
Jobs Added Last Year: 81 (+14.8%)
Transportation - truck

MAYTAG CORPORATION
403 W. Fourth St. North Phone: 515-792-8000
Newton, IA 50208 Fax: 515-791-8395
Chm & CEO: Leonard A. Hadley
SVP HR: Jon O. Nicholas
Employees: 20,951
Jobs Cut Last Year: 456 (-2.1%)
Appliances - washers & dryers (Maytag, Admiral); ovens & cooktops (Jenn-Air, Magic Chef); vacuums (Hoover)

IOWA

MIDWEST RESOURCES INC.
666 Grand Ave., PO Box 9244   Phone: 515-242-4300
Des Moines, IA 50306-9244   Fax: 515-281-2981
Chm, Pres & CEO: Russell E. Christiansen
Dir HR: Keith Hartje
Employees: 3,480
Jobs Added Last Year: 475 (+15.8%)
Utility - electric power

THE UNIVERSITY OF IOWA
105 Jessup Hall   Phone: 319-335-0062
Iowa City, IA 52242   Fax: 319-335-2951
Pres: Hunter R. Rawlings III
Dir Personnel: Marvin Lynch
Employees: 22,410
Jobs Added Last Year: –
University

PIONEER HI-BRED INTERNATIONAL, INC.
700 Capital Sq., 400 Locust St.   Phone: 515-248-4800
Des Moines, IA 50309   Fax: 515-245-3650
Chm & Pres: Thomas N. Urban
HR Dir: Karen Johnsen
Employees: 4,847
Jobs Added Last Year: 40 (+.8%)
Agricultural operations - genetic hybrids of corn, sorghum, sunflowers & vegetables

WINNEBAGO INDUSTRIES, INC.
PO Box 152   Phone: 515-582-3535
Forest City, IA 50436   Fax: 515-582-6966
Pres & CEO: Fred Dohrmann
Personnel Dir: John Green
Employees: 2,770
Jobs Added Last Year: 240 (+9.5%)
Automotive - mobile homes, van conversions & RVs

PRINCIPAL FINANCIAL GROUP
711 High St.   Phone: 515-247-5111
Des Moines, IA 50392   Fax: 515-247-5930
Chm & CEO: G. David Hurd
VP HR: Donald Keown
Employees: 13,583
Jobs Added Last Year: 758 (+5.9%)
Insurance - life

YOUNKERS, INC.
Seventh & Walnut Sts.   Phone: 515-244-1112
Des Moines, IA 50397   Fax: 515-246-3170
Chm & CEO: W. Thomas Gould
SVP HR: Tom Amerman
Employees: 8,100
Jobs Added Last Year: 0
Retail - department stores in Iowa & Nebraska

KANSAS

ADVANCED FINANCIAL, INC.
5425 Martindale   Phone: 913-441-2466
Shawnee, KS 66218   Fax: 913-441-3284
Chm & Pres: Norman L. Peterson
Exec Asst HR: Susie Cole
Employees: 71
Jobs Added Last Year: 11 (+18.3%)
Financial - mortgages & related services

APPLEBEE'S INTERNATIONAL, INC.
4551 W. 107th St., Ste. 100   Phone: 913-967-4000
Overland Park, KS 66207-4031   Fax: 913-967-8102
Chm & CEO: Abe J. Gustin, Jr.
EVP & Chief Admin Off (HR): Ronald B. Reck
Employees: 4,600
Jobs Added Last Year: 2,200 (+91.7%)
Retail - restaurants

ATCHISON CASTING CORPORATION
400 S. Fourth St.   Phone: 913-367-2121
Atchison, KS 66002-0188   Fax: 913-367-2130
Chm & CEO: Hugh H. Aiken
VP HR: Gene N. Brackin
Employees: 1,336
Jobs Added Last Year: 667 (+99.7%)
Steel - large castings for trains & other transportation equipment

THE COLEMAN COMPANY, INC.
250 N. St. Francis   Phone: 316-261-3211
Wichita, KS 67202   Fax: 316-261-3400
Chm & CEO: Michael N. Hammes
VP HR: Kathy J. Smith
Employees: 3,275
Jobs Added Last Year: 375 (+12.9%)
Leisure & recreational products - outdoor & camping equipment

FOURTH FINANCIAL CORPORATION
100 N. Broadway   Phone: 316-261-4444
Wichita, KS 67202   Fax: 316-261-2111
Chm & CEO: Darrell G. Knudson
VP (HR): Kay Walton
Employees: 2,666
Jobs Added Last Year: 611 (+29.7%)
Banks - Midwest

KOCH INDUSTRIES, INC.
4111 E. 37th St. North   Phone: 316-832-5500
Wichita, KS 67220   Fax: 316-832-5739
Chm & CEO: Charles G. Koch
Dir HR: R. A. Pohlman
Employees: 12,000
Jobs Added Last Year: 0
Oil & gas - integrated; chemicals; minerals; agriculture

LABONE, INC.
10310 W. 84th Terrace   Phone: 913-888-8397
Lenexa, KS 66214   Fax: 913-888-0771
Chm & CEO: Bert H. Hood
VP HR: Judy Von Feldt
Employees: 531
Jobs Added Last Year: 71 (+15.4%)
Medical & dental supplies

LONE STAR STEAKHOUSE & SALOON
224 E. Douglas, Ste. 700   Phone: 316-264-8899
Wichita, KS 67202   Fax: 316-264-5988
Chm & CEO: Jamie B. Coulter
VP Personnel Dev: Jeffrey Johnson
Employees: 5,300
Jobs Added Last Year: –
Retail - steakhouses

OTR EXPRESS INC.
804 N. Meadowbrook Dr.   Phone: 913-829-1616
Olathe, KS 66062   Fax: 913-829-0622
Pres: William P. Ward
VP Compensation & Ben: Janice K. Ward
Employees: 450
Jobs Added Last Year: 134 (+42.4%)
Transportation - truck

PURITAN-BENNETT CORPORATION
9401 Indian Creek Pkwy.   Phone: 913-661-0444
Overland Park, KS 66210   Fax: 913-661-0234
Pres & CEO: Burton A. Dole, Jr.
VP HR: Fran Stowell
Employees: 2,700
Jobs Added Last Year: 100 (+3.8%)
Medical instruments - blood-gas monitors & respiratory monitoring systems (CliniVision) for aircraft

KANSAS

SEABOARD CORPORATION
9000 W. 67th St., PO Box 2972   Phone: 913-676-8800
Shawnee Mission, KS 66201   Fax: 617-244-5463
Pres: H. Harry Bresky
Dir HR: Doug Schult
Employees: 10,891
Jobs Cut Last Year: 1,982 (-15.4%)
Food - meat products

VT INC.
8500 Shawnee Mission Pkwy.   Phone: 913-432-6400
Merriam, KS 66202   Fax: 913-789-1039
Co-CEO: Cecil Van Tuyl
VP Personnel: John A. Morford
Employees: 3,682
Jobs Added Last Year: 1,182 (+47.3%)
Retail - auto, aircraft & boat dealerships

SPRINT CORPORATION [11560]
2330 Shawnee Mission Pkwy.   Phone: 913-624-3000
Westwood, KS 66205   Fax: 913-624-3281
Chm & CEO: William T. Esrey
SVP HR: I. Benjamin Watson
Employees: 50,000
Jobs Cut Last Year: 2,200 (-4.2%)
Telecommunications services - #3 US long distance carrier; cellular & local telephone services

YELLOW CORPORATION [15192]
10777 Barkley Ave.   Phone: 913-967-4300
Overland Park, KS 66207   Fax: 913-344-3433
Pres & CEO: George E. Powell III
Dir Emp Ben: Harold Marshall
Employees: 35,000
Jobs Added Last Year: 8,200 (+30.6%)
Transportation - trucks

▼ **Med Search** http://www.medsearch.com

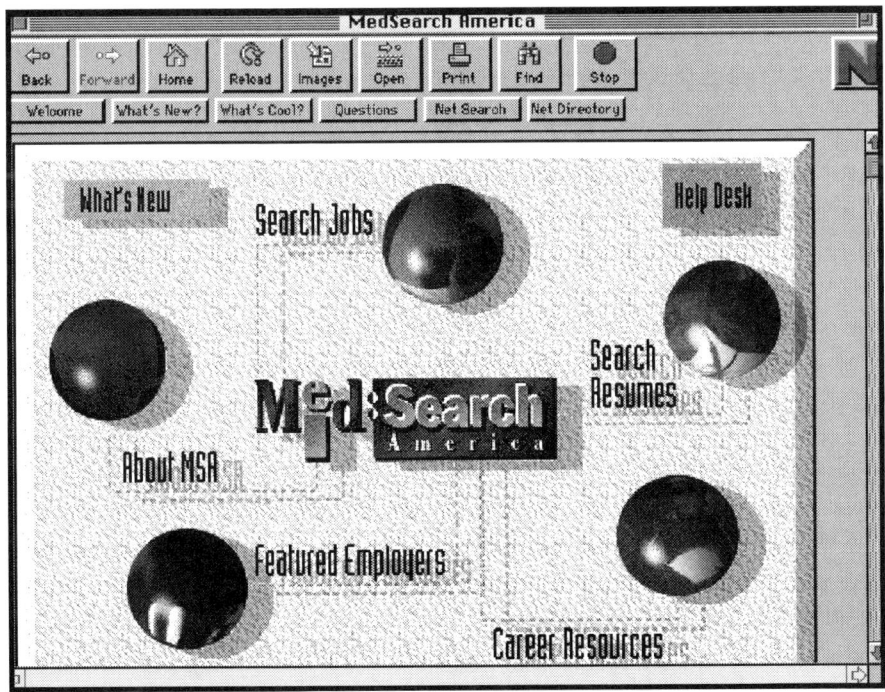

KENTUCKY

ASHLAND, INC.
1000 Ashland Dr. Phone: 606-329-3333
Russell, KY 41169 Fax: 606-329-5274
Chm & CEO: John R. Hall
Admin VP HR: Philip W. Block
Employees: 31,600
Jobs Cut Last Year: 200 (-.6%)
Oil refining & marketing

LONG JOHN SILVER'S RESTAURANTS, INC.
101 Jerrico Dr. Phone: 606-263-6000
Lexington, KY 40579 Fax: 606-263-6680
Pres & CEO: Clyde E. Culp
VP HR: Wayne Hougland
Employees: 18,100
Jobs Cut Last Year: 1,145 (-5.9%)
Retail - seafood restaurants

BROWN-FORMAN CORPORATION
850 Dixie Hwy. Phone: 502-585-1100
Louisville, KY 40210 Fax: 502-774-7876
Pres & CEO: Owsley Brown II
SVP, Exec Dir HR & Info Svcs: Russell Buzby
Employees: 7,100
Jobs Added Last Year: 400 (+6%)
Beverages - alcoholic (Jack Daniels, Korbel); china & crystal (Lennox & Gorham); luggage (Hartmann)

PAPA JOHN'S INTERNATIONAL, INC.
11492 Bluegrass Pkwy. Phone: 502-266-5200
Louisville, KY 40299-2334 Fax: 502-266-2925
Chm & CEO: John H. Schnatter
VP HR: Carol A. Trask
Employees: 2,102
Jobs Added Last Year: 1,087 (+107.1%)
Retail - restaurants

COLUMBIA/HCA HEALTHCARE CORP.
201 W. Main St. Phone: 502-572-2000
Louisville, KY 40202 Fax: 502-572-2120
Pres & CEO: Richard L. Scott
SVP HR: Neil C. Hemphill
Employees: 131,600
Jobs Cut Last Year: 2,100 (-1.6%)
Hospitals - nation's largest for-profit hospital chain & largest operator of outpatient surgery centers

PROVIDIAN CORPORATION
400 W. Market St. Phone: 502-560-2000
Louisville, KY 40202 Fax: 502-560-2550
Chm, Pres & CEO: Irving W. Bailey II
SVP HR & Corp Comm: John Rogers
Employees: 9,360
Jobs Added Last Year: 60 (+.6%)
Insurance - underwriters of life & annuity, accident & health & property & casualty insurance

DOLLAR GENERAL CORPORATION
427 Beech St. Phone: 502-237-5444
Scottsville, KY 42164 Fax: 502-237-3213
Chm, Pres & CEO: Cal Turner, Jr.
VP Dev (HR): Walter Carter
Employees: 10,300
Jobs Added Last Year: 2,300 (+28.8%)
Retail - discount & variety

RALLY'S HAMBURGERS, INC.
10002 Shelbyville Rd., Ste. 150 Phone: 502-245-8900
Louisville, KY 40223 Fax: 502-245-7407
Pres, CEO & COO: Wayne M. Albritton
VP Admin (HR): Butch Dulaney
Employees: 7,100
Jobs Added Last Year: 600 (+9.2%)
Retail - double drive-through hamburger restaurants

HUMANA INC.
The Humana Bldg., 500 W. Main St. Phone: 502-580-1000
Louisville, KY 40202 Fax: 502-580-3615
Chm & CEO: David A. Jones
VP HR: Robert A. Horrar
Employees: 65,800
Jobs Cut Last Year: 4,700 (-6.7%)
Health maintenance organization

RES-CARE, INC.
1300 Embassy Sq. Phone: 502-491-3464
Louisville, KY 40299-1842 Fax: 502-491-4825
Pres & CEO: Ronald G. Geary
VP HR: Diana Fornear
Employees: 5,000
Jobs Added Last Year: 1,094 (+28%)
Training centers for the physically & mentally disabled; Job Corps training centers

KENTUCKY

STEEL TECHNOLOGIES INC.
15415 Shelbyville Rd.   Phone: 502-245-2110
Louisville, KY 40245   Fax: 502-245-3821
Pres & CEO: Merwin J. Ray
HR Mgr: Peyton Badgett
Employees: 424
Jobs Added Last Year: 70 (+19.8%)
Metal processing & fabrication

THE UNIVERSITY OF KENTUCKY
111 Administration Bldg.   Phone: 606-257-9000
Lexington, KY 40506   Fax: 606-257-4000
Pres: Charles T. Wethington,, Jr.
Dir HR: James Webb
Employees: 12,021
Jobs Added Last Year: —
University

TRANS FINANCIAL BANCORP, INC.
500 E. Main St.   Phone: 502-781-5000
Bowling Green, KY 42101   Fax: 502-843-1016
Chm & Pres: Douglas M. Lester
SVP HR: Roger Lundin
Employees: 800
Jobs Added Last Year: 207 (+34.9%)
Banks - Southeast

VENCOR, INC.
400 W. Market St., Ste. 3300   Phone: 502-569-7300
Louisville, KY 40202   Fax: 502-569-7499
Pres & CEO: W. Bruce Lunsford
Dir HR: Cecilia Hagan
Employees: 3,680
Jobs Added Last Year: 2,045 (+125.1%)
Hospitals - long-term care for the chronically ill

▼ **Papyrus** http://www.Britain.EU.net/vendor/jobs/main.html

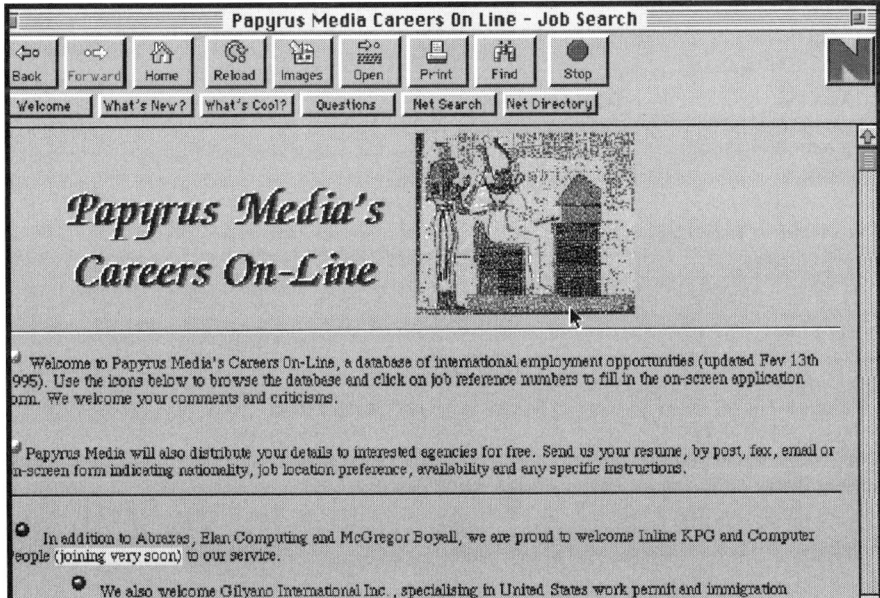

LOUISIANA

ALBEMARLE CORPORATION
451 Florida Blvd. Phone: 504-388-8180
Baton Rouge, LA 70801 Fax: 504-388-8065
Chm & CEO: F. D. Gottwald, Jr.
VP HR: Fred Speno
Employees: 3,700
Jobs Cut Last Year: 100 (-2.6%)
Chemicals - ibuprofen & chemicals used to produce plastics, detergents, pharmaceuticals & synthetic lubricants

CAMPO ELECTRONICS
800 Distributors Row Phone: 504-733-4522
Harahan, LA 70123-3210 Fax: 504-736-8503
Chm, Pres & CEO: Anthony P. Campo
Dir HR: Bonnie Kinerd
Employees: 890
Jobs Added Last Year: 190 (+27.1%)
Retail - name-brand consumer electronics, major appliances & home office technology

CENTURY TELEPHONE ENTERPRISES 10315
100 Century Park Dr. Phone: 318-388-9500
Monroe, LA 71203 Fax: 318-388-9651
VC, Pres & CEO: Glen F. Post III
VP HR: Ray B. Finney
Employees: 2,800
Jobs Added Last Year: 422 (+17.7%)
Utility - telephone

ENTERGY CORPORATION 10524
225 Baronne St. Phone: 504-529-5262
New Orleans, LA 70112 Fax: 504-569-4265
Chm & CEO: Edwin Lupberger
Manager Emp Rel: Joseph Hotard
Employees: 16,679
Jobs Added Last Year: 4,222 (+33.9%)
Utility - electric power

FREEPORT-MCMORAN INC.
1615 Poydras St. Phone: 504-582-4000
New Orleans, LA 70112 Fax: 504-582-1847
Chm & CEO: James R. Moffett
Dir HR: Robert Gettys
Employees: 7,658
Jobs Cut Last Year: 299 (-3.8%)
Fertilizers

K&B
K&B Plaza, Lee Circle Phone: 504-586-1234
New Orleans, LA 70130 Fax: 504-585-4535
CEO & Chm: Sydney J. Besthoff III
VP Ops (HR): Bruce Fiegenschue
Employees: 4,500
Jobs Added Last Year: 300 (+7.1%)
Retail - drug stores

LOUISIANA LAND AND EXPLORATION COMPANY
909 Poydras St. Phone: 504-566-6500
New Orleans, LA 70112 Fax: 504-566-6891
Chm, Pres & CEO: H. Leighton Steward
Dir HR: C. A. Zackary
Employees: 827
Jobs Added Last Year: 118 (+16.6%)
Oil & gas - integrated

MCDERMOTT INTERNATIONAL, INC. 10972
1450 Poydras St. Phone: 504-587-5400
New Orleans, LA 70112-6050 Fax: 504-587-6433
Chm & CEO: Robert E. Howson
Dir HR: L. J. Sannino
Employees: 23,000
Jobs Cut Last Year: 3,000 (-11.5%)
Diversified operations - power generation systems & equipment; marine construction services

PICCADILLY CAFETERIAS, INC.
3232 Sherwood Forest Blvd. Phone: 504-293-9440
Baton Rouge, LA 70816 Fax: 504-296-8370
Chm: Paul W. Murrill
EVP HR: Joe Polito
Employees: 7,300
Jobs Cut Last Year: 300 (-3.9%)
Retail - restaurants

PLAYERS INTERNATIONAL INC.
800 Bilbo St. Phone: 318-437-1560
Lake Charles, LA 70601 Fax: 318-437-1565
Chm & CEO: Edward J. Fishman
No central personnel officer
Employees: 1,955
Jobs Added Last Year: 1,064 (+119.4%)
Leisure & recreational services - riverboat casinos

LOUISIANA

RAMSAY HEALTH CARE, INC.
639 Loyola Ave., Ste. 1700   Phone: 504-525-2505
New Orleans, LA 70113   Fax: 504-585-0505
VC & CEO: Gregory H. Browne
Dir HR: Shannon Dishiara
Employees: 2,273
Jobs Added Last Year: 418 (+22.5%)
Health care - psychiatric services

STEWART ENTERPRISES, INC.
110 Veterans Memorial Blvd.   Phone: 504-837-5880
Metairie, LA 70005   Fax: 504-835-5833
VC & CEO: Joseph P. Henican III
Dir Personnel & Admin: Edward L. Baucom
Employees: 5,000
Jobs Added Last Year: 1,400 (+38.9%)
Funeral services, cemeteries & mausoleums

SCHWEGMANN GIANT SUPER MARKETS
PO Box 26099   Phone: 504-947-9921
New Orleans, LA 92121   Fax: 504-942-5407
Chm, Pres & CEO: John F. Schwegmann
Dir HR: Lee Janies
Employees: 2,315
Jobs Added Last Year: 1,374 (+146%)
Retail - supermarkets

TIDEWATER INC.
1440 Canal St.   Phone: 504-568-1010
New Orleans, LA 70112   Fax: 504-566-4582
Chm, Pres & CEO: William C. O'Malley
VP Gen Counsel (HR): Cliff Laborde
Employees: 6,900
Jobs Added Last Year: 36 (+.5%)
Oil & gas - offshore drilling

SHAW GROUP INC.
11100 Mead Rd.   Phone: 504-296-1140
Baton Rouge, LA 70816   Fax: 504-296-1199
Chm, Pres & CEO: James M. Bernhard, Jr.
HR Dir: P. J. Bourgeois
Employees: 1,300
Jobs Added Last Year: 200 (+18.2%)
Steel - pipes & tubes

TURNER INDUSTRIES, LTD.
8687 United Plaza Blvd., Ste. 500   Phone: 504-922-5050
Baton Rouge, LA 70809   Fax: 504-355-9270
Chm & CEO: Bert S. Turner
EVP HR: Thomas Turner
Employees: 6,500
Jobs Added Last Year: —
Construction - industrial construction & maintenance, including antipollution upgrades to refineries & chemical plants

MAINE

BATH IRON WORKS CORPORATION
700 Washington St. Phone: 207-443-3311
Bath, ME 04530 Fax: 207-442-1567
Pres: Duane D. Fitzgerald
HR: Stephen Wilson
Employees: 9,000
Jobs Added Last Year: 0
Boat building

L.L. BEAN, INC.
Casco St. Phone: 207-865-4761
Freeport, ME 04033 Fax: 207-865-6738
Pres & CEO: Leon A. Gorman
VP HR: Bob Peixotto
Employees: 3,500
Jobs Added Last Year: 0
Retail - mail order outdoor sporting goods & clothing

HANNAFORD BROS. CO. INC.
145 Pleasant Hill Rd. Phone: 207-883-2911
Scarborough, ME 04074 Fax: 207-885-3165
Pres & CEO: Hugh G. Farrington
SVP HR: Michael J. Strout
Employees: 17,000
Jobs Added Last Year: 2,500 (+17.2%)
Retail - supermarkets

UNUM CORPORATION
2211 Congress St. Phone: 207-770-2211
Portland, ME 04122 Fax: 207-770-6933
Chm, Pres & CEO: James F. Orr II
SVP HR Division: Terry P. Cohen
Employees: 7,200
Jobs Added Last Year: 1,440 (+25%)
Insurance - multiline & misc.

IDEXX LABORATORIES, INC.
One IDEXX Dr. Phone: 207-856-0300
Westbrook, ME 04092 Fax: 207-856-0346
Chm & CEO: David E. Shaw
Dir HR: Jo Braley
Employees: 374
Jobs Added Last Year: 56 (+17.6%)
Biomedical & genetic products - biodetection systems

MARYLAND

BALTIMORE GAS AND ELECTRIC COMPANY
Charles Center Phone: 410-234-5000
Baltimore, MD 21201 Fax: 410-234-5126
Pres & CEO: Christian H. Poindexter
VP Gen Svcs (HR): John Files
Employees: 10,018
Jobs Cut Last Year: 83 (-.8%)
Utility - electric power

COSMETIC CENTER, INC.
8839 Greenwood Place Phone: 301-497-6800
Savage, MD 20763 Fax: 301-497-6632
CEO: Mark S. Weinstein
No central personnel officer
Employees: 1,090
Jobs Added Last Year: 175 (+19.1%)
Cosmetics & toiletries

THE BLACK & DECKER CORPORATION
701 E. Joppa Rd. Phone: 410-716-3900
Towson, MD 21286 Fax: 410-716-2933
Chm, Pres & CEO: Nolan D. Archibald
VP HR: Leonard A. Strom
Employees: 37,300
Jobs Cut Last Year: 1,500 (-3.9%)
Tools - power tools, small appliances & hardware

CROWN BOOKS CORPORATION
3300 75th Ave. Phone: 301-731-1200
Landover, MD 20785-1599 Fax: 301-731-1340
Pres & CEO: Glenn E. Hemmerle
VP HR: Dan Garcia
Employees: 3,010
Jobs Added Last Year: 535 (+21.6%)
Retail - bookstores (#3 chain in the US)

CATERAIR INTERNATIONAL CORP.
6550 Rock Spring Dr. Phone: 301-897-7800
Bethesda, MD 20817 Fax: 301-897-7893
Chm, Pres & CEO: Daniel J. Altobello
SVP HR: David B. Workman
Employees: 21,000
Jobs Cut Last Year: 850 (-3.9%)
Food - preparation & distribution of airline meals

DART GROUP CORPORATION
3300 75th Ave. Phone: 301-731-1200
Landover, MD 20785 Fax: 301-731-1340
Chm: Herbert H. Haft
No central personnel officer
Employees: 11,170
Jobs Added Last Year: 1,370 (+14%)
Retail - discount auto parts (Trak Auto); bookstores (Crown Books); supermarkets (50% of Shoppers Food Warehouse)

CLARK ENTERPRISES, INC.
7500 Old Georgetown Rd. Phone: 301-657-7100
Bethesda, MD 20814 Fax: 301-657-7263
Chm & CEO: A. James Clark
Dir Compensation & Ben: Andrea Danko-Koenig
Employees: 5,000
Jobs Added Last Year: 0
Diversified operations - construction; communications; real estate

DAVCO RESTAURANTS INC.
1657 Crofton Blvd. Phone: 410-721-3770
Crofton, MD 21114 Fax: 410-793-0754
Chm, Pres & CEO: Ronald D. Kirstien
SVP HR: Richard H. Borchers
Employees: 7,000
Jobs Added Last Year: 1,500 (+27.3%)
Retail - restaurants (#1 Wendy's franchisee)

COMSAT CORPORATION
6560 Rock Spring Dr. Phone: 301-214-3000
Bethesda, MD 20817 Fax: 301-214-7100
CEO: Bruce L. Crockett
VP HR & Organizational Dev: Steven F. Bell
Employees: 2,800
Jobs Added Last Year: 1,155 (+70.2%)
Telecommunications services - communications satellite services

DIGICON
6903 Rockledge Dr., Ste. 600 Phone: 301-564-6400
Bethesda, MD 20817 Fax: 301-564-6076
Pres & CEO: John J. Wu
Dir HR: David L. Vernon
Employees: 380
Jobs Added Last Year: 115 (+43.4%)
Computers - programming, software development & network services

MARYLAND

F & E RESOURCE SYSTEMS TECHNOLOGY, INC.
5800 Chemical Rd.   Phone: 410-354-3000
Baltimore, MD 21226   Fax: 410-354-3110
Chm, Pres & CEO: Ronald W. Pickett
Office Mgr (HR): Lydia Davis
Employees: 110
Jobs Added Last Year: 93 (+547.1%)
Pollution control - waste recycling, incineration & composting

INTEGRATED HEALTH SERVICES, INC.
10065 Red Run Blvd.   Phone: 410-998-8400
Owings Mills, MD 21117   Fax: 410-998-8714
Chm & CEO: Robert N. Elkins
VP HR: Jan Zdanis
Employees: 22,000
Jobs Added Last Year: 11,100 (+101.8%)
Medical services - subacute & postacute health care services

GIANT FOOD INC.
6300 Sheriff Rd.   Phone: 301-341-4100
Landover, MD 20785   Fax: 301-341-4804
Chm & CEO: Israel Cohen
SVP Labor Rel & Personnel: Roger D. Olson
Employees: 24,500
Jobs Added Last Year: 800 (+3.4%)
Retail - supermarkets in Washington, DC & Baltimore metropolitan areas

THE JOHNS HOPKINS UNIVERSITY INC.
3400 N. Charles St.   Phone: 410-516-8000
Baltimore, MD 21218   Fax: 410-516-8900
Pres: William C. Richardson
VP HR: James R. Jones III
Employees: 17,397
Jobs Added Last Year: –
University

HANGER ORTHOPEDIC GROUP, INC.
8200 Wisconsin Ave.   Phone: 301-986-0701
Bethesda, MD 20814   Fax: 301-986-0702
CEO: Ronald J. Manganiello
Dir HR: Ada Brady
Employees: 600
Jobs Added Last Year: 100 (+20%)
Medical products - prosthetic & orthotic products & services

LEGG MASON, INC.
111 S. Calvert St.   Phone: 410-539-0000
Baltimore, MD 21202   Fax: 410-539-4096
Chm, Pres & CEO: Raymond A. Mason
VP HR: Gail Reichard
Employees: 2,652
Jobs Added Last Year: 216 (+8.9%)
Financial - investment bankers

HECHINGER COMPANY
3500 Pennsy Dr.   Phone: 301-341-1000
Landover, MD 20785-1691   Fax: 301-925-3906
Pres & CEO: John W. Hechinger, Jr.
SVP HR: Carol A. Stevens
Employees: 18,000
Jobs Added Last Year: 1,000 (+5.9%)
Building products - retail

LOCKHEED MARTIN CORPORATION
6801 Rockledge Dr.   Phone: 301-897-6000
Bethesda, MD 20817-1877   Fax: 301-897-6704
Chm & CEO: Daniel M. Tellep
VP HR: Robert B. Corlett
Employees: 24,100
Jobs Added Last Year: 35,300 (+21.6%)
Aerospace - missiles & space systems, aeronautical systems & technology services

HOST MARRIOTT CORPORATION
10400 Fernwood Rd.   Phone: 301-380-9000
Bethesda, MD 20817   Fax: 301-897-9014
Pres & CEO: Stephen F. Bollenbach
SVP HR: Noel Ferguson
Employees: 24,000
Jobs Added Last Year: 1,000 (+4.3%)
Hotel ownership; food & merchandise concessions

MANOR CARE, INC.
10750 Columbia Pike   Phone: 301-681-9400
Silver Spring, MD 20901   Fax: 301-905-4062
Chm, Pres & CEO: Stewart Bainum, Jr.
SVP HR: Charles A. Shields
Employees: 24,100
Jobs Added Last Year: 1,100 (+4.8%)
Nursing homes; hotel & motel franchisor (Clarion, Comfort, Econo Lodge, Friendship, Quality, Rodeway & Sleep Inns)

MARYLAND

MARRIOTT INTERNATIONAL, INC.
10400 Fernwood Rd. Phone: 301-380-3000
Bethesda, MD 20817 Fax: 301-897-9014
Chm, Pres & CEO: J.W. "Bill" Marriott, Jr.
SVP HR: Clifford J. Ehrlich
Employees: 163,440
Jobs Cut Last Year: 2,560 (-1.5%)
Hotels & motels (Courtyard, Fairfield Inn, Marriott & Residence Inn)

MID ATLANTIC MEDICAL SERVICES INC.
4 Taft Ct. Phone: 301-294-5140
Rockville, MD 20850 Fax: 301-762-1430
Chm, CEO & Pres: George T. Jochum
Sr. Dir HR: Gloria Stem
Employees: 726
Jobs Added Last Year: 253 (+53.5%)
Health care - outpatient & home

MCCORMICK & COMPANY, INC.
18 Loveton Circle Phone: 410-771-7301
Sparks, MD 21152-6000 Fax: 410-771-7462
Pres & CEO: H. Eugene Blattman
VP HR: Karen D. Weatherholtz
Employees: 8,000
Jobs Cut Last Year: 600 (-7%)
Food - seasonings & flavorings; plastic packaging

PERDUE FARMS INCORPORATED
PO Box 1537 Phone: 410-543-3000
Salisbury, MD 21801 Fax: 410-543-3874
Chm & CEO: James A. Perdue
VP HR: Tom Moyers
Employees: 13,800
Jobs Added Last Year: 500 (+3.8%)
Food - poultry processing

MERCANTILE BANKSHARES CORPORATION
2 Hopkins Plaza Phone: 410-237-5900
Baltimore, MD 21203 Fax: 410-237-5854
Chm & CEO: H. Furlong Baldwin
VP (HR): Hal E. Hamil
Employees: 2,713
Jobs Cut Last Year: 11 (-.4%)
Banks - Northeast

PHH CORPORATION
11333 McCormick Rd. Phone: 410-771-3600
Hunt Valley, MD 21031-1000 Fax: 410-771-1123
Chm, Pres & CEO: Robert D. Kunisch
VP HR, Gen Counsel & Asst Sec: Samuel H. Wright
Employees: 4,930
Jobs Added Last Year: 130 (+2.7%)
Leasing

MERRY-GO-ROUND ENTERPRISES
3300 Fashion Way Phone: 410-538-1000
Joppa, MD 21085 Fax: 410-538-1001
Chm & CEO: Thomas Shull
VP HR: Jeffrey A. Austin
Employees: 14,970
Jobs Added Last Year: 1,059 (+7.6%)
Retail - apparel stores (Merry-Go-Round, Chess King, Cignal, Dejaiz & Atttivo)

RWD TECHNOLOGIES, INC.
10480 Little Patuxent Pkwy. Phone: 410-730-4377
Columbia, MD 21044-3530 Fax: 410-964-0039
Pres: Robert Deutsch
Dir HR: James Sinclair
Employees: 332
Jobs Added Last Year: 108 (+48.2%)
Computers - training & documentation services, performance support & manufacturing production systems

MICROS SYSTEMS, INC.
12000 Baltimore Ave. Phone: 301-210-6000
Beltsville, MD 20705-1291 Fax: 301-210-3334
Pres & CEO: A. L. Giannopoulous
Mgr HR: Cathy Rensel
Employees: 385
Jobs Added Last Year: 86 (+28.8%)
Business services point-of-sale & property management information systems

RYLAND GROUP, INC.
11000 Broken Land Pkwy. Phone: 410-715-7000
Columbia, MD 21044 Fax: 410-715-7909
Chm, Pres & CEO: R. Chad Dreier
SVP HR: Robert M. Paul
Employees: 3,270
Jobs Added Last Year: 176 (+5.7%)
Building - residential & commercial

MARYLAND

SHOPPERS FOOD WAREHOUSE CORP.
4600 Forbes Blvd. Phone: 301-306-8600
Lanham, MD 20706 Fax: 301-306-9600
Chm, Pres & CEO: Kenneth Herman
Exec Dir HR: Steve Niven
Employees: 3,900
Jobs Added Last Year: 231 (+6.3%)
Retail - discount supermarkets

THE UNIVERSITY OF MARYLAND SYSTEM
3300 Metzerott Rd. Phone: 301-445-1905
Adelphi, MD 20783 Fax: 301-445-2761
Chancellor: Donald N. Langenberg
Dir HR: Karen Farber
Employees: 20,000
Jobs Added Last Year: –
University

SUNBELT BEVERAGE CORPORATION
2330 W. Joppa Rd., Ste. 330 Phone: 410-832-7740
Lutherville, MD 21093 Fax: 410-832-7730
Pres & CEO: Charles E. Andrews
Dir HR: Ronald Meliker
Employees: 1,700
Jobs Added Last Year: –
Beverages - wine & spirits

USF&G CORPORATION
100 Light St. Phone: 410-547-3000
Baltimore, MD 21202 Fax: 410-625-5682
Chm, Pres & CEO: Norman P. Blake, Jr.
SVP HR: Amy P. Marks
Employees: 6,500
Jobs Cut Last Year: 1,000 (-13.3%)
Insurance - property & casualty & life

T. ROWE PRICE ASSOCIATES, INC.
100 E. Pratt St. Phone: 410-547-2000
Baltimore, MD 21202 Fax: 410-385-2026
Mng Dir, Pres & CEO: George J. Collins
Dir HR: Andy Goresh
Employees: 1,665
Jobs Added Last Year: 127 (+8.3%)
Financial - investment management (mutual funds)

WASHINGTON HOMES, INC.
1802 Brightseat Rd. Phone: 301-772-8900
Landover, MD 20785-4235 Fax: 301-772-1380
CEO: Geaton A. DeCesaris, Jr.
No central personnel officer
Employees: 304
Jobs Added Last Year: 88 (+40.7%)
Building - residential & commercial

UNC INC.
175 Admiral Cochrane Dr. Phone: 410-266-7333
Annapolis, MD 21401-7394 Fax: 410-266-5706
Chm, Pres & CEO: Dan A. Colussy
VP HR: Gerald J. Knapp
Employees: 6,430
Jobs Added Last Year: 3,047 (+90.1%)
Aerospace - aircraft equipment

MASSACHUSETTS

ABIOMED, INC.
33 Cherry Hill Dr.   Phone: 508-777-5410
Danvers, MA 01923   Fax: 508-777-8411
Chm: David M. Lederman
VP Fin & Admin (HR): John Farrow
Employees: 81
Jobs Added Last Year: 13 (+19.1%)
Medical & dental instruments - cardiac assist devices & periodontal screening systems

ADVANTAGEHEALTH CORPORATION
304 Cambridge Rd.   Phone: 617-935-2500
Woburn, MA 01801   Fax: 617-935-7451
Chm & CEO: Raymond J. Dunn III
Dir HR: Gary Pollard
Employees: 4,000
Jobs Added Last Year: 900 (+29%)
Health care - outpatient & home

AEROVOX, INC.
370 Faunce Corner Rd.   Phone: 508-995-8000
North Dartmouth, MA 02747-1287   Fax: 508-994-9635
Chm, Pres & CEO: Clifford H. Tuttle
Dir HR: Frank Zych
Employees: 932
Jobs Added Last Year: 148 (+18.9%)
Electrical components - capacitors

ALLMERICA FINANCIAL
440 Lincoln St.   Phone: 508-855-1000
Worcester, MA 01653   Fax: 508-853-6332
Pres & CEO: John F. O'Brien
VP HR: Bruce C. Anderson
Employees: 3,429
Jobs Added Last Year: —
Insurance - life

ALLMERICA PROPERTY & CASUALTY COS., INC.
440 Lincoln St.   Phone: 508-855-1000
Worcester, MA 01653   Fax: 508-856-9092
Pres & CEO: John F. O'Brien
Dir HR: Ellen Beerzen
Employees: 4,700
Jobs Added Last Year: 2,130 (+82.9%)
Insurance - property & casualty

ALPHA-BETA TECHNOLOGY, INC.
One Innovation Dr.   Phone: 508-798-6900
Worcester, MA 01605   Fax: 508-754-2579
CEO: Spiro Jamas
VP HR: Ed Fiander
Employees: 125
Jobs Added Last Year: 54 (+76.1%)
Drugs

AMERICAN BILTRITE INC.
57 River St.   Phone: 617-237-6655
Wellesley Hills, MA 02181   Fax: 617-237-6880
Chm & CEO: Roger S. Marcus
VP Fin & CFO (HR): Gilbert K. Gailius
Employees: 600
Jobs Added Last Year: 100 (+20%)
Building products

AMERICAN MEDICAL RESPONSE, INC.
67 Batterymarch St.   Phone: 617-261-1600
Boston, MA 02110   Fax: 617-261-1610
Chm, Pres & CEO: Paul M. Verrochi
Corp Dir HR: David B. Stiffler
Employees: 4,388
Jobs Added Last Year: 2,168 (+97.7%)
Medical services - emergency & nonemergency transport services

ANALOG DEVICES, INC.
One Technology Way, PO Box 9106   Phone: 617-329-4700
Norwood, MA 02062-9106   Fax: 617-326-8703
Chm & CEO: Ray Stata
VP HR: Ross Brown
Employees: 5,300
Jobs Added Last Year: 100 (+1.9%)
Electrical components - semiconductors for telecommunications applications

APPLIED EXTRUSION TECHNOLOGIES, INC.
96 Swampscott Rd.   Phone: 508-744-8000
Salem, MA 01970   Fax: 508-744-4464
CEO: Thomas E. Williams
HR Mgr: Kay Ywuc
Employees: 1,100
Jobs Added Last Year: 838 (+319.8%)
Rubber & plastic products

MASSACHUSETTS

APPLIED SCIENCE & TECHNOLOGY INC.
35 Cabot Rd.   Phone: 617-933-5560
Woburn, MA 01801   Fax: 617-933-0750
Chm, Pres & CEO: Richard S. Post
CFO (HR): John M. Tarrh
Employees: 93
Jobs Added Last Year: 23 (+32.9%)
Machinery - microwave power & plasma generators; thin film equipment for the production of semiconductors

ARCH COMMUNICATIONS GROUP, INC.
1800 W. Park Dr., Ste. 250   Phone: 508-898-0962
Westborough, MA 01581   Fax: 508-836-3626
Chm, Pres & CEO: C. Edward Baker, Jr.
Exec Asst to CEO (HR): Molly Dubois
Employees: 580
Jobs Added Last Year: 148 (+34.3%)
Telecommunications services - paging systems

ARROW AUTOMOTIVE INDUSTRIES, INC.
3 Speen St.   Phone: 508-872-3711
Framingham, MA 01701   Fax: 508-872-2045
Pres & CEO: Jim L. Osment
VP HR: Terry Reynolds
Employees: 1,656
Jobs Added Last Year: 114 (+7.4%)
Automotive & trucking - replacement parts

ARTHUR D. LITTLE INC.
25 Acorn Park   Phone: 617-498-5000
Cambridge, MA 02140   Fax: 617-498-7200
Pres & CEO: Charles R. LaMantia
SVP (HR): Alan Friedman
Employees: 2,600
Jobs Added Last Year: 200 (+8.3%)
Technology & product development; environmental, health & safety consulting

AUGAT INC.
89 Forbes Blvd., PO Box 448   Phone: 508-543-4300
Mansfield, MA 02048   Fax: 508-543-7019
Pres & CEO: William R. Fenoglio
Corp VP HR: Richard J. Eaton
Employees: 3,900
Jobs Cut Last Year: 200 (-4.9%)
Electrical connectors

AVID TECHNOLOGY, INC.
One Park West   Phone: 508-640-6789
Tewksbury, MA 01876   Fax: 508-640-1366
Pres & CEO: Curt A. Rawley
VP HR: Judith M. Oppenheim
Employees: 408
Jobs Added Last Year: 165 (+67.9%)
Computers - digital software-based video & audio editing systems

BACHMAN INFORMATION SYSTEMS, INC.
8 New England Executive Park   Phone: 617-273-9003
Burlington, MA 01803   Fax: 617-229-9904
Pres & CEO: Peter J. Boni
Dir HR: Maria Fraguso
Employees: 341
Jobs Added Last Year: 103 (+43.3%)
Computer-aided software engineering products

BAIN & COMPANY
2 Copley Place   Phone: 617-572-2000
Boston, MA 02117-0897   Fax: 617-572-2427
CEO: Thomas J. Tierney
Dir HR: Elizabeth Corcoran
Employees: 1,000
Jobs Added Last Year: 100 (+11.1%)
Consulting - management

BANK OF BOSTON CORPORATION
100 Federal St.   Phone: 617-434-2200
Boston, MA 02110   Fax: 617-575-2232
Chm & CEO: Ira Stepanian
Exec Dir HR: Helen G. Drinan
Employees: 18,644
Jobs Cut Last Year: 815 (-4.2%)
Banks - Northeast

BAYBANKS, INC.
175 Federal St.   Phone: 617-482-1040
Boston, MA 02110   Fax: 617-482-0733
Chm & Pres: William M. Crozier, Jr.
Dir HR: Hedy Veith
Employees: 5,571
Jobs Added Last Year: 44 (+.8%)
Banks - Northeast

MASSACHUSETTS

BERKSHIRE REALTY CO.
470 Atlantic Ave. Phone: 617-423-2233
Boston, MA 02210 Fax: 617-423-8919
Chm & CEO: George Krupp
Dir HR: Jim Jackson
Employees: 208
Jobs Added Last Year: 101 (+94.4%)
Real estate investment trust

BERTUCCI'S INC.
14 Audubon Rd. Phone: 617-246-6700
Wakefield, MA 01801 Fax: 617-246-2224
Chm & Pres: Joseph Crugnale
VP HR: Chris Harrington
Employees: 3,185
Jobs Added Last Year: 780 (+32.4%)
Retail - restaurants (Bertucci's Brick Oven Pizzeria & Bertucci's Menucci pizza take-out & delivery)

BIG Y FOODS INC.
280 Chestnut St. Phone: 413-784-0600
Springfield, MA 01102 Fax: 413-732-8475
SVP & CEO: Donald H. D'Amour
Dir Personnel: Donald Trella
Employees: 4,500
Jobs Added Last Year: —
Retail - supermarkets

BIRD CORPORATION
980 Washington St., Ste. 124N Phone: 617-461-1414
Dedham, MA 02026-6714 Fax: 617-461-1618
CEO: Joseph Vecchiolla
No central personnel officer
Employees: 886
Jobs Added Last Year: 82 (+10.2%)
Building products - roofing materials

BOSE CORPORATION
100 Mountain Rd. Phone: 508-879-7330
Framingham, MA 01701 Fax: 508-872-6541
Chm & CEO: Amar G. Bose
VP HR: David Merchant
Employees: 3,100
Jobs Added Last Year: 100 (+3.3%)
Audio & video home products - high-end loudspeakers & auto sound systems

BOSTON EDISON COMPANY
800 Boylston St. Phone: 617-424-2000
Boston, MA 02199 Fax: 617-424-2929
Chm & CEO: Thomas J. May
SVP HR: John J. Higgins, Jr.
Employees: 4,418
Jobs Cut Last Year: 122 (-2.7%)
Utility - electric power

BOSTON SCIENTIFIC CORPORATION
480 Pleasant St. Phone: 617-923-1720
Watertown, MA 02172-2407 Fax: 617-923-0677
Pres & CEO: Peter M. Nicholas
VP HR: Jamie Rubin
Employees: 2,349
Jobs Added Last Year: 298 (+14.5%)
Medical instruments - catheters & other precision medical devices used in reduced-incision surgery

BOSTON TECHNOLOGY, INC.
100 Quannapowitt Pkwy. Phone: 617-246-9000
Wakefield, MA 01880 Fax: 617-245-6516
Pres & CEO: John C. W. Taylor
Asst VP (HR): Donna Callahan
Employees: 347
Jobs Added Last Year: 60 (+20.9%)
Telecommunications equipment - voice messaging system (CO ACCESS)

BRADLEES, INC.
One Bradlees Circle Phone: 617-380-8000
Braintree, MA 02184 Fax: 617-380-5915
Chm & CEO: Mark A. Cohen
SVP HR: Randall E. Dickerson
Employees: 14,000
Jobs Cut Last Year: 2,000 (-12.5%)
Retail - discount & variety

CABOT CORPORATION
75 State St. Phone: 617-345-0100
Boston, MA 02109 Fax: 617-342-6103
Chm & CEO: Samuel W. Bodman
VP HR: Karen Morrissey
Employees: 5,400
Jobs Added Last Year: 100 (+1.9%)
Chemicals - carbon black & fumed silica; thermoplastic concentrates & specialty compounds

MASSACHUSETTS

CHIPCOM CORPORATION
11002
118 Turnpike Rd.
Southborough, MA 01772
Pres & CEO: John Robert Held
VP HR: John C. Meyer
Employees: 567
Jobs Added Last Year: 159 (+39%)
Computers - hubs for networks
Phone: 508-460-8900
Fax: 508-460-8950

CUMBERLAND FARMS INC.
777 Dedham St.
Canton, MA 02021
Pres: Lily H. Bentas
VP HR: Foster G. Macrides
Employees: 7,500
Jobs Added Last Year: —
Retail - convenience stores; gas distribution
Phone: 617-828-4900
Fax: 617-828-5246

CLEAN HARBORS, INC.
1200 Crown Colony Dr.
Quincy, MA 02169
CEO: Alan S. McKim
Dir HR: Kate Creagh
Employees: 1,500
Jobs Added Last Year: 100 (+7.1%)
Pollution control equipment & services
Phone: 617-849-1800
Fax: 617-786-8589

DAKA INTERNATIONAL, INC.
55 Ferncroft Rd.
Danvers, MA 01923
CEO: William H. Baumhauer
SVP HR: Louis A. Kaucic
Employees: 13,903
Jobs Added Last Year: 3,653 (+35.6%)
Retail - restaurants (Fuddruckers) & contract food service
Phone: 508-774-9115
Fax: 508-750-1414

CML GROUP, INC.
10262
524 Main St.
Acton, MA 01720
Chm & CEO: Charles M. Leighton
No central personnel officer
Employees: 6,806
Jobs Added Last Year: 1,193 (+21.3%)
Retail - apparel (Britches) exercise equipment (NordicTrack), gardening equipment, nature stores (The Nature Company)
Phone: 508-264-4155
Fax: 508-264-4073

DATA GENERAL CORPORATION
10436
4400 Computer Dr.
Westboro, MA 01580
Pres & CEO: Ronald L. Skates
VP Admin (HR): Paul Guzzi
Employees: 5,800
Jobs Cut Last Year: 700 (-10.8%)
Computers - servers, storage products & services
Phone: 508-898-5000
Fax: 508-366-1319

CONNELL LIMITED PARTNERSHIP
One International Place, 31st Fl.
Boston, MA 02110
Chm & CEO: William F. Connell
VP HR: Maurice Keller
Employees: 3,100
Jobs Added Last Year: 46 (+1.5%)
Metal products - industrial equipment
Phone: 617-737-2700
Fax: 617-737-1617

DATAWARE TECHNOLOGIES INC.
16443
222 Third St.
Cambridge, MA 02142
Pres, Chm & CEO: Kurt Mueller
Office Mgr (HR): Sue Martin
Employees: 237
Jobs Added Last Year: 128 (+117.4%)
Computers - retrieval software for CD-ROM applications
Phone: 617-621-0820
Fax: 617-621-0307

CONTINENTAL CABLEVISION, INC.
The Pilot House, Lewis Wharf
Boston, MA 02110
Chm & CEO: Amos B. Hostetter, Jr.
SVP HR: Andrew J. Dixon, Jr.
Employees: 7,000
Jobs Added Last Year: 0
Cable TV
Phone: 617-742-9500
Fax: 617-742-0530

DEMOULAS SUPER MARKETS INC.
875 East St.
Tewksbury, MA 01876
Pres & CEO: Arthur T. Demoulas
VP Store Ops (HR): William F. Marsden
Employees: 9,000
Jobs Added Last Year: —
Retail - supermarkets
Phone: 508-851-8000
Fax: 508-851-3942

MASSACHUSETTS

DESIGNS, INC.
1244 Boylston St. Phone: 617-739-6722
Chestnut Hill, MA 01267 Fax: 617-277-3516
Pres & CEO: Joel H. Reichman
VP HR: Mary Ann Chenell
Employees: 2,230
Jobs Added Last Year: 230 (+11.5%)
Retail - apparel & shoes

DIGITAL EQUIPMENT CORPORATION
146 Main St. Phone: 508-493-5111
Maynard, MA 01754-2571 Fax: 508-493-8780
Pres & CEO: Robert B. Palmer
VP HR: Richard Farrahar
Employees: 94,200
Jobs Cut Last Year: 19,600 (-17.2%)
Computers - minicomputers, microprocessors, PCs, software & consulting services

DM MANAGEMENT COMPANY
25 Recreation Park Dr. Phone: 617-740-2718
Hingham, MA 02043 Fax: 617-749-8523
Pres & CEO: Samuel L. Shanaman
Dir Corp Rel (HR): Carol Maher
Employees: 276
Jobs Added Last Year: 86 (+45.3%)
Retail - mail order women's apparel (The Very Thing!, Nicole Summers & J. Jill, Ltd.)

DYNATECH CORPORATION
3 New England Executive Park Phone: 617-272-6100
Burlington, MA 01803-5087 Fax: 617-272-2304
CEO: John F. Reno
Dir HR: John A. Mixon
Employees: 3,200
Jobs Added Last Year: 100 (+3.2%)
Test & measurement instruments for the telecommunications industry

EATON VANCE CORPORATION
24 Federal St. Phone: 617-482-8260
Boston, MA 02110 Fax: 617-482-2396
Pres: M. Dozier Gardner
VP & Dir HR: Benjamin A. Rowland
Employees: 356
Jobs Added Last Year: 85 (+31.4%)
Financial - mutual fund management

EG&G, INC.
45 William St. Phone: 617-237-5100
Wellesley, MA 02181 Fax: 617-431-4255
Chm, Pres & CEO: John M. Kucharski
VP HR: Richard F. Murphy
Employees: 32,000
Jobs Cut Last Year: 2,000 (-5.9%)
Instruments - optoelectronics & mechanical components to the automotive, medical & aerospace industries

EMC CORPORATION
171 South St. Phone: 508-435-1000
Hopkinton, MA 01748-9103 Fax: 508-435-5222
Pres & CEO: Michael C. Ruettgers
VP HR: Brian P. O'Connell
Employees: 2,452
Jobs Added Last Year: 952 (+63.5%)
Computers - redundant arrays of independent hard disk (RAID) storage systems

FMR CORPORATION
82 Devonshire St. Phone: 617-570-7000
Boston, MA 02109 Fax: 617-720-3836
Chm, Pres & CEO: Edward C. Johnson III
SVP Admin (HR): Jerry Lieberman
Employees: 12,900
Jobs Added Last Year: 3,900 (+43.3%)
Financial - mutual fund management & discount brokerage (Fidelity Investments); magazine publishing (*Worth*)

FTP SOFTWARE, INC.
2 High St. Phone: 508-685-4000
North Andover, MA 01845 Fax: 508-659-6557
Pres & CEO: David H. Zirkle
Dir HR: Charlotte H. Evans
Employees: 408
Jobs Added Last Year: 208 (+104%)
Computers - internetworking software

GENETICS INSTITUTE, INC.
87 CambridgePark Dr. Phone: 617-876-1170
Cambridge, MA 02140 Fax: 617-498-8838
Pres & CEO: Gabriel Schmergel
VP HR & Ops: Zoltan Csimma
Employees: 1,015
Jobs Added Last Year: 309 (+43.8%)
Biomedical & genetic products

181

MASSACHUSETTS

GENOME THERAPEUTICS CORPORATION
100 Beaver St.   Phone: 617-893-5007
Waltham, MA 02154   Fax: 617-275-0043
Chm, Pres & CEO: Robert J. Hennessey
VP Fin, Treas & CFO (HR): Fenel M. Eloi
Employees: 80
Jobs Added Last Year: 12 (+17.6%)
Biomedical & genetic products

GENZYME CORPORATION
One Kendall Sq.   Phone: 617-252-7500
Cambridge, MA 02139-1562   Fax: 617-252-7600
Chm, Pres & CEO: Henri A. Termeer
SVP HR: John V. Heffernan
Employees: 1,724
Jobs Added Last Year: 238 (+16%)
Biomedical & genetic products

THE GILLETTE COMPANY
Prudential Tower Bldg.   Phone: 617-421-7000
Boston, MA 02199   Fax: 617-421-7123
Chm & CEO: Alfred M. Zeien
SVP Personnel & Admin: Robert E. DiCenso
Employees: 33,400
Jobs Added Last Year: 2,500 (+8.1%)
Cosmetics & toiletries; shaving equipment; small appliances (Braun); stationery products (Parker & Waterman)

GROUND ROUND RESTAURANTS, INC.
35 Braintree Hill Office Park   Phone: 617-380-3100
Braintree, MA 02184   Fax: 617-380-3168
Chm, Pres & CEO: Michael P. O'Donnell
VP HR: Elizabeth Brennan Baker
Employees: 9,700
Jobs Added Last Year: 500 (+5.4%)
Retail - restaurants

HAEMONETICS CORPORATION
400 Wood Rd.   Phone: 617-848-7100
Braintree, MA 02184-9114   Fax: 617-848-5106
CEO: John F. White
Dir HR: Brigid A. Makes
Employees: 1,109
Jobs Added Last Year: 107 (+10.7%)
Medical products - blood processing systems

HARCOURT GENERAL, INC.
27 Boylston St.   Phone: 617-232-8200
Chestnut Hill, MA 02167   Fax: 617-738-4007
Pres, CEO & COO: Robert J. Tarr, Jr.
Dir HR: Gerald T. Hughes
Employees: 20,742
Jobs Cut Last Year: 9,424 (-31.2%)
Diversified operations - retail apparel (Nieman Marcus, Bergdorf Goodman); publishing (Harcourt Brace)

HARVARD COMMUNITY HEALTH PLAN, INC.
10 Brookline Place West   Phone: 617-731-8210
Brookline, MA 02146   Fax: 617-730-4695
Pres & CEO: Manuel M. Ferris
VP HR: Larry Gibson
Employees: 6,489
Jobs Added Last Year: —
Health maintenance organization

HILLS DEPARTMENT STORES, INC.
15 Dan Rd.   Phone: 617-821-1000
Canton, MA 02021   Fax: 617-821-4379
Pres & CEO: Michael Bozic
VP HR: Larry Miller
Employees: 21,500
Jobs Added Last Year: 1,700 (+8.6%)
Retail - discount & variety

HOLOGIC, INC.
590 Lincoln St.   Phone: 617-890-2300
Waltham, MA 02154   Fax: 617-890-8031
Chm & CEO: S. David Ellenbogen
Mgr HR: Nancy Bubeck
Employees: 154
Jobs Added Last Year: 31 (+25.2%)
Medical instruments - X-ray systems

IMMULOGIC PHARMACEUTICAL CORPORATION
610 Lincoln St.   Phone: 617-466-6000
Waltham, MA 02154   Fax: 617-577-8686
Pres & CEO: Robert J. Gerety
VP HR: Kevin Lawler
Employees: 135
Jobs Added Last Year: 29 (+27.4%)
Biomedical & genetic products

MASSACHUSETTS

INTERNATIONAL DATA GROUP
One Exeter Plaza, 15th Fl. Phone: 617-534-1200
Boston, MA 02116 Fax: 617-262-2300
Chm & CEO: Patrick J. McGovern
Dir HR: Martha Stephens
Employees: 7,000
Jobs Added Last Year: 1,400 (+25%)
Publishing - computer publications (*PC World*); market research, trade shows

IONICS, INC.
65 Grove St. Phone: 617-926-2500
Watertown, MA 02172 Fax: 617-926-4304
CEO: Arthur L. Goldstein
Dir HR: Marianne Manzon-Winsser
Employees: 1,100
Jobs Added Last Year: 100 (+10%)
Filtration products

IPSWICH SAVINGS BANK
23 Market St. Phone: 508-356-2971
Ipswich, MA 01938 Fax: 508-356-9732
Pres & CEO: David L. Grey
HR Dir: Dorothy Bergmann
Employees: 51
Jobs Added Last Year: 8 (+18.6%)
Banks - Northeast

J. BAKER, INC.
555 Turnpike St. Phone: 617-828-9300
Canton, MA 02021 Fax: 617-821-4867
CEO: Jerry M. Socol
VP HR: Virginia Pitts
Employees: 6,402
Jobs Added Last Year: 390 (+6.5%)
Retail - shoe concessions in department stores

JOHN HANCOCK MUTUAL LIFE
PO Box 111 Phone: 617-572-6000
Boston, MA 02117 Fax: 617-572-6451
Chm & CEO: Stephen L. Brown
VP Corp HR: A. Page Palmer
Employees: 16,500
Jobs Added Last Year: 2,597 (+18.7%)
Insurance - life

KEANE, INC.
10 City Sq. Phone: 617-241-9200
Boston, MA 02129-3798 Fax: 617-241-9507
Pres: John F. Keane
VP HR: Edward Sagrue
Employees: 4,300
Jobs Added Last Year: 1,937 (+82%)
Computers - software design, integration & management services for corporation & health care facilities

LIBERTY MUTUAL INSURANCE GROUP
175 Berkeley St. Phone: 617-357-9500
Boston, MA 02117 Fax: 617-350-7648
Chm & CEO: Gary L. Countryman
Dir HR: Julie Baumgartner
Employees: 22,000
Jobs Added Last Year: 3,000 (+15.8%)
Insurance - multiline & employee benefits services

LOJACK CORPORATION
333 Elm St. Phone: 617-326-4700
Dedham, MA 02026 Fax: 617-326-7255
Pres & CEO: C. Michael Daley
Ben Mgr: Mark Bornemann
Employees: 216
Jobs Added Last Year: 39 (+22%)
Data collection & systems

LOTUS DEVELOPMENT CORPORATION
55 Cambridge Pkwy. Phone: 617-577-8500
Cambridge, MA 02142 Fax: 617-693-1299
Chm, Pres & CEO: Jim P. Manzi
VP HR: Russell J. Campanello
Employees: 4,738
Jobs Added Last Year: 338 (+7.7%)
Computers - spreadsheet (1-2-3), graphics, communications (cc:Mail, Notes) & word processing (Ami Pro) software

MASSACHUSETTS INSTITUTE OF TECHNOLOGY
77 Massachusetts Ave. Phone: 617-253-1000
Cambridge, MA 02139 Fax: 617-253-8000
Pres & CEO: Charles M. Vest
VP & Dir Personnel: Joan Rice
Employees: 10,826
Jobs Added Last Year: —
University

An in-depth profile of this company is available by fax. Call 800-510-4452 and use your touch-tone phone to put in the 5-digit code at the prompt. Only $2.95 each with your credit card. See page 12 for more details.

MASSACHUSETTS

MASSBANK CORPORATION
123 Haven St. Phone: 617-944-5000
Reading, MA 01867 Fax: 617-458-4154
Pres & CEO: Gerard H. Brandi
SVP (HR): Donna West
Employees: 159
Jobs Added Last Year: 83 (+109.2%)
Banks - Northeast

MEDISENSE, INC.
266 Second Ave. Phone: 617-895-6000
Waltham, MA 02154 Fax: 617-890-8971
Pres & CEO: Robert L. Coleman
Corp Dir HR: Larraine L. Levine
Employees: 818
Jobs Added Last Year: 120 (+17.2%)
Medical instruments - blood glucose monitoring systems

MILLIPORE CORPORATION
80 Ashby Rd. Phone: 617-275-9200
Bedford, MA 01730-2271 Fax: 617-275-5550
Chm, Pres & CEO: John A. Gilmartin
VP HR: Glenda Burkhart
Employees: 5,772
Jobs Cut Last Year: 3 (-.1%)
Filtration products

NEIMAN MARCUS GROUP, INC.
27 Boylston St. Phone: 617-232-0760
Chestnut Hill, MA 02167 Fax: 617-738-4007
Pres & CEO: Robert J. Tarr, Jr.
VP HR: Gerald Hughes
Employees: 10,600
Jobs Added Last Year: 700 (+7.1%)
Retail - major department stores (Nieman Marcus, Bergdorf Goodman, Contempo Casuals); mail order (Horchow)

THE NEW ENGLAND
501 Boylston St. Phone: 617-578-2000
Boston, MA 02116 Fax: 617-578-3776
Chm & CEO: Robert A. Shafto
SVP HR: Gail E. Weber
Employees: 2,600
Jobs Added Last Year: —
Insurance - life

NEW ENGLAND ELECTRIC CO.
25 Research Dr. Phone: 508-366-9011
Westborough, MA 01582 Fax: 508-836-0276
Pres & CEO: John W. Rowe
VP & Dir HR: David Kennedy
Employees: 5,124
Jobs Added Last Year: 155 (+3.1%)
Utility - electric power

NORTHEAST UTILITIES
174 Brush Hill Ave. Phone: 413-785-5871
West Springfield, MA 01090-0010 Fax: 413-787-9352
Pres & CEO: Bernard M. Fox
SVP HR & Administrative Svcs: Cheryl W. Grise
Employees: 9,697
Jobs Cut Last Year: 443 (-4.4%)
Utility - electric power

NUTRAMAX PRODUCTS, INC.
9 Blackburn Dr. Phone: 508-283-1800
Gloucester, MA 01930 Fax: 508-283-4067
Pres & CEO: Donald E. Lepone
Mgr HR: Katheryn Goodick
Employees: 500
Jobs Added Last Year: 100 (+25%)
Cosmetics & toiletries - private label health & personal care products

OAK INDUSTRIES INC.
1000 Winter St. Phone: 617-890-0400
Waltham, MA 02154 Fax: 617-890-8585
Pres & CEO: William S. Antle III
SVP HR: John D. Richardson
Employees: 2,620
Jobs Added Last Year: 367 (+16.3%)
Electrical products - controls & components, quartz crystals

PARAMETRIC TECHNOLOGY CORP.
128 Technology Dr. Phone: 617-894-7111
Waltham, MA 02154 Fax: 617-891-1069
Pres & CEO: Steven C. Walske
Dir HR: Carl Ockerbloom
Employees: 899
Jobs Added Last Year: 374 (+71.2%)
Computers - computer-aided design software

MASSACHUSETTS

PAUL REVERE CORPORATION
18 Chestnut St.   Phone: 508-799-4441
Worcester, MA 01608   Fax: 508-792-6337
Pres & CEO: Charles E. Soule
VP HR: Kathy Hessel
Employees: 3,218
Jobs Added Last Year: 37 (+1.2%)
Insurance - accident & health

POLAROID CORPORATION
549 Technology Sq.   Phone: 617-577-2000
Cambridge, MA 02139   Fax: 617-386-3118
Chm, Pres & CEO: I. MacAllister Booth
VP HR: Michael LeBlanc
Employees: 12,048
Jobs Cut Last Year: 311 (-2.5%)
Photographic equipment & supplies - cameras & film, medical imaging systems

PERSEPTIVE BIOSYSTEMS, INC.
38 Sidney St.   Phone: 617-621-1787
Cambridge, MA 02139   Fax: 617-621-6973
Pres & CEO: Noubar B. Afeyan
Dir HR: Stacy Radar
Employees: 569
Jobs Added Last Year: 341 (+149.6%)
Medical instruments - diagnostics

PRI AUTOMATION, INC.
805 Middlesex Tpke.   Phone: 508-663-8555
Billerica, MA 01821   Fax: 508-663-9755
Pres & CEO: Mordechai Wiesler
Dir HR: Diane DeLucia
Employees: 384
Jobs Added Last Year: 128 (+50%)
Machinery - semiconductor factory automation systems

PHOENIX TECHNOLOGIES LTD.
846 University Ave.   Phone: 617-551-4000
Norwood, MA 02062-3950   Fax: 617-551-3750
CEO: Ronald D. Fisher
Dir HR: Cathy Newman
Employees: 389
Jobs Added Last Year: 80 (+25.9%)
Computers - operating system software for PCs

PROGRESS SOFTWARE CORPORATION
14 Oak Park   Phone: 617-280-4000
Bedford, MA 01730   Fax: 617-275-4595
Pres & CEO: Joseph W. Alsop
Dir HR: Robert Clancy
Employees: 629
Jobs Added Last Year: 177 (+39.2%)
Computers - database management software

PICTURETEL CORPORATION
222 Rosewood Dr.   Phone: 508-762-5000
Danvers, MA 01923   Fax: 508-762-5245
Chm, Pres & CEO: Norman Gaut
VP HR: Lawrence A. Bortstein
Employees: 811
Jobs Added Last Year: 140 (+20.9%)
Telecommunications equipment - video conferencing

RAYTHEON COMPANY
141 Spring St.   Phone: 617-862-6600
Lexington, MA 01273   Fax: 617-860-2172
Chm & CEO: Dennis J. Picard
SVP Law, HR, Corp Admin & Sec: Christopher L. Hoffman
Employees: 63,800
Jobs Cut Last Year: 100 (-.2%)
Diversified operations - defense electronics; energy & environmental products; corporate jets; appliances

PIONEER GROUP, INC.
60 State St.   Phone: 617-742-7825
Boston, MA 02109   Fax: 617-422-4274
Pres & CEO: John F. Cogan, Jr.
Mgr HR: Bob Nicoson
Employees: 857
Jobs Added Last Year: 291 (+51.4%)
Financial - investment management

REEBOK INTERNATIONAL LTD.
100 Technology Center Dr.   Phone: 617-341-5000
Stoughton, MA 02072   Fax: 617-341-5087
Chm, Pres & CEO: Paul B. Fireman
Dir Emp Rel: Mary Hassan
Employees: 4,700
Jobs Added Last Year: 200 (+4.4%)
Shoes & related apparel - athletic

MASSACHUSETTS

ROBERTSON-CECO CORPORATION
222 Berkeley St. Phone: 617-424-5500
Boston, MA 02116 Fax: 617-424-5555
VC & CEO: Michael E. Heisley
VP & Treas (HR): Stephen P. Bishop
Employees: 3,100
Jobs Added Last Year: 50 (+1.6%)
Diversified operations - building products; metal buildings; door products

SOFTKEY INTERNATIONAL INC.
201 Broadway Phone: 617-494-1200
Cambridge, MA 02139-1955 Fax: 617-494-1219
CEO: Michael Perik
Dir HR: Mary De Saint Croix
Employees: 450
Jobs Added Last Year: 316 (+235.8%)
Computers - consumer software including word processing, education & entertainment products

SPECTRAN CORPORATION
50 Hall Rd. Phone: 508-347-2261
Sturbridge, MA 01566 Fax: 508-347-2747
Pres & CEO: Raymond E. Jaeger
HR Supervisor: Sue Jowett
Employees: 149
Jobs Added Last Year: 25 (+20.2%)
Fiber optics

STAPLES, INC.
100 Pennsylvania Ave. Phone: 508-370-8500
Framingham, MA 01701 Fax: 508-370-8955
Chm & CEO: Thomas G. Stemberg
VP HR: Cathy J. Wells
Employees: 9,658
Jobs Cut Last Year: 630 (-6.1%)
Retail - discount office equipment & supplies

STATE STREET BOSTON CORPORATION
225 Franklin St. Phone: 617-786-3000
Boston, MA 02110 Fax: 617-654-4006
Pres & CEO: Marshall N. Carter
VP HR: Nancy Murphy
Employees: 9,338
Jobs Added Last Year: 1,017 (+12.2%)
Banks - Northeast

THE STOP & SHOP COMPANIES, INC.
1385 Hancock St. Phone: 617-380-8000
Quincy, MA 02169 Fax: 617-380-5915
Chm, Pres & CEO: Robert G. Tobin
VP HR: Daniel P. Corcoran
Employees: 30,000
Jobs Added Last Year: 3,000 (+11.1%)
Retail - supermarkets

STRATUS COMPUTER, INC.
55 Fairbanks Blvd. Phone: 508-460-2000
Marlborough, MA 01752 Fax: 508-481-8945
Pres & CEO: William E. Foster
VP HR: John F. Young
Employees: 2,610
Jobs Cut Last Year: 12 (-.5%)
Computers - fault-tolerant minicomputers

THE STRIDE RITE CORPORATION
5 Cambridge Center Phone: 617-491-8800
Cambridge, MA 02142 Fax: 617-864-1372
Chm, Pres & CEO: Robert C. Siegel
VP HR: John McMahon
Employees: 3,800
Jobs Added Last Year: 500 (+15.2%)
Shoes & related apparel

SYRATECH CORPORATION
175 McClellan Hwy. Phone: 617-561-2200
East Boston, MA 02128-9114 Fax: 617-561-0275
Chm & CEO: Leonard Florence
Dir HR: Susan Fedo
Employees: 1,140
Jobs Added Last Year: 113 (+11%)
Housewares

SYSTEM RESOURCES CORPORATION
128 Wheeler Rd. Phone: 617-270-9228
Burlington, MA 01803 Fax: 617-272-2589
Pres: Samir A. Desai
Emp Svcs Mgr: Susan Griffin
Employees: 370
Jobs Added Last Year: 50 (+15.6%)
Computers - software development, information systems, systems integration

MASSACHUSETTS

TALBOTS INC.
175 Beal St. Phone: 617-749-7600
Hingham, MA 02043 Fax: 617-741-4369
Pres & CEO: Arnold B. Zetcher
VP HR: Stuart Stolper
Employees: 5,200
Jobs Added Last Year: 392 (+8.2%)
Retail - apparel & shoes

THERMO VOLTEK CORPORATION
470 Wildwood St., PO Box 2878 Phone: 617-622-1000
Woburn, MA 01888-1799 Fax: 617-622-1123
CEO: John W. Wood, Jr.
Dir HR: Fred Florio
Employees: 138
Jobs Added Last Year: 70 (+102.9%)
Electronics - measuring instruments

TELEBIT CORPORATION
One Executive Dr. Phone: 508-441-2181
Chelmsford, MA 01824 Fax: 508-656-9304
CEO: James D. Norrod
Dir HR: Joe Musumano
Employees: 225
Jobs Added Last Year: 41 (+22.3%)
Telecommunications equipment - data transmission products

THE TJX COMPANIES, INC.
770 Cochituate Rd. Phone: 508-390-1000
Framingham, MA 01701-4630 Fax: 508-390-3635
Pres & CEO: Bernard Cammarata
VP HR: Mark O. Jacobson
Employees: 36,000
Jobs Added Last Year: 3,000 (+9.1%)
Retail - discount & variety

TERADYNE, INC.
321 Harrison Ave. Phone: 617-482-2700
Boston, MA 02118 Fax: 617-422-2910
Chm & Pres: Alexander V. d'Arbeloff
Corp Dir Personnel: James Dawson
Employees: 4,000
Jobs Cut Last Year: 100 (-2.4%)
Electronics - semiconductor & circuit board test equipment

TOWN & COUNTRY CORPORATION
25 Union St. Phone: 617-884-8500
Chelsea, MA 02150 Fax: 617-889-1473
CEO: C. William Carey
Dir HR: Pam Brown
Employees: 2,500
Jobs Added Last Year: 0
Precious metals & jewelry

THERMEDICS INC.
470 Wildwood St., PO Box 2999 Phone: 617-938-3786
Woburn, MA 01888-1799 Fax: 617-933-4476
Pres & CEO: John W. Wood, Jr.
Personnel Dir: Susan Stander
Employees: 554
Jobs Added Last Year: 206 (+59.2%)
Medical products - medical-grade plastics, drug-delivery systems, wound dressings

THE UNIVERSITY OF MASSACHUSETTS
18 Tremont St. Phone: 617-287-7000
Boston, MA 02108 Fax: 617-287-7044
Pres: Michael K. Hooker
Dir Labor Affairs: Roy Milbury
Employees: 12,935
Jobs Added Last Year: —
University

THERMO ELECTRON CORPORATION
81 Wyman St., PO Box 9046 Phone: 617-622-1000
Waltham, MA 02254-9046 Fax: 617-622-1207
Chm, Pres & CEO: George N. Hatsopoulos
Dir HR: Fred Florao
Employees: 8,800
Jobs Added Last Year: 1,300 (+17.3%)
Diversified operations - monitoring instruments; alternative energy power systems; waste recycling; refrigeration systems

UNO RESTAURANT CORPORATION
100 Charles Park Rd. Phone: 617-323-9200
West Roxbury, MA 02132 Fax: 617-323-4252
Chm & CEO: Aaron D. Spencer
SVP HR & Training: Thomas W. Gathers
Employees: 3,833
Jobs Added Last Year: 518 (+15.6%)
Retail - restaurants (Pizzeria Uno)

MASSACHUSETTS

VERTEX PHARMACEUTICALS, INC.
40 Allston St. Phone: 617-576-3111
Cambridge, MA 02139-4211 Fax: 617-576-2109
Pres & CEO: Joshua S. Boger
Recruiting Coordinator: Laura Engles
Employees: 113
Jobs Added Last Year: 21 (+22.8%)
Drugs

WATTS INDUSTRIES, INC.
815 Chestnut St. Phone: 508-688-1811
North Andover, MA 01845-6098 Fax: 508-794-1848
Chm & CEO: Timothy P. Horne
No central personnel officer
Employees: 3,300
Jobs Added Last Year: 650 (+24.5%)
Instruments - control

VMARK SOFTWARE, INC.
30 Speen St. Phone: 508-879-3311
Framingham, MA 01701-1800 Fax: 508-879-3332
Pres & CEO: James J. Capeless
Dir HR: Sally N. Burke
Employees: 185
Jobs Added Last Year: 58 (+45.7%)
Computers - UNIX software for commercial applications (DATABASE)

XTRA CORPORATION
60 State St. Phone: 617-367-5000
Boston, MA 02109 Fax: 617-227-2190
Pres & CEO: Lewis Rubin
Dir Personnel: Marion Ewell
Employees: 798
Jobs Added Last Year: 243 (+43.8%)
Transportation - equipment & leasing

WABAN, INC.
One Mercer Rd. Phone: 508-651-6500
Natick, MA 01760 Fax: 508-651-6623
Pres & CEO: Herbert J. Zarkin
VP HR: Tom Davis
Employees: 19,000
Jobs Added Last Year: 1,800 (+10.5%)
Retail - warehouse (BJ's Wholesale) & home improvement (HomeClub)

XYLOGICS, INC.
53 Third Ave. Phone: 617-272-8140
Burlington, MA 01803 Fax: 617-273-5392
Pres & CEO: Bruce I. Sachs
HR Supervisor: Dolores Kelly
Employees: 203
Jobs Added Last Year: 50 (+32.7%)
Computers - remote-access networking products (Annex)

WANG LABORATORIES, INC.
One Industrial Ave. Phone: 508-459-5000
Lowell, MA 01851 Fax: 508-458-8969
Chm, Pres & CEO: Joseph M. Tucci
SVP HR & Ops Support: James J. Hogan
Employees: 16,792
Jobs Added Last Year: 3,942 (+30.7%)
Computers - software for imaging & networking

MICHIGAN

AMERIWOOD INDUSTRIES INTERNATIONAL
171 Monroe Ave., Ste. 600　　Phone: 616-336-9400
Grand Rapids, MI 49503　　Fax: 616-336-9401
Pres & CEO: Joseph J. Miglore
Corp HR Dir: Rich L. Compton
Employees: 725
Jobs Added Last Year: 75 (+11.5%)
Furniture

AMWAY CORPORATION
7575 Fulton St. East　　Phone: 616-676-6000
Ada, MI 49355　　Fax: 616-676-7102
Chm: Jay Van Andel
VP HR: Dwight A. Sawyer
Employees: 11,000
Jobs Added Last Year: 0
Retail - multitier seller of household, personal care, health & fitness products

ARBOR DRUGS, INC.
3331 W. Big Beaver Rd.　　Phone: 810-643-9420
Troy, MI 48084　　Fax: 810-637-1636
Chm, Pres & CEO: Eugene Applebaum
VP HR: Ronald F. Haase
Employees: 5,200
Jobs Added Last Year: 800 (+18.2%)
Retail - drug stores

CHAMPION ENTERPRISES, INC.
2701 University Dr., Ste. 320　　Phone: 810-340-9090
Auburn Hills, MI 48326　　Fax: 810-340-9345
Chm, Pres & CEO: Walter R. Young, Jr.
Dir HR: Michael King
Employees: 3,800
Jobs Added Last Year: 1,000 (+35.7%)
Building - mobile homes & RVs

CHEMICAL FINANCIAL CORPORATION
333 E. Main St.　　Phone: 517-631-3310
Midland, MI 48640　　Fax: 517-839-5337
Chm & CEO: Alan W. Ott
Asst VP & HR Off: Joseph Torrence
Employees: 965
Jobs Added Last Year: 100 (+11.6%)
Banks - Midwest

CHRYSLER CORPORATION
12000 Chrysler Dr.　　Phone: 313-956-5741
Highland Park, MI 48288-1919　　Fax: 313-956-3747
Chm & CEO: Robert J. Eaton
VP Corp Personnel: James P. Holden
Employees: 128,000
Jobs Added Last Year: 0
Automotive manufacturing - cars & trucks (Chrysler, Plymouth, Jeep, Dodge, Eagle); car rental (Thrifty, Dollar, Snappy)

CMS ENERGY CORPORATION
330 Town Center Dr.　　Phone: 313-436-9200
Dearborn, MI 48126　　Fax: 313-436-9225
Chm & CEO: William T. McCormick, Jr.
Exec Dir HR: John F. Drake
Employees: 10,500
Jobs Added Last Year: 347 (+3.4%)
Utility - electric power (Consumers Power Company)

COMERICA INC.
100 Renaissance Center　　Phone: 313-222-4000
Detroit, MI 48243　　Fax: 313-222-6067
Chm & CEO: Eugene A. Miller
EVP HR: Richard Collister
Employees: 13,187
Jobs Cut Last Year: 878 (-6.2%)
Banks - Midwest

COMPUWARE CORPORATION
31440 Northwestern Hwy.　　Phone: 810-737-7300
Farmington Hills, MI 48334-2564　　Fax: 810-737-1822
Chm & CEO: Peter Karmanos, Jr.
SVP (HR): W. James Prowse
Employees: 3,321
Jobs Added Last Year: 754 (+29.4%)
Computers - mainframe programming & client-server software

CROWLEY, MILNER AND COMPANY
2301 W. Lafayette　　Phone: 313-962-2400
Detroit, MI 48216　　Fax: 313-962-2529
Pres & CEO: Dennis P. Callahan
Mgr HR: Clara Loria
Employees: 1,265
Jobs Added Last Year: 115 (+10%)
Retail - regional department stores

MICHIGAN

DETROIT DIESEL CORPORATION
13400 Outer Dr. West Phone: 313-592-5000
Detroit, MI 48239-4001 Fax: 313-592-7580
Pres & CEO: Roger S. Penske
VP HR: Paul Walters
Employees: 5,200
Jobs Added Last Year: 1,755 (+50.9%)
Engines - diesel

DETROIT EDISON COMPANY
2000 Second Ave. Phone: 313-237-8000
Detroit, MI 48226-1279 Fax: 313-237-8828
Pres & CEO: John E. Lobbia
VP HR: Haven Cockerham
Employees: 8,819
Jobs Cut Last Year: 364 (-4%)
Utility - electric power

THE DETROIT MEDICAL CENTER
4201 St. Antoine Blvd. Phone: 313-745-5192
Detroit, MI 48201 Fax: 313-993-0438
Pres & CEO: David J. Campbell
VP HR: Dan Zuhlke
Employees: 14,384
Jobs Added Last Year: —
Hospitals

DOMINO'S PIZZA, INC.
30 Frank Lloyd Wright Dr. Phone: 313-930-3030
Ann Arbor, MI 48106 Fax: 313-668-4614
Pres: Thomas S. Monaghan
Dir HR: Mitch Srail
Employees: 20,000
Jobs Added Last Year: 0
Retail - pizza delivery & carryout

DONNELLY CORPORATION
414 E. 40th St. Phone: 616-786-7000
Holland, MI 49423-5368 Fax: 616-786-6034
Pres & CEO: J. Dwane Baumgardner
Mgr HR: Joanne Duquette
Employees: 2,650
Jobs Added Last Year: 250 (+10.4%)
Automotive & trucking - original equipment

DOUGLAS & LOMASON COMPANY
24600 Hollywood Ct. Phone: 810-478-7800
Farmington Hills, MI 48335-1671 Fax: 810-478-5189
Chm, Pres & CEO: Harry A. Lomason II
VP HR: Ollie V. Cheatham
Employees: 5,697
Jobs Cut Last Year: 120 (-2.1%)
Metal products - automotive & other industries

THE DOW CHEMICAL COMPANY
2030 Dow Center Phone: 517-636-1000
Midland, MI 48674 Fax: 517-636-1830
Chm & CEO: Frank P. Popoff
SVP HR: Joseph L. Downey
Employees: 55,436
Jobs Cut Last Year: 5,917 (-9.6%)
Chemicals - diversified

DOW CORNING CORPORATION
2200 W. Salzburg Rd. Phone: 517-496-4000
Midland, MI 48686 Fax: 517-496-4511
Pres & CEO: Richard A. Hazleton
Dir HR: James Chittick
Employees: 8,000
Jobs Added Last Year: —
Chemicals - specialty (fire protection, silicon); lubricants

DURAKON INDUSTRIES, INC.
2101 N. Lapeer Rd. Phone: 810-664-0850
Lapeer, MI 48446 Fax: 810-667-7733
Pres: William Webster
No central personnel officer
Employees: 505
Jobs Added Last Year: 93 (+22.6%)
Automotive & trucking - replacement parts

F & M DISTRIBUTORS, INC.
25800 Sherwood Rd. Phone: 810-758-1400
Warren, MI 48091-4160 Fax: 810-758-7939
Pres & CEO: Dale Ward
Field Training & Recruiting (HR): Mark Brabaw
Employees: 4,370
Jobs Cut Last Year: 61 (-1.4%)
Retail - discount & variety

MICHIGAN

FEDERAL-MOGUL CORPORATION
26555 Northwestern Hwy. Phone: 810-354-7700
Southfield, MI 48034 Fax: 810-354-8950
Chm & CEO: Dennis J. Gormley
VP HR: James M. Eastman
Employees: 16,200
Jobs Added Last Year: 1,800 (+12.5%)
Automotive & trucking - replacement parts

FIRST OF AMERICA BANK CORPORATION
211 S. Rose St. Phone: 616-376-9000
Kalamazoo, MI 49007 Fax: 616-376-8224
Pres & CEO: Daniel R. Smith
SVP HR: Richard Washburn
Employees: 13,330
Jobs Added Last Year: 390 (+3%)
Banks - Midwest

FLINT INK CORPORATION
25111 Glendale Ave. Phone: 313-538-6800
Detroit, MI 48239 Fax: 313-538-1828
Chm & CEO: H. Howard Flint II
VP HR: Glenn T. Autry
Employees: 2,585
Jobs Added Last Year: 385 (+17.5%)
Chemicals - printing ink

FORD MOTOR COMPANY
The American Rd. Phone: 313-322-3000
Dearborn, MI 48121-1899 Fax: 313-845-0570
Chm, Pres & CEO: Alexander J. Trotman
VP Emp Rel: John A. Hall
Employees: 322,213
Jobs Cut Last Year: 3,120 (-1%)
Automotive manufacturing - cars & trucks (Ford, Lincoln, Mercury, Jaguar); car rental (Hertz); financial services

FRETTER, INC.
12501 E. Grand River Rd. Phone: 810-220-5000
Brighton, MI 48116-8326 Fax: 810-220-5681
Pres: John B. Hurley
Controller (HR): Paul Mattei
Employees: 1,699
Jobs Added Last Year: 529 (+45.2%)
Retail - consumer electronics stores (Fretter, YES, Dash Concepts, Fred Schmid Appliance & Silo)

GENERAL MOTORS CORPORATION
3044 W. Grand Blvd. Phone: 313-556-5000
Detroit, MI 48202-3091 Fax: 313-556-5108
Pres & CEO: John L. Smith, Jr.
VP Personnel: Gerald A. Knechtel
Employees: 710,800
Jobs Cut Last Year: 39,200 (-5.2%)
Automotive manufacturing - cars & trucks (Buick, Cadillac, Chevrolet, Oldsmobile, Pontiac, Saturn); finance & insurance

GENTEX CORPORATION
600 N. Centennial St. Phone: 616-772-1800
Zeeland, MI 49464 Fax: 616-772-7348
Chm & CEO: Fred Bauer
Dir HR: John Van Haitsma
Employees: 558
Jobs Added Last Year: 115 (+26%)
Automotive & trucking - original equipment

GUARDIAN INDUSTRIES CORP.
43043 W. Nine Mile Rd. Phone: 810-347-0100
Northville, MI 48167 Fax: 810-349-5995
Pres & CEO: William Davidson
Dir Personnel: Kenneth Battjes
Employees: 10,000
Jobs Added Last Year: 0
Glass products - flat glass, fiberglass insulation, plastics

HAWORTH, INC.
One Haworth Ctr. Phone: 616-393-3000
Holland, MI 49423 Fax: 616-393-1570
Chm & CEO: Richard G. Haworth
VP HR: Randy Evans
Employees: 7,000
Jobs Added Last Year: 1,000 (+16.7%)
Furniture - office

HAYES WHEELS INTERNATIONAL, INC.
38481 Huron River Dr. Phone: 313-941-2000
Romulus, MI 48174 Fax: 313-942-7783
CEO: Ranko Cucuz
VP HR: Larry Karenko
Employees: 3,000
Jobs Added Last Year: 200 (+7.1%)
Automotive & trucking - steel & aluminum wheel rims

 An in-depth profile of this company is available by fax. Call 800-510-4452 and use your touch-tone phone to put in the 5-digit code at the prompt. Only $2.95 each with your credit card. See page 12 for more details.

MICHIGAN

HERMAN MILLER, INC.
855 E. Main Ave.
Zeeland, MI 49464
Pres & CEO: J. Kermit Campbell
VP People: Craig Schrotenboer
Employees: 5,446
Jobs Cut Last Year: 42 (-.8%)
Furniture - office
Phone: 616-654-3300
Fax: 616-654-3632

KMART CORPORATION
3100 W. Big Beaver Rd.
Troy, MI 48084
Pres & CEO: Joseph E. Antonini
VP HR: Michael T. Macik
Employees: 344,000
Jobs Cut Last Year: 14,000 (-3.9%)
Retail - discount stores, bookstores (Borders, Waldenbooks), home improvement stores (Builders Square)
Phone: 810-643-1000
Fax: 810-643-5249

HOWELL INDUSTRIES, INC.
17515 W. 9 Mile Rd., Ste. 650
Southfield, MI 48075
CEO & CFO: Morton Schiff
HR Dir: Richard Decker
Employees: 325
Jobs Added Last Year: 75 (+30%)
Automotive & trucking - original equipment
Phone: 810-424-8220
Fax: 810-424-8131

KNAPE & VOGT MANUFACTURING COMPANY
2700 Oak Industrial Dr. NE
Grand Rapids, MI 49505
Chm, Pres & CEO: Raymond E. Knape
Dir HR: Steve McCarthy
Employees: 1,150
Jobs Added Last Year: 67 (+6.2%)
Furniture
Phone: 616-459-3311
Fax: 616-459-3290

INTERNATIONAL CONTROLS CORP.
2016 N. Pitcher St.
Kalamazoo, MI 49007
Pres & CEO: David R. Markin
VP HR: Marsha Koestner
Employees: 5,055
Jobs Added Last Year: —
Diversified operations - truck trailer manufacturing; auto stamping; insurance
Phone: 616-343-6121
Fax: 616-343-2244

KYSOR INDUSTRIAL CORPORATION
One Madison Ave.
Cadillac, MI 49601-9785
Chm & CEO: George R. Kempton
Mgr Compensation & Ben: Kent Rosenau
Employees: 2,212
Jobs Added Last Year: 318 (+16.8%)
Automotive & trucking - original equipment
Phone: 616-779-7500
Fax: 616-775-2661

JACOBSON STORES INC.
3333 Sargent Rd.
Jackson, MI 49201
Chm: Mark K. Rosenfeld
VP Personnel: James K. Delaney
Employees: 5,700
Jobs Added Last Year: 450 (+8.6%)
Retail - regional department stores
Phone: 517-764-6400
Fax: 517-764-6427

LA-Z-BOY CHAIR COMPANY
1284 N. Telegraph Rd.
Monroe, MI 48161-3390
Chm, Pres & CEO: Charles T. Knabusch
VP HR: Lou Roussey
Employees: 8,724
Jobs Added Last Year: 571 (+7%)
Furniture
Phone: 313-242-1444
Fax: 313-241-4422

KELLOGG COMPANY
One Kellogg Sq.
Battle Creek, MI 49016-3599
Chm & CEO: Arnold G. Langbo
SVP HR: Robert L. Creviston
Employees: 16,151
Jobs Cut Last Year: 400 (-2.4%)
Food - cereals (Rice Crispies, Fruit Loops), baked goods (Eggo, Pop-Tarts)
Phone: 616-961-2000
Fax: 616-961-2871

LEAR SEATING CORPORATION
21557 Telegraph Rd.
Southfield, MI 48034
CEO: Kenneth L. Way
VP HR: Bill Ludwig
Employees: 18,470
Jobs Added Last Year: 3,970 (+27.4%)
Automotive & trucking - automobile seats
Phone: 810-746-1500
Fax: 810-746-1722

MICHIGAN

LITTLE CAESAR ENTERPRISES, INC.
2211 Woodward Ave. Phone: 313-983-6000
Detroit, MI 48201 Fax: 313-983-6494
Pres & CEO: Michael Ilitch
Dir HR: Darrell Snygg
Employees: 92,000
Jobs Added Last Year: 6,000 (+7%)
Retail - pizza restaurants; sports arenas; pro sports teams (Detroit Red Wings, Detroit Tigers)

MANATRON, INC.
2970 S. Ninth St. Phone: 616-375-5300
Kalamazoo, MI 49009 Fax: 616-375-9826
Chm, Pres & CEO: Allen F. Peat
Dir HR: Mary Gedhart
Employees: 192
Jobs Added Last Year: 42 (+28%)
Computers - data processing systems primarily for city, county, township & state governments

MASCO CORPORATION
21001 Van Born Rd. Phone: 313-274-7400
Taylor, MI 48180 Fax: 313-374-6787
Chm & CEO: Richard A. Manoogian
VP HR: David G. Wesenberg
Employees: 45,000
Jobs Added Last Year: 1,900 (+4.4%)
Building products - plumbing, cabinets, hardware; home furnishings

MASCOTECH, INC.
21001 Van Born Rd. Phone: 313-274-7405
Taylor, MI 48180 Fax: 313-374-6666
Chm & CEO: Richard A. Manoogian
VP HR: Dave Wesenburg
Employees: 12,200
Jobs Cut Last Year: 600 (-4.7%)
Automotive & trucking - powertrain & chassis parts; engineering services to car makers

MAXCO, INC.
1118 Centennial Way Phone: 517-321-3130
Lansing, MI 48917 Fax: 517-321-1022
Chm: Max A. Coon
Dir HR: Carl Fry
Employees: 1,000
Jobs Added Last Year: 300 (+42.9%)
Machinery - construction & mining

MCCLAIN INDUSTRIES, INC.
6200 Elmridge Rd. Phone: 810-264-3611
Sterling Heights, MI 48310 Fax: 810-264-2229
Pres & CEO: Kenneth D. McClain
Corp Sec (HR): Carl Jaworski
Employees: 635
Jobs Added Last Year: 68 (+12%)
Transportation - equipment & leasing

MCN CORPORATION
500 Griswold St. Phone: 313-256-5500
Detroit, MI 48226 Fax: 313-256-5871
Chm, Pres & CEO: Alfred R. Glancy III
Dir HR: John C. Elzerman
Employees: 3,966
Jobs Added Last Year: 98 (+2.5%)
Utility - gas distribution

MEIJER, INC.
2929 Walker Ave. NW Phone: 616-453-6711
Grand Rapids, MI 49504 Fax: 616-791-2572
Chm Exec Committee: Fred Meijer
SVP Personnel: Windy Ray
Employees: 60,000
Jobs Added Last Year: 10,000 (+20%)
Retail - supermarkets, discount & retail stores

MERCY HEALTH SERVICES
34605 W. 12 Mile Rd. Phone: 810-489-6000
Farmington Hills, MI 48331 Fax: 810-485-6932
Pres & CEO: Judith C. Pelham
VP HR: Shirley Hughes
Employees: 24,362
Jobs Added Last Year: —
Hospitals

NATIONAL TECHTEAM, INC.
22000 Garrison Ave. Phone: 313-277-2277
Dearborn, MI 48124-2306 Fax: 313-277-6409
CEO, Chm & Pres: William F. Coyro, Jr.
Dir HR: Kris Munroe
Employees: 449
Jobs Added Last Year: 226 (+101.3%)
Computers - software technical support services & training for software makers & large companies

MICHIGAN

NBD BANCORP, INC.
611 Woodward Ave.   Phone: 313-225-1000
Detroit, MI 48226   Fax: 313-225-2109
Chm & CEO: Verne G. Istock
SVP HR: Fred J. Johns
Employees: 17,836
Jobs Cut Last Year: 880 (-4.7%)
Banks - Midwest

PULTE CORPORATION
33 Bloomfield Hills Pkwy.   Phone: 810-647-2750
Bloomfield Hills, MI 48304   Fax: 810-433-4598
Pres & CEO: Robert K. Burgess
VP HR: Mike O'Brien
Employees: 2,700
Jobs Added Last Year: 724 (+36.6%)
Building - residential & commercial

NEWCOR, INC.
1825 S. Woodward, Ste. 240   Phone: 810-253-2400
Bloomfield Hills, MI 48302   Fax: 810-253-2413
Pres & CEO: Richard A. Smith
VP HR & Sec: Thomas D. Parker
Employees: 904
Jobs Added Last Year: 154 (+20.5%)
Machinery - general industrial

R.P. SCHERER CORPORATION
2075 W. Big Beaver Rd.   Phone: 810-649-0900
Troy, MI 48084   Fax: 810-649-2079
Chm & Co-CEO: John P. Cashman
Office Mgr (HR): Sherryl Shewach
Employees: 3,100
Jobs Added Last Year: 452 (+17.1%)
Medical products - drug delivery systems

OLD KENT FINANCIAL CORPORATION
One Vandenberg Center   Phone: 616-771-5000
Grand Rapids, MI 49503   Fax: 616-771-1119
Pres & CEO: John C. Canepa
VP HR: Thomas P. Merchant
Employees: 4,570
Jobs Cut Last Year: 30 (-.7%)
Banks - Midwest

RGIS INVENTORY SPECIALISTS
805 Oakwood Dr.   Phone: 810-651-2511
Rochester, MI 48307   Fax: 810-651-6787
Partner & Owner: Raymond J. Nicholson
Personnel: Susan Kingman
Employees: 20,000
Jobs Added Last Year: —
Business services - inventory taking

PENSKE CORPORATION
13400 Outer Dr. West   Phone: 313-592-5000
Detroit, MI 48239   Fax: 313-592-5256
Chm, Pres & CEO: Roger S. Penske
VP Personnel: Robert Carter
Employees: 11,500
Jobs Added Last Year: 0
Diversified operations - auto dealerships, truck leasing & rental; diesel engine manufacturing

ROUGE STEEL CO.
3001 Miller Rd.   Phone: 313-390-6877
Dearborn, MI 48121-1699   Fax: 313-323-2270
Chm & CEO: Carl L. Valdiserri
Dir HR: Mark Belliston
Employees: 3,225
Jobs Added Last Year: —
Steel - flat-rolled & electrogalvanized

PERRIGO COMPANY
117 Water St.   Phone: 616-673-8451
Allegan, MI 49010   Fax: 616-673-7534
Chm & CEO: Michael J. Jandernoa
VP HR: Mike Stewart
Employees: 3,879
Jobs Added Last Year: 285 (+7.9%)
Cosmetics & toiletries

SAGA COMMUNICATIONS INC.
73 Kercheval Ave.   Phone: 313-886-7070
Grosse Pointe Farms, MI 48236-3603   Fax: 313-886-7150
Chm, Pres & CEO: Edward K. Christian
SVP, Treas & CFO (HR): Norman L. McKee
Employees: 530
Jobs Added Last Year: 130 (+32.5%)
Broadcasting - radio & TV

MICHIGAN

SIMPSON INDUSTRIES, INC.
32100 Telegraph Rd., Ste. 120 Phone: 810-540-6200
Birmingham, MI 48025-2453 Fax: 810-540-7484
Pres & CEO: Roy E. Parrott
VP HR: James T. Strahley
Employees: 1,935
Jobs Added Last Year: 167 (+9.4%)
Automotive & trucking - original equipment

SPARTAN MOTORS, INC.
1000 Reynolds Rd. Phone: 517-543-6400
Charlotte, MI 48813 Fax: 517-543-7727
Chm & CEO: George W. Sztykiel
Dir Personnel: Janine Nierenberger
Employees: 500
Jobs Added Last Year: 112 (+28.9%)
Automotive & trucking - original equipment

SPX CORPORATION
700 Terrace Point Dr. Phone: 616-724-5000
Muskegon, MI 49443-3301 Fax: 616-724-5720
Chm & CEO: Dale A. Johnson
VP HR: Stephen A. Lison
Employees: 8,500
Jobs Cut Last Year: 100 (-1.2%)
Automotive & trucking - original equipment

STEELCASE INC.
901 44th St. SE Phone: 616-247-2710
Grand Rapids, MI 49508 Fax: 616-246-9015
Pres & CEO: James P. Hackett
VP HR: Dan Wiljanen
Employees: 17,800
Jobs Added Last Year: 0
Furniture - office furniture & equipment (world's largest)

STRYKER CORPORATION
2725 Fairfield Rd. Phone: 616-385-2600
Kalamazoo, MI 49002 Fax: 616-385-1062
CEO: John W. Brown
No central personnel officer
Employees: 2,906
Jobs Added Last Year: 458 (+18.7%)
Medical instruments - surgical products; physical therapy centers; maternity beds

TECUMSEH PRODUCTS COMPANY
100 E. Patterson St. Phone: 517-423-8411
Tecumseh, MI 49286 Fax: 517-423-8760
Pres & CEO: Todd W. Herrick
VP Investor Rel (HR): Wallace Stubbs
Employees: 12,800
Jobs Added Last Year: 233 (+1.9%)
Engines for lawn & recreational equipment; pumps; HVAC blowers

THORN APPLE VALLEY, INC.
18700 W. Ten Mile Rd. Phone: 810-552-0700
Southfield, MI 48075 Fax: 810-552-0986
CEO: Henry S. Dorfman
EVP Fresh Pork & HR: Edward E. Boan
Employees: 3,400
Jobs Added Last Year: 100 (+3%)
Food - meat & poultry products

TRIMAS CORPORATION
315 E. Eisenhower Pkwy. Phone: 313-747-7025
Ann Arbor, MI 48108 Fax: 313-747-6565
Pres: Brian P. Campbell
VP & Controller (HR): William E. Meyers
Employees: 3,400
Jobs Added Last Year: 600 (+21.4%)
Metal products - fasteners

UNITED AMERICAN HEALTHCARE CORPORATION
1155 Brewery Park Blvd. Phone: 313-393-0200
Detroit, MI 48207 Fax: 313-393-7940
Chm & CEO: Julius V. Combs
Asst VP Corp Admin (HR): Elizabeth Griffin
Employees: 508
Jobs Added Last Year: 176 (+53%)
Medical services

UNIVERSAL FOREST PRODUCTS INC.
2801 E. Beltline NE Phone: 616-364-6161
Grand Rapids, MI 49505 Fax: 616-361-7534
CEO: William G. Currie
VP Corp Svcs (HR): James A. Overbeek
Employees: 2,106
Jobs Added Last Year: 488 (+30.2%)
Building products - wood

 An in-depth profile of this company is available by fax. Call 800-510-4452 and use your touch-tone phone to put in the 5-digit code at the prompt. Only $2.95 each with your credit card. See page 12 for more details.

MICHIGAN

THE UNIVERSITY OF MICHIGAN
503 Thompson St. Phone: 313-764-1817
Ann Arbor, MI 48109 Fax: 313-747-3529
Pres: James J. Duderstadt
Exec Dir HR: Jackie McClain
Employees: 37,013
Jobs Added Last Year: —
University

THE UPJOHN COMPANY
7000 Portage Rd. Phone: 616-323-4000
Kalamazoo, MI 49001 Fax: 616-323-7034
Chm & CEO: John L. Zabriskie
SVP HR: Robert B. Hughes
Employees: 18,600
Jobs Cut Last Year: 200 (-1.1%)
Drugs, animal health care

VALASSIS COMMUNICATIONS, INC.
36111 Schoolcraft Rd. Phone: 313-591-3000
Livonia, MI 48150 Fax: 313-591-4994
Pres & CEO: David A. Brandon
Mgr HR: Angela Morin
Employees: 1,261
Jobs Added Last Year: 161 (+14.6%)
Printing - commercial lithographic & coupons

WHIRLPOOL CORPORATION
2000 M-63 Phone: 616-923-5000
Benton Harbor, MI 49022-2692 Fax: 616-923-3568
Chm & CEO: David R. Whitwam
VP HR & Asst Sec: Ed R. Dunn
Employees: 39,590
Jobs Added Last Year: 1,070 (+2.8%)
Appliances - washers & dryers, refrigerators, stoves, air conditioners & mixers (KitchenAid)

WOLOHAN LUMBER CO.
1740 Midland Rd. Phone: 517-793-4532
Saginaw, MI 48603 Fax: 517-793-4582
Pres & CEO: James L. Wolohan
VP HR: Bill Stark
Employees: 2,400
Jobs Added Last Year: 500 (+26.3%)
Building products - retail & wholesale

WOLVERINE WORLD WIDE, INC.
9341 Courtland Dr. Phone: 616-866-5500
Rockford, MI 49351 Fax: 616-866-0257
Pres & CEO: Geoffrey Bloom
VP HR: Robert Sedrowski
Employees: 4,761
Jobs Added Last Year: 14 (+.3%)
Shoes & related apparel

X-RITE, INC.
3100 44th St. SW Phone: 616-534-7663
Grandville, MI 49418 Fax: 616-534-9212
Chm & CEO: D. Ted Thompson
Dir HR: Beth Baumgartner
Employees: 520
Jobs Added Last Year: 222 (+74.5%)
Instruments - control

MINNESOTA

ADC TELECOMMUNICATIONS, INC.
4900 W. 78th St. Phone: 612-938-8080
Minneapolis, MN 55435 Fax: 612-946-3292
Chm, Pres & CEO: William J. Cadogan
VP HR: Pamela J. Nichols
Employees: 2,644
Jobs Added Last Year: 182 (+7.4%)
Telecommunications equipment - cable management, transmission & networking communications equipment

ADVANCE CIRCUITS, INC.
5929 Baker Rd., Sre. 470 Phone: 612-988-8700
Minnetonka, MN 55345 Fax: 612-988-8727
Pres & CEO: Robert W. Heller
Dir HR: Richard A. Rodgers
Employees: 1,103
Jobs Added Last Year: 184 (+20%)
Electrical components - printed circuit boards for use in computers & telecommunications equipment

AIRTRAN CORPORATION
7501 26th Ave. South Phone: 612-726-5151
Minneapolis, MN 55450 Fax: 612-725-4901
CEO: Robert D. Swenson
Dir HR: Dan Shehan
Employees: 1,333
Jobs Added Last Year: 367 (+38%)
Transportation - passenger & freight airline

ALLIANT TECHSYSTEMS INC.
600 Second St. NE Phone: 612-931-6000
Hopkins, MN 55343-8384 Fax: 612-939-5920
Pres & CEO: Richard Schwartz
VP Admin (HR): John Buck
Employees: 4,900
Jobs Added Last Year: 400 (+8.9%)
Weapons & weapon systems

ALLINA HEALTH SYSTEM
2810 57th Ave. North Phone: 612-574-7800
Minneapolis, MN 55430 Fax: 612-574-7953
Exec Off: Gordon M. Sprenger
HR Off: Mark G. Mishek
Employees: 15,600
Jobs Added Last Year: —
Hospitals - nonprofit health care delivery system

ANDERSEN CORP.
100 Fourth Ave. North Phone: 612-439-5150
Bayport, MN 55003 Fax: 612-430-5107
VC, Pres & CEO: Jerold W. Wulf
Mgr HR: Paul Wiemerslage
Employees: 4,000
Jobs Added Last Year: 500 (+14.3%)
Building products - windows, patio doors

APOGEE ENTERPRISES, INC.
7900 Xerxes Ave. South, Ste. 1800 Phone: 612-835-1874
Minneapolis, MN 55431-1159 Fax: 612-835-3196
Chm & CEO: Donald W. Goldfus
Corp Ben Mgr (HR): Mary Lehnert
Employees: 5,863
Jobs Added Last Year: 505 (+9.4%)
Glass products - building & automotive products

ARCTCO, INC.
600 Brooks Ave. South Phone: 218-681-8558
Thief River Falls, MN 56701 Fax: 218-681-3162
Pres & CEO: Christopher A. Twomey
HR Mgr: Melba Laidley
Employees: 1,250
Jobs Added Last Year: 350 (+38.9%)
Snowmobiles (Arctic Cat) & accessories, personal watercraft (Barracuda, Daytona)

AUTOMOTIVE INDUSTRIES HOLDING, INC.
4508 IDS Center Phone: 612-332-6828
Minneapolis, MN 55402 Fax: 612-332-2012
CEO: Fred Sommer
VP HR: Dan Clinton
Employees: 4,100
Jobs Added Last Year: 1,167 (+39.8%)
Automotive & trucking - original equipment

BEMIS CO., INC.
222 S. Ninth St., Ste. 2300 Phone: 612-376-3000
Minneapolis, MN 55402-4099 Fax: 612-376-3180
CEO: John H. Roe
VP HR: Larry Schwanke
Employees: 7,700
Jobs Cut Last Year: 100 (-1.3%)
Containers - paper & plastic

MINNESOTA

BEST BUY CO., INC.
7075 Flying Cloud Dr.
Eden Prarie, MN 55344
Chm & CEO: Richard M. Schulze
VP HR & Gen Counsel: Joseph M. Joyce
Employees: 15,200
Jobs Added Last Year: 5,600 (+58.3%)
Retail - consumer electronics
Phone: 612-947-2000
Fax: 612-947-2422

CERIDIAN CORPORATION
8100 34th Ave. South
Minneapolis, MN 55425-1640
Chm, Pres & CEO: Lawrence Perlman
EVP Personnel: Glenn W. Jeffrey
Employees: 7,600
Jobs Cut Last Year: 1,200 (-13.6%)
Computers - mainframe
Phone: 612-853-8100
Fax: 612-853-7173

BRAUN'S FASHIONS CORPORATION
2400 Xenium Ln.
Plymouth, MN 55441
Chm & CEO: Nicholas H. Cook
Dir HR: Lori Leonard
Employees: 1,550
Jobs Added Last Year: 250 (+19.2%)
Retail - apparel & shoes
Phone: 612-551-5000
Fax: 612-551-5199

CHRONIMED, INC.
13911 Ridgedale Dr.
Minnetonka, MN 55305
CEO: Maurice R. Taylor II
Dir HR: Dolly Sollie
Employees: 184
Jobs Added Last Year: 63 (+52.1%)
Medical products, drugs & nutritional products distribution
Phone: 612-541-0239
Fax: 612-451-4969

BUFFETS, INC.
10260 Viking Dr., Ste. 100
Eden Prairie, MN 55344
Chm & CEO: Roe H. Hatlen
VP HR: Laura Zauner
Employees: 13,900
Jobs Added Last Year: 3,400 (+32.4%)
Retail - restaurants in the midwestern & southern US (Old Country Buffet & Country Buffet)
Phone: 612-942-9760
Fax: 612-942-9658

COMMUNICATIONS SYSTEMS, INC.
213 S. Main St.
Hector, MN 55342
Chm, Pres & CEO: Curtis A. Sampson
Dir HR: Janice Weikly
Employees: 1,160
Jobs Added Last Year: 270 (+30.3%)
Telecommunications equipment - voice & data processing equipment
Phone: 612-848-6231
Fax: 612-848-2702

CARGILL, INCORPORATED
15407 McGinty Rd.
Minnetonka, MN 55440
Chm & CEO: Whitney MacMillan
SVP HR: Everett MacLennan
Employees: 70,700
Jobs Added Last Year: 700 (+1%)
Food - trading & processing; steel; animal feeds; salt (Leslie)
Phone: 612-475-7575
Fax: 612-475-6208

COMPUTER NETWORK TECHNOLOGY CORP.
6600 Wedgwood Rd.
Maple Grove, MN 55311-3640
CEO: C. McKenzie Lewis III
Senior HR Mgr: Holly Kennedy
Employees: 224
Jobs Added Last Year: 50 (+28.7%)
Computers - network products for LAN & WAN systems
Phone: 612-550-8000
Fax: 612-550-8800

CARLSON COMPANIES, INC.
Carlson Pkwy.
Minneapolis, MN 55459
Chm, Pres & CEO: Curtis L. Carlson
VP HR: Terry M. Butorac
Employees: 41,000
Jobs Cut Last Year: 8,350 (-16.9%)
Business services - travel, hospitality (Radisson) & restaurants (T.G.I. Friday's)
Phone: 612-540-5000
Fax: 612-540-5832

CONTROL DATA SYSTEMS, INC.
4201 Lexington Ave. North
Arden Hills, MN 55126-6198
CEO: James E. Ousley
Dir HR: Ruth A. Rich
Employees: 3,140
Jobs Added Last Year: —
Computers - systems integration & consulting
Phone: 612-482-2401
Fax: 612-482-2230

MINNESOTA

CRAY RESEARCH, INC.
655-A Lone Oak Dr.
Eagan, MN 55121
Pres & COO: Robert H. Ewald
VP HR: Karen G. Clary
Employees: 4,960
Jobs Added Last Year: 65 (+1.3%)
Computers - supercomputers
Phone: 612-683-7100
Fax: 612-683-7299

DIGI INTERNATIONAL INC.
6400 Flying Cloud Dr.
Eden Prairie, MN 55344
Pres & CEO: Ervin F. Kamm, Jr.
No central personnel officer
Employees: 430
Jobs Added Last Year: 97 (+29.1%)
Computers - networking systems that allow video terminals to connect to a server
Phone: 612-943-9020
Fax: 612-943-5396

DAIG CORPORATION
14901 DeVeau Place
Minnetonka, MN 55345
Chm & CEO: John J. Fleischhacker
No central personnel officer
Employees: 233
Jobs Added Last Year: 38 (+19.5%)
Medical products - minimally invasive surgical instruments
Phone: 612-933-4700
Fax: 612-933-0307

DIGITAL BIOMETRICS, INC.
5600 Rowland Rd., Ste. 205
Minnetonka, MN 55343-4315
CEO: Jack A. Klingert
VP & CFO (HR): Donald E. Berg
Employees: 60
Jobs Added Last Year: 9 (+17.6%)
Computers - inkless live-scan fingerprint system
Phone: 612-932-0888
Fax: 612-932-7181

DAMARK INTERNATIONAL, INC.
7101 Winnetka Ave. North
Brooklyn Park, MN 55428
Chm & CEO: Mark A. Cohn
VP HR: Linda Medin
Employees: 1,036
Jobs Added Last Year: 414 (+66.6%)
Retail - mail order excess inventory of consumer electronics, computers & home office equipment
Phone: 612-531-0066
Fax: 612-531-0481

DONALDSON COMPANY, INC.
1400 W. 94th St., PO Box 1299
Minneapolis, MN 55440
CEO: William A. Hodder
Dir HR: John E. Thames
Employees: 4,417
Jobs Added Last Year: 161 (+3.8%)
Air & liquid filters
Phone: 612-887-3131
Fax: 612-887-3155

DAYTON HUDSON CORPORATION
777 Nicollet Mall
Minneapolis, MN 55402
Chm & CEO: Robert Ulrich
SVP Personnel: Edwin H. Wingate
Employees: 174,000
Jobs Added Last Year: 4,000 (+2.4%)
Retail - major department stores (Dayton's, Hudson's, Marshall Field's, Mervyn's); discount stores (Target)
Phone: 612-370-6948
Fax: 612-370-5502

ECOLAB INC.
Ecolab Center
St. Paul, MN 55102
Chm & CEO: Pierson M. Grieve
VC & CFO (HR): Michael E. Shannon
Employees: 7,600
Jobs Added Last Year: 200 (+2.7%)
Building - cleaning & landscaping services
Phone: 612-293-2233
Fax: 612-225-3059

DELUXE CORPORATION
1080 W. County Rd. F
St. Paul, MN 55126-8201
Chm, Pres & CEO: Harold V. Haverty
VP HR: Terence J. Quigley
Employees: 17,748
Jobs Added Last Year: 348 (+2%)
Paper - business forms, check printing; electronic funds transfer software
Phone: 612-483-7111
Fax: 612-481-4163

EMPI, INC.
1275 Grey Fox Rd.
St. Paul, MN 55112
Pres & CEO: Joseph E. Laptewicz, Jr.
Dir HR: Shawn Fahenson
Employees: 418
Jobs Added Last Year: 196 (+88.3%)
Medical instruments - diagnostic equipment, biomedical devices
Phone: 612-636-6600
Fax: 612-639-2405

MINNESOTA

FASTENAL COMPANY
2001 Theurer Blvd. Phone: 507-454-5374
Winona, MN 55987 Fax: 507-454-6542
Pres & CEO: Robert A. Kierlin
Dir HR: Terry Hanley
Employees: 878
Jobs Added Last Year: 230 (+35.5%)
Building products - retail threaded fasteners & power tools (FastTool)

FINGERHUT COMPANIES, INC.
4400 Baker Rd. Phone: 612-932-3100
Minnetonka, MN 55343 Fax: 612-932-3292
Chm, Pres & CEO: Theodore Deikel
SVP HR: William J. Colucci
Employees: 8,500
Jobs Added Last Year: 500 (+6.3%)
Retail - mail order & direct

FIRST BANK SYSTEM, INC.
601 Second Ave. South Phone: 612-973-2300
Minneapolis, MN 55402 Fax: 612-973-2351
CEO: John F. Grundhofer
EVP (HR): Robert H. Sayre
Employees: 14,000
Jobs Added Last Year: 1,700 (+13.8%)
Banks - Midwest

FOURTH SHIFT CORPORATION
7900 International Dr., Ste. 450 Phone: 612-851-1500
Minneapolis, MN 55425 Fax: 612-851-1560
Chm & CEO: Marion M. Stuckey
Mgr HR: Renee Conklin
Employees: 278
Jobs Added Last Year: 117 (+72.7%)
Computers - accounting & manufacturing management software

FSI INTERNATIONAL, INC.
322 Lake Hazeltine Dr. Phone: 612-448-5440
Chaska, MN 55318 Fax: 612-448-2825
Pres & CEO: Joel A. Elftmann
VP HR: Tim Krieg
Employees: 399
Jobs Added Last Year: 90 (+29.1%)
Machinery - automated wafer-processing equipment

FUNCO INC.
10120 W. 76th St. Phone: 612-946-8883
Minneapolis, MN 55344 Fax: 612-946-7251
Chm, Pres & CEO: David R. Pomije
VP Retail Ops & HR: Jeffery R. Gatesmith
Employees: 614
Jobs Added Last Year: 274 (+80.6%)
Retail - used videogames (FuncoLand)

G&K SERVICES, INC.
505 Waterford Park, Ste. 455 Phone: 612-546-7440
Minneapolis, MN 55441 Fax: 612-546-7872
Chm: Richard Fink
Dir HR: Lynn Weiss
Employees: 4,500
Jobs Added Last Year: 952 (+26.8%)
Linen supply & laundering - uniforms

GENERAL MILLS, INC.
One General Mills Blvd. Phone: 612-540-2311
Minneapolis, MN 55440 Fax: 612-540-4925
Chm & CEO: H. Brewster Atwater, Jr.
VP HR: Keith R. Sieck
Employees: 121,290
Jobs Added Last Year: 9,789 (+8.8%)
Food - cereals, snack foods, prepared mixes & frostings

GFI AMERICA, INC
2815 Blaisdell Ave. South Phone: 612-872-6262
Minneapolis, MN 55408-2312 Fax: 612-870-4955
Chm, Pres & CEO: Robert D. Goldberger
Dir HR: Luis McKibbin
Employees: 1,200
Jobs Added Last Year: 200 (+20%)
Food - meatpacking

GRAND CASINOS, INC.
13705 First Ave. North Phone: 612-449-9092
Minneapolis, MN 55441 Fax: 612-449-9353
Chm & CEO: Lyle Berman
VP HR: Jeffrey Wagner
Employees: 6,300
Jobs Added Last Year: 3,800 (+152%)
Leisure & recreational services - casinos

MINNESOTA

GREEN TREE FINANCIAL CORPORATION
345 St. Peter St.
St. Paul, MN 55102-1639
Phone: 612-293-3400
Fax: 612-293-3503
Chm & CEO: Lawrence M. Coss
VP HR: Barbara Didrickson
Employees: 1,323
Jobs Added Last Year: 117 (+9.7%)
Financial - mortgages & related services

GROW BIZ INTERNATIONAL, INC.
4200 Dahlberg Dr.
Minneapolis, MN 55422-4783
Phone: 612-520-8500
Fax: 612-520-8410
Pres & CEO: Ronald G. Olson
Dir HR: Patricia Knott
Employees: 149
Jobs Added Last Year: 30 (+25.2%)
Business services - franchise sports, toy, computer & CD disc stores that sell, buy, trade & consign used & new merchandise

H. B. FULLER CO.
2400 Energy Park Dr.
St. Paul, MN 55108
Phone: 612-645-3401
Fax: 612-645-6936
Chm & CEO: Anthony L. Andersen
VP (HR): James A. Metts
Employees: 6,400
Jobs Added Last Year: 400 (+6.7%)
Chemicals - specialty

HEI, INC.
1495 Steiger Lake Ln.
Victoria, MN 55386
Phone: 612-443-2500
Fax: 612-443-2668
Pres & CEO: Eugene W. Courtney
No central personnel officer
Employees: 160
Jobs Added Last Year: 30 (+23.1%)
Electrical components - optoelectronic components, optical card readers

HOLIDAY COS.
4567 W. 80th St.
Bloomington, MN 55437
Phone: 612-830-8700
Fax: 612-830-8864
Chm: Ronald Erickson
Dir HR: Bob Nye
Employees: 5,000
Jobs Added Last Year: 1,200 (+31.6%)
Retail - convenience stores & grocery wholesaling

HONEYWELL INC.
Honeywell Plaza
Minneapolis, MN 55408
Phone: 612-951-1000
Fax: 612-951-0137
Chm & CEO: Michael R. Bonisgnore
VP HR: James Porter
Employees: 52,300
Jobs Cut Last Year: 3,100 (-5.6%)
Diversified operations - industrial & environmental control systems; avionics

HORMEL FOODS CORPORATION
One Hormel Place
Austin, MN 55912-3680
Phone: 507-437-5611
Fax: 507-437-5489
Pres & CEO: Joel W. Johnson
VP HR: James A. Jorgenson
Employees: 9,500
Jobs Cut Last Year: 1,300 (-12%)
Food - luncheon meat (Spam), chili, beef stew, hash, bacon, ham, franks & other foods, including salsa

HUTCHINSON TECHNOLOGY INC.
40 W. Highland Park
Hutchinson, MN 55350
Phone: 612-587-3797
Fax: 612-587-1892
CEO: Jeffrey W. Green
Dir HR: Rebecca Albrecht
Employees: 4,575
Jobs Added Last Year: 467 (+11.4%)
Computers - Mechanical suspension assembly arms for hard disk drives

IN HOME HEALTH, INC.
601 Lakeshore Pkwy., Ste. 500
Minnetonka, MN 55305-5214
Phone: 612-449-7500
Fax: 612-449-7599
Pres & CEO: Judy M. Figge
COO & VP (HR): Cathy R. Reeves
Employees: 5,150
Jobs Added Last Year: 310 (+6.4%)
Health care - outpatient & home

INTER-REGIONAL FINANCIAL GROUP, INC.
60 S. Sixth St.
Minneapolis, MN 55402-4422
Phone: 612-371-7750
Fax: 612-371-7755
Pres & CEO: Irving Weiser
EVP HR: Mary M. Melbo
Employees: 3,190
Jobs Added Last Year: 240 (+8.1%)
Financial - investment brokerage

MINNESOTA

INTERNATIONAL MULTIFOODS CORPORATION
33 S. Sixth St., PO Box 2942　　Phone: 612-340-3300
Minneapolis, MN 55402-0942　　Fax: 612-340-3338
Chm, Pres & CEO: Anthony Luiso
VP HR: Robert Maddocks
Employees: 8,390
Jobs Added Last Year: 49 (+.6%)
Food - flour & grain

KAHLER REALTY CORPORATION
20 SW Second Ave.　　Phone: 507-282-2581
Rochester, MN 55902　　Fax: 507-285-2772
CEO: Harold W. Milner
VP HR: Sam Workman
Employees: 3,175
Jobs Added Last Year: 425 (+15.5%)
Hotels & motels

LAND O' LAKES, INC.
4001 Lexington Ave. North　　Phone: 612-481-2222
Arden Hills, MN 55126　　Fax: 612-481-2022
Pres & CEO: Jack Gherty
VP HR: Jack Martin
Employees: 5,700
Jobs Added Last Year: 700 (+14%)
Food - dairy products

LASERMASTER TECHNOLOGIES, INC.
7156 Shady Oak Rd.　　Phone: 612-941-8687
Eden Prairie, MN 55344　　Fax: 612-941-8652
CEO: Melvin L. Master
Dir HR: Mary Paige
Employees: 484
Jobs Added Last Year: 162 (+50.3%)
Computers - laser printers & display systems

LAWSON ASSOCIATES, INC.
1300 Godward Street　　Phone: 612-379-8086
Minneapolis, MN 55413　　Fax: 612-379-7141
Pres & CEO: Richard Lawson
HR Mgr: Wanda Fischer
Employees: 580
Jobs Added Last Year: 205 (+54.7%)
Computers - client/server business applications software

LECTEC CORPORATION
10701 Red Circle Dr.　　Phone: 612-933-2291
Minnetonka, MN 55343　　Fax: 612-933-4808
Chm, Pres & CEO: Thomas E. Brunelle
No central personnel officer
Employees: 63
Jobs Added Last Year: 14 (+28.6%)
Medical instruments - diagnostic & monitoring electrodes, medical tapes

LIFE USA HOLDING, INC.
300 S. Hwy. 169　　Phone: 612-546-7386
Minneapolis, MN 55426　　Fax: 612-525-6000
Chm & CEO: Robert W. MacDonald
VP HR: Lorrie Frankewicz
Employees: 323
Jobs Added Last Year: 50 (+18.3%)
Insurance - life

LIFECORE BIOMEDICAL, INC.
3515 Lyman Blvd.　　Phone: 612-368-4300
Chaska, MN 55318　　Fax: 612-368-3411
CEO: James W. Bracke
VP Corp Admin (HR): Colleen Olsen
Employees: 105
Jobs Added Last Year: 23 (+28%)
Biomedical & genetic products

MAYO FOUNDATION
Mayo Clinic　　Phone: 507-284-2511
Rochester, MN 55905　　Fax: 507-284-8713
Pres & CEO: Robert R. Waller
HR: Greg Warner
Employees: 21,770
Jobs Added Last Year: 1,155 (+5.6%)
Hospitals

MEDTRONIC, INC.
7000 Central Ave. NE　　Phone: 612-574-4000
Minneapolis, MN 55432　　Fax: 612-574-4879
Pres & CEO: William W. George
SVP HR: Janet S. Fiola
Employees: 8,709
Jobs Added Last Year: 375 (+4.5%)
Medical instruments - pacemakers & related cardiovascular products

MINNESOTA

MERRILL CORPORATION
One Merrill Circle Phone: 612-646-4501
St. Paul, MN 55108-5267 Fax: 612-649-1348
Pres & CEO: John W. Castro
VP HR: Kathleen A. Larkin
Employees: 1,618
Jobs Added Last Year: 577 (+55.4%)
Printing - commercial for corporate & financial markets

NASH-FINCH COMPANY
7600 France Ave. South Phone: 612-832-0534
Minneapolis, MN 55440-0355 Fax: 612-924-4854
CEO: Alfred Flaten
Dir HR: Edgar Timberlane
Employees: 12,402
Jobs Added Last Year: 514 (+4.3%)
Food - wholesale to supermarkets

MILES HOMES, INC.
4700 Nathan Ln. Phone: 612-553-8300
Plymouth, MN 55446-0106 Fax: 612-553-8449
CEO: Peter R. DeGeorge
VP Ops (HR): Bob Reiner
Employees: 444
Jobs Added Last Year: 208 (+88.1%)
Building products - building plans, packaged building materials; construction financing

NORSTAN, INC.
6900 Wedgwood Rd., Ste. 150 Phone: 612-420-1100
Maple Grove, MN 55311 Fax: 612-420-1178
Chm, CEO & Pres: Paul Baszucki
VP HR: Karen Clary
Employees: 1,703
Jobs Added Last Year: 110 (+6.9%)
Telecommunications equipment - integrated voice, video, data & image communications equipment

3M
3M Center Phone: 612-733-1110
St. Paul, MN 55144-1000 Fax: 612-733-9973
Chm & CEO: Livio D. DeSimone
VP HR: Richard A. Lidstad
Employees: 86,016
Jobs Cut Last Year: 1,276 (-1.5%)
Diversified operations - information & imaging equipment; consumer products

NORTHERN STATES POWER CO.
414 Nicollet Mall Phone: 612-330-5500
Minneapolis, MN 55401 Fax: 612-330-2900
Chm & CEO: James J. Howard
VP HR: Cynthia L. Lesher
Employees: 7,880
Jobs Cut Last Year: 351 (-4.3%)
Utility - electric power

MTS SYSTEMS CORPORATION
14000 Technology Dr. Phone: 612-937-4000
Eden Prairie, MN 55344-2290 Fax: 612-937-4515
Chm, Pres & CEO: Donald M. Sullivan
HR Mgr: Bruce Hebeisen
Employees: 1,557
Jobs Added Last Year: 110 (+7.6%)
Electronics - measuring instruments

NORTHWEST AIRLINES CORPORATION
5101 Northwest Dr. Phone: 612-726-2111
St. Paul, MN 55111-3034 Fax: 612-726-3942
Pres & CEO: John H. Dasburg
SVP Corp Comm, Advertising & HR: Christopher E. Clouser
Employees: 43,358
Jobs Cut Last Year: 1,097 (-2.5%)
Transportation - airline

MUSICLAND GROUP INC.
10400 Yellow Circle Dr. Phone: 612-931-8000
Minnetonka, MN 55343 Fax: 612-931-8300
Chm, Pres & CEO: Jack W. Eugster
VP HR & Admin: Charles E. Baker
Employees: 13,000
Jobs Added Last Year: 2,000 (+18.2%)
Retail - prerecorded music & video

NORWEST CORPORATION
Sixth & Marquette Phone: 612-667-1234
Minneapolis, MN 55479 Fax: 612-667-5185
Pres & CEO: Richard M. Kovacevich
SVP HR: Stephen W. Hansen
Employees: 35,000
Jobs Added Last Year: 6,000 (+20.7%)
Banks - Midwest

An in-depth profile of this company is available by fax. Call 800-510-4452 and use your touch-tone phone to put in the 5-digit code at the prompt. Only $2.95 each with your credit card. See page 12 for more details.

MINNESOTA

OLYMPIC FINANCIAL LTD.
7825 Washington Ave. South   Phone: 612-942-9880
Minneapolis, MN 55439-2444   Fax: 612-942-6730
CEO: Jeffrey C. Mack
VP HR: Mary West
Employees: 218
Jobs Added Last Year: 120 (+122.4%)
Financial - consumer loans

PATTERSON DENTAL COMPANY
1100 E. 80th St.   Phone: 612-686-1600
Minneapolis, MN 55420   Fax: 612-686-9331
Pres: Peter L. Frechette
Dir HR: Mary Martins
Employees: 2,342
Jobs Added Last Year: 744 (+46.6%)
Dental supply distribution

PENTAIR, INC.
1500 County Rd., Ste. B2 West   Phone: 612-636-7920
St. Paul, MN 55113-3105   Fax: 612-639-5251
Chm, Pres & CEO: Winslow H. Buxton
VP HR: Deb Knutson
Employees: 9,800
Jobs Added Last Year: 1,500 (+18.1%)
Paper & paper products

PET FOOD WAREHOUSE, INC.
600 S. Hwy. 169   Phone: 612-542-0123
St. Louis Park, MN 55426-1011   Fax: 612-542-0094
CEO: Patrick A. Labriola
HR Admin: Pat Connelly
Employees: 294
Jobs Added Last Year: 94 (+47%)
Retail - pet supplies

PIPER JAFFRAY COMPANIES INC.
222 S. Ninth St.   Phone: 612-342-6000
Minneapolis, MN 55402-3804   Fax: 612-342-6996
Chm & CEO: Addison L. Piper
Dir HR: Edward M. Caillier
Employees: 2,658
Jobs Added Last Year: 231 (+9.5%)
Financial - brokerage services

REGIS CORPORATION
7201 Metro Blvd.   Phone: 612-947-7777
Edina, MN 55439   Fax: 612-947-7600
Chm & CEO: Myron Kunin
No central personnel officer
Employees: 15,500
Jobs Added Last Year: 1,000 (+6.9%)
Retail - mall-based hair & beauty salons (Regis Hairstylists, MasterCuts); retail hair care products (Trade Secret)

RELIASTAR FINANCIAL CORPORATION
20 Washington Ave. South   Phone: 612-372-5432
Minneapolis, MN 55401   Fax: 612-342-3966
Chm & CEO: John G. Turner
VP HR: Adair C. Peterson
Employees: 2,687
Jobs Added Last Year: 125 (+4.9%)
Insurance - life

RIMAGE CORPORATION
7725 Washington Ave. South   Phone: 612-944-8144
Minneapolis, MN 55439-2423   Fax: 612-944-7808
Pres: David Suden
Office Mgr (HR): Renee Dallman
Employees: 162
Jobs Added Last Year: 82 (+102.5%)
Computers - diskette duplication & finishing systems

SCHWAN'S SALES ENTERPRISES, INC.
115 W. College Dr.   Phone: 507-532-3274
Marshall, MN 56258   Fax: 507-537-8145
Pres & CEO: Alfred Schwan
Head of Personnel: Larry Gibbs
Employees: 6,000
Jobs Added Last Year: –
Food - home delivery of food

SCIMED LIFE SYSTEMS, INC.
One Scimed Place   Phone: 612-494-1700
Maple Grove, MN 55311-1566   Fax: 612-494-1550
Chm & CEO: Dale A. Spencer
VP HR: Charles M. Bolton
Employees: 1,848
Jobs Added Last Year: 533 (+40.5%)
Medical instruments - artery-cleaning angioplasty catheters used in coronary therapy

MINNESOTA

ST. PAUL COMPANIES, INC.
385 Washington St. Phone: 612-221-7911
St. Paul, MN 55102 Fax: 612-221-8294
Chm & CEO: Douglas W. Leatherdale
SVP HR: Greg A. Lee
Employees: 13,200
Jobs Added Last Year: 1,000 (+8.2%)
Insurance - property & casualty

UNITED HEALTHCARE CORPORATION
9900 Bren Rd. East Phone: 612-936-1300
Minnetonka, MN 55343 Fax: 612-931-9655
Chm, Pres & CEO: William W. McGuire
VP HR & Administrative Svcs: Bob Backes
Employees: 6,502
Jobs Added Last Year: 1,702 (+35.5%)
Insurance - long-term health care

SUPERVALU INC.
11840 Valley View Rd. Phone: 612-828-4000
Eden Prairie, MN 55344 Fax: 612-828-8998
Chm, Pres & CEO: Michael W. Wright
SVP HR: Ronald C. Tortelli
Employees: 42,500
Jobs Added Last Year: 500 (+1.2%)
Food - wholesale; supermarkets

UNIVERSITY OF MINNESOTA
202 Morrill Hall, 100 Church St. SE Phone: 612-625-5000
Minneapolis, MN 55445 Fax: 612-626-1332
Pres & Chancellor: Nils Hasselmo
Assoc VP HR: Carol Carrier
Employees: 18,212
Jobs Added Last Year: —
University

TAYLOR CORPORATION
1725 Roecrest Dr. Phone: 507-625-2828
North Mankato, MN 56003 Fax: 507-625-2988
CEO: Glen Taylor
Personnel Administrator: Marie Eckert
Employees: 7,000
Jobs Added Last Year: —
Printing - commercial

VENTURIAN CORPORATION
1600 Second St. South Phone: 612-931-2500
Hopkins, MN 55343 Fax: 612-931-2402
CEO: Gary B. Rappaport
Dir HR: Judy Winker
Employees: 179
Jobs Added Last Year: 109 (+155.7%)
Diversified operations - security; communications; engineering services

TCF FINANCIAL CORPORATION
801 Marquette Ave., Ste. 302 Phone: 612-661-6500
Minneapolis, MN 55402 Fax: 612-332-1753
CEO: William A. Cooper
Dir HR: Becky Curture
Employees: 3,500
Jobs Added Last Year: 1,000 (+40%)
Banks - Midwest

WEST PUBLISHING CO.
610 Opperman Dr. Phone: 612-687-7000
Eagan, MN 55123 Fax: 612-687-5827
Chm & CEO: Dwight D. Opperman
HR: Barbara Christenson
Employees: 5,600
Jobs Added Last Year: 300 (+5.7%)
Publishing - law & college textbooks & on-line service

TORO COMPANY
8111 Lyndale Ave. South Phone: 612-888-8801
Bloomington, MN 55420 Fax: 612-887-8258
Chm & CEO: Kendrick B. Melrose
VP HR & Administrative Svcs: Karen M. Meyer
Employees: 3,434
Jobs Added Last Year: 317 (+10.2%)
Tools - lawn & garden equipment

ZYTEC CORPORATION
7575 Market Place Dr. Phone: 612-941-1100
Eden Prairie, MN 55344 Fax: 612-829-1837
Chm, Pres & CEO: Ronald D. Schmidt
Dir HR: Annette Cramer
Employees: 1,020
Jobs Added Last Year: 246 (+31.8%)
Electrical components - power supplies for computers & other electronic equipment

MISSISSIPPI

CASINO AMERICA, INC.
711 Washington Loop   Phone: 601-436-7000
Biloxi, MS 39530   Fax: 601-435-5998
Pres & CEO: James E. Ernst
VP HR: Robert Boone
Employees: 3,975
Jobs Added Last Year: 1,875 (+89.3%)
Leisure & recreational services - riverboat casinos

HANCOCK HOLDING COMPANY
One Hancock Plaza   Phone: 601-868-4715
Gulfport, MS 39501   Fax: 601-868-4675
Pres & CEO: Leo W. Seal, Jr.
VC (HR): George Schloegel
Employees: 1,103
Jobs Added Last Year: 88 (+8.7%)
Banks - Southeast

CASINO MAGIC CORPORATION
711 Casino Magic Dr.   Phone: 601-467-9257
Bay St. Louis, MS 39520-1808   Fax: 601-467-7998
CEO: Marlin F. Torguson
VP HR: Kathy Innaurato
Employees: 3,150
Jobs Added Last Year: 1,650 (+110%)
Leisure & recreational services - casinos in Mississippi & South Dakota

JITNEY-JUNGLE STORES OF AMERICA, INC.
453 N. Mill St.   Phone: 601-948-0361
Jackson, MS 39202   Fax: 601-352-0483
Chm, Pres & CEO: W. H. Holman, Jr.
SVP HR: Jerry Jones
Employees: 10,000
Jobs Added Last Year: —
Retail - supermarkets

DEPOSIT GUARANTY CORPORATION
PO Box 1200   Phone: 601-354-8564
Jackson, MS 39215-1200 Fax: 601-354-8192
Chm: E. B. Robinson, Jr.
SVP & Dir HR: Susan S. Cain
Employees: 2,800
Jobs Added Last Year: 282 (+11.2%)
Banks - Southeast

KLLM TRANSPORT SERVICES, INC.
3475 Lakeland Dr.   Phone: 601-939-2545
Jackson, MS 39208   Fax: 601-936-7151
Acting CEO: Benny Lee
Corp VP HR & Risk Mgmt: Irene Howard
Employees: 1,886
Jobs Added Last Year: 579 (+44.3%)
Transportation - truck

FIRST MISSISSIPPI CORPORATION
700 North St.   Phone: 601-948-7550
Jackson, MS 39202-3095 Fax: 601-949-0228
Chm & CEO: J. Kelley Williams
Dir HR: Dennis Watford
Employees: 1,215
Jobs Added Last Year: 73 (+6.4%)
Ferrtilizers; specialty chemicals; gold mining; combustion & thermal plasma equipment

LDDS COMMUNICATIONS, INC.
515 E. Amite St.   Phone: 601-360-8600
Jackson, MS 39201-2702 Fax: 601-360-8616
Pres & CEO: Bernard J. Ebbers
VP HR & Admin: Dennis Sickle
Employees: 4,379
Jobs Added Last Year: 1,939 (+79.5%)
Telecommunications services - #4 long distance carrier in the US

HANCOCK FABRICS, INC.
3406 W. Main St., PO Box 2400 Phone: 601-842-2834
Tupelo, MS 38803-2400   Fax: 601-842-2834
Chm, Pres & CEO: Morris O. Jarvis
VP Personnel: Dave Jenson
Employees: 7,100
Jobs Cut Last Year: 300 (-4.1%)
Retail - fabric & notions

MAGNA BANCORP, INC.
100 W. Front St.   Phone: 601-545-4700
Hattiesburg, MS 39401 Fax: 601-583-7132
CEO: Robert S. Duncan
Dir HR: Barbara S. Ellender
Employees: 1,274
Jobs Added Last Year: 159 (+14.3%)
Financial - savings & loans

MISSISSIPPI

MISSISSIPPI CHEMICAL CORPORATION
Owen Cooper Bldg., Hwy. 49 East   Phone: 601-746-4131
Yazoo City, MS 39194   Fax: 601-746-9158
Pres & CEO: Charles O. Dunn
SVP Fin & Admin (HR): William F. Hawkins
Employees: 1,179
Jobs Added Last Year: 219 (+22.8%)
Fertilizers - nitrogen

TRUSTMARK CORPORATION
248 E. Capitol St.   Phone: 601-354-5111
Jackson, MS 39205   Fax: 601-949-2355
Chm & CEO: Frank R. Day
SVP HR: Robert G. Spring
Employees: 2,202
Jobs Added Last Year: 210 (+10.5%)
Banks - Southeast

SANDERSON FARMS, INC.
225 N. 13th Ave., PO Box 988   Phone: 601-649-4030
Laurel, MS 39441-0988   Fax: 601-426-1461
Pres & CEO: Joe F. Sanderson, Jr.
Dir HR: Jesse Walters
Employees: 3,817
Jobs Added Last Year: 1,413 (+58.8%)
Food - meat products

▼ Skill Search http://www.internet-is.com/skillsearch/index.html

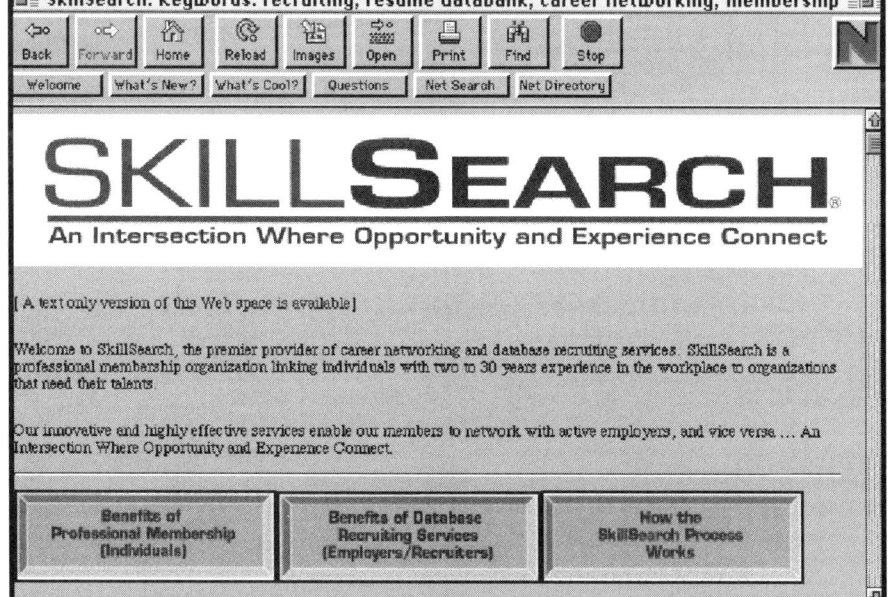

MISSOURI

A.G. EDWARDS, INC.
One N. Jefferson Ave. Phone: 314-289-3000
St. Louis, MO 63103 Fax: 314-289-3565
Chm, Pres & CEO: Benjamin F. Edwards III
VP & Dir Personnel: Ron Hoenninger
Employees: 10,206
Jobs Added Last Year: 719 (+7.6%)
Financial - investment bankers

AMC ENTERTAINMENT INC.
106 W. 14th St., PO Box 419615 Phone: 816-221-4000
Kansas City, MO 64141-6615 Fax: 816-421-5744
Chm & CEO: Stanley H. Durwood
Pres & Vice Chm (HR): Edward D. Durwood
Employees: 8,047
Jobs Added Last Year: 1,847 (+29.8%)
Motion pictures & services - theaters

ANGELICA CORPORATION
424 S. Woods Mill Rd. Phone: 314-854-3800
Chesterfield, MO 63017-3406 Fax: 314-854-3890
Chm & Pres: Lawrence J. Young
VP HR: John S. Aleman
Employees: 9,500
Jobs Added Last Year: 500 (+5.6%)
Linen supply & related - uniforms

ANHEUSER-BUSCH COMPANIES, INC.
One Busch Place Phone: 314-577-2000
St. Louis, MO 63118 Fax: 314-577-2900
Chm & Pres: August A. Busch III
VP Corp HR: William L. Rammes
Employees: 43,345
Jobs Cut Last Year: 1,445 (-3.2%)
Beverages - beer (Budweiser, Michelob); snacks (Eagle); bread; theme parks; St. Louis Cardinals

BELDEN INC.
7701 Forsyth Blvd., Ste. 800 Phone: 314-854-8000
St. Louis, MO 63105 Fax: 314-854-8001
Chm, Pres & CEO: C. Baker Cunningham
VP HR: Cathy O. Staples
Employees: 2,800
Jobs Added Last Year: 100 (+3.7%)
Wire & cable products

BHA GROUP, INC.
8800 E. 63rd St. Phone: 816-356-8400
Kansas City, MO 64133 Fax: 816-353-1873
Pres & CEO: James E. Lund
HR Dir: Rick Lindquist
Employees: 580
Jobs Added Last Year: 93 (+19.1%)
Aftermarket parts & technical services for the industrial air pollution control market

BLACK AND VEATCH
8400 Ward Pkwy. Phone: 913-339-2000
Kansas City, MO 64114 Fax: 913-339-3817
Chm & CEO: P. J. Adam
Dir HR: Dave H. Lillard
Employees: 4,900
Jobs Added Last Year: –
Construction - power plants, wastewater treatment systems & hydrocarbon processing facilities

BOATMEN'S BANCSHARES, INC.
800 Market St. Phone: 314-466-6000
St. Louis, MO 63101 Fax: 314-466-4235
Chm, Pres & CEO: John Morton III
SVP HR: Arthur J. Fleischer
Employees: 14,370
Jobs Added Last Year: 961 (+7.2%)
Banks - Midwest

BROWN GROUP, INC.
8300 Maryland Ave. Phone: 314-854-4000
St. Louis, MO 63105 Fax: 314-854-4274
Chm, Pres & CEO: B. A. Bridgewater, Jr
Dir Personnel: Steve Scanlan
Employees: 22,000
Jobs Cut Last Year: 1,000 (-4.3%)
Shoes & related apparel

BUTLER MANUFACTURING CO.
BMA Tower, Penn Valley Park Phone: 816-968-3000
Kansas City, MO 64141 Fax: 816-968-3279
Chm & CEO: Robert H. West
VP Admin (HR): John W. Huey
Employees: 3,500
Jobs Added Last Year: 436 (+14.2%)
Building products - pre-engineered nonresidential metal buildings

MISSOURI

CERNER CORPORATION
2800 Rockcreek Pkwy. Phone: 816-221-1024
Kansas City, MO 64117-2551 Fax: 816-474-1742
Chm & CEO: Neal L. Patterson
VP Admin (HR): John Reedy
Employees: 653
Jobs Added Last Year: 148 (+29.3%)
Computers - software for health care providers

CITATION COMPUTER SYSTEMS, INC.
424 S. Woods Mill Rd., Ste. 200 Phone: 314-579-7900
Chesterfield, MO 63017 Fax: 314-579-7990
Pres & CEO: Kenneth R. Brown
Dir HR: Ann Prenatt
Employees: 214
Jobs Added Last Year: 56 (+35.4%)
Computers - LAN-based information systems software for hospitals & nursing homes

CLARK USA, INC.
8182 Maryland Ave. Phone: 314-854-9696
St. Louis, MO 63105 Fax: 314-854-1580
Pres, CEO & COO: Paul D. Melnuk
Dir HR & Mktg: Julie Hubbard
Employees: 5,700
Jobs Added Last Year: —
Oil refining & marketing

COMMERCE BANCSHARES, INC.
1000 Walnut St. Phone: 816-234-2000
Kansas City, MO 64106 Fax: 816-234-2019
Chm, Pres, CEO & CFO: David W. Kemper
VP HR: Rowland Ransom
Employees: 4,792
Jobs Added Last Year: 387 (+8.8%)
Banks - Midwest

CPI CORPORATION
1706 Washington Ave. Phone: 314-231-1575
St. Louis, MO 63103 Fax: 314-621-9286
CEO: Alyn V. Essman
EVP HR: Fran Scheper
Employees: 8,900
Jobs Added Last Year: 1,100 (+14.1%)
Photographic equipment & supplies

DATASTORM TECHNOLOGIES INC.
3212 Lemone Industrial Blvd. Phone: 314-443-3282
Columbia, MO 65205 Fax: 314-875-0595
Pres: Bruce Barkelew
Mgr HR: Jill Sievers
Employees: 244
Jobs Added Last Year: 74 (+43.5%)
Computers - data communications software (ProComm Plus)

DIMAC CORPORATION
One Corporate Woods Dr. Phone: 314-344-8000
Bridgeton, MO 63044-3838 Fax: 314-344-8099
Pres & CEO: Michael T. McSweeney
SVP HR & Admin: Michael Z. Sincoff
Employees: 1,100
Jobs Added Last Year: 145 (+15.2%)
Business services - direct marketing

EDISON BROTHERS STORES, INC.
501 N. Broadway Phone: 314-331-6000
St. Louis, MO 63102-2196 Fax: 314-331-7200
Chm: Andrew E. Newman
SVP HR: Eric A. Freesmeier
Employees: 24,200
Jobs Added Last Year: 200 (+.8%)
Retail - women's shoes & clothing, men's clothing, restaurant/entertainment operations

EDWARD D. JONES & CO.
12555 Manchester Rd. Phone: 314-851-2000
St. Louis, MO 63131 Fax: 314-851-3728
CEO: John W. Bachmann
Dir HR: Bob Pearce
Employees: 8,330
Jobs Added Last Year: —
Financial - securities brokerage, real estate

EMERSON ELECTRIC CO.
8000 W. Florissant Ave. Phone: 314-553-2000
St. Louis, MO 63136 Fax: 314-553-3527
Chm & CEO: Charles F. Knight
VP HR: C. T. Kelly
Employees: 73,900
Jobs Added Last Year: 2,300 (+3.2%)
Machinery - electric motors, hand-held tools & misc. electric equipment

MISSOURI

ENTERPRISE RENT-A-CAR CO. [40145]
8850 Ladue Rd. Phone: 314-863-7000
St. Louis, MO 63124 Fax: 314-863-7621
Pres & CEO: Andrew C. Taylor
VP HR: Jerry Spector
Employees: 14,000
Jobs Added Last Year: 5,500 (+64.7%)
Leasing - #2 US car rental company

EXPRESS SCRIPTS, INC. [15773]
1400 Riverport Dr. Phone: 314-770-1666
Maryland Heights, MO 63046 Fax: 314-770-0303
Pres & CEO: Barrett A. Toan
Dir HR: Karen Matteuzzi
Employees: 710
Jobs Added Last Year: 360 (+102.9%)
Medical services - pharmacy benefit management

FALCON PRODUCTS, INC.
9387 Dielman Industrial Dr. Phone: 314-991-9200
St. Louis, MO 63132 Fax: 314-991-9295
Chm & CEO: Franklin A. Jacobs
HR Dir: John F. Becker
Employees: 1,300
Jobs Added Last Year: 486 (+59.7%)
Furniture - tables, booths, chairs, sheet metal kitchen equipment

FARMLAND INDUSTRIES, INC. [40149]
3315 N. Oak Trafficway Phone: 816-459-6000
Kansas City, MO 64116 Fax: 816-459-6979
Pres & CEO: H. D. Cleberg
VP HR: Holly McCoy
Employees: 8,155
Jobs Added Last Year: 539 (+7.1%)
Diversified operations - meat packing; petroleum refining

GENERAL AMERICAN LIFE INSURANCE COMPANY
700 Market St. Phone: 314-231-1700
St. Louis, MO 63101 Fax: 314-525-5760
CEO: Richard A. Liddy
Dir HR: Marsha McMillen
Employees: 2,700
Jobs Added Last Year: –
Insurance - life

GRAYBAR ELECTRIC COMPANY, INC. [40182]
34 N. Meramec Ave. Phone: 314-727-3900
St. Louis, MO 63105 Fax: 314-727-8218
Pres & CEO: Edward A. McGrath
VP HR: Jack F. Van Pelt
Employees: 5,100
Jobs Added Last Year: 400 (+8.5%)
Electrical products - wholesale

H&R BLOCK, INC. [10689]
4410 Main St. Phone: 816-753-6900
Kansas City, MO 64111 Fax: 816-753-5346
Chm: Thomas M. Bloch
Asst VP & Dir HR: Nicki Gustin
Employees: 82,800
Jobs Added Last Year: 800 (+1%)
Financial - tax preparation; on-line information network (Compuserve)

HALLMARK CARDS, INC. [40196]
2501 McGee St. Phone: 816-274-5111
Kansas City, MO 64108 Fax: 816-274-8513
Pres & CEO: Irvine O. Hockaday, Jr.
VP HR: Lowell J. Mayone
Employees: 12,600
Jobs Added Last Year: 113 (+.9%)
Greeting cards; crayons (Binney & Smith); real estate

HARMON INDUSTRIES, INC.
1300 Jefferson Ct. Phone: 816-229-3345
Blue Springs, MO 64015 Fax: 816-229-0556
Pres, CEO & COO: Bjorn Olsson
VP HR: Ronald G. Breshears
Employees: 1,000
Jobs Added Last Year: 110 (+12.4%)
Transportation - equipment & leasing

INSITUFORM MID-AMERICA, INC.
17988 Edison Ave. Phone: 314-532-6137
Chesterfield, MO 63005 Fax: 314-537-1214
CEO: Jerome Kalishman
VP HR: Jack Boatman
Employees: 569
Jobs Added Last Year: 244 (+75.1%)
Wastewater systems repair

MISSOURI

INTERCO INCORPORATED
101 S. Hanley Rd. Phone: 314-863-1100
St. Louis, MO 63105-3493 Fax: 314-863-5306
Chm, Pres & CEO: Richard B. Loynd
Ops Dir (HR): Robert Haas
Employees: 20,045
Jobs Added Last Year: 295 (+1.5%)
Furniture (Broyhill & Lane)

KANSAS CITY SOUTHERN INDUSTRIES, INC.
114 W. 11th St. Phone: 816-556-0303
Kansas City, MO 64105-1804 Fax: 816-556-0297
Pres & CEO: Landon H. Rowland
VP HR: Hugh Salmons
Employees: 7,470
Jobs Added Last Year: 1,399 (+23%)
Transportation - rail

INTERSTATE BAKERIES CORPORATION
12 E. Armour Blvd. Phone: 816-561-6600
Kansas City, MO 64111 Fax: 816-561-6600
Chm & CEO: Charles A. Sullivan
Dir HR: Russell Baker
Employees: 14,000
Jobs Added Last Year: 0
Food - bakery products (Butternut, Holsum, Merita, Mrs. Karl's & Sweetheart)

KELLWOOD COMPANY
600 Kellwood Pkwy. Phone: 314-576-3100
St. Louis, MO 63178 Fax: 314-576-3180
Chm, Pres & CEO: William J. McKenna
VP HR: F. Lee Fox
Employees: 15,400
Jobs Added Last Year: 600 (+4.1%)
Apparel, bedding & camping equipment, including tents & sleeping bags

JACK HENRY & ASSOCIATES, INC.
663 Hwy. 60, PO Box 807 Phone: 417-235-6652
Monett, MO 65708 Fax: 417-235-8406
CEO: Terry W. Thompson
VP HR: Mike Wallace
Employees: 183
Jobs Added Last Year: 29 (+18.8%)
Computers - outsourcing & system integration services software for the retail banking industry

LEGGETT & PLATT, INC.
One Leggett Rd. Phone: 417-358-8131
Carthage, MO 64836 Fax: 417-358-8449
Chm & CEO: Harry M. Cornell, Jr.
VP Personnel: John A. Hale
Employees: 13,000
Jobs Added Last Year: 1,600 (+14%)
Furniture - components for the bedding & home furniture industry

JEFFERSON SMURFIT CORPORATION
8182 Maryland Ave. Phone: 314-746-1100
St. Louis, MO 63105-3786 Fax: 314-746-1281
Pres & CEO: James E. Terrill
Dir HR: Bob Hardie
Employees: 16,600
Jobs Added Last Year: —
Diversified operations - containerboard & recycled cylinder board; wastepaper recycling; newsprint mills; house paneling

MALLINCKRODT GROUP INC.
7733 Forsyth Blvd. Phone: 314-854-5200
St. Louis, MO 63105-1820 Fax: 314-854-5380
Pres & CEO: C. Ray Holman
VP Organization & HR: Beverly L. Hays
Employees: 10,200
Jobs Added Last Year: 200 (+2%)
Diversified operations - human & animal health care products; medical devices; specialty chemicals

JOHN Q. HAMMONS HOTELS, INC.
300 John Q. Hammons Pkwy. Phone: 417-864-6573
Springfield, MO 65806 Fax: 417-864-8900
Chm & CEO: John Q. Hammons
EVP Fin, CFO, Treas (HR): Mel J. Volmert
Employees: 5,800
Jobs Added Last Year: —
Hotels & motels franchisee (Embassy Suites & Holiday Inn)

MARION MERRELL DOW INC.
9300 Ward Pkwy. Phone: 816-966-4000
Kansas City, MO 64114-0480 Fax: 816-966-3270
Chm & CEO: Fred W. Lyons, Jr.
VP HR: Richard J. Bailey, Jr.
Employees: 9,827
Jobs Added Last Year: 19 (+.2%)
Drugs (Nicoderm & Seldane); consumer products (Cepacol, Gaviscon & Cepastat)

MISSOURI

MARITZ INC.
1375 N. Highway Dr.   Phone: 314-827-4000
Fenton, MO 63099   Fax: 314-827-5505
Chm & CEO: William E. Maritz
SVP HR: Terry Goring
Employees: 6,080
Jobs Added Last Year: 80 (+1.3%)
Business services - market research, travel services & training

MARK VII, INC.
10100 NW Executive Hills Blvd.   Phone: 816-891-0500
Kansas City, MO 64153   Fax: 816-891-7373
Chm, Pres & CEO: R. C. Matney
No central personnel officer
Employees: 282
Jobs Added Last Year: 107 (+61.1%)
Transportation - freight brokerage & logistics management

MAVERICK TUBE CORPORATION
400 Chesterfield Center   Phone: 314-537-1314
Chesterfield, MO 63017   Fax: 314-537-1363
Pres & CEO: Gregg M. Eisenberg
Ben Mgr: Jill Westhoff
Employees: 640
Jobs Added Last Year: 83 (+14.9%)
Oil field machinery & equipment

THE MAY DEPARTMENT STORES CO.   10969
611 Olive St.   Phone: 314-342-6300
St. Louis, MO 63101   Fax: 314-342-4461
Chm & CEO: David C. Farrell
SVP HR: Douglas J. Giles
Employees: 113,000
Jobs Added Last Year: 2,000 (+1.8%)
Retail - department stores (Foley's, Hecht's & Lord & Taylor) & shoe stores (Payless)

MCDONNELL DOUGLAS CORP.   10975
PO Box 516   Phone: 314-232-0232
St. Louis, MO 63166-0516   Fax: 314-234-3826
CEO: Harry C. Stonecipher
VP Ben: Michael R. Becker
Employees: 70,016
Jobs Cut Last Year: 17,361 (-19.9%)
Aerospace - aircraft equipment, defense electronics, financial services

MEDICINE SHOPPE INTERNATIONAL, INC.
1100 N. Lindbergh   Phone: 314-993-6000
St. Louis, MO 63132   Fax: 314-569-9780
CEO: David A. Abrahamson
Personnel Mgr: Vivian Rebert
Employees: 267
Jobs Added Last Year: 74 (+38.3%)
Retail - drug stores

MERCANTILE BANCORPORATION INC.
PO Box 524   Phone: 314-425-2525
St. Louis, MO 63166-0524   Fax: 314-425-1286
CEO: Thomas H. Jacobsen
EVP (HR): Jon Pierce
Employees: 4,839
Jobs Added Last Year: 422 (+9.6%)
Banks - Midwest

MID-AMERICA DAIRYMEN, INC.
3253 E. Chestnut Expwy.   Phone: 417-865-7100
Springfield, MO 65802   Fax: 417-865-1093
CEO: Gary E. Hanman
Dir HR: Ray Silvey
Employees: 3,500
Jobs Added Last Year: —
Food - dairy products

MONSANTO COMPANY   11010
800 N. Lindbergh Blvd.   Phone: 314-694-1000
St. Louis, MO 63167   Fax: 314-694-7625
Chm & CEO: Richard J. Mahoney
Corp VP HR: Teresa E. McCaslin
Employees: 30,019
Jobs Cut Last Year: 3,778 (-11.2%)
Chemicals - fat substitutes, artificial sweetener (NutraSweet), herbicides, industrial chemicals, pharmaceuticals

O'REILLY AUTOMOTIVE, INC.
233 S. Patterson   Phone: 417-862-6708
Springfield, MO 65801   Fax: 417-869-8903
Pres & CEO: David E. O'Reilly
Dir HR: Steve Pope
Employees: 1,790
Jobs Added Last Year: 361 (+25.3%)
Retail - auto parts

MISSOURI

PAYLESS CASHWAYS INC.
Two Pershing Sq., 2300 Main Phone: 816-234-6000
Kansas City, MO 64141-0466 Fax: 816-234-6142
Chm & CEO: David Stanley
SVP HR: E. J. Holland, Jr.
Employees: 18,100
Jobs Added Last Year: 300 (+1.7%)
Building products - home improvement centers

PULITZER PUBLISHING COMPANY
900 N. Tucker Blvd. Phone: 314-340-8000
St. Louis, MO 63101 Fax: 314-340-3125
Chm & CEO: Michael E. Pulitzer
Dir HR: Preston Vanderford
Employees: 2,950
Jobs Added Last Year: 50 (+1.7%)
Publishing - newspapers (*The St. Louis Post-Dispatch* & *The* (Tucson) *Arizona Daily Star*); TV & radio broadcasting

RALCORP HOLDINGS, INC.
PO Box 618 Phone: 314-982-1000
St. Louis, MO 63188-0618 Fax: 314-982-4074
Pres & Co-CEO: Richard A. Pearce
VP HR: Jack Owazarczak
Employees: 7,100
Jobs Added Last Year: 600 (+9.2%)
Food - cereal, baby food, crackers & cookies; coupon redemption services; ski resorts

RALSTON PURINA GROUP
Checkerboard Sq. Phone: 314-982-1000
St. Louis, MO 63164 Fax: 314-982-2134
Chm, Pres & CEO: William P. Stiritz
VP Dir of Admin (HR): Charles Sommer
Employees: 31,703
Jobs Cut Last Year: 27,519 (-46.5%)
Diversified operations - pet food; batteries (Eveready, Energizer)

REHABCARE CORPORATION
7733 Forsyth Blvd., Ste. 1700 Phone: 314-863-7422
St. Louis, MO 63105 Fax: 314-863-0769
Pres & CEO: James M. Usdan
SVP HR: Stephen J. Toth
Employees: 1,220
Jobs Added Last Year: 370 (+43.5%)
Health care - outpatient & home

RELIV INTERNATIONAL INC.
136 Chesterfield Industrial Phone: 314-537-9715
St. Louis, MO 63006-0405 Fax: 314-537-9753
Chm, Pres & CEO: Robert L. Montgomery
HR Mgr: Fred Nielson
Employees: 102
Jobs Added Last Year: 22 (+27.5%)
Vitamins & nutritional products

RIVAL CO.
800 E. 101st Terrace Phone: 816-943-4100
Kansas City, MO 64131 Fax: 816-943-4123
Pres & CEO: Thomas K. Manning
Dir Personnel: Sheila Butler
Employees: 2,000
Jobs Added Last Year: 100 (+5.3%)
Appliances - household

ROOSEVELT FINANCIAL GROUP, INC.
900 Roosevelt Pkwy. Phone: 314-532-6200
Chesterfield, MO 63017 Fax: 314-532-6292
Pres & CEO: Stanley J. Bradshaw
EVP (HR): Daniel G. O'Donnell
Employees: 1,250
Jobs Added Last Year: 659 (+111.5%)
Financial - savings & loans

SCHNUCK MARKETS INC.
11420 Lackland Rd. Phone: 314-994-9900
St. Louis, MO 63146 Fax: 314-994-4465
Chm & CEO: Craig D. Schnuck
VP HR: William Jones
Employees: 14,000
Jobs Added Last Year: —
Retail - supermarkets

SIGMA-ALDRICH CORPORATION
3050 Spruce St. Phone: 314-771-5765
St. Louis, MO 63103 Fax: 800-325-5052
CEO & Chm: Tom Cori
VP HR: Terry Colvin
Employees: 4,291
Jobs Added Last Year: 99 (+2.4%)
Chemicals - specialty

MISSOURI

SPARTECH CORPORATION
7733 Forsythe, Ste. 1450 Phone: 314-721-4242
Clayton, MO 63105 Fax: 314-721-1447
Pres & CEO: Bradley B. Buechler
VP Fin & CFO (HR): David B. Mueller
Employees: 1,200
Jobs Added Last Year: 675 (+128.6%)
Rubber & plastic products - polystyrene extrusion

SSM HEALTH CARE SYSTEM INC.
477 N. Lindbergh Blvd. Phone: 314-994-7800
St. Louis, MO 63141 Fax: 314-994-7900
CEO: Sister Mary Jean Ryan
SVP HR: Steven Barney
Employees: 16,051
Jobs Added Last Year: —
Hospitals

THERMADYNE HOLDINGS CORPORATION
101 South Hanley Rd. Phone: 314-721-5573
St. Louis, MO 63101 Fax: 314-721-4822
CEO: James N. Mills
Dir HR: Larry Bacon
Employees: 3,000
Jobs Added Last Year: 0
Machinery - metal cutting & welding; floor cleaning equipment; thermal spray systems

TRANS WORLD AIRLINES, INC.
1 City Center, 515 N. 6th Street Phone: 314-589-3000
St. Louis, MO 63101 Fax: 314-589-3126
Pres & CEO: Jeffrey H. Erickson
SVP Emp Rel: Charles J. Thibaudeau
Employees: 26,100
Jobs Added Last Year: 600 (+2.4%)
Transportation - airline

UNION ELECTRIC COMPANY
1901 Chouteau Ave. Phone: 314-621-3222
St. Louis, MO 63103 Fax: 314-554-3268
Pres & CEO: C.W. Mueller
VP HR: Herbert W. Loeh
Employees: 6,417
Jobs Cut Last Year: 177 (-2.7%)
Utility - electric power

UNITED MISSOURI BANCSHARES, INC.
1010 Grand Ave., PO Box 419226 Phone: 816-556-7000
Kansas City, MO 64141-6226 Fax: 816-421-5411
Chm & CEO: R. Crosby Kemper
SVP HR: Jim Rawlings
Employees: 3,057
Jobs Added Last Year: 132 (+4.5%)
Banks - Midwest

UNITOG COMPANY
101 W. 11th St. Phone: 816-474-7000
Kansas City, MO 64105 Fax: 816-842-1336
Pres & CEO: Randolph K. Rolf
VP HR: John W. Hall
Employees: 3,200
Jobs Added Last Year: 329 (+11.5%)
Linen supply & related services

THE UNIVERSITY OF MISSOURI SYSTEM
321 University Hall Phone: 314-882-6211
Columbia, MO 65211 Fax: 314-882-2721
Pres: George A. Russell
Asst Vice Chancellor HR: Karen Touzeau
Employees: 17,060
Jobs Added Last Year: —
University

UTILICORP UNITED INC.
911 Main, Ste. 3000 Phone: 816-421-6600
Kansas City, MO 64105 Fax: 816-691-3590
Chm, Pres & CEO: Richard C. Green, Jr.
VP (HR): Joseph J. Colosimo
Employees: 4,700
Jobs Added Last Year: 100 (+2.2%)
Utility - electric power

VENTURE STORES, INC.
2001 E. Terra Ln. Phone: 314-281-5500
O'Fallon, MO 63366-0110 Fax: 314-281-5152
Chm & CEO: Julian M. Seeherman
SVP HR: Coleman H. Peterson
Employees: 16,000
Jobs Added Last Year: 700 (+4.6%)
Retail - discount & variety

MONTANA

BUTTREY FOOD AND DRUG STORES COMPANY
601 Sixth St. SW   Phone: 406-761-3401
Great Falls, MT 59404   Fax: 406-761-1295
Pres & CEO: Joseph H. Fernandez
VP HR: John E. Sullivan
Employees: 3,233
Jobs Cut Last Year: 437 (-11.9%)
Retail - convenience stores

ENERGY WEST, INCORPORATED
One First Ave. South, PO Box 2229   Phone: 406-791-7500
Great Falls, MT 59403-2229   Fax: 406-791-7560
CEO: Larry D. Geske
Dir HR: John C. Allen
Employees: 131
Jobs Added Last Year: 35 (+36.5%)
Utility - gas distribution

MONTANA POWER COMPANY
40 E. Broadway   Phone: 406-723-5421
Butte, MT 59701-9989   Fax: 406-496-5099
Chm & CEO: Daniel T. Berube
Dir Compensation & Labor Rel (HR): Daniel Kaluza
Employees: 4,089
Jobs Cut Last Year: 50 (-1.2%)
Utility - electric power

RIBI IMMUNOCHEM RESEARCH, INC.
553 Old Corvallis Rd.   Phone: 406-363-6214
Hamilton, MT 59840-3131   Fax: 406-363-6129
Pres & CEO: Robert E. Ivy
Dir HR: Sue Kerner
Employees: 78
Jobs Added Last Year: 18 (+30%)
Biomedical & genetic products

SEMITOOL, INC.
655 W Reserve Dr.   Phone: 406-752-2107
Kalispell, MT 59901   Fax: 406-452-2107
Chm, Pres & CEO: Ray F. Thompson
Personnel Mgr: Vicki Billmayer
Employees: 523
Jobs Added Last Year: 273 (+109.2%)
Machinery - semiconductor manufacturing equipment

WASHINGTON CORPORATIONS
101 International Dr.   Phone: 406-523-1300
Missoula, MT 59807   Fax: 406-721-4794
Pres: Dorn Parkinson
Personnel Mgr: Jim Brouelette
Employees: 3,650
Jobs Added Last Year: –
Diversified operations - construction; mining; public utilities

NEBRASKA

ACCEPTANCE INSURANCE COMPANIES INC.
222 South 15th St., Ste. 600 North   Phone: 402-344-8800
Omaha, NE 68102-1628   Fax: 402-341-0792
CEO: Kenneth C. Coon
HR Dir: Dawn Wetherell
Employees: 564
Jobs Added Last Year: 59 (+11.7%)
Insurance - property & casualty

AMERICAN BUSINESS INFORMATION
5711 S. 86th Circle   Phone: 402-593-4500
Omaha, NE 68127   Fax: 402-331-5481
Chm & CEO: Vinod Gupta
HR Mgr: Janet Boswell
Employees: 621
Jobs Added Last Year: 109 (+21.3%)
Business services - business-to-business marketing information

BEEFAMERICA, INC.
14748 W. Center Rd., Ste. 201   Phone: 402-330-1899
Omaha, NE 68144   Fax: 402-330-2684
Pres & CEO: Robert R. Norton
Dir HR: Dean Miller
Employees: 1,600
Jobs Added Last Year: 100 (+6.7%)
Food - beef packing & processing

BERKSHIRE HATHAWAY INC.
1440 Kiewit Plaza   Phone: 402-346-1400
Omaha, NE 68131   Fax: 402-536-3030
Chm & CEO: Warren E. Buffett
VP, CFO &Treas (HR): Marc D. Hamburg
Employees: 22,000
Jobs Added Last Year: 0
Diversified operations - insurance; candy; home furnishings; cleaning systems

THE BUCKLE, INC.
2407 W. 24th St.   Phone: 308-236-8491
Kearney, NE 68847   Fax: 308-236-4493
Chm & CEO: Daniel J. Hirschfeld
No central personnel officer
Employees: 2,300
Jobs Added Last Year: 300 (+15%)
Retail - apparel & shoes

CONAGRA, INC.
One ConAgra Dr.   Phone: 402-595-4000
Omaha, NE 68102-5001   Fax: 402-595-4595
Chm & CEO: Philip B. Fletcher
SVP Fin, Corp Sec & Risk Off (HR): L. B. Thomas
Employees: 83,000
Jobs Added Last Year: 2,213 (+2.7%)
Food - packaged food (Chun King & Healthy Choice) & meat products (Armour, Butterball & Eckrich)

DATA TRANSMISSION NETWORK CORPORATION
9110 W. Dodge Rd., Ste. 200   Phone: 402-390-2328
Omaha, NE 68114   Fax: 402-390-7188
Pres & CEO: Roger R. Brodersen
Personnel Administrator: Gerald Pigg
Employees: 400
Jobs Added Last Year: 160 (+66.7%)
Business services - on-line business information

FIRST DATA CORPORATION
11718 Nicholas St.   Phone: 402-222-5563
Omaha, NE 68154   Fax: 402-222-7212
Chm & CEO: Henry C. "Ric" Duques
SVP HR: Donald F. Crowley
Employees: 19,300
Jobs Cut Last Year: 100 (-.5%)
Financial - credit card processing

IBP, INC.
IBP Ave., PO Box 515   Phone: 402-494-2061
Dakota City, NE 68731   Fax: 402-241-2063
Chm, Pres & CEO: Robert L. Peterson
Asst VP Personnel: Richard A. Jochum
Employees: 29,200
Jobs Added Last Year: 1,700 (+6.2%)
Food - fresh beef & pork meat products

INACOM, INC.
10810 Farnam Dr.   Phone: 402-392-3900
Omaha, NE 68154   Fax: 402-392-7209
Pres & CEO: Bill L. Fairfield
VP Corp Resources (HR): Larry Sazzini
Employees: 1,883
Jobs Added Last Year: 574 (+43.9%)
Computers - retail hardware & software

NEBRASKA

MFS COMMUNICATIONS COMPANY, INC.
3555 Farnam St., Ste. 200 Phone: 402-271-2890
Omaha, NE 68131 Fax: 402-271-2971
Chm & CEO: James Q. Crowe
SVP HR: Michael Frank
Employees: 926
Jobs Added Last Year: 361 (+63.9%)
Telecommunications services - local access voice, data & other services

PAMIDA INC.
8800 F St. Phone: 402-339-2400
Omaha, NE 68127 Fax: 402-596-7330
Pres & CEO: Steven S. Fishman
VP HR: Paul Kanutson
Employees: 6,100
Jobs Added Last Year: 200 (+3.4%)
Retail - discount & variety

PETER KIEWIT SONS', INC.
1000 Kiewit Plaza Phone: 402-342-2052
Omaha, NE 68131 Fax: 402-271-2829
Chm & Pres: Walter Scott, Jr.
VP HR: Brad Chapman
Employees: 10,620
Jobs Added Last Year: 3,020 (+39.7%)
Construction - heavy; coal mining; telecommunications

WERNER ENTERPRISES, INC.
Interstate 80 & Hwy. 50 Phone: 402-895-6640
Omaha, NE 68137 Fax: 402-895-1387
Chm, Pres & CEO: Clarence L. Werner
Dir HR: Doug Pedersen
Employees: 4,235
Jobs Added Last Year: 457 (+12.1%)
Transportation - truck

▼ Air Physics http://www.aip.org/aip/careers/careers.html

NEVADA

AMERCO
1325 Airmotive Way, Ste. 100   Phone: 702-688-6300
Reno, NV 89502-3239   Fax: 702-688-6338
Chm, Pres & CEO: Edward J. Shoen
VP HR: Richard Renckly
Employees: 11,300
Jobs Added Last Year: 400 (+3.7%)
Leasing - truck & trailer rental (U-Haul International); insurance (Ponderosa Holdings)

AMERISTAR CASINOS INC.
PO Box 259   Phone: 702-755-6011
Jackpot, NV 89825   Fax: 702-755-2724
Chm, Pres & CEO: Craig H. Neilsen
Corp VP HR: John R. Sims
Employees: 2,148
Jobs Added Last Year: 1,127 (+110.4%)
Leisure & recreational services - casinos in Jackpot, NV (Cactus Pete's, Horseshu)

ANCHOR GAMING
815 Pilot Rd., Ste. G   Phone: 702-896-7568
Las Vegas, NV 89119   Fax: 702-896-6331
CEO: Stanley E. Fulton
Office Mgr (HR): Suzy Delzer
Employees: 586
Jobs Added Last Year: 161 (+37.9%)
Leisure & recreational products - casinos, gaming machines & gaming machine routes

BOOMTOWN, INC.
PO Box 399   Phone: 702-345-8680
Verdi, NV 89439-0399   Fax: 702-345-2327
Chm & CEO: Timothy J. Parrott
VP HR: Donald Dixon
Employees: 4,100
Jobs Added Last Year: 3,067 (+296.9%)
Leisure & recreational services - casino in Reno

BOYD GAMING CORPORATION
2950 S. Industrial Rd.   Phone: 702-792-7200
Las Vegas, NV 89109   Fax: 702-792-7266
CEO: W. S. Boyd
Dir HR: Cathy Shanklin
Employees: 10,000
Jobs Added Last Year: 3,400 (+51.5%)
Leisure & recreational services - casino-hotels in Las Vegas (Stardust, Sam's Town, Fremont)

CIRCUS CIRCUS ENTERPRISES, INC.
2880 Las Vegas Blvd. South   Phone: 702-734-0410
Las Vegas, NV 89109-1120   Fax: 702-734-2268
Chm, Pres & CEO: Clyde T. Turner
VP, Controller & Chief Acctg Off (HR): Terry L. Caudill
Employees: 18,400
Jobs Added Last Year: 4,936 (+36.7%)
Leisure & recreational services - casinos (Circus Circus, Excalibur, Luxor)

FREEPORT-MCMORAN COPPER & GOLD INC.
One E. First St., Ste. 1600   Phone: 504-582-4000
Reno, NV 89501   Fax: 504-585-3265
EVP: George A. Mealey
Dir HR: Robert Gettys
Employees: 7,270
Jobs Added Last Year: 2,287 (+45.9%)
Metals - nonferrous

HARVEYS CASINO RESORTS
Hwy. 50 and Stateline Ave.   Phone: 702-588-2411
Lake Tahoe, NV 89449   Fax: 702-588-6643
Pres & CEO: Thomas M. Yturbide
VP HR: Tom Evans
Employees: 2,800
Jobs Added Last Year: 100 (+3.7%)
Leisure & recreational services - casinos & hotels (Harvey's Resort, Hard Rock Hotel)

INTERNATIONAL GAME TECHNOLOGY
5270 Neil Rd., PO Box 10120   Phone: 702-686-1200
Reno, NV 89510-0120   Fax: 702-688-0777
Pres & CEO: John J. Russell
VP Corp HR: Ronald E. Christensen
Employees: 2,100
Jobs Added Last Year: 676 (+47.5%)
Leisure & recreational products - gambling equipment & casinos

LADY LUCK GAMING CORPORATION
206 N. Third St.   Phone: 702-477-3000
Las Vegas, NV 89101   Fax: 702-477-3003
Chm & CEO: Andrew H. Tompkins
Dir Personnel: Marge Isom
Employees: 3,000
Jobs Added Last Year: 670 (+28.8%)
Leisure & recreational services - dockside & land-based casinos in Mississippi

NEVADA

MIRAGE RESORTS, INCORPORATED
3400 Las Vegas Blvd. South   Phone: 702-791-7111
Las Vegas, NV 89109   Fax: 702-792-7646
Chm, Pres & CEO: Stephen A. Wynn
Mgr HR: Art Nathan
Employees: 17,100
Jobs Added Last Year: 4,900 (+40.2%)
Leisure & recreational services - casinos

SHOWBOAT, INC.
2800 Fremont St.   Phone: 702-385-9141
Las Vegas, NV 89104   Fax: 702-385-9163
Chm: J. Kell Houssels III
VP HR: Walter Reid
Employees: 4,670
Jobs Added Last Year: 1,270 (+37.4%)
Leisure & recreational services - casinos, hotels & bowling centers

OASIS RESIDENTIAL, INC.
4041 E. Sunset Rd.   Phone: 702-435-9800
Henderson, NV 89014   Fax: 702-435-9445
Chm & CEO: Robert V. Jones
Dir HR: Billie Marie Norrison
Employees: 384
Jobs Added Last Year: 105 (+37.6%)
Real estate operations - apartment properties

SOUTHWEST GAS CORPORATION
5241 Spring Mountain Rd.   Phone: 702-876-7237
Las Vegas, NV 89102   Fax: 702-873-3820
Pres & CEO: Michael O. Maffie
VP HR: Martha McDonald
Employees: 2,940
Jobs Added Last Year: 2,291 (+353%)
Utility - gas distribution

RIO HOTEL AND CASINO, INC.
3700 W. Flamingo Rd.   Phone: 702-252-7733
Las Vegas, NV 89103   Fax: 702-252-7633
Chm: Anthony A. Marnell II
Dir HR: Karen Brasier
Employees: 2,600
Jobs Added Last Year: 600 (+30%)
Leisure & recreational services - casinos

SWIFT TRANSPORTATION CO., INC.
1455 Hulda Way   Phone: 702-359-5161
Sparks, NV 89431   Fax: 602-352-6303
Chm, Pres & CEO: Jerry C. Moyes
Dir HR: Bruce Taylor
Employees: 4,500
Jobs Added Last Year: 1,300 (+40.6%)
Transportation - truck

NEW HAMPSHIRE

BAILEY CORPORATION
700 Lafayette Rd., PO Box 307   Phone: 603-474-3011
Seabrook, NH 03874   Fax: 603-474-8949
Chm, Pres, CEO & Sec: Roger R. Phillips
Dir HR: John J. Corbett
Employees: 1,813
Jobs Added Last Year: 873 (+92.9%)
Automotive & trucking - moulders & painters of plastic products

CABLETRON SYSTEMS, INC.
35 Industrial Way   Phone: 603-332-9400
Rochester, NH 03867   Fax: 603-332-4616
Pres & CEO: S. Robert Levine
Head HR: Linda Pepin
Employees: 3,663
Jobs Added Last Year: 1,038 (+39.5%)
Computers - LAN hubs

FISHER SCIENTIFIC INTERNATIONAL, INC.
Liberty Ln.   Phone: 603-929-2650
Hampton, NH 03842   Fax: 603-926-0222
Pres & CEO: Paul M. Montrone
Mgr Emp Ben: Sherry Lovdon
Employees: 4,200
Jobs Added Last Year: 1,000 (+31.3%)
Scientific instruments, supplies & equipment

GENERAL CHEMICAL CORP.
Liberty Ln.   Phone: 603-926-5911
Hampton, NH 03842   Fax: 603-929-2404
Chm & CEO: Michael Dingman
VP HR: Sherry Loudon
Employees: 3,700
Jobs Added Last Year: 130 (+3.6%)
Chemicals & industrial products

HEALTHSOURCE, INC.
2 College Park Dr.   Phone: 603-268-7000
Hooksett, NH 03106   Fax: 603-268-7905
Pres & CEO: Norman C. Payson
VP HR: Richard E. Merkle
Employees: 1,500
Jobs Added Last Year: 900 (+150%)
Health maintenance organization

HOWTEK, INC.
21 Park Ave.   Phone: 603-882-5200
Hudson, NH 03051   Fax: 603-880-3843
CEO: David R. Bothwell
Dir Corp Svcs (HR): Connie Webster
Employees: 122
Jobs Added Last Year: 36 (+41.9%)
Computers - color monitors & related peripheral equipment

NASHUA CORPORATION
44 Franklin St., PO Box 2002   Phone: 603-880-2323
Nashua, NH 03061-2002   Fax: 603-880-5671
Pres & CEO: William E. Mitchell
VP HR: Bruce Wright
Employees: 4,000
Jobs Cut Last Year: 100 (-2.4%)
Diversified operations - coated paper; computer products; photofinishing

PC CONNECTION
6 Mill St.   Phone: 603-446-3383
Marlow, NH 03456   Fax: 603-446-7796
CEO: Patricia Gallup
Dir HR: Ronda Farrington
Employees: 800
Jobs Added Last Year: 350 (+77.8%)
Computers - mail order PCs & peripherals

SOFTDESK, INC.
7 Liberty Hill Rd.   Phone: 603-428-3199
Henniker, NH 03242   Fax: 603-428-7665
Chm, Pres, CEO & Treas: David C. Arnold
Dir HR: Robin Pullo
Employees: 173
Jobs Added Last Year: 39 (+29.1%)
Computers - technical application software for professionals in architectural, engineering & construction industries

STANDEX INTERNATIONAL CORPORATION
6 Manor Pkwy.   Phone: 603-893-9701
Salem, NH 03079   Fax: 603-893-7324
Chm & CEO: Thomas L. King
Dir Ind Rel & Emp Ben: James Mettling
Employees: 5,000
Jobs Added Last Year: 300 (+6.4%)
Diversified operations - food service equipment; educational & religious publishing (Standard)

NEW HAMPSHIRE

TIMBERLAND CO.
200 Domain Dr.
Stratham, NH 03885
Pres & CEO: Sidney W. Swartz
VP HR: Lisa Letizio
Employees: 6,000
Jobs Added Last Year: 0
Shoes & boots

Phone: 603-772-9500
Fax: 603-773-1640

INTERNATIONAL LTD.
One Tyco Park
Exeter, NH 03833
Chm, Pres & CEO: L. Dennis Kozlowski
VP Mktg, Advertising, PR & HR: David P. Brownell
Employees: 24,000
Jobs Added Last Year: 0
Diversified operations - fire protection; packaging products; electrical components; flow control products

Phone: 603-778-9700
Fax: 603-778-7700

▼ **Jobs in Consulting** http://www.cob.ohio-state.edu/dept/fin/consult.htm

NEW JERSEY

A. L. PHARMA INC.
One Executive Dr., PO Box 1399 Phone: 201-947-7774
Fort Lee, NJ 07024 Fax: 201-947-5541
Chm & CEO: Einar W. Sissener
Mgr HR: Loraine Catarcio
Employees: 2,760
Jobs Added Last Year: 860 (+45.3%)
Drugs - generic

ALLIEDSIGNAL INC.
101 Columbia Rd., PO Box 4000 Phone: 201-455-2000
Morristown, NJ 07962-2497 Fax: 201-455-4807
Chm & CEO: Lawrence A. Bossidy
SVP HR: Donald J. Redlinger
Employees: 86,400
Jobs Cut Last Year: 2,900 (-3.2%)
Diversified operations - aerospace, automotive & engineered products

AMERICAN HOME PRODUCTS CORP.
5 Giralda Farms Phone: 201-660-5000
Madison, NJ 07940-0874 Fax: 201-660-6048
Chm, Pres & CEO: John R. Stafford
SVP (HR): Stanley F. Barshay
Employees: 51,399
Jobs Added Last Year: 746 (+1.5%)
Drugs (Anacin, Dristan, Chapstick, Centrum); canned food (Chef Boyardee); herbicides

AMERICAN STANDARD COMPANIES
1 Centennial Ave. Phone: 908-980-6000
Piscataway, NJ 08855-6820 Fax: 908-980-6120
Chm, Pres & CEO: Emmanuel A. Kampouris
VP HR: Adrian B. Deshotel
Employees: 38,500
Jobs Added Last Year: 2,500 (+6.9%)
Building products - bathroom & kitchen fixtures & fittings; air conditioning systems; auto braking systems

AMERICAN WATER WORKS COMPANY, INC.
1025 Laurel Oak Rd. Phone: 609-346-8200
Voorhees, NJ 08043 Fax: 609-346-8360
Pres & CEO: George W. Johnstone
VP HR: Richard Strahalman
Employees: 4,062
Jobs Added Last Year: 18 (+.4%)
Utility - water supply

AUTOINFO, INC.
1600 Rte. 208 Phone: 201-703-0500
Fair Lawn, NJ 07410 Fax: 201-703-1777
Chm & CEO: Jason Bacher
No central personnel officer
Employees: 150
Jobs Added Last Year: 30 (+25%)
Computers - communications & database services to the auto parts salvage, auto insurance & other related industries

AUTOMATIC DATA PROCESSING, INC.
One ADP Blvd. Phone: 201-994-5000
Roseland, NJ 07068-1728 Fax: 201-994-5387
Chm & CEO: Josh S. Weston
VP HR: Richard C. Berke
Employees: 22,000
Jobs Added Last Year: 1,000 (+4.8%)
Business services - payroll & on-line information services

BECTON, DICKINSON AND COMPANY
One Becton Dr. Phone: 201-847-6800
Franklin Lakes, NJ 07417-1880 Fax: 201-847-6475
Chm, Pres & CEO: Clateo Castellini
VP HR: Rosemary Mede
Employees: 18,600
Jobs Cut Last Year: 400 (-2.1%)
Medical supplies - needles, syringes, IVs & diagnostic equipment

BED BATH & BEYOND, INC.
715 Morris Ave. Phone: 201-379-1520
Springfield, NJ 07081 Fax: 201-379-1731
Chm & CEO: Warren Eisenberg
Dir HR: Wayne Sarrow
Employees: 3,200
Jobs Added Last Year: 800 (+33.3%)
Retail - bed & bath furnishings

BELL COMMUNICATIONS RESEARCH INC.
290 W. Mt. Pleasant Ave. Phone: 201-740-3000
Livingston, NJ 07039 Fax: 201-740-6877
Pres & CEO: George H. Heilmeier
VP HR: Robert A. Meese
Employees: 6,624
Jobs Cut Last Year: 584 (-8.1%)
Engineering - telecommunications R&D services

NEW JERSEY

THE BISYS GROUP, INC.
150 Clove Rd.   Phone: 201-812-8600
Little Falls, NJ 07424   Fax: 201-812-1217
Chm & CEO: Lynn J. Mangum
SVP HR: Mark J. Rybarczyk
Employees: 1,000
Jobs Added Last Year: 375 (+60%)
Business services - data processing outsourcing for banks

CAMBREX CORPORATION
One Meadowlands Plaza   Phone: 201-804-3000
East Rutherford, NJ 07073   Fax: 201-804-9852
Chm & CEO: Cyril C. Baldwin, Jr.
VP Admin (HR): Steven Klosk
Employees: 746
Jobs Added Last Year: 163 (+28%)
Chemicals - diversified

BLOCK DRUG CO., INC.
257 Cornelison Ave.   Phone: 201-434-3000
Jersey City, NJ 07302   Fax: 201-434-5739
Chm: Leonard Block
Dir HR: Nancy Sharko
Employees: 3,491
Jobs Cut Last Year: 14 (-.4%)
Toothpaste & toothbrushes, medicated shampoo, sleep-aid tablets & cleaning products

CAMPBELL SOUP COMPANY
Campbell Place   Phone: 609-342-4800
Camden, NJ 08103-1799   Fax: 609-342-3878
Pres & CEO: David W. Johnson
VP HR: Edward F. Walsh
Employees: 44,378
Jobs Cut Last Year: 2,542 (-5.4%)
Food - canned soups, salsa, cookies, candy, meat, prepared foods & pickles

BRANDON SYSTEMS CORPORATION
One Harmon Plaza   Phone: 201-392-0800
Secaucus, NJ 07094   Fax: 201-392-0405
Chm & CEO: Ira B. Brown
Dir HR: Robert J. Hanas
Employees: 5,745
Jobs Cut Last Year: 144 (-2.4%)
Computers - programming & technical support services

CELGENE CORPORATION
7 Powder Horn Dr.   Phone: 908-271-1001
Warren, NJ 07059   Fax: 908-271-4184
Chm & CEO: Richard G. Wright
Mgr HR: Lisa Desnoyers
Employees: 73
Jobs Added Last Year: 27 (+58.7%)
Chemicals - specialty

BURLINGTON COAT FACTORY WAREHOUSE
1830 Rte. 130   Phone: 609-387-7800
Burlington, NJ 08016   Fax: 609-387-7071
CEO: Monroe G. Milstein
HR Mgr: Kyle Gonzales
Employees: 12,800
Jobs Added Last Year: 2,500 (+24.3%)
Retail - apparel & shoes

CHECKPOINT SYSTEMS, INC.
550 Grove Rd., PO Box 188   Phone: 609-848-1800
Thorofare, NJ 08086   Fax: 609-848-0937
Pres & CEO: Kevin P. Dowd
Personnel Mgr: Joanne Nacuchio
Employees: 1,300
Jobs Added Last Year: 331 (+34.2%)
Protection - electronic security systems for commercial applications

C. R. BARD, INC.
730 Central Ave.   Phone: 908-277-8000
Murray Hill, NJ 07974   Fax: 908-277-8240
Pres & COO: William H. Longfield
VP HR: Mark Sickles
Employees: 8,450
Jobs Cut Last Year: 400 (-4.5%)
Medical & dental supplies

THE CHUBB CORPORATION
15 Mountain View Rd.   Phone: 908-903-2000
Warren, NJ 07061-1615   Fax: 908-580-2027
Chm & CEO: Dean R. O'Hare
SVP & Managing Dir HR: Janice Tomlinson
Employees: 10,600
Jobs Added Last Year: 400 (+4%)
Insurance - property & casualty

NEW JERSEY

COLLECTIVE BANCORP, INC.
158 Philadelphia Ave. Phone: 609-625-1110
Egg Harbor City, NJ 08215 Fax: 609-965-4381
Chm, Pres & CEO: Thomas H. Hamilton
VP HR: Peter E. Iacobelli
Employees: 1,084
Jobs Added Last Year: 159 (+17.2%)
Financial - savings & loans

COMMERCE BANCORP, INC.
1701 Rte. 70 East Phone: 609-751-9000
Cherry Hill, NJ 08034-5400 Fax: 609-751-9260
Pres: Vernon W. Hill II
VP (HR): Robert Earl
Employees: 772
Jobs Added Last Year: 631 (+447.5%)
Banks - Northeast

CPC INTERNATIONAL INC.
International Plaza Phone: 201-894-4000
Englewood Cliffs, NJ 07632-9976 Fax: 201-894-2186
Chm, Pres & CEO: Charles R. Shoemate
VP HR: Richard P. Bergeman
Employees: 39,000
Jobs Added Last Year: 1,000 (+2.6%)
Food - soup, pastas, baked goods

CYTEC INDUSTRIES INC.
5 Garret Mountain Plaza Phone: 201-357-3100
West Paterson, NJ 07424-1599 Fax: 201-357-3058
Chm, Pres & CEO: Darryl D. Fry
VP Emp Rel: James W. Hirsch
Employees: 5,200
Jobs Added Last Year: —
Specialty chemicals for water treatment & the appliance, automotive, paper industries

DIALOGIC CORPORATION
300 Littleton Rd. Phone: 201-993-3000
Parsippany, NJ 07054 Fax: 201-993-3093
Pres & CEO: Howard G. Bubb
VP HR: Steven Wentzell
Employees: 370
Jobs Added Last Year: 67 (+22.1%)
Telecommunications equipment - hardware & software signal computing components for call processing systems

ECCS INC.
One Sheila Dr. Phone: 908-747-6995
Tinton Falls, NJ 07724 Fax: 908-747-6542
Pres & CEO: J. L. Shay
Dir HR: Sharon Wallace
Employees: 157
Jobs Added Last Year: 43 (+37.7%)
Computers - mass storage peripherals

ENGELHARD CORPORATION
101 Wood Ave. Phone: 908-205-6000
Iselin, NJ 08830 Fax: 908-321-1161
Pres & CEO: Orin R. Smith
VP HR: William M. Dugle
Employees: 5,750
Jobs Cut Last Year: 280 (-4.6%)
Chemicals - specialty; engineered materials & precious metals management services

ENZON, INC.
40 Kingsbridge Rd. Phone: 908-980-4500
Piscataway, NJ 08854-3998 Fax: 908-980-5911
Pres & CEO: Pete Tombros
No central personnel officer
Employees: 244
Jobs Added Last Year: 125 (+105%)
Biomedical & genetic products

FEDERAL PAPER BOARD COMPANY, INC.
75 Chestnut Ridge Rd. Phone: 201-391-1776
Montvale, NJ 07645 Fax: 201-307-6125
Pres & CEO: John R. Kennedy
HR Mgr: Barry Smedstad
Employees: 6,850
Jobs Added Last Year: 50 (+.7%)
Paper & paper products

FIRST FIDELITY BANCORPORATION
550 Broad St. Phone: 201-565-3200
Newark, NJ 07102 Fax: 201-565-3359
Chm, Pres & CEO: Anthony P. Terracciano
EVP HR: William A. Karmen
Employees: 12,000
Jobs Added Last Year: 1,400 (+13.2%)
Banks; insurance & stock brokerage; automobile & equipment leasing

NEW JERSEY

FOSTER WHEELER CORPORATION
Perryville Corporate Park   Phone: 908-730-4000
Clinton, NJ 08809-4000   Fax: 908-730-4959
Chm, Pres & CEO: Richard J. Swift
VP HR & Admin: James E. Schessler
Employees: 9,350
Jobs Cut Last Year: 630 (-6.3%)
Diversified - engineering & construction, energy equipment & power systems

GAF CORP
1361 Alps Rd.   Phone: 201-628-3000
Wayne, NJ 07470   Fax: 201-628-3311
Chm & CEO: Samuel J. Heyman
VP HR: Jim Strupa
Employees: 4,350
Jobs Added Last Year: 73 (+1.7%)
Diversified operations - building products; chemicals

GBC TECHNOLOGIES, INC.
444 Kelley Dr.   Phone: 609-767-2500
Berlin, NJ 08009   Fax: 609-753-1123
CEO & Pres: Norman M. Some
HR Mgr: Julie Katz
Employees: 183
Jobs Added Last Year: 51 (+38.6%)
Computers - wholesale

GENERAL PUBLIC UTILITIES CORPORATION
100 Interpace Pkwy.   Phone: 201-263-6500
Parsippany, NJ 07054   Fax: 201-263-6822
Chm & CEO: James R. Leva
VP HR: Richard Postweiler
Employees: 11,939
Jobs Cut Last Year: 30 (-.3%)
Utility - electric power

GENLYTE GROUP INC.
100 Lighting Way   Phone: 201-864-3000
Secaucus, NJ 07096   Fax: 201-392-3784
Pres & CEO: Larry Powers
VP Admin (HR): Donna Ratliff
Employees: 2,840
Jobs Cut Last Year: 135 (-4.5%)
Building products - lighting fixtures

THE GRAND UNION HOLDINGS CORPORATION
201 Willowbrook Blvd.   Phone: 201-890-6000
Wayne, NJ 07470   Fax: 201-890-6671
Pres & CEO: Joseph J. McCaig
SVP Personnel: Charles Barrett
Employees: 18,500
Jobs Added Last Year: —
Retail - supermarkets

GREAT ATLANTIC & PACIFIC TEA CO. [10673]
2 Paragon Dr.   Phone: 201-573-9700
Montvale, NJ 07645   Fax: 201-930-8106
Chm & CEO: James Wood
VP HR: H. Nelson Lewis
Employees: 94,000
Jobs Cut Last Year: 600 (-.6%)
Retail - supermarkets

HANDEX ENVIRONMENTAL RECOVERY, INC.
500 Campus Dr.   Phone: 908-536-8500
Morganville, NJ 07751   Fax: 908-536-7751
Chm & CEO: Curtis L. Smith, Jr.
Dir HR: Camille Sorensen
Employees: 600
Jobs Added Last Year: 129 (+27.4%)
Pollution control - groundwater cleanup

HARVARD INDUSTRIES, INC.
Central Ave.   Phone: 908-938-9000
Farmingdale, NJ 07727   Fax: 908-919-2482
Chm, Pres & CEO: Vincent J. Jaimoli
VP HR: James Luci
Employees: 5,619
Jobs Added Last Year: 19 (+.3%)
Diversified operations - automotive parts; aerospace fasteners; furniture

HOME STATE HOLDINGS INC.
One Harding Rd.   Phone: 908-219-6600
Red Bank, NJ 07701   Fax: 908-219-5936
CEO: Robert Abidor
VP HR: Gerry Dohanyos
Employees: 65
Jobs Added Last Year: 12 (+22.6%)
Insurance - property & casualty

NEW JERSEY

HOOPER HOLMES, INC.
170 Mt. Airy Rd.　　　Phone: 908-766-5000
Basking Ridge, NJ 07920　　Fax: 908-766-5073
Pres & CEO: James M. McNamee
VP HR: Frank Steiner
Employees: 10,500
Jobs Added Last Year: 3,311 (+46.1%)
Health care - home

HOVNANIAN K ENTERPRISES, INC.
10 Hwy. 35, PO Box 500　　Phone: 908-747-7800
Red Bank, NJ 07701　　Fax: 908-747-7159
CEO & Chm: Kevork S. Hovnanian
SVP Admin & Sec (HR): Timothy Mason
Employees: 1,070
Jobs Added Last Year: 270 (+33.8%)
Building - residential

HUBCO, INC.
1000 MacArthur Blvd.　　Phone: 201-348-2300
Mahwah, NJ 07430　　Fax: 201-348-0689
Pres & CEO: Kenneth T. Neilson
SVP (HR): Karen A. Foley
Employees: 703
Jobs Added Last Year: 247 (+54.2%)
Banks - Northeast

I-STAT CORPORATION
303 College Rd. East　　Phone: 609-243-9300
Princeton, NJ 08540　　Fax: 609-243-9311
Pres & CEO: William P. Moffitt
Dir HR: Bill Beattie
Employees: 271
Jobs Added Last Year: 55 (+25.5%)
Medical instruments - blood analysis products

INDUCTOTHERM INDUSTRIES
10 Indel Ave.　　Phone: 609-267-9000
Rancocas, NJ 08073　　Fax: 609-267-0497
Chm, CEO & Pres: Henry M. Rowan
VP Admin (HR): David Broddock
Employees: 4,384
Jobs Added Last Year: 221 (+5.3%)
Machinery - general industrial

INGERSOLL-RAND COMPANY
200 Chestnut Ridge Rd.　　Phone: 201-573-0123
Woodcliff Lake, NJ 07675　　Fax: 201-573-3448
Chm, Pres & CEO: James E. Perrella
Dir HR: Donald H. Rice
Employees: 35,143
Jobs Cut Last Year: 165 (-.5%)
Machinery - general industrial, engineered equipment & bearings, locks & tools

J & J SNACK FOODS CORP.
6000 Central Hwy.　　Phone: 609-665-9533
Pennsauken, NJ 08109　　Fax: 609-665-6359
Chm, Pres & CEO: Gerald B. Shreiber
HR Admin: Valerie Bianchi
Employees: 1,700
Jobs Added Last Year: 650 (+61.9%)
Food - snack foods & baked goods; beverages

J. M. HUBER CORPORATION
333 Thornall St.　　Phone: 908-549-8600
Edison, NJ 08818　　Fax: 908-549-2239
Chm, Pres & CEO: Peter T. Francis
VP HR: Joseph P. Matturro
Employees: 3,000
Jobs Added Last Year: —
Diversified operations - natural resources; plastics; electronics; ink

JOHNSON & JOHNSON
One Johnson & Johnson Plaza　　Phone: 908-524-0400
New Brunswick, NJ 08933　　Fax: 908-214-0332
Chm & CEO: Ralph S. Larsen
VP Admin (HR): Roger S. Fine
Employees: 81,600
Jobs Cut Last Year: 3,300 (-3.9%)
Drugs; baby shampoo, pain killers, bandages, toothbrushes, powders & soap; clinical diagnostics

LECHTERS, INC.
One Cape May St.　　Phone: 201-481-1100
Harrison, NJ 07029-9998　　Fax: 201-481-5493
VC, CEO & Acting Pres: Steen Kanter
VP HR: Sevesti Dimitropoulos
Employees: 5,360
Jobs Added Last Year: 667 (+14.2%)
Retail - discount housewares

NEW JERSEY

MAYFAIR SUPERMARKETS INC.
681 Newark Ave. Phone: 908-352-6400
Elizabeth, NJ 07208 Fax: 908-352-0103
Chm & Pres: Stanley P. Kaufelt
VP HR: John Kovaleski
Employees: 4,200
Jobs Added Last Year: –
Retail - supermarkets

MERCK & CO., INC.
One Merck Dr., PO Box 100 Phone: 908-423-1000
Whitehouse Station, NJ 08889-0100 Fax: 908-594-4662
CEO: Raymond V. Gilmartin
VP HR: Steven M. Darien
Employees: 47,100
Jobs Added Last Year: 8,700 (+22.7%)
Drugs - cardiovasculars, antibiotics, anti-ulcerants; mail-order pharmacy

METROLOGIC INSTRUMENTS, INC.
Coles Rd. at Rte. 42 Phone: 609-228-8100
Blackwood, NJ 08012 Fax: 609-228-6673
Chm, Pres & CEO: C. Harry Knowles
Dir HR: John Patten
Employees: 260
Jobs Added Last Year: 30 (+13%)
Optical character recognition - bar code scanning equipment

METROMEDIA COMPANY
One Meadowlands Plaza Phone: 201-804-6400
East Rutherford, NJ 07073 Fax: 201-804-6540
Gen Partner, Chm, Pres & CEO: John W. Kluge
Dir HR: Beverly Scoggins
Employees: 20,000
Jobs Cut Last Year: 400 (-2%)
Diversified operations - restaurants (Bennigan's, Bonanza, Ponderosa, Steak and Ale); entertainment (Orion Pictures)

THE MONEY STORE INC.
2840 Morris Ave. Phone: 908-686-2000
Union, NJ 07083 Fax: 908-686-6907
Pres & CEO: Marc Turtletaub
VP HR: Denise Morgan
Employees: 1,375
Jobs Added Last Year: 325 (+31%)
Financial - home equity, Small Business Administration loans & government-guaranteed student loans

MULTICARE COS INC.
411 Hackensack Ave. Phone: 201-488-8818
Hackensack, NJ 07601-6328 Fax: 201-525-5954
Chm & Co-CEO: Moshael J. Strauss
VP HR: Ronald G. Clarendon
Employees: 4,800
Jobs Added Last Year: 1,050 (+28%)
Medical services - nursing, subacute care & rehabilitation therapies

THE NEWARK GROUP, INC.
20 Jackson Dr. Phone: 908-276-4000
Cranford, NJ 07016 Fax: 908-276-2888
Chm & CEO: Edward K. Mullen
VP (HR): Carl R. Crook
Employees: 2,900
Jobs Added Last Year: 200 (+7.4%)
Paper & paper products - recycled paperboard & converted products

NEXTEL COMMUNICATIONS, INC.
201 Rte. 17 North Phone: 201-438-1400
Rutherford, NJ 07070 Fax: 201-438-5540
VC & CEO: Wayland R. Hicks
Dir HR: Lane Foster
Employees: 773
Jobs Added Last Year: 223 (+40.5%)
Telecommunications services - mobile radio wireless communication services

NUI CORPORATION
550 Rte. 202-206, PO Box 760 Phone: 908-781-0500
Bedminster, NJ 07921-0760 Fax: 908-781-0718
Chm & CEO: John Kean
VP HR: Thomas J. Lynch
Employees: 1,011
Jobs Added Last Year: 52 (+5.4%)
Utility - gas distribution

PATHMARK STORES, INC.
301 Blair Rd. Phone: 908-499-3000
Woodbridge, NJ 07095 Fax: 908-499-3072
Chm & CEO: Jack Futterman
VP HR: Maureen McGurl
Employees: 28,000
Jobs Added Last Year: 1,000 (+3.7%)
Retail - supermarkets, drug stores & home improvement centers

An in-depth profile of this company is available by fax. Call 800-510-4452 and use your touch-tone phone to put in the 5-digit code at the prompt. Only $2.95 each with your credit card. See page 12 for more details.

NEW JERSEY

PETRIE RETAIL, INC.
70 Enterprise Ave. Phone: 201-866-3600
Secaucus, NJ 07094 Fax: 201-866-2355
CEO: Allan Laufgraben
SVP HR: Pat Hughes
Employees: 19,500
Jobs Added Last Year: 2,000 (+11.4%)
Retail - women's apparel (Petrie, Marianne, Stuarts, Jean Nicole, G&G & Winkelman's)

PRIME HOSPITALITY CORPORATION
700 Rte. 46 East Phone: 201-882-1010
Fairfield, NJ 07004 Fax: 201-882-8577
Pres & CEO: David A. Simon
SVP HR: Denise Driscoll
Employees: 5,500
Jobs Added Last Year: 800 (+17%)
Hotels (Wellesley Inns & AmeriSuites; Marriott, Radisson, Sheraton, Holiday Inn, Ramada & Howard Johnson licensee)

PRINCETON UNIVERSITY
One Nassau Hall Phone: 609-258-3000
Princeton, NJ 08544 Fax: 609-258-1294
Pres: Harold T. Shapiro
VP HR: Audrey S. Smith
Employees: 4,931
Jobs Added Last Year: —
University

THE PRUDENTIAL INSURANCE CO.
751 Broad St. Phone: 201-802-6000
Newark, NJ 07102 Fax: 201-802-6092
Chm, Pres & CEO: Robert C. Winters
SVP HR: Donald C. Mann
Employees: 105,534
Jobs Added Last Year: 4,534 (+4.5%)
Insurance - health & life; securities brokerage; residential real estate brokerage

PUBLIC SERVICE ENTERPRISE GROUP
80 Park Plaza, PO Box 1171 Phone: 201-430-7000
Newark, NJ 07101-1171 Fax: 201-430-5983
Chm, Pres & CEO: E. James Ferland
VP HR: M. Peter Mellet
Employees: 13,115
Jobs Added Last Year: 0
Utility - electric & gas power

RESORTS INTERNATIONAL, INC.
1133 Boardwalk Phone: 609-344-6000
Atlantic City, NJ 08401 Fax: 609-340-6284
EVP: Christopher D. Whitney
VP HR: Michelle Perna
Employees: 7,400
Jobs Added Last Year: 200 (+2.8%)
Leisure & recreational services - casinos

RF POWER PRODUCTS, INC.
502 Gibbsboro-Marlton Rd. Phone: 609-751-0033
Vorhees, NJ 08043 Fax: 609-751-2960
Chm, Pres & CEO: Joseph Stach
Mgr HR: Susan Johnston
Employees: 105
Jobs Added Last Year: 30 (+40%)
Electrical products - radio frequency power systems, matching networks & other peripheral products

ROBERTS PHARMACEUTICAL CORPORATION
6 Industrial Way West Phone: 908-389-1182
Eatontown, NJ 07724 Fax: 908-389-1014
Chm, Pres & CEO: Robert A. Vukovich
VP Administrative Svcs & HR: Laura J. DiMichele
Employees: 500
Jobs Added Last Year: 48 (+10.6%)
Drugs

SCHERING-PLOUGH CORPORATION
One Giralda Farms Phone: 201-822-7000
Madison, NJ 07940-7000 Fax: 201-822-7447
Chm & CEO: Robert P. Luciano
SVP HR: Gordon C. O'Brien
Employees: 21,600
Jobs Added Last Year: 500 (+2.4%)
Drugs & consumer health care products (Dr. Scholl's & Coppertone)

THE SCORE BOARD, INC.
1951 Old Cuthbert Rd. Phone: 609-354-9000
Cherry Hill, NJ 08034 Fax: 609-354-8402
Chm, Pres & CEO: Kenneth Goldin
HR Dir: Jim Preston
Employees: 283
Jobs Added Last Year: 73 (+34.8%)
Leisure & recreational products - sports picture cards

NEW JERSEY

SEALED AIR CORPORATION
Park 80 East Phone: 201-791-7600
Saddle Brook, NJ 07662-5291 Fax: 201-368-2674
Pres & CEO: T. J. Dermot Dunphy
Mgr Emp Ben: Heidi Calcagno
Employees: 2,750
Jobs Added Last Year: 30 (+1.1%)
Containers - packaging & cushioning materials including padded mailing envelopes (Jiffy) & food packaging products

SYNETIC, INC.
669 River Dr. Phone: 201-703-3400
Elmwood Pk, NJ 07407 Fax: 201-703-3401
Chm: Martin J. Wygod
No central personnel officer
Employees: 1,090
Jobs Added Last Year: 740 (+211.4%)
Plastic products used in pen tips, home water filters & beauty aids

TOPS APPLIANCE CITY, INC.
45 Brunswick Ave. Phone: 908-248-2850
Edison, NJ 08818 Fax: 908-248-2719
Chm & CEO: Leslie S. Turchin
VP HR: Charles Rosenberg
Employees: 2,100
Jobs Added Last Year: 245 (+13.2%)
Retail - consumer electronics & appliances in New York City metropolitan area

TOYS "R" US, INC.
461 From Rd. Phone: 201-262-7800
Paramus, NJ 07652 Fax: 201-262-7606
VC & CEO: Michael Goldstein
SVP HR: Jeffrey S. Wells
Employees: 55,000
Jobs Cut Last Year: 32,000 (-36.8%)
Retail - toys, children's clothing & books

TRANSTECHNOLOGY CORPORATION
700 Liberty Ave. Phone: 908-964-5666
Union, NJ 07083 Fax: 908-688-8518
Chm, Pres & CEO: Michael J. Berthelot
Dir HR: Monica Lazorchak
Employees: 1,059
Jobs Added Last Year: 227 (+27.3%)
Metal products - fasteners, wire harnesses; helicopter rescue hoist & cargo-hook equipment

TYCO TOYS, INC.
6000 Midlantic Dr. Phone: 609-234-7400
Mt. Laurel, NJ 08054 Fax: 609-273-2885
Chm, Pres & CEO: Richard E. Grey
VP HR: Mary Ann Herron
Employees: 2,800
Jobs Added Last Year: 600 (+27.3%)
Toys - games & hobby products

UJB FINANCIAL CORPORATION
301 Carnegie Center Phone: 609-987-3200
Princeton, NJ 08543-2066 Fax: 609-987-3481
Chm, Pres & CEO: T. Joseph Semrod
EVP (HR): Alfred M. D'Augusta
Employees: 6,135
Jobs Cut Last Year: 84 (-1.4%)
Banks - Northeast

UNION CAMP CORPORATION
1600 Valley Rd. Phone: 201-628-2000
Wayne, NJ 07470 Fax: 201-628-2722
CEO: W. Craig McClelland
VP HR: Russ Boekenheide
Employees: 19,126
Jobs Cut Last Year: 1,027 (-5.1%)
Paper & paperboard, packaging products & wood products; chemicals, flavors & fragrances

UNITED RETAIL GROUP, INC.
365 W. Passaic St. Phone: 201-845-0880
Rochelle Park, NJ 07662 Fax: 201-909-2162
Chm, Pres & CEO: Raphael Benaroya
EVP Organizational Dev (HR): Charles R. Wilkerson
Employees: 4,300
Jobs Added Last Year: 200 (+4.9%)
Retail - women's large-size apparel (Sizes Unlimited, The Avenue)

VITAL SIGNS, INC.
20 Campus Rd. Phone: 201-790-1330
Totowa, NJ 07512 Fax: 201-790-3307
Pres & CEO: Terence D. Wall
Dir HR: Elizabeth Greenberg
Employees: 708
Jobs Added Last Year: 73 (+11.5%)
Medical products - anesthesia & respiratory products

NEW JERSEY

WAKEFERN FOOD CORPORATION
600 York St. Phone: 908-527-3300
Elizabeth, NJ 07207 Fax: 908-906-5215
Chm & CEO: Thomas P. Infusino
VP HR: Marty Glass
Employees: 4,760
Jobs Added Last Year: —
Food - wholesale

WELLMAN, INC.
1040 Broad St., Ste. 302 Phone: 908-542-7300
Shrewsbury, NJ 07702 Fax: 908-542-9344
Pres & CEO: Thomas M. Duff
Dir HR: Steve Lefevre
Employees: 3,600
Jobs Added Last Year: 700 (+24.1%)
Chemicals - plastics

WARNER INSURANCE SERVICES, INC.
17-01 Pollitt Dr. Phone: 201-794-4800
Fair Lawn, NJ 07410 Fax: 201-791-8905
CEO: Harvey Krieger
Mgr HR: Sue Southgate
Employees: 510
Jobs Added Last Year: 52 (+11.4%)
Business services - insurance advisory services

WHEATON INC.
1101 Wheaton Ave. Phone: 609-825-1400
Millville, NJ 08332 Fax: 609-825-8461
Pres & CEO: Robert I. Veghte
VP HR: Thomas Clary
Employees: 6,000
Jobs Added Last Year: 0
Glass & plastic containers

WARNER-LAMBERT COMPANY
201 Tabor Rd. Phone: 201-540-2000
Morris Plains, NJ 07950 Fax: 201-540-3761
Chm & CEO: Melvin R. Goodes
VP HR: Raymond M. Fino
Employees: 35,000
Jobs Added Last Year: 1,000 (+2.9%)
Drugs, consumer & health care products (Halls, Listerine & Rolaids) & confectionery (Certs, Chiclets, Dentyne)

NEW MEXICO

DIAGNOSTEK, INC.
4500 Alexander Blvd. NE Phone: 505-345-8080
Albuquerque, NM 87107 Fax: 505-345-1455
CEO: Nunzio P. DeSantis
Dir HR: Mary D. Ornellas
Employees: 2,500
Jobs Added Last Year: 1,970 (+371.7%)
Medical services - integrated pharmacy management

PUBLIC SERVICE COMPANY OF NEW MEXICO
Alvarado Sq. Phone: 505-848-2700
Albuquerque, NM 87158 Fax: 505-848-2359
Chm: John T. Ackerman
VP HR: Judy Zanotti
Employees: 3,080
Jobs Cut Last Year: 70 (-2.2%)
Utility - electric power

FURR'S SUPERMARKETS, INC.
1730 Montano Rd. NW Phone: 505-344-6525
Albuquerque, NM 87107 Fax: 505-761-0866
CEO: Jan Friederich
VP HR: Delwyn James
Employees: 8,900
Jobs Added Last Year: 2,400 (+36.9%)
Retail - supermarkets

SUN HEALTHCARE GROUP, INC.
5600 Wyoming Blvd. NE Phone: 505-821-3355
Albuquerque, NM 87109 Fax: 505-821-9440
CEO: Andrew L. Turner
SVP HR: Julie Colins
Employees: 8,000
Jobs Added Last Year: 3,010 (+60.3%)
Nursing homes - Alzheimer's disease patient facilities

HORIZON HEALTHCARE CORP.
6001 Indian School Rd. NE Phone: 505-881-4961
Albuquerque, NM 87110 Fax: 505-881-5097
Chm, Pres & CEO: Neal M. Elliott
VP HR: Rodney C. Panyik
Employees: 15,700
Jobs Added Last Year: 6,700 (+74.4%)
Nursing homes; subacute care, pharmacy services, rehabilitation therapies, laboratory services & Alzheimer's care

THERMO INSTRUMENT SYSTEMS INC.
504 Airport Rd., PO Box 2108 Phone: 505-471-3232
Santa Fe, NM 87504-2108 Fax: 505-471-6079
CEO: Arvin H. Smith
HR Admin: Pauline Varele
Employees: 3,652
Jobs Added Last Year: 1,067 (+41.3%)
Instruments - scientific

MESA AIR GROUP
2325 E. 30th St. Phone: 505-327-0271
Farmington, NM 87401 Fax: 505-326-4485
Chm, Pres & CEO: Larry L. Risley
Dir Personnel: Franklin Roberts
Employees: 2,800
Jobs Added Last Year: 260 (+10.2%)
Transportation - regional airline

NEW YORK

"21" INTERNATIONAL HOLDINGS, INC.
153 E. 53rd St., Ste. 5900 Phone: 212-230-0400
New York, NY 10022 Fax: 212-593-1363
Chm & CEO: Marshall S. Cogan
VP & Managing Dir (HR): Barry Zimmerman
Employees: 6,700
Jobs Added Last Year: 2,200 (+48.9%)
Diversified operations - restaurants (21 Club); foam rubber (Foamex); auto interior parts; auto dealerships

ACC CORP.
39 State St. Phone: 716-987-3000
Rochester, NY 14614 Fax: 716-987-3499
Chm & CEO: Richard T. Aab
HR & Corp Communications: George H. Murray, Jr.
Employees: 352
Jobs Added Last Year: 272 (+340%)
Telecommunications services - long distance services in US, Canada & UK

ACCLAIM ENTERTAINMENT, INC.
71 Audrey Ave. Phone: 516-624-8888
Oyster Bay, NY 11771 Fax: 516-624-2885
Co-Chm & CEO: Gregory Fischbach
VP Planning & Ops (HR): John Ma
Employees: 193
Jobs Added Last Year: 60 (+45.1%)
Computers - videogame cartridges

ADVANCE PUBLICATIONS, INC.
950 Fingerboard Rd. Phone: 718-981-1234
Staten Island, NY 10305 Fax: 718-981-1415
Chm & CEO: Samuel I. "Si" Newhouse, Jr.
No central personnel officer
Employees: 19,000
Jobs Added Last Year: 0
Publishing - newspapers, books (Random House), magazines (Conde Nast); cable TV

ALBANY INTERNATIONAL CORPORATION
1373 Broadway Phone: 518-445-2200
Albany, NY 12204 Fax: 518-445-2265
Pres & CEO: Francis L. McKone
Dir HR: Barry D. Jessee
Employees: 5,286
Jobs Cut Last Year: 392 (-6.9%)
Paper & paper products

ALEXANDER & ALEXANDER SERVICES INC.
1211 Avenue of the Americas Phone: 212-840-8500
New York, NY 10036 Fax: 212-840-5900
Chm & CEO: Frank G. Zarb
VP Corp HR: Thomas Soper III
Employees: 14,500
Jobs Cut Last Year: 1,100 (-7.1%)
Insurance - brokerage & management consulting

ALLEGHANY CORPORATION
Park Avenue Plaza Phone: 212-752-1356
New York, NY 10055 Fax: 212-759-8149
Pres & CEO: John J. Burns, Jr.
No central personnel officer
Employees: 10,237
Jobs Added Last Year: 1,237 (+13.7%)
Financial - title insurance & financial services

ALLEGHENY POWER SYSTEM, INC.
12 E. 49th St. Phone: 212-752-2121
New York, NY 10017-1028 Fax: 212-836-4340
Chm, Pres & CEO: Klaus Bergman
VP HR: Richard J. Gagliardi
Employees: 5,157
Jobs Added Last Year: 3,200 (+163.5%)
Utility - electric power

ALLOU HEALTH & BEAUTY CARE, INC.
50 Emjay Blvd. Phone: 516-273-4000
Brentwood, NY 11717 Fax: 516-273-5318
Chm & CEO: Victor Jacobs
Dir Personnel: Kathy Calzente
Employees: 180
Jobs Added Last Year: 30 (+20%)
Cosmetics & toiletries - wholesale

ALPINE GROUP, INC.
1790 Broadway Phone: 212-757-3333
New York, NY 10019-1412 Fax: 212-757-3423
Chm & CEO: Steven S. Elbaum
Office Mgr (HR): Elaine McKee
Employees: 434
Jobs Added Last Year: 366 (+538.2%)
Chemicals - specialty

NEW YORK

AMBAC INC.
One State St. Plaza Phone: 212-668-0340
New York, NY 10004 Fax: 212-509-9190
Chm, Pres & CEO: Phillip B. Lassiter
SVP HR & Admin: Janice A. Reals
Employees: 492
Jobs Added Last Year: 254 (+106.7%)
Insurance - municipal bond insuror

AMERICAN RETAIL GROUP, INC.
1114 Avenue of the Americas Phone: 212-391-4141
New York, NY 10036 Fax: 212-302-4381
Pres : Roland Brenninkmeyer
VP HR: Tom Elliott
Employees: 17,000
Jobs Added Last Year: –
Retail - apparel

AMERADA HESS CORPORATION
1185 Avenue of the Americas Phone: 212-997-8500
New York, NY 10036 Fax: 212-536-8390
Chm & CEO: Leon Hess
SVP HR: Neal Gelfand
Employees: 10,173
Jobs Cut Last Year: 90 (-.9%)
Oil & gas - integrated

AMREP CORPORATION
10 Columbus Circle Phone: 212-705-4700
New York, NY 10019 Fax: 212-705-4740
Chm, Pres & CEO: Anthony B. Gliedman
Office Mgr (HR): Pat Bradley
Employees: 1,100
Jobs Added Last Year: 169 (+18.2%)
Building - residential & commercial

AMERICAN EXPRESS COMPANY
World Financial Center Phone: 212-640-2000
New York, NY 10285 Fax: 212-619-9802
Chm & CEO: Harvey Golub
EVP Quality & HR: Joseph W. Keilty
Employees: 64,654
Jobs Cut Last Year: 49,698 (-43.5%)
Business services - debit & credit cards; travel services

ANNTAYLOR STORES CORPORATION
142 W. 57th St. Phone: 212-541-3300
New York, NY 10019 Fax: 212-541-3298
Chm & CEO: Sally Frame Kasaks
SVP HR: Gerri Feemster
Employees: 5,300
Jobs Added Last Year: 1,540 (+41%)
Retail - apparel & shoes

AMERICAN INTERNATIONAL GROUP
70 Pine St. Phone: 212-770-7000
New York, NY 10270 Fax: 212-770-7821
Chm & CEO: Maurice R. Greenberg
SVP HR: Axel I. Freudmann
Employees: 33,000
Jobs Added Last Year: 0
Insurance - property & casualty

ARROW ELECTRONICS, INC.
25 Hub Dr. Phone: 516-391-1300
Melville, NY 11747 Fax: 516-391-1644
Chm, Pres & CEO: Stephen P. Kaufman
VP HR: Thomas F. Hallam
Employees: 5,569
Jobs Added Last Year: 1,938 (+53.4%)
Electronics - parts distribution

AMERICAN RECREATION COMPANY HOLDINGS
48 Mall Dr. Phone: 516-864-2000
Commack, NY 17725 Fax: 516-804-2031
Pres & CEO: Stephen A. Silverstein
Dir HR: Meg O'Mahoney
Employees: 477
Jobs Added Last Year: 370 (+345.8%)
Leisure & recreational products - bicycles (Mongoose, Outrider) & bicycle helmets (Headwinds)

ARTISTIC GREETINGS, INC.
One Komer Center Phone: 607-737-5235
Elmira, NY 14902 Fax: 607-733-4157
CEO: Stuart Komer
Dir HR: George Altimonda
Employees: 725
Jobs Added Last Year: 95 (+15.1%)
Retail - mail order & direct (stationery & gift items)

NEW YORK

ASARCO INCORPORATED
180 Maiden Ln.   Phone: 212-510-2000
New York, NY 10038   Fax: 212-510-1855
Chm, Pres & CEO: Richard de J. Osborne
VP HR: David B. Woodbury
Employees: 8,500
Jobs Cut Last Year: 400 (-4.5%)
Metal ores - copper, lead, zinc, silver & gold mining

AVON PRODUCTS, INC.
9 W. 57th St.   Phone: 212-546-6015
New York, NY 10019   Fax: 212-546-6136
Chm & CEO: James E. Preston
SVP HR: Marcia L. Worthing
Employees: 29,800
Jobs Added Last Year: 100 (+.3%)
Cosmetics & toiletries

ASTRUM INTERNATIONAL CORP.
600 Madison Ave., Ste. 11   Phone: 305-532-2426
New York, NY 10022   Fax: 305-532-2789
Chm & CEO: Steven J. Green
No central personnel officer
Employees: 11,000
Jobs Added Last Year: 0
Diversified operations - luggage (American Tourister & Samsonite); water treatment (Culligan); apparel (McGregor)

THE BANK OF NEW YORK COMPANY
48 Wall St.   Phone: 212-495-1784
New York, NY 10286   Fax: 212-495-1239
Chm & CEO: J. Carter Bacot
SVP Personnel: Frank L. Peterson
Employees: 15,621
Jobs Cut Last Year: 546 (-3.4%)
Banks - Northeast

AT&T CORPORATION
32 Avenue of the Americas   Phone: 212-387-5400
New York, NY 10013-2412   Fax: 212-841-4715
Chm & CEO: Robert E. Allen
SVP HR: Harold W. Burlingame
Employees: 308,700
Jobs Cut Last Year: 4,000 (-1.3%)
Telecommunications services - #1 US long distance carrier; computers (NCR); credit cards (Universal); cellular (McCaw)

BANKERS TRUST NEW YORK CORP.
280 Park Ave.   Phone: 212-250-2500
New York, NY 10017   Fax: 212-454-1704
Chm & CEO: Charles S. Sanford, Jr.
Managing Dir Corp HR: Mark Bieler
Employees: 13,571
Jobs Added Last Year: 654 (+5.1%)
Banks - money center

AVIS, INC.
900 Old Country Rd.   Phone: 516-222-3000
Garden City, NY 11530   Fax: 516-222-4381
Chm & CEO: Joseph V. Vittoria
SVP HR: Donald L. Korn
Employees: 14,000
Jobs Added Last Year: 500 (+3.7%)
Leasing - #3 US car rental company

BARNES & NOBLE, INC.
122 Fifth Ave.   Phone: 212-633-3300
New York, NY 10011-5605   Fax: 212-675-0413
Chm & CEO: Leonard Riggio
VP HR: Don Lapp
Employees: 14,700
Jobs Cut Last Year: 2,300 (-13.5%)
Retail - bookstores (B. Dalton, Barnes & Noble, Bookstop, Bookstar, Doubleday & Scribner's)

AVNET, INC.
80 Cutter Mill Rd.   Phone: 516-466-7000
Great Neck, NY 11021   Fax: 516-466-1203
Chm & CEO: Leon Machiz
VP HR: Robert Cierk
Employees: 8,000
Jobs Added Last Year: 1,500 (+23.1%)
Electronics - parts distribution

BARR LABORATORIES, INC.
2 Quaker Rd., PO Box D2900   Phone: 914-362-1100
Pomona, NY 10970-0519   Fax: 914-353-3476
Chm, Pres & CEO: Bruce L. Downey
VP HR: Catherine F. Higgins
Employees: 342
Jobs Added Last Year: 55 (+19.2%)
Drugs - generic

NEW YORK

BAUSCH & LOMB INCORPORATED
One Chase Sq. Phone: 716-338-6000
Rochester, NY 14601-0054 Fax: 716-338-6007
Chm & CEO: Daniel E. Gill
VP HR: James P. Greenawalt
Employees: 15,900
Jobs Added Last Year: 1,400 (+9.7%)
Medical products - pharmaceuticals, contact lenses & optics

BITWISE DESIGNS, INC.
Rotterdam Industrial Park, Bldg. 50 Phone: 518-356-9741
Schenectady, NY 12306 Fax: 518-356-9749
Pres, CEO & Chm: John Botti
No central personnel officer
Employees: 57
Jobs Added Last Year: 37 (+185%)
Computers - workstations & laptops; peripherals & accessories

THE BEAR STEARNS COMPANIES INC.
245 Park Ave. Phone: 212-272-2000
New York, NY 10167 Fax: 212-272-8239
Pres & CEO: James E. Cayne
Dir Personnel: Stephen Lacoff
Employees: 6,036
Jobs Added Last Year: 163 (+2.8%)
Financial - investment bankers

BOOZ, ALLEN & HAMILTON INC.
101 Park Ave. Phone: 212-697-1900
New York, NY 10178 Fax: 212-551-6732
Chm, Pres & CEO: William F. Stasior
Personnel Dir: Susan Galager
Employees: 5,481
Jobs Added Last Year: 1,781 (+48.1%)
Consulting - management & technology

BESICORP GROUP INC.
1151 Flatbush Rd. Phone: 914-336-7700
Kingston, NY 12401-7011 Fax: 914-336-7172
Chm, Pres & CEO: Michael F. Zinn
Personnel Administrator: Beth Petramale
Employees: 79
Jobs Added Last Year: 29 (+58%)
Energy - alternative & independent power generation

BRISTOL-MYERS SQUIBB COMPANY
345 Park Ave. Phone: 212-546-4000
New York, NY 10154-0037 Fax: 212-546-4020
Pres & CEO: Charles A. Heimbold, Jr.
SVP HR: Charles G. Tharp
Employees: 49,500
Jobs Cut Last Year: 3,100 (-5.9%)
Drugs & medical devices; consumer health care (Bufferin, Excedrin & NoDoz) & personal care products (Clairol)

BHC COMMUNICATIONS, INC.
600 Madison Ave. Phone: 212-421-0200
New York, NY 10022 Fax: 212-935-8462
Chm & Pres: Herbert J. Siegel
No central personnel officer
Employees: 1,163
Jobs Added Last Year: 335 (+40.5%)
Broadcasting - radio & TV

BROOKLYN UNION GAS CO.
One MetroTech Center Phone: 718-403-2000
Brooklyn, NY 11201-3850 Fax: 718-852-4643
CEO: Robert B. Catell
SVP HR: Wallace P. Parker
Employees: 3,711
Jobs Added Last Year: 60 (+1.6%)
Utility - gas distribution

BIG V SUPERMARKETS INC.
176 N. Main St. Phone: 914-651-4411
Florida, NY 10921 Fax: 914-651-7048
Chm & CEO: David Bronstein
VP HR: Tom Hoskison
Employees: 5,000
Jobs Added Last Year: 500 (+11.1%)
Retail - supermarkets

BUSH INDUSTRIES, INC.
One Mason Dr. Phone: 716-665-2000
Jamestown, NY 14702-0460 Fax: 716-665-2074
Chm, Pres & CEO: Paul S. Bush
EVP, COO & CFO (HR): Robert L. Ayres
Employees: 1,700
Jobs Added Last Year: 400 (+30.8%)
Furniture

 An in-depth profile of this company is available by fax. Call 800-510-4452 and use your touch-tone phone to put in the 5-digit code at the prompt. Only $2.95 each with your credit card. See page 12 for more details.

NEW YORK

CABLEVISION SYSTEMS CORPORATION
One Media Crossways
Woodbury, NY 11797
CEO: Charles F. Dolan
Dir HR: Joyce E Mancini
Employees: 3,636
Jobs Added Last Year: 192 (+5.6%)
Cable TV
Phone: 516-364-8450
Fax: 516-496-1780

CARLISLE COMPANIES INC.
250 S. Clinton St., Ste. 201
Syracuse, NY 13202-1258
Pres & CEO: Stephen P. Munn
Mgr Compensation & Ben (HR): Douglas Freeman
Employees: 4,440
Jobs Cut Last Year: 167 (-3.6%)
Rubber & plastic products
Phone: 315-474-2500
Fax: 315-474-2008

CACHE, INC.
1460 Broadway
New York, NY 10036
CEO: Andrew M. Saul
HR Mgr: Carol Garrymore
Employees: 762
Jobs Added Last Year: 154 (+25.3%)
Retail - apparel & shoes
Phone: 212-840-4242
Fax: 212-840-4225

CARTER-WALLACE, INC. 10301
1345 Avenue of the Americas
New York, NY 10105-0021
CEO: Henry H. Hoyt, Jr.
Dir HR: Thomas B. Moorhead
Employees: 4,060
Jobs Added Last Year: 40 (+1%)
Drugs & personal care products including condoms (Trojan) & deodorant (Arrid, Lady's Choice)
Phone: 212-339-5000
Fax: 212-339-5100

CAI WIRELESS SYSTEMS, INC.
14 Corporate Woods Blvd.
Albany, NY 12211
Chm & CEO: Jared E. Abbruzzese
Dir HR: Lynne Parkinson
Employees: 53
Jobs Added Last Year: 31 (+140.9%)
Telecommunications services - wireless system operator
Phone: 518-462-2632
Fax: 518-462-3045

CBS INC. 10256
51 W. 52nd St.
New York, NY 10019-6188
Chm, Pres & CEO: Laurence A. Tisch
SVP HR: Joan Showalter
Employees: 6,500
Jobs Added Last Year: 0
Broadcasting - radio & TV
Phone: 212-975-4321
Fax: 212-975-7133

CANANDAIGUA WINE COMPANY, INC. 11800
116 Buffalo St.
Canandaigua, NY 14424
Pres & CEO: Richard Sands
VP HR: Al Kidd
Employees: 1,950
Jobs Added Last Year: 1,050 (+116.7%)
Beverages - wine (Almaden, Inglenook, Paul Masson, Manischewitz), imported beer & distilled spirits
Phone: 716-394-7900
Fax: 716-394-2027

CDP TECHNOLOGIES, INC.
333 Seventh Ave.
New York, NY 10001
Pres: Mark L. Nelson
Mgr HR: Beatriz Abreu
Employees: 140
Jobs Added Last Year: 41 (+41.4%)
Business services - electronic information retrieval services to major medical centers in the US & Canada
Phone: 212-563-3006
Fax: 212-563-3784

CAPITAL CITIES/ABC, INC. 10290
77 W. 66th St.
New York, NY 10023-6298
Chm & CEO: Thomas S. Murphy
VP & Exec Asst to Chm (HR): William J. Wilkinson
Employees: 19,250
Jobs Added Last Year: 0
Broadcasting - radio & TV; newspaper & magazine publishing; cable programming (A&E, ESPN & Lifetime)
Phone: 212-456-7777
Fax: 212-456-6850

CELADON GROUP INC.
888 Seventh Ave.
New York, NY 10106-1591
Chm & CEO: Stephen Russell
Dir HR: Norma Bennet
Employees: 1,576
Jobs Added Last Year: 405 (+34.6%)
Transportation - long distance trucking, air cargo, domestic freight primarily between the US & Mexico; travel agencies
Phone: 212-977-4447
Fax: 212-315-5281

NEW YORK

THE CHASE MANHATTAN CORP.
One Chase Manhattan Plaza Phone: 212-552-2222
New York, NY 10081-0001 Fax: 212-552-5005
Chm & CEO: Thomas G. Labrecque
EVP HR: John V. Scicutella
Employees: 34,000
Jobs Cut Last Year: 450 (-1.3%)
Banks - money center

COLGATE-PALMOLIVE COMPANY
300 Park Ave. Phone: 212-310-2000
New York, NY 10022-7499 Fax: 212-310-3284
Chm & CEO: Reuben Mark
SVP HR: Douglas M. Reid
Employees: 28,000
Jobs Cut Last Year: 800 (-2.8%)
Soap & cleaning preparations (Ajax, Irish Spring) & personal care products (Mennen); pet food (Hill's)

CHEMICAL BANKING CORPORATION
270 Park Ave. Phone: 212-270-6000
New York, NY 10017-2036 Fax: 212-270-2613
Chm & CEO: Walter V. Shipley
EVP Personnel Rel: Martin H. Zuckerman
Employees: 41,567
Jobs Added Last Year: 1,870 (+4.7%)
Banks - money center

COLTEC INDUSTRIES INC.
430 Park Ave. Phone: 212-940-0400
New York, NY 10022-3597 Fax: 212-319-8345
Chm, Pres & CEO: John W. Guffey, Jr.
EVP Admin (HR): Laurence H. Polsky
Employees: 10,700
Jobs Cut Last Year: 700 (-6.1%)
Diversified operations - aerospace; automotive & industrial components

CHEYENNE SOFTWARE, INC.
3 Expressway Plaza Phone: 516-484-5110
Roslyn Heights, NY 11577 Fax: 516-484-3446
Chm, Pres & CEO: ReiJane Huai
Dir HR: Andy Boyland
Employees: 430
Jobs Added Last Year: 201 (+87.8%)
Computers - backup software for networks

COMMAND SECURITY CORPORATION
Lexington Park Phone: 914-454-3703
LaGrangeville, NY 12540 Fax: 914-454-0075
Chm, Pres & CEO: William C. Vassell
VP (HR): Eugene McDonald
Employees: 5,300
Jobs Added Last Year: 2,800 (+112%)
Protection - guard services

CITICORP
399 Park Ave. Phone: 800-285-3000
New York, NY 10043 Fax: 212-527-3277
Chm: John S. Reed
Senior HR Off: Lawrence R. Phillips
Employees: 81,500
Jobs Added Last Year: 500 (+.6%)
Banks - money center

COMPUTER ASSOCIATES INTL.
One Computer Associates Plaza Phone: 516-342-5224
Islandia, NY 11788-7000 Fax: 516-342-5329
Chm & CEO: Charles B. Wang
SVP HR: Lisa Mars
Employees: 6,900
Jobs Cut Last Year: 300 (-4.2%)
Computers - database & business applications software

CLUB MED, INC.
40 W. 57th St. Phone: 212-977-2100
New York, NY 10019 Fax: 212-977-4086
Chm, Pres & CEO: Serge Trigano
Personnel Mgr: Maggie Moloney
Employees: 6,500
Jobs Added Last Year: 100 (+1.6%)
Leisure & recreational services - resorts

COMVERSE TECHNOLOGY INC.
170 Crossways Park Dr. Phone: 516-677-7200
Woodbury, NY 11797 Fax: 516-677-7355
Pres & CEO: Kobi Alexander
Dir Corp Communication (HR): Paul Baker
Employees: 435
Jobs Added Last Year: 185 (+74%)
Computers - multimedia message management systems

NEW YORK

CONSOLIDATED EDISON COMPANY [10392]
4 Irving Place Phone: 212-460-4600
New York, NY 10003 Fax: 212-982-7816
Chm, Pres & CEO: Eugene R. McGrath
SVP Central Svcs (HR): Thomas J. Galvin
Employees: 17,586
Jobs Cut Last Year: 1,132 (-6%)
Utility - electric power

CORNELL UNIVERSITY
Cornell University Campus Phone: 607-255-2000
Ithaca, NY 14853 Fax: 607-255-0327
Pres: Frank H. Rhodes
Assoc VP HR: Beth Warren
Employees: 9,500
Jobs Added Last Year: –
University

CONTINENTAL CAN CO.
One Aerial Way Phone: 516-822-4940
Syosset, NY 11791 Fax: 516-931-6344
Chm & CEO: Donald J. Bainton
Dir HR: Abdo Yazgi
Employees: 3,712
Jobs Added Last Year: 530 (+16.7%)
Containers - paper & plastic

CORNING INCORPORATED [10409]
One Riverfront Plaza Phone: 607-974-9000
Corning, NY 14831 Fax: 607-974-8551
Chm & CEO: James R. Houghton
EVP HR, Corp Bus Dev & Mktg: Kenneth W. Freeman
Employees: 34,000
Jobs Added Last Year: 2,900 (+9.3%)
Diversified operations - oven-proof glassware & crystal; sunglasses; laboratory services; fiber optics

CONTINENTAL CORPORATION
180 Maiden Ln. Phone: 212-440-3000
New York, NY 10038 Fax: 212-440-7130
Chm & CEO: John P. Mascotte
Corp SVP (HR): Kenneth B. Zeigler
Employees: 13,100
Jobs Added Last Year: –
Insurance - property & casualty

CULBRO CORPORATION
387 Park Ave. South Phone: 212-561-8700
New York, NY 10016 Fax: 212-561-8791
Pres & CEO: Edgar M. Cullman, Sr.
Dir HR: Mary Raffaniello
Employees: 4,050
Jobs Added Last Year: 300 (+8%)
Tobacco

CONTINENTAL GRAIN COMPANY [40104]
277 Park Ave. Phone: 212-207-5100
New York, NY 10172-0002 Fax: 212-207-5181
Chm & CEO: Donald L. Staheli
VP HR: Dwight Coffin
Employees: 15,500
Jobs Added Last Year: 800 (+5.4%)
Food - commodity merchandising & processing

CURATIVE TECHNOLOGIES, INC.
14 Research Way, PO Box 9052 Phone: 516-689-7000
East Setauket, NY 11733-9052 Fax: 516-689-7067
Pres & CEO: Russell B. Whitman
Dir HR: Denise Smith
Employees: 374
Jobs Added Last Year: 74 (+24.7%)
Drugs - human growth factors

COOPERS & LYBRAND L.L.P. [40107]
1251 Avenue of the Americas Phone: 212-536-2000
New York, NY 10020 Fax: 212-536-3145
Chm & CEO: Eugene M. Freedman
VC HR & Strategy: Anthony J. Conti
Employees: 65,500
Jobs Cut Last Year: 800 (-1.2%)
Business services - accounting & consulting

CYGNE DESIGNS INC. [16293]
1372 Broadway Phone: 212-354-6474
New York, NY 10018 Fax: 212-921-8213
Chm & CEO: Bernard M. Manuel
HR Dir: Remy Nicholas
Employees: 1,650
Jobs Added Last Year: 1,370 (+489.3%)
Apparel - women's & juniors' outerwear

NEW YORK

D'ARCY MASIUS BENTON & BOWLES, INC.
1675 Broadway   Phone: 212-468-3622
New York, NY 10019   Fax: 212-468-4385
Chm & CEO: Roy J. Bostock
Dir Personnel: Judith Kemp
Employees: 5,904
Jobs Added Last Year: —
Advertising

DATA BROADCASTING CORPORATION
120 Wall St.   Phone: 212-208-7705
New York, NY 10005   Fax: 212-207-5414
CEO: Douglas B. Smith
Dir HR: Michelle Grossman
Employees: 264
Jobs Added Last Year: 21 (+8.6%)
Business services - real-time stock market quotes, customized portfolio tracking & investor information

DEAN WITTER, DISCOVER & CO.
Two World Trade Center   Phone: 212-392-2222
New York, NY 10048   Fax: 212-392-3118
Chm & CEO: Philip J. Purcell
SVP HR: Michael Cunningham
Employees: 26,564
Jobs Added Last Year: —
Financial - securities brokerage (Dean Witter, Reynolds), investment banker & credit card issuer (Discover)

DELAWARE NORTH COMPANIES INC.
438 Main St.   Phone: 716-858-5000
Buffalo, NY 14202   Fax: 716-858-5479
Chm & CEO: Jeremy M. Jacobs
VP HR: Marlene Jennings-Galla
Employees: 20,000
Jobs Added Last Year: 0
Diversified operations - food services; parimutuels; metals; typography

DIAL-A-MATTRESS FRANCHISE CORP.
31-10 48th Ave.   Phone: 718-472-1200
Long Island City, NY 11101   Fax: 718-472-1310
CEO: Napoleon Barragan
HR Mgr: Zorida Cook
Employees: 267
Jobs Added Last Year: 72 (+36.9%)
Retail - nationwide discount mattress delivery

DOVER CORPORATION
280 Park Ave.   Phone: 212-922-1640
New York, NY 10017-1292   Fax: 212-922-1656
Pres & CEO: Thomas L. Reece
No central personnel officer
Employees: 20,500
Jobs Added Last Year: 1,673 (+8.9%)
Diversified operations - a group of 70 diverse industrial manufacturing companies

DOW JONES & COMPANY, INC.
200 Liberty St.   Phone: 212-416-2000
New York, NY 10281   Fax: 212-732-8356
Chm & CEO: Peter R. Kann
VP Emp Rel: Donald L. Miller
Employees: 10,006
Jobs Added Last Year: 146 (+1.5%)
Publishing - newspapers (*Wall Street Journal, Barron's*) & on-line business information (DJNR, Telerate)

DRESSER-RAND COMPANY
One Baron Steuben Place   Phone: 607-937-6400
Corning, NY 14830   Fax: 607-937-6405
Pres & CEO: Ben R. Stuart
VP HR: Lynn Sanberg
Employees: 7,500
Jobs Added Last Year: —
Machinery - turbocompressors, power turbines & generators

DREW INDUSTRIES INCORPORATED
200 Mamaroneck Ave.   Phone: 914-428-9098
White Plains, NY 10601   Fax: 914-428-4581
Pres & CEO: Leigh J. Abrams
Sec & Treas (HR): Harvey J. Caplan
Employees: 1,177
Jobs Added Last Year: 98 (+9.1%)
Building products - aluminum windows & skylights

EASTMAN KODAK COMPANY
343 State St.   Phone: 716-724-4000
Rochester, NY 14650   Fax: 716-724-0663
Chm, Pres & CEO: George M.C. Fisher
SVP & Dir, Corp HR: Michael P. Morley
Employees: 110,400
Jobs Cut Last Year: 22,200 (-16.7%)
Photographic equipment & copiers

NEW YORK

THE EQUITABLE COMPANIES, INC.
787 Seventh Ave. Phone: 212-554-1234
New York, NY 10019 Fax: 212-315-2825
Chm & CEO: Richard H. Jenrette
VP HR: Janet Friedman
Employees: 13,100
Jobs Added Last Year: 800 (+6.5%)
Insurance - life, financial services (Donaldson, Lufkin & Jenrette)

ERNST & YOUNG LLP
787 Park Ave. Phone: 212-773-3000
New York, NY 10019 Fax: 212-773-1996
Chm: Phil Laskawy
VC HR: Bruce J. Mantia
Employees: 63,500
Jobs Added Last Year: 5,123 (+8.8%)
Business services - accounting & consulting

FAMILY GOLF CENTERS, INC.
225 Broadhollow Rd. Phone: 516-694-1666
Melville, NY 11747 Fax: 516-694-0918
CEO: Dominic Chang
Dir HR: Krishnan P. Thampi
Employees: 133
Jobs Added Last Year: 33 (+33%)
Leisure & recreational services - golf-related recreational facilities

FAY'S, INCORPORATED
7245 Henry Clay Blvd. Phone: 315-451-8000
Liverpool, NY 13088 Fax: 315-451-2470
Chm & CEO: Henry A. Panasci, Jr.
VP Personnel: Donald R. Bregande
Employees: 9,000
Jobs Added Last Year: 1,500 (+20%)
Retail - drug stores

FINLAY ENTERPRISES
521 Fifth Ave. Phone: 212-382-7400
New York, NY 10175 Fax: 212-557-3848
Chm & CEO: Arthur E. Reiner
Pres HR: Joyce Manning
Employees: 7,000
Jobs Added Last Year: —
Retail - jewelry outlets in department stores

FIRST CENTRAL FINANCIAL CORPORATION
266 Merrick Rd. Phone: 516-593-7070
Lynbrook, NY 11563 Fax: 516-593-8880
CEO: Martin J. Simon
VP HR: Ray Barancaccio
Employees: 105
Jobs Added Last Year: 22 (+26.5%)
Insurance - property & casualty

FIRST EMPIRE STATE CORPORATION
One M&T Plaza Phone: 716-842-5445
Buffalo, NY 14240 Fax: 716-842-5177
Chm & Pres: Robert G. Wilmers
SVP (HR): Ray E. Logan
Employees: 4,149
Jobs Cut Last Year: 251 (-5.7%)
Banks - Northeast

FORSTMANN & CO., INC.
1185 Avenue of the Americas Phone: 212-642-6900
New York, NY 10036 Fax: 212-642-6870
Chm, Pres & CEO: Christopher L. Schaller
VP HR: Robert Christian
Employees: 3,000
Jobs Added Last Year: 0
Textiles - wool & wool-blend fabrics

FRONTIER INSURANCE GROUP, INC.
195 Lake Louise Marie Rd. Phone: 914-796-2100
Rock Hill, NY 12775-8000 Fax: 914-796-1902
Pres & Chm: Walter A. Rhulen
SVP HR: Renee Schivera
Employees: 442
Jobs Added Last Year: 79 (+21.8%)
Insurance - property & casualty

GENOVESE DRUG STORES, INC.
80 Marcus Dr. Phone: 516-420-1900
Melville, NY 11747 Fax: 516-845-8378
Chm & Pres: Leonard Genovese
VP (HR): Sue Crickmore
Employees: 4,200
Jobs Added Last Year: 635 (+17.8%)
Retail - drug stores

NEW YORK

THE GOLDMAN SACHS GROUP, LP
85 Broad St. Phone: 212-902-1000
New York, NY 10004 Fax: 212-902-3925
Sr Partner & Chm of Mgmt Comm: Jon Corzine
Partner, Personnel: Jonathan L. Cohen
Employees: 9,000
Jobs Added Last Year: 2,000 (+28.6%)
Financial - investment banking & securities brokerage

GROW GROUP, INC.
200 Park Ave. Phone: 212-599-4400
New York, NY 10166 Fax: 212-286-0940
Pres & CEO: Russell Banks
Treas & CFO (HR): Frank V. Esser
Employees: 2,800
Jobs Added Last Year: 800 (+40%)
Paints & allied products

THE GOLUB CORPORATION
501 Duanesburg Rd. Phone: 518-355-5000
Schenectady, NY 12306 Fax: 518-355-0843
Chm & CEO: Lewis Golub
VP HR: Curt Hopkins
Employees: 8,000
Jobs Added Last Year: 145 (+1.8%)
Retail - supermarkets (Price Chopper) & convenience stores (Mini Chopper)

THE GUARDIAN LIFE INSURANCE CO.
201 Park Ave. South Phone: 212-598-8000
New York, NY 10003 Fax: 212-598-8813
Chm & CEO: Arthur V. Ferrara
VP HR: Douglas C. Kramer
Employees: 7,502
Jobs Added Last Year: –
Insurance - multiline & misc.

GOULDS PUMPS, INC.
240 Fall St. Phone: 315-568-2811
Seneca Falls, NY 13148 Fax: 315-568-2418
Pres & CEO: Thomas C. McDermott
VP HR: Mary Ann Lambertsen
Employees: 4,200
Jobs Cut Last Year: 100 (-2.3%)
Machinery - centrifugal pumps

HANDY & HARMAN
250 Park Ave. Phone: 212-661-2400
New York, NY 10177 Fax: 212-309-0691
Chm & CEO: Richard N. Daniel
No central personnel officer
Employees: 4,478
Jobs Added Last Year: 145 (+3.3%)
Precious metals & jewelry

GRAFF PAY-PER-VIEW INC.
536 Broadway Phone: 212-941-1434
New York, NY 10012 Fax: 212-941-4746
Chm & CEO: J. Roger Faherty
Dir Office Svcs (HR): Joan Simari
Employees: 63
Jobs Added Last Year: 33 (+110%)
Cable TV - adult entertainment & pay-per-view movie channels

THE HEARST CORPORATION
959 Eighth Ave. Phone: 212-649-2000
New York, NY 10019 Fax: 212-765-3528
Pres & CEO: Frank A. Bennack, Jr.
VP & Dir HR: Kenneth A. Feldman
Employees: 15,000
Jobs Added Last Year: 2,000 (+15.4%)
Publishing - magazines (*Esquire*, *Good Housekeeping*), newspapers & books; broadcasting & cable TV

GRAHAM-FIELD HEALTH PRODUCTS, INC.
400 Rabro Dr. East Phone: 516-582-5900
Hauppauge, NY 11788 Fax: 516-582-5608
Chm & CEO: Irwin Selinger
No central personnel officer
Employees: 670
Jobs Added Last Year: 134 (+25%)
Medical instruments - diagnostic & surgical instruments, home health care products

HELMSLEY ENTERPRISES, INC.
60 E. 42nd St. Phone: 212-687-6400
New York, NY 10165 Fax: 212-687-6437
Chm, Pres & CEO: Harry B. Helmsley
Mgr HR: Jennie Voscina
Employees: 13,000
Jobs Added Last Year: 0
Real estate operations - brokerage & management; hotels

NEW YORK

HOME HOLDINGS INC.
59 Maiden Ln. Phone: 212-530-6600
New York, NY 10038-4548 Fax: 212-530-6143
Pres & CEO: Lars H. Thunell
SVP HR: Albert Morton
Employees: 5,500
Jobs Added Last Year: 1,400 (+34.1%)
Insurance - property & casualty

HOMECARE MANAGEMENT, INC.
80 Air Park Dr. Phone: 516-981-0034
Ronkonkoma, NY 11779 Fax: 516-981-0522
Chm & Pres: Clifford E. Hotte
Personnel & HR Dir: Virginia Belloise
Employees: 194
Jobs Added Last Year: 109 (+128.2%)
Health care - outpatient & home, pharmaceutical supplies

HUDSON GENERAL CORPORATION
111 Great Neck Rd. Phone: 516-487-8610
Great Neck, NY 11021 Fax: 516-487-4855
Chm & Pres: Jay B. Langner
Dir Insurance & HR: Robert Cavalier
Employees: 3,300
Jobs Added Last Year: 300 (+10%)
Transportation - aircraft ground handling, fueling, ground transportation & related services

INFORMATION BUILDERS, INC.
1250 Broadway, 38th Floor Phone: 212-736-4433
New York, NY 10001-3782 Fax: 212-967-6406
Pres: Gerald D. Cohen
HR Mgr: Lila Goldberg
Employees: 1,750
Jobs Added Last Year: 150 (+9.4%)
Computers - database software (Focus)

INNODATA CORPORATION
95 Rockwell Place Phone: 718-625-7750
Brooklyn, NY 11217 Fax: 718-522-9235
Pres: Barry Hertz
Ops Mgr (HR): Jack Cohen
Employees: 2,550
Jobs Added Last Year: 869 (+51.7%)
Data collection & systems

INSTRUMENT SYSTEMS CORPORATION
100 Jericho Quadrangle Phone: 516-938-5544
Jericho, NY 11753 Fax: 516-938-5644
CEO: Harvey R. Blau
Office Mgr (HR): Susan Roland
Employees: 2,900
Jobs Added Last Year: 100 (+3.6%)
Diversified operations - customized plastic films; garage doors

INTEGRATED WASTE SERVICES, INC.
201 Ganson St. Phone: 716-852-2345
Buffalo, NY 14203 Fax: 716-852-2474
Pres & CEO: James H. Williams
HR Dir: Joseph Williams
Employees: 570
Jobs Added Last Year: 279 (+95.9%)
Pollution control - solid waste management

INTERNATIONAL BUSINESS MACHINES
Armonk, NY 10504 Phone: 914-765-1900
Chm & CEO: Louis V. Gerstner, Jr. Fax: 914-765-4190
Dir HR: J. Thomas Bouchard
Employees: 256,207
Jobs Cut Last Year: 45,335 (-15%)
Computers - mainframes, minis, micros, processors, software, services & peripherals

INTL. FLAVORS & FRAGRANCES
521 W. 57th St. Phone: 212-765-5500
New York, NY 10019-2960 Fax: 212-708-7132
Chm & Pres: Eugene P. Grisanti
VP & Corp Dir HR: William A. Myers, Jr.
Employees: 4,371
Jobs Added Last Year: 129 (+3%)
Chemicals - specialty

INTERNATIONAL IMAGING MATERIALS INC.
310 Commerce Dr. Phone: 716-691-6333
Amherst, NY 14228-2396 Fax: 716-691-3895
Pres & CEO: John W. O'Leary
HR Dir: Susan R. Stamp
Employees: 550
Jobs Added Last Year: 56 (+11.3%)
Office automation - thermal transfer ribbons

NEW YORK

INTERNATIONAL PAPER COMPANY
2 Manhattanville Rd.   Phone: 914-397-1500
Purchase, NY 10577   Fax: 914-397-1596
Chm & CEO: John A. Georges
SVP HR: Robert M. Byrnes
Employees: 72,500
Jobs Cut Last Year: 500 (-.7%)
Paper & paper products; specialty products; wood & timber

INTERPUBLIC GROUP OF COMPANIES, INC.
1271 Avenue of the Americas   Phone: 212-399-8000
New York, NY 10020   Fax: 212-399-8130
Pres & CEO: Philip H. Geier, Jr.
SVP HR: Kent Kroeber
Employees: 17,600
Jobs Added Last Year: 800 (+4.8%)
Advertising

INVESTMENT TECHNOLOGY GROUP, INC.
900 Third Ave.   Phone: 212-755-6800
New York, NY 10022   Fax: 212-444-6290
Pres: Raymond L. Killian, Jr.
VP Admin (HR): Susan Nelson
Employees: 69
Jobs Added Last Year: 62 (+885.7%)
Financial - automated securities trade execution & analysis services

ITT CORPORATION
1330 Avenue of the Americas   Phone: 212-258-1000
New York, NY 10019-5490   Fax: 212-258-1037
Chm, Pres & CEO: Rand V. Araskog
SVP & Dir HR: Ralph W. Pausig
Employees: 98,000
Jobs Cut Last Year: 8,000 (-7.5%)
Diversified operations - insurance; automotive components; hotels; electronic components; directory publishing

J. CREW GROUP INC.
625 Sixth Ave.   Phone: 212-886-2500
New York, NY 10011   Fax: 212-886-2666
Chm & CEO: Arthur Cinader
VP HR: Carol Dudgeon
Employees: 6,400
Jobs Added Last Year: 987 (+18.2%)
Retail - mail order & retail apparel

J.P. MORGAN & CO. INCORPORATED
60 Wall St.   Phone: 212-483-2323
New York, NY 10260-0060   Fax: 212-648-5193
Chm & CEO: Dennis Weatherstone
Managing Dir HR: Herbert J. Hefke
Employees: 15,193
Jobs Added Last Year: 825 (+5.7%)
Banks - money center

JEAN PHILIPPE FRAGRANCES, INC.
551 Fifth Ave.   Phone: 212-983-2640
New York, NY 10176   Fax: 212-983-4197
Chm & CEO: Jean Madar
Personnel Dir: Henry Dominentz
Employees: 107
Jobs Added Last Year: 37 (+52.9%)
Cosmetics & toiletries - imitation designer fragrances

JOHNSON & HIGGINS
125 Broad St.   Phone: 212-574-7000
New York, NY 10004   Fax: 212-574-7190
Chm, Pres & CEO: David A. Olsen
Mgr HR: James R. Reardon
Employees: 9,200
Jobs Added Last Year: 500 (+5.7%)
Insurance - risk management consulting, insurance brokerage

K-III COMMUNICATIONS CORP.
745 Fifth Ave.   Phone: 212-745-0100
New York, NY 10151   Fax: 212-745-0169
Chm & CEO: William F. Reilly
VP HR: Michaelanne C. Discepolo
Employees: 4,500
Jobs Added Last Year: 1,055 (+30.6%)
Publishing - periodicals (*New York* & *Seventeen*) & books (*World Almanac*); educational TV programming (Channel One)

KIMCO DEVELOPMENT CORPORATION
1044 Northern Blvd.   Phone: 516-484-5858
Roslyn, NY 11576   Fax: 516-484-5637
CEO: Milton Cooper
HR Dir & Controller: Toni Calandrino
Employees: 124
Jobs Added Last Year: 53 (+74.6%)
Real estate operations

NEW YORK

KING KULLEN GROCERY COMPANY INC.
1194 Prospect Ave. Phone: 516-333-7100
Westbury, NY 11590 Fax: 516-333-7929
Chm & CEO: John B. Cullen
Dir Labor & Personnel: Thomas Nagle
Employees: 4,500
Jobs Added Last Year: 0
Retail - supermarkets

LIZ CLAIBORNE, INC.
1441 Broadway Phone: 212-354-4900
New York, NY 10018 Fax: 212-719-9049
Chm & CEO: Jerome A. Chazen
HR Ops: Jorge Figueredo
Employees: 7,900
Jobs Added Last Year: 500 (+6.8%)
Apparel - women's & men's; cosmetics

KPMG PEAT MARWICK L.L.P.
767 Fifth Ave. Phone: 212-909-5000
New York, NY 10153 Fax: 212-909-5299
Chm & CEO: Jon C. Madonna
HR Partner: Mary L. Dupont
Employees: 72,000
Jobs Cut Last Year: 4,200 (-5.5%)
Business services - accounting & consulting

LOEWS CORPORATION
667 Madison Ave. Phone: 212-545-2000
New York, NY 10021-8087 Fax: 212-545-2498
Chm & Co-CEO: Laurence A. Tisch
VP Personnel: Kenneth Abrams
Employees: 27,100
Jobs Cut Last Year: 1,000 (-3.6%)
Diversified operations - insurance (CNA); tobacco (Kent, Newport, True); hotels (Loews); watches (Bulova)

LEFRAK ORGANIZATION INC.
97-77 Queens Blvd. Phone: 718-459-9021
Rego Park, NY 11374 Fax: 718-897-0688
Chm: Samuel J. LeFrak
HR: Cheryl Jensen
Employees: 18,000
Jobs Added Last Year: 0
Real estate development & management; entertainment; oil & gas exploration

THE LONG ISLAND RAILROAD CO., INC.
Jamaica Station Phone: 718-990-7400
Jamaica, NY 11435 Fax: 718-990-7633
Pres & CEO: Charles W. Hoppe
VP HR: Susan Romeo
Employees: 6,250
Jobs Added Last Year: –
Transportation - rail

LEHMAN BROTHERS HOLDINGS INC.
3 World Financial Center Phone: 212-526-7000
New York, NY 10285 Fax: 212-526-7165
Chm & CEO: Richard S. Fuld
Managing Dir HR: Maryanne Rasmussen
Employees: 9,300
Jobs Added Last Year: –
Financial - investment bankers

LORAL CORPORATION
600 Third Ave. Phone: 212-697-1105
New York, NY 10016 Fax: 212-661-8988
Chm & CEO: Bernard L. Schwartz
VP Admin (HR): Stephen L. Jackson
Employees: 32,600
Jobs Added Last Year: 8,100 (+33.1%)
Electronics - military

LIUSKI INTERNATIONAL, INC.
10 Hub Dr. Phone: 516-454-8220
Melville, NY 11747 Fax: 516-454-8266
CEO: Hsing-Yen Liu
Corp Personnel Dir: Roslyn Bush
Employees: 520
Jobs Added Last Year: 119 (+29.7%)
Computers - peripheral distribution; PC (Magitronic) manufacture

MACANDREWS & FORBES HOLDINGS
35 E. 62nd St. Phone: 212-688-9000
New York, NY 10021 Fax: 212-572-8400
Chm & CEO: Ronald O. Perelman
Dir Facilities (HR): Christine Castari
Employees: 23,500
Jobs Cut Last Year: 2,200 (-8.6%)
Diversified operations - cosmetics (Revlon); banking; publishing (Marvel); outdoor equipment; boats; cigars

NEW YORK

MAPINFO CORPORATION
One Global View Phone: 518-285-6000
Troy, NY 12180 Fax: 518-274-6066
Pres & CEO: Brian D. Owen
HR Dir: Joe Clement
Employees: 210
Jobs Added Last Year: 65 (+44.8%)
Computers - desktop mapping software

MARIETTA CORPORATION
37 Huntington St. Phone: 607-753-6746
Cortland, NY 13045 Fax: 607-753-7456
Pres & CEO: Stephen D. Tannen
Mgr HR: Gail M. Sechrist
Employees: 698
Jobs Added Last Year: 111 (+18.9%)
Cosmetics & toiletries - miniature soaps, shampoos & personal care items for hotel rooms

MARK IV INDUSTRIES, INC.
501 John James Audubon Pkwy. Phone: 716-689-4972
Amherst, NY 14226-0801 Fax: 716-689-6098
Chm & CEO: Salvatore H. Alfiero
Mgr Welfare Ben & Corp Office HR: Christine Werth
Employees: 12,500
Jobs Added Last Year: 700 (+5.9%)
Diversified operations - transportation; process control equipment; professional audio

MARSH & MCLENNAN COS., INC.
1166 Avenue of the Americas Phone: 212-345-5000
New York, NY 10036-2774 Fax: 212-345-4838
Chm & CEO: A. J. "Ian" C. Smith
SVP HR & Admin: Francis N. Bonsignore
Employees: 25,600
Jobs Cut Last Year: 200 (-.8%)
Insurance - brokerage, consulting, investment management

MARVEL ENTERTAINMENT GROUP
387 Park Ave. South Phone: 212-696-0808
New York, NY 10016 Fax: 212-576-8598
CEO: William C. Bevins, Jr.
Dir HR: Jacquelyn Green
Employees: 1,475
Jobs Added Last Year: 597 (+68%)
Publishing - comic books, sports trading cards

MCCRORY CORPORATION
667 Madison Ave. Phone: 212-735-9500
New York, NY 10021 Fax: 212-735-9450
Chm & CEO: Meshulam Riklis
SVP HR & Info Technology: Tom Russell
Employees: 7,000
Jobs Added Last Year: —
Retail - discount & variety stores

MCGRAW-HILL, INC.
1221 Avenue of the Americas Phone: 212-512-2000
New York, NY 10020 Fax: 212-512-4871
Chm & CEO: Joseph L. Dionne
VP HR: Patrick Pavelski
Employees: 15,661
Jobs Added Last Year: 2,268 (+16.9%)
Publishing - magazines (*Business Week*), books & electronic; financial services (Standard & Poor's); broadcasting

MCKINSEY & COMPANY, INC.
55 E. 52nd St. Phone: 212-446-7000
New York, NY 10022 Fax: 212-688-8575
Mng Dir: Rajat Gupta
Principal & Personnel Dir: Jerome Vascellaro
Employees: 5,560
Jobs Added Last Year: 60 (+1.1%)
Consulting - management

MELVILLE CORPORATION
One Theall Rd. Phone: 914-925-4000
Rye, NY 10580 Fax: 914-925-4026
Chm & CEO: Stanley P. Goldstein
SVP HR: Jerald L. Maurer
Employees: 111,082
Jobs Cut Last Year: 4,562 (-3.9%)
Retail - shoes (Thom McAn), apparel (Marshalls), drugs (CVS), health & beauty aids & toys (Kay-Bee)

MERRILL LYNCH & CO., INC.
World Financial Ctr., 250 Vesey St. Phone: 212-449-1000
New York, NY 10281-1332 Fax: 212-236-4384
Chm & CEO: Daniel P. Tully
SVP HR: Patrick J. Walsh
Employees: 41,900
Jobs Added Last Year: 1,800 (+4.5%)
Financial - securities brokerage, investment banking, asset management, insurance

 An in-depth profile of this company is available by fax. Call 800-510-4452 and use your touch-tone phone to put in the 5-digit code at the prompt. Only $2.95 each with your credit card. See page 12 for more details.

NEW YORK

METROPOLITAN LIFE INSURANCE CO.
One Madison Ave. Phone: 212-578-2211
New York, NY 10010 Fax: 212-578-3320
Chm & CEO: Harry Kamen
SVP HR: Anne E. Hayden
Employees: 55,000
Jobs Cut Last Year: 2,000 (-3.5%)
Insurance - life; real estate brokerage (Century 21)

THE MUTUAL LIFE INSURANCE CO. OF NY
1740 Broadway Phone: 212-708-2000
New York, NY 10019 Fax: 212-708-2056
Chm & CEO: Michael I. Roth
Dir HR: Catherine Gushue
Employees: 3,400
Jobs Added Last Year: —
Insurance - life

MONRO MUFFLER BRAKE, INC.
2340 Brighton-Henrietta Rd. Phone: 716-427-2280
Rochester, NY 14623 Fax: 716-427-2295
Pres & CEO: Jack M. Gallagher
HR Mgr: Gail Ryan
Employees: 1,258
Jobs Added Last Year: 170 (+15.6%)
Retail - undercar repair service, located primarily in the northeast US

NAI TECHNOLOGIES, INC.
60 Plant Ave. Phone: 516-582-6500
Hauppauge, NY 11788 Fax: 516-582-8652
Pres & CEO: Robert A. Carlson
Corp Dir HR: Len Stanton
Employees: 560
Jobs Added Last Year: 160 (+40%)
Computers - peripheral equipment & ruggedized computers.

MONTEFIORE MEDICAL CENTER
111 E. 210th St. Phone: 718-920-4321
Bronx, NY 10467 Fax: 718-405-0651
Pres: Spencer Foreman
SVP HR: Donald G. Revelle
Employees: 10,500
Jobs Added Last Year: —
Hospitals

NATHAN'S FAMOUS, INC.
1400 Old Country Rd. Phone: 516-338-8500
Westbury, NY 11590-5119 Fax: 516-338-7220
Chm & CEO: Howard M. Lorber
Dir HR: Karen Brown
Employees: 537
Jobs Added Last Year: 177 (+49.2%)
Retail - hot dog restaurants, carts & kiosks

MOOG INC.
Seneca St. & Jamison Rd. Phone: 716-652-2000
East Aurora, NY 14052-0018 Fax: 716-687-4457
Pres: Robert T. Brady
Mgr HR: Jack Keebler
Employees: 3,140
Jobs Added Last Year: 316 (+11.2%)
Aerospace - aircraft equipment

NATIONWIDE CELLULAR SERVICE, INC.
20 E. Sunrise Hwy. Phone: 516-568-2000
Valley Stream, NY 11582 Fax: 516-568-0554
CEO & Chm: Stephen Katz
Dir HR: Miny Durando
Employees: 451
Jobs Added Last Year: 83 (+22.6%)
Telecommunications services

MORGAN STANLEY GROUP INC.
1251 Avenue of the Americas Phone: 212-703-4000
New York, NY 10020 Fax: 212-703-6503
Chm & Mng Dir: Richard B. Fisher
Dir HR: William Higgins
Employees: 8,173
Jobs Cut Last Year: 6,920 (-45.5%)
Financial - investment banking, merchant banking, stock brokerage

NEW YORK LIFE INSURANCE CO.
51 Madison Ave. Phone: 212-576-7000
New York, NY 10010 Fax: 212-576-6794
Chm & CEO: Harry G. Hohn
SVP HR: George J. Trapp
Employees: 17,169
Jobs Cut Last Year: 237 (-1.4%)
Insurance - life

NEW YORK

NEW YORK POWER AUTHORITY
1633 Broadway Phone: 212-468-6000
New York, NY 10019 Fax: 212-468-6040
Pres & CEO: S. David Freeman
VP HR: Deborah Estrin
Employees: 3,500
Jobs Added Last Year: 0
Utility - electric power

NYNEX CORPORATION
1113 Westchester Ave. Phone: 914-644-7600
White Plains, NY 10604 Fax: 212-921-2684
Pres & CEO: Ivan G. Seidenberg
VP HR: Donald J. Sacco
Employees: 76,200
Jobs Cut Last Year: 6,300 (-7.6%)
Utility - telephone; publishing

NEW YORK STATE ELECTRIC & GAS CORP.
PO Box 3287 Phone: 607-347-4131
Ithaca, NY 14852-3287 Fax: 607-347-4034
Chm, Pres & CEO: James A. Carrigg
VP Consumer Communication & HR Svcs: Carl Johnson
Employees: 4,888
Jobs Added Last Year: 46 (+1%)
Utility - electric power

OGDEN CORPORATION
2 Pennsylvania Plaza Phone: 212-868-6100
New York, NY 10121 Fax: 212-868-5714
Pres & CEO: R. Richard Ablon
VP HR: David Belka
Employees: 41,800
Jobs Cut Last Year: 1,200 (-2.8%)
Diversified operations - facility management & maintenance; in-flight catering; hazardous waste disposal; aviation services

THE NEW YORK TIMES COMPANY
229 W. 43rd St. Phone: 212-556-1234
New York, NY 10036 Fax: 212-556-3722
Chm & CEO: Arthur Ochs Sulzberger
SVP Broadcasting, Corp Dev & HR: Katherine P. Darrow
Employees: 13,000
Jobs Added Last Year: 2,900 (+28.7%)
Publishing - newspapers (*New York Times, Boston Globe*), magazines (*McCall's*); broadcasting

OMNICOM GROUP INC.
437 Madison Ave. Phone: 212-415-3600
New York, NY 10022 Fax: 212-415-3530
Pres & CEO: Bruce Crawford
HR Mgr: Leslie Chiocco
Employees: 14,400
Jobs Added Last Year: 1,900 (+15.2%)
Advertising

NIAGARA MOHAWK POWER CORPORATION
300 Erie Blvd. West Phone: 315-474-1511
Syracuse, NY 13202 Fax: 315-428-5101
Chm & CEO: William E. Davis
SVP HR: David J. Arrington
Employees: 11,500
Jobs Cut Last Year: 600 (-5%)
Utility - electric power

ONBANCORP, INC.
101 S. Salina St., PO Box 4983 Phone: 315-424-4400
Syracuse, NY 13221-4983 Fax: 315-442-1877
Chm, Pres & CEO: Robert J. Bennett
VP (HR): Thomas Delduchetto
Employees: 1,450
Jobs Added Last Year: 292 (+25.2%)
Banks - Northeast

NU HORIZONS ELECTRONIC CORPORATION
6000 New Horizons Blvd. Phone: 516-226-6000
Amityville, NY 11701 Fax: 516-226-6140
CEO: Irving Lubman
Personnel Mgr: Patty Englert
Employees: 140
Jobs Added Last Year: 23 (+19.7%)
Electronics - parts distribution

ONEIDA LTD.
Kenwood Ave. Phone: 315-361-3636
Oneida, NY 13421-2829 Fax: 315-361-3700
CEO: William D. Matthews
VP HR: Darwin Johnston
Employees: 5,500
Jobs Added Last Year: 0
Housewares, tableware & china; industrial wire

NEW YORK

OXFORD RESOURCES CORPORATION
270 S. Service Rd.   Phone: 516-777-8000
Melville, NY 11747   Fax: 516-777-8440
Chm & CEO: Michael C. Pascucci
Dir HR: Patricia Folan
Employees: 334
Jobs Added Last Year: 54 (+19.3%)
Leasing - autos

PAINE WEBBER GROUP INC.
1285 Avenue of the Americas   Phone: 212-713-2000
New York, NY 10019   Fax: 212-713-4924
Chm & CEO: Donald B. Marron
EVP Admin (HR): Ronald M. Schwartz
Employees: 14,400
Jobs Added Last Year: 800 (+5.9%)
Financial - investment banking, retail sales, asset management, capital markets

PALL CORPORATION
2200 Northern Blvd.   Phone: 516-484-5400
East Hills, NY 11548   Fax: 516-484-3529
Chm & CEO: Eric Krasnoff
Corp Emp: Geri Schwalb
Employees: 6,200
Jobs Cut Last Year: 100 (-1.6%)
Filtration products

PARSONS & WHITTEMORE, INC.
4 International Dr.   Phone: 914-937-9009
Rye Brook, NY 10573   Fax: 914-937-2259
Pres & CEO: Arthur L. Schwartz
Mgr HR: Richard Martin
Employees: 1,800
Jobs Added Last Year: 300 (+20%)
Diversified operations - pulp & paper; industrial machinery

PAXAR CORPORATION
275 N. Middletown Rd.   Phone: 914-735-9200
Pearl River, NY 10965   Fax: 914-735-9037
Pres & CEO: Arthur Hershaft
VP HR: Todd Barnett
Employees: 1,492
Jobs Added Last Year: 523 (+54%)
Machinery - electronic & hot-stamp printers

PAYCHEX, INC.
911 Panorama Trail South   Phone: 716-385-6666
Rochester, NY 14625-0397   Fax: 716-383-3428
Chm, Pres & CEO: B. Thomas Golisano
Dir HR: Rick Girard
Employees: 3,100
Jobs Added Last Year: 300 (+10.7%)
Business services - payroll processing

THE PENN TRAFFIC COMPANY
1200 State Fair Blvd.   Phone: 315-453-7284
Syracuse, NY 13221-4737   Fax: 315-453-0474
Pres & CEO: John T. Dixon
Dir Emp Rel: Eilleen O'Rourke
Employees: 25,800
Jobs Added Last Year: 1,233 (+5%)
Retail - supermarkets (Insalaco, P&C, Riverside & Bi-Lo)

PEPSICO, INC.
Purchase, NY 10577-1444   Phone: 914-253-2000
Chm & CEO: D. Wayne Calloway   Fax: 914-253-2070
SVP Personnel: J. Roger King
Employees: 423,000
Jobs Added Last Year: 51,000 (+13.7%)
Beverages - soft drinks; snack foods (Frito-Lay); restaurants (KFC, Pizza Hut, Taco Bell)

PFIZER INC.
235 E. 42nd St.   Phone: 212-573-2323
New York, NY 10017-5755   Fax: 212-573-7851
Chm & CEO: William C. Steere, Jr.
VP Personnel: Bruce R. Ellig
Employees: 40,500
Jobs Cut Last Year: 200 (-.5%)
Diversified operations - drugs; surgical devices; animal health products; chemicals & minerals; consumer products

PHILIP MORRIS COMPANIES INC.
120 Park Ave.   Phone: 212-880-5000
New York, NY 10017   Fax: 212-878-2165
CEO: Geoffrey C. Bible
SVP HR & Admin: Larry A. Gates
Employees: 173,000
Jobs Added Last Year: 12,000 (+7.5%)
Tobacco (Marlboro); food (Kraft); beer (Miller)

NEW YORK

PHILLIPS-VAN HEUSEN CORPORATION
1290 Avenue of the Americas   Phone: 212-541-5200
New York, NY 10104   Fax: 212-247-5309
Chm, Pres & CEO: Bruce J. Klatsky
Dir HR: Barbara Burkepile
Employees: 13,100
Jobs Cut Last Year: 300 (-2.2%)
Apparel - men's & boys

PLY GEM INDUSTRIES, INC.
777 Third Ave.   Phone: 212-832-1550
New York, NY 10017   Fax: 212-888-0472
Chm & CEO: Jeffrey S. Silverman
No central personnel officer
Employees: 4,000
Jobs Added Last Year: 600 (+17.6%)
Building products - specialty products for the home-improvement industry

POLO/RALPH LAUREN CORP.
650 Madison Ave.   Phone: 212-318-7000
New York, NY 10022   Fax: 212-318-5780
Chm & CEO: Ralph Lauren
Dir HR: Karen Rosenback
Employees: 3,000
Jobs Added Last Year: 200 (+7.1%)
Apparel, home furnishings & accessories

THE PORT AUTHORITY OF NY AND NEW JERSEY
One World Trade Center   Phone: 212-435-7000
New York, NY 10048   Fax: 212-435-4660
Chm: Kathleen A. Donovan
Dir HR: Louis J. LaCapra
Employees: 9,200
Jobs Added Last Year: –
Diversified operations - airport, rail passenger, bus terminal & marine terminal operations; cargo handling

PRICE WATERHOUSE LLP
1251 Avenue of the Americas   Phone: 212-819-5000
New York, NY 10020   Fax: 212-790-6620
Chm: Shaun F. O'Malley
VC HR: Richard P. Kearns
Employees: 50,122
Jobs Added Last Year: 1,341 (+2.7%)
Business services - accounting & consulting

PROFESSIONAL SPORTS CARE MANAGEMENT
550 Mamaroneck Ave.   Phone: 914-777-2400
Harrison, NY 10528   Fax: 914-777-2420
Pres & CEO: Russell F. Warren, Jr.
Dir Corp Comm (HR): Melanie Johnson
Employees: 335
Jobs Added Last Year: 208 (+163.8%)
Health care - outpatient physical therapy clinics in New York, New Jersey & Connecticut

PSC INC.
770 Basket Rd.   Phone: 716-265-1600
Webster, NY 14580-0448   Fax: 716-265-1689
Chm, Pres & CEO: L. Michael Hone
VP HR: Mary A. Gallahan
Employees: 330
Jobs Added Last Year: 80 (+32%)
Data collection & systems - bar-code scanning equipment

QUANTUM RESTAURANT GROUP, INC.
3333 New Hyde Park Rd., Ste. 210   Phone: 516-627-1815
New Hyde Park, NY 11042   Fax: 516-627-1898
Chm & CEO: Allen J. Bernstein
VP HR: Agnes Longarzo
Employees: 3,143
Jobs Added Last Year: 718 (+29.6%)
Retail - restaurants (Morton's of Chicago, Mick's, Peasant & Bertolini's)

THE READER'S DIGEST ASSOCIATION
Reader's Digest Rd.   Phone: 914-238-1000
Pleasantville, NY 10570-7000   Fax: 914-238-4559
Pres & CEO: James P. Shadt
SVP HR: Joseph M. Grecky
Employees: 6,700
Jobs Cut Last Year: 600 (-8.2%)
Publishing - periodicals, books, records & videos

RELIANCE GROUP HOLDINGS, INC.
55 E. 52nd St.   Phone: 212-909-1100
New York, NY 10055   Fax: 212-909-1864
Pres & CEO: Saul P. Steinberg
Asst VP Admin Svcs (HR): Eilene Boom
Employees: 9,675
Jobs Added Last Year: 325 (+3.5%)
Insurance - multiline & misc.

NEW YORK

RENCO GROUP INC.
45 Rockefeller Plaza Phone: 212-541-6000
New York, NY 10111 Fax: 212-541-6197
Pres & CEO: Ira L. Rennert
EVP HR: Marvin Koenig
Employees: 7,000
Jobs Added Last Year: 1,000 (+16.7%)
Diversified operations - steel; furniture; cages; all-terrain vehicles (Hummer)

RICH PRODUCTS CORPORATION
1150 Niagara St. Phone: 716-878-8000
Buffalo, NY 14213 Fax: 716-878-8266
Chm: Robert E. Rich, Sr.
VP HR: Brian Townson
Employees: 7,000
Jobs Added Last Year: 0
Diversified operations - frozen foods; minor league baseball teams; broadcasting

RJR NABISCO, INC.
1301 Avenue of the Americas Phone: 212-258-5600
New York, NY 10019-6013 Fax: 212-969-9173
Chm & CEO: Charles M. Harper
SVP HR & Admin: Gerald I. Angowitz
Employees: 66,500
Jobs Added Last Year: 3,500 (+5.6%)
Tobacco (Camel, Doral, Salem & Winston) & food (Oreo, Ritz, Chips Ahoy!, Triscuits, A.1. Steak Sauce, Grey Poupon)

RVSI, INC.
425 Rabro Dr. East Phone: 516-273-9700
Hauppauge, NY 11788 Fax: 516-273-1167
Pres & CEO: Pat V. Costa
Dir HR: Pat Jennison
Employees: 116
Jobs Added Last Year: 28 (+31.8%)
Video equipment

SAKS HOLDINGS, INC.
12 Eighth St. Phone: 212-753-4000
New York, NY 10017 Fax: 212-940-5789
Chm & CEO: Paul W. Soldatos
SVP HR: Owen Dorsey
Employees: 12,000
Jobs Added Last Year: —
Retail - department stores (Saks Fifth Avenue)

SALANT CORPORATION
1114 Avenue of the Americas Phone: 212-221-7500
New York, NY 10036 Fax: 212-221-5363
Chm, Pres & CEO: Nicholas P. DiPaolo
Personnel Mgr: Gloria Adams
Employees: 4,150
Jobs Added Last Year: 150 (+3.8%)
Apparel - men's & boys'

SALOMON INC
7 World Trade Center Phone: 212-783-7000
New York, NY 10048 Fax: 212-783-2110
Chm & CEO: Robert E. Denham
Managing Dir HR: Ed Weihenmayer
Employees: 8,640
Jobs Added Last Year: 9 (+.1%)
Financial - investment banking & securities trading; oil refining & marketing

SBARRO, INC.
763 Larkfield Rd. Phone: 516-864-0200
Commack, NY 11725 Fax: 516-462-9058
Chm, Pres & CEO: Mario Sbarro
VP HR Personnel: Jim O'Shea
Employees: 8,200
Jobs Added Last Year: 800 (+10.8%)
Retail - restaurants

SCHLUMBERGER NV
277 Park Ave. Phone: 212-350-9400
New York, NY 10172-0266 Fax: 212-350-9564
Chm, Pres & CEO: D. Euan Baird
VP Personnel: Pierre E. Bismuth
Employees: 48,000
Jobs Cut Last Year: 3,000 (-5.9%)
Oil & gas - field services; measurement systems

SCHOLASTIC CORPORATION
555 Broadway Phone: 212-343-6100
New York, NY 10012-3999 Fax: 212-505-3377
Chm, Pres & CEO: Richard Robinson
VP HR: Katherine Ryden
Employees: 3,918
Jobs Added Last Year: 522 (+15.4%)
Publishing - books & periodicals

NEW YORK

SEVENSON ENVIRONMENTAL SERVICES INC.
2749 Lockport Rd., PO Box 396   Phone: 716-284-0431
Niagara Falls, NY 14302   Fax: 716-284-7645
Pres & CEO: Michael A. Elia
No central personnel officer
Employees: 429
Jobs Added Last Year: 265 (+161.6%)
Pollution control - construction site remediation

SHOREWOOD PACKAGING CORPORATION
55 Engineers Ln.   Phone: 516-694-2900
Farmingdale, NY 11735   Fax: 516-752-9369
Chm & CEO: Paul B. Shore
No central personnel officer
Employees: 2,200
Jobs Added Last Year: 1,000 (+83.3%)
Paper & paper products - packaging for consumer goods

SKADDEN, ARPS, SLATE, MEAGHER & FLOM
919 Third Ave.   Phone: 212-371-6000
New York, NY 10022   Fax: 212-735-2000
CEO: Robert C. Sheehan
Dir HR: Laurel Henschel
Employees: 3,200
Jobs Added Last Year: 200 (+6.7%)
Law firm

STANDARD MICROSYSTEMS CORPORATION
80 Arkay Dr.   Phone: 516-273-3100
Hauppauge, NY 11788   Fax: 516-273-5550
Pres & CEO: Victor F. Trizzino
VP HR: Ernest W. Stern
Employees: 728
Jobs Added Last Year: 79 (+12.2%)
Computers - LAN interface cards

STANDARD MOTOR PRODUCTS, INC.
37-18 Northern Blvd.   Phone: 718-392-0200
Long Island City, NY 11101   Fax: 718-729-4549
CEO: Bernard Fife
VP HR: Sanford Kay
Employees: 3,450
Jobs Added Last Year: 50 (+1.5%)
Automotive & trucking - replacement parts

STARRETT HOUSING CORPORATION
909 Third Ave.   Phone: 212-751-3100
New York, NY 10022   Fax: 212-759-7699
Chm: Paul M. Lstein
Dir HR: Evelyn Fuerman
Employees: 1,200
Jobs Added Last Year: 100 (+9.1%)
Building - residential & commercial

STATE UNIVERSITY OF NEW YORK
State University Plaza   Phone: 518-443-5313
Albany, NY 12246   Fax: 518-443-5322
Chancellor: Joseph C. Burke
Assoc Vice Chancellor HR: Thomas Mannix
Employees: 47,964
Jobs Added Last Year: —
University

STUDENT LOAN CORPORATION
99 Garnsey Rd.   Phone: 716-248-7187
Pittsford, NY 14534   Fax: 716-248-7007
Pres & CEO: S. C. Biklen
VP & Dir Total Quality Mgmt (HR): Lynn A. Schaeffer
Employees: 800
Jobs Added Last Year: 135 (+20.3%)
Financial - consumer loans

TEACHERS INSURANCE AND ANNUITY
730 Third Ave.   Phone: 212-490-9000
New York, NY 10017   Fax: 212-916-6231
Chm & CEO: John H. Biggs
EVP HR: Matina S. Horner
Employees: 4,000
Jobs Added Last Year: 200 (+5.3%)
Financial - pensions (TIAA); insurance (CREF)

40457

TEXACO INC.
2000 Westchester Ave.   Phone: 914-253-4000
White Plains, NY 10650   Fax: 914-253-7753
Chm & CEO: Alfred C. DeCrane, Jr.
VP HR: John D. Ambler
Employees: 32,514
Jobs Cut Last Year: 5,068 (-13.5%)
Oil & gas - integrated

11458

NEW YORK

TIFFANY & CO.
727 Fifth Ave. Phone: 212-755-8000
New York, NY 10022 Fax: 212-605-4465
Chm & CEO: William R. Chaney
VP HR: Michael H. Mitchell
Employees: 3,300
Jobs Added Last Year: 167 (+5.3%)
Retail - luxury jewelry stores

TOWERS PERRIN
245 Park Ave. Phone: 212-309-3400
New York, NY 10167 Fax: 212-309-3760
Chm, Pres & CEO: John T. Lynch
Mgr HR: Ken Ranftle
Employees: 5,000
Jobs Added Last Year: 270 (+5.7%)
Consulting & reinsurance

TIME WARNER INC. 11482
75 Rockefeller Plaza Phone: 212-484-8000
New York, NY 10019 Fax: 212-484-8734
Chm, Pres & CEO: Gerald M. Levin
VP HR & Admin: Carolyn McCandless
Employees: 50,000
Jobs Added Last Year: 6,000 (+13.6%)
Publishing - periodicals & books; films (Warner Brothers); cable systems; cable programming; music (Atlantic, Elektra)

TRANS WORLD ENTERTAINMENT CORPORATION
38 Corporate Circle Phone: 518-452-1242
Albany, NY 12203 Fax: 518-452-3547
Pres & CEO: Robert J. Higgins
Dir HR: Bert Tobin
Employees: 4,000
Jobs Added Last Year: 0
Retail - prerecorded music & videotapes

TISHMAN REALTY & CONSTRUCTION CO. INC.
666 Fifth Ave. Phone: 212-399-3600
New York, NY 10103 Fax: 212-957-9791
Chm & CEO: John Tishman
Dir Personnel: Gina Perrone
Employees: 575
Jobs Added Last Year: 65 (+12.7%)
Building - management services & hotel management

TRANSMATION, INC.
977 Mt. Read Blvd. Phone: 716-254-9000
Rochester, NY 14606 Fax: 716-254-0273
Pres & Chm: William J. Berk
VP HR & Asst Sec: John A. DeVoldre
Employees: 218
Jobs Added Last Year: 10 (+4.8%)
Instruments - industrial process monitoring

TLC BEATRICE INTERNATIONAL 40466
9 W. 57th St. Phone: 212-756-8900
New York, NY 10019 Fax: 212-888-3093
Chm & CEO: Loida Lewis
Dir HR: Rene S. Meily
Employees: 4,700
Jobs Added Last Year: 0
Food - wholesale & retail distribution, grocery product marketing & manufacturing, primarily in Europe

THE TRAVELERS INC. 16727
65 E. 55th St. Phone: 212-891-8900
New York, NY 10022 Fax: 212-891-8910
Chm & CEO: Sanford I. Weill
SVP HR: Barry L. Mannes
Employees: 65,000
Jobs Added Last Year: 35,000 (+116.7%)
Insurance - property & casualty; retail brokerage (Smith Barney Shearson)

TOPPS COMPANY, INC.
One Whitehall St. Phone: 212-376-0300
New York, NY 10004 Fax: 212-376-0573
Chm: Arthur T. Shorin
VP Admin (HR): William G. O'Connor
Employees: 1,350
Jobs Added Last Year: 150 (+12.5%)
Food - confectionery

TRUMP ORGANIZATION 40473
725 Fifth Ave. Phone: 212-832-2000
New York, NY 10022 Fax: 212-935-0141
Chm: Donald J. Trump
No central personnel officer
Employees: 15,000
Jobs Added Last Year: 0
Diversified operations - hotels (Plaza); casinos (Trump Taj Mahal); real estate (Trump Tower & Empire State Building)

NEW YORK

U.S. HOMECARE CORPORATION
141 S. Central Ave. Phone: 914-946-9601
Hartsdale, NY 10530 Fax: 914-946-1005
Pres & CEO: G. Robert O'Brien
Dir HR: Elaine Arbizo
Employees: 4,000
Jobs Added Last Year: 300 (+8.1%)
Health care - outpatient & home

UNIVERSITY OF ROCHESTER
Administration Bldg. Phone: 716-275-2121
Rochester, NY 14627 Fax: 716-275-2190
Pres & CEO: Thomas Jackson
Dir Personnel: B E Donbaugh
Employees: 11,249
Jobs Added Last Year: —
University

U.S. TRUST CORPORATION
114 W. 47th St. Phone: 212-852-1000
New York, NY 10036 Fax: 212-852-1140
Chm & CEO: H. Marshall Schwarz
SVP HR: Patricia McGuire
Employees: 2,500
Jobs Added Last Year: 299 (+13.6%)
Banks - Northeast

VARITY CORPORATION
672 Delaware Ave. Phone: 716-888-8000
Buffalo, NY 14209 Fax: 716-888-8010
Chm & CEO: Victor Rice
VP Mgmt Resourcing (HR): Arthur A. Rogers
Employees: 13,110
Jobs Cut Last Year: 916 (-6.5%)
Diversified operations - tractors; engines; automotive parts

UIS, INC.
600 5th Ave., 27th Fl. Phone: 212-581-7660
New York, NY 10020 Fax: 212-581-7517
Chm, Pres & CEO: Andrew E. Pietrini
Dir HR: Joseph F. Arrigo
Employees: 7,258
Jobs Added Last Year: 158 (+2.2%)
Automotive & trucking - replacement parts; iron & steel forgings; candy (Necco Wafers)

VIACOM INC.
1515 Broadway Phone: 212-258-6000
New York, NY 10036 Fax: 212-258-6597
Pres & CEO: Frank J. Biondi, Jr.
SVP HR: Robert C. Greenberg
Employees: 17,500
Jobs Added Last Year: 12,500 (+250%)
Diversified operations - broadcasting; film; cable TV (MTV, VH-1); publishing; video rentals (Blockbuster); theme parks

UNITED STATES BANKNOTE CORP.
51 W. 52nd St. Phone: 212-582-9200
New York, NY 10019 Fax: 212-582-9201
Chm & CEO: Morris Weissman
Head Personnel: Serge Droujinsky
Employees: 2,335
Jobs Added Last Year: 1,155 (+97.9%)
Printing - coupons, securities

WEGMANS FOOD MARKETS INC.
1500 Brooks Ave. Phone: 716-328-2550
Rochester, NY 14624 Fax: 716-464-4626
Chm & CEO: Robert B. Wegman
Dir HR: Gerald Pierce
Employees: 21,100
Jobs Added Last Year: 14,700 (+229.7%)
Retail - supermarkets

UNITEL VIDEO, INC.
515 W. 57th St. Phone: 212-265-3600
New York, NY 10019 Fax: 212-765-5801
CEO: John Hoffman
No central personnel officer
Employees: 489
Jobs Added Last Year: 233 (+91%)
Motion pictures & services - studio & mobile production, video editing

WESTVACO CORPORATION
299 Park Ave. Phone: 212-688-5000
New York, NY 10171 Fax: 212-318-5050
Pres & CEO: John A. Luke, Jr.
VP Personnel: Jack Furnas
Employees: 14,170
Jobs Cut Last Year: 270 (-1.9%)
Paper & paper products

An in-depth profile of this company is available by fax. Call 800-510-4452 and use your touch-tone phone to put in the 5-digit code at the prompt. Only $2.95 each with your credit card. See page 12 for more details.

NEW YORK

WITCO CORPORATION
520 Madison Ave.
New York, NY 10022-4236
Chm & CEO: William R. Toller
VP HR: Clark E. Tucker
Employees: 8,161
Jobs Cut Last Year: 280 (-3.3%)
Chemicals - diversified

Phone: 212-605-3800
Fax: 212-605-3660

YOUNG & RUBICAM INC. 40537
285 Madison Ave.
New York, NY 10017-6486
Pres & CEO: Peter A. Georgescu
Dir HR: Raquel Suarez
Employees: 9,846
Jobs Cut Last Year: 276 (-2.7%)
Advertising & communications

Phone: 212-210-3000
Fax: 212-210-9073

WOOLWORTH CORPORATION 10538
233 Broadway
New York, NY 10279-0003
Chm & CEO: Roger N. Farah
VP HR: Patricia A. Peck
Employees: 111,000
Jobs Cut Last Year: 34,000 (-23.4%)
Retail - discount & variety, athletic footwear (Foot Locker)

Phone: 212-553-2000
Fax: 212-553-2042

ZIFF-DAVIS PUBLISHING COMPANY 40541
One Park Ave.
New York, NY 10016
Chm & CEO: Eric Hippeau
Dir HR: Fred Staudmyer
Employees: 4,300
Jobs Added Last Year: 200 (+4.9%)
Publishing - #1 US computer magazine publisher (*PC Week, PC Magazine, Computer Shopper*)

Phone: 212-503-3500
Fax: 212-503-4599

▼ **ESPAN** http://www.espan.com

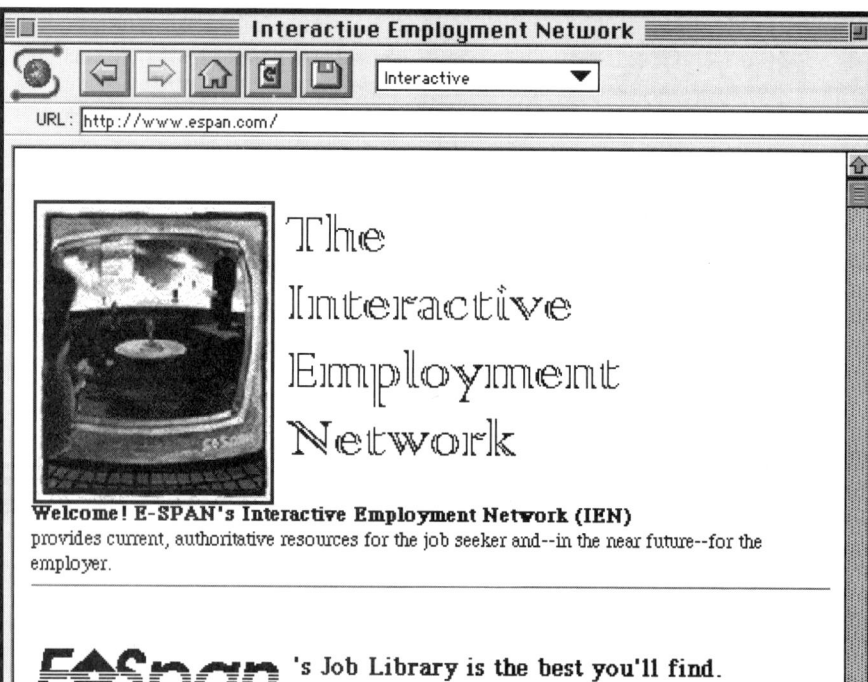

NORTH CAROLINA

AMERICAN STUDIOS, INC.
11001 Park Charlotte Blvd. Phone: 704-588-4351
Charlotte, NC 28273 Fax: 704-588-7844
Chm & CEO: Randy J. Bates
VP HR: Susan Nixon
Employees: 3,000
Jobs Added Last Year: 1,400 (+87.5%)
Retail - portrait photography in discount stores

COASTAL HEALTHCARE GROUP, INC.
2828 Croasdaile Dr. Phone: 919-383-0355
Durham, NC 27705 Fax: 919-383-6463
Chm, Pres & CEO: Steven M. Scott
VP Emp Rel & Compensation: Robert Elder
Employees: 4,401
Jobs Added Last Year: 1,321 (+42.9%)
Medical services - physician contract management for hospitals

BB&T FINANCIAL CORPORATION
223 W. Nash St. Phone: 919-399-4291
Wilson, NC 27893 Fax: 919-399-4260
Chm & CEO: John A. A. Allison IV
SVP (HR): Henry M. Skinner, Jr.
Employees: 4,105
Jobs Added Last Year: 10 (+.2%)
Banks - Southeast

COCA-COLA BOTTLING CO. CONSOLIDATED
1900 Rexford Rd. Phone: 704-551-4400
Charlotte, NC 28211 Fax: 704-551-4646
VC & CEO: J. Frank Harrison III
VP (HR): Robert T. Pettus
Employees: 5,000
Jobs Added Last Year: 1,100 (+28.2%)
Beverages - soft drink bottling

BELK STORES SERVICES, INC.
2801 W. Tyvola Rd. Phone: 704-357-1000
Charlotte, NC 28217 Fax: 704-357-1876
Chm: John M. Belk
SVP HR: Thomas M. Belk, Jr.
Employees: 18,000
Jobs Cut Last Year: 1,000 (-5.3%)
Retail - regional department stores

CONE MILLS CORPORATION
1201 Maple St. Phone: 910-379-6220
Greensboro, NC 27405 Fax: 910-379-6287
Pres & CEO: J. Patrick Danahy
VP (HR): James S. Butner
Employees: 8,101
Jobs Added Last Year: 266 (+3.4%)
Textiles - mill products

BURLINGTON INDUSTRIES, INC.
3330 W. Friendly Ave. Phone: 910-379-2000
Greensboro, NC 27410 Fax: 910-379-4504
Chm & CEO: George W. Henderson
VP HR & Public Rel: J. Kenneth Lesley
Employees: 23,800
Jobs Added Last Year: 200 (+.8%)
Textiles - mill products

DUKE POWER COMPANY
422 S. Church St. Phone: 704-594-0887
Charlotte, NC 28242-0001 Fax: 704-382-3814
Chm & CEO: William H. Grigg
VP HR: James R. Bavis
Employees: 18,274
Jobs Cut Last Year: 453 (-2.4%)
Utility - electric power

CATO CORPORATION
8100 Denmark Rd. Phone: 704-554-8510
Charlotte, NC 28273-5975 Fax: 704-551-7200
CEO: Wayland H. Cato, Jr.
EVP HR: Stephen R. Clark
Employees: 2,800
Jobs Added Last Year: 400 (+16.7%)
Retail - apparel

FAMILY DOLLAR STORES, INC.
10401 Old Monroe Rd. Phone: 704-847-6961
Matthews, NC 28205 Fax: 704-847-5534
Chm, CEO & CFO: Leon Levine
VP HR: Terry A. Cozort
Employees: 15,900
Jobs Cut Last Year: 700 (-4.2%)
Retail - discount & variety (soft goods)

 An in-depth profile of this company is available by fax. Call 800-510-4452 and use your touch-tone phone to put in the 5-digit code at the prompt. Only $2.95 each with your credit card. See page 12 for more details.

NORTH CAROLINA

FIRST CITIZENS BANCSHARES, INC.
239 Fayetteville St. Phone: 919-755-7000
Raleigh, NC 27601 Fax: 919-755-7277
CEO: Lewis R. Holding
Dir HR: James D. Bucci
Employees: 3,971
Jobs Added Last Year: 185 (+4.9%)
Banks - Southeast

GOODMARK FOODS, INC.
6131 Falls of Neuse Rd. Phone: 919-790-9940
Raleigh, NC 27609 Fax: 919-790-6535
Chm & CEO: Ron E. Doggett
Dir HR: Clinton H. Neal, Jr.
Employees: 1,016
Jobs Added Last Year: 69 (+7.3%)
Food - meat snacks (Slim Jim, Pemmican, Penrose & Smokey Mountain) & packaged lunch meat (Jesse Jones)

FIRST UNION CORPORATION
One First Union Center Phone: 704-374-6565
Charlotte, NC 28288-0013 Fax: 704-374-2140
Chm & CEO: Edward Crutchfield, Jr.
EVP HR: Don R. Johnson
Employees: 32,861
Jobs Added Last Year: 9,402 (+40.1%)
Banks - Southeast

GUILFORD MILLS, INC.
4925 W. Market St. Phone: 910-316-4000
Greensboro, NC 27407 Fax: 910-316-4059
Pres & CEO: Charles A. Hayes
VP HR: Ron Houser
Employees: 5,410
Jobs Added Last Year: 871 (+19.2%)
Textiles - warp knit fabrics

FOOD LION, INC.
2110 Executive Dr. Phone: 704-633-8250
Salisbury, NC 28145-1330 Fax: 704-636-5024
Chm, Pres & CEO: Tom E. Smith
VP HR: Eugene R. McKinley
Employees: 65,494
Jobs Added Last Year: 5,773 (+9.7%)
Retail - supermarkets in the Southeast & mid-Atlantic states & Texas & Oklahoma

HENDRICK AUTOMOTIVE GROUP
6000 Monroe Rd., Ste. 100 Phone: 704-568-5550
Charlotte, NC 28218 Fax: 704-568-5550
Pres & CEO: J. R. Hendrick III
Dir HR: Suzanne Wrenn
Employees: 4,500
Jobs Added Last Year: 1,000 (+28.6%)
Diversified operations - auto dealerships; sportswear; motorsports

GALEY & LORD, INC.
PO Box 35528 Phone: 910-665-3000
Greensboro, NC 27425-0528 Fax: 910-665-3113
Chm & CEO: Arthur C. Wiener
Office Mgr (HR): Terrence Bowman
Employees: 4,100
Jobs Added Last Year: 721 (+21.3%)
Textiles - wrinkle-resistant cotton mill products

INGLES MARKETS, INCORPORATED
PO Box 6676 Phone: 704-669-2941
Asheville, NC 28816 Fax: 704-669-3667
Chm & CEO: Robert P. Ingle
HR Mgr: Pat Boyd
Employees: 9,432
Jobs Added Last Year: 1,237 (+15.1%)
Retail - supermarkets

GLENAYRE TECHNOLOGIES, INC.

4201 Congress St., Ste. 455 Phone: 704-553-0038
Charlotte, NC 28209 Fax: 704-553-0524
CEO: Ramon D. Arrizzone
Corp Dir HR: Beverly Cox
Employees: 900
Jobs Added Last Year: 129 (+16.7%)
Telecommunications equipment - mobile paging & messaging systems

INSTEEL INDUSTRIES, INC.
1373 Boggs Dr. Phone: 910-786-2141
Mt. Airy, NC 27030 Fax: 910-786-2144
Pres & CEO: H. O. Woltz II
VP Admin & Sec (HR): Gary D. Kniskern
Employees: 1,013
Jobs Added Last Year: 68 (+7.2%)
Wire & cable products - welded wire fabric used to reinforce concrete & high carbon & industrial wire

NORTH CAROLINA

INTEGON CORPORATION
500 W. Fifth St.
Winston-Salem, NC 27152
Chm, Pres & CEO: James T. Lambie
VP HR: John Beattie
Employees: 625
Phone: 910-770-2000
Fax: 910-770-2942
Jobs Added Last Year: 183 (+41.4%)
Insurance - property & casualty

LOWE'S COMPANIES, INC.
PO Box 1111
North Wilkesboro, NC 28656-0001
Pres & CEO: Leonard G. Herring
VP HR: Perry Jennings
Employees: 28,843
Phone: 919-651-4000
Fax: 919-651-4766
Jobs Added Last Year: 7,574 (+35.6%)
Building products - warehouse retail outlets

INVESTOR'S MANAGEMENT CORPORATION
5151 Glenwood Ave.
Raleigh, NC 27626
Chm: James H. Maynard
VP HR: Paul Weder
Employees: 9,400
Phone: 919-781-9130
Fax: 919-881-4485
Jobs Added Last Year: —
Retail - restaurants (Golden Corral & Ragazzi)

NATIONSBANK CORPORATION
NationsBank Corporate Center
Charlotte, NC 28255
Chm & CEO: Hugh L. McColl, Jr.
Principal Corp Off for Personnel: Charles J. Cooley
Employees: 57,463
Phone: 704-386-5000
Fax: 704-386-6444
Jobs Added Last Year: 6,635 (+13.1%)
Banks - money center

JEFFERSON-PILOT CORPORATION
100 N. Greene St.
Greensboro, NC 27401
Pres & CEO: David A. Stonecipher
SVP HR: Hoyt Phillips
Employees: 3,850
Phone: 910-691-3441
Fax: 910-691-3938
Jobs Added Last Year: 3,350 (+670%)
Insurance - life

NUCOR CORPORATION
2100 Rexford Rd.
Charlotte, NC 28211
Chm & CEO: F. Kenneth Iverson
Personnel Svcs Mgr: Jim Coblin
Employees: 5,900
Phone: 704-366-7000
Fax: 704-362-4208
Jobs Added Last Year: 100 (+1.7%)
Steel - minimill production

LADD FURNITURE, INC.
One Plaza Center, Box HP-3
High Point, NC 27261-1500
Chm & CEO: Richard R. Allen
Dir HR: Keith Gsell
Employees: 7,700
Phone: 910-889-0333
Fax: 910-889-5839
Jobs Added Last Year: 1,030 (+15.4%)
Furniture

OAKWOOD HOMES CORPORATION
2225 S. Holden Rd.
Greensboro, NC 27417-0386
Pres & CEO: Nicholas J. St. George
VP HR: Tom Brinkley
Employees: 1,880
Phone: 910-855-2400
Fax: 910-632-3224
Jobs Added Last Year: 590 (+45.7%)
Building - manufactured homes

LANCE, INC.
8600 S. Boulevard
Charlotte, NC 28232
Chm & CEO: J. William Disher
VP Admin (HR): T.B. Horack
Employees: 5,860
Phone: 704-554-1421
Fax: 704-554-5586
Jobs Cut Last Year: 56 (-.9%)
Food - snack foods

OLD DOMINION FREIGHT LINE, INC.
1730 Westchester Dr.
High Point, NC 27260
Chm & CEO: Earl E. Congdon
Dir Personnel & Safety: Brian Stoddard
Employees: 3,823
Phone: 910-889-5000
Fax: 910-802-5221
Jobs Added Last Year: 1,205 (+46%)
Transportation - shipping

NORTH CAROLINA

PCA INTERNATIONAL, INC.
815 Matthews-Mint Hill Rd. Phone: 704-847-8011
Matthews, NC 28105 Fax: —
Chm, Pres & CEO: John Grosso
VP HR: Richard Brunson
Employees: 3,700
Jobs Added Last Year: 300 (+8.8%)
Retail - portrait photographs

UNIFI, INC.
7201 W. Friendly Rd. Phone: 910-294-4410
Greensboro, NC 27410 Fax: 910-316-5422
CEO: William T. Kretzer
Dir HR: Raymond Hunt
Employees: 6,000
Jobs Added Last Year: 279 (+4.9%)
Textiles - mill products

RUDDICK CORPORATION
2000 Two First Union Center Phone: 704-372-5404
Charlotte, NC 28282 Fax: 704-372-6409
Pres: John W. Copeland
VP Personnel, Harris Teeter: C. Lavette Teeter, Sr.
Employees: 19,090
Jobs Added Last Year: 1,590 (+9.1%)
Retail - supermarkets (Harris Teeter); sewing thread; business forms, labels & other printed material; venture capital

UNITED DOMINION INDUSTRIES INC.
2300 One First Union Center Phone: 704-347-6800
Charlotte, NC 28202-6039 Fax: 704-347-6900
Chm & CEO: William R. Holland
VP HR: Timothy J. Verhagen
Employees: 12,000
Jobs Added Last Year: 300 (+2.6%)
Diversified operations - prefabricated metal buildings; aerospace components; construction; engineering

SCHWITZER, INC.
Hwy. 191, Brevard Rd. Phone: 704-684-4000
Asheville, NC 28813 Fax: 704-684-4114
Pres & CEO: Gary G. Dillon
Dir HR: John Carter
Employees: 1,150
Jobs Added Last Year: 150 (+15%)
Automotive & trucking - turbochargers & other equipment for diesel & gasoline engines

VANGUARD CELLULAR SYSTEMS, INC.
2002 Pisgah Church Rd., Ste. 300 Phone: 910-282-3690
Greensboro, NC 27455-3314 Fax: 910-545-2265
Pres & CEO: Haynes G. Griffin
VP HR & Quality Dev: Neva Reavis
Employees: 1,000
Jobs Added Last Year: 206 (+25.9%)
Telecommunications services - cellular phone systems

SOUTHERN NATIONAL CORPORATION
200 W. Second St. Phone: 910- 773-7221
Winston-Salem, NC 27101 Fax: 910- 607-7049
Chm, Pres & CEO: L. Glenn Orr, Jr.
SVP & Group Executive HR: Robert E. Williams
Employees: 3,795
Jobs Added Last Year: 1,163 (+44.2%)
Banks - Southeast

WACHOVIA CORPORATION
301 N. Main St. Phone: 910-770-5000
Winston-Salem, NC 27150 Fax: 910-770-5959
Pres & CEO: L. M. Baker, Jr.
Dir Personnel: Hector McEachern
Employees: 15,531
Jobs Cut Last Year: 633 (-3.9%)
Banks - Southeast

TEXFI INDUSTRIES, INC.
5400 Glenwood Ave., Ste. 215 Phone: 919-783-4736
Raleigh, NC 27612 Fax: 919-783-4739
VC & CEO: William L. Remley
No central personnel officer
Employees: 4,400
Jobs Cut Last Year: 4 (-.1%)
Textiles - woven finished & narrow elastic fabrics, spun yarns & other apparel products

WELCOME HOME, INC.
309-D Raleigh St. Phone: 910-791-4312
Wilmington, NC 28412 Fax: 910-791-4945
CEO: Thomas H. Quinn
Dir HR: Karen Farris
Employees: 1,034
Jobs Added Last Year: 230 (+28.6%)
Retail - home furnishings & accessories

OHIO

ABS INDUSTRIES, INC.
Interstate Sq., Ste. 300   Phone: 216-946-2274
Willoughby, OH 44094   Fax: 216-946-8298
Pres & CEO: William J. McCarthy
Corp Sec & Dir HR: Robert A. Nappi
Employees: 564
Jobs Added Last Year: 262 (+86.8%)
Automotive & trucking - hitchballs, transmission & drive components, suspension parts

AMERICAN GREETINGS CORP.
One American Rd.   Phone: 216-252-7300
Cleveland, OH 44144   Fax: 216-252-6519
Chm & CEO: Morry Weiss
SVP HR: Harvey Levin
Employees: 36,600
Jobs Added Last Year: 5,200 (+16.6%)
Greeting cards & gift items

ACME-CLEVELAND CORPORATION
PO Box 5639, 1242 East 49th St.   Phone: 216-432-5400
Cleveland, OH 44114   Fax: 216-432-5401
Chm, Pres & CEO: David L. Swift
VP HR: Diane O. McDaniel
Employees: 1,283
Jobs Added Last Year: 231 (+22%)
Diversified operations - metal working; telecommunications; electronics

ARBOR HEALTH CARE COMPANY
1100 Shawnee Rd., PO Box 840   Phone: 419-227-3000
Lima, OH 45802-0840   Fax: 419-227-3499
Chm, Pres & CEO: Pier C. Borra
Ben & Personnel Coordinator: Cindy Mohler
Employees: 3,498
Jobs Added Last Year: 308 (+9.7%)
Nursing homes - high-intensity care facilities

ALLEN GROUP INC.
25101 Chagrin Blvd., Ste. 350   Phone: 216-765-5800
Beachwood, OH 44122-5619   Fax: 216-765-0410
Pres & CEO: Robert G. Paul
No central personnel officer
Employees: 3,000
Jobs Added Last Year: 600 (+25%)
Heavy duty radiators & heat exchangers for trucks; specialized antennas; test & service products

BANC ONE CORPORATION
100 E. Broad St.   Phone: 614-248-5944
Columbus, OH 43271-0251   Fax: 614-248-5624
Chm & CEO: John B. McCoy
SVP Personnel & Admin: Michael W. Hager
Employees: 45,300
Jobs Added Last Year: 12,600 (+38.5%)
Banks - money center

AMERICAN ELECTRIC POWER CO.
One Riverside Plaza   Phone: 614-223-1000
Columbus, OH 43215   Fax: 614-223-1823
Pres & CEO: E. Linn Draper
SVP HR: Ronald A. Petti
Employees: 20,007
Jobs Cut Last Year: 834 (-4%)
Utility - electric power

BAREFOOT INC.
450 W. Wilson Bridge Rd.   Phone: 614-846-1800
Worthington, OH 43085   Fax: 614-846-5142
Pres & Co-CEO: Patrick J. Norton
No central personnel officer
Employees: 1,700
Jobs Added Last Year: 325 (+23.6%)
Lawn care services

AMERICAN FINANCIAL CORP.
One E. Fourth St.   Phone: 513-579-2121
Cincinnati, OH 45202   Fax: 513-579-2580
Chm & CEO: Carl H. Lindner
VP HR: Lawrence Otto
Employees: 60,350
Jobs Cut Last Year: 440 (-.7%)
Diversified operations - insurance; food products (Chiquita); media

BATTELLE MEMORIAL INSTITUTE
505 King Ave.   Phone: 614-424-6424
Columbus, OH 43201   Fax: 614-424-5263
Pres & CEO: Douglas E. Olesen
SVP HR: Robert W. Smith, Jr.
Employees: 8,400
Jobs Cut Last Year: 153 (-1.8%)
Engineering - R&D services

OHIO

BEARINGS, INC.
3600 Euclid Ave.
Cleveland, OH 44115-2515
CEO: John C. Dannemiller
Dir HR: Robert C. Stinson
Employees: 4,056
Jobs Added Last Year: 70 (+1.8%)
Metal products - distribution

Phone: 216-881-8900
Fax: 216-881-8988

BRENLIN GROUP
670 W. Market St.
Akron, OH 44303
Chm & CEO: David L. Brennan
VP HR: Stephen J. Tomasko
Employees: 3,800
Jobs Cut Last Year: 200 (-5%)
Metal processing & fabrication (steel); plastics

Phone: 216-762-2420
Fax: 216-762-4604

BELDEN & BLAKE CORPORATION
5200 Stoneham Rd.
North Canton, OH 44720-1543
Chm & CEO: Henry S. Belden IV
Mgr HR: James C. Ewing
Employees: 435
Jobs Added Last Year: 92 (+26.8%)
Oil & gas - production

Phone: 216-499-1660
Fax: 216-497-5463

CAMELOT MUSIC INC.
8000 Freedom Ave., NW
Canton, OH 44720-2282
CEO: Jack Rogers
VP HR: Don Groom
Employees: 3,000
Jobs Added Last Year: 400 (+15.4%)
Retail - music & video stores

Phone: 216-494-2282
Fax: 216-494-0394

THE B.F. GOODRICH CO.
3925 Embassy Pkwy.
Akron, OH 44333-1799
CEO: John D. Ong
Dir HR: Harold D. Mason
Employees: 13,416
Jobs Added Last Year: 41 (+.3%)
Chemicals - diversified

Phone: 216-374-3985
Fax: 216-374-2333

CARDINAL HEALTH, INC.
655 Metro Place South, Ste. 925
Dublin, OH 43017
Chm & CEO: Robert D. Walter
SVP HR: Carole W. Tomko
Employees: 3,700
Jobs Added Last Year: 2,300 (+164.3%)
Drugs & sundries - wholesale

Phone: 614-761-8700
Fax: 614-761-8919

BOB EVANS FARMS, INC.
3776 S. High St.
Columbus, OH 43207
Chm, CEO & Sec: Daniel E. Evans
Group VP Admin & HR: James B. Radebaugh
Employees: 23,800
Jobs Added Last Year: 4,800 (+25.3%)
Retail - sausages; restaurants

Phone: 614-491-2225
Fax: 614-492-4949

CASTECH ALUMINUM GROUP INC.
753 W. Waterloo Rd.
Akron, OH 44314
Pres & CEO: Norman E. Wells, Jr.
Mgr HR: Joy Lang
Employees: 850
Jobs Added Last Year: 120 (+16.4%)
Metal processing & fabrication - cast aluminum sheet from recycled metal

Phone: 216-848-5555
Fax: 216-753-0689

BORDEN, INC.
180 E. Broad St.
Columbus, OH 43215-3799
Chm, Pres & CEO: C. Robert Kidder
VP HR: Randy D. Kautto
Employees: 41,900
Jobs Added Last Year: 0
Food - dairy products, pasta & pasta sauce, potato chips & snacks; glue; packaging & industrial products

Phone: 614-225-4000
Fax: 614-225-3382

CENTERIOR ENERGY CORPORATION
6200 Oak Tree Blvd.
Independence, OH 44131
Chm, Pres & CEO: Robert J. Farling
Dir HR: John Paganie
Employees: 6,800
Jobs Added Last Year: 52 (+.8%)
Utility - electric power

Phone: 216-447-3100
Fax: 216-447-3240

OHIO

CENTRAL RESERVE LIFE CORP.
17800 Royalton Rd. Phone: 216-572-2400
Strongsville, OH 44136 Fax: 216-572-4500
Pres & CEO: Fred Lick, Jr.
SVP HR: Robert S. Zarick
Employees: 471
Jobs Added Last Year: 63 (+15.4%)
Insurance - accident & health

CHEMED CORPORATION
255 E. Fifth St. Phone: 513-762-6900
Cincinnati, OH 45202-4726 Fax: —
CEO: Edward L. Hutton
VP HR: David G. Sparks
Employees: 3,856
Jobs Added Last Year: 531 (+16%)
Diversified - service enterprises including janitorial & medical/dental supplies

CHEMPOWER, INC.
807 E. Turkeyfoot Lake Rd. Phone: 216-896-4202
Akron, OH 44319 Fax: 216-896-1866
Pres: Toomas J. Kukk
Investor Rel (HR): Beth Yare
Employees: 682
Jobs Added Last Year: 120 (+21.4%)
Pollution control - asbestos abatement

CHIQUITA BRANDS INTERNATIONAL
250 E. Fifth St. Phone: 513-784-8011
Cincinnati, OH 45202 Fax: 513-784-8030
Chm & CEO: Carl H. Lindner
VP HR: Jean B. Lapointe
Employees: 45,000
Jobs Added Last Year: 0
Food - fruit (primarily bananas) & vegetable products

CINCINNATI BELL INC.
201 E. Fourth St., PO Box 2301 Phone: 513-397-9900
Cincinnati, OH 45201 Fax: 513-421-5973
Pres & CEO: John T. LaMacchia
SVP HR & Admin: Thomas A. Cruz
Employees: 14,700
Jobs Added Last Year: 3,500 (+31.3%)
Utility - telephone

CINCINNATI MILACRON INC.
4701 Marburg Ave. Phone: 513-841-8100
Cincinnati, OH 45209 Fax: 513-841-8991
Chm & CEO: Daniel J. Meyer
VP HR: Theodore Mauser
Employees: 8,427
Jobs Added Last Year: 2,292 (+37.4%)
Machine tools & related products

CINERGY CORP.
139 E. Fourth St. Phone: 513-381-2000
Cincinnati, OH 45202 Fax: 513-287-1321
Chm, Pres & CEO: Jackson H. Randolph
Mgr Staffing & Emp Dev: Michelle Hanna
Employees: 5,000
Jobs Added Last Year: —
Utility - electric power (holding company for PSI Resources, Inc. & Cincinnati Gas & Electric Co.)

CINTAS CORPORATION
6800 Cintas Blvd. Phone: 513-459-1200
Cincinnati, OH 45262 Fax: 513-573-4130
Chm & CEO: Richard T. Farmer
VP HR: Scott Farmer
Employees: 7,797
Jobs Added Last Year: 1,411 (+22.1%)
Linen supply & related services - uniform rental & sale

CITICASTERS INC.
One E. Fourth St. Phone: 513-562-8000
Cincinnati, OH 45202 Fax: 513-721-8413
CEO: John P. Zanotti
VP HR: Suzanne J. Cook
Employees: 1,800
Jobs Added Last Year: 200 (+12.5%)
Broadcasting - radio & TV

CLEVELAND-CLIFFS INC.
1100 Superior Ave. Phone: 216-694-5700
Cleveland, OH 44114-2589 Fax: 216-694-4880
Chm, Pres & CEO: M. Thomas Moore
VP HR: Richard F. Novak
Employees: 5,973
Jobs Cut Last Year: 415 (-6.5%)
Iron ores

OHIO

COLE NATIONAL CORPORATION
5915 Landerbrook Dr.   Phone: 216-449-4100
Cleveland, OH 44124   Fax: 216-461-3489
Chm & CEO: Jeffrey A. Cole
Mgr HR: Ken Braun
Employees: 8,300
Jobs Added Last Year: 4,000 (+93%)
Retail - optical products & services (Cole Vision); specialty gifts (Things Remembered); key copying & watch repair

COMAIR HOLDINGS, INC.
PO Box 75021   Phone: 606-525-2550
Cincinnati, OH 45275   Fax: 606-525-3420
CEO: David R. Mueller
Dir HR: Linda E. Noble
Employees: 2,375
Jobs Added Last Year: 141 (+6.3%)
Transportation - airline (Delta Connection); aviation school

COMMERCIAL INTERTECH CORPORATION
1775 Logan Ave.   Phone: 216-746-8011
Youngstown, OH 44505   Fax: 216-746-1148
Pres & CEO: Paul J. Powers
VP HR: Jack Savage
Employees: 3,720
Jobs Cut Last Year: 140 (-3.6%)
Metal products - hydraulic components, filters, metal stampings

CONSOLIDATED STORES CORPORATION
300 Phillipi Rd., PO Box 28512   Phone: 614-278-6800
Columbus, OH 43228   Fax: 614-278-6676
Chm & CEO: William G. Kelley
SVP Info Svcs & HR: Steve Bromet
Employees: 18,000
Jobs Added Last Year: 2,000 (+12.5%)
Retail - discount & variety

COOKER RESTAURANT CORPORATION
1530 Bethel Rd.   Phone: 614-457-8500
Columbus, OH 43220   Fax: 614-442-2120
Chm & CEO: G. Arthur Seelbinder
Dir HR: Jeff Karla
Employees: 2,250
Jobs Added Last Year: 625 (+38.5%)
Retail - restaurants

COOPER TIRE & RUBBER COMPANY
Lima & Western Aves.   Phone: 419-423-1321
Findlay, OH 45840   Fax: 419-424-4108
Chm, Pres & CEO: Patrick W. Rooney
Dir Emp Rel & Dev: Darrell L. Wolfe
Employees: 7,872
Jobs Added Last Year: 265 (+3.5%)
Rubber tires

CORRPRO COS INC.
1055 W. Smith Rd.   Phone: 216-723-5082
Medina, OH 44256   Fax: 216-722-7654
Chm & CEO: Joseph W. Rog
VP HR & Investor Rel: Robert M. Adamov
Employees: 662
Jobs Added Last Year: 320 (+93.6%)
Industrial maintenance - corrosion control engineering services, systems & equipment

D.I.Y. HOME WAREHOUSE, INC.
5811 Canal Rd., Ste. 180   Phone: 216-328-5100
Valley View, OH 44125   Fax: 216-328-5114
Pres: Clifford L. Reynolds
VP HR: Marilyn Hayden
Employees: 800
Jobs Added Last Year: 660 (+471.4%)
Building products - retail

DANA CORPORATION
4500 Dorr St.   Phone: 419-535-4500
Toledo, OH 43615   Fax: 419-535-4643
Chm, Pres, CEO & COO: Southwood J. Morcott
HR Mgr: Pat Gahagan
Employees: 36,000
Jobs Added Last Year: 1,000 (+2.9%)
Automotive & trucking - original equipment for trucks; fluid power systems

DEBARTOLO REALTY CORPORATION
7620 Market St.   Phone: 216-758-7292
Youngstown, OH 44513   Fax: 216-758-3598
Chm & CEO: Edward J. DeBartolo, Jr.
EVP Personnel: Marie Denise DeBartolo York
Employees: 12,000
Jobs Added Last Year: –
Real estate investment trust

OHIO

DEVELOPERS DIVERSIFIED REALTY CORP.
34555 Chagrin Blvd.　　　Phone: 216-247-4700
Moreland Hills, OH 44022　Fax: 216-247-0434
Pres & CEO: Scott A. Wolstein
EVP & COO (HR): James A. Schoff
Employees: 110
Jobs Added Last Year: 17 (+18.3%)
Real estate operations

EATON CORPORATION
Eaton Center　　　　　　Phone: 216-523-5000
Cleveland, OH 44114-2584　Fax: 216-523-4787
Chm & CEO: William E. Butler
VP HR: Susan J. Cook
Employees: 38,000
Jobs Added Last Year: 0
Automotive & trucking - original equipment

DIEBOLD, INC.
PO Box 8230　　　　　　Phone: 216-489-4000
Canton, OH 44711-8230　Fax: 216-489-4104
Chm, Pres & CEO: Robert W. Mahoney
VP HR: Charles B. Scheurer
Employees: 4,202
Jobs Added Last Year: 227 (+5.7%)
Computers - automated banking transaction machines

EDWARD J. DEBARTOLO CORP.
7620 Market St.　　　　Phone: 216-758-7292
Youngstown, OH 44513　Fax: 216-758-3598
CEO: Edward J. DeBartolo, Jr.
Dir HR: Marie Denise DeBartolo York
Employees: 15,000
Jobs Added Last Year: 1,000 (+7.1%)
Real estate development & management

DPL INC.
Courthouse Plaza SW　　Phone: 513-224-6000
Dayton, OH 45402　　　Fax: 513-259-7385
Chm, Pres & CEO: Peter H. Forster
Mgr HR: Ellen Leffak
Employees: 3,147
Jobs Cut Last Year: 56 (-1.7%)
Utility - electric power

THE ELDER-BEERMAN STORES CORP.
3155 El-Bee Rd.　　　　Phone: 513-296-2700
Dayton, OH 45439　　　Fax: 513-296-2915
Chm & CEO: Milton E. Hartley
SVP HR: Patricia Gifford
Employees: 8,700
Jobs Added Last Year: 100 (+1.2%)
Retail - regional department stores

DRUG EMPORIUM, INC.
155 Hidden Ravines Dr.　Phone: 614-548-7080
Powell, OH 43065　　　Fax: 614-548-6541
Chm, CEO & Pres: David L. Kriegel
VP Admin (HR): Jane Lagusch
Employees: 6,100
Jobs Added Last Year: 800 (+15.1%)
Retail - drug stores

FABRI-CENTERS OF AMERICA, INC.
5555 Darrow Rd.　　　　Phone: 216-656-2600
Hudson, OH 44236　　Fax: 216-463-6675
Chm & CEO: Alan Rosskamm
SVP HR: Rosalind Thompson
Employees: 11,400
Jobs Added Last Year: 1,100 (+10.7%)
Retail - fabric & notions

DURIRON COMPANY, INC.
3100 Research Blvd.　　Phone: 513-476-6100
Dayton, OH 45420　　　Fax: 513-476-6247
Pres & CEO: William M. Jordan
HR Mgr: Julie Trey
Employees: 2,575
Jobs Added Last Year: 235 (+10%)
Machinery - general industrial

FEDERATED DEPARTMENT STORES
Seven W. Seventh St.　　Phone: 513-579-7000
Cincinnati, OH 45202　Fax: 513-579-7555
Chm & CEO: Allen I. Questrom
SVP & Dir HR: Thomas G. Cody
Employees: 67,300
Jobs Cut Last Year: 5,700 (-7.8%)
Retail - department stores (Bloomingdale's, Macy's, Lazarus, Bon Marche & Jordan Marsh)

OHIO

FERRO CORPORATION
1000 Lakeside Ave. Phone: 216-641-8580
Cleveland, OH 44144-1183 Fax: 216-566-1464
Pres & CEO: Albert C. Bersticker
Dir HR: Paul Richard
Employees: 6,627
Jobs Cut Last Year: 639 (-8.8%)
Paints & allied products - coatings, ceramics, plastics & chemicals

FIFTH THIRD BANCORP
38 Fountain Sq. Plaza Phone: 513-579-5300
Cincinnati, OH 45263 Fax: 513-741-8909
Pres & CEO: George A. Schaefer, Jr.
VP HR: Dan Keefe
Employees: 4,987
Jobs Added Last Year: 828 (+19.9%)
Banks - Midwest

FIGGIE INTERNATIONAL INC.
4420 Sherwin Rd. Phone: 216-953-2700
Willoughby, OH 44094 Fax: 216-951-1724
Pres & CEO: John P. "Jack" Reilly
Dir HR: Bill Sickman
Employees: 12,600
Jobs Cut Last Year: 2,000 (-13.7%)
Diversified operations - vacuum cleaners; fire trucks; insurance; real estate

FIRST MERIT CORPORATION
800 First National Tower Phone: 216-384-8000
Akron, OH 44308 Fax: 216-253-1849
Pres & CEO: Howard L. Flood
SVP HR: Christopher J. Maurer
Employees: 2,726
Jobs Cut Last Year: 21 (-.8%)
Banks - Midwest

FRISCH'S RESTAURANTS, INC.
2800 Gilbert Ave. Phone: 513-961-2660
Cincinnati, OH 45206 Fax: 513-559-5160
Pres & CEO: Craig F. Maier
VP HR: Ronald E. Heineman
Employees: 6,300
Jobs Added Last Year: 600 (+10.5%)
Retail - restaurants (Big Boy, Hardee's licensee)

FUTURE HEALTHCARE INC.
201 E. Fourth St., Ste. 19 Phone: 513-651-2525
Cincinnati, OH 45202-4118 Fax: 513-784-1642
Pres, CEO & Chm: John D. Peckskamp, Jr.
Dir HR: Gene Wells
Employees: 167
Jobs Added Last Year: 70 (+72.2%)
Medical services - clinical testing of drugs for pharmaceutical companies

GENCORP INC.
175 Ghent Rd. Phone: 216-869-4200
Fairlawn, OH 44333-3300 Fax: 216-869-4211
Chm & CEO: John B. Yasinsky
VP HR: Gary J. Goberville
Employees: 13,300
Jobs Cut Last Year: 600 (-4.3%)
Diversified operations - defense products; polymer products for the auto industry

GIBSON GREETINGS, INC.
2100 Section Rd. Phone: 513-841-6600
Cincinnati, OH 45237 Fax: 513-841-6739
Chm, Pres & CEO: Benjamin J. Sottile
VP HR: Stephen M. Sweeney
Employees: 9,400
Jobs Added Last Year: 600 (+6.8%)
Greeting cards & gift wrapping

THE GOODYEAR TIRE & RUBBER CO.
1144 E. Market St. Phone: 216-796-2121
Akron, OH 44316 Fax: 216-796-2222
Chm & CEO: Stanley C. Gault
VP HR: Mike L. Burns
Employees: 91,754
Jobs Cut Last Year: 3,958 (-4.1%)
Rubber products - tires & industrial; automotive services; oil pipeline

HEALTH CARE AND RETIREMENT CORPORATION
One SeaGate Phone: 419-247-5000
Toledo, OH 43604-2616 Fax: 419-247-2839
Pres: Paul A. Ormand
Dir HR: Gary Banjamin
Employees: 16,500
Jobs Cut Last Year: 100 (-.6%)
Health care - outpatient & home

OHIO

HEALTH-MOR INC.
3500 Payne Ave. Phone: 216-432-1990
Cleveland, OH 44114 Fax: 216-432-0250
Chm & CEO: Kirk W. Foley
Dir HR: Wayne F. Dow
Employees: 1,159
Jobs Added Last Year: 340 (+41.5%)
Appliances - vacuum cleaners; metal fabricating

HOLOPHANE CORPORATION
250 E. Broad St., Ste. 1400 Phone: 614-224-3134
Columbus, OH 43215 Fax: 614-341-2142
Chm & CEO: John R. DallePezze
VP HR: Robert Taylor
Employees: 1,443
Jobs Added Last Year: 357 (+32.9%)
Building products - lighting fixtures

HUFFY CORPORATION
225 Byers Rd. Phone: 513-866-6251
Miamisburg, OH 45342 Fax: 513-865-5470
Chm, Pres & CEO: Richard L. Molen
VP HR: George A. Plotner
Employees: 6,421
Jobs Added Last Year: 567 (+9.7%)
Leisure & recreational products - bicycles, lawn & garden tools, basketball equipment; inventory services

HUNTINGTON BANCSHARES INCORPORATED
Huntington Center Phone: 614-476-8300
Columbus, OH 43287 Fax: 614-476-8029
Chm & CEO: Frank Wobst
VP & Dir HR: Les Ridout
Employees: 8,395
Jobs Added Last Year: 356 (+4.4%)
Banks - Midwest

INSILCO CORPORATION
425 Metro Place North Phone: 614-792-0468
Dublin, OH 43017 Fax: 614-791-3197
Pres & CEO: Robert L. Smialek
VP HR: Les Jacobs
Employees: 5,300
Jobs Cut Last Year: 100 (-1.9%)
Diversified operations - metal fabricating; electronics; communications; office supplies (Rolodex)

INVACARE CORPORATION
899 Cleveland St., PO Box 4028 Phone: 216-329-6000
Elyria, OH 44036-2125 Fax: 216-366-6160
Chm, Pres & CEO: A. Malachi Mixon III
VP HR: Richard A. Sayers II
Employees: 3,042
Jobs Added Last Year: 112 (+3.8%)
Medical products - mobility products & home medical equipment for people with disabilities

THE J. M. SMUCKER COMPANY
One Strawberry Ln. Phone: 216-682-3000
Orrville, OH 44667-0280 Fax: 216-684-3370
Chm, CEO & CFO: Paul H. Smucker
Dir HR: Bob Ellis
Employees: 2,600
Jobs Added Last Year: 650 (+33.3%)
Food - jams, jellies & other fruit-related products

JACOR COMMUNICATIONS, INC.
201 E. Fifth St., Ste. 1300 Phone: 513-621-1300
Cincinnati, OH 45202 Fax: 513-621-0090
Pres: Randy Michaels
CFO (HR): R. Christopher Weber
Employees: 675
Jobs Added Last Year: 101 (+17.6%)
Broadcasting - radio & TV

KEYCORP
127 Public Square Phone: 216-689-3000
Cleveland, OH 44114-1306 Fax: 216-689-0519
Chm & CEO: Victor J. Riley, Jr.
SVP HR: Robert M. Haas
Employees: 29,983
Jobs Added Last Year: 866 (+3%)
Banks - money center

THE KROGER CO.
1014 Vine St. Phone: 513-762-4000
Cincinnati, OH 45202-1100 Fax: 513-762-4454
Chm & CEO: Joseph A. Pichler
Group VP Labor Rel & HR: Tom Murphy
Employees: 190,000
Jobs Added Last Year: 0
Retail - supermarkets & convenience stores

OHIO

LANCASTER COLONY CORPORATION
37 W. Broad St. Phone: 614-224-7141
Columbus, OH 43215 Fax: 614-469-8219
CEO & Chm: John B. Gerlach
Corp Counsel (HR): David Segal
Employees: 5,000
Jobs Added Last Year: 700 (+16.3%)
Diversified operations - specialty foods; automotive products; glassware & candles

LINCOLN ELECTRIC COMPANY
22801 St. Clair Ave. Phone: 216-481-8100
Cleveland, OH 44117 Fax: 216-486-1751
Chm & CEO: Donald F. Hastings
VP HR: Paul Beddia
Employees: 2,700
Jobs Added Last Year: 32 (+1.2%)
Machinery - welding & cutting equipment

LEASEWAY TRANSPORTATION CORPORATION
3700 Park East Dr. Phone: 216-765-5500
Beachwood, OH 44122 Fax: 216-765-5077
Pres & CEO: Richard A. Damsel
VP HR: Robert Plantz
Employees: 8,000
Jobs Added Last Year: 0
Transportation - truck & related services

LSI INDUSTRIES INC.
10000 Alliance Rd. Phone: 513-793-3200
Cincinnati, OH 45242 Fax: 513-433-7715
Chm & Pres: Robert J. Ready
VP HR: Ed Kombrinck
Employees: 900
Jobs Added Last Year: 300 (+50%)
Building products - lighting fixtures

LESCO, INC.
20005 Lake Rd. Phone: 216-333-9250
Rocky River, OH 44116 Fax: 216-333-6832
Chm, Pres & CEO: William A. Foley
VP HR: Rhonda P. Lawson
Employees: 688
Jobs Added Last Year: 84 (+13.9%)
Fertilizers, turf protection products & grass seed; turf care service centers; golf course fairway & greens mowers

THE LTV CORPORATION
25 W. Prospect Ave. Phone: 216-622-5000
Cleveland, OH 44115 Fax: 216-622-4610
Chm, Pres & CEO: David H. Hoag
SVP Personnel & Corp Affairs: Roger A. Dunn
Employees: 15,700
Jobs Cut Last Year: 2,200 (-12.3%)
Steel - production; oil & gas drilling equipment

LIBBEY INC.
420 Madison Ave. Phone: 419-727-2100
Toledo, OH 43604 Fax: 419-727-2253
Chm & CEO: John F. Meier
VP HR: George W. Templin
Employees: 3,500
Jobs Added Last Year: 600 (+20.7%)
Glass products

LUBRIZOL CORPORATION
29400 Lakeland Blvd. Phone: 216-943-4200
Wickliffe, OH 44092 Fax: 216-943-5337
CEO: L. E. Coleman
No central personnel officer
Employees: 4,613
Jobs Added Last Year: 4 (+.1%)
Oil refining & marketing

THE LIMITED, INC.
3 Limited Pkwy., PO Box 16000 Phone: 614-479-7000
Columbus, OH 43216 Fax: 614-479-7080
Chm & Pres: Leslie H. Wexner
EVP & Dir HR: Arnold F. Kanarick
Employees: 97,200
Jobs Cut Last Year: 3,200 (-3.2%)
Retail - apparel (Lerner New York, Express, Abercrombie & Fitch, Victoria's Secret) & bath products (Bath & Body Works)

MAX & ERMA'S RESTAURANTS, INC.
4849 Evanswood Dr. Phone: 614-431-5800
Columbus, OH 43229 Fax: 614-431-4111
Pres, CEO & Chm: Todd B. Barnum
VP Mktg & Strategic Dev (HR): Karen Brennan
Employees: 2,442
Jobs Added Last Year: 205 (+9.2%)
Retail - casual dining restaurants

OHIO

MCDONALD & COMPANY SECURITIES, INC.
800 Superior Ave., Ste. 2100   Phone: 216-443-2300
Cleveland, OH 44114   Fax: 216-443-2699
Pres & CEO: William B. Summers, Jr.
Mgr HR: Tom Clevidence
Employees: 1,100
Jobs Added Last Year: 160 (+17%)
Financial - investment bankers

THE MEAD CORPORATION
Courthouse Plaza NE   Phone: 513-495-6323
Dayton, OH 45463   Fax: 513-461-2424
Chm & CEO: Steven C. Mason
VP HR: Charles J. Mazza
Employees: 19,600
Jobs Cut Last Year: 800 (-3.9%)
Paper & paper products - packaging, school & office products

MEDUSA CORPORATION
Lee & Monticello Blvd.   Phone: 216-371-4000
Cleveland Heights, OH 44118   Fax: 216-371-2912
Chm & CEO: Robert S. Evans
VP HR: Richard A. Brown
Employees: 1,184
Jobs Added Last Year: 254 (+27.3%)
Construction - cement & concrete

MERCANTILE STORES COMPANY, INC.
9450 Seward Rd.   Phone: 513-881-8000
Fairfield, OH 45014   Fax: 513-881-8689
Chm & CEO: David L. Nichols
Dir HR: Lou Ripley
Employees: 30,000
Jobs Added Last Year: 0
Retail - regional department stores in the Midwest, South, Colorado & Montana

MERCY HEALTH SYSTEM
2335 Grandview Ave.   Phone: 513-221-2736
Cincinnati, OH 45206   Fax: 513-559-3835
CEO: Sister Marjorie Bosse
SVP HR: Ronald J. Baril
Employees: 15,739
Jobs Added Last Year: —
Hospitals

MERIDIAN DIAGNOSTICS, INC.
3471 River Hills Dr.   Phone: 513-271-3700
Cincinnati, OH 45244   Fax: 513-271-3762
CEO: Jerry L. Ryan
HR Dir: Marlene Cook
Employees: 130
Jobs Added Last Year: 31 (+31.3%)
Medical products - immunodiagnostic test kits

MTD PRODUCTS INC.
PO Box 368022   Phone: 216-225-2600
Valley City, OH 44136   Fax: 216-225-0896
Chm & CEO: Curtis E. Moll
VP HR: Mike Murray
Employees: 4,850
Jobs Added Last Year: 250 (+5.4%)
Machinery - outdoor power equipment

NACCO INDUSTRIES, INC.
5875 Landerbrook Dr.   Phone: 216-449-9600
Mayfield Heights, OH 44124-4017   Fax: 216-449-9581
Pres & CEO: Alfred M. Rankin, Jr.
Personnel Mgr: Sue Taylor
Employees: 10,250
Jobs Added Last Year: 749 (+7.9%)
Diversified operations - forklifts; small appliances; coal

NATIONAL CITY CORPORATION
1900 E. Ninth St.   Phone: 216-575-2000
Cleveland, OH 44114-3484   Fax: 216-575-3332
CEO: Edward B. Brandon
Dir HR: Shelley J. Seifert
Employees: 19,960
Jobs Added Last Year: 1,194 (+6.4%)
Banks - Midwest

NATIONWIDE INSURANCE ENTERPRISE
One Nationwide Plaza   Phone: 614-249-7111
Columbus, OH 43215   Fax: 614-249-9071
Chm, Pres & CEO: D. Richard McFerson
VP HR: Susan A. Wolken
Employees: 32,583
Jobs Added Last Year: 83 (+.3%)
Insurance - multiline (Nationwide, Wausau)

OHIO

NORDSON CORPORATION
28601 Clemens Rd. Phone: 216-892-1580
Westlake, OH 44145 Fax: 216-892-9507
Pres & CEO: William P. Madar
VP HR: Bruce H. Fields
Employees: 3,281
Jobs Added Last Year: 179 (+5.8%)
Machinery - general industrial

OFFICEMAX, INC.
3605 Warrensville Center Rd. Phone: 216-921-6900
Shaker Heights, OH 44122 Fax: 216-283-3365
Pres & CEO: Michael Feuer
Divisional VP & HR: Suzanne Forsythe
Employees: 13,500
Jobs Added Last Year: 2,300 (+19.5%)
Retail - #2 US deep-discount office products superstore operator

OHIO CASUALTY CORPORATION
136 N. Third St. Phone: 513-867-3000
Hamilton, OH 45025 Fax: 513-867-3215
Pres & CEO: Lauren N. Patch
VP HR: Rick Thomas
Employees: 5,100
Jobs Added Last Year: 300 (+6.3%)
Insurance - property & casualty

OHIO EDISON CO.
76 S. Main St. Phone: 216-384-5100
Akron, OH 44308-1890 Fax: 216-384-5791
Pres & CEO: W. R. Holland
Mgr HR: Tom Kayuha
Employees: 6,263
Jobs Added Last Year: 1,214 (+24%)
Utility - electric power

THE OHIO STATE UNIVERSITY
190 N. Oval Mall Phone: 614-292-2424
Columbus, OH 43210 Fax: 614-292-1231
Pres: Gordon Gee
VP HR: Linda Tom
Employees: 29,576
Jobs Added Last Year: –
University

OWENS-CORNING FIBERGLAS CORP.
Fiberglas Tower Phone: 419-248-8000
Toledo, OH 43659 Fax: 419-248-5337
Chm & CEO: Glen H. Hiner
SVP HR: Robert D. Heddens
Employees: 16,200
Jobs Cut Last Year: 200 (-1.2%)
Building products - insulation, roofing; industrial materials; resins; textile yarns

OWENS-ILLINOIS, INC.
One SeaGate Phone: 419-247-5000
Toledo, OH 43666 Fax: 419-247-2839
Chm & CEO: Joseph H. Lemieux
Dir HR Mgmt: Gary Benjamin
Employees: 28,900
Jobs Cut Last Year: 4,500 (-13.5%)
Glass products - containers & specialized; plastics & closures

PARK-OHIO INDUSTRIES, INC.
600 Tower E., 20600 Chagrin Blvd. Phone: 216-991-9700
Cleveland, OH 44122 Fax: 216-991-9317
Chm & CEO: Edward P. Crawford
Dir HR: Betty Buris
Employees: 1,889
Jobs Added Last Year: 696 (+58.3%)
Metal products - fabrication

PARKER HANNIFIN CORPORATION
17325 Euclid Ave. Phone: 216-531-3000
Cleveland, OH 44112 Fax: 216-531-6525
Pres & CEO: Duane E. Collins
VP HR: Daniel T. Garey
Employees: 26,730
Jobs Added Last Year: 1,084 (+4.2%)
Instruments - control

PHAR-MOR INC.
20 Federal Plaza West Phone: 216-746-6641
Youngstown, OH 44501 Fax: 216-740-2915
CEO: Antonio C. Alvarez
VP HR: Robert C. Miller
Employees: 10,000
Jobs Added Last Year: –
Retail - discount drug & variety stores

OHIO

PREMIER INDUSTRIAL CORPORATION
4500 Euclid Ave. Phone: 216-391-8300
Cleveland, OH 44103 Fax: 216-391-8327
Pres & CEO: Morton L. Mandel
VP HR: Bob Mason
Employees: 4,300
Jobs Cut Last Year: 100 (-2.3%)
Electronics - parts distribution

THE PROCTER & GAMBLE COMPANY
One Procter & Gamble Plaza Phone: 513-983-1100
Cincinnati, OH 45202 Fax: 513-562-2062
Chm & CEO: Edwin L. Artzt
SVP HR: Benjamin L. Bethell
Employees: 96,500
Jobs Cut Last Year: 7,000 (-6.8%)
Soap & cleaning preparations, personal care products (Head & Shoulders), food & beverages

PROGRESSIVE CORPORATION
6000 Parkland Blvd. Phone: 216-464-8000
Mayfield Heights, OH 44124 Fax: 216-446-7097
Chm, Pres & CEO: Peter B. Lewis
VP HR: Tiona Thompson
Employees: 6,101
Jobs Added Last Year: 510 (+9.1%)
Insurance - property & casualty

REPUBLIC ENGINEERED STEELS, INC.
410 Oberlin Rd. SW Phone: 800-331-9420
Massillon, OH 44648 Fax: 216-837-6083
Chm, Pres & CEO: Russell Maier
VP HR: Rick Miller
Employees: 4,400
Jobs Added Last Year: —
Steel - engineered bars

REVCO D.S., INC.
1925 Enterprise Pkwy. Phone: 216-425-9811
Twinsburg, OH 44087 Fax: 216-487-6539
Pres & CEO: D. Dwayne Hoven
SVP HR: Douglas W. Coffey
Employees: 18,000
Jobs Added Last Year: 1,200 (+7.1%)
Retail - drug stores

REYNOLDS AND REYNOLDS CO.
115 S. Ludlow St. Phone: 513-443-2000
Dayton, OH 45402 Fax: 513-449-4416
Chm, Pres & CEO: David R. Holmes
VP HR: Tom Momchilov
Employees: 5,140
Jobs Cut Last Year: 496 (-8.8%)
Paper - business forms; software for automotive & medical markets

RISER FOODS, INC.
5300 Richmond Rd. Phone: 216-292-7000
Bedford Heights, OH 44146 Fax: 216-591-2640
Chm & CEO: Anthony C. Rego
VP HR: Frank A. Zeiher
Employees: 5,000
Jobs Added Last Year: 500 (+11.1%)
Retail - supermarkets (Rini-Rego Stop-n-Shop); wholesale food distribution (American Seaway Foods); private label ice cream

ROADWAY SERVICES, INC.
1077 Gorge Blvd., PO Box 88 Phone: 216-384-8184
Akron, OH 44309-0088 Fax: 216-258-6042
Chm & CEO: Joseph M. Clapp
VP Admin & Treas (HR): John P. Chandler
Employees: 46,600
Jobs Added Last Year: 7,600 (+19.5%)
Transportation - truck

ROBBINS & MYERS, INC.
1400 Kettering Tower Phone: 513-222-2610
Dayton, OH 45423-1400 Fax: 513-225-3314
Pres & CEO: Daniel W. Duval
Dir HR & Corp Rel: Hugh E. Becker
Employees: 2,226
Jobs Added Last Year: 1,611 (+262%)
Machinery - fluid handling & motion control

ROBERD'S, INC.
1100 E. Central Ave. Phone: 513-859-5127
West Carrollton, OH 45449-1888 Fax: 513-859-8125
Chm, Pres & CEO: Kenneth W. Fletcher
Asst Treas (HR): Wayne B. Howdens
Employees: 1,650
Jobs Added Last Year: 250 (+17.9%)
Retail - home furnishings, furniture, appliances & electronics

OHIO

ROTO-ROOTER, INC.
255 E. Fifth St. Phone: 513-762-6690
Cincinnati, OH 45202-4726 Fax: 513-762-6590
Pres & CEO: William R. Griffin
VP HR: Dan Mollaun
Employees: 2,700
Jobs Added Last Year: 440 (+19.5%)
Building - sewer & drain cleaning maintenance & services

THE SHERWIN-WILLIAMS COMPANY
101 Prospect Ave. NW Phone: 216-566-2000
Cleveland, OH 44115-1075 Fax: 216-566-3310
Chm & CEO: John G. Breen
VP HR: Thomas Kroeger
Employees: 17,200
Jobs Added Last Year: 253 (+1.5%)
Paints & allied products

RPM, INC.
2628 Pearl Rd., PO Box 777 Phone: 216-273-5090
Medina, OH 44258 Fax: 216-225-8743
CEO: Thomas C. Sullivan
No central personnel officer
Employees: 3,500
Jobs Added Last Year: 0
Paints & allied products

THE STANDARD PRODUCTS CO.
2130 W. 110th St. Phone: 216-281-8300
Cleveland, OH 44102 Fax: 216-281-0126
Chm & CEO: James S. Reid, Jr.
VP HR: John C. Brandmahl
Employees: 10,343
Jobs Added Last Year: 1,313 (+14.5%)
Rubber & plastic - parts for automotive, construction, appliance & marine industries

RUBBERMAID INCORPORATED
1147 Akron Rd. Phone: 216-264-6464
Wooster, OH 44691-6000 Fax: 216-287-2739
Chm & CEO: Wolfgang R. Schmitt
SVP HR: Thomas W. Ward
Employees: 11,978
Jobs Added Last Year: 682 (+6%)
Rubber & plastic products - consumer & industrial

STANDARD REGISTER COMPANY
600 Albany St. Phone: 513-434-1000
Dayton, OH 45401 Fax: 513-443-1239
Pres & CEO: Peter S. Redding
Asst VP HR: John E. Scarpelli
Employees: 6,180
Jobs Added Last Year: 456 (+8%)
Paper - business forms

SCHOTTENSTEIN STORES CORPORATION
1800 Moler Rd. Phone: 614-221-9200
Columbus, OH 43207 Fax: 614-449-0403
Chm & CEO: Jay Schottenstein
VP HR: Herbert E. Minkin
Employees: 15,000
Jobs Added Last Year: 0
Retail - home furnishings & department stores

STAR BANC CORPORATION
425 Walnut St. Phone: 513-632-4000
Cincinnati, OH 45202 Fax: 513-632-5512
Pres & CEO: Jerry A. Grundhofer
SVP & Dir HR: Steve Smith
Employees: 3,540
Jobs Cut Last Year: 153 (-4.1%)
Banks - Midwest

SEAWAY FOOD TOWN, INC.
1020 Ford St. Phone: 419-893-9401
Maumee, OH 43537 Fax: 419-891-4214
Chm & CEO: Wallace D. Iott
Dir Emp Rel: Charles North
Employees: 4,500
Jobs Cut Last Year: 360 (-7.4%)
Retail - supermarkets

STERIS CORPORATION
9450 Pineneedle Dr. Phone: 216-354-2600
Mentor, OH 44060 Fax: 216-639-4457
Chm, Pres, CEO & Treas: Bill R. Sanford
VP Admin (HR): Gerard Reiz
Employees: 318
Jobs Added Last Year: 131 (+70.1%)
Medical products - sterilizers for surgical equipment

OHIO

STRUCTURAL DYNAMICS RESEARCH CORP.
2000 Eastman Dr. Phone: 513-576-2400
Milford, OH 45150-2789 Fax: 513-576-2734
Pres & CEO: Albert F. Peter
SVP HR: Edward Neenan
Employees: 1,154
Jobs Added Last Year: 113 (+10.9%)
Computers - computer-aided engineering software

SUN TELEVISION & APPLIANCES, INC.
1583 Alum Creek Dr. Phone: 614-445-8401
Columbus, OH 43209 Fax: 614-444-0849
CEO: Macy T. Block
Dir HR: Getitia Matheny
Employees: 2,100
Jobs Added Last Year: 430 (+25.7%)
Retail - consumer electronics

TELXON CORPORATION
3330 W. Market St. Phone: 216-867-3700
Akron, OH 44333 Fax: 216-869-2220
Chm & CEO, COO: Robert F. Meyerson
Dir HR: Meg Pais
Employees: 1,650
Jobs Added Last Year: 235 (+16.6%)
Computers - portable & wireless transaction systems

THOR INDUSTRIES, INC.
419 W. Pike St. Phone: 513-596-6849
Jackson Center, OH 45334 Fax: 513-596-6092
Chm, Pres & CEO: Wade F. B. Thompson
Chief Admin Off (HR): Walter Bennett
Employees: 2,807
Jobs Added Last Year: 686 (+32.3%)
Automotive - RVs (Airstream, Ambassador, Four Winds & General Coach) & small & mid-sized buses

THRIFTWAY FOOD & DRUG
4901 Hunt Rd. Phone: 513-984-0500
Cincinnati, OH 45242 Fax: 513-984-8644
CEO: Richard E. Lindner
Dir HR: James Krbec
Employees: 3,900
Jobs Added Last Year: 100 (+2.6%)
Retail - grocery & drug stores

THE TIMKEN COMPANY
1835 Dueber Ave. SW Phone: 216-438-3000
Canton, OH 44706-2798 Fax: 216-438-3452
Pres & CEO: Joseph F. Toot, Jr.
VP HR & Logistics: Stephen A. Perry
Employees: 15,985
Jobs Cut Last Year: 744 (-4.4%)
Metal processing & fabrication

TRANZONIC COMPANIES
30195 Chagrin Blvd. Phone: 216-831-5757
Pepper Pike, OH 44124 Fax: 216-831-5647
Chm & CEO: Robert S. Reitman
No central personnel officer
Employees: 1,088
Jobs Added Last Year: 805 (+284.5%)
Paper products - personal care, industrial & medical

TRINOVA CORPORATION
3000 Strayer Phone: 419-867-2200
Maumee, OH 43537-0050 Fax: 419-867-2547
CEO: Darryl F. Allen
Dir HR: Debra Schaefer
Employees: 15,923
Jobs Cut Last Year: 1,773 (-10%)
Machinery - general industrial

TRW INC.
1900 Richmond Rd. Phone: 216-291-7000
Cleveland, OH 44124 Fax: 216-291-7629
Chm & CEO: Joseph T. Gorman
EVP HR, Comm & Info Resources: Howard V. Knicely
Employees: 61,200
Jobs Cut Last Year: 2,900 (-4.5%)
Diversified operations - automotive products; space & defense products, information systems; consumer credit information

THE UNITED STATES SHOE CORP.
One Eastwood Dr. Phone: 513-527-7000
Cincinnati, OH 45227-1127 Fax: 513-561-2007
Pres & CEO: Bannus B. Hudson
VP HR: James P. Maloney
Employees: 38,000
Jobs Cut Last Year: 3,000 (-7.3%)
Retail - shoes (Easy Spirit, Bandolino & Selby), apparel (Casual Corner), optical products (Lenscrafters)

An in-depth profile of this company is available by fax. Call 800-510-4452 and use your touch-tone phone to put in the 5-digit code at the prompt. Only $2.95 each with your credit card. See page 12 for more details.

271

OHIO

VALUE CITY DEPARTMENT STORES, INC.
3241 Westerville Rd. Phone: 614-471-4722
Columbus, OH 43224 Fax: 614-478-2253
Chm & CEO: Jay L. Schottenstein
VP HR: Herbert E. Minkin
Employees: 10,000
Jobs Added Last Year: 400 (+4.2%)
Retail - regional department stores

WENDY'S INTERNATIONAL, INC.
4288 W. Dublin-Granville Rd. Phone: 614-764-3100
Dublin, OH 43017-0256 Fax: 614-764-3459
Pres, CEO & COO: Gordon F. Teter
SVP HR: Kathleen A. McGinnis
Employees: 43,000
Jobs Added Last Year: 1,000 (+2.4%)
Retail - fast-food restaurants

VICTORIA FINANCIAL CORPORATION
5915 Landerbrook Dr. Phone: 216-461-3461
Cleveland, OH 44124-4058 Fax: 216-461-0958
Pres & CEO: Kenneth R. Rosen
Dir HR: John Pospistl
Employees: 144
Jobs Added Last Year: 20 (+16.1%)
Insurance - multiline & misc.

WESTFIELD COMPANIES
One Park Circle Phone: 216-887-0101
Westfield Center, OH 44251 Fax: 216-887-0840
Pres & CEO: R. C. Blair
VP HR: R. D. Sondles
Employees: 1,840
Jobs Added Last Year: 122 (+7.1%)
Insurance - multiline

WAXMAN INDUSTRIES, INC.
24460 Aurora Rd. Phone: 216-439-1830
Bedford Heights, OH 44146 Fax: 216-439-8678
Chm & Co-CEO: Melvin Waxman
SVP Ops (HR): John R. Peters
Employees: 1,211
Jobs Added Last Year: 148 (+13.9%)
Building products - plumbing, electrical & hardware

WORTHINGTON INDUSTRIES, INC.
1205 Dearborn Dr. Phone: 614-438-3210
Columbus, OH 43085 Fax: 614-438-3136
VC & CEO: John P. McConnell
VP Personnel: Thomas L. Hockman
Employees: 7,700
Jobs Added Last Year: 700 (+10%)
Metal processing & fabrication - flat rolled steel coils; injection molded plastic products

OKLAHOMA

BANCFIRST CORPORATION
101 N. Broadway, Ste. 200　　Phone: 405-270-1000
Oklahoma City, OK 73102-8401　　Fax: 405-270-1089
CEO: David E. Rainbolt
VP HR: J. Michael Rogers
Employees: 515
Jobs Added Last Year: 421 (+447.9%)
Financial - savings & loans

CMI CORPORATION
Interstate 40 and Morgan Rd.　　Phone: 405-787-6020
Oklahoma City, OK 73101　　Fax: 405-491-2417
Chm: Bill Swisher
HR Mgr: Richard H. Cole
Employees: 952
Jobs Added Last Year: 177 (+22.8%)
Machinery - material handling

DEVON ENERGY CORPORATION
20 N. Broadway, Ste. 1500　　Phone: 405-235-3611
Oklahoma City, OK 73102-8260　　Fax: 405-552-4550
Pres & CEO: J. Larry Nichols
Personnel Mgr: Gary May
Employees: 182
Jobs Added Last Year: 66 (+56.9%)
Oil & gas - US exploration & production

EATERIES INC.
3240 W. Britton Rd., Ste. 202　　Phone: 405-755-3607
Oklahoma City, OK 73120　　Fax: 405-751-7348
CEO: Vincent F. Orza
HR Mgr: Meline Schwartz-Towler
Employees: 2,300
Jobs Added Last Year: 300 (+15%)
Retail - family-style restaurants (Garfield's) & sports bars

FLEMING COMPANIES, INC.　　10587
6301 Waterford Blvd.　　Phone: 405-840-7200
Oklahoma City, OK 73126-0647　　Fax: 405-841-8149
Chm, Pres & CEO: Robert E. Stauth
Dir HR: Larry A. Wagner
Employees: 23,300
Jobs Added Last Year: 500 (+2.2%)
Food - wholesale to supermarkets

HALE HALSELL CO.
9111 E. Pine St.　　Phone: 918-835-4484
Tulsa, OK 74158-2898　　Fax: 918-835-3979
Pres: Robert Hawk
Personnel Mgr: Paul Bradley
Employees: 5,320
Jobs Added Last Year: 1,241 (+30.4%)
Food - wholesale

HAROLD'S STORES, INC.
765 Asp Ave.　　Phone: 405-329-4045
Norman, OK 73069　　Fax: 405-366-2588
CEO: Rebecca Powell Casey
Chm (HR): Harold G. Powell
Employees: 950
Jobs Added Last Year: 185 (+24.2%)
Retail - apparel & shoes

HELMERICH & PAYNE, INC.
Utica at 21st St.　　Phone: 918-742-5531
Tulsa, OK 74114　　Fax: 918-742-0237
Pres & CEO: Hans Helmerich
Dir HR: Todd Sprague
Employees: 2,787
Jobs Added Last Year: 398 (+16.7%)
Oil & gas - US exploration & production

HOMELAND HOLDING CORPORATION
400 NE 36th St.　　Phone: 405-557-5500
Oklahoma City, OK 73105　　Fax: 405-557-5600
Pres & CEO: Max E. Raydon
Dir HR: Prentess Alletag
Employees: 6,000
Jobs Added Last Year: —
Retail - supermarkets

KERR-MCGEE CORPORATION　　10852
Kerr-McGee Center　　Phone: 405-270-1313
Oklahoma City, OK 73125　　Fax: 405-270-3029
Chm & CEO: Frank A. McPherson
VP HR: Jean B. Wallace
Employees: 5,812
Jobs Cut Last Year: 54 (-.9%)
Oil & gas - integrated

OKLAHOMA

LOUIS DREYFUS NATURAL GAS CORPORATION
14000 Quail Springs Pkwy. Phone: 405-749-1300
Oklahoma City, OK 73134 Fax: 405-749-9385
CEO: S. B. Rich, Jr.
Mgr HR: Rebecca Perot-Tripp
Employees: 300
Jobs Added Last Year: 75 (+33.3%)
Oil & gas - US exploration & production

QUIKTRIP CORPORATION
901 N. Mingo Rd. Phone: 918-836-8551
Tulsa, OK 74101 Fax: 918-834-4117
Chm & CEO: Chester Cadieux
VP HR: Jim Denny
Employees: 2,500
Jobs Added Last Year: 300 (+13.6%)
Retail - gasoline convenience stores

LOWRANCE ELECTRONICS, INC.
12000 E. Skelly Dr. Phone: 918-437-6881
Tulsa, OK 74128 Fax: 918-234-1702
CEO: Darrell J. Lowrance
VP HR: Sue Chase
Employees: 729
Jobs Added Last Year: 262 (+56.1%)
Leisure & recreational products - sonars for boating

SILVERADO FOODS, INC.
7312 E. 38th St. Phone: 918-627-7783
Tulsa, OK 74145 Fax: 918-627-7784
Chm & CEO: Lawrence D. Field
VP (HR): Angela Swift
Employees: 550
Jobs Added Last Year: 249 (+82.7%)
Food - gourmet & snack foods

MAPCO PETROLEUM INC.
1800 S. Baltimore Ave. Phone: 918-581-1800
Tulsa, OK 74119 Fax: 918-599-3634
Chm & CEO: James E. Barnes
SVP HR: Jack D. Maynard
Employees: 6,001
Jobs Added Last Year: 16 (+.3%)
Oil & gas - production & pipeline

SONIC CORP.
101 Park Ave. Phone: 405-280-7654
Oklahoma City, OK 73102 Fax: 405-272-8298
Chm, Pres & CEO: C. Stephen Lynn
Personnel Dir: Marcy Vickers
Employees: 4,141
Jobs Added Last Year: 1,017 (+32.6%)
Retail - drive-in hamburger restaurants

PARKER DRILLING CO.
Eight E. Third St. Phone: 918-585-8221
Tulsa, OK 74103 Fax: 918-585-1058
Pres & CEO: Robert L. Parker Jr.
Mgr HR: Gloria West
Employees: 2,106
Jobs Added Last Year: 322 (+18%)
Oil & gas - field services

UNITED VIDEO SATELLITE GROUP INC.
7140 S. Lewis Ave. Phone: 918-488-4000
Tulsa, OK 74136-5422 Fax: 918-663-6228
Chm & CEO: Lawrence Flinn, Jr.
VP HR: Suzanne Shepherd
Employees: 500
Jobs Added Last Year: 149 (+42.5%)
Telecommunications services - satellite-delivered video, audio, data & program services to cable TV systems

PHILLIPS PETROLEUM COMPANY
Phillips Bldg. Phone: 918-661-6600
Bartlesville, OK 74004 Fax: 918-661-7636
Chm & CEO: Wayne W. Allen
SVP Corp Rel & Svcs (HR): J. Bryan Whitworth
Employees: 19,400
Jobs Cut Last Year: 2,000 (-9.3%)
Oil & gas - integrated

THE WILLIAMS COMPANIES, INC.
One Williams Center Phone: 918-588-2000
Tulsa, OK 74172 Fax: 918-588-2296
Pres & CEO: Keith E. Bailey
VP HR: John C. Fischer
Employees: 7,189
Jobs Added Last Year: 394 (+5.8%)
Oil & gas - production & pipeline

OREGON

CFI PROSERVICES, INC.
220 NW Second Ave. Phone: 503-274-7280
Portland, OR 97209 Fax: 503-274-7284
Chm & CEO: Matthew W. Chapman
Dir HR: Kathy Holmquist
Employees: 290
Jobs Added Last Year: 120 (+70.6%)
Computers - electronic banking software for financial institutions

COLUMBIA SPORTSWEAR
6600 N. Baltimore Phone: 503-286-3676
Portland, OR 97203 Fax: 503-289-6602
CEO: Tim Boyle
Dir HR: Bill Baumann
Employees: 800
Jobs Added Last Year: 100 (+14.3%)
Apparel - outerwear including ski jackets, raincoats & fishing vests

ELECTRO SCIENTIFIC INDUSTRIES, INC.
13900 NW Science Park Dr. Phone: 503-641-4141
Portland, OR 97229-5497 Fax: 503-643-4873
Pres & CEO: Donald R. VanLuvanee
Dir HR: Robert C. Cimino
Employees: 600
Jobs Added Last Year: 80 (+15.4%)
Lasers - trimming & memory repair systems, test & production equipment for manufacturers of miniature capacitors

FRED MEYER, INC.
3800 SE 22nd Ave. Phone: 503-232-8844
Portland, OR 97202 Fax: 503-233-4535
Chm & CEO: Robert G. Miller
SVP HR: Keith W. Lovett
Employees: 25,000
Jobs Added Last Year: 1,000 (+4.2%)
Retail - regional hypermarts

THE GREENBRIER COMPANIES, INC.
One Centerpointe Dr. Phone: 503-684-7000
Lake Oswego, OR 97035 Fax: 503-684-7553
CEO: William A. Furman
Dir HR: Jeannie Wakayama-Onchi
Employees: 1,764
Jobs Added Last Year: 136 (+8.4%)
Transportation - double-stack railcars, intermodal transportation equipment & services to the railroad industry

LOUISIANA-PACIFIC CORPORATION
111 SW Fifth Ave. Phone: 503-221-0800
Portland, OR 97204-3699 Fax: 503-796-0204
Chm, Pres & CEO: Harry A. Merlo
No central personnel officer
Employees: 13,000
Jobs Added Last Year: 1,500 (+13%)
Building products - wood

NIKE, INC.
One Bowerman Dr. Phone: 503-671-6453
Beaverton, OR 97005-6453 Fax: 503-671-6300
Chm & CEO: Philip H. Knight
Dir HR: Jim Fredericks
Employees: 9,600
Jobs Added Last Year: 1,800 (+23.1%)
Shoes & related apparel - athletic

OREGON STEEL MILLS, INC.
1000 SW Broadway, Ste. 2200 Phone: 503-223-9228
Portland, OR 97203 Fax: 503-240-5291
Chm, Pres & CEO: Thomas B. Boklund
VP Emp Rel: Jack C. Longbine
Employees: 3,060
Jobs Added Last Year: 1,571 (+105.5%)
Steel - specialty alloys

PACIFICORP
700 NE Multnomah Phone: 503-731-2000
Portland, OR 97232-4116 Fax: 503-731-2136
Pres & CEO: Frederick W. Buckman
VP HR: Mike Pittman
Employees: 13,635
Jobs Added Last Year: 542 (+4.1%)
Utility - electric power

PLANAR SYSTEMS INC.
1400 NW Compton Dr. Phone: 503-690-1100
Beaverton, OR 97006 Fax: 503-690-1244
Pres & CEO: James M. Hurd
Dir HR: Iris Newman
Employees: 450
Jobs Added Last Year: 91 (+25.3%)
Electrical products - electroluminescent flat-panel displays, primarily for use in industrial & medical systems

OREGON

POPE & TALBOT, INC.
1500 SW First Ave. Phone: 503-228-9161
Portland, OR 97201 Fax: 503-220-2755
Chm, Pres & CEO: Peter T. Pope
VP HR: Richard N. Moffitt
Employees: 3,100
Jobs Added Last Year: 100 (+3.3%)
Paper & paper products

RENTRAK CORPORATION
7227 NE 55th Ave. Phone: 503-284-7581
Portland, OR 97218 Fax: 503-288-1563
Pres & CEO: Ron Berger
Corp Dir HR: Maureen Haggerty
Employees: 156
Jobs Added Last Year: 30 (+23.8%)
Leisure & recreational services - prerecorded videotapes

PORTLAND GENERAL CORPORATION
121 SW Salmon St. Phone: 503-464-8800
Portland, OR 97204 Fax: 503-464-2233
Pres & CEO: Ken L. Harrison
VP HR: Don Kielblock
Employees: 3,253
Jobs Added Last Year: 96 (+3%)
Utility - electric power

ROSEBURG FOREST PRODUCTS CO.
PO Box 1088 Phone: 503-679-3311
Roseburg, OR 97470 Fax: 503-679-9683
CEO: Kenneth Ford
VP HR: Alyn Ford
Employees: 3,500
Jobs Added Last Year: —
Forest products

PRECISION CASTPARTS CORPORATION
4600 SE Harney Dr. Phone: 503-777-3881
Portland, OR 97206 Fax: 503-777-7632
CEO: William C. McCormick
No central personnel officer
Employees: 3,993
Jobs Cut Last Year: 348 (-8%)
Aerospace - aircraft equipment

SCHNITZER STEEL INDUSTRIES, INC.
3200 NW Yeon Ave. Phone: 503-224-9900
Portland, OR 97210 Fax: 503-323-2804
CEO: Leonard Schnitzer
VP HR: Andrew Lipay
Employees: 909
Jobs Added Last Year: 109 (+13.6%)
Scrap recycling & steel production

R. B. PAMPLIN CORPORATION
900 SW 5th Ave., Ste. 1800 Phone: 503-248-1133
Portland, OR 97204 Fax: 503-245-1175
Chm & CEO: Robert B. Pamplin, Sr.
No central personnel officer
Employees: 5,728
Jobs Added Last Year: 0
Diversified operations - textiles; concrete & asphalt

SEQUENT COMPUTER SYSTEMS, INC.
15450 SW Koll Pkwy. Phone: 503-626-5700
Beaverton, OR 97006-6063 Fax: 503-578-9890
Chm & CEO: Karl C. "Casey" Powell, Jr.
VP HR: Julie A. Sackett
Employees: 1,700
Jobs Added Last Year: 100 (+6.3%)
Computers - parallel processing UNIX-based systems

RADISYS CORPORATION
15025 SW Koll Pkwy Phone: 503-646-1800
Beaverton, OR 97006 Fax: 503-646-1850
Pres & CEO: Glen Myers
Dir HR: Mark Skiba
Employees: 105
Jobs Added Last Year: 44 (+72.1%)
Computers - embedded microcomputers for industrial applications

STANDARD INSURANCE CO.
1100 SW 6th Ave. Phone: 503-321-7000
Portland, OR 97204 Fax: 503-321-7935
Pres & CEO: Ronald E. Timpe
Corp Sec (HR): Ivy E. Lenz
Employees: 1,600
Jobs Added Last Year: 100 (+6.7%)
Insurance - accident & health

OREGON

THRIFTY PAYLESS INC.
9275 SW Peyton Ln. Phone: 213-251-6000
Wilsonville, OR 97070 Fax: 213-386-3079
Pres & CEO: Tim R. McAlear
SVP HR: Jeannette Stone
Employees: 30,000
Jobs Added Last Year: 0
Retail - drug & sporting goods stores

WILLAMETTE INDUSTRIES, INC.
1300 SW Fifth Ave. Phone: 503-227-5581
Portland, OR 97201 Fax: 503-273-5601
Chm & CEO: William Swindells
VP HR: Linda Tenny
Employees: 12,040
Jobs Added Last Year: 40 (+.3%)
Paper & paper products

TRM COPY CENTERS CORPORATION
5515 SE Milwaukie Ave. Phone: 503-231-0230
Portland, OR 97202 Fax: 503-231-3771
Pres & CEO: Edwin S. Chan
Dir HR: Ken Wolfe
Employees: 535
Jobs Added Last Year: 85 (+18.9%)
Business services - photocopy centers

WTD INDUSTRIES, INC.
10260 SW Greenburg Rd., Ste. 900 Phone: 503-246-3440
Portland, OR 97223 Fax: 503-245-4229
CEO: Bruce L. Engel
VP Admin (HR): Robert Riecke
Employees: 1,250
Jobs Added Last Year: 150 (+13.6%)
Building products - lumber & veneer

U. S. BANCORP
111 SW Fifth Ave. Phone: 503-275-6111
Portland, OR 97204 Fax: 503-275-3452
VC & CEO: Gerry B. Cameron
EVP HR: Judy Rice
Employees: 12,863
Jobs Added Last Year: 883 (+7.4%)
Banks - West

PENNSYLVANIA

84 LUMBER COMPANY
Rte. 519 Phone: 412-228-8820
Eighty Four, PA 15384 Fax: 412-225-2530
CEO: Joseph A. Hardy, Sr.
Dir HR: Steve Cherry
Employees: 3,500
Jobs Added Last Year: 300 (+9.4%)
Building products - retail

ALCO STANDARD CORPORATION
PO Box 834 Phone: 215-296-8000
Valley Forge, PA 19482 Fax: 215-296-8419
Pres & CEO: John E. Stuart
Dir Corp MIS & HR: Elizabeth H. Barrett
Employees: 28,500
Jobs Added Last Year: 5,000 (+21.3%)
Paper products & office equipment

ADELPHIA COMMUNICATIONS CORPORATION
5 W. Third St., PO Box 472 Phone: 814-274-9830
Coudersport, PA 16915 Fax: 814-274-8631
Chm, Pres & CEO: John J. Rigas
VP HR: Orby G. Kelley, Jr.
Employees: 2,486
Jobs Added Last Year: 940 (+60.8%)
Cable TV

ALLEGHENY HEALTH, EDUCATION AND RESEARCH
320 E. North Ave. Phone: 412-359-3131
Pittsburgh, PA 15212 Fax: 412-359-6606
Pres & CEO: Sherif S. Abdelhak
Dir HR: Kasper Bauer
Employees: 14,018
Jobs Added Last Year: —
Hospitals

ADVANTA CORPORATION
300 Welsh Rd. Phone: 215-657-4000
Horsham, PA 19044 Fax: 215-956-0268
Chm & CEO: Dennis Alter
VP HR: John B. Hofmann
Employees: 1,327
Jobs Added Last Year: 245 (+22.6%)
Financial - credit card issuance

ALUMINUM COMPANY OF AMERICA
425 Sixth Ave., Alcoa Bldg. Phone: 412-553-4545
Pittsburgh, PA 15219-1850 Fax: 412-553-4498
Chm & CEO: Paul H. O'Neill
EVP HR: Ronald R. Hoffman
Employees: 63,400
Jobs Cut Last Year: 200 (-.3%)
Metals - nonferrous

AIR PRODUCTS AND CHEMICALS, INC.
7201 Hamilton Blvd. Phone: 610-481-4911
Allentown, PA 18195-1501 Fax: 610-481-5900
Chm, Pres & CEO: Harold A. Wagner
VP HR: Joseph P. McAndrew
Employees: 13,300
Jobs Cut Last Year: 800 (-5.7%)
Chemicals - industrial gases & related equipment; specialty & intermediate chemicals; environmental & energy systems

AMERICAN EAGLE OUTFITTERS, INC.
150 Thornhill Dr., PO Box 788 Phone: 412-776-4857
Warrendale, PA 15095 Fax: 412-776-9758
Chm & CEO: Jay L. Schottenstein
VP HR: Michael E. Bergdahl
Employees: 4,307
Jobs Added Last Year: 837 (+24.1%)
Retail - casual apparel, shoes & accessories

AIRGAS, INC.
100 Matsonford Rd., Ste. 550 Phone: 610-687-5253
Radnor, PA 19087-4579 Fax: 610-687-1052
Chm & CEO: Peter McCausland
Dir HR: Don Daemer
Employees: 3,600
Jobs Added Last Year: 800 (+28.6%)
Chemicals - compressed gas distribution for industrial, medical & specialty uses

AMETEK, INC.
Station Sq. Phone: 610-647-2121
Paoli, PA 19301 Fax: 610-296-3412
Chm & CEO: Walter E. Blankley
Corp Dir HR: Robert Zuzack
Employees: 6,000
Jobs Cut Last Year: 200 (-3.2%)
Electrical products - electromechanical devices, process equipment & precision instruments

PENNSYLVANIA

AMP INCORPORATED
PO Box 3608　　　　　　　Phone: 717-564-0100
Harrisburg, PA 17105-3608　Fax: 717-780-6348
Pres & CEO: William J. Hudson, Jr.
VP Global HR: Philip G. Guarneschelli
Employees: 26,900
Jobs Added Last Year: 1,800 (+7.2%)
Electrical connectors that link communications & computer systems

AMSCO INTERNATIONAL, INC.
500 Grant St., Ste. 5000　　Phone: 412-338-6500
Pittsburgh, PA 15219　　　　Fax: 412-338-6501
Pres & CEO: Daniel P. Barry
VP HR & Admin: Gregory R. Spencer
Employees: 4,370
Jobs Added Last Year: 209 (+5%)
Medical products - decontamination & infection control products

APOGEE, INC.
1018 W. Ninth Ave., Ste. 202　Phone: 610-992-7670
King of Prussia, PA 19406-9233　Fax: 610-992-0483
CEO: John H. Foster
Dir HR: Jane P. Stanton
Employees: 319
Jobs Added Last Year: 83 (+35.2%)
Health care - outpatient mental health group practices

ARAMARK CORPORATION
1101 Market St.　　　　　Phone: 215-238-3000
Philadelphia, PA 19107　　Fax: 215-238-3333
Chm, Pres & CEO: Joseph Neubauer
SVP Corp Comm (HR): James E. Ksansnak
Employees: 131,000
Jobs Added Last Year: 7,000 (+5.6%)
Diversified operations - food services; uniform rentals; child care services; magazine distribution

ARCO CHEMICAL COMPANY
3801 W. Chester Pike　　　Phone: 610-359-2000
Newtown Square, PA 19073　Fax: 610-359-2722
Pres & CEO: Alan R. Hirsig
VP HR: Frank Welsh
Employees: 4,309
Jobs Added Last Year: 89 (+2.1%)
Chemicals - specialty

ARMSTRONG WORLD INDUSTRIES
313 W. Liberty St.　　　　Phone: 717-397-0611
Lancaster, PA 17604-3001　Fax: 717-396-2126
Chm, Pres & CEO: George A. Lorch
VP & Dir HR: John N. Jordin
Employees: 21,000
Jobs Cut Last Year: 2,500 (-10.6%)
Building products - tile, flooring, insulation & adhesives

ARNOLD INDUSTRIES INC.
625 S. Fifth Ave.　　　　Phone: 717-274-2521
Lebanon, PA 17042　　　Fax: 717-274-5593
Chm & Pres: Edward H. Arnold
VP HR: Andy Kerlik
Employees: 2,600
Jobs Added Last Year: 1,300 (+100%)
Transportation - truck

ASPLUNDH TREE EXPERT CO.
708 Blair Mill Rd.　　　　Phone: 215-784-4200
Willow Grove, PA 19090　Fax: 215-784-4493
Pres & CEO: Christopher B. Asplundh
HR: William Hughes
Employees: 14,500
Jobs Added Last Year: 0
Business services - tree trimming

BELL ATLANTIC CORPORATION
1717 Arch St.　　　　　Phone: 215-963-6000
Philadelphia, PA 19103　Fax: 215-963-6470
VC, Pres & CEO: James G. Cullen
VP HR: Charles W. Crist
Employees: 73,600
Jobs Added Last Year: 2,200 (+3.1%)
Utility - telephone; cable TV & interactive multimedia

BETHLEHEM STEEL CORPORATION
1170 Eighth Ave.　　　　Phone: 610-694-2424
Bethlehem, PA 18016-7699　Fax: 610-694-1509
Chm & CEO: Curtis H. Barnette
VP HR: Benjamin C. Boylston
Employees: 20,700
Jobs Cut Last Year: 4,200 (-16.9%)
Steel - production

PENNSYLVANIA

BETZ LABORATORIES, INC.
4636 Somerton Rd. Phone: 215-355-3300
Trevose, PA 19047 Fax: 215-953-5544
Pres & CEO: William R. Cook
VP HR: June B. Barry
Employees: 4,050
Jobs Cut Last Year: 65 (-1.6%)
Chemicals - specialty

CABLE DESIGN TECHNOLOGIES CORPORATION
Foster Plaza 7, 661 Andersen Dr. Phone: 412-937-2300
Pittsburgh, PA 15220 Fax: 412-937-9690
Pres & CEO: P. M. Olson
Dir HR: Jack Winter
Employees: 748
Jobs Added Last Year: 123 (+19.7%)
Wire & cable products - high-performance copper & fiber-optic data transmission cables

BLACK BOX CORPORATION
1000 Park Dr. Phone: 412-746-5500
Lawrence, PA 15055 Fax: 412-746-0746
Pres & CEO: Jeffery M. Boetticher
Dir Human Dev: Kathy Bullions
Employees: 615
Jobs Added Last Year: 134 (+27.9%)
Retail - mail order communications, networking & related computer connectivity products

CABOT MEDICAL CORPORATION
2021 Cabot Blvd. West Phone: 215-752-8300
Langhorne, PA 19047 Fax: 215-750-0161
CEO & Pres: Warren G. Wood
Dir HR: Judy Smoyer
Employees: 376
Jobs Added Last Year: 180 (+91.8%)
Medical products - gynecological & surgery devices

BLAIR CORPORATION
220 Hickory St. Phone: 814-723-3600
Warren, PA 16366 Fax: 814-726-6123
Pres & Chm: Murray K. McComas
No central personnel officer
Employees: 2,250
Jobs Added Last Year: 150 (+7.1%)
Retail - mail order & direct (apparel & home furnishings)

CARPENTER TECHNOLOGY CORPORATION
101 W. Bern St. Phone: 610-208-2000
Reading, PA 19612 Fax: 610-208-3579
Chm, Pres & CEO: Robert W. Cardy
VP Human & Administrative Svcs: Robert W. Lodge
Employees: 3,697
Jobs Added Last Year: 359 (+10.8%)
Steel - specialty alloys

BON-TON STORES, INC.
2801 E. Market St. Phone: 717-757-7660
York, PA 17402 Fax: 717-751-3198
Chm & CEO: M. Thomas Grumbacher
SVP HR: Theodore Johnson
Employees: 4,800
Jobs Cut Last Year: 100 (-2%)
Retail - regional department stores

CASTLE ENERGY CORPORATION
100 Matsonford Rd., Ste. 250 Phone: 610-995-9400
Radnor, PA 19087 Fax: 610-995-2477
Chm & CEO: Joseph L. Castle II
Dir HR: David Williamson
Employees: 808
Jobs Added Last Year: 406 (+101%)
Oil & gas - US exploration & production

C-COR ELECTRONICS, INC.
60 Decibel Rd. Phone: 814-238-2461
State College, PA 16801 Fax: 814-238-4065
Chm & CEO: Richard E. Perry
Dir HR: Edwin Childs
Employees: 1,010
Jobs Added Last Year: 485 (+92.4%)
Telecommunications equipment - data transmission systems

CEDAR GROUP, INC.
1000 Conshohocken Rd., Ste. 400 Phone: 514-634-3551
Conshohocken, PA 19428-1070 Fax: 514-634-2448
Chm, Pres & CEO: Michel L. Marengere
Dir HR: Carmen Sd-cyr
Employees: 97
Jobs Added Last Year: 73 (+304.2%)
Metal products - fasteners

PENNSYLVANIA

CENTRAL SPRINKLER CORPORATION
451 N. Cannon Ave. Phone: 215-362-0700
Lansdale, PA 19446 Fax: 215-362-5385
CEO, Sec & Treas: George G. Meyer
Mgr HR: Charles Whitney
Employees: 710
Jobs Added Last Year: 180 (+34%)
Protection - automatic fire sprinkler heads, valves & other components

CHARMING SHOPPES, INC.
450 Winks Ln. Phone: 215-245-9100
Bensalem, PA 19020 Fax: 215-638-6873
Chm & CEO: David V. Wachs
EVP & Corp Dir HR: Anthony A. DeSabato
Employees: 15,200
Jobs Added Last Year: 3,000 (+24.6%)
Retail - apparel & shoes

CIGNA CORPORATION
One Liberty Place Phone: 215-761-1000
Philadelphia, PA 19192-1550 Fax: 215-761-5515
Chm & CEO: Wilson H. Taylor
EVP HR & Svcs: Donald M. Levinson
Employees: 50,600
Jobs Cut Last Year: 1,655 (-3.2%)
Insurance - property & casualty & health

CMAC INVESTMENT CORPORATION
8 Penn Center Phone: 215-564-6600
Philadelphia, PA 19103 Fax: 215-564-5020
Chm, Pres & CEO: F. P. Filipps
Dir HR: William Marlin
Employees: 310
Jobs Added Last Year: 70 (+29.2%)
Insurance - multiline & misc.

COMCAST CORPORATION
1500 Market St. Phone: 215-665-1700
Philadelphia, PA 19102 Fax: 215-981-7790
Pres: Brian L. Roberts
VP HR: Paul Gillert
Employees: 5,391
Jobs Added Last Year: 64 (+1.2%)
Cable TV

CONRAIL, INC.
2001 Market St. Phone: 215-209-4000
Philadelphia, PA 19101 Fax: 215-209-5567
Chm, Pres & CEO: James A. Hagen
VP HR Dev: Frank H. Nichols
Employees: 25,406
Jobs Added Last Year: 26 (+.1%)
Transportation - rail; hazardous waste handling

CONSOL ENERGY INC.
1800 Washington Rd. Phone: 412-831-4000
Pittsburgh, PA 15241 Fax: 412-831-4916
Pres & CEO: B. R. Brown
VP HR: Buck Hyler
Employees: 10,036
Jobs Added Last Year: —
Coal

CONSOLIDATED NATURAL GAS COMPANY
625 Liberty Ave. Phone: 412-227-1000
Pittsburgh, PA 15222-3199 Fax: 412-227-1304
Chm & CEO: George A. Davidson, Jr.
VP HR & Administrative Svcs: Joseph S. Usaj
Employees: 7,625
Jobs Added Last Year: 10 (+.1%)
Utility - gas distribution

CONTINENTAL MEDICAL SYSTEMS
600 Wilson Ln., PO Box 715 Phone: 717-790-8300
Mechanicsburg, PA 17055-0715 Fax: 717-766-8277
CEO: Rocco A. Ortenzio
Dir HR: Frank Fritsch
Employees: 14,000
Jobs Added Last Year: 500 (+3.7%)
Nursing homes

CORESTATES FINANCIAL CORPORATION
PO Box 7618 Phone: 215-973-3827
Philadelphia, PA 19101-7618 Fax: 215-786-7693
Chm & CEO: Terrence A. Larsen
No central personnel officer
Employees: 13,526
Jobs Added Last Year: 2,544 (+23.2%)
Banks - Northeast

PENNSYLVANIA

CROWN HOLDING COMPANY
Pasquerilla Plaza Phone: 814-536-4441
Johnstown, PA 15901 Fax: 814-535-9343
Chm & CEO: Frank J. Pasquerilla
Dir Admin (HR): Donald Zucco
Employees: 9,000
Jobs Added Last Year: —
Real estate operations - shopping malls, motels

DENTSPLY INTERNATIONAL INC.
570 W. College Ave. Phone: 717-845-7511
York, PA 17405 Fax: 717-846-0256
Chm & CEO: Burton C. Borgelt
Corp Dir HR: James R. Wingert
Employees: 4,600
Jobs Added Last Year: 1,060 (+29.9%)
Medical equipment - x-ray products

CROWN CORK & SEAL COMPANY
9300 Ashton Rd. Phone: 215-698-5100
Philadelphia, PA 19136 Fax: 215-676-7245
Chm, Pres & CEO: William J. Avery
VP HR: Gary L. Burgess
Employees: 21,254
Jobs Added Last Year: 876 (+4.3%)
Containers - metal & plastic; packaging machinery

EXIDE CORPORATION
645 Penn St., PO Box 14205 Phone: 610-378-0500
Reading, PA 19612-4205 Fax: 610-378-0315
Chm, Pres & CEO: Arthur M. Hawkins
VP HR: Jack J. Sosiak
Employees: 5,641
Jobs Added Last Year: 1,435 (+34.1%)
Automotive & trucking - car batteries

CSS INDUSTRIES, INC.
1845 Walnut St., Ste. 800 Phone: 215-569-9900
Philadelphia, PA 19103 Fax: 215-569-9979
Chm, Pres & CEO: Jack Farber
Mgr Admin (HR): Jacqueline Tully
Employees: 3,066
Jobs Added Last Year: 1,021 (+49.9%)
Paper & paper products - decorative paper products

FIRST COMMONWEALTH FINANCIAL CORP.
22 N. Sixth St. Phone: 412-349-7220
Indiana, PA 15701 Fax: 412-349-6427
Pres & CEO: Joseph E. O'Dell
HR Administrator: Thad C. Clements
Employees: 1,040
Jobs Added Last Year: 134 (+14.8%)
Banks - Northeast

DAY & ZIMMERMANN INCORPORATED
1818 Market St. Phone: 610-299-8295
Philadelphia, PA 19103 Fax: 610-975-6666
Chm, Pres & CEO: Harold L. "Spike" Yoh, Jr.
VP HR: Anthony G. Natale
Employees: 12,000
Jobs Added Last Year: 400 (+3.4%)
Consulting & engineering

FOAMEX INTERNATIONAL INC.
1000 Columbia Ave. Phone: 610-859-3000
Linwood, PA 19061 Fax: 610-859-3162
Chm & CEO: Marshall S. Cogan
VP HR: Donald Mallo
Employees: 5,400
Jobs Added Last Year: 1,135 (+26.6%)
Rubber & plastic products - polyurethane foam

DEB SHOPS, INC.
9401 Blue Grass Rd. Phone: 215-676-6000
Philadelphia, PA 19114 Fax: 215-969-2830
Chm & CEO: Marvin Rounick
Dir HR: Pat Okun
Employees: 3,400
Jobs Added Last Year: 200 (+6.3%)
Retail - apparel & shoes

FRANCISCAN HEALTH SYSTEM
One MacIntyre Dr. Phone: 215-358-3950
Aston, PA 19014 Fax: 215-358-4207
Pres & CEO: Ronald R. Aldrich
VP HR: Edward T. Kane
Employees: 14,000
Jobs Added Last Year: —
Hospitals

PENNSYLVANIA

GENERAL NUTRITION COMPANIES, INC.
921 Penn Ave. Phone: 412-288-4600
Pittsburgh, PA 15222 Fax: 412-288-2074
Pres & CEO: William E. Watts
Dir HR: Ilene Scott
Employees: 6,402
Jobs Added Last Year: 702 (+12.3%)
Retail - vitamins

HARSCO CORPORATION
350 Poplar Church Rd. Phone: 717-763-7064
Camp Hill, PA 17001-8888 Fax: 717-763-6424
Chm, Pres & CEO: Derek C. Hathaway
VP HR: Richard Hawkins
Employees: 14,200
Jobs Added Last Year: 3,700 (+35.2%)
Metal processing & fabrication

GENESIS HEALTH VENTURES, INC.
148 W. State St. Phone: 610-444-6350
Kennett Square, PA 19348 Fax: 610-444-3365
Chm & CEO: Michael R. Walker
Dir HR: James Tabak
Employees: 14,500
Jobs Added Last Year: 6,500 (+81.3%)
Health care - outpatient & home

HEALTHCARE SERVICES GROUP, INC.
2643 Huntingdon Pike Phone: 215-938-1661
Huntingdon Valley, PA 19006 Fax: 215-938-1590
Chm & CEO: Daniel P. McCartney
Payroll Admin (HR): Nick Marino
Employees: 8,880
Jobs Added Last Year: 1,040 (+13.3%)
Building - maintenance & services

GERIATRIC & MEDICAL COMPANIES, INC.
5601 Chestnut St. Phone: 215-476-2250
Philadelphia, PA 19139 Fax: 215-748-8862
Chm, Pres & CEO: Daniel Veloric
VP Legal & HR & Asst Sec: James J. Wankmiller
Employees: 4,150
Jobs Added Last Year: 263 (+6.8%)
Nursing homes; medical transport services; medical home care services; pharmacy services

HERLEY INDUSTRIES, INC.
10 Industry Dr. Phone: 717-397-2777
Lancaster, PA 17603 Fax: 717-397-4475
CEO: Lee N. Blatt
Dir Personnel: Patricia Walsh
Employees: 322
Jobs Added Last Year: 189 (+142.1%)
Electronics - military

GIANT EAGLE INC.
101 Kappa Dr. Phone: 412-963-6200
Pittsburgh, PA 15238 Fax: 412-963-0374
Chm & CEO: David S. Shapira
VP Personnel: Raymond A. Huber
Employees: 11,800
Jobs Added Last Year: –
Retail - supermarkets

HERSHEY FOODS CORPORATION
100 Crystal A Dr. Phone: 717-534-6799
Hershey, PA 17033 Fax: 717-534-4078
Chm & CEO: Kenneth L. Wolfe
VP HR: Sharon A. Lambly
Employees: 14,300
Jobs Added Last Year: 600 (+4.4%)
Food - confectionery

H. J. HEINZ COMPANY
600 Grant St. Phone: 412-456-5700
Pittsburgh, PA 15219 Fax: 412-237-5377
Chm, Pres & CEO: Anthony J.F. O'Reilly
VP Organization Dev & Admin (HR): George C. Greer
Employees: 35,700
Jobs Cut Last Year: 2,000 (-5.3%)
Food - ketchup, tuna (StarKist), pet food (9-Lives), diet program (Weight Watchers)

HUNT MANUFACTURING CO.
230 S. Broad St. Phone: 215-732-7700
Philadelphia, PA 19102-4167 Fax: 215-876-5331
Chm & CEO: Ronald J. Naples
VP HR: John W. Carney
Employees: 2,000
Jobs Added Last Year: 100 (+5.3%)
Office & art materials

PENNSYLVANIA

INTEGRA FINANCIAL CORPORATION
4 PPG Place Phone: 412-644-7669
Pittsburgh, PA 15222-5408 Fax: 412-261-7279
Chm & CEO: William F. Roemer
VP HR: Mary York
Employees: 4,025
Jobs Added Last Year: 120 (+3.1%)
Banks - Northeast

INTEGRATED CIRCUIT SYSTEMS, INC.
2435 Blvd. of the Generals Phone: 610-630-5300
Norristown, PA 19403 Fax: 610-666-1099
CEO: David Fear
Mgr HR: Thomas Halphen
Employees: 279
Jobs Added Last Year: 63 (+29.2%)
Electrical components - integrated circuits

INTELLIGENT ELECTRONICS, INC.
411 Eagleview Blvd. Phone: 215-458-5500
Exton, PA 19341 Fax: 215-458-8454
Chm & CEO: Richard D. Sanford
Mgr HR: Linda Cahill
Employees: 809
Jobs Added Last Year: 283 (+53.8%)
Computers - retail & wholesale

JLG INDUSTRIES, INC.
JLG Drive Phone: 717-485-5161
McConnellsburg, PA 17233-9502 Fax: 717-485-6417
Pres & CEO: L. David Black
VP HR: Samuel D. Swope
Employees: 1,324
Jobs Added Last Year: 310 (+30.6%)
Machinery - elevating work platforms & truck-mounted materials handling equipment

JONES APPAREL GROUP, INC.
250 Rittenhouse Circle Phone: 215-785-4000
Bristol, PA 19007 Fax: 215-785-1795
Chm & CEO: Sidney Kimmel
Dir HR: Aida Tejero-DeColli
Employees: 1,475
Jobs Added Last Year: 315 (+27.2%)
Apparel - women's & juniors outerwear

KENNAMETAL INC.
Westmoreland Airport, PO Box 231 Phone: 412-539-5000
Latrobe, PA 15650 Fax: 412-539-4629
Pres & CEO: Robert L. McGeehan
Dir HR: Timothy D. Hudson
Employees: 6,600
Jobs Added Last Year: 1,700 (+34.7%)
Machine tools & related products for the metalworking, mining & highway construction industries

KEYSTONE FINANCIAL, INC.
One Keystone Plaza, PO Box 3660 Phone: 717-233-1555
Harrisburg, PA 17105-3660 Fax: 717-231-5759
Pres & CEO: Carl L. Campbell
SVP & Dir HR: Gerry E. Aumiller
Employees: 2,507
Jobs Added Last Year: 276 (+12.4%)
Banks - Northeast

KULICKE AND SOFFA INDUSTRIES, INC.
2101 Blair Mill Rd. Phone: 215-784-6000
Willow Grove, PA 19090 Fax: 215-659-7588
Chm & CEO: C. Scott Kulicke
HR Mgr: Chad Weimer
Employees: 1,035
Jobs Added Last Year: 124 (+13.6%)
Machinery - semiconductor assembly systems, including wafer dicing & die & wire bonding systems

LUKENS INC.
50 S. First Ave. Phone: 610-383-2000
Coatesville, PA 19320-0911 Fax: 610-383-3093
Chm & CEO: R. William Van Sant
VP HR: Richard D. Luzzi
Employees: 4,769
Jobs Added Last Year: 529 (+12.5%)
Steel - specialty alloys

MARLTON TECHNOLOGIES, INC.
111 Presidential Blvd. Phone: 610-664-6900
Bala Cynwyd, PA 19004 Fax: 610-664-6900
Pres & CEO (HR): Robert B. Ginsburg
Employees: 150
Jobs Added Last Year: 25 (+20%)
Business services - trade show exhibit design & on-line information services

PENNSYLVANIA

MASLAND CORPORATION
50 Spring Rd. Phone: 717-249-1866
Carlisle, PA 17013 Fax: 717-258-7576
Chm & CEO: William J. Branch
VP HR: Richard G. Sears
Employees: 3,600
Jobs Added Last Year: 600 (+20%)
Automotive & trucking - carpet & vinyl interior products

MASTECH SYSTEMS CORPORATION
2090 Greentree Rd., 1st Fl. Phone: 412-279-6400
Pittsburgh, PA 15220 Fax: 412-279-6870
Chm: Sunil Wadhwani
Dir HR: Rajeev Srinastava
Employees: 1,200
Jobs Added Last Year: 450 (+60%)
Computers - systems integration services & custom programming

MELLON BANK CORPORATION
One Mellon Bank Center Phone: 412-234-5000
Pittsburgh, PA 15258-0001 Fax: 412-234-6265
Chm, Pres & CEO: Frank V. Cahouet
EVP HR: D. Michael Roark
Employees: 21,400
Jobs Added Last Year: 3,400 (+18.9%)
Banks - Northeast

MERIDIAN BANCORP, INC.
35 N. Sixth St. Phone: 610-655-2000
Reading, PA 19601 Fax: 610-655-2492
Pres & CEO: George W. Grosz
EVP HR: R. William Holland
Employees: 6,917
Jobs Added Last Year: 1,064 (+18.2%)
Banks - Northeast

MICHAEL BAKER CORPORATION
420 Rouser Rd., Bldg. 3 Phone: 412-269-6300
Coraopolis, PA 15108 Fax: 412-269-2534
CEO: Charles I. Homan
VP HR: Frederick J. Slack
Employees: 3,863
Jobs Added Last Year: 949 (+32.6%)
Engineering - R&D services; operations & maintenance services

MYLAN LABORATORIES INC.
1030 Century Bldg., 130 Seventh St. Phone: 412-232-0100
Pittsburgh, PA 15222 Fax: 412-232-0123
Chm, Pres & CEO: Milan Puskar
Dir HR: Robert Myers
Employees: 1,037
Jobs Added Last Year: 527 (+103.3%)
Drugs - generic

NATIONAL PENN BANCSHARES, INC.
Philadelphia & Reading Aves. Phone: 610-367-6001
Boyertown, PA 19512 Fax: 610-369-6349
Pres & CEO: Lawrence T. Jilk, Jr.
VP & HR Mgr: Earl J. Houseknecht
Employees: 615
Jobs Added Last Year: 106 (+20.8%)
Banks - Northeast

NOVACARE, INC.
1016 W. Ninth Ave. Phone: 610-992-7200
King of Prussia, PA 19406 Fax: 610-992-3328
Chm & CEO: John H. Foster
SVP HR: Arthur T. "Bud" Locilento, Jr.
Employees: 11,512
Jobs Added Last Year: 3,762 (+48.5%)
Medical services - hospital, outpatient & home therapy & rehabilitation services

OWOSSO CORPORATION
100 Front St., Ste. 1400 Phone: 610-834-0222
West Conshohocken, PA 19428 Fax: 610-834-8664
Chm & CEO: George B. Lemmon, Sr.
EVP Corp Dev, Treas & Sec (HR): George B. Lemmon, Jr.
Employees: 976
Jobs Added Last Year: 191 (+24.3%)
Machinery - electric motors & electromechanical timers, heat transfer coils & replacement camshaft bearings

PECO ENERGY CO.
2301 Market St., PO Box 8699 Phone: 215-841-4000
Philadelphia, PA 19101 Fax: 215-841-6830
Chm & CEO: Joseph F. Paquette, Jr.
VP HR: Bruce Allhouse
Employees: 9,391
Jobs Cut Last Year: 378 (-3.9%)
Utility - electric power

 An in-depth profile of this company is available by fax. Call 800-510-4452 and use your touch-tone phone to put in the 5-digit code at the prompt. Only $2.95 each with your credit card. See page 12 for more details.

PENNSYLVANIA

PENN MUTUAL LIFE INSURANCE CO.
Independence Sq. Phone: 215-956-8000
Philadelphia, PA 19172 Fax: 215-956-8347
Chm & CEO: John E. Tait
VP HR: Catherine B. Strauss
Employees: 1,110
Jobs Added Last Year: 210 (+23.3%)
Insurance - life

PPG INDUSTRIES, INC.
One PPG Place Phone: 412-434-3131
Pittsburgh, PA 15272 Fax: 412-434-2448
Chm & CEO: Jerry E. Dempsey
SVP HR: Russell L. Crane
Employees: 31,400
Jobs Cut Last Year: 900 (-2.8%)
Chemicals - diversified; glass; coatings & resins; biomedical products

PENNSYLVANIA POWER & LIGHT COMPANY
Two N. Ninth St. Phone: 610-774-5151
Allentown, PA 18101-1179 Fax: 610-774-4198
Chm, Pres & CEO: William F. Hecht
VP HR & Dev: Robert S. Gombos
Employees: 7,500
Jobs Cut Last Year: 177 (-2.3%)
Utility - electric power

QUAD SYSTEMS CORPORATION
Two Electronic Dr. Phone: 215-657-6202
Horsham, PA 19044 Fax: 215-657-5013
Pres & CEO: David W. Smith
HR Dir: Craig Walker
Employees: 292
Jobs Added Last Year: 76 (+35.2%)
Machinery - printed circuit board surface mount assembly equipment

THE PEP BOYS - MANNY, MOE & JACK
3111 W. Allegheny Ave. Phone: 215-229-9000
Philadelphia, PA 19132 Fax: 215-226-2323
Chm, Pres & CEO: Mitchell G. Leibovitz
VP HR: Roger A. Rendin
Employees: 14,895
Jobs Added Last Year: 1,504 (+11.2%)
Retail - auto parts

RENAL TREATMENT CENTERS INC.
1180 W. Swedesford Rd. Phone: 610-644-4796
Berwyn, PA 19312 Fax: 610-889-7415
Pres & CEO: Robert L. Mayer, Jr.
Dir HR: Dick Fitzgerald
Employees: 616
Jobs Added Last Year: 249 (+67.8%)
Health care - outpatient dialysis treatments to patients with end-stage kidney failure

PIERCING PAGODA, INC.
3910 Adler Place Phone: 610-691-0437
Bethlehem, PA 18002 Fax: 610-694-9077
CEO: Richard H. Penske
Dir HR: Beverly Hamrick
Employees: 1,419
Jobs Added Last Year: 79 (+5.9%)
Retail - jewelry kiosk stores

RESPIRONICS, INC.
1001 Murry Ridge Dr. Phone: 412-733-0200
Murrysville, PA 15668-8550 Fax: 412-733-0299
Pres & CEO: Dennis S. Meteny
Mgr HR: William Decker
Employees: 1,187
Jobs Added Last Year: 226 (+23.5%)
Medical products - respiratory products

PNC BANK CORPORATION
Fifth Ave. & Wood St. Phone: 412-762-2666
Pittsburgh, PA 15265 Fax: 412-762-6238
Chm & CEO: Thomas H. O'Brien
SVP HR: Susan B. Bohn
Employees: 21,100
Jobs Added Last Year: 3,300 (+18.5%)
Banks - Northeast

RIGHT MANAGEMENT CONSULTANTS
1818 Market St. Phone: 215-988-1588
Philadelphia, PA 19103-3614 Fax: 215-988-9112
Chm & CEO: Richard J. Pinola
Mgr HR: Sally Barlow
Employees: 501
Jobs Added Last Year: 181 (+56.6%)
Consulting - outplacement services

HOOVER'S MASTERLIST OF AMERICA'S TOP 2,500 EMPLOYERS

PENNSYLVANIA

RITE AID CORPORATION
30 Hunter Ln. Phone: 717-761-2633
Camp Hill, PA 17011 Fax: 717-975-5871
Chm & CEO: Alex Grass
SVP Personnel: Robert R. Souder
Employees: 27,364
Jobs Cut Last Year: 386 (-1.4%)
Retail - discount drug stores in the eastern US

SERVISTAR CORP.
PO Box 1510 Phone: 412-283-4567
Butler, PA 16003 Fax: 412-284-6320
Pres & CEO: Paul E. Pentz
SVP HR: Russell A. Thomas
Employees: 2,200
Jobs Added Last Year: 193 (+9.6%)
Building products - retail & wholesale

ROHM AND HAAS COMPANY
100 Independence Mall West Phone: 215-592-3000
Philadelphia, PA 19106-2399 Fax: 215-592-3377
Chm & CEO: J. Lawrence Wilson
VP HR: Marisa Guerin
Employees: 12,203
Jobs Cut Last Year: 782 (-6%)
Chemicals - diversified

SOFTMART, INC.
467 Creamery Way Phone: 610-524-7440
Exton, PA 19341 Fax: 610-363-1438
Pres & CEO: A. Richard Sloane
VP HR: Brenda Reis
Employees: 450
Jobs Added Last Year: 250 (+125%)
Computers - supplier of business software, networks, peripherals & consulting services

SAFEGUARD SCIENTIFICS, INC.
435 Devon Park Dr. Phone: 610-293-0600
Wayne, PA 19087 Fax: 610-293-0601
Chm, Pres & CEO: Warren V. Musser
Dir Corp Admin (HR): Gerald M. Hogan
Employees: 3,140
Jobs Added Last Year: 690 (+28.2%)
Financial - investments in technology companies

SOVEREIGN BANCORP, INC.
1130 Berkshire Blvd. Phone: 610-320-8400
Wyomissing, PA 19610 Fax: 610-320-8448
Pres & CEO: Jay S. Sidhu
Dir Team Member Svcs (HR): Sandra J. Penney
Employees: 1,280
Jobs Added Last Year: 294 (+29.8%)
Financial - savings & loans

SCOTT PAPER COMPANY
Scott Plaza Phone: 610-522-5000
Philadelphia, PA 19113 Fax: 610-522-5129
Chm & CEO: Albert J. Dunlap
Dir HR: Barbara A. Rice
Employees: 26,900
Jobs Added Last Year: 400 (+1.5%)
Paper & paper products - personal, printing & publishing paper

SPECTRUM CONTROL, INC.
6000 W. Ridge Rd. Phone: 814-835-4000
Erie, PA 16506 Fax: 814-455-2550
CEO: John L. Johnston
Dir HR: Robert McKenna
Employees: 584
Jobs Added Last Year: 169 (+40.7%)
Electrical products - electromagnetic compatability products

SELAS CORPORATION OF AMERICA
PO Box 200 Phone: 215-646-6600
Dresher, PA 19025 Fax: 215-646-3536
CEO & Pres: Stephen F. Ryan
Dir HR: Robert Mason
Employees: 210
Jobs Added Last Year: 120 (+133.3%)
Diversified operations - heat processing products; tire holders

STRAWBRIDGE & CLOTHIER
801 Market St. Phone: 215-629-6000
Philadelphia, PA 19107 Fax: 215-629-7835
Chm: Francis Strawbridge III
VP Personnel: David W. Strawbridge
Employees: 15,298
Jobs Added Last Year: 1,945 (+14.6%)
Retail - regional department stores

PENNSYLVANIA

SUN COMPANY, INC.
10 Penn Center, 1801 Market St. Phone: 215-977-3000
Philadelphia, PA 19103-1699 Fax: 215-977-3409
Chm, Pres & CEO: Robert H. Campbell
VP HR: Albert Little
Employees: 14,500
Jobs Added Last Year: 281 (+2%)
Oil refining & marketing

UGI CORPORATION
PO Box 858 Phone: 610-337-1000
Valley Forge, PA 19482 Fax: 610-992-3259
CEO: James A. Sutton
Dir HR: Starr Keat
Employees: 3,520
Jobs Added Last Year: 130 (+3.8%)
Utility - gas distribution

TELEFLEX INC.
630 W. Germantown Pike Phone: 610-834-6301
Plymouth Meeting, PA 19462 Fax: 610-834-8307
Chm & CEO: Lennox K. Black
VP HR: Robert D. Boldt
Employees: 7,920
Jobs Added Last Year: 1,000 (+14.5%)
Instruments - control

UNION PACIFIC CORPORATION
Martin Towers, Eighth & Eaton Aves. Phone: 610-861-3200
Bethlehem, PA 18018 Fax: 610-861-3220
Chm & CEO: Drew Lewis
SVP HR: Ursula F. Fairbairn
Employees: 47,126
Jobs Added Last Year: 1,087 (+2.4%)
Transportation - rail & trucking; natural resources; waste management

TOLL BROTHERS, INC.
3103 Philmont Ave. Phone: 215-938-8000
Huntingdon Valley, PA 19006-4298 Fax: 215-938-8010
Chm & CEO: Robert I. Toll
Dir HR: Jon Downs
Employees: 1,061
Jobs Added Last Year: 188 (+21.5%)
Building - residential & commercial

UNISYS CORPORATION
PO Box 500 Phone: 215-986-4011
Blue Bell, PA 19424-0001 Fax: 215-986-6850
Chm & CEO: James A. Unruh
VP HR: Thomas E. McKinnon
Employees: 49,000
Jobs Cut Last Year: 5,300 (-9.8%)
Computers - mainframes, workstations, software

TUSCARORA PLASTICS, INC.
800 Fifth Ave. Phone: 412-843-8200
New Brighton, PA 15066 Fax: 412-847-2140
Pres & CEO: John P. O'Leary, Jr.
HR Mgr: Irene McAllister
Employees: 1,045
Jobs Added Last Year: 140 (+15.5%)
Containers - custom molded products for protective packaging

UNIVERSAL HEALTH SERVICES, INC.
367 S. Gulph Rd. Phone: 610-768-3300
King of Prussia, PA 19406 Fax: 610-768-3336
Chm, Pres & CEO: Alan B. Miller
VP HR: Eileen Bove
Employees: 9,700
Jobs Added Last Year: 600 (+6.6%)
Hospitals

U.S. HEALTHCARE, INC.
980 Jolly Rd. Phone: 215-628-4800
Blue Bell, PA 19422 Fax: 215-283-6579
Pres: Leonard Abramson
VP HR: Rob Rosend
Employees: 3,409
Jobs Added Last Year: 564 (+19.8%)
Health maintenance organization

URBAN OUTFITTERS INC.
1809 Walnut St. Phone: 215-564-2313
Philadelphia, PA 19103 Fax: 215-568-1549
Pres & CEO: Richard A. Hayne
HR Mgr: Melanie Kirk
Employees: 1,066
Jobs Added Last Year: 466 (+77.7%)
Retail - apparel & home furnishings for Generation X

PENNSYLVANIA

US FOODSERVICE INC.
1065 Hwy 315, Ste. 203　　Phone: 717-822-0902
Wilkes-Barre, PA 18702　　Fax: 717-822-0909
Chm & CEO: Frank H. Bevevino
VP Admin (HR): William Griffin
Employees: 3,646
Jobs Cut Last Year: 79 (-2.1%)
Food - wholesale to restaurants

VISHAY INTERTECHNOLOGY, INC.
63 Lincoln Hwy.　　Phone: 610-644-1300
Malvern, PA 19355-2120　　Fax: 610-296-0657
Chm & CEO: Felix Zandman
VP & Sec (HR): William J. Spires
Employees: 16,000
Jobs Added Last Year: 1,600 (+11.1%)
Electronics - fixed resistors & capacitors

USX CORP. - DELHI GROUP
600 Grant St.　　Phone: 412-433-1121
Pittsburgh, PA 15219-4776　　Fax: 412-433-5733
Chm & CEO: Charles A. Corry
VP Emp Rel: Thomas W. Sterling III
Employees: 21,527
Jobs Added Last Year: 48 (+.2%)
Oil & gas - gas pipelines

WAWA INC.
260 Baltimore Pike　　Phone: 610-358-8000
Wawa, PA 19063　　Fax: 610-358-8878
Pres & CEO: Richard D. Wood
Dir HR: Vincent P. Anderson
Employees: 2,200
Jobs Added Last Year: 300 (+15.8%)
Retail - convenience stores

USX CORP. - MARATHON GROUP
600 Grant St.　　Phone: 412-433-1121
Pittsburgh, PA 15219-4776　　Fax: 412-433-5733
VC, Marathon Group; Pres, Marathon Oil: Victor G. Beghini
VP HR & Environment, Marathon Oil: Kenneth L. Matheny
Employees: 21,914
Jobs Cut Last Year: 896 (-3.9%)
Oil & gas - integrated

WEIS MARKETS, INC.
1000 S. Second St.　　Phone: 717-286-4571
Sunbury, PA 17801　　Fax: 717-286-3286
Co-Chm: Sigfried Weis
Dir Emp Rel: Alan Corcoran
Employees: 16,000
Jobs Added Last Year: 2,000 (+14.3%)
Retail - supermarkets

USX CORP. - U.S. STEEL GROUP
600 Grant St.　　Phone: 412-433-1121
Pittsburgh, PA 15219-4776　　Fax: 412-433-5733
Chm & CEO: Charles A. Corry
VP Emp Rel: Thomas W. Sterling III
Employees: 21,527
Jobs Added Last Year: 48 (+.2%)
Steel - production

WESTINGHOUSE ELECTRIC CORP.
Westinghouse Bldg., 11 Stanwix St.　　Phone: 412-244-2000
Pittsburgh, PA 15222-1384　　Fax: 412-642-3404
Chm & CEO: Michael H. Jordan
SVP Corp HR & Total Quality: James S. Moore
Employees: 101,654
Jobs Cut Last Year: 7,396 (-6.8%)
Diversified operations - electronic systems; power systems; broadcasting

V. F. CORPORATION
1047 North Park Rd.　　Phone: 610-378-1151
Wyomissing, PA 19610　　Fax: 610-375-9371
Chm & CEO: Lawrence R. Pugh
VP HR & Admin: Harold E. Addis
Employees: 62,000
Jobs Added Last Year: 5,000 (+8.8%)
Apparel - jeans (Lee & Wrangler), sportswear (Jantzen), work clothes, intimate apparel & children's clothes

YORK INTERNATIONAL CORPORATION
631 S. Richland Ave.　　Phone: 717-771-7890
York, PA 17403　　Fax: 717-771-6476
Chm, Pres & CEO: Robert N. Pokelwaldt
VP HR: Wayne J. Kennedy
Employees: 13,800
Jobs Added Last Year: 1,300 (+10.4%)
Building products - a/c & heating

RHODE ISLAND

AFC CABLE SYSTEMS, INC.
50 Kennedy Plaza, Ste. 1250 Phone: 401-453-2000
Providence, RI 02903 Fax: 401-453-2009
Pres & CEO: Harry M. Crump
HR Mgr: Edward J. Verissino
Employees: 625
Jobs Added Last Year: 130 (+26.3%)
Wire & cable products - custom & modular electrical cable systems

AMERICAN POWER CONVERSION
132 Fairgrounds Rd. Phone: 401-789-5735
West Kingston, RI 02892 Fax: 401-789-3710
Chm, Pres & CEO: Rodger B. Dowdell,, Jr.
Emp Coordinator: Georgina Rivera-Santos
Employees: 914
Jobs Added Last Year: 183 (+25%)
Electrical products - uninterruptible power supplies & battery backup for computer systems

AMTROL INC.
1400 Division Rd. Phone: 401-884-6300
West Warwick, RI 02893-1008 Fax: 401-885-2567
CEO: Chester H. Kirk
Corp Personnel Mgr: Michael A. Montigny
Employees: 1,100
Jobs Added Last Year: 100 (+10%)
Metal products

BROWN & SHARPE MANUFACTURING COMPANY
Precision Park, 200 Frenchtown Rd. Phone: 401-886-2000
North Kingstown, RI 02852-1700 Fax: 401-886-2762
Pres & CEO: Fred M. Stuber
Dir HR: Ralph Chase
Employees: 2,500
Jobs Added Last Year: 957 (+62%)
Electronics - measuring instruments

BUGABOO CREEK STEAK HOUSE, INC.
1275 Wampanoag Trail Phone: 401-433-5500
East Providence, RI 02915 Fax: 401-433-5986
Chm, Pres & CEO: Edward P. Grace III
VP HR: Corinne A. Sylvia
Employees: 465
Jobs Added Last Year: 150 (+47.6%)
Retail - restaurants

FLEET FINANCIAL GROUP, INC.
50 Kennedy Plaza Phone: 401-278-5800
Providence, RI 02903 Fax: 401-278-5801
Chm, Pres & CEO: J. Terrence Murray
SVP HR: Anne Szostak
Employees: 26,000
Jobs Cut Last Year: 1,500 (-5.5%)
Banks - Northeast

GTECH HOLDINGS CORPORATION
55 Technology Way Phone: 401-392-1000
West Greenwich, RI 02817 Fax: 401-392-1234
Co-Chm & CEO: Guy B. Snowden
VP HR: Stephen A. Davidson
Employees: 4,000
Jobs Added Last Year: 900 (+29%)
Leisure & recreation services - lottery & gambling systems; electronic delivery of government entitlements

HASBRO, INC.
1027 Newport Ave. Phone: 401-431-8697
Pawtucket, RI 02861 Fax: 401-727-5433
Chm, Pres & CEO: Alan G. Hassenfeld
SVP HR: Sherry Turner
Employees: 12,500
Jobs Added Last Year: 1,500 (+13.6%)
Toys - games & hobby products, infant products

OUTLET COMMUNICATIONS, INC.
23 Kenney Dr. Phone: 401-455-9200
Cranston, RI 02920 Fax: 401-455-9216
Chm, Pres & CEO: James G. Babb
Corp Administrator (HR): Joanne Scheneil
Employees: 400
Jobs Added Last Year: 105 (+35.6%)
Broadcasting - radio & TV

TEXTRON INC.
40 Westminster St. Phone: 401-421-2800
Providence, RI 02903 Fax: 401-421-2878
Chm & CEO: James F. Hardymon
EVP Admin & Chief HR Off: William F. Wayland
Employees: 56,000
Jobs Added Last Year: 2,000 (+3.7%)
Diversified operations - industrial products; auto parts; finance & insurance; helicopters (Bell) & aircraft (Cessna)

SOUTH CAROLINA

BUILDERS TRANSPORT, INC.
2029 W. DeKalb St. Phone: 803-432-1400
Camden, SC 29020-7005 Fax: 803-425-1721
VC & CEO: Stanford M. Dinstein
VP HR: John W. Pryor
Employees: 3,950
Jobs Added Last Year: 514 (+15%)
Transportation - truck

CONSO PRODUCTS COMPANY
513 N. Duncan Bypass, PO Box 326 Phone: 803-427-9004
Union, SC 29379 Fax: 803-427-8820
Pres & CEO: J. Cary Findlay
Dir HR: Sharon O'Dell
Employees: 1,177
Jobs Added Last Year: 523 (+80%)
Textiles - decorative trimmings for the home furnishings industry

DELTA WOODSIDE INDUSTRIES, INC.
233 N. Main St., Ste. 200 Phone: 803-232-8301
Greenville, SC 29601 Fax: 803-232-6164
Pres & CEO: E. Erwin Maddrey II
VP & Sec (HR): Jane H. Greer
Employees: 8,500
Jobs Added Last Year: 600 (+7.6%)
Apparel

FLAGSTAR COMPANIES, INC.
203 E. Main St. Phone: 803-597-8700
Spartanburg, SC 29319-9966 Fax: 803-597-8780
Chm & CEO: Jerome J. Richardson
SVP HR: Edna K. Morris
Employees: 123,000
Jobs Added Last Year: 7,000 (+6%)
Retail - food service (Canteen) & restaurants (Denny's, Quincy's El Pollo Loco, Hardee's franchisee)

GREENWOOD MILLS
PO Drawer 1017 Phone: 803-229-2571
Greenwood, SC 29648 Fax: 803-229-1111
Chm: James C. Self, Jr.
SVP HR: Bill Whaley
Employees: 7,000
Jobs Cut Last Year: 200 (-2.8%)
Textiles - denim, other fabrics

INSIGNIA FINANCIAL GROUP INC.
PO Box 1089 Phone: 803-239-1000
Greenville, SC 29602 Fax: 803-239-1032
Chm & CEO: A. L. Farkas
SVP HR: S. Richard Sargent
Employees: 7,600
Jobs Added Last Year: 4,000 (+111.1%)
Real estate operations

THE INTERTECH GROUP INC.
4838 Jenkins Ave. Phone: 803-744-5174
North Charleston, SC 29406 Fax: 803-747-4092
CEO: Jerry Zucker
Dir HR: Al Tiedemann
Employees: 5,850
Jobs Added Last Year: —
Chemicals - distribution

JPS TEXTILE GROUP INC.
555 N. Pleasantburg Dr., Ste. 202 Phone: 803-239-3900
Greenville, SC 29607 Fax: 803-271-9939
Chm & CEO: Steven M. Friedman
VP HR: Monnie L. Broome
Employees: 8,000
Jobs Added Last Year: 0
Textiles - mill products

KEMET CORPORATION
2835 Kemet Way Phone: 803-963-6300
Simpsonville, SC 29681-9555 Fax: 803-963-6322
Pres: David E. Maguire
VP HR: Glen Stears
Employees: 7,700
Jobs Added Last Year: 500 (+6.9%)
Electrical components - capacitors

LIBERTY CORPORATION
PO Box 789 Phone: 803-268-8111
Greenville, SC 29602 Fax: 803-292-4411
Pres & CEO: W. Hayne Hipp
VP Quality & Operating VP HR: Kathy Blackwell
Employees: 3,282
Jobs Added Last Year: 118 (+3.7%)
Insurance - life

SOUTH CAROLINA

MILLIKEN & CO.
920 Milliken Rd.
Spartanburg, SC 29303
Chm & CEO: Roger Milliken
VP HR: Tommy Hodge
Employees: 14,000
Jobs Added Last Year: 0
Textiles - mill products
Phone: 803-573-2020
Fax: 803-573-2100

RESOURCE BANCSHARES MORTGAGE GROUP
7909 Parklane Rd.
Columbia, SC 29223
Pres & CEO: Edward J. Sebastian
Dir HR: Mike Watson
Employees: 350
Jobs Added Last Year: 49 (+16.3%)
Financial - mortgages & related services
Phone: 803-741-3000
Fax: 803-741-3583

MULTIMEDIA, INC.
PO Box 1688
Greenville, SC 29602
Chm & CEO: Donald D. Sbarra
VP Personnel Ben: Clyde Baucom
Employees: 4,442
Jobs Added Last Year: 642 (+16.9%)
Broadcasting - radio & TV
Phone: 803-298-4373
Fax: 803-298-4271

RYAN'S FAMILY STEAK HOUSES, INC.
405 Lancaster Ave., PO Box 100
Greer, SC 29652
Chm, Pres & CEO: Charles D. Way
VP HR: James R. Hart
Employees: 14,500
Jobs Added Last Year: 500 (+3.6%)
Retail - restaurants
Phone: 803-879-1000
Fax: 803-877-0974

ONE PRICE CLOTHING STORES, INC.
Hwy. 290, Commerce Park
Duncan, SC 29334
Chm & CEO: Henry D. Jacobs, Jr.
VP HR: Rebecca Luce
Employees: 3,723
Jobs Added Last Year: 894 (+31.6%)
Retail - apparel & shoes
Phone: 803-439-6666
Fax: 803-439-9584

SCANA CORPORATION
1426 Main St.
Columbia, SC 29201
Chm, Pres & CEO: Lawrence Gressette, Jr.
VP HR: M. K. Phalen
Employees: 4,788
Jobs Cut Last Year: 61 (-1.3%)
Utility - electric power
Phone: 803-748-3000
Fax: 803-733-2435

ONEITA INDUSTRIES, INC.
Hwy. 41, Conifer St.
Andrews, SC 29510
Chm & Pres: Robert M. Gintel
HR Dir: Michelle Deese
Employees: 3,400
Jobs Added Last Year: 300 (+9.7%)
Apparel
Phone: 803-264-5225
Fax: 803-264-4262

SONOCO PRODUCTS COMPANY
N. Second St., PO Box 160
Hartsville, SC 29550-0160
Chm & CEO: Charles W. Coker
HR Mgr: Grady Weaver
Employees: 16,472
Jobs Added Last Year: 692 (+4.4%)
Containers - paper
Phone: 803-383-7000
Fax: 803-339-6078

PIEMONTE FOODS INC.
400 Augusta St.
Greenville, SC 29604
Pres & CEO: Virgil L. Clark
Personnel Mgr: Robin Barnett
Employees: 346
Jobs Added Last Year: 83 (+31.6%)
Food - pizza crusts & toppings
Phone: 803-242-0424
Fax: 803-235-0239

SPRINGS INDUSTRIES, INC.
205 N. White St., PO Box 70
Fort Mill, SC 29715
Chm, Pres & CEO: Walter Y. Elisha
VP HR: Richard D. Foster
Employees: 20,300
Jobs Cut Last Year: 600 (-2.9%)
Textiles - home furnishings, finished fabrics, industrial fabrics
Phone: 803-547-1500
Fax: 803-547-1636

SOUTH DAKOTA

DAKOTAH, INC.
One N. Park Ln. Phone: 605-345-4646
Webster, SD 57274-0120 Fax: 605-345-3327
Chm, Pres & CEO: George C. Whyte
Mgr HR: Sharon Jurgens
Employees: 366
Jobs Added Last Year: 4 (+1.1%)
Textiles - home furnishings

RAVEN INDUSTRIES, INC.
205 E. 6th St., PO Box 1007 Phone: 605-336-2750
Sioux Falls, SD 57117-5107 Fax: 605-335-0268
Pres: David A. Christensen
VP Corp Svcs (HR): Gary Conradi
Employees: 1,435
Jobs Added Last Year: 119 (+9%)
Diversified operations - plastics; electronics; sewn products

GATEWAY 2000 INC.
610 Gateway Dr., PO Box 2000 Phone: 605-232-2000
North Sioux City, SD 57049-2000 Fax: 605-232-2023
Chm, Pres & CEO: Theodore W. Waitt
Dir HR: Dwayne Rideout
Employees: 2,832
Jobs Added Last Year: 1,463 (+106.9%)
Computers - mail-order microcomputers & software

SODAK GAMING, INC.
405 E. Omaha Phone: 605-341-5400
Rapid City, SD 57701 Fax: 605-341-1443
Chm & CEO: Michael G. Wordeman
Mgr HR: Jim Swaggart
Employees: 110
Jobs Added Last Year: 37 (+50.7%)
Leisure & recreational products - slot & gaming machines

▼ **Job Web** http://www.jobweb.com

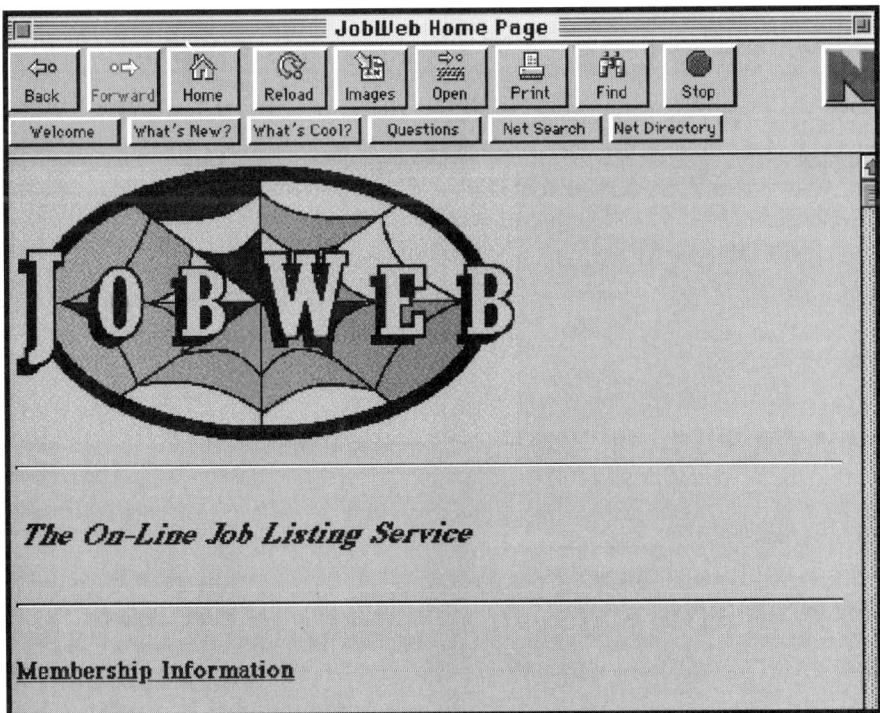

TENNESSEE

A+ COMMUNICATIONS, INC.
2416 Hillsboro Rd. Phone: 615-385-4500
Nashville, TN 37212-3700 Fax: 615-385-4265
CEO: Elliot H. Singer
Dir HR: Earl Posey
Employees: 803
Jobs Added Last Year: 164 (+25.7%)
Telecommunications services - wireless mobile communications (paging) services

ADVOCAT, INC.
7108 Crossroads Blvd., Ste. 313 Phone: 615-370-9255
Brentwood, TN 37027 Fax: 615-373-9865
CEO: Charles W. Birkett
Dir HR: Robert Rice
Employees: 3,100
Jobs Added Last Year: 0
Nursing homes & retirement centers

ARCADIAN PARTNERS, L.P.
6750 Poplar Ave., Ste. 600 Phone: 901-758-5200
Memphis, TN 38138-7419 Fax: 901-758-5206
Pres & CEO: J. Douglas Campbell
VP Admin (HR): Charles W. Lance
Employees: 1,316
Jobs Added Last Year: 275 (+26.4%)
Fertilizers - nitrogen

ASTEC INDUSTRIES, INC.
4101 Jerome Ave., PO Box 72787 Phone: 615-867-4210
Chattanooga, TN 37407 Fax: 615-867-4127
Chm, Pres & CEO: J. Don Brock
No central personnel officer
Employees: 1,185
Jobs Added Last Year: 125 (+11.8%)
Machinery - material handling

AUTOZONE, INC.
3030 Poplar Ave. Phone: 901-325-4600
Memphis, TN 38111 Fax: 901-325-4773
Chm & CEO: Joseph R. Hyde III
VP HR: Francis C. Brown III
Employees: 15,700
Jobs Added Last Year: 2,500 (+18.9%)
Auto parts - retail

CATHERINES STORES CORPORATION
3742 Lamar Ave. Phone: 901-363-3900
Memphis, TN 38118 Fax: 901-794-9726
Pres & CEO: Bernard J. Wein
VP HR: Betty Jewett
Employees: 2,040
Jobs Added Last Year: 805 (+65.2%)
Retail - apparel & shoes

CLAYTON HOMES, INC.
623 Market St. Phone: 615-595-4700
Knoxville, TN 37902 Fax: 615-595-4703
Chm & CEO: James L. Clayton
Dir HR: Greg Stanley
Employees: 3,955
Jobs Added Last Year: 386 (+11.3%)
Building - vertically integrated manufactured homes company (builds, sells, finances & insures)

CORRECTIONS CORP. OF AMERICA
102 Woodmont Blvd. Phone: 615-292-3100
Nashville, TN 37205 Fax: 615-269-8635
VC, Pres & CEO: Doctor R. Crants
Dir Personnel: Shirley Harbison
Employees: 2,279
Jobs Added Last Year: 156 (+7.3%)
Protection - prison construction & operation

COVENANT TRANSPORT, INC.
1320 E. 23rd St. Phone: 615-629-0393
Chattanooga, TN 37404 Fax: 615-624-7985
CEO: David R. Parker
Dir Safety (HR): David Frady
Employees: 1,950
Jobs Added Last Year: 353 (+22.1%)
Transportation - long-haul trucking

CRACKER BARREL
Hartmann Dr., PO Box 787 Phone: 615-444-5533
Lebanon, TN 37088-0787 Fax: 615-443-6780
Chm, Pres & CEO: Dan W. Evins
Dir HR: Wayne Jerkins
Employees: 21,796
Jobs Added Last Year: 3,761 (+20.9%)
Retail - restaurants & gift shops in the central & southern US

TENNESSEE

DIXIE YARNS, INC.
1100 S. Watkins St. Phone: 615-698-2501
Chattanooga, TN 37404 Fax: 615-493-7353
Chm, Pres & CEO: Daniel K. Frierson
VP HR: W. Derek Davis
Employees: 7,300
Jobs Added Last Year: 1,500 (+25.9%)
Textiles - mill products

FIRST TENNESSEE NATIONAL CORPORATION
165 Madison Ave. Phone: 901-523-5630
Memphis, TN 38103 Fax: 901-523-4354
Pres & CEO: Ronald Terry
VP HR: Bob Zizina
Employees: 5,653
Jobs Added Last Year: 1,444 (+34.3%)
Banks - Southeast

DYERSBURG FABRICS INC.
1315 Philips St. Phone: 901-285-2323
Dyersburg, TN 38024 Fax: 901-286-3474
Pres & CEO: T. Eugene McBride
Dir HR: Allen Tillman
Employees: 1,518
Jobs Added Last Year: 398 (+35.5%)
Apparel

FRED'S, INC.
4300 New Getwell Rd. Phone: 901-365-8880
Memphis, TN 38118 Fax: 901-365-8865
CEO: Michael J. Hayes
VP HR: Paul Upchurch
Employees: 3,800
Jobs Added Last Year: 300 (+8.6%)
Retail - discount & variety

EASTMAN CHEMICAL COMPANY
100 N. Eastman Rd. Phone: 615-229-2000
Kingsport, TN 37660 Fax: 615-229-1351
Chm & CEO: Earnest W. Deavenport, Jr.
VP HR, Communications & Public Affairs: William G. Adams
Employees: 18,043
Jobs Cut Last Year: 414 (-2.2%)
Chemicals - polyesters, olefins, organic chemistry & cellulose chemistry

GAYLORD ENTERTAINMENT CO.
2802 Opryland Dr. Phone: 615-885-1000
Nashville, TN 37214 Fax: 615-316-6570
Chm & CEO: Earl W. Wendell
Dir Corp HR: Elwyn Taylor
Employees: 9,100
Jobs Added Last Year: 2,300 (+33.8%)
Leisure & recreational products - musical show park, convention/resort complex; TV stations & cable networks

FEDERAL EXPRESS CORPORATION
2005 Corporate Ave. Phone: 901-395-3382
Memphis, TN 38132 Fax: 901-795-1027
Chm, Pres & CEO: Frederick W. Smith
SVP & Chief Personnel Off: James A. Perkins
Employees: 101,000
Jobs Added Last Year: 6,000 (+6.3%)
Transportation - air freight

GENESCO INC.
1415 Murfreesboro Rd. Phone: 615-367-7000
Nashville, TN 37217-2895 Fax: 615-367-8179
Chm, Pres & CEO: David M. Chamberlain
Dir HR: Steve Little
Employees: 6,950
Jobs Added Last Year: 400 (+6.1%)
Shoes & related apparel

FIRST AMERICAN CORPORATION
First American Center Phone: 615-748-2000
Nashville, TN 37237 Fax: 615-781-7851
Pres & CEO: Dennis C. Bottorff
Dir HR: John W. Smithwick
Employees: 3,465
Jobs Added Last Year: 390 (+12.7%)
Banks - Southeast

GOODY'S FAMILY CLOTHING, INC.
400 Goody's Ln. Phone: 615-966-2000
Knoxville, TN 37933 Fax: 615-675-1940
Pres & CEO: Robert M. Goodfriend
Dir Corp HR: Hazel Moxim
Employees: 6,000
Jobs Added Last Year: 1,175 (+24.4%)
Retail - apparel & shoes

TENNESSEE

HEALTHTRUST, INC., THE HOSPITAL COMPANY
4525 Harding Rd. Phone: 615-383-4444
Nashville, TN 37205 Fax: 615-298-6377
Chm, Pres & CEO: R. Clayton McWhorter
VP HR: Yolanda D. Chelsey
Employees: 33,000
Jobs Added Last Year: –
Hospitals

M.S. CARRIERS, INC.
3171 Directors Row Phone: 901-332-2500
Memphis, TN 38116 Fax: 901-344-4599
Chm & CEO: Michael S. Starnes
Dir HR: Ken Stonebrook
Employees: 3,000
Jobs Added Last Year: 823 (+37.8%)
Transportation - truck

HEALTHWISE OF AMERICA, INC. 16990
102 Woodmont Blvd., Ste. 110 Phone: 615-385-4666
Nashville, TN 37205 Fax: 615-383-0104
Chm & CEO: Ken Melkus
Dir HR: Robin Corey
Employees: 205
Jobs Added Last Year: 58 (+39.5%)
Health maintenance organization - operates in smaller communities in the eastern US

MCKEE FOODS CORPORATION
10260 McKee Rd. Phone: 615-238-7111
Collegedale, TN 37315 Fax: 615-238-7170
Pres & CEO: Ellsworth D. McKee
VP HR: Blair Lake
Employees: 4,400
Jobs Cut Last Year: 100 (-2.2%)
Food - snacks

INGRAM INDUSTRIES INC. 40233
4400 Harding Rd. Phone: 615-298-8200
Nashville, TN 37205 Fax: 615-298-8242
Chm & CEO: E. Bronson Ingram
VP HR: W. Michael Head
Employees: 9,658
Jobs Added Last Year: 1,251 (+14.9%)
Diversified - wholesale books & microcomputer software; drilling equipment; barge service; insurance

MORGAN KEEGAN, INC.
Fifty Front St. Phone: 901-524-4100
Memphis, TN 38103 Fax: 901-524-4158
Pres & CEO: Allen B. Morgan, Jr.
VP HR: Jane Benaar
Employees: 1,088
Jobs Added Last Year: 210 (+23.9%)
Financial - investment bankers

THE KRYSTAL COMPANY
One Union Sq. Phone: 615-757-1550
Chattanooga, TN 37402 Fax: 615-757-1590
Chm & CEO: Carl D. Long
VP HR: James W. Compton
Employees: 8,900
Jobs Added Last Year: 300 (+3.5%)
Retail - restaurants

NORTH AMERICAN ADVANCED MATERIALS
120 Sherlake Dr. Phone: 615-691-2170
Knoxville, TN 37922 Fax: 615-531-7663
Pres & CEO: Dennis Johnson
Quality Assurance Mgr (HR): Margie Hensley
Employees: 79
Jobs Added Last Year: 11 (+16.2%)
Ceramics & ceramic products

LIFE CARE CENTERS OF AMERICA
3570 Keith St. NW Phone: 615-472-9585
Cleveland, TN 37320 Fax: 615-339-8337
Chm & Pres: Forrest L. Preston
VP Professional Dev & HR: Mark Gibson
Employees: 18,000
Jobs Added Last Year: –
Nursing homes

O'CHARLEY'S INC.
3038 Sidco Dr. Phone: 615-256-8500
Nashville, TN 37204 Fax: 615-256-8443
CEO: Gregory L. Burns
HR Off: Carol Arrowood
Employees: 2,770
Jobs Cut Last Year: 30 (-1.1%)
Retail - restaurants

TENNESSEE

OLAN MILLS
PO Box 23456
Chattanooga, TN 37422
Chm: Olan Mills II
Dir HR: Terry Blunt
Employees: 13,300
Jobs Cut Last Year: 700 (-5%)
Retail - portrait photography studios

Phone: 615-622-5141
Fax: 615-624-4815

PROFFITT'S, INC.
115 N. Calderwood, PO Box 388
Alcoa, TN 37701
Chm & CEO: R. Brad Martin
Dir HR: Phyllis Moyers
Employees: 8,700
Jobs Added Last Year: 6,400 (+278.3%)
Retail - regional department stores

Phone: 615-983-7000
Fax: 615-981-6336

ORNDA HEALTHCORP
3401 West End Ave., Ste. 700
Nashville, TN 37203
Chm, Pres & CEO: Charles N. Martin
VP HR: James Johnson
Employees: 15,900
Jobs Added Last Year: 5,600 (+54.4%)
Hospitals

Phone: 615-383-8599
Fax: 615-783-1270

THE PROMUS COMPANIES INC.
1023 Cherry Rd.
Memphis, TN 38117
Pres, CEO & COO: Philip G. Satre
SVP HR & Comm: Ben C. Peternell
Employees: 23,100
Jobs Added Last Year: 100 (+.4%)
Hotels & motels, casinos

Phone: 901-762-8600
Fax: 901-762-8637

PERFORMANCE FOOD GROUP COMPANY
25 Century Blvd., Ste. 509
Nashville, TN 37214
Pres: Robert C. Sledd
VP (HR): David Sober
Employees: 1,250
Jobs Added Last Year: 100 (+8.7%)
Food - wholesale to restaurants

Phone: 615-391-0112
Fax: 615-391-3547

PROVIDENT LIFE AND ACCIDENT INS. CO.
One Fountain Sq.
Chattanooga, TN 37402
Pres & CEO: J. Harold Chandler
SVP HR: Alberto J. Morales
Employees: 4,284
Jobs Cut Last Year: 246 (-5.4%)
Insurance - accident & health

Phone: 615-755-1011
Fax: 615-755-7013

PERKINS FAMILY RESTAURANTS, L.P.
6075 Poplar Ave., Ste. 800
Memphis, TN 38119-4709
CEO: Donald N. Smith
VP HR: Jeanne A. Scott
Employees: 8,500
Jobs Added Last Year: 1,100 (+14.9%)
Retail - restaurants

Phone: 901-766-6400
Fax: 901-766-6482

QUORUM HEALTH GROUP, INC.
155 Franklin Rd., Ste. 401
Brentwood, TN 37027
Pres & CEO: James E. Dalton, Jr.
VP Corp Svcs (HR): C. Thomas Neill
Employees: 8,500
Jobs Added Last Year: 4,700 (+123.7%)
Hospitals & hospital management

Phone: 615-371-7979
Fax: 615-371-4853

PHYCOR, INC.
30 Burton Hills Blvd., Ste. 500
Nashville, TN 37215
Pres & CEO: Joseph C. Hutts
Office Mgr (HR): Ann Ayers
Employees: 5,500
Jobs Added Last Year: 2,500 (+83.3%)
Medical services - medical practice management

Phone: 615-665-9066
Fax: 615-665-9088

REHABILITY CORPORATION
111 Westwood Place, Ste. 210
Brentwood, TN 37027
Pres & CEO: William F. Youree
VP HR: Dennis Buchanan
Employees: 3,700
Jobs Added Last Year: 532 (+16.8%)
Health care - outpatient & home

Phone: 615-377-2937
Fax: 615-371-0002

TENNESSEE

REN CORPORATION - USA
6820 Charlotte Pike Phone: 615-353-4200
Nashville, TN 37209 Fax: 615-353-1635
Pres & CEO: Lawrence J. Centella
VP HR: Glen R. Kielley
Employees: 1,385
Jobs Added Last Year: 142 (+11.4%)
Health care - outpatient & home

SERVICE MERCHANDISE COMPANY
7100 Service Merchandise Dr. Phone: 615-660-6000
Brentwood, TN 37027 Fax: 615-660-7912
Chm, Pres & CEO: Raymond Zimmerman
Administrative VP Assoc Rel: Rod Jeffries
Employees: 22,879
Jobs Added Last Year: 679 (+3.1%)
Retail - catalog showrooms

SHONEY'S, INC.
1727 Elm Hill Pike Phone: 615-391-5201
Nashville, TN 37210 Fax: 615-231-2531
Chm & CEO: Taylor H. Henry
EVP HR: H. Benny Ball
Employees: 30,000
Jobs Added Last Year: 0
Retail - restaurants

SOFAMOR DANEK GROUP, INC.
3092 Directors Row Phone: 901-396-2695
Memphis, TN 38131 Fax: 901-396-2699
Chm & CEO: E. R. Pickard
HR Dir: Philippe Tijou
Employees: 615
Jobs Added Last Year: 309 (+101%)
Medical products - spinal implant devices

TENNESSEE VALLEY AUTHORITY
400 W. Summit Hill Dr. Phone: 615-632-2101
Knoxville, TN 37902 Fax: 615-632-6783
Chm: Craven Crowell
Employment Svcs Mgr: Kathleen Branson
Employees: 18,974
Jobs Cut Last Year: 519 (-2.7%)
Utility - electric power

THOMAS & BETTS CORPORATION
1555 Lynnfield Rd. Phone: 901-682-7766
Memphis, TN 38119 Fax: 901-685-1988
CEO: T. Kevin Dunnigan
VP HR: David Myler
Employees: 8,000
Jobs Added Last Year: 500 (+6.7%)
Electrical connectors

UNION PLANTERS CORPORATION
7130 Goodlett Farms Pkwy. Phone: 901-383-6000
Cordova, TN 38018 Fax: 901-383-6974
CEO: Benjamin W. Rawlins, Jr.
VP HR: Faye Weakley
Employees: 2,960
Jobs Added Last Year: 633 (+27.2%)
Banks - Southeast

THE UNIVERSITY OF TENNESSEE
305 Student Services Bldg. Phone: 615-974-2105
Knoxville, TN 37996 Fax: 615-974-6341
Pres: Joseph E. Johnson
Dir HR: Lola Dodge
Employees: 14,967
Jobs Added Last Year: —
University

VANDERBILT UNIVERSITY
110 21st Ave. South Phone: 615-322-7311
Nashville, TN 37203 Fax: 615-343-7286
Chancellor: Joe B. Wyatt
Assoc Vice Chancellor HR: H. Clint Davidson
Employees: 11,781
Jobs Added Last Year: —
University

VOLUNTEER CAPITAL CORPORATION
3401 West End Ave. Phone: 615-269-1900
Nashville, TN 37202 Fax: 615-269-1999
Chm, Pres & CEO: Lonnie J. Stout II
No central personnel officer
Employees: 1,950
Jobs Added Last Year: 300 (+18.2%)
Retail - restaurants

TEXAS

A. H. BELO CORPORATION
400 S. Record St. Phone: 214-977-6606
Dallas, TX 75202 Fax: 214-977-6603
Chm, Pres & CEO: Robert W. Decherd
HR Dir: Jeff Lamb
Employees: 2,788
Jobs Added Last Year: 161 (+6.1%)
Broadcasting - radio & TV; newspapers (*Dallas Morning News*)

ACE CASH EXPRESS, INC.
1231 Greenway Dr., Ste. 800 Phone: 214-550-5000
Irving, TX 75038-7594 Fax: 214-550-5150
Pres & CEO: Donald H. Neustadt
VP HR: Sherry Detwiler
Employees: 867
Jobs Added Last Year: 150 (+20.9%)
Financial - check-cashing services

ALAMO GROUP, INC.
1502 E. Walnut Phone: 210-379-1480
Seguin, TX 78155 Fax: 210-379-0864
CEO: Oran Logan
Personnel Mgr: Gabrielle Garcia
Employees: 1,040
Jobs Added Last Year: 308 (+42.1%)
Machinery - tractor-mounted farm equipment

ALLWASTE, INC.
5151 San Felipe, Ste. 1600 Phone: 713-623-8777
Houston, TX 77056 Fax: 713-625-7087
Pres & CEO: Robert M. Chiste
Dir Admin & Info Svcs (HR): Richard White
Employees: 3,634
Jobs Added Last Year: 59 (+1.7%)
Pollution control - industrial remediation services

AMBER'S STORES, INC.
11035 Switzer Ave. Phone: 214-349-5300
Dallas, TX 75238 Fax: 214-349-2572
Chm, Pres & CEO: Ron Craft
Dir HR: Larry Burton
Employees: 1,000
Jobs Added Last Year: 226 (+29.2%)
Retail - arts & crafts & picture framing

AMERICAN MEDICAL ELECTRONICS, INC.
250 E. Arapahoe Rd. Phone: 214-918-8300
Richardson, TX 75081 Fax: 214-918-8480
Pres & CEO: John F. Clifford
VP HR: LaVonne M. Chimbel
Employees: 240
Jobs Added Last Year: 32 (+15.4%)
Medical instruments for spinal fusions & recalcitrant bone fractures

AMR CORPORATION   10021
4333 Amon Carter Blvd. Phone: 817-963-1234
Fort Worth, TX 76155 Fax: 817-967-9641
Chm, Pres & CEO: Robert L. Crandall
VP Emp Rel (HR): Jane G. Allen
Employees: 118,900
Jobs Cut Last Year: 400 (-.3%)
Transportation - American Airlines

AMRE, INC.
8585 N. Stemmons Fwy. Phone: 214-819-7000
Dallas, TX 75247 Fax: 214-658-6100
Pres & CEO: V. James Sardo
VP HR: Walker T. Williams
Employees: 3,324
Jobs Added Last Year: 74 (+2.3%)
Building products - doors & trim

AMRESCO, INC.
1845 Woodall Rodgers Fwy. Phone: 214-953-7700
Dallas, TX 75201-2268 Fax: 214-969-5478
CEO & Chm: Robert H. Lutz
Dir HR: Ronald Castleman
Employees: 1,430
Jobs Added Last Year: 998 (+231%)
Consulting - management consulting; apartment building operations

AMTECH CORPORATION   15217
17304 Preston Rd., Ste. E100 Phone: 214-733-6600
Dallas, TX 75252 Fax: 214-733-6699
Pres & CEO: G. Russell Mortenson
VP HR: Joe Crumpton
Employees: 362
Jobs Added Last Year: 90 (+33.1%)
Wireless electronic identification systems, primarily for the transportation & toll road industries

TEXAS

ARMY & AIR FORCE EXCHANGE [40039]
3911 S. Walton Walker Blvd. Phone: 214-312-2011
Dallas, TX 75236 Fax: 214-312-3000
Commander & CEO: Albin G. Wheeler
HR: Michael R. Cunningham
Employees: 72,562
Jobs Cut Last Year: 3,022 (-4%)
Retail - post & base exchanges at military bases

ASSOCIATED MILK PRODUCERS, INC. [40044]
6609 Blanco Rd. Phone: 512-340-9100
San Antonio, TX 78216 Fax: 512-340-9158
Pres: Irvin J. Elkin
HR Mgr: Charlie Warren
Employees: 4,199
Jobs Cut Last Year: 165 (-3.8%)
Food - dairy products

AUSTIN INDUSTRIES INC.
PO Box 1590 Phone: 214-443-5500
Dallas, TX 75221 Fax: 214-443-5581
Pres & CEO: William T. Solomon
Dir HR: Rob Brewer
Employees: 5,500
Jobs Added Last Year: 500 (+10%)
Building - commercial & industrial

BANCTEC, INC.
4435 Spring Valley Rd. Phone: 214-450-7700
Dallas, TX 75244 Fax: 214-450-7867
Chm & CEO: Grahame N. Clark, Jr.
SVP HR: Jim Wimberley
Employees: 1,860
Jobs Added Last Year: 160 (+9.4%)
Optical character recognition

BJ SERVICES COMPANY
5500 NW Central Dr. Phone: 713-462-4239
Houston, TX 77092 Fax: 713-895-5851
CEO: J. W. Stewart
Dir HR: Stephen A. Wright
Employees: 2,629
Jobs Cut Last Year: 3 (-.1%)
Oil & gas - pressure pumping services

THE BOMBAY COMPANY, INC. [16119]
550 Bailey Ave., Ste. 700 Phone: 817-347-8200
Fort Worth, TX 76107 Fax: 817-332-7066
Pres & CEO: Robert E. M. Nourse
VP HR: William S. Goodlatte
Employees: 4,200
Jobs Added Last Year: 1,300 (+44.8%)
Retail - traditionally styled furniture, prints & accessories; country furnishings & accessories (Alex & Ivy)

BRINKER INTERNATIONAL, INC. [10330]
6820 LBJ Fwy. Phone: 214-980-9917
Dallas, TX 75240 Fax: 214-770-9593
Chm & CEO: Norman E. Brinker
VP HR: Janet A. Coen
Employees: 29,000
Jobs Added Last Year: 1,000 (+3.6%)
Retail - restaurants (Chili's, Grady's, Romano's Macaroni Grill, Spageddies, Cozymel's & On the Border)

BROOKSHIRE BROTHERS INCORPORATED
1201 Ellen Trout Dr. Phone: 409-634-8155
Lufkin, TX 75901 Fax: 409-634-8646
CEO: Eugene Brookshire
Dir HR: Tim Hale
Employees: 5,000
Jobs Added Last Year: —
Retail - supermarkets (Budget Chopper & Brookshire Brothers Inc.)

BROOKSHIRE GROCERY COMPANY
1600 SW Loop 323 Phone: 903-534-3000
Tyler, TX 75701 Fax: 903-534-3272
Pres & CEO: James G. Hardin
EVP HR: Tim Brookshire
Employees: 3,200
Jobs Added Last Year: —
Retail - supermarkets (Brookshire Grocery Co. & Super 1 Food Stores)

BROWNING-FERRIS INDUSTRIES, INC. [10343]
757 N. Eldridge, PO Box 3151 Phone: 713-870-8100
Houston, TX 77253 Fax: 713-870-7844
Chm & CEO: William D. Ruckelshaus
VP HR & Emp Rel: Susan J. Piller
Employees: 37,000
Jobs Added Last Year: 5,400 (+17.1%)
Pollution control - waste disposal

TEXAS

BURLINGTON NORTHERN INC.
777 Main St. Phone: 817-878-2000
Fort Worth, TX 76102-5384 Fax: 817-878-2377
Chm & CEO: Gerald Grinstein
EVP Emp Rel: James B. Dagnon
Employees: 30,502
Jobs Cut Last Year: 702 (-2.2%)
Transportation - rail

CELEBRITY, INC.
PO Box 6666 Phone: 903-561-3981
Tyler, TX 75711 Fax: 903-581-2887
CEO: Robert H. Patterson, Jr.
VP Ops (HR): Roger Craft
Employees: 489
Jobs Added Last Year: 213 (+77.2%)
Wholesale trade

BUSINESS RECORDS CORP. HOLDING CO.
1111 W. Mockingbird, Ste. 1400 Phone: 214-905-2590
Dallas, TX 75247 Fax: 214-905-2303
CEO: Perry E. Esping
Dir HR: Laura Stelter
Employees: 1,200
Jobs Added Last Year: 418 (+53.5%)
Office automation

CELLSTAR CORPORATION
1730 Briercroft Dr. Phone: 214-323-0600
Carrollton, TX 75006-7426 Fax: 214-994-1516
Chm & CEO: Alan H. Goldfield
Dir HR: Barbara O'Neal
Employees: 1,061
Jobs Added Last Year: 354 (+50.1%)
Retail - cellular telephones & auto security systems

CALTEX PETROLEUM CORPORATION
125 E. John Carpenter Fwy. Phone: 214-830-1000
Irving, TX 75602 Fax: 214-830-1156
Chm, Pres & CEO: Patrick J. Ward
VP HR: E. M. Schmidt
Employees: 7,800
Jobs Added Last Year: 200 (+2.6%)
Oil & gas - refining & marketing

CENTEX CORPORATION
3333 Lee Pkwy., Ste. 1200 Phone: 214-559-6500
Dallas, TX 75219 Fax: 214-559-6750
Chm & CEO: Laurence E. Hirsch
Dir Emp Rel: Diane Clifton
Employees: 8,430
Jobs Added Last Year: 1,930 (+29.7%)
Building - residential & commercial

CAMCO INTERNATIONAL INC.
7030 Ardmore Phone: 713-747-4000
Houston, TX 77054 Fax: 713-747-6751
Pres & CEO: Gary D. Nicholson
EVP Corp HR: Tom Everett
Employees: 4,513
Jobs Added Last Year: 30 (+.7%)
Oil & gas - field services

CENTRAL AND SOUTH WEST SERVICES CORP.
1616 Woodall Rodgers Fwy. Phone: 214-777-1000
Dallas, TX 75266 Fax: 214-777-3716
Chm & CEO: E. Brooks
HR Consultant: Diana Wright
Employees: 8,057
Jobs Cut Last Year: 538 (-6.3%)
Utility - electric power

CASH AMERICA INTERNATIONAL, INC.
1600 W. 7th St. Phone: 817-335-1100
Fort Worth, TX 76102-2599 Fax: 817-335-1119
CEO: Jack R. Daugherty
Dir HR: David F. Johns
Employees: 1,830
Jobs Added Last Year: 130 (+7.6%)
Financial - pawn shops

CHIEF AUTO PARTS INCORPORATED
15303 Dallas Pkwy. Phone: 214-404-1114
Dallas, TX 75248 Fax: 214-991-9259
Pres: David H. Eisenberg
Mgr HR: Lynn Ashly
Employees: 5,000
Jobs Added Last Year: —
Auto parts - retail

An in-depth profile of this company is available by fax. Call 800-510-4452 and use your touch-tone phone to put in the 5-digit code at the prompt. Only $2.95 each with your credit card. See page 12 for more details.

TEXAS

CLEAR CHANNEL COMMUNICATIONS, INC.
200 Concord Plaza, Ste. 600 Phone: 210-822-2828
San Antonio, TX 78216 Fax: 210-822-2299
Pres & CEO: L. Lowry Mays
VP & Controller (HR): Herbert W. Hill, Jr.
Employees: 1,061
Jobs Added Last Year: 348 (+48.8%)
Broadcasting - radio & TV

CLIFFS DRILLING COMPANY
1200 Smith St., Ste. 300 Phone: 713-651-9426
Houston, TX 77002 Fax: 713-651-9466
Chm & Pres: Douglas E. Swanson
Treas (HR): Ed O. Davis
Employees: 478
Jobs Added Last Year: 152 (+46.6%)
Oil & gas - offshore drilling

CLUB CORPORATION INTERNATIONAL
3030 LBJ Fwy., Ste 700 Phone: 214-888-7308
Dallas, TX 75234 Fax: 214-888-7583
Chm & CEO: Robert H. Dedman
SVP HR: Dorothy Lawrence
Employees: 13,000
Jobs Added Last Year: 1,000 (+8.3%)
Leisure & recreational services - private clubs, resorts

THE COASTAL CORPORATION 10358
Coastal Tower, 9 Greenway Plaza Phone: 713-877-1400
Houston, TX 77046-0995 Fax: 713-877-6754
Chm & CEO: Oscar S. Wyatt, Jr.
VP Emp Rel: E. C. Simpson
Employees: 16,300
Jobs Added Last Year: 300 (+1.9%)
Oil & gas - production & pipeline

COMMERCIAL METALS COMPANY
7800 Stemmons Fwy. Phone: 214-689-4300
Dallas, TX 75247 Fax: 214-689-4320
Pres & CEO: Stanley A. Rabin
SVP Admin (HR): Bert Romberg
Employees: 4,314
Jobs Added Last Year: 410 (+10.5%)
Metal processing & fabrication

COMMUNITY HEALTH SYSTEMS, INC.
3707 FM 1960 West, Ste. 500 Phone: 713-537-5230
Houston, TX 77068-5704 Fax: 713-537-9265
Pres & CEO: E. Thomas Chaney
Mgr HR: Tara Wineinger
Employees: 5,000
Jobs Added Last Year: 2,000 (+66.7%)
Hospitals

COMPAQ COMPUTER CORPORATION 10381
20555 SH 249 Phone: 713-370-0670
Houston, TX 77070 Fax: 713-374-1740
Pres & CEO: Eckhard Pfeiffer
VP HR: Jerry G. Welch
Employees: 10,541
Jobs Cut Last Year: 759 (-6.7%)
Computers - mini & micro

COMPUCOM SYSTEMS, INC. 13060
10100 N. Central Expwy. Phone: 214-265-3600
Dallas, TX 75231-1800 Fax: 214-265-5220
Pres & CEO: Edward R. Anderson
VP Assoc Svcs (HR): Mark S. Esselman
Employees: 1,542
Jobs Added Last Year: 386 (+33.4%)
Computers - retail to corporate customers

COMPUSA INC. 15490
14951 N. Dallas Pkwy. Phone: 214-383-4000
Dallas, TX 75240 Fax: 214-383-4276
Pres & CEO: James Halpin
VP HR, Training & Admin: Paul B. Poyfair
Employees: 4,402
Jobs Added Last Year: 1,635 (+59.1%)
Computers - superstore chain

CONTINENTAL AIRLINES HOLDINGS 41903
2929 Allen Pkwy., Ste. 2010 Phone: 713-834-5000
Houston, TX 77019-2156 Fax: 713-834-2087
Pres & COO: Gordon Bethune
SVP HR: David A. Loeser
Employees: 43,100
Jobs Added Last Year: 4,800 (+12.5%)
Transportation - airline

TEXAS

THE CONTINUUM COMPANY, INC.
9500 Arboretum Blvd. Phone: 512-345-5700
Austin, TX 78759-6399 Fax: 512-338-7041
Pres & CEO: W. Michael Long
HR Dev Mgr: Deborah Stafford
Employees: 2,519
Jobs Added Last Year: 1,410 (+127.1%)
Computers - insurance industry software & services

COOPER INDUSTRIES, INC.
1001 Fannin St., Ste. 4000 Phone: 713-739-5400
Houston, TX 77002 Fax: 713-739-5555
Chm & CEO: Robert Cizik
SVP HR: Carl J. Plesnicher, Jr.
Employees: 49,500
Jobs Cut Last Year: 3,400 (-6.4%)
Diversified operations - electrical products; electrical power equipment, tools & hardware; automotive products

COUNTY SEAT STORES INC.
17950 Preston Rd., Ste. 1000 Phone: 214-248-5100
Dallas, TX 75252 Fax: 214-248-5214
CEO: Barry J. C. Parker
Dir HR: Tom Grissom
Employees: 6,864
Jobs Added Last Year: —
Retail - specialty apparel

CYBERONICS, INC.
17448 Hwy. 3, Ste. 100 Phone: 713-332-1375
Webster, TX 77598-4135 Fax: 713-332-3615
Pres & CEO: Allen W. Hill
VP Fin & Admin & CFO (HR): John K. Bakewell
Employees: 51
Jobs Added Last Year: 7 (+15.9%)
Medical instruments - nerve stimulation

CYRIX CORPORATION
2703 N. Central Expwy. Phone: 214-994-8387
Richardson, TX 75080-2010 Fax: 214-699-9857
Pres & CEO: Gerald "Jerry" D. Rogers
Dir HR: Margaret Quinn
Employees: 229
Jobs Added Last Year: 89 (+63.6%)
Electrical components - math coprocessor & 486-clone microprocessors

D. R. HORTON, INC.
1901 Ascension Blvd., Ste. 100 Phone: 817-856-8200
Arlington, TX 76006 Fax: 817-856-8249
CEO: Donald R. Horton
Mgr HR: Mary Ledbetter
Employees: 461
Jobs Added Last Year: 135 (+41.4%)
Building - residential & commercial

DELL COMPUTER CORPORATION
9505 Arboretum Blvd. Phone: 512-338-4400
Austin, TX 78759 Fax: 512-728-3653
Chm & CEO: Michael S. Dell
VP HR: Savino R. Ferrales
Employees: 5,980
Jobs Added Last Year: 1,330 (+28.6%)
Computers - mini & micro

DESTEC ENERGY, INC.
2500 City West Blvd., Ste. 150 Phone: 713-735-4000
Houston, TX 77042-3020 Fax: 713-735-4201
Pres & CEO: Charles F. Goff
VP HR, Comm & Quality: Gerald Crone
Employees: 667
Jobs Added Last Year: 61 (+10.1%)
Energy - cogeneration & coal gasification

DIAMOND SHAMROCK, INC.
9830 Colonnade Blvd. Phone: 210-641-6800
San Antonio, TX 78230 Fax: 210-641-8687
Chm, Pres & CEO: Roger R. Hemminghaus
VP HR: Penelope R. Viteo
Employees: 6,300
Jobs Added Last Year: 300 (+5%)
Oil refining & marketing

DRESSER INDUSTRIES, INC.
2001 Ross Ave. Phone: 214-740-6000
Dallas, TX 75201 Fax: 214-740-6584
Chm & CEO: John J. Murphy
VP HR: Paul M. Bryant
Employees: 25,926
Jobs Cut Last Year: 1,454 (-5.3%)
Oil field machinery & equipment

An in-depth profile of this company is available by fax. Call 800-510-4452 and use your touch-tone phone to put in the 5-digit code at the prompt. Only $2.95 each with your credit card. See page 12 for more details.

303

TEXAS

DSC COMMUNICATIONS CORPORATION
1000 Coit Rd. Phone: 214-519-3000
Plano, TX 75075-5813 Fax: 214-519-2322
Pres & CEO: James L. Donald
VP HR: Dan Allman
Employees: 3,301
Jobs Added Last Year: 39 (+1.2%)
Telecommunications equipment - digital switching, transmission, access & private network system products

THE DWYER GROUP, INC.
1010 N. University Parks Dr. Phone: 817-756-2122
Waco, TX 76707 Fax: 817-752-0661
Chm, Pres & CEO: Donald J. Dwyer
Treas & CFO (HR): Douglas Holsted
Employees: 122
Jobs Added Last Year: 39 (+47%)
Business services - franchise business operations (Rainbow International, Mr. Rooter, General Business Services, Aire-Serv)

E-SYSTEMS, INC.
6250 LBJ Fwy., PO Box 66028 Phone: 214-661-1000
Dallas, TX 75266-0248 Fax: 214-661-8508
Chm & CEO: A. Lowell Lawson
Dir HR: Rick Huntley
Employees: 16,700
Jobs Cut Last Year: 1,900 (-10.2%)
Electronics - military

E-Z SERVE CORPORATION
2550 North Loop West Phone: 713-684-4300
Houston, TX 77092 Fax: 713-684-4367
Chm & Pres: Neil H. McLaurin
VP HR: Robert L. Howell
Employees: 3,103
Jobs Added Last Year: 87 (+2.9%)
Oil refining & marketing

EL CHICO RESTAURANTS, INC.
12200 Stemmons, Ste. 100 Phone: 214-241-5500
Dallas, TX 75234 Fax: 214-888-8198
Pres & CEO: Wallace A. Jones
Dir HR: Alice M. Kain
Employees: 4,000
Jobs Added Last Year: 450 (+12.7%)
Retail - restaurants

ELECTRONIC DATA SYSTEMS CORP.
5400 Legacy Dr. Phone: 214-604-6000
Plano, TX 75024-3199 Fax: 214-645-6798
Chm, Pres & CEO: Lester M. Alberthal, Jr.
SVP Personnel: G. Stuart Reeves
Employees: 70,000
Jobs Cut Last Year: 500 (-.7%)
Computers - outsourcing, consulting & system design services

ELJER INDUSTRIES, INC.
17120 Dallas Pkwy., Ste. 205 Phone: 214-407-2600
Dallas, TX 75248 Fax: 214-407-2789
Pres & CEO: Scott G. Arbuckle
VP HR: Chet Wachenhuth
Employees: 3,750
Jobs Cut Last Year: 50 (-1.3%)
Building products - plumbing fixtures, including sinks, bathtubs & toilets

ENERGY VENTURES, INC.
5 Post Oak Park, Ste. 1760 Phone: 713-297-8400
Houston, TX 77027-3415 Fax: 713-963-9785
Pres: Bernard J. Duroc-Danner
Off Mgr & Dir HR: Diana Lambert
Employees: 2,000
Jobs Added Last Year: 300 (+17.6%)
Oil & gas - field services

ENRON CORPORATION
1400 Smith St. Phone: 713-853-6161
Houston, TX 77002-7369 Fax: 713-853-3129
Chm & CEO: Kenneth L. Lay
VP HR: Philip J. Bazelides
Employees: 7,100
Jobs Cut Last Year: 680 (-8.7%)
Oil & gas - production & pipeline

ERC INDUSTRIES, INC.
2906 Holmes Rd. Phone: 713-733-9301
Houston, TX 77051 Fax: 713-731-1183
Pres & Sec: Richard H. Rau
No central personnel officer
Employees: 265
Jobs Added Last Year: 98 (+58.7%)
Oil & gas - oilfield wellhead equipment

TEXAS

EVERGREEN MEDIA CORPORATION
433 E. Las Colinas Blvd. Phone: 214-869-9020
Irving, TX 75039 Fax: 214-869-3671
Chm & CEO: Scott K. Ginsburg
CFO (HR): Matthew E. Devine
Employees: 534
Jobs Added Last Year: 221 (+70.6%)
Broadcasting - radio

FINA, INC.
8350 N. Central Expwy. Phone: 214-750-2400
Dallas, TX 75206 Fax: 214-750-2355
Pres & CEO: Ronald W. Haddock
Gen Mgr HR: Bill Bonnett
Employees: 3,224
Jobs Cut Last Year: 145 (-4.3%)
Oil refining & marketing

EXXON CORPORATION
225 E. John W. Carpenter Fwy. Phone: 214-444-1000
Irving, TX 75062-2298 Fax: 214-444-1505
Chm & CEO: Lee R. Raymond
VP HR: Daniel S. Sanders
Employees: 91,000
Jobs Cut Last Year: 4,000 (-4.2%)
Oil & gas - integrated

FOSSIL, INC.
11052 Grader St. Phone: 214-348-7400
Dallas, TX 75238-2401 Fax: 214-348-1366
Chm & CEO: Tom Kartsotis
Dir HR: Shane Winkles
Employees: 370
Jobs Added Last Year: 136 (+58.1%)
Precious metals & jewelry - fashion watches

EZCORP, INC.
1901 Capital Pkwy. Phone: 512-314-3400
Austin, TX 78746-7617 Fax: 512-314-3404
Pres & CEO: Vincent A. Lambiase
Dir HR: Jim Penny
Employees: 1,404
Jobs Added Last Year: 485 (+52.8%)
Financial - pawn shops (EZ Pawn)

THE FREEMAN COMPANIES
8801 Ambassador Row Phone: 214-638-6450
Dallas, TX 75247-4622 Fax: 214-905-0957
CEO: Donald S. Freeman, Jr.
Dir HR: Dan Camp
Employees: 18,205
Jobs Added Last Year: –
Business services - trade show & convention arrangements, exhibit construction, equipment rental & leasing

FARAH INC.
8889 Gateway West Phone: 915-593-4444
El Paso, TX 79925-6519 Fax: 915-593-4203
Chm & CEO: Richard C. Allender
Dir HR: Frank C. Marroquin
Employees: 5,508
Jobs Added Last Year: 208 (+3.9%)
Apparel - men & boys

FROZEN FOOD EXPRESS INDUSTRIES, INC.
318 Cadiz St. Phone: 214-630-8090
Dallas, TX 75207 Fax: 214-819-5625
CEO: Stoney M. Stubbs, Jr.
Dir Fin (HR): Bart Bartholomew
Employees: 1,822
Jobs Added Last Year: 288 (+18.8%)
Transportation - refrigerated carrier of perishable goods

FIESTA MART INC.
5235 Katy Fwy. Phone: 713-869-5060
Houston, TX 77007 Fax: 713-869-8210
Chm & CEO: Donald L. Bonham
Dir HR: Juanita Elizando
Employees: 6,500
Jobs Added Last Year: 500 (+8.3%)
Retail - supermarkets

GOLF ENTERPRISES, INC.
1603 LBJ Fwy., Ste. 810 Phone: 214-247-1199
Dallas, TX 75234 Fax: 214-247-3806
CEO: Robert H. Williams
Dir HR: Fran Adams
Employees: 1,400
Jobs Added Last Year: 300 (+27.3%)
Real estate operations - public, resort & country club golf course operations

An in-depth profile of this company is available by fax. Call 800-510-4452 and use your touch-tone phone to put in the 5-digit code at the prompt. Only $2.95 each with your credit card. See page 12 for more details.

TEXAS

GRANT GEOPHYSICAL, INC.
10615 Shadow Wood Dr.   Phone: 713-398-9503
Houston, TX 77043   Fax: 713-932-4475
Pres & CEO: George W. Tilley
Mgr HR: Sue Woelfel
Employees: 2,066
Jobs Added Last Year: 156 (+8.2%)
Oil & gas - field services

HAGGAR CORPORATION
6113 Lemmon Ave.   Phone: 214-352-8481
Dallas, TX 75209-5715   Fax: 214-956-0367
Chm & CEO: J. M. Haggar III
VP HR: George Greer
Employees: 6,400
Jobs Added Last Year: 300 (+4.9%)
Apparel - men's trousers, suits, & separates

GREYHOUND LINES, INC.
15110 N. Dallas Pkwy., Ste. 600   Phone: 214-789-7000
Dallas, TX 75248   Fax: 214-387-1874
Pres & CEO: Craig R. Lentzsch
VP HR: Dan Weston
Employees: 11,500
Jobs Added Last Year: 1,800 (+18.6%)
Transportation - bus

HALLIBURTON COMPANY
3600 Lincoln Plaza   Phone: 214-978-2600
Dallas, TX 75201   Fax: 214-978-2611
Chm & CEO: Thomas H. Cruikshank
VP Admin (HR): Karen S. Stuart
Employees: 64,700
Jobs Cut Last Year: 4,500 (-6.5%)
Diversified operations - heavy construction (Brown & Root); oil & gas field services; insurance

GULF STATES UTILITIES CO.
350 Pine St.   Phone: 409-838-6631
Beaumont, TX 77701   Fax: 409-839-3077
Pres & CEO: Joseph L. Donnelly
VP HR & Admin: Rick Landy
Employees: 4,867
Jobs Added Last Year: 24 (+.5%)
Utility - electric power

THE HALLWOOD GROUP INCORPORATED
3710 Rawlins St., Ste. 1500   Phone: 214-528-5588
Dallas, TX 75219-4236   Fax: 214-528-8855
Chm: Anthony J. Gumbiner
Dir HR: Donna Henton
Employees: 1,152
Jobs Added Last Year: 226 (+24.4%)
Financial - business services

GULFMARK INTERNATIONAL, INC.
5 Post Oak Park, Ste. 1170   Phone: 713-963-9522
Houston, TX 77027   Fax: 713-963-9796
Chm: David J. Butters
Controller (HR): Elizabeth Brumley
Employees: 337
Jobs Added Last Year: 122 (+56.7%)
Oil & gas - field services

HARTE-HANKS COMMUNICATIONS, INC.
200 Concord Plaza Dr., Ste. 800   Phone: 210-829-9000
San Antonio, TX 78216   Fax: 210-829-9403
Pres & CEO: Larry Franklin
No central personnel officer
Employees: 6,150
Jobs Added Last Year: 325 (+5.6%)
Diversified operations - newspaper publishing; television broadcasting; direct mail

H. E. BUTT GROCERY COMPANY
646 S. Main Ave.   Phone: 210-246-8000
San Antonio, TX 78204   Fax: 210-246-8169
Chm, Pres & CEO: Charles C. Butt
VP HR: Louis M. Laguardia
Employees: 19,772
Jobs Added Last Year: 7,772 (+64.8%)
Retail - supermarkets

HASTINGS BOOKS, MUSIC & VIDEO, INC.
3601 Plains Blvd., PO Box 35350   Phone: 806-376-6251
Amarillo, TX 79120   Fax: 806-374-0093
Chm, Pres & CEO: John H. Marmaduke
Dir Assoc Dev (HR): Dan Crunk
Employees: 3,500
Jobs Added Last Year: 700 (+25%)
Retail - prerecorded music & books; video rental

TEXAS

HEALTHCARE AMERICA, INC.
912 Capital of Texas Hwy. South Phone: 512-329-8821
Austin, TX 78746 Fax: 512-314-5254
Pres & CEO: Kevin P. Sheehan
Dir HR: Jay Gemperle
Employees: 2,249
Jobs Added Last Year: 782 (+53.3%)
Hospitals

HOLLYWOOD CASINO CORPORATION
13455 Noel Rd., Ste. LB 48 Phone: 214-386-9777
Dallas, TX 75240 Fax: 214-386-7411
Pres & CEO: Jack E. Pratt
No central personnel officer
Employees: 4,700
Jobs Added Last Year: 50 (+1.1%)
Leisure & recreational services - casinos

HERITAGE MEDIA CORPORATION
13355 Noel Rd., Ste. 1500 Phone: 214-702-7380
Dallas, TX 75240 Fax: 214-702-7382
Pres & CEO: David N. Walthall
Mgr HR: Amy Kruckemeyer
Employees: 16,300
Jobs Added Last Year: 1,000 (+6.5%)
Broadcasting - radio & TV

HORNBECK OFFSHORE SERVICES, INC.
7707 Harborside Phone: 409-744-9500
Galveston, TX 77554 Fax: 409-744-0201
CEO, Chm & Pres: Larry D. Hornbeck
Personnel Dir: Tim Zeringue
Employees: 400
Jobs Added Last Year: 100 (+33.3%)
Oil & gas - offshore drilling

HI-LO AUTOMOTIVE, INC.
2575 W. Bellfort Phone: 713-663-6700
Houston, TX 77054 Fax: 713-663-9296
Pres & CEO: T. Michael Young
VP HR: Ed Fabritiis
Employees: 2,586
Jobs Added Last Year: 203 (+8.5%)
Auto parts - retail & wholesale

HOUSTON INDUSTRIES INC.
4400 Post Oak Pkwy. Phone: 713-629-3000
Houston, TX 77027 Fax: 713-629-3129
Chm & CEO: Don D. Jordan
VP HR: Susan D. Fabre
Employees: 11,350
Jobs Cut Last Year: 226 (-2%)
Utility - electric power

HILITE INDUSTRIES INC.
1671 S. Broadway Phone: 214-466-0475
Carrollton, TX 75006 Fax: 214-242-2902
VC & CEO: Daniel W. Brady
Dir HR: George Del Rio
Employees: 343
Jobs Added Last Year: 73 (+27%)
Automotive & trucking - brake proportioning valves & electromagnetic clutches

HUNT CONSOLIDATED INC.
1445 Ross at Field Phone: 214-978-8000
Dallas, TX 75202 Fax: 214-978-8888
Chm & CEO: Ray L. Hunt
Dir HR: Chuck Mills
Employees: 2,600
Jobs Added Last Year: —
Oil & gas - petroleum & natural gas extraction

HOGAN SYSTEMS, INC.
5080 Spectrum Dr., Ste. 400E Phone: 214-386-0020
Dallas, TX 75248 Fax: 214-386-0315
Chm, Pres & CEO: Michael H. Anderson
SVP Corp Dev (HR): Dan Johnson
Employees: 475
Jobs Added Last Year: 115 (+31.9%)
Computers - banking software

ICO, INC
100 Glenborough Dr., Ste. 250 Phone: 713-872-4994
Houston, TX 77067 Fax: 713-872-9610
Chm & CEO: James P. Shanahan, Jr.
VP Corp Dev (HR): John Cook
Employees: 960
Jobs Added Last Year: 170 (+21.5%)
Oil field machinery & equipment

TEXAS

IMCO RECYCLING
5215 N. O'Connor Blvd.   Phone: 214-869-6575
Irving, TX 75039   Fax: 214-869-6556
Pres, Chm & CEO: Frank Romanelli
VP & Treas (HR): James B. Walburg
Employees: 428
Jobs Added Last Year: 106 (+32.9%)
Metal processing & fabrication - aluminum recycling

INFOMART
1950 Stemmons Fwy   Phone: 214-746-3500
Dallas, TX 75207-3199   Fax: 214-746-3501
Pres & Gen Mgr: Tom Jones
Dir HR: Susan Lauderdale
Employees: 150
Jobs Added Last Year: 40 (+36.4%)
Computers - industry market center for computer companies

INPUT/OUTPUT, INC.
12300 Parc Crest Dr.   Phone: 713-933-3339
Stafford, TX 77477-2416   Fax: 713-240-2419
Pres, Chm & CEO: Gary D. Owens
HR Dir: Lacy Rice
Employees: 449
Jobs Added Last Year: 239 (+113.8%)
Electronics - measuring instruments

INTERVOICE, INC.
17811 Waterview Pkwy.   Phone: 214-454-8000
Dallas, TX 75252   Fax: 214-907-1079
Chm & CEO: Daniel D. Hammond
Dir HR: H. Don Brown
Employees: 394
Jobs Added Last Year: 65 (+19.8%)
Telecommunications equipment - phone-call automation equipment

J. C. PENNEY COMPANY, INC.
6501 Legacy Dr.   Phone: 214-431-1000
Plano, TX 75024-3698   Fax: 214-431-1977
CEO: James E. Oesterreicher
VP & Dir Personnel: Jay F. Hundley
Employees: 193,000
Jobs Added Last Year: 1,000 (+.5%)
Retail - major department stores, catalog stores & drug stores

JUSTIN INDUSTRIES, INC.
2821 W. Seventh St.   Phone: 817-336-5125
Fort Worth, TX 76107   Fax: 817-390-2477
Chm & CEO: John Justin
VP HR: John Bennett
Employees: 5,102
Jobs Added Last Year: 517 (+11.3%)
Diversified operations - boots (Tony Lama); building materials (Acme Brick); evaporative coolers; publishing (Northland)

KAISER ALUMINUM CORPORATION
5847 San Felipe, Ste. 2600   Phone: 713-267-3777
Houston, TX 77057   Fax: 713-267-3710
Chm & CEO: George T. Haymaker, Jr.
Dir Corp Personnel: James P. McKnight
Employees: 9,500
Jobs Cut Last Year: 629 (-6.2%)
Metals - nonferrous

KANEB SERVICES, INC.
2400 Lakeside Blvd.   Phone: 214-699-4000
Richardson, TX 75082   Fax: 214-699-4025
Chm, Pres & CEO: John R. Barnes
Dir HR: William Kettler
Employees: 2,026
Jobs Added Last Year: 304 (+17.7%)
Oil & gas - production & pipeline

KENT ELECTRONICS CORPORATION
7433 Harwin Dr.   Phone: 713-780-7770
Houston, TX 77036-2015   Fax: 713-978-5890
Chm & CEO: Morrie K. Abramson
Mgr HR: Pam Huffman
Employees: 808
Jobs Added Last Year: 139 (+20.8%)
Electrical components - wire, cable & electronic connectors & components

KEYSTONE INTERNATIONAL, INC.
9600 W. Gulf Bank Dr.   Phone: 713-466-1176
Houston, TX 77040   Fax: 713-937-5453
Chm & CEO: Raymond A. LeBlanc
Dir HR: Kathy Ruf
Employees: 4,200
Jobs Added Last Year: 100 (+2.4%)
Instruments - flow control

TEXAS

KIMBERLY-CLARK CORPORATION
DFW Airport Station Phone: 214-830-1200
Dallas, TX 75261-9100 Fax: 214-830-1490
Chm & CEO: Wayne R. Sanders
VP HR: Bruce J. Olsen
Employees: 42,131
Jobs Cut Last Year: 771 (-1.8%)
Paper & paper products - facial tissues (Kleenex), diapers (Huggies), tampons (Tampax), towels & napkins

KIRBY CORPORATION
1775 St. James Place, Ste. 300 Phone: 713-629-9370
Houston, TX 77056-3453 Fax: 713-964-2200
CEO: George A. Peterkin, Jr.
Dir HR: Jack Simms
Employees: 1,875
Jobs Added Last Year: 150 (+8.7%)
Diversified operations - petrochemical transport; diesel repair; insurance

KITTY HAWK, INC.
1515 W. 20th St. Phone: 214-456-2200
Dallas, TX 76261 Fax: 214-456-2259
Chm & CEO: M. Tom Christopher
Dir HR: Lena Knolton
Employees: 204
Jobs Added Last Year: 129 (+172%)
Transportation - air-charter management & cargo services

LA QUINTA INNS, INC.
112 E. Pecan St., PO Box 2636 Phone: 210-302-6000
San Antonio, TX 78299-2636 Fax: 210-302-6263
Pres & CEO: Gary L. Mead
VP HR: Robert T. Foley
Employees: 6,500
Jobs Added Last Year: 400 (+6.6%)
Hotels & motels - budget accomodations primarily in Texas & other sunbelt states

LANDMARK GRAPHICS CORPORATION
15150 Memorial Dr. Phone: 713-560-1000
Houston, TX 77079-4304 Fax: 713-560-1410
Pres & CEO: Robert P. Peebler
VP Dir HR: Daniel Casaccia
Employees: 613
Jobs Added Last Year: 103 (+20.2%)
Computers - geoscientific exploration software

LANDRY'S SEAFOOD RESTAURANTS
1400 Post Oak Blvd., Ste. 1010 Phone: 713-850-1010
Houston, TX 77056 Fax: 713-623-4702
Pres & CEO: Tilman J. Fertitta
HR Dir: Rex E. Lee
Employees: 1,323
Jobs Added Last Year: 273 (+26%)
Retail - seafood restaurants in Texas & Louisiana

LENNOX INTERNATIONAL INC.
2100 Lake Park Blvd. Phone: 214-497-5017
Richardson, TX 75080 Fax: 214-497-5299
Chm & CEO: John W. Norris, Jr.
EVP HR: Harry Ashenhurst
Employees: 8,000
Jobs Added Last Year: 500 (+6.7%)
Building products - a/c & heating

LINCOLN PROPERTY COMPANY
500 N. Akard, Ste. 3300 Phone: 214-740-3300
Dallas, TX 75201 Fax: 214-740-3313
Chm & CEO: Mack Pogue
Dir HR: Connie Rutledge
Employees: 4,200
Jobs Cut Last Year: 200 (-4.5%)
Real estate development & management

LIVING CENTERS OF AMERICA, INC.
15415 Katy Fwy., Ste. 800 Phone: 713-578-4600
Houston, TX 77094 Fax: 713-578-4735
Pres & CEO: Edward L. Kuntz
Dir HR: Tom Gillson
Employees: 17,800
Jobs Added Last Year: 300 (+1.7%)
Nursing homes

LOMAS FINANCIAL CORPORATION
1600 Viceroy Dr. Phone: 214-879-4000
Dallas, TX 75235 Fax: 214-879-5589
CEO: Eric D. Booth
SVP HR: Jim Alleman
Employees: 2,244
Jobs Added Last Year: 106 (+5%)
Financial - real estate investment management

TEXAS

LUBY'S CAFETERIAS, INC.
2211 NE Loop 410
San Antonio, TX 78265-3069
Pres & CEO: Ralph Erben
VP Mgmt Personnel: David W. Simpson
Employees: 9,600
Jobs Added Last Year: 600 (+6.7%)
Retail - cafeterias

Phone: 210-654-9000
Fax: 210-654-3211

MEDIANEWS GROUP INC.
4888 Loop Central Dr., Ste. 525
Houston, TX 77081
VC, Pres & CEO: William D. Singleton
Dir HR: Pat Angel
Employees: 7,950
Jobs Added Last Year: 7 (+.1%)
Publishing - newspapers (*The Houston Post*)

Phone: 713-295-3800
Fax: 713-295-3893

MARINE DRILLING COMPANIES, INC.
14141 Southwest Fwy., Ste 2500
Sugar Land, TX 77478
Chm, Pres & CEO: William O. Keyes
Personnel Supervisor: Gayle Schmidt
Employees: 800
Jobs Added Last Year: 100 (+14.3%)
Oil & gas - field services

Phone: 713-491-2002
Fax: 713-565-2002

MEDICALCONTROL, INC.
9649 Webb Chapel Rd.
Dallas, TX 75220
Pres & CEO: John W. Hunt
Dir Corp Svcs (HR): Cindy Orie
Employees: 73
Jobs Added Last Year: 19 (+35.2%)
Health maintenance organization

Phone: 214-352-2666
Fax: 214-352-5777

MARY KAY COSMETICS INC.
8787 Stemmons Fwy.
Dallas, TX 75247
Chm & CEO: Richard R. Rogers
SVP HR: Amy Digeso
Employees: 2,400
Jobs Added Last Year: 300 (+14.3%)
Cosmetics

Phone: 214-630-8787
Fax: 214-905-5699

THE MEN'S WEARHOUSE, INC.
5803 Glenmont Dr.
Houston, TX 77081
Chm, Pres & CEO: George Zimmer
VP Admin (HR): Julie Maciag
Employees: 2,545
Jobs Added Last Year: 779 (+44.1%)
Retail - men's clothing stores

Phone: 713-664-3692
Fax: 713-664-1957

MAXXAM INC.
5847 San Felipe, Ste. 2600
Houston, TX 77257-2887
Chm & CEO: Charles E. Hurwitz
Dir HR: Sharon Romere
Employees: 13,795
Jobs Added Last Year: 1,416 (+11.4%)
Diversified operations - forest products; real estate development; aluminum

Phone: 713-975-7600
Fax: 713-267-3701

MICHAELS STORES, INC.
5931 Campus Circle Dr.
Irving, TX 75063
Chm & CEO: Sam Wyly
VP Personnel: Donald C. Toby
Employees: 10,040
Jobs Added Last Year: 4,730 (+89.1%)
Retail - arts & crafts

Phone: 214-714-7000
Fax: 214-714-7155

MAXXIM MEDICAL, INC.
104 Industrial Blvd.
Sugar Land, TX 77478
Chm, Pres & CEO: Kenneth W. Davidson
HR Mgr: Donna Hustis
Employees: 2,282
Jobs Added Last Year: 482 (+26.8%)
Medical products - physical therapy & pain management products

Phone: 713-240-5588
Fax: 713-240-2577

MINYARD FOOD STORES INC.
777 Freeport Pkwy.
Coppell, TX 75019
Pres & CEO: J. L. "Sonny" Williams
Dir HR: Alan Vaughan
Employees: 6,200
Jobs Added Last Year: —
Retail - supermarkets

Phone: 214-393-8700
Fax: 214-462-9407

TEXAS

MITCHELL ENERGY & DEVELOPMENT CORP.
2001 Timberloch Place   Phone: 713-377-5500
The Woodlands, TX 77380   Fax: 713-377-6910
Chm & CEO: George P. Mitchell
SVP HR: Clyde Black
Employees: 2,900
Jobs Added Last Year: 75 (+2.7%)
Oil & gas - US exploration & production; real estate development (Woodlands)

NABORS INDUSTRIES, INC.
515 W. Greens Rd., Ste. 1200   Phone: 713-874-0035
Houston, TX 77067   Fax: 713-872-5205
Chm & CEO: Eugene M. Isenberg
VP Admin (HR): Daniel McLachlin
Employees: 5,700
Jobs Added Last Year: 2,532 (+79.9%)
Oil & gas - land drilling services

NATIONAL CONVENIENCE STORES INC.
100 Waugh Dr.   Phone: 713-863-2200
Houston, TX 77007   Fax: 713-880-0579
Pres & CEO: V. H. Van Horn
No central personnel officer
Employees: 5,300
Jobs Added Last Year: 700 (+15.2%)
Retail - convenience stores (Stop N Go)

NCH CORPORATION
2727 Chemsearch Blvd.   Phone: 214-438-0211
Irving, TX 75062   Fax: 214-438-0186
Pres & CEO: Irvin L. Levy
VP HR: Neil Thomas
Employees: 10,378
Jobs Added Last Year: 280 (+2.8%)
Soap & cleaning preparations

NCI BUILDING SYSTEMS, INC.
7301 Fairview   Phone: 713-466-7788
Houston, TX 77041   Fax: 713-466-3194
Pres & CEO: Johnie Schulte, Jr.
Dir HR: Karen Rosales
Employees: 907
Jobs Added Last Year: 426 (+88.6%)
Building products - prefabricated steel kits used to build schools, auto dealerships, shopping centers & restaurants

NORAM ENERGY CORP
PO Box 2628   Phone: 713-654-5699
Houston, TX 77252-2628   Fax: 713-654-7511
Chm, Pres & CEO: T. Milton Honer
SVP HR & Administrative Svcs: Rick L. Spurlock
Employees: 6,880
Jobs Cut Last Year: 27 (-.4%)
Utility - gas distribution

NORWOOD PROMOTIONAL PRODUCTS INC.
817 N. Frio St.   Phone: 210-227-7629
San Antonio, TX 78207-5702   Fax: 210-224-5531
CEO: Frank P. Krasovec
VP HR: Mark McBurmett
Employees: 1,066
Jobs Added Last Year: 409 (+62.3%)
Business services - promotional items imprinted with name or logo of advertiser

NUEVO ENERGY COMPANY
1221 Lamar, Ste. 1600   Phone: 713-652-0706
Houston, TX 77010   Fax: 713-655-1866
Pres, CEO & COO: Michael D. Watford
VP Admin (HR): Carolyn Driesbach
Employees: 630
Jobs Added Last Year: 80 (+14.5%)
Oil & gas - US exploration & production

OCEANEERING INTERNATIONAL, INC.
16001 Park Ten Place, Ste. 600   Phone: 713-578-8868
Houston, TX 77084   Fax: 713-578-5243
Chm & CEO: John R. Huff
Mgr Compensation & Ben: Sheila Jaynes
Employees: 1,950
Jobs Added Last Year: 150 (+8.3%)
Oil & gas - field services

OLD AMERICA STORES, INC.
811 N. Collins Fwy.   Phone: 903-532-5549
Howe, TX 75459   Fax: 903-532-6708
Pres & CEO: Richard Tredinnick
Dir HR: Cindy Young
Employees: 2,300
Jobs Added Last Year: 400 (+21.1%)
Retail - arts & crafts stores

 An in-depth profile of this company is available by fax. Call 800-510-4452 and use your touch-tone phone to put in the 5-digit code at the prompt. Only $2.95 each with your credit card. See page 12 for more details.

TEXAS

PAGING NETWORK, INC.
4965 Preston Park Blvd.   Phone: 214-985-4100
Plano, TX 75093   Fax: 214-985-6711
Pres & CEO: Terry L. Scott
VP HR: Levy H. Curry
Employees: 4,000
Jobs Added Last Year: 1,330 (+49.8%)
Telecommunications services - #1 paging service in US

PIER 1 IMPORTS, INC.
301 Commerce St., Ste. 600   Phone: 817-878-8000
Fort Worth, TX 76102   Fax: 817-878-7883
Chm & CEO: Clark A. Johnson
VP HR: Mitch Weatherly
Employees: 8,227
Jobs Added Last Year: 393 (+5%)
Retail - imported apparel & home furnishings

PANCHO'S MEXICAN BUFFET, INC.
3500 Noble Ave., PO Box 7407   Phone: 817-831-0081
Fort Worth, TX 76111-0407   Fax: 817-838-1480
Pres & CEO: Hollis Taylor
VP HR: David Dixon
Employees: 3,967
Jobs Added Last Year: 436 (+12.3%)
Retail - restaurants

PILGRIM'S PRIDE CORPORATION
110 S. Texas St.   Phone: 903-855-1000
Pittsburg, TX 75686-0093   Fax: 903-856-7505
CEO: Lonnie A. Pilgrim
SVP HR: Ray Gameson
Employees: 10,700
Jobs Added Last Year: 400 (+3.9%)
Food - poultry products

PANHANDLE EASTERN CORP.
5400 Westheimer Ct., PO Box 1642   Phone: 713-627-5400
Houston, TX 77251-1642   Fax: 713-627-4145
Chm & CEO: Dennis R. Hendrix
VP HR: Dan R. Hennig
Employees: 4,900
Jobs Cut Last Year: 100 (-2%)
Oil & gas - production & pipeline

PLAINS RESOURCES INC.
1600 Smith St.   Phone: 713-654-1414
Houston, TX 77002   Fax: 713-654-1523
Pres & CEO: Greg L. Armstrong
VP HR: Susie Peters
Employees: 209
Jobs Added Last Year: 109 (+109%)
Oil & gas - US exploration & production

PENNZOIL COMPANY
PO Box 2967, Pennzoil Place   Phone: 713-546-4000
Houston, TX 77252-2967   Fax: 713-546-6639
Chm, Pres & CEO: James L. Pate
VP HR: Harry C. Mitchell
Employees: 9,901
Jobs Added Last Year: 776 (+8.5%)
Oil & gas - integrated; automotive products

POOL ENERGY SERVICES CO.
10375 Richmond Ave.   Phone: 713-954-3000
Houston, TX 77042   Fax: 713-954-3319
Pres & CEO: James T. Jongebloed
VP HR: Louis E. Dupre
Employees: 4,519
Jobs Cut Last Year: 189 (-4%)
Oil & gas - field services

PHYSICIAN RELIANCE NETWORK, INC.
3320 Live Oak, Ste. 700   Phone: 214-828-0377
Dallas, TX 75204   Fax: 214-826-8109
CEO: Merrick H. Reese
Dir HR: Sheila Deason
Employees: 392
Jobs Added Last Year: 239 (+156.2%)
Medical services - cancer-treatment practice management

POWELL INDUSTRIES, INC.
PO Box 12818   Phone: 713-944-6900
Houston, TX 77217   Fax: 713-947-4435
Pres & CEO: Thomas W. Powell
Dir HR: Robert J. Murphy
Employees: 857
Jobs Added Last Year: 111 (+14.9%)
Machinery - electrical

TEXAS

PRATT HOTEL CORPORATION
13455 Noel Rd., Ste. LB 48　　Phone: 214-386-9777
Dallas, TX 75240　　Fax: 214-386-7411
CEO: Jack E. Pratt
No central personnel officer
Employees: 3,200
Jobs Added Last Year: 100 (+3.2%)
Hotels & motels

RIVIANA FOODS INC.
2777 Allen Pkwy.　　Phone: 713-529-3251
Houston, TX 77019　　Fax: 713-529-1661
Pres & CEO: Joseph A. Hafner, Jr.
VP HR: Jack Nolingberg
Employees: 2,645
Jobs Added Last Year: 245 (+10.2%)
Food - rice milling, canning & baking

RAILTEX, INC.
4040 Broadway, Ste. 200　　Phone: 210-841-7600
San Antonio, TX 78209-3745　　Fax: 210-841-7693
Chm, Pres & CEO: Bruce M. Flohr
VP HR: Eamonn F. Grant
Employees: 466
Jobs Added Last Year: 189 (+68.2%)
Transportation - short-line freight railroad

SAMMONS ENTERPRISES, INC.
300 Crescent Ct., Ste. 700　　Phone: 214-855-2800
Dallas, TX 75201　　Fax: 214-855-2899
Pres & CEO: Robert W. Korba
Dir Welfare Benefit Plans (HR): Pam Fain
Employees: 4,000
Jobs Added Last Year: 100 (+2.6%)
Diversified operations - insurance; cable TV; industrial equipment

RANDALLS FOOD MARKETS
3663 Briarpark Dr.　　Phone: 713-268-3500
Houston, TX 77042　　Fax: 713-268-3601
Chm, Pres & CEO: Robert Randall Onstead, Jr.
VP HR: Jan Gillespie
Employees: 9,600
Jobs Added Last Year: 1,800 (+23.1%)
Retail - Texas supermarkets

SANIFILL, INC.
2777 Allen Pkwy., Ste. 700　　Phone: 713-942-6200
Houston, TX 77019　　Fax: 713-942-6322
Chm & CEO: Lorne D. Bain
Dir Admin (HR): Ken Rose
Employees: 1,000
Jobs Added Last Year: 350 (+53.8%)
Pollution control - solid waste disposal

REDMAN INDUSTRIES INC.
2550 Walnut Hill Ln., Ste. 200　　Phone: 214-353-3600
Dallas, TX 75229-5672　　Fax: 214-350-5927
Pres: Robert M. Linton
EVP HR & CFO: Fergus J. Walker, Jr.
Employees: 3,634
Jobs Added Last Year: 420 (+13.1%)
Building - manufactured homes

SBC COMMUNICATIONS, INC.
175 E. Houston　　Phone: 210-821-4105
San Antonio, TX 78299-2933　　Fax: 210-351-2071
Chm & CEO: Edward E. Whitacre, Jr.
SEVP HR: Richard A. Harris
Employees: 59,400
Jobs Cut Last Year: 100 (-.2%)
Utility - telephone service (Southwestern Bell); cellular telephone services, long distance advertising

RF MONOLITHICS, INC.
4441 Sigma Rd.　　Phone: 214-233-2903
Dallas, TX 75244　　Fax: 214-387-8148
Pres & CEO: Gary A. Anderson
Dir HR: Diana Handler
Employees: 377
Jobs Added Last Year: 139 (+58.4%)
Electrical components - radio frequency components & modules; digital clocks

SEMATECH, INC.
2706 Montopolis Dr.　　Phone: 512-356-3500
Austin, TX 78741　　Fax: 512-356-3083
Pres & CEO: William Spencer
Dir HR: Mike Foster
Employees: 841
Jobs Added Last Year: 99 (+13.3%)
Engineering - R&D services, semiconductor technology

313

TEXAS

SERV-TECH, INC. [12638]
5200 Cedar Crest Blvd. Phone: 713-644-9974
Houston, TX 77087 Fax: 713-644-0731
CEO: Richard L. Daerr
Dir HR: Cheryl Cummings
Employees: 1,016
Jobs Added Last Year: 199 (+24.4%)
Oil & gas - cleaning & maintenance services

SERVICE CORPORATION INTERNATIONAL
1929 Allen Pkwy. Phone: 713-522-5141
Houston, TX 77019 Fax: 713-525-5586
Chm & CEO: Robert L. Waltrip
SVP Admin (HR): Jack L. Stoner
Employees: 11,818
Jobs Added Last Year: 3,702 (+45.6%)
Funeral homes & cemeteries

SHELL OIL COMPANY [41841]
One Shell Plaza Phone: 713-241-6161
Houston, TX 77002 Fax: 713-241-6781
Pres & CEO: Philip J. Carroll
VP HR: B. E. Levan
Employees: 22,212
Jobs Cut Last Year: 3,096 (-12.2%)
Oil & gas - integrated

SHOWBIZ PIZZA TIME, INC.
4441 W. Airport Fwy. Phone: 214-258-8507
Irving, TX 75015 Fax: 214-258-8545
Chm & CEO: Richard M. Frank
VP (HR): Catherine Kreston
Employees: 13,500
Jobs Added Last Year: 1,500 (+12.5%)
Retail - restaurants

SOFTWARE SPECTRUM, INC. [15128]
2140 Merritt Dr. Phone: 214-840-6600
Garland, TX 75041 Fax: 214-864-7878
Chm & CEO: Judy O. Sims
HR Dir: Sally Brecht
Employees: 514
Jobs Added Last Year: 126 (+32.5%)
Computers - retail software direct to companies

SOUTHDOWN, INC.
1200 Smith St., Ste. 2400 Phone: 713-650-6200
Houston, TX 77002 Fax: 713-653-6815
Pres & CEO: Clarence C. Comer
Dir HR: L. Ross Buckner
Employees: 2,600
Jobs Added Last Year: 0
Construction - cement & concrete

THE SOUTHLAND CORPORATION [41970]
2711 N. Haskell Ave. Phone: 214-828-7011
Dallas, TX 75204-2906 Fax: 214-822-7848
Pres & CEO: Clark J. Matthews II
VP HR: David M. Finley
Employees: 32,406
Jobs Cut Last Year: 3,240 (-9.1%)
Retail - convenience stores

SOUTHWEST AIRLINES CO. [11377]
PO Box 36611 Phone: 214-904-4000
Dallas, TX 75235-1611 Fax: 214-904-4200
Chm, Pres & CEO: Herbert D. Kelleher
VP People: Margaret Ann Rhoades
Employees: 15,175
Jobs Added Last Year: 3,778 (+33.1%)
Transportation - airline

SPECIALTY RETAILERS INC.
10201 Main St. Phone: 713-667-5601
Houston, TX 77025 Fax: 713-669-2708
Pres & CEO: Carl Tooker
VP HR: Jack Chipperfield
Employees: 8,000
Jobs Added Last Year: —
Retail - apparel (Palais Royal, Beall's, Fashion Bar)

SPORT SUPPLY GROUP, INC.
1901 Diplomat Phone: 214-484-9484
Dallas, TX 75234 Fax: 214-243-0149
CEO: Michael J. Blumenfeld
Dir HR: Joe Holt
Employees: 492
Jobs Added Last Year: 165 (+50.5%)
Leisure & recreational products - sports equipment

TEXAS

STAR ENTERPRISE
12700 Northborough Dr. Phone: 713-874-7000
Houston, TX 77067 Fax: 713-874-7760
Pres & CEO: Lester A. Wilkes
Dir HR: Floyd Chaney
Employees: 5,000
Jobs Added Last Year: 0
Oil refining & marketing (Texaco-Aramco joint venture)

SYNERCOM TECHNOLOGY, INC.
2500 City West Blvd., Ste. 1100 Phone: 713-954-7000
Houston, TX 77042 Fax: 713-785-0880
Pres & CEO: William Engel
Chief Admin Off (HR): Robert Ubank
Employees: 241
Jobs Added Last Year: 95 (+65.1%)
Computers - database management software

STERLING INFORMATION GROUP
515 Capital of Texas Hwy. South Phone: 512-327-0090
Austin, TX 78746-4305 Fax: 512-327-0197
CEO: Chip Wolfe
VP HR: Leslie Martinich
Employees: 55
Jobs Added Last Year: 13 (+31%)
Computers - software consulting services

SYSCO CORPORATION
1390 Enclave Pkwy. Phone: 713-584-1390
Houston, TX 77077-2099 Fax: 713-584-1188
CEO, Pres & COO: Bill M. Lindig
VP Emp Relations: Mike Nichols
Employees: 26,000
Jobs Added Last Year: 1,800 (+7.4%)
Food - wholesale to restaurants

STERLING SOFTWARE, INC.
8080 N. Central Expwy., Ste. 1100 Phone: 214-891-8600
Dallas, TX 75206 Fax: 214-739-0535
Pres & CEO: Sterling L. Williams
No central personnel officer
Employees: 3,000
Jobs Added Last Year: 200 (+7.1%)
Computers - software & network services; automated program design software

TANDY BRANDS, INC.
690 E. Lamar Blvd., Ste. 200 Phone: 817-548-0090
Arlington, TX 76011 Fax: 817-548-1144
CEO: J. S. B. Jenkins
Emp Ben Mgr: Jan Bland
Employees: 470
Jobs Added Last Year: 136 (+40.7%)
Leather & related products

STEVENS GRAPHICS CORPORATION
5500 Airport Fwy. Phone: 817-831-3911
Fort Worth, TX 76113 Fax: 817-838-4344
Chm & CEO: Paul I. Stevens
Office Mgr (HR): Claudia Teague
Employees: 650
Jobs Added Last Year: 125 (+23.8%)
Machinery - printing presses

TANDY CORPORATION
1800 One Tandy Center Phone: 817-390-3700
Fort Worth, TX 76102 Fax: 817-390-2774
Chm, Pres & CEO: John V. Roach
VP HR: George Berger
Employees: 42,000
Jobs Added Last Year: 5,000 (+13.5%)
Retail - consumer electronics (Radio Shack, Computer City, McDuff, VideoConcepts, The Edge, Incredible Universe)

STEWART & STEVENSON SERVICES, INC.
2707 N. Loop West Phone: 713-868-7700
Houston, TX 77008 Fax: 713-868-7692
Pres & CEO: Bob H. O'Neal
VP HR & Risk Mgmt: Bobby Brown
Employees: 3,400
Jobs Added Last Year: 550 (+19.3%)
Engines - adaptation of diesel & jet engines for power plants & vehicles

TANDYCRAFTS, INC.
1400 Everman Pkwy. Phone: 817-551-9600
Fort Worth, TX 76140 Fax: 817-551-9795
Pres & CEO: Jerry L. Roy
EVP & CFO (HR): Michael J. Walsh
Employees: 4,000
Jobs Added Last Year: 1,400 (+53.8%)
Diversified operations - retail outlets; leather products; frames; furniture

TEXAS

TARRANT DISTRIBUTORS INC.
9835 Genard Rd.   Phone: 713-690-8888
Houston, TX 77041   Fax: 713-690-1169
Chm: N. B. Strauss
Dir HR: Rose Clark
Employees: 350
Jobs Added Last Year: 100 (+40%)
Wholesale distribution - alcoholic beverages

THE TEXAS A&M UNIVERSITY SYSTEM
State Headquarters Building   Phone: 409-845-4331
College Station, TX 77843   Fax: 409-862-2679
Chancellor: Barry P. Thompson
Vice Chancellor Fin & Ops (HR): Richard Lindsay
Employees: 19,000
Jobs Added Last Year: —
University

TEJAS POWER CORPORATION
200 WestLake Park Blvd.   Phone: 713-597-6200
Houston, TX 77079   Fax: 713-584-8212
CEO: Larry W. Bickle
Dir HR: Marianne Finch
Employees: 90
Jobs Added Last Year: 13 (+16.9%)
Oil & gas - production & pipeline

TEXAS INDUSTRIES, INC.
1341 W. Mockingbird Ln.   Phone: 214-647-6700
Dallas, TX 75247   Fax: 214-647-3878
CEO: Robert D. Rogers
Dir HR: Brooke E. Brewer
Employees: 2,700
Jobs Added Last Year: 0
Diversified operations - steel; concrete; cement

TEMPLE-INLAND INC.
303 S. Temple Dr., Drawer N   Phone: 409-829-2211
Diboll, TX 75941   Fax: 409-829-1366
Chm & CEO: Clifford J. Grum
VP HR: Herb George
Employees: 15,000
Jobs Added Last Year: 500 (+3.4%)
Containers & containerboard; bleached paperboard; building products

TEXAS INSTRUMENTS INC.   [11462]
13500 N. Central Expwy.   Phone: 214-995-2551
Dallas, TX 75265-5474   Fax: 214-995-3340
Chm, Pres & CEO: Jerry R. Junkins
VP HR: Charles F. Nielson
Employees: 59,048
Jobs Cut Last Year: 1,529 (-2.5%)
Electrical components - semiconductors; printers; laptop computers; defense systems

TEMTEX INDUSTRIES, INC.
3010 LBJ Fwy., Ste. 650   Phone: 214-484-1845
Dallas, TX 75234   Fax: 214-241-1452
CEO: Edwin R. Buford
No central personnel officer
Employees: 473
Jobs Added Last Year: 122 (+34.8%)
Diversified operations - face brick for home & commercial use; bomb fins & other defense hardware

TEXAS UTILITIES COMPANY   [11464]
2001 Bryan Tower   Phone: 214-812-4600
Dallas, TX 75201   Fax: 214-812-4079
Chm & CEO: Jerry Farrington
VP Personnel: Pitt Pittman
Employees: 10,859
Jobs Added Last Year: 172 (+1.6%)
Utility - electric power

TENNECO INC.   [11455]
Tenneco Bldg., PO Box 2511   Phone: 713-757-2131
Houston, TX 77252-2511   Fax: 713-757-1410
Chm, Pres, CEO & COO: Dana G. Mead
SVP HR: Steve Smith
Employees: 75,000
Jobs Cut Last Year: 4,000 (-5.1%)
Diversified operations - natural gas pipelines; shipbuilding; auto parts; chemicals; packaging

TRACOR INC.
6500 Tracor Ln.   Phone: 512-926-2800
Austin, TX 78725-2000   Fax: 512-929-2241
Chm, Pres & CEO: James B. Skaggs
VP HR: Murray Shaw
Employees: 8,900
Jobs Added Last Year: 5,500 (+161.8%)
Electronics - defense countermeasure systems; technical support & services

TEXAS

TRIANGLE PACIFIC CORPORATION
16803 Dallas Pkwy. Phone: 214-931-3000
Dallas, TX 75248 Fax: 214-931-3284
CEO: Floyd F. Sherman
Dir HR: Jennifer Wisdom
Employees: 3,545
Jobs Added Last Year: 233 (+7%)
Building products - wood

TUESDAY MORNING CORPORATION
14621 Inwood Rd. Phone: 214-387-3562
Dallas, TX 75244 Fax: 214-387-2344
Chm & CEO: Lloyd L. Ross
Dir HR: Debbie Steenrod
Employees: 2,895
Jobs Added Last Year: 18 (+.6%)
Retail - discount & variety

TRINITY INDUSTRIES, INC.
2525 Stemmons Fwy. Phone: 214-689-0592
Dallas, TX 75207-2401 Fax: 214-689-0501
Chm, Pres & CEO: W. Ray Wallace
VP HR: Jack Cunningham
Employees: 14,700
Jobs Added Last Year: 2,100 (+16.7%)
Metal products - railcars, marine products, construction products, pressure & nonpressure containers

TYLER CORPORATION
3200 San Jacinto Tower Phone: 214-754-7800
Dallas, TX 75201 Fax: 214-969-9352
Pres & CEO: Joseph F. McKinney
Corp Sec (HR): Sandy Shepherd
Employees: 3,470
Jobs Added Last Year: 25 (+.7%)
Diversified operations - cast iron pipe & fittings; retail auto parts

TRISM, INC.
301 Commerce St. Phone: 817-335-1791
Fort Worth, TX 76102 Fax: 817-335-1913
Pres & CEO: M. L. Lawrence
Sec, Gen Counsel & VP HR: Mike May
Employees: 2,442
Jobs Added Last Year: 144 (+6.3%)
Transportation - truck

U.S. LONG DISTANCE CORPORATION
9311 San Pedro, Ste. 300 Phone: 210-525-9009
San Antonio, TX 78216-4476 Fax: 210-525-0389
Chm & CEO: Parris H. Holmes, Jr.
VP HR: David S. Horne
Employees: 904
Jobs Added Last Year: 250 (+38.2%)
Telecommunications services - long distance telephone service

TSX CORPORATION
5-D Butterfield Trail Phone: 915-772-4400
El Paso, TX 79906 Fax: 915-778-9930
Chm, Pres & CEO: William H. Lambert
Dir HR: Wes Schotten
Employees: 850
Jobs Added Last Year: 150 (+21.4%)
Fiber optics - high technology distribution equipment & advertising insertion equipment

ULTRAK, INC.
1220 Champion Circle Phone: 214-280-9675
Carrollton, TX 75006 Fax: 214-280-9674
CEO: George Broady
HR Dir: Patty Cramer
Employees: 123
Jobs Added Last Year: 90 (+272.7%)
Video equipment - closed circuit TV systems

TUCKER DRILLING COMPANY, INC.
PO Box 1876 Phone: 915-655-6773
San Angelo, TX 76902 Fax: 915-653-4873
Chm & Pres: Larry J. Tucker
Dir Personnel: Janet Herode
Employees: 203
Jobs Added Last Year: 97 (+91.5%)
Oil & gas - US exploration & production

UNITED MERIDIAN CORPORATION
1201 Louisiana, Ste. 1400 Phone: 713-654-9110
Houston, TX 77002 Fax: 713-653-5124
CEO: John B. Brock
Dir HR: Paul Priest
Employees: 215
Jobs Added Last Year: 79 (+58.1%)
Oil & gas - US exploration & production

An in-depth profile of this company is available by fax. Call 800-510-4452 and use your touch-tone phone to put in the 5-digit code at the prompt. Only $2.95 each with your credit card. See page 12 for more details.

317

TEXAS

THE UNIVERSITY OF TEXAS SYSTEM
O. Henry Hall
Austin, TX 78701
Chancellor: William H. Cunningham
Dir, System Personnel Office: Trennis Jones
Employees: 71,109
Jobs Added Last Year: –
University
Phone: 512-499-4201
Fax: 512-499-4215

WESTCOTT COMMUNICATIONS, INC.
1303 Marsh Ln.
Carrollton, TX 75006
CEO: Carl Westcott
Dir HR: Ellen Hillis
Employees: 406
Jobs Added Last Year: 112 (+38.1%)
Motion pictures & services - satellite broadcast training films
Phone: 214-417-4100
Fax: 214-417-4933

USA WASTE SERVICES, INC.
5000 Quorum Dr., Ste. 300
Dallas, TX 75240
CEO: John E. Drury
Exec Asst (HR): Diana Neal
Employees: 650
Jobs Added Last Year: 250 (+62.5%)
Pollution control - solid waste management, trash disposal & landfill operations
Phone: 214-233-4212
Fax: 214-385-1757

WHOLE FOODS MARKET, INC.
1705 Capital of Texas Hwy.
Austin, TX 78746
Chm & CEO: John Mackey
No central personnel officer
Employees: 4,150
Jobs Added Last Year: 1,800 (+76.6%)
Retail - natural food stores
Phone: 512-328-7541
Fax: 512-328-5482

USAA
9800 Fredericksburg Rd.
San Antonio, TX 78288
Chm & CEO: Robert T. Herres
SVP HR: William B. Tracy
Employees: 15,905
Jobs Added Last Year: 1,238 (+8.4%)
Insurance - multiline for consumers; brokerage services; mutual funds; banking; retirement plans & services
Phone: 210-498-2211
Fax: 210-498-9940

H. B. ZACHRY COMPANY
527 W. Harding Blvd.
San Antonio, TX 78221
Chm & CEO: Henry B. Zachry, Jr.
VP HR: Steve Hoech
Employees: 8,000
Jobs Added Last Year: –
Building - general contracting
Phone: 210-922-1213
Fax: 210-927-8060

VALHI, INC.
5430 LBJ Fwy., Ste. 1700
Dallas, TX 75240-1700
Chm & CEO: Harold C. Simmons
Personnel Mgr: Kathy Brownlee
Employees: 11,810
Jobs Cut Last Year: 1,015 (-7.9%)
Diversified operations - chemicals; refined sugar; forest products
Phone: 214-233-1700
Fax: 214-385-0586

ZALE CORPORATION
901 W. Walnut Hill Ln.
Irving, TX 75038-1003
Chm & CEO: Robert DiNicola
SVP HR: A. Herschel Kranitz
Employees: 9,500
Jobs Added Last Year: –
Retail - jewelry stores (Zales, Gordon's, Bailey Banks & Biddle)
Phone: 214-580-4000
Fax: 214-580-5336

WEATHERFORD INTERNATIONAL INC.
1360 Post Oak Blvd., Ste. 1000
Houston, TX 77056
Chm, Pres & CEO: Philip Burguieres
VP HR: John Nicholson
Employees: 2,871
Jobs Added Last Year: 1,628 (+131%)
Oil & gas - field services
Phone: 713-439-9400
Fax: 713-621-0994

ZAPATA CORPORATION
One Riverway, PO Box 4240
Houston, TX 77210
Chm, Pres & CEO: Malcolm I. Glazer
Mgr HR: Vivian Schott
Employees: 1,600
Jobs Added Last Year: 400 (+33.3%)
Oil & gas - natural gas services including gathering, compression, processing & marketing
Phone: 713-940-6100
Fax: 713-226-6052

UTAH

AMERICAN STORES COMPANY
709 E. South Temple Phone: 801-539-0112
Salt Lake City, UT 84102 Fax: 801-531-0768
Pres & CEO: Victor L. Lund
SVP HR: Scott Bergeson
Employees: 127,000
Jobs Cut Last Year: 6,000 (-4.5%)
Retail - supermarkets

HUNTSMAN CHEMICAL CORP.
2000 Eagle Gate Tower Phone: 801-532-5200
Salt Lake City, UT 84111 Fax: 801-536-1581
Chm & CEO: Jon Meade Huntsman
VP HR: Winston H. Conners
Employees: 5,000
Jobs Added Last Year: 1,100 (+28.2%)
Chemicals - diversified

FIRST SECURITY CORPORATION
79 S. Main St., PO Box 30006 Phone: 801-246-5706
Salt Lake City, UT 84130-0006 Fax: 801-359-6928
Chm & CEO: Spencer F. Eccles
SVP & Dir HR: Tad Jeppesen
Employees: 6,318
Jobs Added Last Year: 1,331 (+26.7%)
Banks - West

INTERMOUNTAIN HEALTH CARE, INC.
36 S. State St. Phone: 801-442-3587
Salt Lake City, UT 84111 Fax: 801-442-3728
Pres & CEO: Scott S. Parker
VP HR: Gary Hart
Employees: 18,000
Jobs Added Last Year: —
Hospitals

FLYING J INC.
50 W. 990 South Phone: 801-734-6400
Brigham City, UT 84302 Fax: 801-734-6556
Chm: O. Jay Call
Dir Personnel: Robert O. Langford
Employees: 6,300
Jobs Added Last Year: 1,800 (+40%)
Oil & gas - integrated

JB'S RESTAURANTS, INC.
1010 W. 2610 South Phone: 801-974-4300
Salt Lake City, UT 84119 Fax: 801-974-4385
Pres & CEO: Don M. McLomas
SVP HR & Franchising: George Gehling
Employees: 4,700
Jobs Added Last Year: 200 (+4.4%)
Retail - JB's buffet restaurants

FRANKLIN QUEST CO.
2200 W. Parkway Blvd. Phone: 801-975-1776
Salt Lake City, UT 84119-2331 Fax: 801-977-1431
Chm & CEO: Hyrum W. Smith
HR Mgr: Daken Tanner
Employees: 1,438
Jobs Added Last Year: 427 (+42.2%)
Business services - productivity seminars, business calendars & planners

MERIT MEDICAL SYSTEMS, INC.
1600 W. Merit Parkway Phone: 801-253-1600
South Jordon, UT 84095 Fax: 801-253-1688
CEO: Fred P. Lampropoulos
Dir Organizational Dev (HR): Brent Bowen
Employees: 503
Jobs Added Last Year: 195 (+63.3%)
Medical products - disposable proprietary products for cardiology & radiology

GENEVA STEEL
10 S. Geneva Rd. Phone: 801-227-9000
Vineyard, UT 84058 Fax: 801-227-9090
CEO: Joseph A. Cannon
VP HR: Carl Ramnitz
Employees: 2,680
Jobs Added Last Year: 80 (+3.1%)
Steel - production

NATURE'S SUNSHINE PRODUCTS
75 E. 1700 South Phone: 801-342-4300
Provo, UT 84606 Fax: 801-342-4305
Pres & CEO: Alan D. Kennedy
VP HR: Bruno Vassel III
Employees: 588
Jobs Added Last Year: 148 (+33.6%)
Vitamins, nutritional & personal care products - direct sales

UTAH

NOVELL, INC.
1555 N. Technology Way Phone: 801-429-7000
Orem, UT 84057 Fax: 801-429-5775
Chm, Pres & CEO: Robert J. Frankenberg
SVP HR: Ernest J. Harris
Employees: 7,914
Jobs Added Last Year: 3,579 (+82.6%)
Computers - network & word-processing software (WordPerfect)

SKYWEST AIRLINES, INC.
444 S. River Rd. Phone: 801-634-3000
St. George, UT 84770-2086 Fax: 801-634-2330
Pres & CEO: Jerry C. Atkin
VP HR: R. Dale Merrill
Employees: 2,079
Jobs Added Last Year: 285 (+15.9%)
Transportation - airline (SkyWest Airlines, Scenic Airlines); car rental franchises (Avis)

QUESTAR CORPORATION
180 E. First South Phone: 801-534-5000
Salt Lake City, UT 84147 Fax: 801-534-5166
Pres: R. D. Cash
No central personnel officer
Employees: 2,659
Jobs Added Last Year: 49 (+1.9%)
Utility - gas distribution

SMITH'S FOOD & DRUG CENTERS, INC.
1550 S. Redwood Rd. Phone: 801-974-1400
Salt Lake City, UT 84104 Fax: 801-974-1662
Chm & CEO: Jeffrey P. Smith
SVP HR: Rich Bylski
Employees: 19,000
Jobs Added Last Year: 1,000 (+5.6%)
Retail - supermarkets

SINCLAIR OIL CORPORATION
550 E. South Temple St. Phone: 801-524-2700
Salt Lake City, UT 84102 Fax: 801-524-2773
Pres: Robert E. Holding
Dir HR: Wendel White
Employees: 3,000
Jobs Added Last Year: 0
Diversified operations - oil refineries; ski resorts; hotels; gas stations

THIOKOL CORPORATION
2475 Washington Blvd. Phone: 801-629-2000
Ogden, UT 84401 Fax: 801-629-2420
Pres & CEO: James R. Wilson
EVP HR & Admin: James E. McNulty
Employees: 8,000
Jobs Cut Last Year: 1,300 (-14%)
Aerospace - solid rocket motors, propulsion & missile-launching systems

VERMONT

BEN & JERRY'S HOMEMADE, INC.
Junction of Rts. 2 & 100   Phone: ~~802-244-6957~~
North Moretown, VT 05660   Fax: 802-244-5944
Pres & CEO: Robert Holland, Jr.   802-651-9600
Dir HR: Keith Hunt
Employees: 500   *Tracy*
Jobs Added Last Year: 54 (+12.1%)   *Burns*
Food - premium ice cream

FUND AMERICAN ENTERPRISES HOLDINGS, INC.
The 1820 House   Phone: 802-649-3633
Norwich, VT 05055-0850   Fax: 802-649-2240
Chm, Pres & CEO: John J. Byrne
No central personnel officer
Employees: 3,000
Jobs Cut Last Year: 67 (-2.2%)
Financial - investment management

C&S WHOLESALE GROCERS INC.
Old Ferry Rd.   Phone: 802-257-4371
Brattleboro, VT 05301   Fax: 802-257-6727
Chm, Pres & CEO: Richard B. Cohen
VP HR: Mitchell Davis
Employees: 1,500
Jobs Added Last Year: 200 (+15.4%)
Food - wholesale

▼ *Career Magazine* http://www.careermag.com/careermag/

VIRGINIA

AMERICA ONLINE, INC.
8619 Westwood Center Dr. Phone: 703-448-8700
Vienna, VA 22182-2285 Fax: 703-448-0793
Pres & CEO: Stephen M. Case
HR Off: Anita Faircloth
Employees: 527
Jobs Added Last Year: 291 (+123.3%)
Computers - on-line information

CACI INTERNATIONAL INC.
1100 N. Glebe Rd. Phone: 703-841-7800
Arlington, VA 22201 Fax: 703-841-7882
Chm, Pres & CEO: J. P. London
SVP Administrative Svcs (HR): William Clancy
Employees: 3,069
Jobs Added Last Year: 769 (+33.4%)
Computers - services

AMERICAN MANAGEMENT SYSTEMS
4050 Legato Rd. Phone: 703-267-8000
Fairfax, VA 22033 Fax: 703-267-8123
CEO: Paul A. Brands
Dir HR: Judy Blair
Employees: 3,800
Jobs Added Last Year: 600 (+18.8%)
Computers - management consulting, software programming, systems design & development

CADMUS COMMUNICATIONS CORPORATION
6620 W. Broad St., Ste. 500 Phone: 804-287-5680
Richmond, VA 23230 Fax: 804-287-5230
Chm, Pres & CEO: C. Stephenson Gillispie, Jr.
VP HR: Gregory Moyer
Employees: 2,400
Jobs Added Last Year: 620 (+34.8%)
Printing - commercial; marketing & publishing

ATLANTIC COAST AIRLINES INC.
One Export Dr. Phone: 703-406-6500
Sterling, VA 20164 Fax: 703-406-6599
CEO: C. Edward Acker
Dir Admin & Sales (HR): Angie M. Shermer
Employees: 1,324
Jobs Added Last Year: 273 (+26%)
Transportation - airline

CARPENTER CO.
5016 Monument Ave. Phone: 804-359-0800
Richmond, VA 23261 Fax: 804-353-0694
Chm & CEO: Stanley F. Pauley
Dir Personnel: David Harned
Employees: 6,905
Jobs Added Last Year: 310 (+4.7%)
Chemicals - specialty; polyurethane foam

BASSETT FURNITURE INDUSTRIES, INC.
PO Box 626 Phone: 703-629-7511
Bassett, VA 24055 Fax: 703-629-6333
Pres & COO: Glenn Hunsucker
VP & Dir Personnel: Jim Philpott
Employees: 7,800
Jobs Added Last Year: 400 (+5.4%)
Furniture

CHESAPEAKE CORPORATION
1021 E. Cary St., PO Box 2350 Phone: 804-697-1000
Richmond, VA 23218-2350 Fax: 804-697-1199
Chm & CEO: J. Carter Fox
VP HR: Thomas A. Smith
Employees: 5,062
Jobs Added Last Year: 23 (+.5%)
Paper & paper products - containerboard, linerboard & corrugated packaging materials

BEST PRODUCTS CO. INC.
PO Box 26303 Phone: 804-261-2000
Richmond, VA 23260 Fax: 804-261-2250
Chm, Pres & CEO: Stewart M. Kasen
VP HR: Wayne Tennent
Employees: 5,000
Jobs Added Last Year: —
Retail - catalog showrooms (general merchandise & jewelry)

CIRCUIT CITY STORES, INC.
9950 Mayland Dr. Phone: 804-527-4000
Richmond, VA 23233-1464 Fax: 804-527-4164
Pres & CEO: Richard L. Sharp
SVP HR: William E. Zierden
Employees: 23,625
Jobs Added Last Year: 6,990 (+42%)
Retail - consumer electronics

VIRGINIA

CRESTAR FINANCIAL CORPORATION
919 E. Main St., PO Box 26665 Phone: 804-782-5000
Richmond, VA 23261-6665 Fax: 804-782-5815
CEO: Richard G. Tilghman
EVP & Mgmt Resources Dir (HR): James J. Kelley
Employees: 7,000
Jobs Added Last Year: 424 (+6.4%)
Banks - Southeast

GANNETT CO., INC.
1100 Wilson Blvd. Phone: 703-284-6000
Arlington, VA 22234 Fax: 703-558-4697
Chm, Pres & CEO: John J. Curley
SVP Personnel: Madelyn P. Jennings
Employees: 36,500
Jobs Cut Last Year: 200 (-.5%)
Publishing - newspapers; radio & TV broadcasting

CSX CORPORATION
One James Center, 901 E. Cary St. Phone: 804-782-1400
Richmond, VA 23219 Fax: 804-782-1409
Chm, Pres & CEO: John W. Snow
SVP Emp Rel: Donald D. Davis
Employees: 47,063
Jobs Cut Last Year: 534 (-1.1%)
Transportation - rail; container ships (Sea-Land); barges (American Commercial)

GENERAL DYNAMICS CORPORATION
3190 Fairview Park Dr. Phone: 703-876-3000
Falls Church, VA 22042-4523 Fax: 703-876-3125
Chm, Pres & CEO: James R. Mellor
VP HR: Ralph W. Kiger
Employees: 30,500
Jobs Cut Last Year: 26,300 (-46.3%)
Weapons & weapon systems - nuclear submarines; armored vehicles

DOMINION RESOURCES, INC.
901 E. Byrd St., PO Box 26532 Phone: 804-775-5700
Richmond, VA 23261-6532 Fax: 804-775-5819
Chm, Pres & CEO: Thos. E. Capps
VP HR: Robert E. Rigsby
Employees: 12,057
Jobs Cut Last Year: 160 (-1.3%)
Utility - electric power

GENICOM CORPORATION
14800 Conference Center Dr. Phone: 703-949-1000
Chantilly, VA 22021-3806 Fax: 703-949-1185
Pres & CEO: Paul T. Winn
VP HR: Bruce Meyer
Employees: 2,395
Jobs Added Last Year: 248 (+11.6%)
Computers - printers

DYNCORP
2000 Edmund Halley Dr. Phone: 703-264-0330
Reston, VA 22091 Fax: 703-264-8600
Pres & CEO: Daniel R. Bannister
Dir HR: Ronald R. Geiger
Employees: 22,000
Jobs Added Last Year: 2,200 (+11.1%)
Business services - technical & professional

HEILIG-MEYERS CO.
2235 Staples Mill Rd. Phone: 804-359-9171
Richmond, VA 23230 Fax: 804-254-1498
Chm & CEO: William C. DeRusha
SVP HR & Training: Ronald M. Ragland
Employees: 10,536
Jobs Added Last Year: 2,686 (+34.2%)
Retail - home furnishings & appliances in the rural Southeast & Midwest

FIRST VIRGINIA BANKS, INC.
6400 Arlington Blvd. Phone: 703-241-4000
Falls Church, VA 22042-2336 Fax: 703-241-3464
Chm, Pres & CEO: Barry J. Fitzpatrick
Asst VP HR: Terrance Bayly
Employees: 5,155
Jobs Added Last Year: 604 (+13%)
Banks - Southeast

ICF KAISER INTERNATIONAL, INC.
9300 Lee Hwy. Phone: 703-934-3600
Fairfax, VA 22031 Fax: 703-934-9740
Chm & CEO: James O. Edwards
SVP HR: Marcy Romm
Employees: 5,700
Jobs Added Last Year: 1,700 (+42.5%)
Engineering - R&D services

VIRGINIA

INTL. FAMILY ENTERTAINMENT
1000 Centerville Tpke. Phone: 804-523-7301
Virginia Beach, VA 23463 Fax: 804-523-7878
Pres & CEO: Timothy B. Robertson
Dir Personnel: Carol Kleiber
Employees: 692
Jobs Added Last Year: 412 (+147.1%)
Broadcasting - cable TV network (The Family Channel), TV production, TV syndication (*Bob Newhart, Mary Tyler Moore*)

FELD PRODUCTIONS, INC.
8607 Westwood Center Dr. Phone: 703-448-4000
Vienna, VA 22182 Fax: 703-448-4100
Pres: Kenneth Feld
Dir HR: Connie Kepple
Employees: 2,500
Jobs Added Last Year: 0
Leisure & recreational services - Ringling Brothers & Barnum & Bailey Circus, Siegfried & Roy & Walt Disney's World on Ice

JAMES RIVER CORPORATION
120 Tredegar St. Phone: 804-644-5411
Richmond, VA 23219 Fax: 804-649-4428
Chm, Pres & CEO: Robert C. Williams
SVP HR: Daniel J. Girvan
Employees: 35,000
Jobs Cut Last Year: 3,000 (-7.9%)
Paper & paper products; packaging; paperware (Dixie) & paper towels (Brawny)

JEFFERSON BANKSHARES, INC.
123 E. Main St. Phone: 804-972-1100
Charlottesville, VA 22902 Fax: 804-972-1419
Pres & CEO: O. Kenton McCartney
SVP & HR Dir: Susan Stafford
Employees: 1,272
Jobs Added Last Year: 87 (+7.3%)
Banks - Southeast

K-VA-T FOOD STORES, INC.
329 N. Main St. Phone: 703-935-4587
Grundy, VA 24614 Fax: 703-935-4587
Chm & CEO: Jack C. Smith
VP HR & Security: William L. Neely
Employees: 3,673
Jobs Added Last Year: 41 (+1.1%)
Retail - supermarkets

LAWYERS TITLE INSURANCE CORPORATION
6630 W. Broad St. Phone: 804-281-6700
Richmond, VA 23260 Fax: 804-282-5453
CEO: Charles H. Foster, Jr.
Mgr HR: Bob Martin
Employees: 3,429
Jobs Added Last Year: 477 (+16.2%)
Financial - title insurance

LEGENT CORPORATION
575 Herndon Pkwy. Phone: 703-708-3000
Herndon, VA 22070-5526 Fax: 703-708-3668
Chm, Pres & CEO: Jere L. Stead
HR Mgr: Sue Ratcliffe
Employees: 2,700
Jobs Added Last Year: 300 (+12.5%)
Computers - systems management software

LITTLEFIELD, ADAMS & CO.
1302 Rockland Ave. NW Phone: 703-366-2451
Roanoke, VA 24012 Fax: 210-829-0618
CEO: John Stuth
Controller (HR): Greg Shaff
Employees: 205
Jobs Added Last Year: 145 (+241.7%)
Apparel

MARS, INC.
6885 Elm St. Phone: 703-821-4900
McLean, VA 22101 Fax: 703-448-9678
Chm, CEO & Co-Pres: Forrest E. Mars, Jr.
Sec (HR): E. J. Stegeman
Employees: 27,000
Jobs Cut Last Year: 1,000 (-3.6%)
Food - confectionery (Milky Way, Dove), pet food (Kal Kan) & rice (Uncle Ben's)

MEDIA GENERAL, INC.
333 E. Grace St. Phone: 804-649-6000
Richmond, VA 23219 Fax: 804-649-6898
Chm, Pres & CEO: J. Stewart Bryan II
Dir Administrative Svcs (HR): Edward C. Tosh
Employees: 7,300
Jobs Added Last Year: 0
Publishing - newspapers & business information

VIRGINIA

MOBIL CORPORATION
3225 Gallows Rd. Phone: 703-846-3000
Fairfax, VA 22037-0001 Fax: 703-846-4669
Chm, Pres, CEO & COO: Lucio A. Noto
Mgr HR: Douglas O. Fitzsimmons
Employees: 61,900
Jobs Cut Last Year: 1,800 (-2.8%)
Oil & gas - integrated; packaging films; fabricated plastics

ORBITAL SCIENCES CORPORATION
21700 Atlantic Blvd. Phone: 703-406-5000
Dulles, VA 20166 Fax: 703-406-3502
Chm, Pres & CEO: David W. Thompson
VP HR: Stephen Parker
Employees: 1,123
Jobs Added Last Year: 254 (+29.2%)
Aerospace - aircraft & space launch equipment

NAVY EXCHANGE SYSTEM
3280 Virginia Beach Blvd. Phone: 804- 463-6200
Virginia Beach, VA 23452 Fax: 804-631-3659
Commander: John T. Kavanaugh
Dir HR: Michael Marchesani
Employees: 22,000
Jobs Cut Last Year: 387 (-1.7%)
Retail - network of retail outlets serving Navy personnel & their families, reservists & retirees

PHP HEALTHCARE
4900 Seminary Rd., 12th Fl. Phone: 703-998-7808
Alexandria, VA 22311 Fax: 703-758-3600
Chm & Pres: Charles H. Robbins
VP HR: John Bucur
Employees: 2,800
Jobs Added Last Year: 450 (+19.1%)
Health care - outpatient & home

NETWORK IMAGING CORPORATION
500 Huntmar Park Dr. Phone: 703-478-2260
Herndon, VA 22070 Fax: 703-478-0147
Pres & CEO: Robert P. Bernardi
VP HR: Karen Alden
Employees: 425
Jobs Added Last Year: 301 (+242.7%)
Computers - graphics

PRIMARK CORPORATION
8251 Greensboro Dr., Ste. 700 Phone: 703-790-7600
McLean, VA 22102 Fax: 703-790-7677
Chm & Pres: Joseph E. Kasputys
Dir Personnel: Diane Robson
Employees: 3,339
Jobs Added Last Year: 1,468 (+78.5%)
Diversified operations - leasing services; ground transport; mortgage banking

NORFOLK SOUTHERN CORPORATION
3 Commercial Place Phone: 804-629-2680
Norfolk, VA 23510-2191 Fax: 804-629-2798
Chm, Pres & CEO: David R. Goode
VP Personnel: Paul Austin
Employees: 29,304
Jobs Cut Last Year: 831 (-2.8%)
Transportation - rail & truck (North American Van Lines)

REYNOLDS METALS COMPANY
6601 W. Broad St. Phone: 804-281-2000
Richmond, VA 23261-7003 Fax: 804-281-3695
Chm & CEO: Richard G. Holder
EVP HR & External Affairs: Donald T. Cowles
Employees: 29,000
Jobs Cut Last Year: 300 (-1%)
Metals - aluminum, including cans & wrap

O'SULLIVAN CORPORATION
1944 Valley Ave., PO Box 3510 Phone: 703-667-6666
Winchester, VA 22604 Fax: 703-722-2695
CEO: Arthur H. Bryant II
HR Mgr: Rick Pomeroy
Employees: 2,100
Jobs Added Last Year: 200 (+10.5%)
Rubber & plastic products - molded plastic parts for automotive & other industries

ROWE FURNITURE CORPORATION
239 Rowan St. Phone: 703-389-8671
Salem, VA 24153 Fax: 703-389-8217
Pres & CEO: Gerald M. Birnbach
Corp Dir HR: John Clark
Employees: 1,000
Jobs Added Last Year: 100 (+11.1%)
Furniture

VIRGINIA

S&K FAMOUS BRANDS, INC.
11100 W. Broad St.   Phone: 804-346-2500
Richmond, VA 23294-1800   Fax: 804-346-2627
Chm & CEO: Stuart C. Siegel
VP HR: Gray Rawlings
Employees: 1,350
Jobs Added Last Year: 150 (+12.5%)
Retail - apparel & shoes

SIGNET BANKING CORPORATION
7 N. Eighth St.   Phone: 804-747-2000
Richmond, VA 23219   Fax: 804-771-7599
Chm & CEO: Robert M. Freeman
Dir HR: Harold N. Taylor
Employees: 5,828
Jobs Added Last Year: 96 (+1.7%)
Banks - Southeast

SMITHFIELD COMPANIES, INC.
311 County St., Ste. 203   Phone: 804-399-3100
Portsmouth, VA 23704   Fax: 804-399-0916
Chm, Pres & CEO: Richard S. Fuller
No central personnel officer
Employees: 365
Jobs Added Last Year: 70 (+23.7%)
Food - meat processing & dry-cured hams (Smithfield Hams & Joyner)

SMITHFIELD FOODS, INC.
501 N. Church St.   Phone: 804-357-4321
Smithfield, VA 23430   Fax: 804-357-1331
CEO: Joseph W. Luter III
Personnel: Herbert DeGoft
Employees: 8,000
Jobs Added Last Year: 1,000 (+14.3%)
Food - pork products (Patrick Cudahy, Gwaltney, Esskay & Smithfield)

STANLEY FURNITURE COMPANY INC.
Rte. 57   Phone: 703-627-2000
Stanleytown, VA 24168   Fax: 703-629-5114
CEO: Albert L. Prillaman
No central personnel officer
Employees: 3,000
Jobs Added Last Year: 200 (+7.1%)
Furniture

TFC ENTERPRISES INC.
240 Corporate Blvd.   Phone: 804-466-1222
Norfolk, VA 23502   Fax: 804-455-5574
Pres & CEO: George R. Kouri
VP HR: Nancy Hawkins
Employees: 400
Jobs Added Last Year: 100 (+33.3%)
Financial - auto loans, primarily to armed forces personnel

TULTEX CORPORATION
22 E. Church St., PO Box 5191   Phone: 703-632-2961
Martinsville, VA 24115   Fax: 703-632-8658
CEO: Charles W. Davis, Jr.
Dir HR: Randolph Rollins
Employees: 7,500
Jobs Added Last Year: 1,100 (+17.2%)
Apparel - activewear

UNIVERSAL CORPORATION
Hamilton & Broad Sts.   Phone: 804-359-9311
Richmond, VA 23260   Fax: 804-254-3584
Chm & CEO: Henry H. Harrell
Corp Dir HR: Mike Oberschmidt, Jr.
Employees: 25,000
Jobs Added Last Year: 0
Tobacco; lumber & building products; agricultural products

USAIR GROUP, INC.
2345 Crystal Dr.   Phone: 703-418-5306
Arlington, VA 22227   Fax: 703-418-5307
Chm & CEO: Seth E. Schofield
SVP HR: John P. Frestel, Jr.
Employees: 48,500
Jobs Cut Last Year: 400 (-.8%)
Transportation - airline

THE WHITLOCK GROUP
4120 Cox Rd.   Phone: 804-273-9200
Glen Allen, VA 23060   Fax: 804-273-9905
Pres: John D. Whitlock
No central personnel officer
Employees: 210
Jobs Added Last Year: 123 (+141.4%)
Computers - information, media, presentation, broadcast & security services

WASHINGTON

ADVANCED TECHNOLOGY LABORATORIES, INC.
22100 Bothell Hwy. SE Phone: 206-487-7000
Bothell, WA 98012 Fax: 206-487-7970
CEO: Dennis C. Fill
No central personnel officer
Employees: 2,650
Jobs Cut Last Year: 50 (-1.9%)
Medical instruments

CELLULAR TECHNICAL SERVICES COMPANY, INC.
2401 Fourth Ave. Phone: 206-443-6400
Seattle, WA 98121-1438 Fax: 206-443-1550
Chm: Stephen Katz
Pres & COO (HR): Robert Dahut
Employees: 59
Jobs Added Last Year: 11 (+22.9%)
Integrated real-time information management systems for the cellular communications industry

AIRBORNE FREIGHT CORPORATION
3101 Western Ave., PO Box 662 Phone: 206-285-4600
Seattle, WA 98111 Fax: 206-281-7615
Chm & CEO: Robert S. Cline
SVP HR: Richard G. Goodwin
Employees: 16,800
Jobs Added Last Year: 1,100 (+7%)
Transportation - air express

EAGLE HARDWARE & GARDEN
101 Andover Park East, Ste. 200 Phone: 206-431-5740
Tukwila, WA 98188 Fax: 206-241-7184
Chm & CEO: David J. Heersperger
Dir HR: Brian Price
Employees: 2,400
Jobs Added Last Year: 1,100 (+84.6%)
Building products - home improvement centers in the Pacific Northwest, western Canada & Hawaii

ALASKA AIR GROUP, INC.
19300 Pacific Hwy. South Phone: 206-431-7040
Seattle, WA 98188 Fax: 206-433-3366
Chm, Pres & CEO: John F. Kelly
VP HR: Timothy R. Metcalf
Employees: 8,458
Jobs Cut Last Year: 208 (-2.4%)
Transportation - airline (Alaska Airlines, Horizon Air)

ERNST HOME CENTER, INC.
1511 Sixth Ave. Phone: 206-621-6700
Seattle, WA 98101 Fax: 206-626-6837
CEO: Hal Smith
Dir HR: Sue Alford
Employees: 3,250
Jobs Added Last Year: —
Building products - home improvement, hardware & garden centers

ASYMETRIX CORP.
110 110th Ave NE, Ste. 700 Phone: 206-426-0501
Bellevue, WA 98004-5840 Fax: 206-455-3071
Chm & CEO: Paul Allen
Dir HR: Shirley Carder
Employees: 270
Jobs Added Last Year: 30 (+12.5%)
Computers - multimedia applications development (ToolBook) & database customizing software

FLUKE CORPORATION
6920 Seaway Blvd. Phone: 206-347-6100
Everett, WA 98203 Fax: 206-356-5116
Chm & CEO: William G. Parzybok, Jr.
Dir HR: Patrick O'Hara
Employees: 2,583
Jobs Added Last Year: 369 (+16.7%)
Electronics - test tools

THE BOEING COMPANY
7755 E. Marginal Way South Phone: 206-655-2121
Seattle, WA 98108 Fax: 206-655-7004
Chm & CEO: Frank A. Shrontz
VP HR: Larry G. McKean
Employees: 123,000
Jobs Cut Last Year: 19,000 (-13.4%)
Aerospace - commercial & military aircraft equipment

FOURGEN SOFTWARE INC.
115 NE 100th St. Phone: 206-522-0055
Seattle, WA 98125 Fax: 206-522-0053
Pres & CEO: Gary Gagliardi
HR Mgr: Megan Kimsey
Employees: 115
Jobs Added Last Year: 31 (+36.9%)
Computers - supply chain management & financial software

WASHINGTON

GROUP HEALTH COOPERATIVE OF PUGET SOUND
521 Wall St. Phone: 206-448-6460
Seattle, WA 98121 Fax: 206-448-6755
Pres & CEO: Phillip M. Nudelman
VP HR: Brenda Tolbert
Employees: 9,000
Jobs Added Last Year: —
Health maintenance organization

KEY TRONIC CORPORATION
4424 N. Sullivan Rd. Phone: 509-928-8000
Spokane, WA 99216 Fax: 509-927-5248
CEO: Stanley Hiller, Jr.
Dir HR: Keith C. Clement
Employees: 2,244
Jobs Added Last Year: 159 (+7.6%)
Computers - keyboards & input devices

HEART TECHNOLOGY, INC.
17425 NE Union Hill Rd. Phone: 206-889-6160
Redmond, WA 98052-3376 Fax: 206-867-5466
CEO: David C. Auth
HR Mgr: Karen Grosz
Employees: 294
Jobs Added Last Year: 110 (+59.8%)
Medical products - drill for clogged arteries (Rotablator)

LANOGA CORPORATION
17946 NE 65th St. Phone: 206-883-4125
Redmond, WA 98052 Fax: 206-882-2959
Pres & CEO: Daryl Nagel
No central personnel officer
Employees: 2,975
Jobs Added Last Year: 75 (+2.6%)
Building products

HILLHAVEN CORPORATION
1148 Broadway Plaza Phone: 206-572-4901
Tacoma, WA 98402 Fax: 206-756-4745
CEO: Bruce L. Busby
SVP HR & Support Svcs: Kris Scoumperdis
Employees: 38,100
Jobs Cut Last Year: 700 (-1.8%)
Nursing homes

LONGVIEW FIBRE COMPANY
PO Box 639 Phone: 206-425-1550
Longview, WA 98632 Fax: 206-425-3116
Chm, Pres & CEO: Richard P. Wollenberg
Personnel Mgr: L.L. Metzler
Employees: 3,750
Jobs Added Last Year: 250 (+7.1%)
Paper & paper products - shipping containers, merchandise & grocery bags; containerboard & paper; tree farms

IMMUNEX CORPORATION 13742
51 University St. Phone: 206-587-0430
Seattle, WA 98101 Fax: 206-587-0606
Chm & CEO: Edward V. Fritzky
VP HR: Anita Williamson
Employees: 782
Jobs Added Last Year: 187 (+31.4%)
Biomedical & genetic products - cancer & immune-deficiency therapies

MICROSOFT CORPORATION 14120
One Microsoft Way Phone: 206-882-8080
Redmond, WA 98052-6399 Fax: 206-883-8101
Chm & CEO: William H. Gates III
VP HR: Michael R. Murray
Employees: 15,257
Jobs Added Last Year: 827 (+5.7%)
Computers - operating environments (MS-DOS, Windows) & application software (Excel, Word); CD-ROM publishing

INTERLINQ SOFTWARE CORPORATION
11255 Kirkland Way Phone: 206-827-1112
Kirkland, WA 98033-6361 Fax: 206-827-0927
CFO & Interim Pres (HR): Stephen A. Yount
Employees: 183
Jobs Added Last Year: 40 (+28%)
Computers - mortgage loan management software (MortgageWare)

NORDSTROM, INC. 14261
1501 Fifth Ave. Phone: 206-628-2111
Seattle, WA 98101-1603 Fax: 206-628-1795
Co-President: Raymond A. Johnson
VP HR: Charles Dudley
Employees: 33,000
Jobs Added Last Year: 0
Retail - department stores

WASHINGTON

OMEGA ENVIRONMENTAL, INC.
19805 N. Creek Pkwy. Phone: 206-486-4800
Bothell, WA 98041-3005 Fax: 206-486-1532
Pres & CEO: David C. Kravitz
VP HR: Jerry Gutman
Employees: 650
Jobs Added Last Year: 460 (+242.1%)
Pollution control - installation & removal of underground storage tanks

PACCAR INC.
777 106th Ave. NE Phone: 206-455-7400
Bellevue, WA 98004 Fax: 206-453-4900
Chm & CEO: Charles M. Pigott
VP Emp Rel: Laurie L. Baker
Employees: 11,800
Jobs Added Last Year: 823 (+7.5%)
Trucks - medium & heavy (Kenworth, Peterbilt); winches & oilfield pumps; auto parts stores (Grand Auto)

PRICE/COSTCO, INC.
10809-120th Ave N.E. Phone: 206-803-8100
Kirkland, WA 98033 Fax: 206-803-8103
Pres & CEO: James D. Sinegal
VP & Dir HR/Risk Mgmt: John Matthews
Employees: 40,000
Jobs Cut Last Year: 3,000 (-7%)
Retail - discount warehouse clubs

QUALITY FOOD CENTERS, INC.
10112 NE 10th St. Phone: 206-455-3761
Bellevue, WA 98004 Fax: 206-462-2159
Chm & CEO: Stuart M. Sloan
No central personnel officer
Employees: 2,900
Jobs Added Last Year: 300 (+11.5%)
Retail - supermarkets

RED LION INNS LIMITED PARTNERSHIP
4001 Main St. Phone: 206-696-0001
Vancouver, WA 98663 Fax: 206-696-4964
Pres & CEO: David J. Johnson
Dir Employment: Susan Rivenbark
Employees: 11,000
Jobs Added Last Year: —
Hotels & motels

SAFECO CORPORATION
SAFECO Plaza Phone: 206-545-5000
Seattle, WA 98185 Fax: 206-545-5995
Chm, Pres & CEO: Roger H. Eigsti
VP HR: Darryl Sabin
Employees: 7,000
Jobs Cut Last Year: 300 (-4.1%)
Insurance - property & casualty

SERVICES GROUP OF AMERICA INC.
4025 Delridge Way SW Phone: 206-933-5000
Seattle, WA 98106 Fax: 206-933-5279
Chm: Thomas J. Stewart
Dir HR: Jacqueline Steven
Employees: 3,000
Jobs Added Last Year: 0
Food - distribution; insurance & real estate

SIMPSON INVESTMENT CO.
1201 Third Ave., Ste. 4900 Phone: 206-224-5000
Seattle, WA 98101 Fax: 206-224-5060
Chm: William G. Reed, Jr.
VP HR: Cynthia Sonstelie
Employees: 7,600
Jobs Added Last Year: 600 (+8.6%)
Building products - lumber, logging, plywood doors

STARBUCKS CORPORATION
2203 Airport Way South Phone: 206-447-1575
Seattle, WA 98134 Fax: 206-682-7570
Chm, Pres & CEO: Howard Schultz
SVP HR: Sharon Elliott
Employees: 4,585
Jobs Added Last Year: 1,732 (+60.7%)
Retail - coffee & other beverages

STERLING FINANCIAL CORPORATION
N. 120 Wall St. Phone: 509-458-3711
Spokane, WA 99201 Fax: 509-624-4233
Chm & CEO: Harold B. Gilkey
VP & HR Mgr: Debby J. Ogan
Employees: 494
Jobs Added Last Year: 115 (+30.3%)
Financial - savings & loans

WASHINGTON

UNIVAR CORPORATION
6100 Carillon Point Phone: 206-889-3400
Kirkland, WA 98033 Fax: 206-889-4100
Pres & CEO: James W. Bernard
VP HR: Drew McAfee
Employees: 3,250
Jobs Cut Last Year: 75 (-2.3%)
Chemicals - diversified

UTILX CORPORATION
22404 66th Ave. South Phone: 206-395-0200
Kent, WA 98032-4801 Fax: 206-395-1040
Pres & CEO: Craig E. Davis
Dir HR: Isaiah Brown, Jr.
Employees: 426
Jobs Added Last Year: 95 (+28.7%)
Business services - specialized underground pipe & cable repair for utilities

WALKER RICHER & QUINN INC.
1500 Dexter Ave N. Phone: 206-217-7500
Seattle, WA 98109-3051 Fax: 206-217-0380
CEO & Pres: Doug Walker
Mgr Human Svcs: Char Harrington
Employees: 400
Jobs Added Last Year: 175 (+77.8%)
Computers - software to connect open & proprietary systems

WALL DATA, INC.
11332 122nd Way NE Phone: 206-814-9255
Kirkland, WA 98034-6931 Fax: 206-814-4300
Chm, Pres & CEO: James Simpson
Mgr HR: Lynn Sederholm
Employees: 388
Jobs Added Last Year: 167 (+75.6%)
Computers - software to connect PCs & mainframes

WASHINGTON MUTUAL, INC.
1201 Third Ave. Phone: 206-461-2000
Seattle, WA 98101 Fax: 206-554-2604
Pres: Kerry K. Killinger
EVP (HR): Liane Wilson
Employees: 4,857
Jobs Added Last Year: 174 (+3.7%)
Financial - savings & loans

WEYERHAEUSER COMPANY
Tacoma, WA 98477 Phone: 206-924-2345
Pres & CEO: John W. Creighton, Jr. Fax: 206-924-7407
SVP HR: Steven R. Hill
Employees: 36,748
Jobs Cut Last Year: 2,274 (-5.8%)
Building products - wood; pulp & paper; financial services; real estate

WEST VIRGINIA

HORIZON BANCORP INC.
One Park Ave. Phone: 304-255-7000
Beckley, WV 25802 Fax: 304-255-7329
Pres: Philip L. McLaughlin
VP HR: Myra Crook
Employees: 260
Jobs Added Last Year: 116 (+80.6%)
Banks - Southeast

UNITED BANKSHARES, INC.
Fifth & Avery Sts. Phone: 304-424-8800
Parkersburg, WV 26102 Fax: 304-348-8479
Chm: Richard M. Adams
SVP (HR): Jack Stokes
Employees: 889
Jobs Added Last Year: 93 (+11.7%)
Banks - Southeast

MCJUNKIN CORPORATION
PO Box 513 Phone: 304-348-5211
Charleston, WV 25322 Fax: 304-348-4922
CEO: H. B. Wehrle III
Dir HR: William E. Board
Employees: 1,372
Jobs Added Last Year: 127 (+10.2%)
Electrical products - piping & electrical equipment; oil & gas field equipment

WEIRTON STEEL CORPORATION
400 Three Springs Dr. Phone: 304-797-2000
Weirton, WV 26062 Fax: 304-797-2821
Chm & CEO: Herbert Elish
SVP HR: William C. Brenneisen
Employees: 6,542
Jobs Cut Last Year: 437 (-6.3%)
Steel - flat-rolled

ONE VALLEY BANCORP OF WEST VIRGINIA, INC.
PO Box 1793 Phone: 304-348-7000
Charleston, WV 25326 Fax: 304-348-7306
Pres & CEO: J. Holmes Morrison
SVP HR: Bernice J. Deem
Employees: 2,200
Jobs Added Last Year: 562 (+34.3%)
Banks - Southeast

WESBANCO, INC.
One Bank Plaza Phone: 304-234-9000
Wheeling, WV 26003 Fax: 304-232-3795
Pres & CEO: Edward M. George
Dir HR: John W. Moore, Jr.
Employees: 775
Jobs Added Last Year: 352 (+83.2%)
Banks - Southeast

STEEL OF WEST VIRGINIA, INC.
17th St. & Second Ave. Phone: 304-696-8200
Huntington, WV 25703 Fax: 304-529-1479
Pres: Robert L. Bunting, Jr.
VP HR: Larry Gue
Employees: 539
Jobs Added Last Year: 107 (+24.8%)
Steel - production

WISCONSIN

A. O. SMITH CORPORATION
PO Box 23972 Phone: 414-359-4000
Milwaukee, WI 53223-0972 Fax: 414-359-4180
Chm & CEO: Robert J. O'Toole
Corp Dir HR: Randy White
Employees: 10,000
Jobs Added Last Year: 600 (+6.4%)
Automotive & trucking - original equipment

ABT BUILDING PRODUCTS CORPORATION
One Neenah Center, Ste. 600 Phone: 414-751-8611
Neenah, WI 54956-3070 Fax: 414-751-0370
Chm, Pres & CEO: George T. Brophy
Corp Dir HR: Thomas J. Kelly
Employees: 1,435
Jobs Added Last Year: 415 (+40.7%)
Building products - paneling & siding

AMERICAN FAMILY MUTUAL INSURANCE CO.
6000 American Pkwy. Phone: 608-243-4921
Madison, WI 53783 Fax: 608-249-0100
Chm & CEO: Dale F. Mathwich
VP HR: Vicki L. Chvala
Employees: 6,373
Jobs Added Last Year: —
Insurance - multiline

APPLIED POWER INC.
13000 W. Silver Spring Dr. Phone: 414-781-6600
Butler, WI 53007 Fax: 414-781-1049
Chm, Pres & CEO: Richard G. Sim
VP HR: Louis Font
Employees: 2,702
Jobs Cut Last Year: 73 (-2.6%)
Machine tools & related products

ASSOCIATED BANC-CORP
112 N. Adams St., PO Box 13307 Phone: 414-433-4384
Green Bay, WI 54307-3307 Fax: 414-433-3261
Chm, Pres & CEO: Harry B. Conlon
VP & HR Dir: Pat O'Keefe
Employees: 1,718
Jobs Added Last Year: 141 (+8.9%)
Banks - Midwest

BANTA CORPORATION
225 Main St. Phone: 414-722-7777
Menasha, WI 54952 Fax: 414-722-6495
Pres & CEO: Donald D. Belcher
VP HR: James Milslagle
Employees: 4,172
Jobs Cut Last Year: 56 (-1.3%)
Printing - commercial

BRIGGS & STRATTON CORPORATION
12301 W. Wirth St. Phone: 414-259-5333
Wauwatosa, WI 53222-2110 Fax: 414-259-5338
Chm & CEO: Frederick T. Stratton, Jr.
VP HR: Gerald E. Zitzer
Employees: 8,583
Jobs Added Last Year: 238 (+2.9%)
Engines - internal combustion

CARSON PIRIE SCOTT & CO.
331 W. Wisconsin Ave. Phone: 414-347-4141
Milwaukee, WI 53203 Fax: 414-278-5748
Pres & CEO: Stanton J. Bluestone
EVP HR: Roger Gaston
Employees: 17,800
Jobs Added Last Year: 3,800 (+27.1%)
Retail - major department stores (Carson Pirie Scott, Bergner's & Boston Store)

CASE CORPORATION
700 State St. Phone: 414-636-6011
Racine, WI 53404 Fax: 414-636-0483
Pres & CEO: Jean-Pierre Rosso
VP HR: Judy Murray
Employees: 16,892
Jobs Cut Last Year: 208 (-1.2%)
Machinery - tractors, combines, cotton pickers, backhoes, excavators & forklifts

CONSOLIDATED PAPERS, INC.
PO Box 8050 Phone: 715-422-3111
Wisconsin Rapids, WI 54495-8050 Fax: 715-422-3469
Pres & CEO: Patrick F. Brennan
Dir HR: Kenneth A. Ebert
Employees: 4,852
Jobs Cut Last Year: 94 (-1.9%)
Paper & paper products

WISCONSIN

FIRSTAR CORPORATION
777 E. Wisconsin Ave.　　　Phone: 414-765-4321
Milwaukee, WI 53202　　　Fax: 414-765-4349
CEO: Roger L. Fitzsimonds
SVP HR: Peggy Page
Employees: 9,133
Jobs Added Last Year: 462 (+5.3%)
Banks - Midwest

FISERV, INC.
255 FIserv Dr.　　　　　　Phone: 414-879-5000
Brookfield, WI 53045　　　Fax: 414-879-5013
Chm & CEO: George D. Dalton
SVP HR: Jack P. Bucalo
Employees: 6,050
Jobs Added Last Year: 1,000 (+19.8%)
Business services - data processing systems & information management

FORT HOWARD CORPORATION
1919 S. Broadway　　　　Phone: 414-435-8821
Green Bay, WI 54304　　　Fax: 414-435-3703
Chm & CEO: Donald H. DeMeuse
VP HR: David K. Wong
Employees: 6,800
Jobs Added Last Year: 200 (+3%)
Paper & products - paper towels (Mardi Gras, So-Dri, Page, Green Forest), bath tissue (Soft'n Gentle)

GANDER MOUNTAIN, INC.
PO Box 128, Hwy. West　　Phone: 414-862-2331
Wilmot, WI 53192　　　　Fax: 414-862-2330
Pres & CEO: Joseph C. Lawler
Dir HR: Milton D. Ancevic
Employees: 1,439
Jobs Added Last Year: 276 (+23.7%)
Retail - mail order of outdoor apparel & equipment

HARLEY-DAVIDSON, INC. `10706`
3700 W. Juneau Ave.　　　Phone: 414-342-4680
Milwaukee, WI 53208　　　Fax: 414-935-4977
Pres & CEO: Richard F. Teerlink
VP HR: C. William Gray
Employees: 6,000
Jobs Added Last Year: 200 (+3.4%)
Motorcycles & related products; RVs

HARNISCHFEGER INDUSTRIES INCORPORATED
13400 Bishops Ln.　　　　Phone: 414-671-4400
Brookfield, WI 53005　　　Fax: 414-671-7604
Chm & CEO: Jeffery T. Grade
VP HR: Joseph A. Podawiltz, Jr.
Employees: 13,000
Jobs Added Last Year: 2,200 (+20.4%)
Machinery - mining (Joy Technologies), material handling & papermaking (Beloit Corp.)

HEIN-WERNER CORPORATION
2120 N. Pewaukee Rd.　　Phone: 414-542-6611
Waukesha, WI 53187　　　Fax: 414-542-4884
Chm & Pres: Joseph L. Dindorf
VP HR: Michael Koons
Employees: 566
Jobs Added Last Year: 64 (+12.7%)
Machine tools & related products

J.J. KELLER & ASSOCIATES
3003 W. Breezewood Ln.　Phone: 414-722-2848
Neenah, WI 54957-0368　Fax: 414-727-7522
Pres & CEO: R. L. Keller
Corp Personnel Mgr: Anthony M. LaMalfo
Employees: 700
Jobs Added Last Year: 100 (+16.7%)
Printing - publications & printing services

JASON INCORPORATED
411 E. Wisconsin Ave., Ste. 2500　Phone: 414-277-9300
Milwaukee, WI 53202　　Fax: 414-277-9445
Chm & Pres (HR): Vincent L. Martin
Employees: 2,140
Jobs Added Last Year: 417 (+24.2%)
Automotive & trucking - original equipment

JOHNSON CONTROLS, INC. `10825`
5757 N. Green Bay Ave.　Phone: 414-228-1200
Milwaukee, WI 53201-0591　Fax: 414-228-2302
Chm, Pres & CEO: James H. Keyes
VP HR: Susan F. Davis
Employees: 54,800
Jobs Added Last Year: 4,700 (+9.4%)
Diversified operations - building controls; automotive products; plastics & batteries

WISCONSIN

JOURNAL COMMUNICATIONS
PO Box 661   Phone: 414-224-2000
Milwaukee, WI 53201   Fax: 414-224-2599
CEO: Robert Kahlor
Dir HR: Daniel Harmsen
Employees: 5,200
Jobs Added Last Year: 459 (+9.7%)
Publishing - newspapers; broadcasting; printing; telecommunications

KOHL'S CORPORATION
N54 W13600 Woodale Dr.   Phone: 414-783-5800
Menomenee, WI 53051   Fax: 414-783-6501
Chm: William Kellogg
VP (HR): Margaretta Cullen
Employees: 14,900
Jobs Added Last Year: 960 (+6.9%)
Retail - supermarkets

KOHLER CO.
444 Highland Dr.   Phone: 414-457-4441
Kohler, WI 53044   Fax: 414-459-1665
Chm & Pres: Herbert V. Kohler, Jr.
VP HR: Kenneth W. Conger
Employees: 14,000
Jobs Cut Last Year: 257 (-1.8%)
Building products - plumbing products; generators & engines; fine furniture

LACROSSE FOOTWEAR, INC.
1319 St. Andrew St.   Phone: 608-782-3020
LaCrosse, WI 54603   Fax: 608-782-1733
Pres & CEO: Patrick K. Gantert
HR Mgr: David F. Flaschberger
Employees: 1,617
Jobs Added Last Year: 131 (+8.8%)
Shoes & related apparel - protective footwear (LaCrosse & Danner)

LANDS' END, INC.
Lands' End Ln.   Phone: 608-935-9341
Dodgeville, WI 53595   Fax: 608-935-4260
Pres & CEO: Michael Smith
VP Emp Relations: John F. Keenan
Employees: 6,400
Jobs Cut Last Year: 100 (-1.5%)
Retail - mail order apparel & home furnishings

LUNAR CORPORATION
313 W. Beltline Hwy.   Phone: 608-274-2663
Madison, WI 53713   Fax: 608-274-5374
Pres & CEO: Richard B. Mazess
HR Mgr: Ann Trainor
Employees: 131
Jobs Added Last Year: 28 (+27.2%)
Medical products - bone disease treatment products

MANITOWOC COMPANY, INC.
700 E. Magnolia Ave., Ste. B   Phone: 414-684-4410
Manitowoc, WI 54221-0066   Fax: 414-683-6277
Pres & CEO: Fred M. Butler
Mgr HR: Thomas Musial
Employees: 1,900
Jobs Added Last Year: 100 (+5.6%)
Diversified operations - construction cranes; ship building & repair; ice makers

MARCUS CORPORATION
250 W. Wisconsin Ave.   Phone: 414-272-6020
Milwaukee, WI 53202-4220   Fax: 414-272-0669
Chm, Pres & CEO: Stephen H. Marcus
VP HR: H. Fred Delmenhorst
Employees: 7,500
Jobs Added Last Year: 0
Hotels & motels (Budgetel Inns); movie theaters; resorts; restaurants

MARQUETTE ELECTRONICS, INC.
8200 W. Tower Ave.   Phone: 414-355-5000
Milwaukee, WI 53223   Fax: 414-355-3790
Chm & CEO: Michael J. Cudahy
Dir Personnel: Gordon W. Petersen
Employees: 2,039
Jobs Added Last Year: 544 (+36.4%)
Medical products - critical care monitors

MARSHALL & ILSLEY CORPORATION
770 N. Water St.   Phone: 414-765-7801
Milwaukee, WI 53202   Fax: 414-765-7899
Chm, Pres & CEO: J. B. Wigdale
SVP HR: Gary Strelow
Employees: 6,315
Jobs Added Last Year: 178 (+2.9%)
Banks - Midwest

WISCONSIN

MARTEN TRANSPORT, LTD.
129 Marten St.   Phone: 715-926-4216
Mondovi, WI 54755   Fax: 715-926-4530
Chm, Pres & COO: Roger R. Marten
Dir HR: Rick Saring
Employees: 1,128
Jobs Added Last Year: 120 (+11.9%)
Transportation - truck

NORTHWESTERN MUTUAL LIFE
720 E. Wisconsin Ave.   Phone: 414-271-1444
Milwaukee, WI 53202   Fax: 414-299-7022
Pres & CEO: James D. Ericson
SVP HR & Admin: James W. Ehrenstrom
Employees: 3,500
Jobs Added Last Year: 202 (+6.1%)
Insurance - life

MENARD, INC.
4777 Menard Dr.   Phone: 715-874-5911
Eau Claire, WI 54703   Fax: 715-876-5901
Pres & CEO: John R. Menard
Dir HR, Office Mgr: Terri Jain
Employees: 5,000
Jobs Added Last Year: —
Building products - home improvement centers

OSHKOSH B'GOSH, INC.
112 Otter Ave.   Phone: 414-231-8800
Oshkosh, WI 54901   Fax: 414-231-8621
Pres & CEO: Douglas W. Hyde
VP HR: Donald M. Carlson
Employees: 6,400
Jobs Cut Last Year: 1,300 (-16.9%)
Apparel - children's

MENASHA CORPORATION
1645 Bergstrom Rd.   Phone: 414-751-1000
Neenah, WI 54956   Fax: 414-751-1236
Pres & CEO: Robert D. Bero
VP HR: David H. Rust
Employees: 4,600
Jobs Added Last Year: 600 (+15%)
Paper & paper products - packaging, plastics, forest products & printing

PAYCO AMERICAN CORPORATION
180 N. Executive Dr.   Phone: 414-784-9035
Brookfield, WI 53005   Fax: 414-780-7447
Pres: Neal R. Sparby
VP HR: Pete Pugel
Employees: 3,058
Jobs Cut Last Year: 121 (-3.8%)
Financial - collection services

MODINE MANUFACTURING COMPANY
1500 DeKoven Ave.   Phone: 414-636-1200
Racine, WI 53403   Fax: 414-636-1424
Pres & CEO: Richard T. Savage
Dir HR: Roger L. Hetrick
Employees: 6,800
Jobs Added Last Year: 1,500 (+28.3%)
Automotive & trucking - heat exchangers

QUAD/GRAPHICS, INC.
W224 N3322 Duplainville Rd.   Phone: 414-246-9200
Pewaukee, WI 53072   Fax: 414-246-4322
CEO: Harry V. Quadracci
Dir HR: Emmy Labode
Employees: 7,500
Jobs Added Last Year: 700 (+10.3%)
Printing - commercial

NORTHLAND CRANBERRIES, INC.
800 First Ave. South   Phone: 715-424-4444
Wisconsin Rapids, WI 54494-8020   Fax: 715-422-6800
Pres & CEO: John Swendrowski
VP Hr & Corp Counsel: David J. Lukas
Employees: 527
Jobs Added Last Year: 369 (+233.5%)
Agricultural operations - cranberry farms

REGAL-BELOIT CORPORATION
200 State St.   Phone: 608-364-8800
Beloit, WI 53511-6254   Fax: 608-365-2182
Pres & CEO: James L. Packard
VP HR: Fritz Hollenbach
Employees: 2,600
Jobs Added Last Year: 400 (+18.2%)
Machinery - power transmission for industrial applications

WISCONSIN

ROUNDY'S INC.
23000 Roundy Dr. Phone: 414-547-7999
Pewaukee, WI 53072 Fax: 414-547-4540
Chm & CEO: John R. Dickson
Mgr HR: Cathy Persch
Employees: 5,000
Jobs Added Last Year: —
Retail - supermarkets

S.C. JOHNSON & SON, INC.
1525 Howe St. Phone: 414-631-2000
Racine, WI 53403 Fax: 414-631-2133
Pres & CEO: William D. George, Jr.
SVP HR & Corp Comm: M. Garvin Shankster
Employees: 13,100
Jobs Added Last Year: 0
Soap & cleaning preparations (Glade, Pledge, Vanish & Windex); insect control (OFF!, Raid)

SCHNEIDER NATIONAL INC.
3101 S. Packerland Dr. Phone: 414-592-2000
Green Bay, WI 54306 Fax: 414-592-3565
Pres : Donald J. Schneider
Mgr HR: Mary Vogel
Employees: 13,950
Jobs Added Last Year: 1,950 (+16.3%)
Transportation - trucks

SENTRY INSURANCE, A MUTUAL COMPANY
1800 Northpoint Dr. Phone: 715-346-6000
Stevens Point, WI 54481 Fax: 715-346-7516
Chm & Pres: Larry C. Ballard
VP HR: Alfred C. Noel
Employees: 4,500
Jobs Added Last Year: —
Insurance - multi line

SHOPKO STORES, INC.
700 Pilgrim Way, PO Box 19060 Phone: 414-497-2211
Green Bay, WI 54307-9060 Fax: 414-496-4133
Pres & CEO: Dale P. Kramer
SVP & Sec (HR): David Liebergen
Employees: 19,000
Jobs Added Last Year: 800 (+4.4%)
Retail - regional department stores in upper Midwest, mountain states & Pacific Northwest

SNAP-ON INCORPORATED
2801 80th St. Phone: 414-656-5200
Kenosha, WI 53141-1410 Fax: 414-656-5123
Chm, Pres & CEO: Robert A. Cornog
VP HR: William R. Whyte
Employees: 9,000
Jobs Added Last Year: 0
Tools - hand-held & power tools, primarily for the automotive industry

SULLIVAN DENTAL PRODUCTS, INC.
10920 W. Lincoln Ave. Phone: 414-321-8881
West Allis, WI 53227 Fax: 414-321-8865
CEO: Robert E. Doering
Mgr HR: Marcy Nightingale
Employees: 575
Jobs Added Last Year: 219 (+61.5%)
Dental supplies & equipment distribution

SYBRON INTERNATIONAL CORPORATION
411 E. Wisconsin Ave. Phone: 414-274-6600
Milwaukee, WI 53202 Fax: 414-274-6561
Chm, Pres & CEO: Kenneth F. Yontz
Dir HR: Eileen A. Short
Employees: 3,900
Jobs Added Last Year: 394 (+11.2%)
Laboratory & dental supplies

UNITED WISCONSIN SERVICES, INC.
401 W. Michigan St. Phone: 414-226-6900
Milwaukee, WI 53203-2896 Fax: 414-226-6229
CEO: Thomas R. Hefty
Dir Personnel: Kathy Potos
Employees: 746
Jobs Added Last Year: 596 (+397.3%)
Insurance - accident & health

UNIVERSAL FOODS CORPORATION
433 E. Michigan St. Phone: 414-271-6755
Milwaukee, WI 53202 Fax: 414-347-3785
CEO: Guy A. Osborn
VP HR: Richard Carney
Employees: 5,450
Jobs Cut Last Year: 474 (-8%)
Food - frozen potato products, cheeses, dehydrated vegetable products

WISCONSIN

THE UNIVERSITY OF WISCONSIN SYSTEM
1220 Linden Dr. Phone: 608-262-2321
Madison, WI 53706 Fax: 608-265-3175
Pres: Katharine C. Lyall
Assoc VP HR: Charles Wright
Employees: 28,606
Jobs Added Last Year: —
University

WISCONSIN ENERGY CORPORATION
231 W. Michigan St. Phone: 414-221-2590
Milwaukee, WI 53201 Fax: 414-221-2010
CEO: Richard A. Abdoo
SVP HR: David Porter
Employees: 5,823
Jobs Added Last Year: 65 (+1.1%)
Utility - electric power

W. H. BRADY CO.
727 W. Glendale Ave. Phone: 414-332-8100
Milwaukee, WI 53201 Fax: 414-332-2887
Pres & CEO: Katherine M. Hudson
VP HR: James M. Sweet
Employees: 2,000
Jobs Added Last Year: 200 (+11.1%)
Chemicals - adhesives, coatings & graphics technologies, including pressure-sensitive tapes & wound-care products

WPL HOLDINGS, INC.
222 W. Washington Ave. Phone: 608-252-3311
Madison, WI 53703 Fax: 608-252-3397
Pres & CEO: Erroll B. Davis, Jr.
VP Info Tech & Admin (HR): Pamela Wegner
Employees: 4,650
Jobs Added Last Year: 1,409 (+43.5%)
Utility - electric power

WAUSAU PAPER MILLS CO.
One Clark's Island Phone: 715-845-5266
Wausau, WI 54402 Fax: 715-848-2652
Chm & CEO: San W. Orr, Jr.
Dir HR, Printing & Writing Div.: Richard D. LaPoint
Employees: 1,695
Jobs Added Last Year: 185 (+12.3%)
Printing, writing & technical paper

WPS RESOURCES CORPORATION
700 N. Adams St., PO Box 19001 Phone: 414-433-1445
Green Bay, WI 54307 Fax: 414-433-1297
Pres & CEO: Daniel A. Bollom
VP HR: B. J. Treml
Employees: 2,600
Jobs Cut Last Year: 79 (-2.9%)
Utility - electric power

WICOR, INC.
626 E. Wisconsin Ave., PO Box 334 Phone: 414-291-7026
Milwaukee, WI 53201 Fax: 414-291-7025
Pres & CEO: George E. Wardeberg
VP HR: Wally Zeddun
Employees: 3,222
Jobs Added Last Year: 44 (+1.4%)
Utility - gas distribution

HOOVER'S MASTERLIST OF AMERICA'S TOP 2,500 EMPLOYERS

THE INDEXES

INDEX OF COMPANIES BY NAME
INDEX OF COMPANIES BY INDUSTRY
INDEX OF COMPANIES BY METROPOLITAN AREA

INDEX OF COMPANIES BY NAME

Symbol
"21" International Holdings, Inc. 232
3Com Corporation 81
3D Systems Corporation 81
The 3DO Company 81
84 Lumber Company 278

A
A+ Communications, Inc. 294
A.G. Edwards, Inc. 208
A. H. Belo Corporation 299
A. L. Pharma Inc. 222
A. O. Smith Corporation 332
Aames Financial Corporation 81
Aaron Rents, Inc. 136
Abaxis, Inc. 81
Abbott Laboratories 145
ABC Rail Products Corporation 145
ABCO Markets Inc. 76
ABIOMED, Inc. 177
ABM Industries Incorporated 81
ABR Information Services, Inc. 127
ABS Industries, Inc. 259
ABT Building Products Corporation 332
ACC Corp. 232
Acceptance Insurance Companies Inc. 216
Access Graphics Inc. 112
Acclaim Entertainment, Inc. 232
Accolade Inc. 81
Ace Cash Express, Inc. 299
Ace Hardware Corporation 145
Acme Metals Incorporated 145
Acme-Cleveland Corporation 259
Acxiom Corporation 79
Adaptec, Inc. 81
ADC Telecommunications, Inc. 197
Adelphia Communications Corporation 278
Adesa Corporation 160
ADFlex Solutions, Inc. 76
Adia 30

Adobe Systems Incorporated 81
Advance Circuits, Inc. 197
Advance Publications, Inc. 232
Advance Ross Corporation 145
Advanced Financial, Inc. 166
Advanced Marketing Services, Inc. 81
Advanced Medical, Inc. 82
Advanced Micro Devices, Inc. 82
Advanced Polymer Systems, Inc. 82
Advanced Technology Laboratories, Inc. 327
Advanced Tissue Sciences, Inc. 82
ADVANTA Corporation 278
AdvantageHEALTH Corporation 177
Advantis 145
Adventist Health System/West 82
ADVO, Inc. 115
Advocat, Inc. 294
Aerovox, Inc. 177
Aetna Life and Casualty Company 115
AFC Cable Systems, Inc. 290
AFLAC Incorporated 136
AGCO Corporation 136
Agouron Pharmaceuticals, Inc. 82
Air Express International Corporation 115
Air Products and Chemicals, Inc. 278
Airborne Freight Corporation 327
Airgas, Inc. 278
AirTouch Communications 82
AirTran Corporation 197
Alamo Group, Inc. 299
Alamo Rent A Car, Inc. 127
Alaska Air Group, Inc. 327
Albany International Corporation 232
Albemarle Corporation 170
Alberto-Culver Company 145

Albertson's, Inc. 144
Alco Standard Corporation 278
Alexander & Alexander Services Inc. 232
Alexander & Baldwin, Inc. 143
Alleghany Corporation 232
Allegheny Health, Education and Research Foundation 278
Allegheny Power System, Inc. 232
Allen Group Inc. 259
Allergan, Inc. 82
Alliant Techsystems Inc. 197
Allied Holdings Inc. 136
AlliedSignal Inc. 222
Allina Health System 197
Allmerica Financial 177
Allmerica Property & Casualty Companies, Inc. 177
Allou Health & Beauty Care, Inc. 232
The Allstate Corporation 145
ALLTEL Corporation 79
Allwaste, Inc. 299
Alpha-Beta Technology, Inc. 177
Alpine Group, Inc. 232
Altera Corporation 82
Aluminum Company of America 278
ALZA Corporation 82
A-Mark Financial Corporation 83
AMBAC Inc. 233
Amber's Stores, Inc. 299
AMC Entertainment Inc. 208
AMDURA Corporation 115
Amerada Hess Corporation 233
AMERCO 218
America Online, Inc. 322
America Service Group, Inc. 123
America West Airlines, Inc. 76
American Automobile Association 127
American Bankers Insurance Group, Inc. 127

INDEX OF COMPANIES BY NAME

American Biltrite Inc. 177
American Brands, Inc. 115
American Buildings Company 72
American Business Information, Inc. 216
American Business Products, Inc. 136
American Cancer Society 136
American Eagle Outfitters, Inc. 278
American Electric Power Company, Inc. 259
American Express Company 233
American Family Mutual Insurance Company 332
American Financial Corporation 259
American Freightways Corporation 79
American Greetings Corporation 259
American Home Products Corporation 222
American International Group, Inc. 233
American Management Systems, Incorporated 322
American Media, Inc. 127
American Medical Electronics, Inc. 299
American Medical Response, Inc. 177
American Power Conversion Corporation 290
American President Companies, Ltd. 83
American Protective Services, Inc. 83
American Recreation Company Holdings, Inc. 233
American Red Cross 125
American Retail Group, Inc. 233
American Standard Companies, Inc. 222
American Stores Company 319
American Studios, Inc. 255
American United Global, Inc. 83

American Vanguard Corporation 83
American Water Works Company, Inc. 222
American White Cross, Inc. 115
Amerihost Properties, Inc. 145
Ameristar Casinos Inc. 218
Ameritech Corporation 145
Ameriwood Industries International Corporation 189
Ames Department Stores, Inc. 115
AMETEK, Inc. 278
Amgen Inc. 83
Amoco Corporation 146
AMP Incorporated 279
Amphenol Corporation 115
AMR Corporation 299
AMRE, Inc. 299
AMREP Corporation 233
AMRESCO, Inc. 299
Amsco International, Inc. 279
AmSouth Bancorporation 72
AMSTED Industries Incorporated 146
Amtech Corporation 299
Amtrol Inc. 290
Amway Corporation 189
Anacomp, Inc. 160
Analog Devices, Inc. 177
Anchor Gaming 218
Andersen Corp. 197
Andrew Corporation 146
Angelica Corporation 208
Anheuser-Busch Companies, Inc. 208
AnnTaylor Stores Corporation 233
The Anschutz Corporation 112
Anthony Industries, Inc. 83
Aon Corporation 146
Apogee Enterprises, Inc. 197
Apogee, Inc. 279
Apollo Group, Inc. 76
Apple Computer, Inc. 83
Apple South, Inc. 136

Applebee's International, Inc. 166
Applied Extrusion Technologies, Inc. 177
Applied Materials, Inc. 83
Applied Power Inc. 332
Applied Science & Technology Inc. 178
ARAMARK Corporation 279
Arbor Drugs, Inc. 189
Arbor Health Care Company 259
Arcadian Partners, L.P. 294
Arch Communications Group, Inc. 178
Archer-Daniels-Midland Company 146
ARCO Chemical Company 279
Arctco, Inc. 197
Argosy Gaming Company 146
Arizona Instrument Corporation 76
Arkansas Best Corporation 79
Armstrong World Industries, Inc. 279
Army & Air Force Exchange Service 300
Arnold Industries Inc. 279
Arrow Automotive Industries, Inc. 178
Arrow Electronics, Inc. 233
Arthur Andersen & Co, S.C. 146
Arthur D. Little Inc. 178
Arthur J. Gallagher & Co. 146
Artisoft, Inc. 76
Artistic Greetings, Inc. 233
Arvin Industries, Inc. 160
ASARCO Incorporated 234
Ashland, Inc. 168
Aspect Telecommunications Corporation 83
Asplundh Tree Expert Co. 279
Associated Banc-Corp 332
Associated Milk Producers, Inc. 300
AST Research, Inc. 84

INDEX OF COMPANIES BY NAME

Astec Industries, Inc. 294
Astrum International Corp. 234
Asymetrix Corp. 327
AT&T Corporation 234
Atchison Casting Corporation 166
Atlanta Gas Light Company 136
Atlantic Coast Airlines Inc. 322
Atlantic Richfield Company 84
Atlantis Group, Inc. 127
Atmel Corporation 84
Augat Inc. 178
Austin Industries Inc. 300
Authentic Fitness Corporation 84
Autodesk, Inc. 84
AutoFinance Group, Inc. 146
AutoInfo, Inc. 222
Automatic Data Processing, Inc. 222
Automotive Industries Holding, Inc. 197
Autotote Corporation 123
AutoZone, Inc. 294
Avatar Holdings, Inc. 127
Avery Dennison Corporation 84
Avid Technology, Inc. 178
Avis, Inc. 234
Avnet, Inc. 234
Avon Products, Inc. 234
Avondale Mills, Inc. 136
Aztar Corporation 76

B

Bachman Information Systems, Inc. 178
Bailey Corporation 220
Bain & Company 178
Baker & McKenzie 146
Baldor Electric Co. 79
Ball Corporation 160
Bally Entertainment Corporation 147
Baltimore Gas and Electric Company 173
Banc One Corporation 259
BancFirst Corporation 273
Bancorp Hawaii, Inc. 143
BancTec, Inc. 300

Bank of Boston Corporation 178
The Bank of New York Company, Inc. 234
BankAmerica Corporation 84
Bankers Trust New York Corporation 234
Banta Corporation 332
Barefoot Inc. 259
Barnes & Noble, Inc. 234
Barnett Banks, Inc. 127
Barr Laboratories, Inc. 234
Barrett Resources Corporation 112
Bashas' Inc. 76
Bassett Furniture Industries, Inc. 322
Bath Iron Works Corporation 172
Battelle Memorial Institute 259
Bausch & Lomb Incorporated 235
Baxter International Inc. 147
Bay Networks Inc. 84
BayBanks, Inc. 178
BB&T Financial Corporation 255
BE Aerospace, Inc. 127
BE&K Inc. 72
The Bear Stearns Companies Inc. 235
Bearings, Inc. 260
Beazer Homes USA, Inc. 136
Bechtel Group, Inc. 84
Beckman Instruments, Inc. 84
Becton, Dickinson and Company 222
Bed Bath & Beyond, Inc. 222
BeefAmerica, Inc. 216
Belden & Blake Corporation 260
Belden Inc. 208
Belk Stores Services, Inc. 255
Bell Atlantic Corporation 279
Bell Communications Research Inc. 222
Bell & Howell Co. 147
Bell Industries, Inc. 85

Bell Microproducts Inc. 85
BellSouth Corporation 137
Bemis Co., Inc. 197
Ben & Jerry's Homemade, Inc. 321
Beneficial Corporation 123
Benihana National Corp. 127
Bergen Brunswig Corporation 85
Berkshire Hathaway Inc. 216
Berkshire Realty Co. 179
Bertucci's Inc. 179
Besicorp Group Inc. 235
Best Buy Co., Inc. 198
Best Products Co. Inc. 322
Bestop, Inc. 112
Bethlehem Steel Corporation 279
Betz Laboratories, Inc. 280
Beverly Enterprises, Inc. 79
The B.F.Goodrich Co. 260
BHA Group, Inc. 208
BHC Communications, Inc. 235
Big B, Inc. 72
Big V Supermarkets Inc. 235
Big Y Foods Inc. 179
Bird Corporation 179
The BISYS Group, Inc. 223
BitWise Designs, Inc. 235
BJ Services Company 300
Black and Veatch 208
Black Box Corporation 280
The Black & Decker Corporation 173
Black Hawk Gaming and Development Co., Inc. 112
Blair Corporation 280
Block Drug Co., Inc. 223
Blount, Inc. 72
Blue Cross and Blue Shield Association 147
Blyth Industries, Inc. 115
BMC West Corporation 144

INDEX OF COMPANIES BY NAME

Boatmen's Bancshares, Inc. 208
Bob Evans Farms, Inc. 260
Boca Research Inc. 128
The Boeing Company 327
Boise Cascade Corporation 144
The Bombay Company, Inc. 300
Bon-Ton Stores, Inc. 280
Books-A-Million, Inc. 72
Boole & Babbage, Inc. 85
Boomtown, Inc. 218
Booz, Allen & Hamilton Inc. 235
Borden, Inc. 260
Borg-Warner Security Corporation 147
Bose Corporation 179
Boston Edison Company 179
Boston Scientific Corporation 179
Boston Technology, Inc. 179
Boyd Bros. Transportation Inc. 72
Boyd Gaming Corporation 218
Bradlees, Inc. 179
Brandon Systems Corporation 223
Braun's Fashions Corporation 198
Breed Technologies, Inc. 128
Brenlin Group 260
Briggs & Stratton Corporation 332
Brinker International, Inc. 300
Bristol-Myers Squibb Company 235
Broadway Stores Inc. 85
Brock Control Systems, Inc. 137
Brooklyn Union Gas Co. 235
Brookshire Brothers Incorporated 300
Brookshire Grocery Company 300
Brown Group, Inc. 208
Brown & Sharpe Manufacturing Company 290

Brown-Forman Corporation 168
Browning-Ferris Industries, Inc. 300
Bruno's, Inc. 72
Brunswick Corporation 147
The Buckle, Inc. 216
Budget Rent a Car Corporation 147
Buffets, Inc. 198
Bugaboo Creek Steak House, Inc. 290
Bugle Boy Industries 85
Builders Transport, Inc. 291
Burlington Coat Factory Warehouse Corporation 223
Burlington Industries, Inc. 255
Burlington Northern Inc. 301
Bush Industries, Inc. 235
Business Records Corporation Holding Co. 301
Butler Manufacturing Co. 208
Buttrey Food and Drug Stores Company 215

C

C. H. Heist Corporation 128
C. R. Bard, Inc. 223
C&S Wholesale Grocers Inc. 321
C-COR Electronics, Inc. 280
Cable Design Technologies Corporation 280
Cabletron Systems, Inc. 220
Cablevision Systems Corporation 236
Cabot Corporation 179
Cabot Medical Corporation 280
Cache, Inc. 236
CACI International Inc. 322
Cadmus Communications Corporation 322
Cagle's, Inc. 137
CAI Wireless Systems, Inc. 236
Caldor Corporation 115

California Microwave, Inc. 85
Callaway Golf Company 85
Caltex Petroleum Corporation 301
Cambrex Corporation 223
Camco International Inc. 301
Camelot Music Inc. 260
Campbell Soup Company 223
Campo Electronics, Appliances & Computers, Inc. 170
Canandaigua Wine Company, Inc. 236
Capital Bancorp 128
Capital Cities/ABC, Inc. 236
Cardinal Health, Inc. 260
Caremark International, Inc. 147
Cargill, Incorporated 198
Carlisle Companies Inc. 236
Carlisle Plastics, Inc. 76
Carlson Companies, Inc. 198
Carmike Cinemas, Inc. 137
Carnival Corporation 128
Carnival Hotels and Casinos 128
Carpenter Co. 322
Carpenter Technology Corporation 280
Carr-Gottstein Foods Co. 75
Carson Pirie Scott & Co. 332
Carter-Wallace, Inc. 236
Case Corporation 332
Casey's General Stores, Inc. 164
Cash America International, Inc. 301
Casino America, Inc. 206
Casino Magic Corporation 206
CasTech Aluminum Group Inc. 260
Castle Energy Corporation 280
Catalina Lighting, Inc. 128
Catalina Marketing Corporation 128

INDEX OF COMPANIES BY NAME

Caterair International Corp. 173
Caterpillar Inc. 147
Catherines Stores Corporation 294
Catholic Healthcare West Inc. 85
Cato Corporation 255
Cavalier Homes of Alabama, Inc. 72
CBI Industries, Inc. 147
CBS Inc. 236
CDP Technologies, Inc. 236
CDW Computer Centers, Inc. 148
Cedar Group, Inc. 280
Celadon Group Inc. 236
Celebrity, Inc. 301
Celex Group Inc. 148
Celgene Corporation 223
Cellstar Corporation 301
Cellular Technical Services Company, Inc. 327
Celtrix Pharmaceuticals, Inc. 85
Centerior Energy Corporation 260
Centex Corporation 301
Central and South West Services Corporation 301
Central Garden & Pet Co. 86
Central Newspapers, Inc. 160
Central Reserve Life Corp. 261
Central Sprinkler Corporation 281
Century Communications Corporation 116
Century Telephone Enterprises, Inc. 170
Ceridian Corporation 198
Cerner Corporation 209
Cerplex Group, Inc. 86
Cerprobe Corporation 76
Certified Grocers of California, Ltd 86
CFI ProServices, Inc. 275
CH2M Hill Cos. 112
Champion Enterprises, Inc. 189
Champion International Corporation 116

The Charles Schwab Corporation 86
Charming Shoppes, Inc. 281
Chart House Enterprises, Inc. 86
Charter Medical Corporation 137
The Chase Manhattan Corporation 237
Checkers Drive-In Restaurants, Inc. 128
Checkpoint Systems, Inc. 223
The Cheesecake Factory Incorporated 86
Chemed Corporation 261
Chemical Banking Corporation 237
Chemical Financial Corporation 189
Chempower, Inc. 261
The Cherry Corporation 148
Chesapeake Corporation 322
Chevron Corporation 86
Cheyenne Software, Inc. 237
Chicago and North Western Transportation Company 148
Chico's FAS, Inc. 128
Chief Auto Parts Incorporated 301
Children's Discovery Centers of America, Inc. 86
Chipcom Corporation 180
Chiquita Brands International, Inc. 261
Chiron Corporation 86
The Chronicle Publishing Company, Inc. 86
Chronimed, Inc. 198
Chrysler Corporation 189
The Chubb Corporation 223
CIBER, Inc. 112
CIGNA Corporation 281
Cincinnati Bell Inc. 261
Cincinnati Milacron Inc. 261
Cinema Ride, Inc. 87
CINergy Corp. 261
Cintas Corporation 261
The Circle K Corporation 77

Circon Corporation 87
Circuit City Stores, Inc. 322
Circuit Systems, Inc. 148
Circus Circus Enterprises, Inc. 218
Cirrus Logic, Inc. 87
Cisco Systems, Inc. 87
CITATION Computer Systems, Inc. 209
Citation Corporation 72
Citicasters Inc. 261
Citicorp 237
CKE Restaurants, Inc. 87
Claire's Stores, Inc. 129
Clark Enterprises, Inc. 173
Clark Equipment Company 160
Clark USA, Inc. 209
Clayton Homes, Inc. 294
Clean Harbors, Inc. 180
Clear Channel Communications, Inc. 302
Cleveland-Cliffs Inc. 261
Cliffs Drilling Company 302
The Clorox Company 87
The Clothestime, Inc. 87
Club Corporation International 302
Club Med, Inc. 237
CMAC Investment Corporation 281
CMI Corporation 273
CML Group, Inc. 180
CMS Energy Corporation 189
CNA Financial Corporation 148
Coachmen Industries, Inc. 160
The Coastal Corporation 302
Coastal Healthcare Group, Inc. 255
Coca-Cola Bottling Co. Consolidated 255
Coca-Cola Bottling Co. of Chicago 148
The Coca-Cola Company 137
Coca-Cola Enterprises Inc. 137
Coeur d'Alene Mines Corporation 144

INDEX OF COMPANIES BY NAME

Cole National Corporation 262
The Coleman Company, Inc. 166
Colgate-Palmolive Company 237
Collective Bancorp, Inc. 224
Colonial Data Technologies Corporation 116
Coltec Industries Inc. 237
The Columbia Gas System, Inc. 123
Columbia Sportswear 275
Columbia/HCA Healthcare Corporation 168
Comair Holdings, Inc. 262
Comcast Corporation 281
Comerica Inc. 189
Command Security Corporation 237
Commerce Bancorp, Inc. 224
Commerce Bancshares, Inc. 209
Commercial Intertech Corporation 262
Commercial Metals Company 302
CommNet Cellular Inc. 112
Communications Systems, Inc. 198
Community Health Systems, Inc. 302
Compaq Computer Corporation 302
Compass Bancshares, Inc. 73
Compression Labs, Incorporated 87
CompuCom Systems, Inc. 302
CompUSA Inc. 302
Computer Associates International, Inc. 237
Computer Network Technology Corporation 198
Computer Sciences Corporation 87
Compuware Corporation 189
COMSAT Corporation 173
Comverse Technology Inc. 237

ConAgra, Inc. 216
Cone Mills Corporation 255
Connecticut Mutual Life Insurance Company 116
Connell Limited Partnership 180
Conner Peripherals, Inc. 87
Conrail, Inc. 281
Conseco, Inc. 160
Conso Products Company 291
CONSOL Energy Inc. 281
Consolidated Edison Company of New York, Inc. 238
Consolidated Freightways, Inc. 88
Consolidated Natural Gas Company 281
Consolidated Papers, Inc. 332
Consolidated Products, Inc. 160
Consolidated Stores Corporation 262
Contel Cellular Inc. 137
Continental Airlines Holdings, Inc. 302
Continental Cablevision, Inc. 180
Continental Can Co. 238
Continental Corporation 238
Continental Grain Company 238
Continental Medical Systems, Inc. 281
The Continuum Company, Inc. 303
Control Data Systems, Inc. 198
Cooker Restaurant Corporation 262
Cooper Development Company 88
Cooper Industries, Inc. 303
Cooper Tire & Rubber Company 262
Coopers & Lybrand L.L.P. 238
CooperSmith Inc. 137
Cordis Corporation 129
CoreStates Financial Corporation 281
Cornell University 238

Cornerstone Imaging Inc. 88
Corning Incorporated 238
Corporate Express, Inc. 112
Corrections Corporation of America 294
Corrpro Cos Inc. 262
Cosmetic Center, Inc. 173
Cotter & Company 148
Coulter Corporation 129
Countrywide Credit Industries, Inc. 88
County Seat Stores Inc. 303
Covenant Transport, Inc. 294
Cox Enterprises, Inc. 137
CPC International Inc. 224
CPI Corporation 209
Cracker Barrel Old Country Store, Inc. 294
Craig Corporation 88
Crane Co. 116
Crawford & Company Risk Management Services 138
Cray Research, Inc. 199
Crestar Financial Corporation 323
Crompton & Knowles Corporation 116
Crowley Maritime Corporation 88
Crowley, Milner and Company 189
Crown Holding Company 282
Crown Books Corporation 173
Crown Cork & Seal Company, Inc. 282
Crown Crafts, Inc. 138
CSS Industries, Inc. 282
CSX Corporation 323
CTS Corporation 160
CUC International Inc. 116
Culbro Corporation 238
Cumberland Farms Inc. 180
Cummins Engine Company, Inc. 161
Curative Technologies, Inc. 238
Cyberonics, Inc. 303

INDEX OF COMPANIES BY NAME

Cygne Designs Inc. 238
Cyprus Amax Minerals Company 112
Cyrix Corporation 303
Cytec Industries Inc. 224

D

D.I.Y. Home Warehouse, Inc. 262
D. R. Horton, Inc. 303
Daig Corporation 199
Dairy Mart Convenience Stores, Inc. 116
DAKA International, Inc. 180
Dakotah, Inc. 293
Damark International, Inc. 199
Dames & Moore, Inc. 88
Dana Corporation 262
Danaher Corporation 125
D'Arcy Masius Benton & Bowles, Inc. 239
Dart Group Corporation 173
Data Broadcasting Corporation 239
Data General Corporation 180
Data Storage Marketing, Inc. 113
Data Transmission Network Corporation 216
Datastorm Technologies Inc. 209
Dataware Technologies Inc. 180
Davco Restaurants Inc. 173
Davidson & Associates, Inc. 88
Day Runner, Inc. 88
Day & Zimmermann Incorporated 282
Dayton Hudson Corporation 199
Dean Foods Company 148
Dean Witter, Discover & Co. 239
Deb Shops, Inc. 282
DeBartolo Realty Corporation 262
Deckers Outdoor Corporation 88
Deere & Company 148
Del Monte Foods Company 89
Del Webb Corporation 77

Delaware North Companies Inc. 239
Delchamps, Inc. 73
Dell Computer Corporation 303
Delmarva Power & Light Company 123
Deloitte & Touche 116
Delrina Corporation 89
Delta Air Lines, Inc. 138
Delta Woodside Industries, Inc. 291
Deluxe Corporation 199
Demoulas Super Markets Inc./Market Basket Inc. 180
Dentsply International Inc. 282
Deposit Guaranty Corporation 206
Designs, Inc. 181
DeSoto, Inc. 149
Destec Energy, Inc. 303
Detroit Diesel Corporation 190
Detroit Edison Company 190
The Detroit Medical Center 190
Developers Diversified Realty Corporation 263
Devon Energy Corporation 273
Devon Group, Inc. 116
DHL Worldwide Express 89
Diagnostek, Inc. 231
The Dial Corp. 77
Dial-A-Mattress Franchise Corporation 239
Dialogic Corporation 224
Diamond Multimedia Systems, Inc. 89
Diamond Shamrock, Inc. 303
Diebold, Inc. 263
Digi International Inc. 199
DIGICON 173
Digital Biometrics, Inc. 199
Digital Communications Technology Corporation 129
Digital Equipment Corporation 181
Dillard Department Stores, Inc. 79

DIMAC Corporation 209
Dionex Corporation 89
Discount Auto Parts, Inc. 129
Discovery Zone, Inc. 149
Diversified Communications Industries, Ltd. 129
Dixie Yarns, Inc. 295
DM Management Company 181
Dole Food Company, Inc. 89
Dollar General Corporation 168
Dominion Resources, Inc. 323
Domino's Pizza, Inc. 190
Donaldson Company, Inc. 199
Donnelly Corporation 190
Dorsey Trailers, Inc. 138
Doubletree Corporation 77
Douglas & Lomason Company 190
Dover Corporation 239
The Dow Chemical Company 190
Dow Corning Corporation 190
Dow Jones & Company, Inc. 239
DPL Inc. 263
Dress Barn, Inc. 117
Dresser Industries, Inc. 303
Dresser-Rand Company 239
Drew Industries Incorporated 239
Dreyer's Grand Ice Cream, Inc. 89
Drug Emporium, Inc. 263
DS Bancor, Inc. 117
DSC Communications Corporation 304
Duchossois Industries, Inc. 149
Duke Power Company 255
The Dun & Bradstreet Corporation 117
Duracell International, Inc. 117
Durakon Industries, Inc. 190

INDEX OF COMPANIES BY NAME

Duriron Company, Inc. 263
The Dwyer Group, Inc. 304
Dyersburg Fabrics Inc. 295
Dynatech Corporation 181
DynCorp 323

E

E.I. du Pont de Nemours and Company 123
E. & J. Gallo Winery 89
The E.W. Scripps Company 123
E-Systems, Inc. 304
E-Z Serve Corporation 304
Eagle Financial Corp. 117
Eagle Food Centers, Inc. 149
Eagle Hardware & Garden, Inc. 327
Earle M. Jorgensen Holding Company, Inc. 89
Eastman Chemical Company 295
Eastman Kodak Company 239
Eateries Inc. 273
Eaton Corporation 263
Eaton Vance Corporation 181
ECCS Inc. 224
Echlin Inc. 117
Eckerd Corporation 129
Ecolab Inc. 199
Edison Brothers Stores, Inc. 209
Edward D. Jones & Co. 209
Edward J. DeBartolo Corporation 263
EG&G, Inc. 181
EIS International, Inc. 117
El Chico Restaurants, Inc. 304
Elco Industries, Inc. 149
The Elder-Beerman Stores Corp. 263
Electro Scientific Industries, Inc. 275
Electromagnetic Sciences, Inc. 138
Electronic Arts Inc. 89
Electronic Data Systems Corporation 304
Electronics for Imaging, Inc. 90
Elek-Tek Inc. 149
Eli Lilly and Company 161
Eljer Industries, Inc. 304
ELXSI Corporation 117
EMC Corporation 181
EMC Insurance Group Inc. 164
Emerson Electric Co. 209
Emory University Inc. 138
Empi, Inc. 199
Encyclopaedia Britannica Inc. 149
Energy Ventures, Inc. 304
Energy West, Incorporated 215
Engelhard Corporation 224
Enron Corporation 304
Entergy Corporation 170
Enterprise Rent-A-Car Co. 210
Environmental Systems Research Institute Inc. 90
Envirotest Systems Corporation 77
Enzon, Inc. 224
EPIC Design Technology, Inc. 90
Equifax Inc. 138
The Equitable Companies, Incorporated 240
Equity Residential Properties Trust 149
ERC Industries, Inc. 304
Ernst Home Center, Inc. 327
Ernst & Young LLP 240
Esprit de Corp. 90
Essex Group Inc. 161
Esstar Inc. 117
Evergreen Media Corporation 305
Excel Industries, Inc. 161
EXECUTONE Information Systems, Inc. 117
Exide Corporation 282
Express Scripts, Inc. 210
Exxon Corporation 305
EZCORP, Inc. 305

F

F & E Resource Systems Technology, Inc. 174
F & M Distributors, Inc. 190
Fabri-Centers of America, Inc. 263
Fair, Isaac and Company, Incorporated 90
Falcon Products, Inc. 210
Falcon Systems Inc. 90
Family Dollar Stores, Inc. 255
Family Golf Centers, Inc. 240
Family Restaurants Inc. 90
Farah Inc. 305
Farmland Industries, Inc. 210
Fastenal Company 200
Fay's, Incorporated 240
Federal Express Corporation 295
Federal National Mortgage Association 125
Federal Paper Board Company, Inc. 224
Federal Signal Corporation 149
Federal-Mogul Corporation 191
Federated Department Stores, Inc. 263
Ferro Corporation 264
FHP International Corporation 90
Fibreboard Corporation 90
Fidelity National Financial, Inc. 90
Fiesta Mart Inc. 305
Fifth Third Bancorp 264
Figgie International Inc. 264
FINA, Inc. 305
Fingerhut Companies, Inc. 200
Finish Line, Inc. 161
Finlay Enterprises 240
First Alabama Bancshares, Inc. 73
First American Corporation 295
First American Financial Corporation 91
First Bank System, Inc. 200

INDEX OF COMPANIES BY NAME

First Brands Corporation 118
First Central Financial Corporation 240
First Chicago Corporation 149
First Citizens BancShares, Inc. 256
First Commonwealth Financial Corporation 282
First Data Corporation 216
First Empire State Corporation 240
First Fidelity Bancorporation 224
First Financial Management Corporation 138
First Hawaiian, Inc. 143
First Interstate Bancorp 91
First Merit Corporation 264
First Mississippi Corporation 206
First Mortgage Corporation 91
First of America Bank Corporation 191
First Security Corporation 319
First Tennessee National Corporation 295
First Union Corporation 256
First Virginia Banks, Inc. 323
Firstar Corporation 333
FIserv, Inc. 333
Fisher Scientific International, Inc. 220
Flagstar Companies, Inc. 291
Flair Corporation 129
Fleet Financial Group, Inc. 290
Fleetwood Enterprises, Inc. 91
Fleming Companies, Inc. 273
Flexsteel Industries, Inc. 164
Flint Ink Corporation 191
Florida Progress Corporation 129
The Florsheim Shoe Company 150

Flowers Industries, Inc. 138
Fluke Corporation 327
Fluor Corporation 91
Flying J Inc. 319
FMC Corporation 150
FMR Corporation 181
Foamex International Inc. 282
Follett Corporation 150
Food Lion, Inc. 256
Foodmaker, Inc. 91
Ford Motor Company 191
Forschner Group, Inc. 118
Forstmann & Co., Inc. 240
Fort Howard Corporation 333
Forum Group, Inc. 161
Fossil, Inc. 305
Foster Poultry Farms Inc. 91
Foster Wheeler Corporation 225
Foundation Health Corporation 91
FourGen Software Inc. 327
Fourth Financial Corporation 166
Fourth Shift Corporation 200
FPL Group, Inc. 129
Franciscan Health System 282
Franklin Quest Co. 319
Franklin Resources, Inc. 91
Fred Meyer, Inc. 275
Fred's, Inc. 295
Freedom Newspapers Inc. 91
The Freeman Companies 305
Freeport-McMoRan Copper & Gold Inc. 218
Freeport-McMoRan Inc. 170
Fresenius USA Inc. 92
Fresh Choice, Inc. 92
Fretter, Inc. 191
Frisch's Restaurants, Inc. 264
Fritz Companies, Inc. 92
Frontier Insurance Group, Inc. 240

Frozen Food Express Industries, Inc. 305
Fruit of the Loom, Inc. 150
FSI International, Inc. 200
FTP Software, Inc. 181
Funco Inc. 200
Fund American Enterprises Holdings, Inc. 321
Furr's Supermarkets, Inc. 231
Future Healthcare Inc. 264

G

G&K Services, Inc. 200
GAF Corp 225
Galey & Lord, Inc. 256
Gander Mountain, Inc. 333
Gannett Co., Inc. 323
The Gap, Inc. 92
Gartner Group Inc. 118
Gates Corporation 113
Gateway 2000 Inc. 293
GATX Corporation 150
Gaylord Container Corporation 150
Gaylord Entertainment Co. 295
GBC Technologies, Inc. 225
GEICO Corporation 125
GenCorp Inc. 264
Genentech, Inc. 92
General American Life Insurance Company 210
General Binding Corporation 150
General Chemical Corp. 220
General Communication, Inc. 75
General Dynamics Corporation 323
General Electric Company 118
General Host Corporation 118
General Instrument Corporation 150
General Mills, Inc. 200
General Motors Corporation 191
General Nutrition Companies, Inc. 283

INDEX OF COMPANIES BY NAME

General Public Utilities Corporation 225
General Signal Corporation 118
Genesco Inc. 295
Genesis Health Ventures, Inc. 283
Genetics Institute, Inc. 181
Geneva Steel 319
GENICOM Corporation 323
Genlyte Group Inc. 225
Genome Therapeutics Corporation 182
Genovese Drug Stores, Inc. 240
Gentex Corporation 191
Genuine Parts Co. 138
Genzyme Corporation 182
The George Washington University 125
Georgia-Pacific Corporation 139
Geriatric & Medical Companies, Inc. 283
GF Industries Inc. 92
GFI America, Inc 200
Giant Eagle Inc. 283
Giant Food Inc. 174
Gibson Greetings, Inc. 264
Gilead Sciences, Inc. 92
The Gillette Company 182
Glenayre Technologies, Inc. 256
GM Hughes Electronics Corporation 92
Gold Kist Inc. 139
Golden Poultry Co., Inc. 139
Golden West Financial Corporation 92
The Goldman Sachs Group, LP 241
Golf Enterprises, Inc. 305
The Golub Corporation 241
The Good Guys, Inc. 92
GoodMark Foods, Inc. 256
Goody's Family Clothing, Inc. 295
The Goodyear Tire & Rubber Company 264
Gottschalks Inc. 93
Goulds Pumps, Inc. 241

Graff Pay-Per-View Inc. 241
Graham-Field Health Products, Inc. 241
W. W. Grainger, Inc. 150
GranCare, Inc. 93
Grand Casinos, Inc. 200
The Grand Union Holdings Corporation 225
Granite Construction Inc. 93
Grant Geophysical, Inc. 306
Graybar Electric Company, Inc. 210
Great American Management & Investment, Inc. 150
The Great Atlantic & Pacific Tea Company, Inc. 225
Great Lakes Aviation Ltd. 164
Great Lakes Chemical Corporation 161
Great Western Financial Corporation 93
Green Tree Financial Corporation 201
The Greenbrier Companies, Inc. 275
Greenwich Air Services Inc. 130
Greenwood Mills 291
Greyhound Lines, Inc. 306
Ground Round Restaurants, Inc. 182
Group Health Cooperative of Puget Sound 328
Grow Biz International, Inc. 201
Grow Group, Inc. 241
Grubb & Ellis Co. 93
GTE Corporation 118
GTECH Holdings Corporation 290
GTI Corporation 93
Guardian Industries Corp. 191
The Guardian Life Insurance Company of America 241
Guidant Corporation 161
Guilford Mills, Inc. 256
Gulf States Utilities Co. 306

GulfMark International, Inc. 306
Gulfstream Aerospace Corporation 139
Gupta Corporation 93
The Gymboree Corporation 93

H

H. B. Fuller Co. 201
H. E. Butt Grocery Company 306
H. F. Ahmanson & Company 93
H. J. Heinz Company 283
H&R Block, Inc. 210
Haemonetics Corporation 182
Haggar Corporation 306
Hale Halsell Co. 273
Halliburton Company 306
Hallmark Cards, Inc. 210
The Hallwood Group Incorporated 306
Hamilton Financial Services Corporation 93
Hancock Fabrics, Inc. 206
Hancock Holding Company 206
Handex Environmental Recovery, Inc. 225
Handy & Harman 241
Hanger Orthopedic Group, Inc. 174
Hannaford Bros. Co. Inc. 172
Harcourt General, Inc. 182
Harley-Davidson, Inc. 333
Harman International Industries, Inc. 125
Harmon Industries, Inc. 210
Harnischfeger Industries Incorporated 333
Harold's Stores, Inc. 273
Harper Group, Inc. 94
Harris Corporation 130
Harsco Corporation 283
Harte-Hanks Communications, Inc. 306
Hartford Steam Boiler Inspection and Ins. Co. 118
Hartmarx Corporation 151
Harvard Community Health Plan, Inc. 182

HOOVER'S MASTERLIST OF AMERICA'S TOP 2,500 EMPLOYERS 349

INDEX OF COMPANIES BY NAME

Harvard Industries, Inc. 225
Harveys Casino Resorts 218
Hasbro, Inc. 290
Hastings Books, Music & Video, Inc. 306
Hawaiian Electric Industries, Inc. 143
Haworth, Inc. 191
Hayes Wheels International, Inc. 191
HBO & Company 139
Health Care and Retirement Corporation 264
Health Management Associates, Inc. 130
Health-Mor Inc. 265
Healthcare America, Inc. 307
Healthcare Services Group, Inc. 283
Healthsource, Inc. 220
HEALTHSOUTH Corporation 73
HealthTrust, Inc., The Hospital Company 296
Healthwise of America, Inc. 296
The Hearst Corporation 241
Heart Technology, Inc. 328
Heartland Express, Inc. 164
Hechinger Company 174
Hecla Mining Company 144
HEI, Inc. 201
Heilig-Meyers Co. 323
Hein-Werner Corporation 333
Helene Curtis Industries, Inc. 151
Helmerich & Payne, Inc. 273
Helmsley Enterprises, Inc. 241
Hendrick Automotive Group 256
Henry Crown and Co. 151
Herbalife International, Inc. 94
Hercules Incorporated 123
Heritage Media Corporation 307

Herley Industries, Inc. 283
Herman Miller, Inc. 192
Hershey Foods Corporation 283
Hewlett-Packard Company 94
Hi-Lo Automotive, Inc. 307
Hilite Industries Inc. 307
Hillenbrand Industries, Inc. 161
Hillhaven Corporation 328
Hills Department Stores, Inc. 182
Hilton Hotels Corporation 94
Hogan Systems, Inc. 307
Holiday Cos. 201
Holiday RV Superstores, Inc. 130
Hollywood Casino Corporation 307
Hologic, Inc. 182
Holophane Corporation 265
Holy Cross Health System 161
The Home Depot, Inc. 139
Home Holdings Inc. 242
Home Shopping Network, Inc. 130
Home State Holdings Inc. 225
Home Theater Products International 94
Homecare Management, Inc. 242
Homeland Holding Corporation 273
Hometown Buffet Inc. 94
HON Industries Inc. 164
Honeywell Inc. 201
Hooper Holmes, Inc. 226
Horizon Bancorp Inc. 331
Horizon Healthcare Corporation 231
Hormel Foods Corporation 201
Hornbeck Offshore Services, Inc. 307
Host Marriott Corporation 174
Household International, Inc. 151

Houston Industries Incorporated 307
Hovnanian K Enterprises, Inc. 226
Howell Industries, Inc. 192
Howtek, Inc. 220
Hubbell Inc. 118
HUBCO, Inc. 226
Hudson Foods, Inc. 79
Hudson General Corporation 242
Huffy Corporation 265
Hughes Markets, Inc. 94
Humana Inc. 168
Hunt Manufacturing Co. 283
Hunt Consolidated Inc. 307
Huntington Bancshares Incorporated 265
Huntsman Chemical Corporation 319
Hutchinson Technology Inc. 201
Hyatt Corporation 151
Hyperion Software Corporation 118
Hy-Vee Food Stores, Inc. 164

I

i-STAT Corporation 226
IBP, Inc. 216
ICF Kaiser International, Inc. 323
ICO, Inc 307
IDEX Corporation 151
IDEXX Laboratories, Inc. 172
IES Industries Inc. 164
IHOP Corporation 94
ILC Technology, Inc. 94
Illinois Central Corporation 151
Illinois Power Company 151
Illinois Tool Works Inc. 151
IMC Global, Inc. 151
IMCO Recycling 308
ImmuLogic Pharmaceutical Corporation 182
Immunex Corporation 328
Imperial Credit Industries, Inc. 94

INDEX OF COMPANIES BY NAME

In Home Health, Inc. 201
InaCom, Inc. 216
Indiana Federal Corporation 162
Inductotherm Industries 226
INFOMART 308
Information Builders, Inc. 242
Information Resources, Inc. 152
Informix Corporation 95
Ingersoll-Rand Company 226
Ingles Markets, Incorporated 256
Ingram Industries Inc. 296
Inland Steel Industries, Inc. 152
Innodata Corporation 242
Inphynet Medical Management Inc. 130
Input/Output, Inc. 308
Insignia Financial Group Inc. 291
Insilco Corporation 265
Insituform Mid-America, Inc. 210
Insteel Industries, Inc. 256
Instrument Systems Corporation 242
Integon Corporation 257
Integra Financial Corporation 284
Integracare Inc. 130
Integrated Circuit Systems, Inc. 284
Integrated Device Technology, Inc. 95
Integrated Health Services, Inc. 174
Integrated Waste Services, Inc. 242
Intel Corporation 95
Intelcom Group, Inc. 113
Intelligent Electronics, Inc. 284
Inter-Regional Financial Group, Inc. 201
Inter-Tel, Inc. 77
INTERCO Incorporated 211
Interface, Inc. 139
Intergraph Corporation 73

Interlake Conveyors Inc. 152
Interlaken Capital Inc. 119
Interlinq Software Corporation 328
Intermet Corporation 139
Intermountain Health Care, Inc. 319
International Business Machines Corporation 242
International Controls Corp. 192
International Data Group 183
International Family Entertainment, Inc. 324
International Flavors & Fragrances Inc. 242
International Game Technology 218
International Imaging Materials Inc. 242
International Multifoods Corporation 202
International Paper Company 243
International Rectifier Corporation 95
International Technology Corporation 95
Interplay Productions Inc. 95
Interpublic Group of Companies, Inc. 243
Interstate Bakeries Corporation 211
The InterTech Group Inc. 291
InterVoice, Inc. 308
Invacare Corporation 265
Investment Technology Group, Inc. 243
Investor's Management Corporation 257
Ionics, Inc. 183
Ipswich Savings Bank 183
IQ Software Corporation 139
Irvin Feld & Kenneth Feld Productions, Inc. 324
Irwin Financial Corporation 162
Island Lincoln-Mercury Inc. 130
Isolyser Company, Inc. 139

ITT Corporation 243
ITT Educational Services, Inc. 162
IVAX Corporation 130
IWC Resources Corporation 162
Iwerks Entertainment Inc. 95

J

J.B. Hunt Transport Services, Inc. 79
J. Baker, Inc. 183
J. C. Penney Company, Inc. 308
J. Crew Group Inc. 243
J.J. Keller & Associates 333
J & J Snack Foods Corp. 226
J. M. Huber Corporation 226
The J. M. Smucker Company 265
J.P. Morgan & Co. Incorporated 243
Jack Henry & Associates, Inc. 211
Jacobs Engineering Group Inc. 95
Jacobson Stores Inc. 192
Jacor Communications, Inc. 265
James River Corporation of Virginia 324
Jan Bell Marketing, Inc. 130
Jason Incorporated 333
JB's Restaurants, Inc. 319
Jean Philippe Fragrances, Inc. 243
Jefferson Bankshares, Inc. 324
Jefferson Smurfit Corporation 211
Jefferson-Pilot Corporation 257
Jitney-Jungle Stores of America, Inc. 206
JLG Industries, Inc. 284
JMB Realty Corporation 152
John H. Harland Company 140
John Hancock Mutual Life Insurance Company 183
John Q. Hammons Hotels, Inc. 211

HOOVER'S MASTERLIST OF AMERICA'S TOP 2,500 EMPLOYERS

INDEX OF COMPANIES BY NAME

The Johns Hopkins University Inc. 174
Johnson Controls, Inc. 333
Johnson & Higgins 243
Johnson & Johnson 226
Johnson Publishing Company, Inc. 152
Jones Apparel Group, Inc. 284
Jones Intercable, Inc. 113
Journal Communications 334
JPS Textile Group Inc. 291
Juno Lighting, Inc. 152
Jupiter Industries, Inc. 152
Justin Industries, Inc. 308

K
K&B 170
K-III Communications Corporation 243
Kahler Realty Corporation 202
Kaiser Aluminum Corporation 308
Kaiser Foundation Health Plan, Inc. 95
Kaman Corporation 119
Kaneb Services, Inc. 308
Kansas City Southern Industries, Inc. 211
Kaufman and Broad Home Corporation 95
Keane, Inc. 183
Kellogg Company 192
Kellwood Company 211
Kelly Services, Inc. 24
KEMET Corporation 291
Kemper Corporation 152
The Kemper National Insurance Companies 152
Kendall-Jackson Winery Ltd. 96
Kennametal Inc. 284
Kent Electronics Corporation 308
Kentek Information Systems, Inc. 113
Kerr-McGee Corporation 273
Key Tronic Corporation 328
KeyCorp 265
Keystone Financial, Inc. 284

Keystone International, Inc. 308
Kimball International, Inc. 162
Kimberly-Clark Corporation 309
Kimco Development Corporation 243
KinderCare Learning Centers, Inc. 73
King Kullen Grocery Company Inc. 244
Kingston Technology Corporation 96
Kirby Corporation 309
Kitty Hawk, Inc. 309
KLLM Transport Services, Inc. 206
Kmart Corporation 192
Knape & Vogt Manufacturing Company 192
Knight-Ridder, Inc. 131
Koch Industries, Inc. 166
Kohl's Corporation 334
Kohler Co. 334
Komag, Incorporated 96
KPMG Peat Marwick L.L.P. 244
The Kroger Co. 265
The Krystal Company 296
Kulicke and Soffa Industries, Inc. 284
K-Va-T Food Stores, Inc. 324
Kysor Industrial Corporation 192

L
L A T Sportswear Inc. 140
L.L. Bean, Inc. 172
La Quinta Inns, Inc. 309
La-Z-Boy Chair Company 192
LabOne, Inc. 166
LaCrosse Footwear, Inc. 334
Ladd Furniture, Inc. 257
Lady Luck Gaming Corporation 218
Lam Research Corporation 96
Lancaster Colony Corporation 266
Lance, Inc. 257
Land O' Lakes, Inc. 202
Landmark Graphics Corporation 309

Landry's Seafood Restaurants, Inc. 309
Lands' End, Inc. 334
Lanoga Corporation 328
LaserMaster Technologies, Inc. 202
Lawson Associates, Inc. 202
Lawyers Title Insurance Corporation 324
LDDS Communications, Inc. 206
Lear Seating Corporation 192
Leaseway Transportation Corporation 266
Lechters, Inc. 226
LecTec Corporation 202
Lee Enterprises, Incorporated 164
Lefrak Organization Inc. 244
LEGENT Corporation 324
Legg Mason, Inc. 174
Leggett & Platt, Inc. 211
Lehman Brothers Holdings Inc. 244
Lennar Corporation 131
Lennox International Inc. 309
Leo Burnett Company, Inc. 152
LESCO, Inc. 266
Levi Strauss Associates Inc. 96
Levitz Furniture Inc. 131
Lexmark International Inc. 119
Libbey Inc. 266
Liberty Corporation 291
Liberty Homes, Inc. 162
Liberty Mutual Insurance Group 183
Life Care Centers of America 296
Life USA Holding, Inc. 202
LifeCore Biomedical, Inc. 202
The Limited, Inc. 266
Lincare Holdings, Inc. 131
Lincoln Electric Company 266
Lincoln National Corporation 162
Lincoln Property Company 309

INDEX OF COMPANIES BY NAME

Linear Technology Corporation 96
Little Caesar Enterprises, Inc. 193
Littlefield, Adams & Co. 324
Litton Industries, Inc. 96
Liuski International, Inc. 244
Living Centers of America, Inc. 309
Liz Claiborne, Inc. 244
Lockheed Martin Corporation 174
Loctite Corporation 119
Loews Corporation 244
Lojack Corporation 183
Lomas Financial Corporation 309
Lone Star Steakhouse & Saloon, Inc. 166
The Long Island Railroad Co., Inc. 244
Long John Silver's Restaurants, Inc. 168
Longhorn Steaks, Inc. 140
Longs Drug Stores Corporation 96
Longview Fibre Company 328
Loral Corporation 244
Lotus Development Corporation 183
Louis Dreyfus Natural Gas Corporation 274
Louisiana Land and Exploration Company 170
Louisiana-Pacific Corporation 275
Lowe's Companies, Inc. 257
Lowrance Electronics, Inc. 274
LR Holdings, Inc. 96
LSI Industries Inc. 266
The LTV Corporation 266
Lubrizol Corporation 266
Luby's Cafeterias, Inc. 310
Lukens Inc. 284
Lunar Corporation 334
LXE Inc. 140
Lykes Bros. Inc. 131
Lynch Corporation 119

M
M.D.C. Holdings, Inc. 113
M.S. Carriers, Inc. 296

Mac Frugal's Bargains - Close-outs, Inc. 96
MacAndrews & Forbes Holdings Inc. 244
MacTemps, Inc. 31
Magma Copper Co. 77
Magna Bancorp, Inc. 206
Mail Boxes Etc. 97
Main St. & Main, Inc. 77
Mallinckrodt Group Inc. 211
Manatron, Inc. 193
Manitowoc Company, Inc. 334
Manor Care, Inc. 174
Manpower, Inc. 26
Manville Corporation 113
MAPCO Petroleum Inc. 274
MapInfo Corporation 245
Marcus Corporation 334
Marietta Corporation 245
Marine Drilling Companies, Inc. 310
Mariner Health Group, Inc. 119
Marion Merrell Dow Inc. 211
Maritz Inc. 212
Mark VII, Inc. 212
Mark IV Industries, Inc. 245
Marlton Technologies, Inc. 284
The Marmon Group, Inc. 153
Marquette Electronics, Inc. 334
Marriott International, Inc. 175
Mars, Inc. 324
Marsh & McLennan Companies, Inc. 245
Marsh Supermarkets, Inc. 162
Marshall & Ilsley Corporation 334
Marten Transport, Ltd. 335
Marvel Entertainment Group, Inc. 245
Mary Kay Cosmetics Inc. 310
Masco Corporation 193
Mascotech, Inc. 193
Mashantucket Pequot Gaming Enterprise Inc. 119

Masland Corporation 285
Massachusetts Institute of Technology 183
MASSBANK Corporation 184
Mastech Systems Corporation 285
Mattel, Inc. 97
Maverick Tube Corporation 212
Max & Erma's Restaurants, Inc. 266
Maxco, Inc. 193
The Maxim Group, Inc. 140
Maxim Integrated Products, Inc. 97
Maxtor Corporation 97
MAXXAM Inc. 310
MAXXIM Medical, Inc. 310
The May Department Stores Company 212
Mayfair Supermarkets Inc. 227
Mayflower Group, Inc. 162
Mayo Foundation 202
Maytag Corporation 164
MBNA 123
McClain Industries, Inc. 193
McClatchy Newspapers, Inc. 97
McCormick & Company, Inc. 175
McCrory Corporation 245
McDermott International, Inc. 170
McDonald & Company Securities, Inc. 267
McDonald's Corporation 153
McDonnell Douglas Corporation 212
McGraw-Hill, Inc. 245
MCI Communications Corporation 125
McJunkin Corporation 331
McKee Foods Corporation 296
McKesson Corporation 97
McKinsey & Company, Inc. 245
MCN Corporation 193
The Mead Corporation 267

INDEX OF COMPANIES BY NAME

Mecklermedia Corporation 119
Medaphis Corporation 140
Media Arts Group, Inc. 97
Media General, Inc. 324
Media Vision Technology Inc. 97
MediaNews Group Inc. 310
Medical Technology Systems, Inc. 131
MedicalControl, Inc. 310
Medicine Shoppe International, Inc. 212
Medicus Systems Corporation 153
MediSense, Inc. 184
Medtronic, Inc. 202
Medusa Corporation 267
Megafoods Stores, Inc. 77
Meijer, Inc. 193
Mellon Bank Corporation 285
Melville Corporation 245
The Men's Wearhouse, Inc. 310
Menard, Inc. 335
Menasha Corporation 335
Mercantile Bancorporation Inc. 212
Mercantile Bankshares Corporation 175
Mercantile Stores Company, Inc. 267
Merck & Co., Inc. 227
Mercury Finance Co. 153
Mercury General Corporation 97
Mercury Interactive Corporation 97
Mercy Health Services 193
Mercy Health System 267
Meridian Bancorp, Inc. 285
Meridian Diagnostics, Inc. 267
Merisel, Inc. 98
Merit Medical Systems, Inc. 319
Merrill Corporation 203
Merrill Lynch & Co., Inc. 245
Merry-Go-Round Enterprises, Inc. 175
Mesa Air Group 231

Metrologic Instruments, Inc. 227
Metromedia Company 227
Metropolitan Life Insurance Company 246
MFS Communications Company, Inc. 217
Michael Baker Corporation 285
Michaels Stores, Inc. 310
Micro Warehouse, Inc. 119
MicroAge Computer Centers, Inc. 77
Microchip Technology, Incorporated 78
Micron Technology, Inc. 144
Micronics Computers, Inc. 98
MICROS Systems, Inc. 175
Microsemi Corporation 98
Microsoft Corporation 328
Mid Atlantic Medical Services Inc. 175
Mid-America Dairymen, Inc. 212
Midwest Resources Inc. 165
Miles Homes, Inc. 203
Milliken & Co. 292
Millipore Corporation 184
Minnesota Mining and Manufacturing Company 203
Minyard Food Stores Inc. 310
Mirage Resorts, Incorporated 219
Mississippi Chemical Corporation 207
Mitchell Energy & Development Corp. 311
MMI Medical, Inc. 98
Mobil Corporation 325
Modine Manufacturing Company 335
Mohawk Industries, Inc. 140
Molex Inc. 153
The Money Store Inc. 227
Monro Muffler Brake, Inc. 246
Monsanto Company 212

Montana Power Company 215
Montefiore Medical Center 246
Montgomery Ward Holding Corp. 153
Moog Inc. 246
Moorman Manufacturing Company 153
Morgan Keegan, Inc. 296
Morgan Stanley Group Inc. 246
Morningstar Inc. 153
Morrison Knudsen Corporation 144
Morrison Restaurants, Inc. 73
Morse Operations 131
Morton International, Inc. 153
Motorola, Inc. 153
Mountasia Entertainment International, Inc. 140
MTD Products Inc. 267
MTS Inc. 98
MTS Systems Corporation 203
Multicare Cos Inc. 227
Multimedia, Inc. 292
Musicland Group Inc. 203
The Mutual Life Insurance Company of New York 246
Mylan Laboratories Inc. 285

N

Nabors Industries, Inc. 311
NACCO Industries, Inc. 267
NAI Technologies, Inc. 246
Nalco Chemical Company 154
Nash-Finch Company 203
Nashua Corporation 220
Nathan's Famous, Inc. 246
National Association of Securities Dealers, Inc. 125
National Bancorp of Alaska, Inc. 75
National City Corporation 267
National Convenience Stores Incorporated 311

354   HOOVER'S MASTERLIST OF AMERICA'S TOP 2,500 EMPLOYERS

INDEX OF COMPANIES BY NAME

National Health Laboratories, Inc. 98
National Home Centers, Inc. 79
National Medical Enterprises, Inc. 98
National Penn Bancshares, Inc. 285
National Railroad Passenger Corporation 125
National RV Holdings Inc. 98
National Semiconductor Corporation 98
National Service Industries, Inc. 140
National Steel Corporation 162
National TechTeam, Inc. 193
National Vision Associates Ltd. 140
NationsBank Corporation 257
Nationwide Cellular Service, Inc. 246
Nationwide Insurance Enterprise 267
Natural Wonders, Inc. 98
Nature's Sunshine Products, Inc. 319
Navistar International Corporation 154
Navy Exchange System 325
NBD Bancorp, Inc. 194
NCH Corporation 311
NCI Building Systems, Inc. 311
Neiman Marcus Group, Inc. 184
NetManage, Inc. 99
Network General Corporation 99
Network Imaging Corporation 325
The New England 184
New England Electric Co. 184
New Image Industries Inc. 99
New United Motor Manufacturing, Inc. 99
New York Life Insurance Company 246
New York Power Authority 247

New York State Electric & Gas Corporation 247
The New York Times Company 247
The Newark Group, Inc. 227
Newcor, Inc. 194
Newell Co. 154
Newmont Gold Company 113
NeXT Computer, Inc. 99
Nextel Communications, Inc. 227
Niagara Mohawk Power Corporation 247
Nichols Research Corporation 73
NICOR Inc. 154
NIKE, Inc. 275
Nine West Group Inc. 119
NIPSCO Industries, Inc. 163
Noise Cancellation Technologies, Inc. 120
NorAm Energy Corp 311
Nordson Corporation 268
Nordstrom, Inc. 328
Norfolk Southern Corporation 325
Norstan, Inc. 203
North American Advanced Materials Corporation 296
North American Mortgage Co. 99
Northeast Utilities 184
Northern States Power Co. 203
Northern Trust Corporation 154
Northland Cranberries, Inc. 335
Northrim Bank 75
Northrop Grumman Corporation 99
Northwest Airlines Corporation 203
Northwestern Mutual Life Insurance Company 335
Northwestern Steel & Wire Company 154
Norwest Corporation 203
Norwood Promotional Products Inc. 311
NovaCare, Inc. 285
Novell, Inc. 320
Novellus Systems, Inc. 99

Nu Horizons Electronic Corporation 247
Nucor Corporation 257
Nuevo Energy Company 311
NUI Corporation 227
NutraMax Products, Inc. 184
NYNEX Corporation 247

O

O'Charley's Inc. 296
O'Reilly Automotive, Inc. 212
O'Sullivan Corporation 325
Oak Industries Inc. 184
Oakwood Homes Corporation 257
Oasis Residential, Inc. 219
Occidental Petroleum Corporation 99
Oceaneering International, Inc. 311
Octel Communications Corporation 99
Office Depot, Inc. 131
OfficeMax, Inc. 268
Ogden Corporation 247
Ohio Casualty Corporation 268
Ohio Edison Co. 268
The Ohio State University 268
Olan Mills 297
Old America Stores, Inc. 311
Old Dominion Freight Line, Inc. 257
Old Kent Financial Corporation 194
Old Republic International Corporation 154
Olin Corporation 120
The Olsten Corporation 28
Olympic Financial Ltd. 204
Omega Environmental, Inc. 329
Omnicom Group Inc. 247
ONBANCorp, Inc. 247
One Price Clothing Stores, Inc. 292
One Valley Bancorp of West Virginia, Inc. 331
Oneida Ltd. 247
Oneita Industries, Inc. 292

INDEX OF COMPANIES BY NAME

Optical Coating Laboratory, Inc. 100
Option Care, Inc. 154
Oracle Systems Corporation 100
Orbit Semiconductor, Inc. 100
Orbital Sciences Corporation 325
Oregon Steel Mills, Inc. 275
OrNda HealthCorp 297
Oshkosh B'Gosh, Inc. 335
OTR Express Inc. 166
Outback Steakhouse, Inc. 131
Outboard Marine Corporation 154
Outlet Communications, Inc. 290
Owens-Corning Fiberglas Corporation 268
Owens-Illinois, Inc. 268
Owosso Corporation 285
Oxbow Corporation 131
Oxford Health Plans, Inc. 120
Oxford Industries, Inc. 141
Oxford Resources Corporation 248

P

PACCAR Inc. 329
Pacific Enterprises 100
Pacific Gas and Electric Company 100
Pacific Holding Co. 100
Pacific Scientific Co. 100
Pacific Sunwear of California, Inc. 100
Pacific Telesis Group 100
PacifiCare Health Systems, Inc. 100
PacifiCorp 275
Pages, Inc. 132
Paging Network, Inc. 312
Paine Webber Group Inc. 248
Pall Corporation 248
PAM Transportation Services, Inc. 80
Pamida Inc. 217
Pancho's Mexican Buffet, Inc. 312
Panhandle Eastern Corporation 312

Papa John's International, Inc. 168
Parametric Technology Corporation 184
ParcPlace Systems, Inc. 101
Park-Ohio Industries, Inc. 268
Parker Drilling Co. 274
Parker Hannifin Corporation 268
Parsons & Whittemore, Inc. 248
Pathmark Stores, Inc. 227
Patrick Industries, Inc. 163
Patterson Dental Company 204
Paul Harris Stores, Inc. 163
Paul Revere Corporation 185
PAXAR Corporation 248
Paychex, Inc. 248
Payco American Corporation 335
Payless Cashways Inc. 213
PC Connection 220
PCA International, Inc. 258
Peco Energy Co. 285
Pediatric Services of America, Inc. 141
Penn Mutual Life Insurance Co. 286
The Penn Traffic Company 248
Pennsylvania Power & Light Company 286
Pennzoil Company 312
Penske Corporation 194
Pentair, Inc. 204
People's Choice TV Corporation 120
Peoples Energy Corporation 154
PeopleSoft, Inc. 101
The Pep Boys - Manny, Moe & Jack 286
Pepper Cos. Inc. 155
PepsiCo, Inc. 248
Perdue Farms Incorporated 175
Performance Food Group Company 297
Perkin-Elmer Corporation 120

Perkins Family Restaurants, L.P. 297
Perrigo Company 194
PerSeptive Biosystems, Inc. 185
Pet Food Warehouse, Inc. 204
Peter Kiewit Sons', Inc. 217
Petrie Retail, Inc. 228
PETsMART, Inc. 78
Pfizer Inc. 248
Phar-Mor Inc. 268
Pharmaceutical Marketing Services Inc. 78
Phelps Dodge Corporation 78
PHH Corporation 175
Philip Morris Companies Inc. 248
Phillips Petroleum Company 274
Phillips-Van Heusen Corporation 249
Phoenix Technologies Ltd. 185
PHP Healthcare 325
PhyCor, Inc. 297
Physician Corporation of America 132
Physician Reliance Network, Inc. 312
Physicians Clinical Laboratory, Inc. 101
Piccadilly Cafeterias, Inc. 170
Pico Products, Inc. 101
PictureTel Corporation 185
Piemonte Foods Inc. 292
Pier 1 Imports, Inc. 312
Piercing Pagoda, Inc. 286
Pilgrim's Pride Corporation 312
Pinkerton's Security & Investigation Services 101
Pinnacle West Capital Corporation 78
Pioneer Group, Inc. 185
Pioneer Hi-Bred International, Inc. 165
Piper Jaffray Companies Inc. 204
Pitney Bowes Inc. 120
Pittston Services Group 120
Pittway Corporation 155

INDEX OF COMPANIES BY NAME

Plains Resources Inc. 312
Planar Systems Inc. 275
Plantronics, Inc. 101
Platinum Software Corporation 101
PLATINUM technology, inc. 155
Players International Inc. 170
Plaza Home Mortgage Corporation 101
Ply Gem Industries, Inc. 249
PMC Inc. 101
PMR Corporation 101
PNC Bank Corporation 286
Polaroid Corporation 185
Pollo Tropical Inc. 132
Polo/Ralph Lauren Corporation 249
Pool Energy Services Co. 312
Pope & Talbot, Inc. 276
The Port Authority of New York and New Jersey 249
Portland General Corporation 276
Post Properties, Inc. 141
Potlatch Corporation 102
Potomac Electric Power Company 125
Powell Industries, Inc. 312
PPG Industries, Inc. 286
Pratt Hotel Corporation 313
Praxair, Inc. 120
Precision Castparts Corporation 276
Precision Standard, Inc. 73
Premark International, Inc. 155
Premier Industrial Corporation 269
PRI Automation, Inc. 185
Price Waterhouse LLP 249
Price/Costco, Inc. 329
Prima Energy Corporation 113
Primark Corporation 325
Prime Hospitality Corporation 228
Princeton University 228

Principal Financial Group 165
The Procter & Gamble Company 269
Professional Sports Care Management, Inc. 249
Proffitt's, Inc. 297
Progress Software Corporation 185
Progressive Corporation 269
The Promus Companies Incorporated 297
Protective Life Corporation 73
Provident Life and Accident Ins. Co. of America 297
Providian Corporation 168
Proxima Corporation 102
The Prudential Insurance Company of America 228
PSC Inc. 249
PSICOR, Inc. 102
Public Service Company of Colorado 113
Public Service Company of New Mexico 231
Public Service Enterprise Group Incorporated 228
Publix Super Markets, Inc. 132
Pueblo Xtra International, Inc. 132
Pulitzer Publishing Company 213
Pulte Corporation 194
Puritan-Bennett Corporation 166
Pyxis Corporation 102

Q

Quad Systems Corporation 286
Quad/Graphics, Inc. 335
The Quaker Oats Company 155
QUALCOMM Incorporated 102
Quality Food Centers, Inc. 329
Quality Products, Inc. 132
Quantum Corporation 102
Quantum Health Resources, Inc. 102

Quantum Restaurant Group, Inc. 249
Questar Corporation 320
Quick & Reilly Group, Inc. 132
QuikTrip Corporation 274
Quixote Corporation 155
Quorum Health Group, Inc. 297

R

R. B. Pamplin Corporation 276
R.P. Scherer Corporation 194
R.R. Donnelley & Sons Company 155
RadiSys Corporation 276
Radius, Inc. 102
RailTex, Inc. 313
Ralcorp Holdings, Inc. 213
Raley's Inc. 102
Rally's Hamburgers, Inc. 168
Ralston Purina Group 213
Ramsay Health Care, Inc. 171
Randalls Food Markets 313
Random Access, Inc. 114
Rational Software Corporation 102
Raven Industries, Inc. 293
Raychem Corporation 103
Raymond James Financial, Inc. 132
Rayonier, Inc. 120
Raytech Corporation 120
Raytheon Company 185
Read-Rite Corporation 103
The Reader's Digest Association, Inc. 249
Red Lion Inns Limited Partnership 329
Redman Industries Inc. 313
Redwood Empire Bancorp 103
Reebok International Ltd. 185
Regal-Beloit Corporation 335
Regency Health Services, Inc. 103
Regis Corporation 204
RehabCare Corporation 213

INDEX OF COMPANIES BY NAME

Rehability Corporation 297
Reliance Group Holdings, Inc. 249
ReliaStar Financial Corporation 204
Reliv International Inc. 213
REN Corporation - USA 298
Renal Treatment Centers Inc. 286
Renco Group Inc. 250
Rentrak Corporation 276
Reptron Electronics, Inc. 132
Republic Engineered Steels, Inc. 269
Res-Care, Inc. 168
Resorts International, Inc. 228
Resource Bancshares Mortgage Group Inc. 292
Respironics, Inc. 286
Revco D.S., Inc. 269
Rexall Sundown, Inc. 132
Reynolds and Reynolds Co. 269
Reynolds Metals Company 325
RF Monolithics, Inc. 313
RF Power Products, Inc. 228
RGIS Inventory Specialists 194
RIBI ImmunoChem Research, Inc. 215
Rich Products Corporation 250
Right Management Consultants, Inc. 286
Rimage Corporation 204
Rio Hotel and Casino, Inc. 219
Riser Foods, Inc. 269
Rite Aid Corporation 287
The Ritz-Carlton Hotel Company, Inc. 141
Rival Co. 213
Riverwood International Corporation 141
Riviana Foods Inc. 313
RJR Nabisco, Inc. 250
Roadway Services, Inc. 269
Robbins & Myers, Inc. 269

Roberd's, Inc. 269
Roberts Pharmaceutical Corporation 228
Robertson-Ceco Corporation 186
Robinson Nugent, Inc. 163
Rock Bottom Restaurants, Inc. 114
Rock-Tenn Co. 141
Rockwell International Corporation 103
Rohm and Haas Company 287
Roll International 103
Rollins, Inc. 141
Rollins Leasing Corporation 123
Roosevelt Financial Group, Inc. 213
Ropak Corporation 103
Roseburg Forest Products Co. 276
Ross Stores, Inc. 103
Rotary International 155
RoTech Medical Corporation 133
Roto-Rooter, Inc. 270
Rotonics Manufacturing Inc. 103
Rouge Steel Co. 194
Roundy's Inc. 336
Rowe Furniture Corporation 325
RPC Energy Services, Inc. 141
RPM, Inc. 270
Rubbermaid Incorporated 270
Ruddick Corporation 258
Rural/Metro Corporation 78
Russell Corporation 74
Rust International Inc. 74
RVSI, Inc. 250
RWD Technologies, Inc. 175
Ryan's Family Steak Houses, Inc. 292
Ryder System, Inc. 133
Rykoff-Sexton, Inc. 103
Ryland Group, Inc. 175

S

S.C. Johnson & Son, Inc. 336
S&K Famous Brands, Inc. 326

SAFECO Corporation 329
Safeguard Scientifics, Inc. 287
Safeskin Corporation 133
Safety Components International, Inc. 104
Safety-Kleen Corporation 155
Safeway Inc. 104
Saga Communications Inc. 194
St. Ives Laboratories, Inc. 104
Saks Holdings, Inc. 250
Salant Corporation 250
Salick Health Care, Inc. 104
Salomon Inc 250
Salt River Project Agricultural Improvement & Power District 78
Sammons Enterprises, Inc. 313
San Diego Gas & Electric Company 104
Sanderson Farms, Inc. 207
Sanifill, Inc. 313
Sara Lee Corporation 155
Savannah Foods & Industries, Inc. 141
Save Mart Supermarkets 104
Sbarro, Inc. 250
SBC Communications, Inc. 313
SCANA Corporation 292
SCEcorp 104
Schering-Plough Corporation 228
Schlumberger NV 250
Schneider National Inc. 336
Schnitzer Steel Industries, Inc. 276
Schnuck Markets Inc. 213
Scholastic Corporation 250
Schottenstein Stores Corporation 270
Schult Homes Corporation 163
Schwan's Sales Enterprises, Inc. 204
Schwegmann Giant Super Markets 171

358   HOOVER'S MASTERLIST OF AMERICA'S TOP 2,500 EMPLOYERS

INDEX OF COMPANIES BY NAME

Schwitzer, Inc. 258
SCI Systems, Inc. 74
Science Applications International Corporation 104
Scientific-Atlanta, Inc. 141
SCIMED Life Systems, Inc. 204
The Score Board, Inc. 228
Scott Paper Company 287
Seaboard Corporation 167
Seagate Technology, Inc. 104
Sealed Air Corporation 229
Sears, Roebuck and Co. 156
Seaway Food Town, Inc. 270
Selas Corporation of America 287
SEMATECH, Inc. 313
Semitool, Inc. 215
Sensormatic Electronics Corporation 133
Sentry Insurance, A Mutual Company 336
Sequent Computer Systems, Inc. 276
Serv-Tech, Inc. 314
Service Corporation International 314
Service Merchandise Company, Inc. 298
ServiceMaster L.P. 156
Services Group of America Inc. 329
SERVISTAR Corp. 287
Sevenson Environmental Services Inc. 251
Shamrock Foods Company Inc. 78
Shaw Group Inc. 171
Shaw Industries, Inc. 142
Shell Oil Company 314
The Sherwin-Williams Company 270
Shoe Carnival, Inc. 163
Shoney's, Inc. 298
ShopKo Stores, Inc. 336
Shoppers Food Warehouse Corp. 176
Shorewood Packaging Corporation 251
ShowBiz Pizza Time, Inc. 314
Showboat, Inc. 219

Sierra Pacific Industries 104
Sierra Semiconductor Corporation 105
Sigma-Aldrich Corporation 213
Signet Banking Corporation 326
Silicon Graphics, Inc. 105
Silicon Valley Group, Inc. 105
Silverado Foods, Inc. 274
J.R. Simplot Company 144
Simpson Industries, Inc. 195
Simpson Investment Co. 329
Sinclair Oil Corporation 320
Sizzler International, Inc. 105
SJW Corporation 105
Skadden, Arps, Slate, Meagher & Flom 251
Skyline Corporation 163
SkyWest Airlines, Inc. 320
Smart & Final Inc. 105
Smith Corona Corporation 121
Smith's Food & Drug Centers, Inc. 320
Smithfield Companies, Inc. 326
Smithfield Foods, Inc. 326
Smithsonian Institution 126
Snap-on Incorporated 336
Sodak Gaming, Inc. 293
Sofamor Danek Group, Inc. 298
Softdesk, Inc. 220
Softkey International Inc. 186
Softmart, Inc. 287
Software Spectrum, Inc. 314
Software Technical Services, Inc. 142
Solectron Corporation 105
Somatix Therapy Corporation 105
Sonic Corp. 274
Sonoco Products Company 292
Sound Advice, Inc. 133

Southdown, Inc. 314
The Southern Company 142
Southern Energy Homes, Inc. 74
Southern National Corporation 258
Southern New England Telecommunications 121
Southern Pacific Rail Corporation 105
The Southland Corporation 314
SouthTrust Corporation 74
Southwest Airlines Co. 314
Southwest Gas Corporation 219
Southwire Company, Inc. 142
Sovereign Bancorp, Inc. 287
Spartan Motors, Inc. 195
Spartech Corporation 214
Special Devices, Inc. 105
Specialty Foods Corp. 156
Specialty Retailers Inc. 314
SpecTran Corporation 186
Spectrum Control, Inc. 287
Spelling Entertainment Group, Inc. 106
Spiegel, Inc. 156
Sport Supply Group, Inc. 314
Sportmart Inc. 156
The Sports Authority, Inc. 133
The Sports Club Company, Inc. 106
Sports & Recreation, Inc. 133
Springs Industries, Inc. 292
Sprint Corporation 167
SPS Transaction Services, Inc. 156
SPX Corporation 195
SSM Health Care System Inc. 214
St. Joe Paper Company 133
St. Paul Companies, Inc. 205

INDEX OF COMPANIES BY NAME

Stac Electronics 106
Standard Insurance Co. 276
Standard Microsystems Corporation 251
Standard Motor Products, Inc. 251
The Standard Products Co. 270
Standard Register Company 270
Standex International Corporation 220
Stanford University Hospital 106
Stanley Furniture Company Inc. 326
The Stanley Works 121
Stant Corporation 163
Staodyn, Inc. 114
Staples, Inc. 186
Star Banc Corporation 270
Star Enterprise 315
Starbucks Corporation 329
Starrett Housing Corporation 251
State Farm Mutual Automobile Insurance Company 156
State Street Boston Corporation 186
State University of New York 251
Stater Bros. Holdings Inc. 106
Steel of West Virginia, Inc. 331
Steel Technologies Inc. 169
Steelcase Inc. 195
Stein Mart, Inc. 133
STERIS Corporation 270
Sterling Financial Corporation 329
Sterling Information Group 315
Sterling Software, Inc. 315
Stevens Graphics Corporation 315
Stewart Enterprises, Inc. 171
Stewart & Stevenson Services, Inc. 315
Stone Container Corporation 156

The Stop & Shop Companies, Inc. 186
Storage Technology Corporation 114
StrataCom Inc. 106
Stratus Computer, Inc. 186
Strawbridge & Clothier 287
The Stride Rite Corporation 186
Structural Dynamics Research Corporation 271
Stryker Corporation 195
Student Loan Corporation 251
Student Loan Marketing Association 126
Sturm, Ruger & Company, Inc. 121
Sullivan Dental Products, Inc. 336
Summit Care Corporation 106
Sun Company, Inc. 288
Sun Healthcare Group, Inc. 231
Sun Microsystems, Inc. 106
Sun Television & Appliances, Inc. 271
Sunbeam-Oster Company, Inc. 133
Sunbelt Beverage Corporation 176
Sunglass Hut International, Inc. 134
Sunrise Medical Inc. 106
SunTrust Banks, Inc. 142
Supercom, Inc. 106
Supercuts, Inc. 107
Superior Industries International, Inc. 107
SUPERVALU Inc. 205
Sweetheart Holdings, Inc. 156
Swift Transportation Co., Inc. 219
Swinerton & Walberg Co. 107
Sybase, Inc. 107
Sybron International Corporation 336
Symantec Corporation 107
Synercom Technology, Inc. 315

Synetic, Inc. 229
Synopsys, Inc. 107
Synovus Financial Corporation 142
Syntellect Inc. 78
Syratech Corporation 186
SYSCO Corporation 315
System Resources Corporation 186
System Software Associates, Inc. 156

T

T. Rowe Price Associates, Inc. 176
Talbots Inc. 187
Tandem Computers Incorporated 107
Tandy Brands, Inc. 315
Tandy Corporation 315
Tandycrafts, Inc. 315
Tarrant Distributors Inc. 316
Taylor Corporation 205
TCF Financial Corporation 205
Teachers Insurance and Annuity Association - College Retirement Equities Fund 251
Tech Data Corporation 134
Teco Energy Corporation 134
Tecumseh Products Company 195
Tejas Power Corporation 316
TELACU Industries 107
Tele-Communications, Inc. 114
Telebit Corporation 187
Teledyne, Inc. 107
Teleflex Inc. 288
Telephone and Data Systems, Inc. 157
Tellabs, Inc. 157
Telxon Corporation 271
Temple-Inland Inc. 316
Temtex Industries, Inc. 316
Tenneco Inc. 316
Tennessee Restaurant Co. 157
Tennessee Valley Authority 298
Teradyne, Inc. 187
Tetra Tech, Inc. 107

INDEX OF COMPANIES BY NAME

Texaco Inc. 251
The Texas A&M University System 316
Texas Industries, Inc. 316
Texas Instruments Incorporated 316
Texas Utilities Company 316
Texfi Industries, Inc. 258
Textron Inc. 290
TFC Enterprises Inc. 326
Thermadyne Holdings Corporation 214
Thermedics Inc. 187
Thermo Electron Corporation 187
Thermo Instrument Systems Inc. 231
Thermo Voltek Corporation 187
Thiokol Corporation 320
Thomas & Betts Corporation 298
Thor Industries, Inc. 271
Thorn Apple Valley, Inc. 195
Three-Five Systems, Inc. 78
Thriftway Food & Drug 271
Thrifty Oil Co. 108
Thrifty PayLess Inc. 277
Tidewater Inc. 171
Tiffany & Co. 252
Timberland Co. 221
Time Warner Inc. 252
The Times Mirror Company 108
The Timken Company 271
Tishman Realty & Construction Co. Inc. 252
Titan Wheel International, Inc. 157
TJ International, Inc. 144
The TJX Companies, Inc. 187
TLC Beatrice International Holdings, Inc. 252
TNT Freightways Corporation 157
Todhunter International, Inc. 134
Toll Brothers, Inc. 288
Tootsie Roll Industries, Inc. 157
Topps Company, Inc. 252

Tops Appliance City, Inc. 229
Torchmark Corporation 74
Toro Company 205
Tosco Corporation 121
Total System Services, Inc. 142
Towers Perrin 252
Town & Country Corporation 187
Toys "R" Us, Inc. 229
TPI Enterprises, Inc. 134
Tracor Inc. 316
Trans Financial Bancorp, Inc. 169
Trans World Airlines, Inc. 214
Trans World Entertainment Corporation 252
Transamerica Corporation 108
Transmation, Inc. 252
TransTechnology Corporation 229
Tranzonic Companies 271
The Travelers Inc. 252
TRC Companies, Inc. 121
Triangle Pacific Corporation 317
Trimark Holdings, Inc. 108
TriMas Corporation 195
Trinity Industries, Inc. 317
TRINOVA Corporation 271
TRISM, Inc. 317
TRM Copy Centers Corporation 277
Truck Components Inc. 157
True North Communications Inc. 157
Trump Organization 252
Trustmark Corporation 207
TRW Inc. 271
TSX Corporation 317
Tucker Drilling Company, Inc. 317
Tuesday Morning Corporation 317
Tultex Corporation 326
Turner Broadcasting System, Inc. 142

Turner Industries, Ltd. 171
Tuscarora Plastics, Inc. 288
Tyco International Ltd. 221
Tyco Toys, Inc. 229
Tyler Corporation 317
Tyson Foods, Inc. 80

U

U. S. Bancorp 277
U.S. Healthcare, Inc. 288
U.S. HomeCare Corporation 253
U.S. Long Distance Corporation 317
U.S. Robotics, Inc. 157
U.S. Trust Corporation 253
U S WEST, Inc. 114
UAL Corporation 157
UGI Corporation 288
UIS, Inc. 253
UJB Financial Corporation 229
Ultimate Electronics, Inc. 114
Ultrak, Inc. 317
Ultramar Corporation 121
UNC Inc. 176
The Unicom Corporation 158
Unifi, Inc. 258
UniHealth America 108
Union Bank 108
Union Camp Corporation 229
Union Carbide Corporation 121
Union Electric Company 214
Union Pacific Corporation 288
Union Planters Corporation 298
Uniroyal Chemical Company, Inc. 121
Unisys Corporation 288
United American Healthcare Corporation 195
United Artists Theatre Circuit, Inc. 114
United Bankshares, Inc. 331
United Dominion Industries Inc. 258

INDEX OF COMPANIES BY NAME

United HealthCare Corporation 205
United Meridian Corporation 317
United Missouri Bancshares, Inc. 214
United Parcel Service of America, Inc. 142
United Retail Group, Inc. 229
United States Banknote Corporation 253
United States Cellular Corporation 158
United States Filter Corporation 108
United States Postal Service 126
The United States Shoe Corporation 271
United States Surgical Corporation 121
United Technologies Corporation 122
United Video Satellite Group Inc. 274
United Waste Systems, Inc. 122
United Wisconsin Services, Inc. 336
Unitel Video, Inc. 253
Unitog Company 214
Univar Corporation 330
Universal Corporation 326
Universal Foods Corporation 336
Universal Forest Products Inc. 195
Universal Health Services, Inc. 288
The University of Alabama 74
University of California 108
The University of Chicago 158
University of Florida 134
University of Illinois 158
The University of Iowa 165
The University of Kentucky 169
The University of Maryland System 176
The University of Massachusetts 187
The University of Michigan 196
University of Minnesota 205
The University of Missouri System 214
University of Rochester 253
University of Southern California 108
The University of Tennessee 298
The University of Texas System 318
The University of Wisconsin System 337
Uno Restaurant Corporation 187
Unocal Corporation 108
UNUM Corporation 172
UOP 158
The Upjohn Company 196
Urban Outfitters Inc. 288
URS Corporation 109
US Foodservice Inc. 289
USA Truck, Inc. 80
USA Waste Services, Inc. 318
USAA 318
USAir Group, Inc. 326
USF&G Corporation 176
USG Corporation 158
UST Inc. 122
USX Corporation - Delhi Group 289
USX Corporation - Marathon Group 289
USX Corporation - U.S. Steel Group 289
UtiliCorp United Inc. 214
UTILX Corporation 330

V

V. F. Corporation 289
Vacu Dry Co. 109
Valassis Communications, Inc. 196
Valhi, Inc. 318
Valley Forge Corporation 109
Value City Department Stores, Inc. 272
Value Health, Inc. 122
Vanderbilt University 298
Vanguard Cellular Systems, Inc. 258
Vans, Inc. 109
Varian Associates, Inc. 109
Varity Corporation 253
Vencor, Inc. 169
Ventritex, Inc. 109
Venture Stores, Inc. 214
Venturian Corporation 205
Vertex Pharmaceuticals, Inc. 188
Viacom Inc. 253
VICORP Restaurants, Inc. 114
Victoria Financial Corporation 272
The Vigoro Corporation 158
Viking Office Products, Inc. 109
ViroGroup, Inc. 134
Vishay Intertechnology, Inc. 289
Vital Signs, Inc. 229
Vitalink Pharmacy Services, Inc. 158
Vivra Inc. 109
VMARK Software, Inc. 188
Volunteer Capital Corporation 298
The Vons Companies, Inc. 109
VT Inc. 167
Vulcan Materials Company 74

W

W. H. Brady Co. 337
W. L. Gore & Associates Inc. 124
W. R. Grace & Co. 134
Waban, Inc. 188
Wabash National Corporation 163
Wachovia Corporation 258
Wackenhut Corporation 134
Wackenhut Corrections Corporation 134
Wakefern Food Corporation 230
Wal-Mart Stores, Inc. 80
Walgreen Co. 158
Walker Richer & Quinn Inc. 330
Wall Data, Inc. 330

INDEX OF COMPANIES BY NAME

Wallace Computer Services, Inc. 158
The Walt Disney Company 109
Walter Industries, Inc. 135
Wang Laboratories, Inc. 188
Warner Insurance Services, Inc. 230
Warner-Lambert Company 230
Warrantech Corporation 122
Washington Corporations 215
Washington Gas Light Co. 126
Washington Homes, Inc. 176
Washington Mutual, Inc. 330
The Washington Post Company 126
Watsco, Inc. 135
Watson Pharmaceuticals Inc. 110
Watts Industries, Inc. 188
Wausau Paper Mills Co. 337
Wawa Inc. 289
Waxman Industries, Inc. 272
Weatherford International Incorporated 318
Webster Financial Corporation 122
Wegmans Food Markets Inc. 253
Weirton Steel Corporation 331
Weis Markets, Inc. 289
Welcome Home, Inc. 258
Wellman, Inc. 230
WellPoint Health Networks Inc. 110
Wells Fargo & Company 110
Wendy's International, Inc. 272
Werner Enterprises, Inc. 217
WesBanco, Inc. 331
West Marine, Inc. 110
West One Bancorp 144
West Publishing Co. 205

Westcott Communications, Inc. 318
Western Atlas, Inc. 110
Western Digital Corporation 110
Western Gas Resources, Inc. 114
Westfield Companies 272
Westinghouse Electric Corporation 289
WestPoint Stevens, Inc. 142
Westvaco Corporation 253
Weyerhaeuser Company 330
Wheaton Inc. 230
Whirlpool Corporation 196
The Whitlock Group 326
Whitman Corporation 159
Whole Foods Market, Inc. 318
Wickes Lumber Company 159
WICOR, Inc. 337
Wilbur-Ellis Company 110
Willamette Industries, Inc. 277
Willcox & Gibbs, Inc. 135
The Williams Companies, Inc. 274
Williams-Sonoma, Inc. 110
Windmere Corporation 135
Winn-Dixie Stores, Inc. 135
Winnebago Industries, Inc. 165
Wisconsin Central Transportation Corporation 159
Wisconsin Energy Corporation 337
Witco Corporation 254
Wm. Wrigley Jr. Company 159
WMX Technologies, Inc. 159
Wolohan Lumber Co. 196
Wolverine World Wide, Inc. 196
Woodhead Industries, Inc. 159

Woodward & Lothrop, Incorporated 126
Woolworth Corporation 254
Worthington Industries, Inc. 272
WPL Holdings, Inc. 337
WPS Resources Corporation 337
WSFS Financial Corporation 124
WTD Industries, Inc. 277
The Wyatt Company 126

X
X-Rite, Inc. 196
Xerox Corporation 122
Xilinx, Inc. 110
Xircom, Inc. 110
XTRA Corporation 188
Xylogics, Inc. 188

Y
Yale University 122
Yellow Corporation 167
York International Corporation 289
Young Men's Christian Association 159
Young & Rubicam Inc. 254
Young's Market Co. 111
Younkers, Inc. 165
Yucaipa Companies 111

Z
H. B. Zachry Company 318
Zale Corporation 318
Zapata Corporation 318
Zebra Technologies Corporation 159
Zeigler Coal Holding Company 159
Zenith Electronics Corporation 159
Ziff-Davis Publishing Company 254
Zytec Corporation 205

INDEX OF COMPANIES BY INDUSTRY

Advertising
D'Arcy Masius Benton & Bowles, Inc. 239
Interpublic Group of Companies, Inc. 243
Leo Burnett Company, Inc. 152
Omnicom Group Inc. 247
True North Communications Inc. 157
Young & Rubicam Inc. 254

Aerospace - aircraft equipment
BE Aerospace, Inc. 127
The Boeing Company 327
Gulfstream Aerospace Corporation 139
Kaman Corporation 119
Lockheed Martin Corporation 174
McDonnell Douglas Corporation 212
Moog Inc. 246
Northrop Grumman Corporation 99
Orbital Sciences Corporation 325
Precision Castparts Corporation 276
Precision Standard, Inc. 73
Rockwell International Corporation 103
Thiokol Corporation 320
UNC Inc. 176

Agricultural
Northland Cranberries, Inc. 335
Pioneer Hi-Bred International, Inc. 165

Apparel
Authentic Fitness Corporation 84
Bugle Boy Industries 85
Columbia Sportswear 275
Cygne Designs Inc. 238
Delta Woodside Industries, Inc. 291
Dyersburg Fabrics Inc. 295
Esprit de Corp. 90
Farah Inc. 305
Fruit of the Loom, Inc. 150

Haggar Corporation 306
Hartmarx Corporation 151
Jones Apparel Group, Inc. 284
Kellwood Company 211
L A T Sportswear Inc. 140
Levi Strauss Associates Inc. 96
Littlefield, Adams & Co. 324
Liz Claiborne, Inc. 244
Oneita Industries, Inc. 292
Oshkosh B'Gosh, Inc. 335
Oxford Industries, Inc. 141
Phillips-Van Heusen Corporation 249
Polo/Ralph Lauren Corporation 249
Russell Corporation 74
Salant Corporation 250
Tultex Corporation 326
V. F. Corporation 289

Appliances
Health-Mor Inc. 265
Maytag Corporation 164
Rival Co. 213
Sunbeam-Oster Company, Inc. 133
Whirlpool Corporation 196
Windmere Corporation 135

Audio & video home products
The 3DO Company 81
Bose Corporation 179
Harman International Industries, Inc. 125
Home Theater Products International 94
Zenith Electronics Corporation 159

Auto parts - retail & wholesale
AutoZone, Inc. 294
Chief Auto Parts Incorporated 301
Discount Auto Parts, Inc. 129
Genuine Parts Co. 138
Hi-Lo Automotive, Inc. 307
Monro Muffler Brake, Inc. 246

O'Reilly Automotive, Inc. 212
The Pep Boys - Manny, Moe & Jack 286
UIS, Inc. 253

Automotive manufacturing
Chrysler Corporation 189
Fleetwood Enterprises, Inc. 91
Ford Motor Company 191
General Motors Corporation 191
Harley-Davidson, Inc. 333
National RV Holdings Inc. 98
Navistar International Corporation 154
New United Motor Manufacturing, Inc. 99
PACCAR Inc. 329
Skyline Corporation 163
Thor Industries, Inc. 271
Winnebago Industries, Inc. 165

Automotive & trucking - original equipment
ABS Industries, Inc. 259
Allen Group Inc. 259
Arvin Industries, Inc. 160
Automotive Industries Holding, Inc. 197
Bailey Corporation 220
Bestop, Inc. 112
Breed Technologies, Inc. 128
Citation Corporation 72
Dana Corporation 262
Donnelly Corporation 190
Dorsey Trailers, Inc. 138
Eaton Corporation 263
Excel Industries, Inc. 161
Exide Corporation 282
Gentex Corporation 191
Hayes Wheels International, Inc. 191
Hilite Industries Inc. 307
Howell Industries, Inc. 192
Intermet Corporation 139
Jason Incorporated 333
Kysor Industrial Corporation 192
Lear Seating Corporation 192
Mascotech, Inc. 193
Masland Corporation 285

INDEX OF COMPANIES BY INDUSTRY

Modine Manufacturing Company 335
Raytech Corporation 120
Safety Components International, Inc. 104
Schwitzer, Inc. 258
Simpson Industries, Inc. 195
A. O. Smith Corporation 332
Spartan Motors, Inc. 195
SPX Corporation 195
Stant Corporation 163
Superior Industries International, Inc. 107
Truck Components Inc. 157
Wabash National Corporation 163

Automotive & trucking - replacement parts
Arrow Automotive Industries, Inc. 178
Durakon Industries, Inc. 190
Echlin Inc. 117
Federal-Mogul Corporation 191
Standard Motor Products, Inc. 251
Valley Forge Corporation 109

Banks - Midwest
Associated Banc-Corp 332
Boatmen's Bancshares, Inc. 208
Chemical Financial Corporation 189
Comerica Inc. 189
Commerce Bancshares, Inc. 209
Fifth Third Bancorp 264
First Bank System, Inc. 200
First Merit Corporation 264
First of America Bank Corporation 191
Firstar Corporation 333
Fourth Financial Corporation 166
Huntington Bancshares Incorporated 265
Indiana Federal Corporation 162
Irwin Financial Corporation 162

Marshall & Ilsley Corporation 334
Mercantile Bancorporation Inc. 212
National City Corporation 267
NBD Bancorp, Inc. 194
Northern Trust Corporation 154
Norwest Corporation 203
Old Kent Financial Corporation 194
Star Banc Corporation 270
TCF Financial Corporation 205
United Missouri Bancshares, Inc. 214

Banks - money center
Banc One Corporation 259
BankAmerica Corporation 84
Bankers Trust New York Corporation 234
The Chase Manhattan Corporation 237
Chemical Banking Corporation 237
Citicorp 237
First Chicago Corporation 149
First Interstate Bancorp 91
KeyCorp 265
J.P. Morgan & Co. Incorporated 243
NationsBank Corporation 257
Wells Fargo & Company 110

Banks - Northeast
Bank of Boston Corporation 178
The Bank of New York Company, Inc. 234
BayBanks, Inc. 178
Commerce Bancorp, Inc. 224
CoreStates Financial Corporation 281
First Commonwealth Financial Corporation 282
First Empire State Corporation 240
First Fidelity Bancorporation 224

Fleet Financial Group, Inc. 290
HUBCO, Inc. 226
Integra Financial Corporation 284
Ipswich Savings Bank 183
Keystone Financial, Inc. 284
MASSBANK Corporation 184
Mellon Bank Corporation 285
Mercantile Bankshares Corporation 175
Meridian Bancorp, Inc. 285
National Penn Bancshares, Inc. 285
ONBANCorp, Inc. 247
PNC Bank Corporation 286
State Street Boston Corporation 186
U.S. Trust Corporation 253
UJB Financial Corporation 229
WSFS Financial Corporation 124

Banks - Southeast
AmSouth Bancorporation 72
Barnett Banks, Inc. 127
BB&T Financial Corporation 255
Capital Bancorp 128
Compass Bancshares, Inc. 73
Crestar Financial Corporation 323
Deposit Guaranty Corporation 206
First Alabama Bancshares, Inc. 73
First American Corporation 295
First Citizens BancShares, Inc. 256
First Tennessee National Corporation 295
First Union Corporation 256
First Virginia Banks, Inc. 323
Hancock Holding Company 206
Horizon Bancorp Inc. 331

HOOVER'S MASTERLIST OF AMERICA'S TOP 2,500 EMPLOYERS

INDEX OF COMPANIES BY INDUSTRY

Jefferson Bankshares, Inc. 324
One Valley Bancorp of West Virginia, Inc. 331
Signet Banking Corporation 326
Southern National Corporation 258
SouthTrust Corporation 74
SunTrust Banks, Inc. 142
Synovus Financial Corporation 142
Trans Financial Bancorp, Inc. 169
Trustmark Corporation 207
Union Planters Corporation 298
United Bankshares, Inc. 331
Wachovia Corporation 258
WesBanco, Inc. 331

Banks - West
Bancorp Hawaii, Inc. 143
First Hawaiian, Inc. 143
First Security Corporation 319
National Bancorp of Alaska, Inc. 75
Northrim Bank 75
Redwood Empire Bancorp 103
U. S. Bancorp 277
Union Bank 108
West One Bancorp 144

Beverages - alcoholic
Anheuser-Busch Companies, Inc. 208
Brown-Forman Corporation 168
Canandaigua Wine Company, Inc. 236
E. & J. Gallo Winery 89
Kendall-Jackson Winery Ltd. 96
Sunbelt Beverage Corporation 176
Todhunter International, Inc. 134

Beverages - soft drinks
Coca-Cola Bottling Co. Consolidated 255
Coca-Cola Bottling Co. of Chicago 148

The Coca-Cola Company 137
Coca-Cola Enterprises Inc. 137
PepsiCo, Inc. 248

Biomedical & genetic products
Advanced Tissue Sciences, Inc. 82
Amgen Inc. 83
Chiron Corporation 86
Enzon, Inc. 224
Genentech, Inc. 92
Genetics Institute, Inc. 181
Genome Therapeutics Corporation 182
Genzyme Corporation 182
IDEXX Laboratories, Inc. 172
ImmuLogic Pharmaceutical Corporation 182
Immunex Corporation 328
LifeCore Biomedical, Inc. 202
RIBI ImmunoChem Research, Inc. 215
Somatix Therapy Corporation 105

Boat building
Bath Iron Works Corporation 172

Broadcasting - radio & TV
A. H. Belo Corporation 299
BHC Communications, Inc. 235
Capital Cities/ABC, Inc. 236
CBS Inc. 236
Citicasters Inc. 261
Clear Channel Communications, Inc. 302
Evergreen Media Corporation 305
Heritage Media Corporation 307
International Family Entertainment, Inc. 324
Jacor Communications, Inc. 265
Multimedia, Inc. 292

Outlet Communications, Inc. 290
People's Choice TV Corporation 120
Pulitzer Publishing Company 213
Saga Communications Inc. 194
Spelling Entertainment Group, Inc. 106

Building - maintenance & services
ABM Industries Incorporated 81
Barefoot Inc. 259
Ecolab Inc. 199
Healthcare Services Group, Inc. 283
Insituform Mid-America, Inc. 210
Roto-Rooter, Inc. 270
ServiceMaster L.P. 156

Building - mobile homes & RV
Cavalier Homes of Alabama, Inc. 72
Champion Enterprises, Inc. 189
Clayton Homes, Inc. 294
Coachmen Industries, Inc. 160
Liberty Homes, Inc. 162
Oakwood Homes Corporation 257
Patrick Industries, Inc. 163
Redman Industries Inc. 313

Building products - a/c & heating
Lennox International Inc. 309
York International Corporation 289

Building products - doors & trim
AMRE, Inc. 299
Andersen Corp. 197

Building products - lighting fixtures
Catalina Lighting, Inc. 128
Genlyte Group Inc. 225
Holophane Corporation 265
Juno Lighting, Inc. 152

INDEX OF COMPANIES BY INDUSTRY

LSI Industries Inc. 266
Building products - misc.
ABT Building Products Corporation 332
American Biltrite Inc. 177
American Buildings Company 72
American Standard Companies, Inc. 222
Armstrong World Industries, Inc. 279
Bird Corporation 179
Butler Manufacturing Co. 208
Drew Industries Incorporated 239
Eljer Industries, Inc. 304
Kohler Co. 334
Lanoga Corporation 328
Manville Corporation 113
Masco Corporation 193
NCI Building Systems, Inc. 311
Owens-Corning Fiberglas Corporation 268
TJ International, Inc. 144
USG Corporation 158
Vulcan Materials Company 74
Waxman Industries, Inc. 272

Building products - retail & wholesale
84 Lumber Company 278
Ace Hardware Corporation 145
BMC West Corporation 144
Cotter & Company 148
D.I.Y. Home Warehouse, Inc. 262
Eagle Hardware & Garden, Inc. 327
Ernst Home Center, Inc. 327
Fastenal Company 200
Hechinger Company 174
The Home Depot, Inc. 139
Lowe's Companies, Inc. 257
Menard, Inc. 335
Miles Homes, Inc. 203
National Home Centers, Inc. 79
Payless Cashways Inc. 213
SERVISTAR Corp. 287

Wickes Lumber Company 159
Wolohan Lumber Co. 196

Building products - wood
Fibreboard Corporation 90
Georgia-Pacific Corporation 139
Louisiana-Pacific Corporation 275
Ply Gem Industries, Inc. 249
Riverwood International Corporation 141
Sierra Pacific Industries 104
Simpson Investment Co. 329
Triangle Pacific Corporation 317
Universal Forest Products Inc. 195
Weyerhaeuser Company 330
WTD Industries, Inc. 277

Building - residential & commercial
AMREP Corporation 233
Austin Industries Inc. 300
Beazer Homes USA, Inc. 136
Centex Corporation 301
D. R. Horton, Inc. 303
Hovnanian K Enterprises, Inc. 226
Kaufman and Broad Home Corporation 95
Pepper Cos. Inc. 155
Pulte Corporation 194
Ryland Group, Inc. 175
Schult Homes Corporation 163
Southern Energy Homes, Inc. 74
Starrett Housing Corporation 251
Swinerton & Walberg Co. 107
Tishman Realty & Construction Co. Inc. 252
Toll Brothers, Inc. 288
Washington Homes, Inc. 176
H. B. Zachry Company 318

Business services
ABR Information Services, Inc. 127
Adesa Corporation 160
Allied Holdings Inc. 136
American Express Company 233
Arthur Andersen & Co, S.C. 146
Asplundh Tree Expert Co. 279
Automatic Data Processing, Inc. 222
The BISYS Group, Inc. 223
Carlson Companies, Inc. 198
CDP Technologies, Inc. 236
Coopers & Lybrand L.L.P. 238
Data Broadcasting Corporation 239
Data Transmission Network Corporation 216
Day Runner, Inc. 88
Deloitte & Touche 116
The Dun & Bradstreet Corporation 117
The Dwyer Group, Inc. 304
DynCorp 323
Equifax Inc. 138
Ernst & Young LLP 240
Fair, Isaac and Company, Incorporated 90
Franklin Quest Co. 319
The Freeman Companies 305
Fritz Companies, Inc. 92
Gartner Group Inc. 118
Grow Biz International, Inc. 201
KPMG Peat Marwick L.L.P. 244
Mail Boxes Etc. 97
Marlton Technologies, Inc. 284
Medaphis Corporation 140
MICROS Systems, Inc. 175
Norwood Promotional Products Inc. 311
Paychex, Inc. 248
Price Waterhouse LLP 249

HOOVER'S MASTERLIST OF AMERICA'S TOP 2,500 EMPLOYERS   367

INDEX OF COMPANIES BY INDUSTRY

RGIS Inventory Specialists 194
SPS Transaction Services, Inc. 156
TRM Copy Centers Corporation 277
UTILX Corporation 330
Warner Insurance Services, Inc. 230

Business services - marketing
ADVO, Inc. 115
American Business Information, Inc. 216
Catalina Marketing Corporation 128
DIMAC Corporation 209
Information Resources, Inc. 152
Maritz Inc. 212
Pharmaceutical Marketing Services Inc. 78

Cable TV
Adelphia Communications Corporation 278
Cablevision Systems Corporation 236
Century Communications Corporation 116
Comcast Corporation 281
Continental Cablevision, Inc. 180
Graff Pay-Per-View Inc. 241
Jones Intercable, Inc. 113
Tele-Communications, Inc. 114
Turner Broadcasting System, Inc. 142

Ceramics & ceramic products
North American Advanced Materials Corporation 296

Charitable organizations
American Cancer Society 136
American Red Cross 125

Chemicals - diversified
The B.F.Goodrich Co. 260
Cambrex Corporation 223
The Dow Chemical Company 190
Dow Corning Corporation 190

Eastman Chemical Company 295
General Chemical Corp. 220
W. R. Grace & Co. 134
Huntsman Chemical Corporation 319
Monsanto Company 212
PPG Industries, Inc. 286
Rohm and Haas Company 287
Union Carbide Corporation 121
Uniroyal Chemical Company, Inc. 121
Univar Corporation 330
Witco Corporation 254

Chemicals - plastics
PMC Inc. 101
Wellman, Inc. 230

Chemicals - specialty
Air Products and Chemicals, Inc. 278
Airgas, Inc. 278
Albemarle Corporation 170
Alpine Group, Inc. 232
American Vanguard Corporation 83
ARCO Chemical Company 279
Betz Laboratories, Inc. 280
W. H. Brady Co. 337
Cabot Corporation 179
Carpenter Co. 322
Celgene Corporation 223
Crompton & Knowles Corporation 116
Cytec Industries Inc. 224
Engelhard Corporation 224
Flint Ink Corporation 191
H. B. Fuller Co. 201
Great Lakes Chemical Corporation 161
Hercules Incorporated 123
International Flavors & Fragrances Inc. 242
The InterTech Group Inc. 291
Morton International, Inc. 153
Nalco Chemical Company 154

Praxair, Inc. 120
Sigma-Aldrich Corporation 213
UOP 158
Wilbur-Ellis Company 110

Coal
CONSOL Energy Inc. 281
Zeigler Coal Holding Company 159

Computers - graphics
Cornerstone Imaging Inc. 88
Electronics for Imaging, Inc. 90
Intergraph Corporation 73
Network Imaging Corporation 325
New Image Industries Inc. 99
Radius, Inc. 102
Silicon Graphics, Inc. 105

Computers - mainframe
Ceridian Corporation 198
Cray Research, Inc. 199
International Business Machines Corporation 242
Sequent Computer Systems, Inc. 276
Unisys Corporation 288

Computers - mini & micro
Apple Computer, Inc. 83
AST Research, Inc. 84
BitWise Designs, Inc. 235
Compaq Computer Corporation 302
Comverse Technology Inc. 237
Data General Corporation 180
Dell Computer Corporation 303
Diebold, Inc. 263
Digital Equipment Corporation 181
Gateway 2000 Inc. 293
Hewlett-Packard Company 94
NAI Technologies, Inc. 246
RadiSys Corporation 276
Stratus Computer, Inc. 186

INDEX OF COMPANIES BY INDUSTRY

Sun Microsystems, Inc. 106
Tandem Computers Incorporated 107
Telxon Corporation 271
Computers - networking
3Com Corporation 81
Artisoft, Inc. 76
Bay Networks Inc. 84
Cabletron Systems, Inc. 220
Cheyenne Software, Inc. 237
Chipcom Corporation 180
Cisco Systems, Inc. 87
Computer Network Technology Corporation 198
Digi International Inc. 199
FTP Software, Inc. 181
Lawson Associates, Inc. 202
NetManage, Inc. 99
Network General Corporation 99
Standard Microsystems Corporation 251
Sterling Software, Inc. 315
StrataCom Inc. 106
Wang Laboratories, Inc. 188
Xircom, Inc. 110
Xylogics, Inc. 188
Computers - nonelectrical components
Hutchinson Technology Inc. 201
Computers - peripheral equipment
Adaptec, Inc. 81
American Power Conversion Corporation 290
Boca Research Inc. 128
Conner Peripherals, Inc. 87
Diamond Multimedia Systems, Inc. 89
Digital Biometrics, Inc. 199
ECCS Inc. 224
EMC Corporation 181
Falcon Systems Inc. 90
GENICOM Corporation 323

Howtek, Inc. 220
Kentek Information Systems, Inc. 113
Key Tronic Corporation 328
Kingston Technology Corporation 96
Komag, Incorporated 96
LaserMaster Technologies, Inc. 202
Lexmark International Inc. 119
Maxtor Corporation 97
Media Vision Technology Inc. 97
Micronics Computers, Inc. 98
Quantum Corporation 102
Read-Rite Corporation 103
Rimage Corporation 204
Seagate Technology, Inc. 104
Stac Electronics 106
Storage Technology Corporation 114
U.S. Robotics, Inc. 157
Western Digital Corporation 110
Computers - retail & wholesale
Access Graphics Inc. 112
CDW Computer Centers, Inc. 148
CompuCom Systems, Inc. 302
CompUSA Inc. 302
Data Storage Marketing, Inc. 113
Elek-Tek Inc. 149
GBC Technologies, Inc. 225
InaCom, Inc. 216
Intelligent Electronics, Inc. 284
Liuski International, Inc. 244
Merisel, Inc. 98
Micro Warehouse, Inc. 119
MicroAge Computer Centers, Inc. 77
PC Connection 220
Random Access, Inc. 114
Softmart, Inc. 287

Software Spectrum, Inc. 314
Supercom, Inc. 106
Tech Data Corporation 134
Computers - services
Acxiom Corporation 79
America Online, Inc. 322
American Management Systems, Incorporated 322
Anacomp, Inc. 160
AutoInfo, Inc. 222
Brandon Systems Corporation 223
CACI International Inc. 322
Cerplex Group, Inc. 86
CIBER, Inc. 112
The Continuum Company, Inc. 303
Control Data Systems, Inc. 198
DIGICON 173
Electronic Data Systems Corporation 304
FIserv, Inc. 333
HBO & Company 139
INFOMART 308
Keane, Inc. 183
Mastech Systems Corporation 285
National TechTeam, Inc. 193
RWD Technologies, Inc. 175
Software Technical Services, Inc. 142
Sterling Information Group 315
The Whitlock Group 326
Computers - software
Acclaim Entertainment, Inc. 232
Accolade Inc. 81
Adobe Systems Incorporated 81
Asymetrix Corp. 327
Autodesk, Inc. 84
Avid Technology, Inc. 178
Bachman Information Systems, Inc. 178
Boole & Babbage, Inc. 85
Brock Control Systems, Inc. 137
Cerner Corporation 209

HOOVER'S MASTERLIST OF AMERICA'S TOP 2,500 EMPLOYERS

INDEX OF COMPANIES BY INDUSTRY

CFI ProServices, Inc. 275
CITATION Computer Systems, Inc. 209
Computer Associates International, Inc. 237
Compuware Corporation 189
Datastorm Technologies Inc. 209
Dataware Technologies Inc. 180
Davidson & Associates, Inc. 88
Delrina Corporation 89
Electronic Arts Inc. 89
Environmental Systems Research Institute Inc. 90
EPIC Design Technology, Inc. 90
FourGen Software Inc. 327
Fourth Shift Corporation 200
Gupta Corporation 93
Hogan Systems, Inc. 307
Hyperion Software Corporation 118
Information Builders, Inc. 242
Informix Corporation 95
Interlinq Software Corporation 328
Interplay Productions Inc. 95
IQ Software Corporation 139
Jack Henry & Associates, Inc. 211
Landmark Graphics Corporation 309
LEGENT Corporation 324
Lotus Development Corporation 183
Manatron, Inc. 193
MapInfo Corporation 245
Medicus Systems Corporation 153
Mercury Interactive Corporation 97
Microsoft Corporation 328
NeXT Computer, Inc. 99
Novell, Inc. 320
Oracle Systems Corporation 100
Parametric Technology Corporation 184

ParcPlace Systems, Inc. 101
PeopleSoft, Inc. 101
Phoenix Technologies Ltd. 185
Platinum Software Corporation 101
PLATINUM technology, inc. 155
Progress Software Corporation 185
Rational Software Corporation 102
Reynolds and Reynolds Co. 269
Softdesk, Inc. 220
Softkey International Inc. 186
Structural Dynamics Research Corporation 271
Sybase, Inc. 107
Symantec Corporation 107
Synercom Technology, Inc. 315
Synopsys, Inc. 107
System Resources Corporation 186
System Software Associates, Inc. 156
VMARK Software, Inc. 188
Walker Richer & Quinn Inc. 330
Wall Data, Inc. 330

Construction - cement & concrete
Medusa Corporation 267
Southdown, Inc. 314

Construction - heavy
BE&K Inc. 72
Bechtel Group, Inc. 84
Black and Veatch 208
CBI Industries, Inc. 147
Fluor Corporation 91
Granite Construction Inc. 93
Jacobs Engineering Group Inc. 95
Morrison Knudsen Corporation 144
Peter Kiewit Sons', Inc. 217
Turner Industries, Ltd. 171

Consulting
AMRESCO, Inc. 299
Arthur D. Little Inc. 178
Bain & Company 178
Booz, Allen & Hamilton Inc. 235
Computer Sciences Corporation 87
Day & Zimmermann Incorporated 282
McKinsey & Company, Inc. 245
Right Management Consultants, Inc. 286
Towers Perrin 252
The Wyatt Company 126

Containers - metal
Crown Cork & Seal Company, Inc. 282

Containers - paper & plastic
Bemis Co., Inc. 197
Continental Can Co. 238
Gaylord Container Corporation 150
Ropak Corporation 103
Sealed Air Corporation 229
Sonoco Products Company 292
Temple-Inland Inc. 316
Tuscarora Plastics, Inc. 288

Cosmetics & toiletries
Alberto-Culver Company 145
Avon Products, Inc. 234
Block Drug Co., Inc. 223
Cosmetic Center, Inc. 173
The Gillette Company 182
Helene Curtis Industries, Inc. 151
Jean Philippe Fragrances, Inc. 243
Marietta Corporation 245
Mary Kay Cosmetics Inc. 310
NutraMax Products, Inc. 184
Perrigo Company 194
St. Ives Laboratories, Inc. 104

Data collection & systems
Innodata Corporation 242
Lojack Corporation 183
PSC Inc. 249

370 HOOVER'S MASTERLIST OF AMERICA'S TOP 2,500 EMPLOYERS

INDEX OF COMPANIES BY INDUSTRY

Diversified operations
"21" International Holdings, Inc. 232
Acme-Cleveland Corporation 259
AlliedSignal Inc. 222
American Brands, Inc. 115
American Financial Corporation 259
The Anschutz Corporation 112
ARAMARK Corporation 279
Astrum International Corp. 234
Atlantis Group, Inc. 127
Bell & Howell Co. 147
Berkshire Hathaway Inc. 216
Chemed Corporation 261
Clark Enterprises, Inc. 173
Coltec Industries Inc. 237
Cooper Development Company 88
Cooper Industries, Inc. 303
Corning Incorporated 238
Crane Co. 116
Delaware North Companies Inc. 239
The Dial Corp. 77
Dover Corporation 239
Duchossois Industries, Inc. 149
E.I. du Pont de Nemours and Company 123
Farmland Industries, Inc. 210
Federal Signal Corporation 149
Figgie International Inc. 264
FMC Corporation 150
Follett Corporation 150
Foster Wheeler Corporation 225
GAF Corp 225
GenCorp Inc. 264
General Electric Company 118
W. L. Gore & Associates Inc. 124
Great American Management & Investment, Inc. 150
Halliburton Company 306

Harcourt General, Inc. 182
Harris Corporation 130
Harte-Hanks Communications, Inc. 306
Harvard Industries, Inc. 225
Hendrick Automotive Group 256
Henry Crown and Co. 151
Hillenbrand Industries, Inc. 161
Honeywell Inc. 201
J. M. Huber Corporation 226
Ingram Industries Inc. 296
Insilco Corporation 265
Instrument Systems Corporation 242
International Controls Corp. 192
ITT Corporation 243
Jefferson Smurfit Corporation 211
Johnson Controls, Inc. 333
Johnson Publishing Company, Inc. 152
Jupiter Industries, Inc. 152
Justin Industries, Inc. 308
Kirby Corporation 309
Lancaster Colony Corporation 266
Litton Industries, Inc. 96
Loews Corporation 244
Lykes Bros. Inc. 131
Lynch Corporation 119
MacAndrews & Forbes Holdings Inc. 244
Mallinckrodt Group Inc. 211
Manitowoc Company, Inc. 334
Mark IV Industries, Inc. 245
The Marmon Group, Inc. 153
MAXXAM Inc. 310
McDermott International, Inc. 170
Menasha Corporation 335
Metromedia Company 227

Minnesota Mining and Manufacturing Company 203
Motorola, Inc. 153
NACCO Industries, Inc. 267
Nashua Corporation 220
National Service Industries, Inc. 140
Newell Co. 154
Ogden Corporation 247
Olin Corporation 120
Oxbow Corporation 131
Pacific Holding Co. 100
R. B. Pamplin Corporation 276
Parsons & Whittemore, Inc. 248
Penske Corporation 194
Pfizer Inc. 248
Pittston Services Group 120
Pittway Corporation 155
The Port Authority of New York and New Jersey 249
Premark International, Inc. 155
Primark Corporation 325
Quality Products, Inc. 132
Quixote Corporation 155
Ralston Purina Group 213
Raven Industries, Inc. 293
Raytheon Company 185
Renco Group Inc. 250
Rich Products Corporation 250
Robertson-Ceco Corporation 186
Rollins, Inc. 141
Sammons Enterprises, Inc. 313
Sara Lee Corporation 155
Selas Corporation of America 287
J.R. Simplot Company 144
Sinclair Oil Corporation 320
Standex International Corporation 220
Tandycrafts, Inc. 315
Teledyne, Inc. 107
Temtex Industries, Inc. 316
Tenneco Inc. 316
Texas Industries, Inc. 316

HOOVER'S MASTERLIST OF AMERICA'S TOP 2,500 EMPLOYERS 371

INDEX OF COMPANIES BY INDUSTRY

Textron Inc. 290
Thermo Electron Corporation 187
Trump Organization 252
TRW Inc. 271
Tyco International Ltd. 221
Tyler Corporation 317
United Dominion Industries Inc. 258
United Technologies Corporation 122
Valhi, Inc. 318
Varity Corporation 253
Venturian Corporation 205
Viacom Inc. 253
Walter Industries, Inc. 135
Washington Corporations 215
Watsco, Inc. 135
Westinghouse Electric Corporation 289
Whitman Corporation 159

Drugs
Abbott Laboratories 145
Advanced Medical, Inc. 82
Agouron Pharmaceuticals, Inc. 82
Alpha-Beta Technology, Inc. 177
American Home Products Corporation 222
Bristol-Myers Squibb Company 235
Carter-Wallace, Inc. 236
Celtrix Pharmaceuticals, Inc. 85
Curative Technologies, Inc. 238
Eli Lilly and Company 161
Gilead Sciences, Inc. 92
Johnson & Johnson 226
Marion Merrell Dow Inc. 211
Merck & Co., Inc. 227
Roberts Pharmaceutical Corporation 228
Schering-Plough Corporation 228
The Upjohn Company 196
Vertex Pharmaceuticals, Inc. 188
Warner-Lambert Company 230

Drugs - generic
A. L. Pharma Inc. 222
Barr Laboratories, Inc. 234
Mylan Laboratories Inc. 285
Watson Pharmaceuticals Inc. 110

Drugs & sundries - wholesale
Allou Health & Beauty Care, Inc. 232
Bergen Brunswig Corporation 85
Cardinal Health, Inc. 260
Chronimed, Inc. 198
McKesson Corporation 97

Electrical components - misc.
ADFlex Solutions, Inc. 76
Advance Circuits, Inc. 197
Aerovox, Inc. 177
The Cherry Corporation 148
Circuit Systems, Inc. 148
CTS Corporation 160
Diversified Communications Industries, Ltd. 129
GTI Corporation 93
HEI, Inc. 201
Integrated Circuit Systems, Inc. 284
KEMET Corporation 291
Kent Electronics Corporation 308
Linear Technology Corporation 96
Maxim Integrated Products, Inc. 97
RF Monolithics, Inc. 313
SCI Systems, Inc. 74
Solectron Corporation 105
Special Devices, Inc. 105
Three-Five Systems, Inc. 78
Zytec Corporation 205

Electrical components - semiconductors
Advanced Micro Devices, Inc. 82
Altera Corporation 82
Analog Devices, Inc. 177
Atmel Corporation 84
Cirrus Logic, Inc. 87
Cyrix Corporation 303

Integrated Device Technology, Inc. 95
Intel Corporation 95
International Rectifier Corporation 95
Microchip Technology, Incorporated 78
Micron Technology, Inc. 144
Microsemi Corporation 98
National Semiconductor Corporation 98
Orbit Semiconductor, Inc. 100
Sierra Semiconductor Corporation 105
Texas Instruments Incorporated 316
Xilinx, Inc. 110

Electrical connectors
AMP Incorporated 279
Amphenol Corporation 115
Augat Inc. 178
Molex Inc. 153
Robinson Nugent, Inc. 163
Thomas & Betts Corporation 298

Electrical products - misc.
AMETEK, Inc. 278
Duracell International, Inc. 117
Graybar Electric Company, Inc. 210
Hubbell Inc. 118
McJunkin Corporation 331
Oak Industries Inc. 184
Planar Systems Inc. 275
Raychem Corporation 103
RF Power Products, Inc. 228
Spectrum Control, Inc. 287
Woodhead Industries, Inc. 159

Electronics - components & systems
Vishay Intertechnology, Inc. 289

Electronics - measuring instruments
Brown & Sharpe Manufacturing Company 290

INDEX OF COMPANIES BY INDUSTRY

Cerprobe Corporation 76
Fluke Corporation 327
Input/Output, Inc. 308
MTS Systems Corporation 203
Pacific Scientific Co. 100
Teradyne, Inc. 187
Thermo Voltek Corporation 187

Electronics - military
E-Systems, Inc. 304
GM Hughes Electronics Corporation 92
Herley Industries, Inc. 283
Loral Corporation 244
Tracor Inc. 316

Electronics - parts distribution
Arrow Electronics, Inc. 233
Avnet, Inc. 234
Bell Industries, Inc. 85
Bell Microproducts Inc. 85
Nu Horizons Electronic Corporation 247
Premier Industrial Corporation 269
Reptron Electronics, Inc. 132

Energy - cogeneration
Besicorp Group Inc. 235
Destec Energy, Inc. 303

Engineering - R&D services
Battelle Memorial Institute 259
Bell Communications Research Inc. 222
CH2M Hill Cos. 112
Dames & Moore, Inc. 88
ICF Kaiser International, Inc. 323
Michael Baker Corporation 285
Nichols Research Corporation 73
Noise Cancellation Technologies, Inc. 120
Science Applications International Corporation 104
SEMATECH, Inc. 313
URS Corporation 109

Engines - internal combustion
Briggs & Stratton Corporation 332
Cummins Engine Company, Inc. 161
Detroit Diesel Corporation 190
Stewart & Stevenson Services, Inc. 315
Tecumseh Products Company 195

Fertilizers
Arcadian Partners, L.P. 294
First Mississippi Corporation 206
Freeport-McMoRan Inc. 170
IMC Global, Inc. 151
LESCO, Inc. 266
Mississippi Chemical Corporation 207
The Vigoro Corporation 158

Fiber optics
SpecTran Corporation 186
TSX Corporation 317

Filtration products
Donaldson Company, Inc. 199
Flair Corporation 129
Ionics, Inc. 183
Millipore Corporation 184
Pall Corporation 248
United States Filter Corporation 108

Financial - business services
Alleghany Corporation 232
AutoFinance Group, Inc. 146
First Data Corporation 216
First Financial Management Corporation 138
H&R Block, Inc. 210
The Hallwood Group Incorporated 306
Investment Technology Group, Inc. 243
Lawyers Title Insurance Corporation 324

National Association of Securities Dealers, Inc. 125
Payco American Corporation 335
Teachers Insurance and Annuity Association - College Retirement Equities Fund 251
Total System Services, Inc. 142
Warrantech Corporation 122

Financial - consumer loans
ADVANTA Corporation 278
Beneficial Corporation 123
Cash America International, Inc. 301
EZCORP, Inc. 305
Household International, Inc. 151
MBNA 123
Mercury Finance Co. 153
The Money Store Inc. 227
Olympic Financial Ltd. 204
Student Loan Corporation 251
Student Loan Marketing Association 126
TFC Enterprises Inc. 326

Financial - investment bankers & brokerages
A.G. Edwards, Inc. 208
The Bear Stearns Companies Inc. 235
The Charles Schwab Corporation 86
Dean Witter, Discover & Co. 239
Edward D. Jones & Co. 209
The Goldman Sachs Group, LP 241
Inter-Regional Financial Group, Inc. 201
Interlaken Capital Inc. 119
Kemper Corporation 152
Legg Mason, Inc. 174
Lehman Brothers Holdings Inc. 244
McDonald & Company Securities, Inc. 267

HOOVER'S MASTERLIST OF AMERICA'S TOP 2,500 EMPLOYERS

INDEX OF COMPANIES BY INDUSTRY

Merrill Lynch & Co., Inc. 245
Morgan Keegan, Inc. 296
Morgan Stanley Group Inc. 246
Paine Webber Group Inc. 248
Piper Jaffray Companies Inc. 204
Quick & Reilly Group, Inc. 132
Raymond James Financial, Inc. 132
Safeguard Scientifics, Inc. 287
Salomon Inc 250

Financial - investment management
Eaton Vance Corporation 181
Franklin Resources, Inc. 91
Fund American Enterprises Holdings, Inc. 321
Lomas Financial Corporation 309
M.D.C. Holdings, Inc. 113
Pioneer Group, Inc. 185
T. Rowe Price Associates, Inc. 176

Financial - mortgage & related services
Aames Financial Corporation 81
Advanced Financial, Inc. 166
Countrywide Credit Industries, Inc. 88
Federal National Mortgage Association 125
First American Financial Corporation 91
First Mortgage Corporation 91
Green Tree Financial Corporation 201
Hamilton Financial Services Corporation 93
Imperial Credit Industries, Inc. 94
North American Mortgage Co. 99
Plaza Home Mortgage Corporation 101
Resource Bancshares Mortgage Group Inc. 292

TELACU Industries 107

Financial - savings & loans
H. F. Ahmanson & Company 93
BancFirst Corporation 273
Collective Bancorp, Inc. 224
DS Bancor, Inc. 117
Eagle Financial Corp. 117
Golden West Financial Corporation 92
Great Western Financial Corporation 93
Magna Bancorp, Inc. 206
Roosevelt Financial Group, Inc. 213
Sovereign Bancorp, Inc. 287
Sterling Financial Corporation 329
Washington Mutual, Inc. 330
Webster Financial Corporation 122

Financial - SBIC & commercial
Ace Cash Express, Inc. 299

Food - canned
Campbell Soup Company 223
Del Monte Foods Company 89
Dole Food Company, Inc. 89
H. J. Heinz Company 283

Food - confectionery
Hershey Foods Corporation 283
Mars, Inc. 324
The J. M. Smucker Company 265
Tootsie Roll Industries, Inc. 157
Topps Company, Inc. 252
Wm. Wrigley Jr. Company 159

Food - dairy products
Associated Milk Producers, Inc. 300
Ben & Jerry's Homemade, Inc. 321
Borden, Inc. 260
Dean Foods Company 148

Dreyer's Grand Ice Cream, Inc. 89
Land O' Lakes, Inc. 202
Mid-America Dairymen, Inc. 212

Food - flour & grain
Archer-Daniels-Midland Company 146
International Multifoods Corporation 202

Food - meat products
BeefAmerica, Inc. 216
Cagle's, Inc. 137
Foster Poultry Farms Inc. 91
GFI America, Inc 200
Gold Kist Inc. 139
Golden Poultry Co., Inc. 139
GoodMark Foods, Inc. 256
Hormel Foods Corporation 201
Hudson Foods, Inc. 79
IBP, Inc. 216
Perdue Farms Incorporated 175
Pilgrim's Pride Corporation 312
Sanderson Farms, Inc. 207
Seaboard Corporation 167
Smithfield Companies, Inc. 326
Smithfield Foods, Inc. 326
Thorn Apple Valley, Inc. 195
Tyson Foods, Inc. 80

Food - misc.
Caterair International Corp. 173
Chiquita Brands International, Inc. 261
ConAgra, Inc. 216
CooperSmith Inc. 137
CPC International Inc. 224
Flowers Industries, Inc. 138
FMR Corporation 181
General Mills, Inc. 200
GF Industries Inc. 92
Interstate Bakeries Corporation 211
J & J Snack Foods Corp. 226

INDEX OF COMPANIES BY INDUSTRY

Kellogg Company 192
Lance, Inc. 257
McCormick & Company, Inc. 175
McKee Foods Corporation 296
Piemonte Foods Inc. 292
The Quaker Oats Company 155
Ralcorp Holdings, Inc. 213
Riviana Foods Inc. 313
Schwan's Sales Enterprises, Inc. 204
Silverado Foods, Inc. 274
Specialty Foods Corp. 156
Universal Foods Corporation 336
Vacu Dry Co. 109

Food - sugar & refining
Savannah Foods & Industries, Inc. 141

Food - wholesale to grocers
C&S Wholesale Grocers Inc. 321
Cargill, Incorporated 198
Certified Grocers of California, Ltd 86
Continental Grain Company 238
Fleming Companies, Inc. 273
Hale Halsell Co. 273
Nash-Finch Company 203
Performance Food Group Company 297
Rykoff-Sexton, Inc. 103
Services Group of America Inc. 329
Shamrock Foods Company Inc. 78
SUPERVALU Inc. 205
TLC Beatrice International Holdings, Inc. 252
Wakefern Food Corporation 230
Young's Market Co. 111

Food - wholesale to restaurants
SYSCO Corporation 315
US Foodservice Inc. 289

Funeral services & related
Service Corporation International 314
Stewart Enterprises, Inc. 171

Furniture
Ameriwood Industries International Corporation 189
Bassett Furniture Industries, Inc. 322
Bush Industries, Inc. 235
Falcon Products, Inc. 210
Flexsteel Industries, Inc. 164
Haworth, Inc. 191
Herman Miller, Inc. 192
HON Industries Inc. 164
INTERCO Incorporated 211
Kimball International, Inc. 162
Knape & Vogt Manufacturing Company 192
La-Z-Boy Chair Company 192
Ladd Furniture, Inc. 257
Leggett & Platt, Inc. 211
Rowe Furniture Corporation 325
Stanley Furniture Company Inc. 326
Steelcase Inc. 195

Glass products
Apogee Enterprises, Inc. 197
Ball Corporation 160
Guardian Industries Corp. 191
Libbey Inc. 266
Owens-Illinois, Inc. 268
Wheaton Inc. 230

Greeting cards & related products
American Greetings Corporation 259
Gibson Greetings, Inc. 264
Hallmark Cards, Inc. 210

Health care - outpatient & home
AdvantageHEALTH Corporation 177
America Service Group, Inc. 123
Apogee, Inc. 279
Caremark International, Inc. 147
Foundation Health Corporation 91
Genesis Health Ventures, Inc. 283
Health Care and Retirement Corporation 264
Homecare Management, Inc. 242
Hooper Holmes, Inc. 226
In Home Health, Inc. 201
Integracare Inc. 130
Mid Atlantic Medical Services Inc. 175
Option Care, Inc. 154
Pediatric Services of America, Inc. 141
PHP Healthcare 325
Professional Sports Care Management, Inc. 249
Ramsay Health Care, Inc. 171
RehabCare Corporation 213
Rehability Corporation 297
REN Corporation - USA 298
Renal Treatment Centers Inc. 286
RoTech Medical Corporation 133
Salick Health Care, Inc. 104
U.S. HomeCare Corporation 253
Vivra Inc. 109

Health maintenance organizations
FHP International Corporation 90
Group Health Cooperative of Puget Sound 328
Harvard Community Health Plan, Inc. 182
Healthsource, Inc. 220
Healthwise of America, Inc. 296
Humana Inc. 168
Kaiser Foundation Health Plan, Inc. 95
MedicalControl, Inc. 310
Oxford Health Plans, Inc. 120
PacifiCare Health Systems, Inc. 100
Physician Corporation of America 132
Summit Care Corporation 106

INDEX OF COMPANIES BY INDUSTRY

U.S. Healthcare, Inc. 288
WellPoint Health
  Networks Inc. 110

Hospitals
Adventist Health System/
  West 82
Allegheny Health,
  Education and Research
  Foundation 278
Allina Health System 197
Catholic Healthcare West
  Inc. 85
Charter Medical
  Corporation 137
Columbia/HCA Healthcare
  Corporation 168
Community Health
  Systems, Inc. 302
The Detroit Medical
  Center 190
Franciscan Health System
  282
Health Management
  Associates, Inc. 130
Healthcare America, Inc.
  307
HEALTHSOUTH
  Corporation 73
HealthTrust, Inc., The
  Hospital Company 296
Holy Cross Health System
  161
Intermountain Health
  Care, Inc. 319
Mariner Health Group,
  Inc. 119
Mayo Foundation 202
Mercy Health Services
  193
Mercy Health System 267
Montefiore Medical Center
  246
National Medical
  Enterprises, Inc. 98
OrNda HealthCorp 297
Quorum Health Group,
  Inc. 297
SSM Health Care System
  Inc. 214
Stanford University
  Hospital 106
UniHealth America 108
Universal Health Services,
  Inc. 288
Vencor, Inc. 169

Hotels & motels
Amerihost Properties, Inc.
  145

Carnival Hotels and
  Casinos 128
Doubletree Corporation
  77
Hilton Hotels Corporation
  94
Host Marriott Corporation
  174
Hyatt Corporation 151
John Q. Hammons Hotels,
  Inc. 211
Kahler Realty Corporation
  202
La Quinta Inns, Inc. 309
Marcus Corporation 334
Marriott International,
  Inc. 175
Pratt Hotel Corporation
  313
Prime Hospitality
  Corporation 228
The Promus Companies
  Incorporated 297
Red Lion Inns Limited
  Partnership 329
The Ritz-Carlton Hotel
  Company, Inc. 141

Housewares
Blyth Industries, Inc. 115
Forschner Group, Inc.
  118
Media Arts Group, Inc. 97
Oneida Ltd. 247
Syratech Corporation 186

Industrial maintenance
Corrpro Cos Inc. 262
C. H. Heist Corporation
  128

Instruments - control
3D Systems Corporation
  81
Arizona Instrument
  Corporation 76
General Signal
  Corporation 118
ILC Technology, Inc. 94
Keystone International,
  Inc. 308
Parker Hannifin
  Corporation 268
Teleflex Inc. 288
Transmation, Inc. 252
Watts Industries, Inc. 188
X-Rite, Inc. 196

Instruments - scientific
Dionex Corporation 89

Dynatech Corporation
  181
EG&G, Inc. 181
Fisher Scientific
  International, Inc. 220
Optical Coating
  Laboratory, Inc. 100
Perkin-Elmer Corporation
  120
Thermo Instrument
  Systems Inc. 231
Varian Associates, Inc.
  109

**Insurance - accident &
health**
Aon Corporation 146
Blue Cross and Blue
  Shield Association 147
Central Reserve Life Corp.
  261
Paul Revere Corporation
  185
Provident Life and
  Accident Ins. Co. of
  America 297
Standard Insurance Co.
  276
United HealthCare
  Corporation 205
United Wisconsin
  Services, Inc. 336

Insurance - brokerage
Alexander & Alexander
  Services Inc. 232
Arthur J. Gallagher & Co.
  146
Johnson & Higgins 243
Marsh & McLennan
  Companies, Inc. 245

Insurance - life
AFLAC Incorporated 136
Allmerica Financial 177
American Bankers
  Insurance Group, Inc.
  127
Connecticut Mutual Life
  Insurance Company 116
Conseco, Inc. 160
The Equitable Companies,
  Incorporated 240
General American Life
  Insurance Company 210
Jefferson-Pilot
  Corporation 257
John Hancock Mutual Life
  Insurance Company 183
Liberty Corporation 291

376 HOOVER'S MASTERLIST OF AMERICA'S TOP 2,500 EMPLOYERS

INDEX OF COMPANIES BY INDUSTRY

Life USA Holding, Inc. 202
Metropolitan Life Insurance Company 246
The Mutual Life Insurance Company of New York 246
The New England 184
New York Life Insurance Company 246
Northwestern Mutual Life Insurance Company 335
Penn Mutual Life Insurance Co. 286
Principal Financial Group 165
Protective Life Corporation 73
Providian Corporation 168
The Prudential Insurance Company of America 228
ReliaStar Financial Corporation 204
Torchmark Corporation 74
Transamerica Corporation 108

Insurance - multiline & misc.
Aetna Life and Casualty Company 115
AMBAC Inc. 233
American Family Mutual Insurance Company 332
CIGNA Corporation 281
CMAC Investment Corporation 281
Fidelity National Financial, Inc. 90
The Guardian Life Insurance Company of America 241
Liberty Mutual Insurance Group 183
Nationwide Insurance Enterprise 267
Reliance Group Holdings, Inc. 249
Sentry Insurance, A Mutual Company 336
UNUM Corporation 172
USAA 318
Victoria Financial Corporation 272
Westfield Companies 272

Insurance - property & casualty
Acceptance Insurance Companies Inc. 216
Allmerica Property & Casualty Companies, Inc. 177
The Allstate Corporation 145
American International Group, Inc. 233
The Chubb Corporation 223
CNA Financial Corporation 148
Continental Corporation 238
Crawford & Company Risk Management Services 138
EMC Insurance Group Inc. 164
First Central Financial Corporation 240
Frontier Insurance Group, Inc. 240
GEICO Corporation 125
Hartford Steam Boiler Inspection and Ins. Co. 118
Home Holdings Inc. 242
Home State Holdings Inc. 225
Integon Corporation 257
The Kemper National Insurance Companies 152
Lincoln National Corporation 162
Mercury General Corporation 97
Ohio Casualty Corporation 268
Old Republic International Corporation 154
Progressive Corporation 269
SAFECO Corporation 329
St. Paul Companies, Inc. 205
State Farm Mutual Automobile Insurance Company 156
The Travelers Inc. 252
USF&G Corporation 176

Lasers - systems & components
Electro Scientific Industries, Inc. 275

Law firms
Baker & McKenzie 146
Skadden, Arps, Slate, Meagher & Flom 251

Leasing
Aaron Rents, Inc. 136
Alamo Rent A Car, Inc. 127
AMERCO 218
Avis, Inc. 234
Budget Rent a Car Corporation 147
Enterprise Rent-A-Car Co. 210
Oxford Resources Corporation 248
PHH Corporation 175
Rollins Leasing Corporation 123
Ryder System, Inc. 133

Leather & related products
Tandy Brands, Inc. 315

Leisure & recreational products
American Recreation Company Holdings, Inc. 233
Anchor Gaming 218
Anthony Industries, Inc. 83
Arctco, Inc. 197
Autotote Corporation 123
Black Hawk Gaming and Development Co., Inc. 112
Brunswick Corporation 147
Callaway Golf Company 85
Cinema Ride, Inc. 87
The Coleman Company, Inc. 166
Gaylord Entertainment Co. 295
Huffy Corporation 265
International Game Technology 218
Lowrance Electronics, Inc. 274
Outboard Marine Corporation 154

INDEX OF COMPANIES BY INDUSTRY

The Score Board, Inc. 228
Sodak Gaming, Inc. 293
Sport Supply Group, Inc. 314
Sturm, Ruger & Company, Inc. 121

Leisure & recreational services
American Automobile Association 127
Ameristar Casinos Inc. 218
Argosy Gaming Company 146
Aztar Corporation 76
Bally Entertainment Corporation 147
Boomtown, Inc. 218
Boyd Gaming Corporation 218
Carnival Corporation 128
Casino America, Inc. 206
Casino Magic Corporation 206
Circus Circus Enterprises, Inc. 218
Club Corporation International 302
Club Med, Inc. 237
Discovery Zone, Inc. 149
Family Golf Centers, Inc. 240
Grand Casinos, Inc. 200
GTECH Holdings Corporation 290
Harveys Casino Resorts 218
Hollywood Casino Corporation 307
Irvin Feld & Kenneth Feld Productions, Inc. 324
Lady Luck Gaming Corporation 218
Mashantucket Pequot Gaming Enterprise Inc. 119
Mirage Resorts, Incorporated 219
Mountasia Entertainment International, Inc. 140
Players International Inc. 170
Rentrak Corporation 276
Resorts International, Inc. 228
Rio Hotel and Casino, Inc. 219

Showboat, Inc. 219
Smithsonian Institution 126
The Sports Club Company, Inc. 106
Young Men's Christian Association 159

Linen supply & related
Angelica Corporation 208
Cintas Corporation 261
G&K Services, Inc. 200
Unitog Company 214

Machine tools & related products
Applied Power Inc. 332
Cincinnati Milacron Inc. 261
Hein-Werner Corporation 333
Kennametal Inc. 284

Machinery - construction & mining
Caterpillar Inc. 147
Harnischfeger Industries Incorporated 333
JLG Industries, Inc. 284
Maxco, Inc. 193

Machinery - electrical
Applied Materials, Inc. 83
Baldor Electric Co. 79
Emerson Electric Co. 209
FSI International, Inc. 200
W. W. Grainger, Inc. 150
Kulicke and Soffa Industries, Inc. 284
Lam Research Corporation 96
MTD Products Inc. 267
Novellus Systems, Inc. 99
Powell Industries, Inc. 312
PRI Automation, Inc. 185
Robbins & Myers, Inc. 269
Semitool, Inc. 215
Silicon Valley Group, Inc. 105

Machinery - farm
AGCO Corporation 136
Alamo Group, Inc. 299
Case Corporation 332
Deere & Company 148

Machinery - general industrial
AMSTED Industries Incorporated 146
Applied Science & Technology Inc. 178
Blount, Inc. 72
Digital Communications Technology Corporation 129
Dresser-Rand Company 239
Duriron Company, Inc. 263
Goulds Pumps, Inc. 241
IDEX Corporation 151
Inductotherm Industries 226
Ingersoll-Rand Company 226
Lincoln Electric Company 266
Newcor, Inc. 194
Nordson Corporation 268
Owosso Corporation 285
PAXAR Corporation 248
Quad Systems Corporation 286
Regal-Beloit Corporation 335
Thermadyne Holdings Corporation 214
TRINOVA Corporation 271
Willcox & Gibbs, Inc. 135

Machinery - material handling
Astec Industries, Inc. 294
Clark Equipment Company 160
CMI Corporation 273
Interlake Conveyors Inc. 152

Machinery - printing
Stevens Graphics Corporation 315

Medical & dental supplies
American White Cross, Inc. 115
Becton, Dickinson and Company 222
C. R. Bard, Inc. 223
LabOne, Inc. 166
National Health Laboratories, Inc. 98
Patterson Dental Company 204

INDEX OF COMPANIES BY INDUSTRY

Safeskin Corporation 133
Sullivan Dental Products, Inc. 336
Sunrise Medical Inc. 106
Sybron International Corporation 336

Medical instruments
Abaxis, Inc. 81
ABIOMED, Inc. 177
Advanced Technology Laboratories, Inc. 327
American Medical Electronics, Inc. 299
Beckman Instruments, Inc. 84
Boston Scientific Corporation 179
Circon Corporation 87
Cordis Corporation 129
Cyberonics, Inc. 303
Dentsply International Inc. 282
Empi, Inc. 199
Fresenius USA Inc. 92
Graham-Field Health Products, Inc. 241
Hologic, Inc. 182
i-STAT Corporation 226
LecTec Corporation 202
MediSense, Inc. 184
Medtronic, Inc. 202
PerSeptive Biosystems, Inc. 185
Puritan-Bennett Corporation 166
SCIMED Life Systems, Inc. 204
Stryker Corporation 195

Medical products
Advanced Polymer Systems, Inc. 82
Allergan, Inc. 82
ALZA Corporation 82
Amsco International, Inc. 279
Bausch & Lomb Incorporated 235
Baxter International Inc. 147
Cabot Medical Corporation 280
Coulter Corporation 129
Daig Corporation 199
Guidant Corporation 161
Haemonetics Corporation 182

Hanger Orthopedic Group, Inc. 174
Heart Technology, Inc. 328
Invacare Corporation 265
Isolyser Company, Inc. 139
IVAX Corporation 130
Lunar Corporation 334
Marquette Electronics, Inc. 334
MAXXIM Medical, Inc. 310
Medical Technology Systems, Inc. 131
Meridian Diagnostics, Inc. 267
Merit Medical Systems, Inc. 319
Pyxis Corporation 102
R.P. Scherer Corporation 194
Respironics, Inc. 286
Sofamor Danek Group, Inc. 298
Staodyn, Inc. 114
STERIS Corporation 270
Thermedics Inc. 187
United States Surgical Corporation 121
Ventritex, Inc. 109
Vital Signs, Inc. 229

Medical services
American Medical Response, Inc. 177
Coastal Healthcare Group, Inc. 255
Diagnostek, Inc. 231
Express Scripts, Inc. 210
Future Healthcare Inc. 264
GranCare, Inc. 93
Inphynet Medical Management Inc. 130
Integrated Health Services, Inc. 174
Lincare Holdings, Inc. 131
MMI Medical, Inc. 98
Multicare Cos Inc. 227
NovaCare, Inc. 285
PhyCor, Inc. 297
Physician Reliance Network, Inc. 312
Physicians Clinical Laboratory, Inc. 101
PMR Corporation 101

PSICOR, Inc. 102
Quantum Health Resources, Inc. 102
Rural/Metro Corporation 78
United American Healthcare Corporation 195
Value Health, Inc. 122
Vitalink Pharmacy Services, Inc. 158

Membership organizations
Rotary International 155

Metal processing & fabrication
Acme Metals Incorporated 145
Brenlin Group 260
CasTech Aluminum Group Inc. 260
Commercial Metals Company 302
Douglas & Lomason Company 190
Harsco Corporation 283
IMCO Recycling 308
Steel Technologies Inc. 169
The Timken Company 271
Worthington Industries, Inc. 272

Metal products - distribution
Bearings, Inc. 260

Metal products - fabrication
AMDURA Corporation 115
Amtrol Inc. 290
Commercial Intertech Corporation 262
Connell Limited Partnership 180
Park-Ohio Industries, Inc. 268
Titan Wheel International, Inc. 157
Trinity Industries, Inc. 317

Metal products - fasteners
Cedar Group, Inc. 280
Elco Industries, Inc. 149
Esstar Inc. 117
Illinois Tool Works Inc. 151

INDEX OF COMPANIES BY INDUSTRY

TransTechnology
  Corporation 229
TriMas Corporation 195
Metals - nonferrous
Aluminum Company of
  America 278
ASARCO Incorporated
  234
Cleveland-Cliffs Inc. 261
Cyprus Amax Minerals
  Company 112
Freeport-McMoRan
  Copper & Gold Inc. 218
Hecla Mining Company
  144
Kaiser Aluminum
  Corporation 308
Magma Copper Co. 77
Newmont Gold Company
  113
Phelps Dodge Corporation
  78
Reynolds Metals Company
  325

Motion pictures & services
AMC Entertainment Inc.
  208
Carmike Cinemas, Inc.
  137
Iwerks Entertainment Inc.
  95
Trimark Holdings, Inc.
  108
United Artists Theatre
  Circuit, Inc. 114
Unitel Video, Inc. 253
The Walt Disney Company
  109
Westcott
  Communications, Inc.
  318

Nursing homes
Advocat, Inc. 294
Arbor Health Care
  Company 259
Beverly Enterprises, Inc.
  79
Continental Medical
  Systems, Inc. 281
Geriatric & Medical
  Companies, Inc. 283
Hillhaven Corporation
  328
Horizon Healthcare
  Corporation 231

Life Care Centers of
  America 296
Living Centers of America,
  Inc. 309
Manor Care, Inc. 174
Regency Health Services,
  Inc. 103
Sun Healthcare Group,
  Inc. 231

Office & art materials
Avery Dennison
  Corporation 84
Hunt Manufacturing Co.
  283

Office automation
Business Records
  Corporation Holding Co.
  301
International Imaging
  Materials Inc. 242

Office equipment & supplies
General Binding
  Corporation 150
Pitney Bowes Inc. 120
Smith Corona
  Corporation 121
Xerox Corporation 122

Oil field machinery & equipment
Dresser Industries, Inc.
  303
ICO, Inc 307
Maverick Tube
  Corporation 212

Oil & gas - field services
BJ Services Company 300
Camco International Inc.
  301
Energy Ventures, Inc. 304
ERC Industries, Inc. 304
Grant Geophysical, Inc.
  306
GulfMark International,
  Inc. 306
Marine Drilling
  Companies, Inc. 310
Nabors Industries, Inc.
  311
Oceaneering
  International, Inc. 311
Parker Drilling Co. 274
Pool Energy Services Co.
  312
RPC Energy Services, Inc.
  141

Schlumberger NV 250
Serv-Tech, Inc. 314
Weatherford International
  Incorporated 318
Western Atlas, Inc. 110

Oil & gas - integrated
Amerada Hess
  Corporation 233
Amoco Corporation 146
Atlantic Richfield
  Company 84
Chevron Corporation 86
Exxon Corporation 305
Flying J Inc. 319
Kerr-McGee Corporation
  273
Koch Industries, Inc. 166
Louisiana Land and
  Exploration Company
  170
Mobil Corporation 325
Occidental Petroleum
  Corporation 99
Pennzoil Company 312
Phillips Petroleum
  Company 274
Shell Oil Company 314
Texaco Inc. 251
Unocal Corporation 108
USX Corporation -
  Marathon Group 289
Zapata Corporation 318

Oil & gas - offshore drilling
Cliffs Drilling Company
  302
Hornbeck Offshore
  Services, Inc. 307
Tidewater Inc. 171

Oil & gas - production & pipeline
Belden & Blake
  Corporation 260
The Coastal Corporation
  302
The Columbia Gas
  System, Inc. 123
Enron Corporation 304
Kaneb Services, Inc. 308
MAPCO Petroleum Inc.
  274
Panhandle Eastern
  Corporation 312
Tejas Power Corporation
  316
USX Corporation - Delhi
  Group 289

INDEX OF COMPANIES BY INDUSTRY

Western Gas Resources, Inc. 114
The Williams Companies, Inc. 274

Oil & gas - US exploration & production
Barrett Resources Corporation 112
Castle Energy Corporation 280
Devon Energy Corporation 273
Helmerich & Payne, Inc. 273
Hunt Consolidated Inc. 307
Louis Dreyfus Natural Gas Corporation 274
Mitchell Energy & Development Corp. 311
Nuevo Energy Company 311
Plains Resources Inc. 312
Prima Energy Corporation 113
Tucker Drilling Company, Inc. 317
United Meridian Corporation 317

Oil refining & marketing
Ashland, Inc. 168
Caltex Petroleum Corporation 301
Clark USA, Inc. 209
Diamond Shamrock, Inc. 303
E-Z Serve Corporation 304
FINA, Inc. 305
Lubrizol Corporation 266
Star Enterprise 315
Sun Company, Inc. 288
Thrifty Oil Co. 108
Tosco Corporation 121
Ultramar Corporation 121

Optical character recognition
BancTec, Inc. 300
Metrologic Instruments, Inc. 227
Zebra Technologies Corporation 159

Paints & allied products
DeSoto, Inc. 149
Ferro Corporation 264

Grow Group, Inc. 241
Loctite Corporation 119
RPM, Inc. 270
The Sherwin-Williams Company 270

Paper - business forms
American Business Products, Inc. 136
Deluxe Corporation 199
John H. Harland Company 140
Standard Register Company 270
Wallace Computer Services, Inc. 158

Paper & paper products
Albany International Corporation 232
Alco Standard Corporation 278
Boise Cascade Corporation 144
Champion International Corporation 116
Chesapeake Corporation 322
Consolidated Papers, Inc. 332
CSS Industries, Inc. 282
Federal Paper Board Company, Inc. 224
Fort Howard Corporation 333
International Paper Company 243
James River Corporation of Virginia 324
Kimberly-Clark Corporation 309
Longview Fibre Company 328
The Mead Corporation 267
The Newark Group, Inc. 227
Pentair, Inc. 204
Pope & Talbot, Inc. 276
Potlatch Corporation 102
Rayonier, Inc. 120
Rock-Tenn Co. 141
Roseburg Forest Products Co. 276
Scott Paper Company 287
Shorewood Packaging Corporation 251
St. Joe Paper Company 133

Stone Container Corporation 156
Sweetheart Holdings, Inc. 156
Tranzonic Companies 271
Union Camp Corporation 229
Wausau Paper Mills Co. 337
Westvaco Corporation 253
Willamette Industries, Inc. 277

Photographic equipment & supplies
CPI Corporation 209
Eastman Kodak Company 239
Polaroid Corporation 185

Pollution control equipment & services
Advance Ross Corporation 145
Allwaste, Inc. 299
BHA Group, Inc. 208
Browning-Ferris Industries, Inc. 300
Chempower, Inc. 261
Clean Harbors, Inc. 180
Envirotest Systems Corporation 77
F & E Resource Systems Technology, Inc. 174
Handex Environmental Recovery, Inc. 225
Integrated Waste Services, Inc. 242
International Technology Corporation 95
Omega Environmental, Inc. 329
Rust International Inc. 74
Safety-Kleen Corporation 155
Sanifill, Inc. 313
Sevenson Environmental Services Inc. 251
Tetra Tech, Inc. 107
TRC Companies, Inc. 121
United Waste Systems, Inc. 122
USA Waste Services, Inc. 318
ViroGroup, Inc. 134
WMX Technologies, Inc. 159

INDEX OF COMPANIES BY INDUSTRY

Precious metals & jewelry
A-Mark Financial
  Corporation 83
Fossil, Inc. 305
Handy & Harman 241
Town & Country
  Corporation 187

Printing - commercial
Banta Corporation 332
Cadmus Communications
  Corporation 322
Devon Group, Inc. 116
R.R. Donnelley & Sons
  Company 155
J.J. Keller & Associates
  333
Merrill Corporation 203
Quad/Graphics, Inc. 335
Taylor Corporation 205
United States Banknote
  Corporation 253
Valassis Communications,
  Inc. 196

Protection - safety equipment & services
American Protective
  Services, Inc. 83
Borg-Warner Security
  Corporation 147
Central Sprinkler
  Corporation 281
Checkpoint Systems, Inc.
  223
Command Security
  Corporation 237
Corrections Corporation
  of America 294
Pinkerton's Security &
  Investigation Services
  101
Sensormatic Electronics
  Corporation 133
Wackenhut Corporation
  134
Wackenhut Corrections
  Corporation 134

Publishing - books
Encyclopaedia Britannica
  Inc. 149
McGraw-Hill, Inc. 245
Pages, Inc. 132
Scholastic Corporation
  250
West Publishing Co. 205

Publishing - newspapers
Advance Publications, Inc.
  232

Central Newspapers, Inc.
  160
The Chronicle Publishing
  Company, Inc. 86
Cox Enterprises, Inc. 137
Dow Jones & Company,
  Inc. 239
Freedom Newspapers Inc.
  91
Gannett Co., Inc. 323
Journal Communications
  334
Knight-Ridder, Inc. 131
Lee Enterprises,
  Incorporated 164
McClatchy Newspapers,
  Inc. 97
Media General, Inc. 324
MediaNews Group Inc.
  310
The New York Times
  Company 247
The E.W. Scripps
  Company 123
The Times Mirror
  Company 108
The Washington Post
  Company 126

Publishing - periodicals
American Media, Inc. 127
The Hearst Corporation
  241
International Data Group
  183
K-III Communications
  Corporation 243
Marvel Entertainment
  Group, Inc. 245
Mecklermedia Corporation
  119
Morningstar Inc. 153
The Reader's Digest
  Association, Inc. 249
Time Warner Inc. 252
Ziff-Davis Publishing
  Company 254

Pumps & seals
American United Global,
  Inc. 83

Real estate development
Avatar Holdings, Inc. 127
Edward J. DeBartolo
  Corporation 263
Lefrak Organization Inc.
  244
Lennar Corporation 131

Lincoln Property
  Company 309

Real estate investment trust
Berkshire Realty Co. 179
DeBartolo Realty
  Corporation 262
Equity Residential
  Properties Trust 149

Real estate operations
Crown Holding Company
  282
Del Webb Corporation 77
Developers Diversified
  Realty Corporation 263
Forum Group, Inc. 161
Golf Enterprises, Inc. 305
Grubb & Ellis Co. 93
Helmsley Enterprises, Inc.
  241
Insignia Financial Group
  Inc. 291
JMB Realty Corporation
  152
Kimco Development
  Corporation 243
Oasis Residential, Inc. 219
Post Properties, Inc. 141

Retail - apparel & shoes
American Eagle Outfitters,
  Inc. 278
American Retail Group,
  Inc. 233
AnnTaylor Stores
  Corporation 233
Braun's Fashions
  Corporation 198
The Buckle, Inc. 216
Burlington Coat Factory
  Warehouse Corporation
  223
Cache, Inc. 236
Catherines Stores
  Corporation 294
Cato Corporation 255
Charming Shoppes, Inc.
  281
Chico's FAS, Inc. 128
The Clothestime, Inc. 87
County Seat Stores Inc.
  303
Deb Shops, Inc. 282
Designs, Inc. 181
Dress Barn, Inc. 117
Edison Brothers Stores,
  Inc. 209

INDEX OF COMPANIES BY INDUSTRY

Finish Line, Inc. 161
The Gap, Inc. 92
Goody's Family Clothing, Inc. 295
Gottschalks Inc. 93
The Gymboree Corporation 93
Harold's Stores, Inc. 273
J. Baker, Inc. 183
The Limited, Inc. 266
Melville Corporation 245
The Men's Wearhouse, Inc. 310
Merry-Go-Round Enterprises, Inc. 175
One Price Clothing Stores, Inc. 292
Pacific Sunwear of California, Inc. 100
Paul Harris Stores, Inc. 163
Petrie Retail, Inc. 228
Ross Stores, Inc. 103
S&K Famous Brands, Inc. 326
Shoe Carnival, Inc. 163
Specialty Retailers Inc. 314
Stein Mart, Inc. 133
Talbots Inc. 187
United Retail Group, Inc. 229
Urban Outfitters Inc. 288

Retail - books, music & video
Barnes & Noble, Inc. 234
Books-A-Million, Inc. 72
Camelot Music Inc. 260
Crown Books Corporation 173
Funco Inc. 200
Hastings Books, Music & Video, Inc. 306
MTS Inc. 98
Musicland Group Inc. 203
Trans World Entertainment Corporation 252

Retail - catalog showrooms
Best Products Co. Inc. 322
Corporate Express, Inc. 112
Service Merchandise Company, Inc. 298

Retail - consumer electronics
Best Buy Co., Inc. 198
Campo Electronics, Appliances & Computers, Inc. 170
Cellstar Corporation 301
Circuit City Stores, Inc. 322
Fretter, Inc. 191
The Good Guys, Inc. 92
Sound Advice, Inc. 133
Sun Television & Appliances, Inc. 271
Tandy Corporation 315
Tops Appliance City, Inc. 229
Ultimate Electronics, Inc. 114

Retail - convenience stores
Buttrey Food and Drug Stores Company 215
Casey's General Stores, Inc. 164
The Circle K Corporation 77
Cumberland Farms Inc. 180
Dairy Mart Convenience Stores, Inc. 116
Holiday Cos. 201
National Convenience Stores Incorporated 311
QuikTrip Corporation 274
The Southland Corporation 314
Wawa Inc. 289

Retail - discount & variety
Ames Department Stores, Inc. 115
Bradlees, Inc. 179
Caldor Corporation 115
Consolidated Stores Corporation 262
Dollar General Corporation 168
F & M Distributors, Inc. 190
Family Dollar Stores, Inc. 255
Fred's, Inc. 295
Hills Department Stores, Inc. 182
Kmart Corporation 192
Lechters, Inc. 226

Mac Frugal's Bargains - Close-outs, Inc. 96
McCrory Corporation 245
Pamida Inc. 217
Pier 1 Imports, Inc. 312
Price/Costco, Inc. 329
The TJX Companies, Inc. 187
Tuesday Morning Corporation 317
Venture Stores, Inc. 214
Waban, Inc. 188
Wal-Mart Stores, Inc. 80
Woolworth Corporation 254

Retail - drugstores
Arbor Drugs, Inc. 189
Big B, Inc. 72
Drug Emporium, Inc. 263
Eckerd Corporation 129
Fay's, Incorporated 240
Genovese Drug Stores, Inc. 240
K&B 170
Longs Drug Stores Corporation 96
Medicine Shoppe International, Inc. 212
Phar-Mor Inc. 268
Revco D.S., Inc. 269
Rite Aid Corporation 287
Thrifty PayLess Inc. 277
Walgreen Co. 158

Retail - home furnishings
The Bombay Company, Inc. 300
Heilig-Meyers Co. 323
Levitz Furniture Inc. 131
Roberd's, Inc. 269
Schottenstein Stores Corporation 270
Welcome Home, Inc. 258

Retail - jewelry stores
Claire's Stores, Inc. 129
Finlay Enterprises 240
Jan Bell Marketing, Inc. 130
Piercing Pagoda, Inc. 286
Tiffany & Co. 252
Zale Corporation 318

Retail - mail order & direct
Amway Corporation 189
Artistic Greetings, Inc. 233

HOOVER'S MASTERLIST OF AMERICA'S TOP 2,500 EMPLOYERS

INDEX OF COMPANIES BY INDUSTRY

L.L. Bean, Inc. 172
Black Box Corporation 280
Blair Corporation 280
CUC International Inc. 116
Damark International, Inc. 199
Dial-A-Mattress Franchise Corporation 239
DM Management Company 181
Fingerhut Companies, Inc. 200
Gander Mountain, Inc. 333
Herbalife International, Inc. 94
Home Shopping Network, Inc. 130
J. Crew Group Inc. 243
Lands' End, Inc. 334
Roll International 103
Spiegel, Inc. 156
Viking Office Products, Inc. 109

Retail - major department stores
Broadway Stores Inc. 85
Carson Pirie Scott & Co. 332
Dayton Hudson Corporation 199
Dillard Department Stores, Inc. 79
Federated Department Stores, Inc. 263
The May Department Stores Company 212
Montgomery Ward Holding Corp. 153
Neiman Marcus Group, Inc. 184
Nordstrom, Inc. 328
J. C. Penney Company, Inc. 308
Saks Holdings, Inc. 250
Sears, Roebuck and Co. 156

Retail - misc.
Amber's Stores, Inc. 299
American Studios, Inc. 255
Army & Air Force Exchange Service 300
Bed Bath & Beyond, Inc. 222

Celex Group Inc. 148
CML Group, Inc. 180
Cole National Corporation 262
Dart Group Corporation 173
Fabri-Centers of America, Inc. 263
General Host Corporation 118
General Nutrition Companies, Inc. 283
Hancock Fabrics, Inc. 206
The Maxim Group, Inc. 140
Michaels Stores, Inc. 310
National Vision Associates Ltd. 140
Natural Wonders, Inc. 98
Navy Exchange System 325
Office Depot, Inc. 131
OfficeMax, Inc. 268
Olan Mills 297
Old America Stores, Inc. 311
PCA International, Inc. 258
Pet Food Warehouse, Inc. 204
PETsMART, Inc. 78
Regis Corporation 204
Sportmart Inc. 156
The Sports Authority, Inc. 133
Sports & Recreation, Inc. 133
Staples, Inc. 186
Sunglass Hut International, Inc. 134
Supercuts, Inc. 107
Toys "R" Us, Inc. 229
West Marine, Inc. 110
Williams-Sonoma, Inc. 110

Retail - new & used cars
Holiday RV Superstores, Inc. 130
Island Lincoln-Mercury Inc. 130
Morse Operations 131
VT Inc. 167

Retail - regional department stores
Belk Stores Services, Inc. 255
Bon-Ton Stores, Inc. 280

Crowley, Milner and Company 189
The Elder-Beerman Stores Corp. 263
Fred Meyer, Inc. 275
Jacobson Stores Inc. 192
Mercantile Stores Company, Inc. 267
Proffitt's, Inc. 297
ShopKo Stores, Inc. 336
Strawbridge & Clothier 287
Value City Department Stores, Inc. 272
Woodward & Lothrop, Incorporated 126
Younkers, Inc. 165

Retail - restaurants
Apple South, Inc. 136
Applebee's International, Inc. 166
Benihana National Corp. 127
Bertucci's Inc. 179
Bob Evans Farms, Inc. 260
Brinker International, Inc. 300
Buffets, Inc. 198
Bugaboo Creek Steak House, Inc. 290
Chart House Enterprises, Inc. 86
Checkers Drive-In Restaurants, Inc. 128
The Cheesecake Factory Incorporated 86
CKE Restaurants, Inc. 87
Consolidated Products, Inc. 160
Cooker Restaurant Corporation 262
Cracker Barrel Old Country Store, Inc. 294
DAKA International, Inc. 180
Davco Restaurants Inc. 173
Domino's Pizza, Inc. 190
Eateries Inc. 273
El Chico Restaurants, Inc. 304
ELXSI Corporation 117
Family Restaurants Inc. 90
Flagstar Companies, Inc. 291

INDEX OF COMPANIES BY INDUSTRY

Foodmaker, Inc. 91
Fresh Choice, Inc. 92
Frisch's Restaurants, Inc. 264
Ground Round Restaurants, Inc. 182
Hometown Buffet Inc. 94
IHOP Corporation 94
Investor's Management Corporation 257
JB's Restaurants, Inc. 319
The Krystal Company 296
Landry's Seafood Restaurants, Inc. 309
Little Caesar Enterprises, Inc. 193
Lone Star Steakhouse & Saloon, Inc. 166
Long John Silver's Restaurants, Inc. 168
Longhorn Steaks, Inc. 140
LR Holdings, Inc. 96
Luby's Cafeterias, Inc. 310
Main St. & Main, Inc. 77
Max & Erma's Restaurants, Inc. 266
McDonald's Corporation 153
Morrison Restaurants, Inc. 73
Nathan's Famous, Inc. 246
O'Charley's Inc. 296
Outback Steakhouse, Inc. 131
Pancho's Mexican Buffet, Inc. 312
Papa John's International, Inc. 168
Perkins Family Restaurants, L.P. 297
Piccadilly Cafeterias, Inc. 170
Pollo Tropical Inc. 132
Quantum Restaurant Group, Inc. 249
Rally's Hamburgers, Inc. 168
Rock Bottom Restaurants, Inc. 114
Ryan's Family Steak Houses, Inc. 292
Sbarro, Inc. 250
Shoney's, Inc. 298
ShowBiz Pizza Time, Inc. 314

Sizzler International, Inc. 105
Sonic Corp. 274
Starbucks Corporation 329
Tennessee Restaurant Co. 157
TPI Enterprises, Inc. 134
Uno Restaurant Corporation 187
VICORP Restaurants, Inc. 114
Volunteer Capital Corporation 298
Wendy's International, Inc. 272

Retail - supermarkets
ABCO Markets Inc. 76
Albertson's, Inc. 144
American Stores Company 319
Bashas' Inc. 76
Big V Supermarkets Inc. 235
Big Y Foods Inc. 179
Brookshire Brothers Incorporated 300
Brookshire Grocery Company 300
Bruno's, Inc. 72
H. E. Butt Grocery Company 306
Carr-Gottstein Foods Co. 75
Craig Corporation 88
Delchamps, Inc. 73
Demoulas Super Markets Inc./Market Basket Inc. 180
Eagle Food Centers, Inc. 149
Fiesta Mart Inc. 305
Food Lion, Inc. 256
Furr's Supermarkets, Inc. 231
Giant Eagle Inc. 283
Giant Food Inc. 174
The Golub Corporation 241
The Grand Union Holdings Corporation 225
The Great Atlantic & Pacific Tea Company, Inc. 225
Hannaford Bros. Co. Inc. 172

Homeland Holding Corporation 273
Hughes Markets, Inc. 94
Hy-Vee Food Stores, Inc. 164
Ingles Markets, Incorporated 256
Jitney-Jungle Stores of America, Inc. 206
King Kullen Grocery Company Inc. 244
Kohl's Corporation 334
The Kroger Co. 265
K-Va-T Food Stores, Inc. 324
Marsh Supermarkets, Inc. 162
Mayfair Supermarkets Inc. 227
Megafoods Stores, Inc. 77
Meijer, Inc. 193
Minyard Food Stores Inc. 310
Pathmark Stores, Inc. 227
The Penn Traffic Company 248
Publix Super Markets, Inc. 132
Pueblo Xtra International, Inc. 132
Quality Food Centers, Inc. 329
Raley's Inc. 102
Randalls Food Markets 313
Riser Foods, Inc. 269
Roundy's Inc. 336
Ruddick Corporation 258
Safeway Inc. 104
Save Mart Supermarkets 104
Schnuck Markets Inc. 213
Schwegmann Giant Super Markets 171
Seaway Food Town, Inc. 270
Shoppers Food Warehouse Corp. 176
Smart & Final Inc. 105
Smith's Food & Drug Centers, Inc. 320
Stater Bros. Holdings Inc. 106
The Stop & Shop Companies, Inc. 186
Thriftway Food & Drug 271

INDEX OF COMPANIES BY INDUSTRY

The Vons Companies, Inc. 109
Wegmans Food Markets Inc. 253
Weis Markets, Inc. 289
Whole Foods Market, Inc. 318
Winn-Dixie Stores, Inc. 135
Yucaipa Companies 111

Rubber & plastic products
Applied Extrusion Technologies, Inc. 177
Carlisle Companies Inc. 236
Carlisle Plastics, Inc. 76
Foamex International Inc. 282
Gates Corporation 113
O'Sullivan Corporation 325
Rotonics Manufacturing Inc. 103
Rubbermaid Incorporated 270
Spartech Corporation 214
The Standard Products Co. 270
Synetic, Inc. 229

Rubber tires
Cooper Tire & Rubber Company 262
The Goodyear Tire & Rubber Company 264

Schools
Apollo Group, Inc. 76
Children's Discovery Centers of America, Inc. 86
Cornell University 238
Emory University Inc. 138
The George Washington University 125
ITT Educational Services, Inc. 162
The Johns Hopkins University Inc. 174
KinderCare Learning Centers, Inc. 73
Massachusetts Institute of Technology 183
The Ohio State University 268
Princeton University 228
Res-Care, Inc. 168
State University of New York 251

The Texas A&M University System 316
The University of Alabama 74
University of California 108
The University of Chicago 158
University of Florida 134
University of Illinois 158
The University of Iowa 165
The University of Kentucky 169
The University of Maryland System 176
The University of Massachusetts 187
The University of Michigan 196
University of Minnesota 205
The University of Missouri System 214
University of Rochester 253
University of Southern California 108
The University of Tennessee 298
The University of Texas System 318
The University of Wisconsin System 337
Vanderbilt University 298
Yale University 122

Shoes & related apparel
Brown Group, Inc. 208
Deckers Outdoor Corporation 88
The Florsheim Shoe Company 150
Genesco Inc. 295
LaCrosse Footwear, Inc. 334
NIKE, Inc. 275
Nine West Group Inc. 119
Reebok International Ltd. 185
The Stride Rite Corporation 186
Timberland Co. 221
The United States Shoe Corporation 271
Vans, Inc. 109
Wolverine World Wide, Inc. 196

Silver mining & processing
Coeur d'Alene Mines Corporation 144

Soap & cleaning preparations
The Clorox Company 87
Colgate-Palmolive Company 237
First Brands Corporation 118
S.C. Johnson & Son, Inc. 336
NCH Corporation 311
The Procter & Gamble Company 269

Steel - pipes & tubes
Shaw Group Inc. 171

Steel - production
Atchison Casting Corporation 166
Bethlehem Steel Corporation 279
Earle M. Jorgensen Holding Company, Inc. 89
Geneva Steel 319
Inland Steel Industries, Inc. 152
The LTV Corporation 266
National Steel Corporation 162
Northwestern Steel & Wire Company 154
Nucor Corporation 257
Republic Engineered Steels, Inc. 269
Rouge Steel Co. 194
Schnitzer Steel Industries, Inc. 276
Steel of West Virginia, Inc. 331
USX Corporation - U.S. Steel Group 289
Weirton Steel Corporation 331

Steel - specialty alloys
Carpenter Technology Corporation 280
Lukens Inc. 284
Oregon Steel Mills, Inc. 275

Telecommunications equipment
ADC Telecommunications, Inc. 197

386 HOOVER'S MASTERLIST OF AMERICA'S TOP 2,500 EMPLOYERS

INDEX OF COMPANIES BY INDUSTRY

Amtech Corporation 299
Andrew Corporation 146
Aspect Telecommunications Corporation 83
Boston Technology, Inc. 179
C-COR Electronics, Inc. 280
California Microwave, Inc. 85
Cellular Technical Services Company, Inc. 327
Colonial Data Technologies Corporation 116
CommNet Cellular Inc. 112
Communications Systems, Inc. 198
Compression Labs, Incorporated 87
Dialogic Corporation 224
DSC Communications Corporation 304
EIS International, Inc. 117
EXECUTONE Information Systems, Inc. 117
General Instrument Corporation 150
Glenayre Technologies, Inc. 256
Inter-Tel, Inc. 77
InterVoice, Inc. 308
LXE Inc. 140
Norstan, Inc. 203
Octel Communications Corporation 99
Pico Products, Inc. 101
PictureTel Corporation 185
Plantronics, Inc. 101
QUALCOMM Incorporated 102
Scientific-Atlanta, Inc. 141
Sprint Corporation 167
Syntellect Inc. 78
Telebit Corporation 187
Tellabs, Inc. 157

Telecommunications services
A+ Communications, Inc. 294
ACC Corp. 232

Advantis 145
AirTouch Communications 82
Arch Communications Group, Inc. 178
AT&T Corporation 234
CAI Wireless Systems, Inc. 236
COMSAT Corporation 173
Contel Cellular Inc. 137
Electromagnetic Sciences, Inc. 138
General Communication, Inc. 75
LDDS Communications, Inc. 206
MCI Communications Corporation 125
MFS Communications Company, Inc. 217
Nationwide Cellular Service, Inc. 246
Nextel Communications, Inc. 227
Paging Network, Inc. 312
U.S. Long Distance Corporation 317
United States Cellular Corporation 158
United Video Satellite Group Inc. 274
Vanguard Cellular Systems, Inc. 258

Textiles - home furnishings
Conso Products Company 291
Crown Crafts, Inc. 138
Dakotah, Inc. 293
Interface, Inc. 139
Mohawk Industries, Inc. 140
Shaw Industries, Inc. 142
Springs Industries, Inc. 292
WestPoint Stevens, Inc. 142

Textiles - mill products
Avondale Mills, Inc. 136
Burlington Industries, Inc. 255
Cone Mills Corporation 255
Dixie Yarns, Inc. 295
Forstmann & Co., Inc. 240
Galey & Lord, Inc. 256

Greenwood Mills 291
Guilford Mills, Inc. 256
JPS Textile Group Inc. 291
Milliken & Co. 292
Texfi Industries, Inc. 258
Unifi, Inc. 258

Tobacco
Culbro Corporation 238
Philip Morris Companies Inc. 248
RJR Nabisco, Inc. 250
Universal Corporation 326
UST Inc. 122

Tools - hand held
The Black & Decker Corporation 173
Danaher Corporation 125
Snap-on Incorporated 336
The Stanley Works 121
Toro Company 205

Toys - games & hobby products
Hasbro, Inc. 290
Mattel, Inc. 97
Tyco Toys, Inc. 229

Transportation - air freight
Air Express International Corporation 115
Airborne Freight Corporation 327
DHL Worldwide Express 89
Federal Express Corporation 295
Harper Group, Inc. 94

Transportation - airlines
AirTran Corporation 197
Alaska Air Group, Inc. 327
America West Airlines, Inc. 76
AMR Corporation 299
Atlantic Coast Airlines Inc. 322
Comair Holdings, Inc. 262
Continental Airlines Holdings, Inc. 302
Delta Air Lines, Inc. 138
Great Lakes Aviation Ltd. 164
Mesa Air Group 231
Northwest Airlines Corporation 203

INDEX OF COMPANIES BY INDUSTRY

SkyWest Airlines, Inc. 320
Southwest Airlines Co. 314
Trans World Airlines, Inc. 214
UAL Corporation 157
USAir Group, Inc. 326

Transportation - bus
Greyhound Lines, Inc. 306

Transportation - equipment & leasing
ABC Rail Products Corporation 145
GATX Corporation 150
Harmon Industries, Inc. 210
McClain Industries, Inc. 193
XTRA Corporation 188

Transportation - rail
Burlington Northern Inc. 301
Chicago and North Western Transportation Company 148
Conrail, Inc. 281
CSX Corporation 323
Illinois Central Corporation 151
Kansas City Southern Industries, Inc. 211
The Long Island Railroad Co., Inc. 244
National Railroad Passenger Corporation 125
Norfolk Southern Corporation 325
RailTex, Inc. 313
Southern Pacific Rail Corporation 105
Union Pacific Corporation 288
Wisconsin Central Transportation Corporation 159

Transportation - services
The Greenbrier Companies, Inc. 275
Greenwich Air Services Inc. 130
Hudson General Corporation 242
Kitty Hawk, Inc. 309
Mark VII, Inc. 212

United States Postal Service 126

Transportation - shipping
Alexander & Baldwin, Inc. 143
American President Companies, Ltd. 83
Crowley Maritime Corporation 88
Old Dominion Freight Line, Inc. 257

Transportation - truck
American Freightways Corporation 79
Arkansas Best Corporation 79
Arnold Industries Inc. 279
Boyd Bros. Transportation Inc. 72
Builders Transport, Inc. 291
Celadon Group Inc. 236
Consolidated Freightways, Inc. 88
Covenant Transport, Inc. 294
Frozen Food Express Industries, Inc. 305
Heartland Express, Inc. 164
J.B. Hunt Transport Services, Inc. 79
KLLM Transport Services, Inc. 206
Leaseway Transportation Corporation 266
M.S. Carriers, Inc. 296
Marten Transport, Ltd. 335
Mayflower Group, Inc. 162
OTR Express Inc. 166
PAM Transportation Services, Inc. 80
Roadway Services, Inc. 269
Schneider National Inc. 336
Swift Transportation Co., Inc. 219
TNT Freightways Corporation 157
TRISM, Inc. 317
United Parcel Service of America, Inc. 142
USA Truck, Inc. 80
Werner Enterprises, Inc. 217

Yellow Corporation 167

Utility - electric power
Allegheny Power System, Inc. 232
American Electric Power Company, Inc. 259
Baltimore Gas and Electric Company 173
Boston Edison Company 179
Centerior Energy Corporation 260
Central and South West Services Corporation 301
CINergy Corp. 261
CMS Energy Corporation 189
Consolidated Edison Company of New York, Inc. 238
Delmarva Power & Light Company 123
Detroit Edison Company 190
Dominion Resources, Inc. 323
DPL Inc. 263
Duke Power Company 255
Entergy Corporation 170
Florida Progress Corporation 129
FPL Group, Inc. 129
General Public Utilities Corporation 225
Gulf States Utilities Co. 306
Hawaiian Electric Industries, Inc. 143
Houston Industries Incorporated 307
IES Industries Inc. 164
Illinois Power Company 151
Midwest Resources Inc. 165
Montana Power Company 215
New England Electric Co. 184
New York Power Authority 247
New York State Electric & Gas Corporation 247
Niagara Mohawk Power Corporation 247

INDEX OF COMPANIES BY INDUSTRY

NIPSCO Industries, Inc. 163
Northeast Utilities 184
Northern States Power Co. 203
Ohio Edison Co. 268
Pacific Gas and Electric Company 100
PacifiCorp 275
Peco Energy Co. 285
Pennsylvania Power & Light Company 286
Pinnacle West Capital Corporation 78
Portland General Corporation 276
Potomac Electric Power Company 125
Public Service Company of Colorado 113
Public Service Company of New Mexico 231
Public Service Enterprise Group Incorporated 228
Salt River Project Agricultural Improvement & Power District 78
San Diego Gas & Electric Company 104
SCANA Corporation 292
SCEcorp 104
The Southern Company 142
Teco Energy Corporation 134
Tennessee Valley Authority 298
Texas Utilities Company 316
The Unicom Corporation 158
Union Electric Company 214
UtiliCorp United Inc. 214
Wisconsin Energy Corporation 337
WPL Holdings, Inc. 337
WPS Resources Corporation 337

Utility - gas distribution
Atlanta Gas Light Company 136
Brooklyn Union Gas Co. 235
Consolidated Natural Gas Company 281

Energy West, Incorporated 215
MCN Corporation 193
NICOR Inc. 154
NorAm Energy Corp 311
NUI Corporation 227
Pacific Enterprises 100
Peoples Energy Corporation 154
Questar Corporation 320
Southwest Gas Corporation 219
UGI Corporation 288
Washington Gas Light Co. 126
WICOR, Inc. 337

Utility - telephone
ALLTEL Corporation 79
Ameritech Corporation 145
Bell Atlantic Corporation 279
BellSouth Corporation 137
Century Telephone Enterprises, Inc. 170
Cincinnati Bell Inc. 261
GTE Corporation 118
Intelcom Group, Inc. 113
NYNEX Corporation 247
Pacific Telesis Group 100
SBC Communications, Inc. 313
Southern New England Telecommunications 121
Telephone and Data Systems, Inc. 157
U S WEST, Inc. 114

Utility - water supply
American Water Works Company, Inc. 222
IWC Resources Corporation 162
SJW Corporation 105

Veterinary products & services
Moorman Manufacturing Company 153

Video equipment
Proxima Corporation 102
RVSI, Inc. 250
Ultrak, Inc. 317

Vitamins & nutritional products
Nature's Sunshine Products, Inc. 319
Reliv International Inc. 213
Rexall Sundown, Inc. 132

Weapons & weapon systems
Alliant Techsystems Inc. 197
General Dynamics Corporation 323

Wholesale distribution - consumer products
Advanced Marketing Services, Inc. 81
Celebrity, Inc. 301
Central Garden & Pet Co. 86
Tarrant Distributors Inc. 316

Wire & cable products
AFC Cable Systems, Inc. 290
Belden Inc. 208
Cable Design Technologies Corporation 280
Essex Group Inc. 161
Insteel Industries, Inc. 256
Southwire Company, Inc. 142

INDEX OF COMPANIES BY METROPOLITAN AREA

Addison, AL
Cavalier Homes of Alabama, Inc. 72
Southern Energy Homes, Inc. 74

Albany, GA
Flowers Industries, Inc. 138

Albany, NY
Albany International Corporation 232
Besicorp Group Inc. 235
BitWise Designs, Inc. 235
CAI Wireless Systems, Inc. 236
The Golub Corporation 241
MapInfo Corporation 245
State University of New York 251
Trans World Entertainment Corporation 252

Albuquerque, NM
Diagnostek, Inc. 231
Furr's Supermarkets, Inc. 231
Horizon Healthcare Corporation 231
Public Service Company of New Mexico 231
Sun Healthcare Group, Inc. 231

Allentown, PA
Air Products and Chemicals, Inc. 278
Bethlehem Steel Corporation 279
Pennsylvania Power & Light Company 286
Piercing Pagoda, Inc. 286
Union Pacific Corporation 288

Amarillo, TX
Hastings Books, Music & Video, Inc. 306

Anchorage, AK
Carr-Gottstein Foods Co. 75
General Communication, Inc. 75
National Bancorp of Alaska, Inc. 75
Northrim Bank 75

Appleton, WI
ABT Building Products Corporation 332
Banta Corporation 332
J.J. Keller & Associates 333
Menasha Corporation 335
Oshkosh B'Gosh, Inc. 335

Asheville, NC
Ingles Markets, Incorporated 256
Schwitzer, Inc. 258

Athens, GA
Apple South, Inc. 136
Avondale Mills, Inc. 136

Atlanta, GA
Aaron Rents, Inc. 136
AGCO Corporation 136
Allied Holdings Inc. 136
American Business Products, Inc. 136
American Cancer Society 136
Atlanta Gas Light Company 136
Beazer Homes USA, Inc. 136
BellSouth Corporation 137
Brock Control Systems, Inc. 137
Cagle's, Inc. 137
Charter Medical Corporation 137
The Coca-Cola Company 137
Coca-Cola Enterprises Inc. 137
Contel Cellular Inc. 137
CooperSmith Inc. 137
Cox Enterprises, Inc. 137
Crawford & Company Risk Management Services 138
Crown Crafts, Inc. 138
Delta Air Lines, Inc. 138
Dorsey Trailers, Inc. 138
Electromagnetic Sciences, Inc. 138
Emory University Inc. 138
Equifax Inc. 138
First Financial Management Corporation 138
Genuine Parts Co. 138

Georgia-Pacific Corporation 139
Gold Kist Inc. 139
Golden Poultry Co., Inc. 139
GranCare, Inc. 93
HBO & Company 139
The Home Depot, Inc. 139
Interface, Inc. 139
Intermet Corporation 139
IQ Software Corporation 139
Isolyser Company, Inc. 139
John H. Harland Company 140
L A T Sportswear Inc. 140
Longhorn Steaks, Inc. 140
LXE Inc. 140
The Maxim Group, Inc. 140
Medaphis Corporation 140
Mohawk Industries, Inc. 140
Mountasia Entertainment International, Inc. 140
National Service Industries, Inc. 140
National Vision Associates Ltd. 140
Oxford Industries, Inc. 141
Pediatric Services of America, Inc. 141
Post Properties, Inc. 141
The Ritz-Carlton Hotel Company, Inc. 141
Riverwood International Corporation 141
Rock-Tenn Co. 141
Rollins, Inc. 141
RPC Energy Services, Inc. 141
Scientific-Atlanta, Inc. 141
Software Technical Services, Inc. 142
The Southern Company 142
Southwire Company, Inc. 142
SunTrust Banks, Inc. 142
Turner Broadcasting System, Inc. 142

INDEX OF COMPANIES BY METROPOLITAN AREA

United Parcel Service of
America, Inc. 142
Atlantic City, NJ
Collective Bancorp, Inc. 224
Resorts International, Inc. 228
Wheaton Inc. 230
Austin, TX
The Continuum Company, Inc. 303
Dell Computer Corporation 303
EZCORP, Inc. 305
Healthcare America, Inc. 307
SEMATECH, Inc. 313
Sterling Information Group 315
Tracor Inc. 316
The University of Texas System 318
Whole Foods Market, Inc. 318
Baltimore, MD
Baltimore Gas and Electric Company 173
The Black & Decker Corporation 173
Davco Restaurants Inc. 173
F & E Resource Systems Technology, Inc. 174
Integrated Health Services, Inc. 174
The Johns Hopkins University Inc. 174
Legg Mason, Inc. 174
McCormick & Company, Inc. 175
Mercantile Bankshares Corporation 175
Merry-Go-Round Enterprises, Inc. 175
PHH Corporation 175
RWD Technologies, Inc. 175
Ryland Group, Inc. 175
Sunbelt Beverage Corporation 176
T. Rowe Price Associates, Inc. 176
UNC Inc. 176
USF&G Corporation 176

Bangor, ME
Bath Iron Works Corporation 172
Baton Rouge, LA
Albemarle Corporation 170
Piccadilly Cafeterias, Inc. 170
Shaw Group Inc. 171
Turner Industries, Ltd. 171
Beaumont, TX
Gulf States Utilities Co. 306
Biloxi, MS
Casino America, Inc. 206
Casino Magic Corporation 206
Hancock Holding Company 206
Birmingham, AL
AmSouth Bancorporation 72
BE&K Inc. 72
Big B, Inc. 72
Books-A-Million, Inc. 72
Bruno's, Inc. 72
Citation Corporation 72
Compass Bancshares, Inc. 73
First Alabama Bancshares, Inc. 73
HEALTHSOUTH Corporation 73
Precision Standard, Inc. 73
Protective Life Corporation 73
Russell Corporation 74
Rust International Inc. 74
SouthTrust Corporation 74
Torchmark Corporation 74
The University of Alabama 74
Vulcan Materials Company 74
Bloomington, IL
State Farm Mutual Automobile Insurance Company 156
Boise, ID
Albertson's, Inc. 144
BMC West Corporation 144

Boise Cascade Corporation 144
Micron Technology, Inc. 144
Morrison Knudsen Corporation 144
J.R. Simplot Company 144
TJ International, Inc. 144
West One Bancorp 144
Boston, MA
ABIOMED, Inc. 177
AdvantageHEALTH Corporation 177
Aerovox, Inc. 177
American Biltrite Inc. 177
American Medical Response, Inc. 177
Analog Devices, Inc. 177
Applied Extrusion Technologies, Inc. 177
Applied Science & Technology Inc. 178
Arch Communications Group, Inc. 178
Arrow Automotive Industries, Inc. 178
Arthur D. Little Inc. 178
Augat Inc. 178
Avid Technology, Inc. 178
Bachman Information Systems, Inc. 178
Bailey Corporation 220
Bain & Company 178
Bank of Boston Corporation 178
BayBanks, Inc. 178
Berkshire Realty Co. 179
Bertucci's Inc. 179
Bird Corporation 179
Bose Corporation 179
Boston Edison Company 179
Boston Scientific Corporation 179
Boston Technology, Inc. 179
Bradlees, Inc. 179
Cabletron Systems, Inc. 220
Cabot Corporation 179
Chipcom Corporation 180
Clean Harbors, Inc. 180
CML Group, Inc. 180
Connell Limited Partnership 180

HOOVER'S MASTERLIST OF AMERICA'S TOP 2,500 EMPLOYERS 391

INDEX OF COMPANIES BY METROPOLITAN AREA

Continental Cablevision, Inc. 180
Cumberland Farms Inc. 180
DAKA International, Inc. 180
Data General Corporation 180
Dataware Technologies Inc. 180
Demoulas Super Markets Inc./Market Basket Inc. 180
Digital Equipment Corporation 181
DM Management Company 181
Dynatech Corporation 181
Eaton Vance Corporation 181
EG&G, Inc. 181
EMC Corporation 181
Fisher Scientific International, Inc. 220
FMR Corporation 181
FTP Software, Inc. 181
General Chemical Corp. 220
Genetics Institute, Inc. 181
Genome Therapeutics Corporation 182
Genzyme Corporation 182
The Gillette Company 182
Ground Round Restaurants, Inc. 182
Haemonetics Corporation 182
Harcourt General, Inc. 182
Harvard Community Health Plan, Inc. 182
Hills Department Stores, Inc. 182
Hologic, Inc. 182
Howtek, Inc. 220
ImmuLogic Pharmaceutical Corporation 182
International Data Group 183
Ionics, Inc. 183
Ipswich Savings Bank 183
J. Baker, Inc. 183
John Hancock Mutual Life Insurance Company 183

Keane, Inc. 183
Liberty Mutual Insurance Group 183
Lojack Corporation 183
Lotus Development Corporation 183
Massachusetts Institute of Technology 183
MASSBANK Corporation 184
MediSense, Inc. 184
Millipore Corporation 184
Nashua Corporation 220
Neiman Marcus Group, Inc. 184
The New England 184
New England Electric Co. 184
NutraMax Products, Inc. 184
Oak Industries Inc. 184
Parametric Technology Corporation 184
PerSeptive Biosystems, Inc. 185
Phoenix Technologies Ltd. 185
PictureTel Corporation 185
Pioneer Group, Inc. 185
Polaroid Corporation 185
PRI Automation, Inc. 185
Progress Software Corporation 185
Reebok International Ltd. 185
Robertson-Ceco Corporation 186
Softkey International Inc. 186
SpecTran Corporation 186
Standex International Corporation 220
Staples, Inc. 186
State Street Boston Corporation 186
The Stop & Shop Companies, Inc. 186
Stratus Computer, Inc. 186
The Stride Rite Corporation 186
Syratech Corporation 186
System Resources Corporation 186
Talbots Inc. 187

Telebit Corporation 187
Teradyne, Inc. 187
Thermedics Inc. 187
Thermo Electron Corporation 187
Thermo Voltek Corporation 187
Timberland Co. 221
The TJX Companies, Inc. 187
Town & Country Corporation 187
Tyco International Ltd. 221
The University of Massachusetts 187
Uno Restaurant Corporation 187
Vertex Pharmaceuticals, Inc. 188
VMARK Software, Inc. 188
Waban, Inc. 188
Wang Laboratories, Inc. 188
Watts Industries, Inc. 188
XTRA Corporation 188
Xylogics, Inc. 188

Buffalo, NY
Delaware North Companies Inc. 239
First Empire State Corporation 240
Integrated Waste Services, Inc. 242
International Imaging Materials Inc. 242
Mark IV Industries, Inc. 245
Moog Inc. 246
Rich Products Corporation 250
Varity Corporation 253

Butte, MT
Montana Power Company 215

Canton, OH
Belden & Blake Corporation 260
Camelot Music Inc. 260
Diebold, Inc. 263
The J. M. Smucker Company 265
Republic Engineered Steels, Inc. 269
Rubbermaid Incorporated 270

392   HOOVER'S MASTERLIST OF AMERICA'S TOP 2,500 EMPLOYERS

INDEX OF COMPANIES BY METROPOLITAN AREA

The Timken Company 271
Cedar Rapids, IA
IES Industries Inc. 164
Champaign-Urbana, IL
University of Illinois 158
Charleston, SC
The InterTech Group Inc. 291
Charleston, WV
McJunkin Corporation 331
One Valley Bancorp of West Virginia, Inc. 331
Charlotte, NC
American Studios, Inc. 255
Belk Stores Services, Inc. 255
Cato Corporation 255
Coca-Cola Bottling Co. Consolidated 255
Duke Power Company 255
Family Dollar Stores, Inc. 255
First Union Corporation 256
Food Lion, Inc. 256
Glenayre Technologies, Inc. 256
Hendrick Automotive Group 256
Lance, Inc. 257
NationsBank Corporation 257
Nucor Corporation 257
PCA International, Inc. 258
Ruddick Corporation 258
Springs Industries, Inc. 292
United Dominion Industries Inc. 258
Charlottesville, VA
Jefferson Bankshares, Inc. 324
Chattanooga, TN
Astec Industries, Inc. 294
Covenant Transport, Inc. 294
Dixie Yarns, Inc. 295
The Krystal Company 296
Life Care Centers of America 296

McKee Foods Corporation 296
Olan Mills 297
Provident Life and Accident Ins. Co. of America 297
Shaw Industries, Inc. 142
Chicago, IL
Abbott Laboratories 145
ABC Rail Products Corporation 145
Ace Hardware Corporation 145
Acme Metals Incorporated 145
Advance Ross Corporation 145
Advantis 145
Alberto-Culver Company 145
The Allstate Corporation 145
Amerihost Properties, Inc. 145
Ameritech Corporation 145
Amoco Corporation 146
AMSTED Industries Incorporated 146
Andrew Corporation 146
Aon Corporation 146
Arthur Andersen & Co, S.C. 146
Arthur J. Gallagher & Co. 146
AutoFinance Group, Inc. 146
Baker & McKenzie 146
Bally Entertainment Corporation 147
Baxter International Inc. 147
Bell & Howell Co. 147
Blue Cross and Blue Shield Association 147
Borg-Warner Security Corporation 147
Brunswick Corporation 147
Budget Rent a Car Corporation 147
Caremark International, Inc. 147
CBI Industries, Inc. 147
CDW Computer Centers, Inc. 148
Celex Group Inc. 148

The Cherry Corporation 148
Chicago and North Western Transportation Company 148
Circuit Systems, Inc. 148
CNA Financial Corporation 148
Coca-Cola Bottling Co. of Chicago 148
Cotter & Company 148
Dean Foods Company 148
DeSoto, Inc. 149
Discovery Zone, Inc. 149
Duchossois Industries, Inc. 149
Elek-Tek Inc. 149
Encyclopaedia Britannica Inc. 149
Equity Residential Properties Trust 149
Federal Signal Corporation 149
First Chicago Corporation 149
The Florsheim Shoe Company 150
FMC Corporation 150
Follett Corporation 150
Fruit of the Loom, Inc. 150
GATX Corporation 150
Gaylord Container Corporation 150
General Binding Corporation 150
General Instrument Corporation 150
W. W. Grainger, Inc. 150
Great American Management & Investment, Inc. 150
Hartmarx Corporation 151
Helene Curtis Industries, Inc. 151
Henry Crown and Co. 151
Household International, Inc. 151
Hyatt Corporation 151
IDEX Corporation 151
Illinois Central Corporation 151
Illinois Tool Works Inc. 151
IMC Global, Inc. 151
Indiana Federal Corporation 162

HOOVER'S MASTERLIST OF AMERICA'S TOP 2,500 EMPLOYERS

INDEX OF COMPANIES BY METROPOLITAN AREA

Information Resources, Inc. 152
Inland Steel Industries, Inc. 152
Interlake Conveyors Inc. 152
JMB Realty Corporation 152
Johnson Publishing Company, Inc. 152
Juno Lighting, Inc. 152
Jupiter Industries, Inc. 152
Kemper Corporation 152
The Kemper National Insurance Companies 152
Leo Burnett Company, Inc. 152
The Marmon Group, Inc. 153
McDonald's Corporation 153
Medicus Systems Corporation 153
Mercury Finance Co. 153
Molex Inc. 153
Montgomery Ward Holding Corp. 153
Morningstar Inc. 153
Morton International, Inc. 153
Motorola, Inc. 153
Nalco Chemical Company 154
Navistar International Corporation 154
NICOR Inc. 154
NIPSCO Industries, Inc. 163
Northern Trust Corporation 154
Old Republic International Corporation 154
Option Care, Inc. 154
Outboard Marine Corporation 154
Peoples Energy Corporation 154
Pepper Cos. Inc. 155
Pittway Corporation 155
PLATINUM technology, inc. 155
Premark International, Inc. 155
The Quaker Oats Company 155
Quixote Corporation 155

R.R. Donnelley & Sons Company 155
Rotary International 155
Safety-Kleen Corporation 155
Sara Lee Corporation 155
Sears, Roebuck and Co. 156
ServiceMaster L.P. 156
Specialty Foods Corp. 156
Spiegel, Inc. 156
Sportmart Inc. 156
SPS Transaction Services, Inc. 156
Stone Container Corporation 156
Sweetheart Holdings, Inc. 156
System Software Associates, Inc. 156
Telephone and Data Systems, Inc. 157
Tellabs, Inc. 157
Tennessee Restaurant Co. 157
TNT Freightways Corporation 157
Tootsie Roll Industries, Inc. 157
True North Communications Inc. 157
U.S. Robotics, Inc. 157
UAL Corporation 157
The Unicom Corporation 158
United States Cellular Corporation 158
The University of Chicago 158
UOP 158
USG Corporation 158
The Vigoro Corporation 158
Vitalink Pharmacy Services, Inc. 158
Walgreen Co. 158
Wallace Computer Services, Inc. 158
Whitman Corporation 159
Wickes Lumber Company 159
Wisconsin Central Transportation Corporation 159
Wm. Wrigley Jr. Company 159

WMX Technologies, Inc. 159
Woodhead Industries, Inc. 159
Young Men's Christian Association 159
Zebra Technologies Corporation 159
Zenith Electronics Corporation 159

Cincinnati, OH

American Financial Corporation 259
Chemed Corporation 261
Chiquita Brands International, Inc. 261
Cincinnati Bell Inc. 261
Cincinnati Milacron Inc. 261
CINergy Corp. 261
Cintas Corporation 261
Citicasters Inc. 261
Comair Holdings, Inc. 262
Federated Department Stores, Inc. 263
Fifth Third Bancorp 264
Frisch's Restaurants, Inc. 264
Future Healthcare Inc. 264
Gibson Greetings, Inc. 264
Hillenbrand Industries, Inc. 161
Jacor Communications, Inc. 265
The Kroger Co. 265
LSI Industries Inc. 266
Mercantile Stores Company, Inc. 267
Mercy Health System 267
Meridian Diagnostics, Inc. 267
Ohio Casualty Corporation 268
The Procter & Gamble Company 269
Roto-Rooter, Inc. 270
Star Banc Corporation 270
Structural Dynamics Research Corporation 271
Thriftway Food & Drug 271
The United States Shoe Corporation 271

INDEX OF COMPANIES BY METROPOLITAN AREA

Cleveland, OH
ABS Industries, Inc. 259
Acme-Cleveland Corporation 259
Allen Group Inc. 259
American Greetings Corporation 259
Bearings, Inc. 260
The B.F.Goodrich Co. 260
Brenlin Group 260
CasTech Aluminum Group Inc. 260
Centerior Energy Corporation 260
Central Reserve Life Corp. 261
Chempower, Inc. 261
Cleveland-Cliffs Inc. 261
Cole National Corporation 262
Corrpro Cos Inc. 262
D.I.Y. Home Warehouse, Inc. 262
Developers Diversified Realty Corporation 263
Eaton Corporation 263
Fabri-Centers of America, Inc. 263
Ferro Corporation 264
Figgie International Inc. 264
First Merit Corporation 264
GenCorp Inc. 264
The Goodyear Tire & Rubber Company 264
Health-Mor Inc. 265
Invacare Corporation 265
KeyCorp 265
Leaseway Transportation Corporation 266
LESCO, Inc. 266
Lincoln Electric Company 266
The LTV Corporation 266
Lubrizol Corporation 266
McDonald & Company Securities, Inc. 267
Medusa Corporation 267
MTD Products Inc. 267
NACCO Industries, Inc. 267
National City Corporation 267
Nordson Corporation 268
OfficeMax, Inc. 268
Ohio Edison Co. 268

Park-Ohio Industries, Inc. 268
Parker Hannifin Corporation 268
Premier Industrial Corporation 269
Progressive Corporation 269
Revco D.S., Inc. 269
Riser Foods, Inc. 269
Roadway Services, Inc. 269
RPM, Inc. 270
The Sherwin-Williams Company 270
The Standard Products Co. 270
STERIS Corporation 270
Telxon Corporation 271
Tranzonic Companies 271
TRW Inc. 271
Victoria Financial Corporation 272
Waxman Industries, Inc. 272
Westfield Companies 272

Coeur d'Alene, ID
Coeur d'Alene Mines Corporation 144
Hecla Mining Company 144

College Station, TX
The Texas A&M University System 316

Columbia, MO
Datastorm Technologies Inc. 209
The University of Missouri System 214

Columbia, SC
Builders Transport, Inc. 291
Resource Bancshares Mortgage Group Inc. 292
SCANA Corporation 292

Columbus, GA
AFLAC Incorporated 136
Carmike Cinemas, Inc. 137
Synovus Financial Corporation 142
Total System Services, Inc. 142
WestPoint Stevens, Inc. 142

Columbus, IN
Arvin Industries, Inc. 160
Cummins Engine Company, Inc. 161
Irwin Financial Corporation 162

Columbus, OH
American Electric Power Company, Inc. 259
Banc One Corporation 259
Barefoot Inc. 259
Battelle Memorial Institute 259
Bob Evans Farms, Inc. 260
Borden, Inc. 260
Cardinal Health, Inc. 260
Consolidated Stores Corporation 262
Cooker Restaurant Corporation 262
Drug Emporium, Inc. 263
Holophane Corporation 265
Huntington Bancshares Incorporated 265
Insilco Corporation 265
Lancaster Colony Corporation 266
The Limited, Inc. 266
Max & Erma's Restaurants, Inc. 266
Nationwide Insurance Enterprise 267
The Ohio State University 268
Schottenstein Stores Corporation 270
Sun Television & Appliances, Inc. 271
Value City Department Stores, Inc. 272
Wendy's International, Inc. 272
Worthington Industries, Inc. 272

Dallas-Fort Worth, TX
A. H. Belo Corporation 299
Ace Cash Express, Inc. 299
Amber's Stores, Inc. 299
American Medical Electronics, Inc. 299
AMR Corporation 299
AMRE, Inc. 299

INDEX OF COMPANIES BY METROPOLITAN AREA

AMRESCO, Inc. 299
Amtech Corporation 299
Army & Air Force Exchange Service 300
Austin Industries Inc. 300
BancTec, Inc. 300
The Bombay Company, Inc. 300
Brinker International, Inc. 300
Burlington Northern Inc. 301
Business Records Corporation Holding Co. 301
Cash America International, Inc. 301
Cellstar Corporation 301
Centex Corporation 301
Central and South West Services Corporation 301
Chief Auto Parts Incorporated 301
Club Corporation International 302
Commercial Metals Company 302
CompuCom Systems, Inc. 302
CompUSA Inc. 302
County Seat Stores Inc. 303
Cyrix Corporation 303
D. R. Horton, Inc. 303
Dresser Industries, Inc. 303
DSC Communications Corporation 304
E-Systems, Inc. 304
El Chico Restaurants, Inc. 304
Electronic Data Systems Corporation 304
Eljer Industries, Inc. 304
Evergreen Media Corporation 305
Exxon Corporation 305
FINA, Inc. 305
Fossil, Inc. 305
The Freeman Companies 305
Frozen Food Express Industries, Inc. 305
Golf Enterprises, Inc. 305
Greyhound Lines, Inc. 306

Haggar Corporation 306
Halliburton Company 306
The Hallwood Group Incorporated 306
Heritage Media Corporation 307
Hilite Industries Inc. 307
Hogan Systems, Inc. 307
Hollywood Casino Corporation 307
Hunt Consolidated Inc. 307
IMCO Recycling 308
INFOMART 308
InterVoice, Inc. 308
J. C. Penney Company, Inc. 308
Justin Industries, Inc. 308
Kaneb Services, Inc. 308
Kimberly-Clark Corporation 309
Kitty Hawk, Inc. 309
Lennox International Inc. 309
Lincoln Property Company 309
Lomas Financial Corporation 309
Mary Kay Cosmetics Inc. 310
MedicalControl, Inc. 310
Michaels Stores, Inc. 310
Minyard Food Stores Inc. 310
NCH Corporation 311
Old America Stores, Inc. 311
Paging Network, Inc. 312
Pancho's Mexican Buffet, Inc. 312
Physician Reliance Network, Inc. 312
Pier 1 Imports, Inc. 312
Pratt Hotel Corporation 313
Redman Industries Inc. 313
RF Monolithics, Inc. 313
Sammons Enterprises, Inc. 313
ShowBiz Pizza Time, Inc. 314
Software Spectrum, Inc. 314
The Southland Corporation 314

Southwest Airlines Co. 314
Sport Supply Group, Inc. 314
Sterling Software, Inc. 315
Stevens Graphics Corporation 315
Tandy Brands, Inc. 315
Tandy Corporation 315
Tandycrafts, Inc. 315
Temtex Industries, Inc. 316
Texas Industries, Inc. 316
Texas Instruments Incorporated 316
Texas Utilities Company 316
Triangle Pacific Corporation 317
Trinity Industries, Inc. 317
TRISM, Inc. 317
Tuesday Morning Corporation 317
Tyler Corporation 317
Ultrak, Inc. 317
USA Waste Services, Inc. 318
Valhi, Inc. 318
Westcott Communications, Inc. 318
Zale Corporation 318

Davenport, IA
Deere & Company 148
Eagle Food Centers, Inc. 149
HON Industries Inc. 164
Lee Enterprises, Incorporated 164

Dayton, OH
DPL Inc. 263
Duriron Company, Inc. 263
The Elder-Beerman Stores Corp. 263
Huffy Corporation 265
The Mead Corporation 267
Reynolds and Reynolds Co. 269
Robbins & Myers, Inc. 269
Roberd's, Inc. 269
Standard Register Company 270

INDEX OF COMPANIES BY METROPOLITAN AREA

Thor Industries, Inc. 271
Decatur, IL
Archer-Daniels-Midland Company 146
Illinois Power Company 151
Denver, CO
Access Graphics Inc. 112
The Anschutz Corporation 112
Barrett Resources Corporation 112
Bestop, Inc. 112
Black Hawk Gaming and Development Co., Inc. 112
CH2M Hill Cos. 112
CIBER, Inc. 112
CommNet Cellular Inc. 112
Corporate Express, Inc. 112
Cyprus Amax Minerals Company 112
Data Storage Marketing, Inc. 113
Gates Corporation 113
Intelcom Group, Inc. 113
Jones Intercable, Inc. 113
Kentek Information Systems, Inc. 113
M.D.C. Holdings, Inc. 113
Manville Corporation 113
Newmont Gold Company 113
Prima Energy Corporation 113
Public Service Company of Colorado 113
Random Access, Inc. 114
Rock Bottom Restaurants, Inc. 114
Staodyn, Inc. 114
Storage Technology Corporation 114
Tele-Communications, Inc. 114
U S WEST, Inc. 114
Ultimate Electronics, Inc. 114
United Artists Theatre Circuit, Inc. 114
VICORP Restaurants, Inc. 114
Western Gas Resources, Inc. 114

Des Moines, IA
Casey's General Stores, Inc. 164
EMC Insurance Group Inc. 164
Hy-Vee Food Stores, Inc. 164
Maytag Corporation 164
Midwest Resources Inc. 165
Pioneer Hi-Bred International, Inc. 165
Principal Financial Group 165
Younkers, Inc. 165
Detroit, MI
Arbor Drugs, Inc. 189
Champion Enterprises, Inc. 189
Chrysler Corporation 189
CMS Energy Corporation 189
Comerica Inc. 189
Compuware Corporation 189
Crowley, Milner and Company 189
Detroit Diesel Corporation 190
Detroit Edison Company 190
The Detroit Medical Center 190
Domino's Pizza, Inc. 190
Douglas & Lomason Company 190
Durakon Industries, Inc. 190
F & M Distributors, Inc. 190
Federal-Mogul Corporation 191
Flint Ink Corporation 191
Ford Motor Company 191
Fretter, Inc. 191
General Motors Corporation 191
Guardian Industries Corp. 191
Hayes Wheels International, Inc. 191
Howell Industries, Inc. 192
Kmart Corporation 192
La-Z-Boy Chair Company 192
Lear Seating Corporation 192

Little Caesar Enterprises, Inc. 193
Masco Corporation 193
Mascotech, Inc. 193
McClain Industries, Inc. 193
MCN Corporation 193
Mercy Health Services 193
National TechTeam, Inc. 193
NBD Bancorp, Inc. 194
Newcor, Inc. 194
Penske Corporation 194
Pulte Corporation 194
R.P. Scherer Corporation 194
RGIS Inventory Specialists 194
Rouge Steel Co. 194
Saga Communications Inc. 194
Simpson Industries, Inc. 195
Thorn Apple Valley, Inc. 195
TriMas Corporation 195
United American Healthcare Corporation 195
The University of Michigan 196
Valassis Communications, Inc. 196
Dubuque, IA
Flexsteel Industries, Inc. 164
Eau Claire, WI
Marten Transport, Ltd. 335
Menard, Inc. 335
El Paso, TX
Farah Inc. 305
TSX Corporation 317
Elmira, NY
Artistic Greetings, Inc. 233
Cornell University 238
Corning Incorporated 238
Dresser-Rand Company 239
New York State Electric & Gas Corporation 247
Erie, PA
Spectrum Control, Inc. 287

HOOVER'S MASTERLIST OF AMERICA'S TOP 2,500 EMPLOYERS

INDEX OF COMPANIES BY METROPOLITAN AREA

Eugene, OR
Roseburg Forest Products Co. 276

Evansville, IN
Shoe Carnival, Inc. 163

Fayetteville, AR
Hudson Foods, Inc. 79
J.B. Hunt Transport Services, Inc. 79
National Home Centers, Inc. 79
PAM Transportation Services, Inc. 80
Tyson Foods, Inc. 80
Wal-Mart Stores, Inc. 80

Florence, SC
Oneita Industries, Inc. 292
Sonoco Products Company 292

Fort Myers, FL
Chico's FAS, Inc. 128
Health Management Associates, Inc. 130
ViroGroup, Inc. 134

Fort Smith, AR
Arkansas Best Corporation 79
Baldor Electric Co. 79
Beverly Enterprises, Inc. 79
USA Truck, Inc. 80

Fort Wayne, IN
Essex Group Inc. 161
Lincoln National Corporation 162

Fresno, CA
Gottschalks Inc. 93

Gainesville, FL
University of Florida 134

Grand Rapids, MI
Ameriwood Industries International Corporation 189
Amway Corporation 189
Donnelly Corporation 190
Gentex Corporation 191
Haworth, Inc. 191
Herman Miller, Inc. 192
Knape & Vogt Manufacturing Company 192
Meijer, Inc. 193
Old Kent Financial Corporation 194

SPX Corporation 195
Steelcase Inc. 195
Universal Forest Products Inc. 195
Wolverine World Wide, Inc. 196
X-Rite, Inc. 196

Great Falls, MT
Buttrey Food and Drug Stores Company 215
Energy West, Incorporated 215

Green Bay, WI
Associated Banc-Corp 332
Fort Howard Corporation 333
Manitowoc Company, Inc. 334
Schneider National Inc. 336
ShopKo Stores, Inc. 336
WPS Resources Corporation 337

Greensboro, NC
Burlington Industries, Inc. 255
Cone Mills Corporation 255
Galey & Lord, Inc. 256
Guilford Mills, Inc. 256
Insteel Industries, Inc. 256
Integon Corporation 257
Jefferson-Pilot Corporation 257
Ladd Furniture, Inc. 257
Oakwood Homes Corporation 257
Old Dominion Freight Line, Inc. 257
Southern National Corporation 258
Unifi, Inc. 258
Vanguard Cellular Systems, Inc. 258
Wachovia Corporation 258

Greenville, SC
Conso Products Company 291
Delta Woodside Industries, Inc. 291
Flagstar Companies, Inc. 291
Greenwood Mills 291
Insignia Financial Group Inc. 291

JPS Textile Group Inc. 291
KEMET Corporation 291
Liberty Corporation 291
Milliken & Co. 292
Multimedia, Inc. 292
One Price Clothing Stores, Inc. 292
Piemonte Foods Inc. 292
Ryan's Family Steak Houses, Inc. 292

Harrisburg, PA
AMP Incorporated 279
Arnold Industries Inc. 279
Continental Medical Systems, Inc. 281
Harsco Corporation 283
Hershey Foods Corporation 283
Keystone Financial, Inc. 284
Masland Corporation 285
Rite Aid Corporation 287

Hartford, CT
ADVO, Inc. 115
Aetna Life and Casualty Company 115
American White Cross, Inc. 115
Ames Department Stores, Inc. 115
Connecticut Mutual Life Insurance Company 116
Dairy Mart Convenience Stores, Inc. 116
Eagle Financial Corp. 117
Hartford Steam Boiler Inspection and Ins. Co. 118
Kaman Corporation 119
Loctite Corporation 119
The Stanley Works 121
TRC Companies, Inc. 121
United Technologies Corporation 122
Value Health, Inc. 122

Hickory, NC
Lowe's Companies, Inc. 257

Honolulu, HI
Alexander & Baldwin, Inc. 143
Bancorp Hawaii, Inc. 143
First Hawaiian, Inc. 143
Hawaiian Electric Industries, Inc. 143

INDEX OF COMPANIES BY METROPOLITAN AREA

Houston, TX
Allwaste, Inc. 299
BJ Services Company 300
Browning-Ferris Industries, Inc. 300
Camco International Inc. 301
Cliffs Drilling Company 302
The Coastal Corporation 302
Community Health Systems, Inc. 302
Compaq Computer Corporation 302
Continental Airlines Holdings, Inc. 302
Cooper Industries, Inc. 303
Cyberonics, Inc. 303
Destec Energy, Inc. 303
E-Z Serve Corporation 304
Energy Ventures, Inc. 304
Enron Corporation 304
ERC Industries, Inc. 304
Fiesta Mart Inc. 305
Grant Geophysical, Inc. 306
GulfMark International, Inc. 306
Hi-Lo Automotive, Inc. 307
Hornbeck Offshore Services, Inc. 307
Houston Industries Incorporated 307
ICO, Inc. 307
Input/Output, Inc. 308
Kaiser Aluminum Corporation 308
Kent Electronics Corporation 308
Keystone International, Inc. 308
Kirby Corporation 309
Landmark Graphics Corporation 309
Landry's Seafood Restaurants, Inc. 309
Living Centers of America, Inc. 309
Marine Drilling Companies, Inc. 310
MAXXAM Inc. 310
MAXXIM Medical, Inc. 310

MediaNews Group Inc. 310
The Men's Wearhouse, Inc. 310
Mitchell Energy & Development Corp. 311
Nabors Industries, Inc. 311
National Convenience Stores Incorporated 311
NCI Building Systems, Inc. 311
NorAm Energy Corp 311
Nuevo Energy Company 311
Oceaneering International, Inc. 311
Panhandle Eastern Corporation 312
Pennzoil Company 312
Plains Resources Inc. 312
Pool Energy Services Co. 312
Powell Industries, Inc. 312
Randalls Food Markets 313
Riviana Foods Inc. 313
Sanifill, Inc. 313
Serv-Tech, Inc. 314
Service Corporation International 314
Shell Oil Company 314
Southdown, Inc. 314
Specialty Retailers Inc. 314
Star Enterprise 315
Stewart & Stevenson Services, Inc. 315
Synercom Technology, Inc. 315
SYSCO Corporation 315
Tarrant Distributors Inc. 316
Tejas Power Corporation 316
Tenneco Inc. 316
United Meridian Corporation 317
Weatherford International Incorporated 318
Zapata Corporation 318

Huntington, WV
Ashland, Inc. 168
Steel of West Virginia, Inc. 331

Huntsville, AL
Intergraph Corporation 73
Nichols Research Corporation 73
SCI Systems, Inc. 74

Indianapolis, IN
Adesa Corporation 160
Anacomp, Inc. 160
Central Newspapers, Inc. 160
Conseco, Inc. 160
Consolidated Products, Inc. 160
Eli Lilly and Company 161
Finish Line, Inc. 161
Forum Group, Inc. 161
Guidant Corporation 161
ITT Educational Services, Inc. 162
IWC Resources Corporation 162
Marsh Supermarkets, Inc. 162
Mayflower Group, Inc. 162
Paul Harris Stores, Inc. 163

Iowa City, IA
Heartland Express, Inc. 164
The University of Iowa 165

Jackson, MI
Jacobson Stores Inc. 192
Tecumseh Products Company 195

Jackson, MS
Deposit Guaranty Corporation 206
First Mississippi Corporation 206
Jitney-Jungle Stores of America, Inc. 206
KLLM Transport Services, Inc. 206
LDDS Communications, Inc. 206
Mississippi Chemical Corporation 207
Trustmark Corporation 207

Jacksonville, FL
Barnett Banks, Inc. 127

INDEX OF COMPANIES BY METROPOLITAN AREA

St. Joe Paper Company 133
Stein Mart, Inc. 133
Winn-Dixie Stores, Inc. 135

Jamestown, NY
Bush Industries, Inc. 235

Johnson City, TN
Eastman Chemical Company 295

Johnstown, PA
Crown Holding Company 282
First Commonwealth Financial Corporation 282

Joplin, MO
Leggett & Platt, Inc. 211

Kalamazoo, MI
First of America Bank Corporation 191
International Controls Corp. 192
Kellogg Company 192
Manatron, Inc. 193
Perrigo Company 194
Stryker Corporation 195
The Upjohn Company 196
Whirlpool Corporation 196

Kansas City, MO-Kansas City, KS
Advanced Financial, Inc. 166
AMC Entertainment Inc. 208
Applebee's International, Inc. 166
Atchison Casting Corporation 166
BHA Group, Inc. 208
Black and Veatch 208
Butler Manufacturing Co. 208
Cerner Corporation 209
Commerce Bancshares, Inc. 209
Farmland Industries, Inc. 210
H&R Block, Inc. 210
Hallmark Cards, Inc. 210
Harmon Industries, Inc. 210
Interstate Bakeries Corporation 211

Kansas City Southern Industries, Inc. 211
LabOne, Inc. 166
Marion Merrell Dow Inc. 211
Mark VII, Inc. 212
OTR Express Inc. 166
Payless Cashways Inc. 213
Puritan-Bennett Corporation 166
Rival Co. 213
Seaboard Corporation 167
Sprint Corporation 167
United Missouri Bancshares, Inc. 214
Unitog Company 214
UtiliCorp United Inc. 214
VT Inc. 167
Yellow Corporation 167

Knoxville, TN
Clayton Homes, Inc. 294
Goody's Family Clothing, Inc. 295
North American Advanced Materials Corporation 296
Proffitt's, Inc. 297
Tennessee Valley Authority 298
The University of Tennessee 298

La Crosse, WI
LaCrosse Footwear, Inc. 334

Lafayette, IN
Great Lakes Chemical Corporation 161
Wabash National Corporation 163

Lake Charles, LA
Players International Inc. 170

Lakeland, FL
Breed Technologies, Inc. 128
Discount Auto Parts, Inc. 129
Publix Super Markets, Inc. 132

Lancaster, PA
Armstrong World Industries, Inc. 279
Herley Industries, Inc. 283

Lansing, MI
Maxco, Inc. 193
Spartan Motors, Inc. 195

Las Vegas, NV
Anchor Gaming 218
Boyd Gaming Corporation 218
Circus Circus Enterprises, Inc. 218
Lady Luck Gaming Corporation 218
Mirage Resorts, Incorporated 219
Oasis Residential, Inc. 219
Rio Hotel and Casino, Inc. 219
Showboat, Inc. 219
Southwest Gas Corporation 219

Lexington, KY
Long John Silver's Restaurants, Inc. 168
The University of Kentucky 169

Lima, OH
Arbor Health Care Company 259
Cooper Tire & Rubber Company 262

Little Rock, AR
Acxiom Corporation 79
ALLTEL Corporation 79
Dillard Department Stores, Inc. 79

Longview, TX
Caltex Petroleum Corporation 301
Pilgrim's Pride Corporation 312

Los Angeles, CA
3D Systems Corporation 81
Aames Financial Corporation 81
Allergan, Inc. 82
A-Mark Financial Corporation 83
American United Global, Inc. 83
American Vanguard Corporation 83
Amgen Inc. 83
Anthony Industries, Inc. 83
AST Research, Inc. 84

INDEX OF COMPANIES BY METROPOLITAN AREA

Atlantic Richfield Company 84
Authentic Fitness Corporation 84
Avery Dennison Corporation 84
Beckman Instruments, Inc. 84
Bell Industries, Inc. 85
Bergen Brunswig Corporation 85
Broadway Stores Inc. 85
Bugle Boy Industries 85
Cerplex Group, Inc. 86
Certified Grocers of California, Ltd 86
The Cheesecake Factory Incorporated 86
Cinema Ride, Inc. 87
CKE Restaurants, Inc. 87
The Clothestime, Inc. 87
Computer Sciences Corporation 87
Countrywide Credit Industries, Inc. 88
Craig Corporation 88
Dames & Moore, Inc. 88
Davidson & Associates, Inc. 88
Day Runner, Inc. 88
Deckers Outdoor Corporation 88
Dole Food Company, Inc. 89
Earle M. Jorgensen Holding Company, Inc. 89
Environmental Systems Research Institute Inc. 90
Family Restaurants Inc. 90
FHP International Corporation 90
Fidelity National Financial, Inc. 90
First American Financial Corporation 91
First Interstate Bancorp 91
First Mortgage Corporation 91
Fleetwood Enterprises, Inc. 91
Fluor Corporation 91
Freedom Newspapers Inc. 91
GM Hughes Electronics Corporation 92
Great Western Financial Corporation 93
H. F. Ahmanson & Company 93
Herbalife International, Inc. 94
Hilton Hotels Corporation 94
Home Theater Products International 94
Hughes Markets, Inc. 94
IHOP Corporation 94
Imperial Credit Industries, Inc. 94
International Rectifier Corporation 95
International Technology Corporation 95
Interplay Productions Inc. 95
Iwerks Entertainment Inc. 95
Jacobs Engineering Group Inc. 95
Kaufman and Broad Home Corporation 95
Kingston Technology Corporation 96
Litton Industries, Inc. 96
Mac Frugal's Bargains - Close-outs, Inc. 96
Mattel, Inc. 97
Mercury General Corporation 97
Merisel, Inc. 98
Microsemi Corporation 98
MMI Medical, Inc. 98
National Medical Enterprises, Inc. 98
National RV Holdings Inc. 98
New Image Industries Inc. 99
Northrop Grumman Corporation 99
Occidental Petroleum Corporation 99
Pacific Enterprises 100
Pacific Holding Co. 100
Pacific Scientific Co. 100
Pacific Sunwear of California, Inc. 100
PacifiCare Health Systems, Inc. 100
Pico Products, Inc. 101
Pinkerton's Security & Investigation Services 101
Platinum Software Corporation 101
Plaza Home Mortgage Corporation 101
PMC Inc. 101
Quantum Health Resources, Inc. 102
Regency Health Services, Inc. 103
Rockwell International Corporation 103
Roll International 103
Ropak Corporation 103
Rotonics Manufacturing Inc. 103
Rykoff-Sexton, Inc. 103
Safety Components International, Inc. 104
St. Ives Laboratories, Inc. 104
Salick Health Care, Inc. 104
SCEcorp 104
Sizzler International, Inc. 105
Smart & Final Inc. 105
Special Devices, Inc. 105
Spelling Entertainment Group, Inc. 106
The Sports Club Company, Inc. 106
Stater Bros. Holdings Inc. 106
Summit Care Corporation 106
Sunrise Medical Inc. 106
Superior Industries International, Inc. 107
TELACU Industries 107
Teledyne, Inc. 107
Tetra Tech, Inc. 107
Thrifty Oil Co. 108
The Times Mirror Company 108
Trimark Holdings, Inc. 108
UniHealth America 108
United States Filter Corporation 108
University of Southern California 108
Unocal Corporation 108

INDEX OF COMPANIES BY METROPOLITAN AREA

Vans, Inc. 109
Viking Office Products, Inc. 109
The Vons Companies, Inc. 109
The Walt Disney Company 109
Watson Pharmaceuticals Inc. 110
WellPoint Health Networks Inc. 110
Western Atlas, Inc. 110
Western Digital Corporation 110
Xircom, Inc. 110
Young's Market Co. 111
Yucaipa Companies 111

Louisville, KY
Brown-Forman Corporation 168
Columbia/HCA Healthcare Corporation 168
Humana Inc. 168
Papa John's International, Inc. 168
Providian Corporation 168
Rally's Hamburgers, Inc. 168
Res-Care, Inc. 168
Robinson Nugent, Inc. 163
Steel Technologies Inc. 169
Vencor, Inc. 169

Madison, WI
American Family Mutual Insurance Company 332
Lands' End, Inc. 334
Lunar Corporation 334
Regal-Beloit Corporation 335
The University of Wisconsin System 337
WPL Holdings, Inc. 337

Manchester, NH
Healthsource, Inc. 220

Melbourne, FL
Harris Corporation 130
Island Lincoln-Mercury Inc. 130

Memphis, TN
Arcadian Partners, L.P. 294

AutoZone, Inc. 294
Catherines Stores Corporation 294
Dyersburg Fabrics Inc. 295
Federal Express Corporation 295
First Tennessee National Corporation 295
Fred's, Inc. 295
M.S. Carriers, Inc. 296
Morgan Keegan, Inc. 296
Perkins Family Restaurants, L.P. 297
The Promus Companies Incorporated 297
Sofamor Danek Group, Inc. 298
Thomas & Betts Corporation 298
Union Planters Corporation 298

Miami, FL
Alamo Rent A Car, Inc. 127
American Bankers Insurance Group, Inc. 127
Atlantis Group, Inc. 127
Avatar Holdings, Inc. 127
Benihana National Corp. 127
Capital Bancorp 128
Carnival Corporation 128
Carnival Hotels and Casinos 128
Catalina Lighting, Inc. 128
Claire's Stores, Inc. 129
Cordis Corporation 129
Coulter Corporation 129
Digital Communications Technology Corporation 129
Greenwich Air Services Inc. 130
Inphynet Medical Management Inc. 130
IVAX Corporation 130
Jan Bell Marketing, Inc. 130
Knight-Ridder, Inc. 131
Lennar Corporation 131
Morse Operations 131
Physician Corporation of America 132
Pollo Tropical Inc. 132

Pueblo Xtra International, Inc. 132
Ryder System, Inc. 133
Sound Advice, Inc. 133
The Sports Authority, Inc. 133
Sunbeam-Oster Company, Inc. 133
Sunglass Hut International, Inc. 134
Wackenhut Corporation 134
Wackenhut Corrections Corporation 134
Watsco, Inc. 135
Willcox & Gibbs, Inc. 135
Windmere Corporation 135

Milwaukee, WI
A. O. Smith Corporation 332
Applied Power Inc. 332
Briggs & Stratton Corporation 332
Carson Pirie Scott & Co. 332
Case Corporation 332
Firstar Corporation 333
FIserv, Inc. 333
Gander Mountain, Inc. 333
Harley-Davidson, Inc. 333
Harnischfeger Industries Incorporated 333
Hein-Werner Corporation 333
Jason Incorporated 333
Johnson Controls, Inc. 333
Journal Communications 334
Kohl's Corporation 334
Kohler Co. 334
Marcus Corporation 334
Marquette Electronics, Inc. 334
Marshall & Ilsley Corporation 334
Modine Manufacturing Company 335
Northwestern Mutual Life Insurance Company 335
Payco American Corporation 335
Quad/Graphics, Inc. 335
Roundy's Inc. 336

INDEX OF COMPANIES BY METROPOLITAN AREA

S.C. Johnson & Son, Inc. 336
Snap-on Incorporated 336
Sullivan Dental Products, Inc. 336
Sybron International Corporation 336
United Wisconsin Services, Inc. 336
Universal Foods Corporation 336
W. H. Brady Co. 337
WICOR, Inc. 337
Wisconsin Energy Corporation 337

Minneapolis-St. Paul, MN
ADC Telecommunications, Inc. 197
Advance Circuits, Inc. 197
AirTran Corporation 197
Alliant Techsystems Inc. 197
Allina Health System 197
Andersen Corp. 197
Apogee Enterprises, Inc. 197
Automotive Industries Holding, Inc. 197
Bemis Co., Inc. 197
Best Buy Co., Inc. 198
Braun's Fashions Corporation 198
Buffets, Inc. 198
Cargill, Incorporated 198
Carlson Companies, Inc. 198
Ceridian Corporation 198
Chronimed, Inc. 198
Communications Systems, Inc. 198
Computer Network Technology Corporation 198
Control Data Systems, Inc. 198
Cray Research, Inc. 199
Daig Corporation 199
Damark International, Inc. 199
Dayton Hudson Corporation 199
Deluxe Corporation 199
Digi International Inc. 199
Digital Biometrics, Inc. 199

Donaldson Company, Inc. 199
Ecolab Inc. 199
Empi, Inc. 199
Fingerhut Companies, Inc. 200
First Bank System, Inc. 200
Fourth Shift Corporation 200
FSI International, Inc. 200
Funco Inc. 200
G&K Services, Inc. 200
General Mills, Inc. 200
GFI America, Inc. 200
Grand Casinos, Inc. 200
Green Tree Financial Corporation 201
Grow Biz International, Inc. 201
H. B. Fuller Co. 201
HEI, Inc. 201
Holiday Cos. 201
Honeywell Inc. 201
Hutchinson Technology Inc. 201
In Home Health, Inc. 201
Inter-Regional Financial Group, Inc. 201
International Multifoods Corporation 202
Land O' Lakes, Inc. 202
LaserMaster Technologies, Inc. 202
Lawson Associates, Inc. 202
LecTec Corporation 202
Life USA Holding, Inc. 202
LifeCore Biomedical, Inc. 202
Medtronic, Inc. 202
Merrill Corporation 203
Miles Homes, Inc. 203
Minnesota Mining and Manufacturing Company 203
MTS Systems Corporation 203
Musicland Group Inc. 203
Nash-Finch Company 203
Norstan, Inc. 203
Northern States Power Co. 203
Northwest Airlines Corporation 203

Norwest Corporation 203
Olympic Financial Ltd. 204
Patterson Dental Company 204
Pentair, Inc. 204
Pet Food Warehouse, Inc. 204
Piper Jaffray Companies Inc. 204
Regis Corporation 204
ReliaStar Financial Corporation 204
Rimage Corporation 204
SCIMED Life Systems, Inc. 204
St. Paul Companies, Inc. 205
SUPERVALU Inc. 205
TCF Financial Corporation 205
Toro Company 205
United HealthCare Corporation 205
University of Minnesota 205
Venturian Corporation 205
West Publishing Co. 205
Zytec Corporation 205

Missoula, MT
RIBI ImmunoChem Research, Inc. 215
Washington Corporations 215

Mobile, AL
Delchamps, Inc. 73
Morrison Restaurants, Inc. 73

Modesto, CA
E. & J. Gallo Winery 89
Foster Poultry Farms Inc. 91
Save Mart Supermarkets 104

Monroe, LA
Century Telephone Enterprises, Inc. 170

Montgomery, AL
American Buildings Company 72
Blount, Inc. 72
Boyd Bros. Transportation Inc. 72
KinderCare Learning Centers, Inc. 73

INDEX OF COMPANIES BY METROPOLITAN AREA

Muncie, IN
Ball Corporation 160
Stant Corporation 163

Nashville, TN
A+ Communications, Inc. 294
Advocat, Inc. 294
Corrections Corporation of America 294
Cracker Barrel Old Country Store, Inc. 294
First American Corporation 295
Gaylord Entertainment Co. 295
Genesco Inc. 295
HealthTrust, Inc., The Hospital Company 296
Healthwise of America, Inc. 296
Ingram Industries Inc. 296
O'Charley's Inc. 296
OrNda HealthCorp 297
Performance Food Group Company 297
PhyCor, Inc. 297
Quorum Health Group, Inc. 297
Rehabilitation Corporation 297
REN Corporation - USA 298
Service Merchandise Company, Inc. 298
Shoney's, Inc. 298
Vanderbilt University 298
Volunteer Capital Corporation 298

New Haven, CT
AMDURA Corporation 115
Amphenol Corporation 115
DS Bancor, Inc. 117
Echlin Inc. 117
Esstar Inc. 117
EXECUTONE Information Systems, Inc. 117
Forschner Group, Inc. 118
General Electric Company 118
Hubbell Inc. 118
People's Choice TV Corporation 120
Raytech Corporation 120

Southern New England Telecommunications 121
Sturm, Ruger & Company, Inc. 121
Yale University 122

New London, CT
Mariner Health Group, Inc. 119
Mashantucket Pequot Gaming Enterprise Inc. 119

New Orleans, LA
Campo Electronics, Appliances & Computers, Inc. 170
Entergy Corporation 170
Freeport-McMoRan Inc. 170
K&B 170
Louisiana Land and Exploration Company 170
McDermott International, Inc. 170
Ramsay Health Care, Inc. 171
Stewart Enterprises, Inc. 171
Tidewater Inc. 171

New York, NY
"21" International Holdings, Inc. 232
A. L. Pharma Inc. 222
Acclaim Entertainment, Inc. 232
Advance Publications, Inc. 232
Air Express International Corporation 115
Alexander & Alexander Services Inc. 232
Alleghany Corporation 232
Allegheny Power System, Inc. 232
AlliedSignal Inc. 222
Allou Health & Beauty Care, Inc. 232
Alpine Group, Inc. 232
AMBAC Inc. 233
Amerada Hess Corporation 233
American Brands, Inc. 115
American Express Company 233

American Home Products Corporation 222
American International Group, Inc. 233
American Retail Group, Inc. 233
American Standard Companies, Inc. 222
AMREP Corporation 233
AnnTaylor Stores Corporation 233
Arrow Electronics, Inc. 233
ASARCO Incorporated 234
Astrum International Corp. 234
AT&T Corporation 234
AutoInfo, Inc. 222
Automatic Data Processing, Inc. 222
Avis, Inc. 234
Avnet, Inc. 234
Avon Products, Inc. 234
The Bank of New York Company, Inc. 234
Bankers Trust New York Corporation 234
Barnes & Noble, Inc. 234
Barr Laboratories, Inc. 234
The Bear Stearns Companies Inc. 235
Becton, Dickinson and Company 222
Bed Bath & Beyond, Inc. 222
Bell Communications Research Inc. 222
BHC Communications, Inc. 235
Big V Supermarkets Inc. 235
The BISYS Group, Inc. 223
Block Drug Co., Inc. 223
Blyth Industries, Inc. 115
Booz, Allen & Hamilton Inc. 235
Brandon Systems Corporation 223
Bristol-Myers Squibb Company 235
Brooklyn Union Gas Co. 235
C. R. Bard, Inc. 223
Cablevision Systems Corporation 236

404   HOOVER'S MASTERLIST OF AMERICA'S TOP 2,500 EMPLOYERS

INDEX OF COMPANIES BY METROPOLITAN AREA

Cache, Inc. 236
Caldor Corporation 115
Cambrex Corporation 223
Capital Cities/ABC, Inc. 236
Carter-Wallace, Inc. 236
CBS Inc. 236
CDP Technologies, Inc. 236
Celadon Group Inc. 236
Celgene Corporation 223
Century Communications Corporation 116
Champion International Corporation 116
The Chase Manhattan Corporation 237
Chemical Banking Corporation 237
Cheyenne Software, Inc. 237
The Chubb Corporation 223
Citicorp 237
Club Med, Inc. 237
Colgate-Palmolive Company 237
Coltec Industries Inc. 237
Computer Associates International, Inc. 237
Comverse Technology Inc. 237
Consolidated Edison Company of New York, Inc. 238
Continental Can Co. 238
Continental Corporation 238
Continental Grain Company 238
Coopers & Lybrand L.L.P. 238
CPC International Inc. 224
Crane Co. 116
Crompton & Knowles Corporation 116
CUC International Inc. 116
Culbro Corporation 238
Curative Technologies, Inc. 238
Cygne Designs Inc. 238
Cytec Industries Inc. 224
D'Arcy Masius Benton & Bowles, Inc. 239
Data Broadcasting Corporation 239

Dean Witter, Discover & Co. 239
Deloitte & Touche 116
Devon Group, Inc. 116
Dial-A-Mattress Franchise Corporation 239
Dialogic Corporation 224
Dover Corporation 239
Dow Jones & Company, Inc. 239
Dress Barn, Inc. 117
Drew Industries Incorporated 239
The Dun & Bradstreet Corporation 117
Duracell International, Inc. 117
ECCS Inc. 224
EIS International, Inc. 117
ELXSI Corporation 117
Engelhard Corporation 224
Enzon, Inc. 224
The Equitable Companies, Incorporated 240
Ernst & Young LLP 240
Family Golf Centers, Inc. 240
Federal Paper Board Company, Inc. 224
Finlay Enterprises 240
First Brands Corporation 118
First Central Financial Corporation 240
First Fidelity Bancorporation 224
Forstmann & Co., Inc. 240
Foster Wheeler Corporation 225
GAF Corp 225
Gartner Group Inc. 118
General Host Corporation 118
General Public Utilities Corporation 225
General Signal Corporation 118
Genlyte Group Inc. 225
Genovese Drug Stores, Inc. 240
The Goldman Sachs Group, LP 241
Graff Pay-Per-View Inc. 241

Graham-Field Health Products, Inc. 241
The Grand Union Holdings Corporation 225
The Great Atlantic & Pacific Tea Company, Inc. 225
Grow Group, Inc. 241
GTE Corporation 118
The Guardian Life Insurance Company of America 241
Handex Environmental Recovery, Inc. 225
Handy & Harman 241
Harvard Industries, Inc. 225
The Hearst Corporation 241
Helmsley Enterprises, Inc. 241
Home Holdings Inc. 242
Home State Holdings Inc. 225
Homecare Management, Inc. 242
Hooper Holmes, Inc. 226
Hovnanian K Enterprises, Inc. 226
HUBCO, Inc. 226
Hudson General Corporation 242
Hyperion Software Corporation 118
Information Builders, Inc. 242
Ingersoll-Rand Company 226
Innodata Corporation 242
Instrument Systems Corporation 242
Interlaken Capital Inc. 119
International Business Machines Corporation 242
International Flavors & Fragrances Inc. 242
International Paper Company 243
Interpublic Group of Companies, Inc. 243
Investment Technology Group, Inc. 243
ITT Corporation 243
J. Crew Group Inc. 243

INDEX OF COMPANIES BY METROPOLITAN AREA

J. M. Huber Corporation 226
J.P. Morgan & Co. Incorporated 243
Jean Philippe Fragrances, Inc. 243
Johnson & Higgins 243
Johnson & Johnson 226
K-III Communications Corporation 243
Kimco Development Corporation 243
King Kullen Grocery Company Inc. 244
KPMG Peat Marwick L.L.P. 244
Lechters, Inc. 226
Lefrak Organization Inc. 244
Lehman Brothers Holdings Inc. 244
Lexmark International Inc. 119
Liuski International, Inc. 244
Liz Claiborne, Inc. 244
Loews Corporation 244
The Long Island Railroad Co., Inc. 244
Loral Corporation 244
Lynch Corporation 119
MacAndrews & Forbes Holdings Inc. 244
Marsh & McLennan Companies, Inc. 245
Marvel Entertainment Group, Inc. 245
Mayfair Supermarkets Inc. 227
McCrory Corporation 245
McGraw-Hill, Inc. 245
McKinsey & Company, Inc. 245
Mecklermedia Corporation 119
Melville Corporation 245
Merck & Co., Inc. 227
Merrill Lynch & Co., Inc. 245
Metromedia Company 227
Metropolitan Life Insurance Company 246
Micro Warehouse, Inc. 119
The Money Store Inc. 227
Montefiore Medical Center 246

Morgan Stanley Group Inc. 246
Multicare Cos Inc. 227
The Mutual Life Insurance Company of New York 246
NAI Technologies, Inc. 246
Nathan's Famous, Inc. 246
Nationwide Cellular Service, Inc. 246
New York Life Insurance Company 246
New York Power Authority 247
The New York Times Company 247
The Newark Group, Inc. 227
Nextel Communications, Inc. 227
Nine West Group Inc. 119
Noise Cancellation Technologies, Inc. 120
Nu Horizons Electronic Corporation 247
NUI Corporation 227
NYNEX Corporation 247
Ogden Corporation 247
Olin Corporation 120
Omnicom Group Inc. 247
Oxford Health Plans, Inc. 120
Oxford Resources Corporation 248
Paine Webber Group Inc. 248
Pall Corporation 248
Parsons & Whittemore, Inc. 248
Pathmark Stores, Inc. 227
PAXAR Corporation 248
PepsiCo, Inc. 248
Perkin-Elmer Corporation 120
Petrie Retail, Inc. 228
Pfizer Inc. 248
Philip Morris Companies Inc. 248
Phillips-Van Heusen Corporation 249
Pitney Bowes Inc. 120
Pittston Services Group 120
Ply Gem Industries, Inc. 249

Polo/Ralph Lauren Corporation 249
The Port Authority of New York and New Jersey 249
Praxair, Inc. 120
Price Waterhouse LLP 249
Prime Hospitality Corporation 228
Professional Sports Care Management, Inc. 249
The Prudential Insurance Company of America 228
Public Service Enterprise Group Incorporated 228
Quantum Restaurant Group, Inc. 249
Rayonier, Inc. 120
The Reader's Digest Association, Inc. 249
Reliance Group Holdings, Inc. 249
Renco Group Inc. 250
RJR Nabisco, Inc. 250
Roberts Pharmaceutical Corporation 228
RVSI, Inc. 250
Saks Holdings, Inc. 250
Salant Corporation 250
Salomon Inc 250
Sbarro, Inc. 250
Schering-Plough Corporation 228
Schlumberger NV 250
Scholastic Corporation 250
Sealed Air Corporation 229
Shorewood Packaging Corporation 251
Skadden, Arps, Slate, Meagher & Flom 251
Smith Corona Corporation 121
Standard Microsystems Corporation 251
Standard Motor Products, Inc. 251
Starrett Housing Corporation 251
Synetic, Inc. 229
Teachers Insurance and Annuity Association - College Retirement Equities Fund 251
Texaco Inc. 251

INDEX OF COMPANIES BY METROPOLITAN AREA

Tiffany & Co. 252
Time Warner Inc. 252
Tishman Realty & Construction Co. Inc. 252
TLC Beatrice International Holdings, Inc. 252
Topps Company, Inc. 252
Tops Appliance City, Inc. 229
Tosco Corporation 121
Towers Perrin 252
Toys "R" Us, Inc. 229
TransTechnology Corporation 229
The Travelers Inc. 252
Trump Organization 252
U.S. HomeCare Corporation 253
U.S. Trust Corporation 253
UIS, Inc. 253
Ultramar Corporation 121
Union Camp Corporation 229
Union Carbide Corporation 121
United Retail Group, Inc. 229
United States Banknote Corporation 253
United States Surgical Corporation 121
United Waste Systems, Inc. 122
Unitel Video, Inc. 253
UST Inc. 122
Viacom Inc. 253
Vital Signs, Inc. 229
Wakefern Food Corporation 230
Warner Insurance Services, Inc. 230
Warner-Lambert Company 230
Warrantech Corporation 122
Wellman, Inc. 230
Westvaco Corporation 253
Witco Corporation 254
Woolworth Corporation 254
Xerox Corporation 122
Young & Rubicam Inc. 254
Ziff-Davis Publishing Company 254

Niagara Falls, NY
Sevenson Environmental Services Inc. 251

Norfolk, VA
International Family Entertainment, Inc. 324
Navy Exchange System 325
Norfolk Southern Corporation 325
Smithfield Companies, Inc. 326
Smithfield Foods, Inc. 326
TFC Enterprises Inc. 326

Ocala, FL
Flair Corporation 129

Oklahoma City, OK
BancFirst Corporation 273
CMI Corporation 273
Devon Energy Corporation 273
Eateries Inc. 273
Fleming Companies, Inc. 273
Harold's Stores, Inc. 273
Homeland Holding Corporation 273
Kerr-McGee Corporation 273
Louis Dreyfus Natural Gas Corporation 274
Sonic Corp. 274

Omaha, NE
Acceptance Insurance Companies Inc. 216
American Business Information, Inc. 216
BeefAmerica, Inc. 216
Berkshire Hathaway Inc. 216
ConAgra, Inc. 216
Data Transmission Network Corporation 216
First Data Corporation 216
InaCom, Inc. 216
MFS Communications Company, Inc. 217
Pamida Inc. 217
Peter Kiewit Sons', Inc. 217
Werner Enterprises, Inc. 217

Orlando, FL
American Automobile Association 127
Holiday RV Superstores, Inc. 130
RoTech Medical Corporation 133

Parkersburg, WV
United Bankshares, Inc. 331

Peoria, IL
Caterpillar Inc. 147

Philadelphia, PA
ADVANTA Corporation 278
Airgas, Inc. 278
Alco Standard Corporation 278
America Service Group, Inc. 123
American Water Works Company, Inc. 222
AMETEK, Inc. 278
Apogee, Inc. 279
ARAMARK Corporation 279
ARCO Chemical Company 279
Asplundh Tree Expert Co. 279
Autotote Corporation 123
Bell Atlantic Corporation 279
Beneficial Corporation 123
Betz Laboratories, Inc. 280
Burlington Coat Factory Warehouse Corporation 223
Cabot Medical Corporation 280
Campbell Soup Company 223
Castle Energy Corporation 280
Cedar Group, Inc. 280
Central Sprinkler Corporation 281
Charming Shoppes, Inc. 281
Checkpoint Systems, Inc. 223
CIGNA Corporation 281
CMAC Investment Corporation 281

INDEX OF COMPANIES BY METROPOLITAN AREA

The Columbia Gas System, Inc. 123
Comcast Corporation 281
Commerce Bancorp, Inc. 224
Conrail, Inc. 281
CoreStates Financial Corporation 281
Crown Cork & Seal Company, Inc. 282
CSS Industries, Inc. 282
Day & Zimmermann Incorporated 282
Deb Shops, Inc. 282
Delmarva Power & Light Company 123
E.I. du Pont de Nemours and Company 123
The E.W. Scripps Company 123
Foamex International Inc. 282
Franciscan Health System 282
GBC Technologies, Inc. 225
Genesis Health Ventures, Inc. 283
Geriatric & Medical Companies, Inc. 283
Healthcare Services Group, Inc. 283
Hercules Incorporated 123
Hunt Manufacturing Co. 283
i-STAT Corporation 226
Inductotherm Industries 226
Integrated Circuit Systems, Inc. 284
Intelligent Electronics, Inc. 284
J & J Snack Foods Corp. 226
Jones Apparel Group, Inc. 284
Kulicke and Soffa Industries, Inc. 284
Lukens Inc. 284
Marlton Technologies, Inc. 284
MBNA 123
Metrologic Instruments, Inc. 227
NovaCare, Inc. 285
Owosso Corporation 285
Peco Energy Co. 285

Penn Mutual Life Insurance Co. 286
The Pep Boys - Manny, Moe & Jack 286
Princeton University 228
Quad Systems Corporation 286
Renal Treatment Centers Inc. 286
RF Power Products, Inc. 228
Right Management Consultants, Inc. 286
Rohm and Haas Company 287
Rollins Leasing Corporation 123
Safeguard Scientifics, Inc. 287
The Score Board, Inc. 228
Scott Paper Company 287
Selas Corporation of America 287
Softmart, Inc. 287
Strawbridge & Clothier 287
Sun Company, Inc. 288
Teleflex Inc. 288
Toll Brothers, Inc. 288
Tyco Toys, Inc. 229
U.S. Healthcare, Inc. 288
UGI Corporation 288
UJB Financial Corporation 229
Unisys Corporation 288
Universal Health Services, Inc. 288
Urban Outfitters Inc. 288
Vishay Intertechnology, Inc. 289
W. L. Gore & Associates Inc. 124
Wawa Inc. 289
WSFS Financial Corporation 124

Phoenix, AZ
ABCO Markets Inc. 76
ADFlex Solutions, Inc. 76
America West Airlines, Inc. 76
Apollo Group, Inc. 76
Arizona Instrument Corporation 76
Aztar Corporation 76
Bashas' Inc. 76
Carlisle Plastics, Inc. 76
Cerprobe Corporation 76

The Circle K Corporation 77
Del Webb Corporation 77
The Dial Corp. 77
Doubletree Corporation 77
Envirotest Systems Corporation 77
Inter-Tel, Inc. 77
Main St. & Main, Inc. 77
Megafoods Stores, Inc. 77
MicroAge Computer Centers, Inc. 77
Microchip Technology, Incorporated 78
PETsMART, Inc. 78
Pharmaceutical Marketing Services Inc. 78
Phelps Dodge Corporation 78
Pinnacle West Capital Corporation 78
Rural/Metro Corporation 78
Salt River Project Agricultural Improvement & Power District 78
Shamrock Foods Company Inc. 78
Syntellect Inc. 78
Three-Five Systems, Inc. 78

Pittsburgh, PA
84 Lumber Company 278
Allegheny Health, Education and Research Foundation 278
Aluminum Company of America 278
American Eagle Outfitters, Inc. 278
Amsco International, Inc. 279
Black Box Corporation 280
Cable Design Technologies Corporation 280
CONSOL Energy Inc. 281
Consolidated Natural Gas Company 281
General Nutrition Companies, Inc. 283
Giant Eagle Inc. 283
H. J. Heinz Company 283
Integra Financial Corporation 284

408 HOOVER'S MASTERLIST OF AMERICA'S TOP 2,500 EMPLOYERS

INDEX OF COMPANIES BY METROPOLITAN AREA

Kennametal Inc. 284
Mastech Systems Corporation 285
Mellon Bank Corporation 285
Michael Baker Corporation 285
Mylan Laboratories Inc. 285
PNC Bank Corporation 286
PPG Industries, Inc. 286
Respironics, Inc. 286
Tuscarora Plastics, Inc. 288
USX Corporation - Delhi Group 289
USX Corporation - Marathon Group 289
USX Corporation - U.S. Steel Group 289
Westinghouse Electric Corporation 289

Pittsfield, MA
Designs, Inc. 181
Raytheon Company 185

Portland, ME
Hannaford Bros. Co. Inc. 172
IDEXX Laboratories, Inc. 172
L.L. Bean, Inc. 172
UNUM Corporation 172

Portland, OR
CFI ProServices, Inc. 275
Columbia Sportswear 275
Electro Scientific Industries, Inc. 275
Fred Meyer, Inc. 275
The Greenbrier Companies, Inc. 275
Longview Fibre Company 328
Louisiana-Pacific Corporation 275
NIKE, Inc. 275
Oregon Steel Mills, Inc. 275
PacifiCorp 275
Planar Systems Inc. 275
Pope & Talbot, Inc. 276
Portland General Corporation 276
Precision Castparts Corporation 276
R. B. Pamplin Corporation 276

RadiSys Corporation 276
Red Lion Inns Limited Partnership 329
Rentrak Corporation 276
Schnitzer Steel Industries, Inc. 276
Sequent Computer Systems, Inc. 276
Standard Insurance Co. 276
Thrifty PayLess Inc. 277
TRM Copy Centers Corporation 277
U. S. Bancorp 277
Willamette Industries, Inc. 277
WTD Industries, Inc. 277

Poughkeepsie, NY
Command Security Corporation 237

Providence, RI
AFC Cable Systems, Inc. 290
American Power Conversion Corporation 290
Amtrol Inc. 290
Brown & Sharpe Manufacturing Company 290
Bugaboo Creek Steak House, Inc. 290
Fleet Financial Group, Inc. 290
GTECH Holdings Corporation 290
Hasbro, Inc. 290
Outlet Communications, Inc. 290
Textron Inc. 290

Quincy, IL
Moorman Manufacturing Company 153
Titan Wheel International, Inc. 157

Raleigh-Durham, NC
Coastal Healthcare Group, Inc. 255
First Citizens BancShares, Inc. 256
GoodMark Foods, Inc. 256
Investor's Management Corporation 257
Texfi Industries, Inc. 258

Rapid City, SD
Sodak Gaming, Inc. 293

Reading, PA
Carpenter Technology Corporation 280
Exide Corporation 282
Meridian Bancorp, Inc. 285
National Penn Bancshares, Inc. 285
Sovereign Bancorp, Inc. 287
V. F. Corporation 289

Redding, CA
Sierra Pacific Industries 104

Reno, NV
AMERCO 218
Boomtown, Inc. 218
Freeport-McMoRan Copper & Gold Inc. 218
Harveys Casino Resorts 218
International Game Technology 218
Swift Transportation Co., Inc. 219

Richmond, VA
Best Products Co. Inc. 322
Cadmus Communications Corporation 322
Carpenter Co. 322
Chesapeake Corporation 322
Circuit City Stores, Inc. 322
Crestar Financial Corporation 323
CSX Corporation 323
Dominion Resources, Inc. 323
Heilig-Meyers Co. 323
James River Corporation of Virginia 324
Lawyers Title Insurance Corporation 324
Media General, Inc. 324
Reynolds Metals Company 325
S&K Famous Brands, Inc. 326
Signet Banking Corporation 326
Universal Corporation 326
The Whitlock Group 326

INDEX OF COMPANIES BY METROPOLITAN AREA

Roanoke, VA
Bassett Furniture Industries, Inc. 322
Littlefield, Adams & Co. 324
Rowe Furniture Corporation 325
Stanley Furniture Company Inc. 326
Tultex Corporation 326

Rochester, MN
Fastenal Company 200
Hormel Foods Corporation 201
Kahler Realty Corporation 202
Mayo Foundation 202

Rochester, NY
ACC Corp. 232
Bausch & Lomb Incorporated 235
Canandaigua Wine Company, Inc. 236
Eastman Kodak Company 239
Monro Muffler Brake, Inc. 246
Paychex, Inc. 248
PSC Inc. 249
Student Loan Corporation 251
Transmation, Inc. 252
University of Rochester 253
Wegmans Food Markets Inc. 253

Rockford, IL
Elco Industries, Inc. 149
Newell Co. 154
Northwestern Steel & Wire Company 154
Truck Components Inc. 157

Sacramento, CA
Adventist Health System/ West 82
Falcon Systems Inc. 90
Foundation Health Corporation 91
McClatchy Newspapers, Inc. 97
MTS Inc. 98
Physicians Clinical Laboratory, Inc. 101
Raley's Inc. 102

Saginaw, MI
Chemical Financial Corporation 189
The Dow Chemical Company 190
Dow Corning Corporation 190
Wolohan Lumber Co. 196

Salt Lake City, UT
American Stores Company 319
First Security Corporation 319
Flying J Inc. 319
Franklin Quest Co. 319
Geneva Steel 319
Huntsman Chemical Corporation 319
Intermountain Health Care, Inc. 319
JB's Restaurants, Inc. 319
Merit Medical Systems, Inc. 319
Nature's Sunshine Products, Inc. 319
Novell, Inc. 320
Questar Corporation 320
Sinclair Oil Corporation 320
SkyWest Airlines, Inc. 320
Smith's Food & Drug Centers, Inc. 320
Thiokol Corporation 320

San Angelo, TX
Tucker Drilling Company, Inc. 317

San Antonio, TX
Alamo Group, Inc. 299
Associated Milk Producers, Inc. 300
Clear Channel Communications, Inc. 302
Diamond Shamrock, Inc. 303
H. E. Butt Grocery Company 306
Harte-Hanks Communications, Inc. 306
La Quinta Inns, Inc. 309
Luby's Cafeterias, Inc. 310
Norwood Promotional Products Inc. 311
RailTex, Inc. 313
SBC Communications, Inc. 313

U.S. Long Distance Corporation 317
USAA 318
H. B. Zachry Company 318

San Diego, CA
Advanced Marketing Services, Inc. 81
Advanced Medical, Inc. 82
Advanced Tissue Sciences, Inc. 82
Agouron Pharmaceuticals, Inc. 82
Callaway Golf Company 85
Chart House Enterprises, Inc. 86
Foodmaker, Inc. 91
GTI Corporation 93
Hometown Buffet Inc. 94
Mail Boxes Etc. 97
National Health Laboratories, Inc. 98
PMR Corporation 101
Proxima Corporation 102
PSICOR, Inc. 102
Pyxis Corporation 102
QUALCOMM Incorporated 102
San Diego Gas & Electric Company 104
Schwegmann Giant Super Markets 171
Science Applications International Corporation 104
Stac Electronics 106

San Francisco, CA
3Com Corporation 81
The 3DO Company 81
Abaxis, Inc. 81
ABM Industries Incorporated 81
Accolade Inc. 81
Adaptec, Inc. 81
Adobe Systems Incorporated 81
Advanced Micro Devices, Inc. 82
Advanced Polymer Systems, Inc. 82
AirTouch Communications 82
Altera Corporation 82
ALZA Corporation 82
American President Companies, Ltd. 83

410 HOOVER'S MASTERLIST OF AMERICA'S TOP 2,500 EMPLOYERS

INDEX OF COMPANIES BY METROPOLITAN AREA

American Protective Services, Inc. 83
Apple Computer, Inc. 83
Applied Materials, Inc. 83
Aspect Telecommunications Corporation 83
Atmel Corporation 84
Autodesk, Inc. 84
BankAmerica Corporation 84
Bay Networks Inc. 84
Bechtel Group, Inc. 84
Bell Microproducts Inc. 85
Boole & Babbage, Inc. 85
California Microwave, Inc. 85
Catholic Healthcare West Inc. 85
Celtrix Pharmaceuticals, Inc. 85
Central Garden & Pet Co. 86
The Charles Schwab Corporation 86
Chevron Corporation 86
Children's Discovery Centers of America, Inc. 86
Chiron Corporation 86
The Chronicle Publishing Company, Inc. 86
Cirrus Logic, Inc. 87
Cisco Systems, Inc. 87
The Clorox Company 87
Compression Labs, Incorporated 87
Conner Peripherals, Inc. 87
Consolidated Freightways, Inc. 88
Cooper Development Company 88
Cornerstone Imaging Inc. 88
Crowley Maritime Corporation 88
Del Monte Foods Company 89
Delrina Corporation 89
DHL Worldwide Express 89
Diamond Multimedia Systems, Inc. 89
Dionex Corporation 89
Dreyer's Grand Ice Cream, Inc. 89

Electronic Arts Inc. 89
Electronics for Imaging, Inc. 90
EPIC Design Technology, Inc. 90
Esprit de Corp. 90
Fair, Isaac and Company, Incorporated 90
Fibreboard Corporation 90
Franklin Resources, Inc. 91
Fresenius USA Inc. 92
Fresh Choice, Inc. 92
Fritz Companies, Inc. 92
The Gap, Inc. 92
Genentech, Inc. 92
GF Industries Inc. 92
Gilead Sciences, Inc. 92
Golden West Financial Corporation 92
The Good Guys, Inc. 92
Granite Construction Inc. 93
Grubb & Ellis Co. 93
Gupta Corporation 93
The Gymboree Corporation 93
Hamilton Financial Services Corporation 93
Harper Group, Inc. 94
Hewlett-Packard Company 94
ILC Technology, Inc. 94
Informix Corporation 95
Integrated Device Technology, Inc. 95
Intel Corporation 95
Kaiser Foundation Health Plan, Inc. 95
Kendall-Jackson Winery Ltd. 96
Komag, Incorporated 96
Lam Research Corporation 96
Levi Strauss Associates Inc. 96
Longs Drug Stores Corporation 96
LR Holdings, Inc. 96
Maxim Integrated Products, Inc. 97
Maxtor Corporation 97
McKesson Corporation 97
Media Arts Group, Inc. 97
Media Vision Technology Inc. 97

Mercury Interactive Corporation 97
Micronics Computers, Inc. 98
National Semiconductor Corporation 98
Natural Wonders, Inc. 98
NetManage, Inc. 99
Network General Corporation 99
New United Motor Manufacturing, Inc. 99
NeXT Computer, Inc. 99
North American Mortgage Co. 99
Novellus Systems, Inc. 99
Octel Communications Corporation 99
Optical Coating Laboratory, Inc. 100
Oracle Systems Corporation 100
Orbit Semiconductor, Inc. 100
Pacific Gas and Electric Company 100
Pacific Telesis Group 100
ParcPlace Systems, Inc. 101
PeopleSoft, Inc. 101
Plantronics, Inc. 101
Potlatch Corporation 102
Quantum Corporation 102
Radius, Inc. 102
Rational Software Corporation 102
Raychem Corporation 103
Read-Rite Corporation 103
Redwood Empire Bancorp 103
Ross Stores, Inc. 103
Safeway Inc. 104
Seagate Technology, Inc. 104
Sierra Semiconductor Corporation 105
Silicon Graphics, Inc. 105
Silicon Valley Group, Inc. 105
SJW Corporation 105
Solectron Corporation 105
Somatix Therapy Corporation 105

INDEX OF COMPANIES BY METROPOLITAN AREA

Southern Pacific Rail Corporation 105
Stanford University Hospital 106
StrataCom Inc. 106
Sun Microsystems, Inc. 106
Supercom, Inc. 106
Supercuts, Inc. 107
Swinerton & Walberg Co. 107
Sybase, Inc. 107
Symantec Corporation 107
Synopsys, Inc. 107
Tandem Computers Incorporated 107
Transamerica Corporation 108
Union Bank 108
University of California 108
URS Corporation 109
Vacu Dry Co. 109
Valley Forge Corporation 109
Varian Associates, Inc. 109
Ventritex, Inc. 109
Vivra Inc. 109
Wells Fargo & Company 110
West Marine, Inc. 110
Wilbur-Ellis Company 110
Williams-Sonoma, Inc. 110
Xilinx, Inc. 110

San Jose, CA
Linear Technology 96

Santa Barbara, CA
Circon Corporation 87

Santa Fe, NM
Thermo Instrument Systems Inc. 231

Savannah, GA
Gulfstream Aerospace Corporation 139
Savannah Foods & Industries, Inc. 141

Scranton, PA
US Foodservice Inc. 289
Weis Markets, Inc. 289

Seattle, WA
Advanced Technology Laboratories, Inc. 327
Airborne Freight Corporation 327
Alaska Air Group, Inc. 327
Asymetrix Corp. 327
The Boeing Company 327
Cellular Technical Services Company, Inc. 327
Eagle Hardware & Garden, Inc. 327
Ernst Home Center, Inc. 327
Fluke Corporation 327
FourGen Software Inc. 327
Group Health Cooperative of Puget Sound 328
Heart Technology, Inc. 328
Hillhaven Corporation 328
Immunex Corporation 328
Interlinq Software Corporation 328
Lanoga Corporation 328
Microsoft Corporation 328
Nordstrom, Inc. 328
Omega Environmental, Inc. 329
PACCAR Inc. 329
Price/Costco, Inc. 329
Quality Food Centers, Inc. 329
SAFECO Corporation 329
Services Group of America Inc. 329
Simpson Investment Co. 329
Starbucks Corporation 329
Univar Corporation 330
UTILX Corporation 330
Walker Richer & Quinn Inc. 330
Wall Data, Inc. 330
Washington Mutual, Inc. 330
Weyerhaeuser Company 330

Sioux City, IA
IBP, Inc. 216

Sioux Falls, SD
Gateway 2000 Inc. 293
Raven Industries, Inc. 293

South Bend, IN
Clark Equipment Company 160
Coachmen Industries, Inc. 160
CTS Corporation 160
Excel Industries, Inc. 161
Holy Cross Health System 161
Liberty Homes, Inc. 162
National Steel Corporation 162
Patrick Industries, Inc. 163
Schult Homes Corporation 163
Skyline Corporation 163

Spokane, WA
Key Tronic Corporation 328
Sterling Financial Corporation 329

Springfield, MA
Big Y Foods Inc. 179
Northeast Utilities 184

Springfield, MO
Jack Henry & Associates, Inc. 211
John Q. Hammons Hotels, Inc. 211
Mid-America Dairymen, Inc. 212
O'Reilly Automotive, Inc. 212

St. Louis, MO
A.G. Edwards, Inc. 208
Angelica Corporation 208
Anheuser-Busch Companies, Inc. 208
Argosy Gaming Company 146
Belden Inc. 208
Boatmen's Bancshares, Inc. 208
Brown Group, Inc. 208
CITATION Computer Systems, Inc. 209
Clark USA, Inc. 209
CPI Corporation 209
DIMAC Corporation 209
Edison Brothers Stores, Inc. 209

INDEX OF COMPANIES BY METROPOLITAN AREA

Edward D. Jones & Co. 209
Emerson Electric Co. 209
Enterprise Rent-A-Car Co. 210
Express Scripts, Inc. 210
Falcon Products, Inc. 210
General American Life Insurance Company 210
Graybar Electric Company, Inc. 210
Insituform Mid-America, Inc. 210
INTERCO Incorporated 211
Jefferson Smurfit Corporation 211
Kellwood Company 211
Mallinckrodt Group Inc. 211
Maritz Inc. 212
Maverick Tube Corporation 212
The May Department Stores Company 212
McDonnell Douglas Corporation 212
Medicine Shoppe International, Inc. 212
Mercantile Bancorporation Inc. 212
Monsanto Company 212
Pulitzer Publishing Company 213
Ralcorp Holdings, Inc. 213
Ralston Purina Group 213
RehabCare Corporation 213
Reliv International Inc. 213
Roosevelt Financial Group, Inc. 213
Schnuck Markets Inc. 213
Sigma-Aldrich Corporation 213
Spartech Corporation 214
SSM Health Care System Inc. 214
Thermadyne Holdings Corporation 214
Trans World Airlines, Inc. 214
Union Electric Company 214
Venture Stores, Inc. 214
Zeigler Coal Holding Company 159

State College, PA
C-COR Electronics, Inc. 280

Syracuse, NY
Carlisle Companies Inc. 236
Fay's, Incorporated 240
Goulds Pumps, Inc. 241
Marietta Corporation 245
Niagara Mohawk Power Corporation 247
ONBANCorp, Inc. 247
The Penn Traffic Company 248

Tampa-St. Petersburg, FL
ABR Information Services, Inc. 127
C. H. Heist Corporation 128
Catalina Marketing Corporation 128
Checkers Drive-In Restaurants, Inc. 128
Eckerd Corporation 129
Florida Progress Corporation 129
Home Shopping Network, Inc. 130
Lincare Holdings, Inc. 131
Lykes Bros. Inc. 131
Medical Technology Systems, Inc. 131
Outback Steakhouse, Inc. 131
Pages, Inc. 132
Quality Products, Inc. 132
Raymond James Financial, Inc. 132
Reptron Electronics, Inc. 132
Sports & Recreation, Inc. 133
Tech Data Corporation 134
Teco Energy Corporation 134
Walter Industries, Inc. 135

Toledo, OH
Dana Corporation 262
Health Care and Retirement Corporation 264
Libbey Inc. 266
Owens-Corning Fiberglas Corporation 268

Owens-Illinois, Inc. 268
Seaway Food Town, Inc. 270
TRINOVA Corporation 271

Tucson, AZ
Artisoft, Inc. 76
Magma Copper Co. 77

Tulsa, OK
Hale Halsell Co. 273
Helmerich & Payne, Inc. 273
Lowrance Electronics, Inc. 274
MAPCO Petroleum Inc. 274
Parker Drilling Co. 274
Phillips Petroleum Company 274
QuikTrip Corporation 274
Silverado Foods, Inc. 274
United Video Satellite Group Inc. 274
The Williams Companies, Inc. 274

Tyler, TX
Brookshire Brothers Incorporated 300
Brookshire Grocery Company 300
Celebrity, Inc. 301
Temple-Inland Inc. 316

Utica, NY
Oneida Ltd. 247

Waco, TX
The Dwyer Group, Inc. 304

Washington, DC
America Online, Inc. 322
American Management Systems, Incorporated 322
American Red Cross 125
Atlantic Coast Airlines Inc. 322
CACI International Inc. 322
Caterair International Corp. 173
Clark Enterprises, Inc. 173
COMSAT Corporation 173
Cosmetic Center, Inc. 173
Crown Books Corporation 173
Danaher Corporation 125

INDEX OF COMPANIES BY METROPOLITAN AREA

Dart Group Corporation 173
DIGICON 173
DynCorp 323
Federal National Mortgage Association 125
First Virginia Banks, Inc. 323
Gannett Co., Inc. 323
GEICO Corporation 125
General Dynamics Corporation 323
GENICOM Corporation 323
The George Washington University 125
Giant Food Inc. 174
Hanger Orthopedic Group, Inc. 174
Harman International Industries, Inc. 125
Hechinger Company 174
Host Marriott Corporation 174
ICF Kaiser International, Inc. 323
Irvin Feld & Kenneth Feld Productions, Inc. 324
LEGENT Corporation 324
Lockheed Martin Corporation 174
Manor Care, Inc. 174
Marriott International, Inc. 175
Mars, Inc. 324
MCI Communications Corporation 125
MICROS Systems, Inc. 175
Mid Atlantic Medical Services Inc. 175
Mobil Corporation 325
National Association of Securities Dealers, Inc. 125
National Railroad Passenger Corporation 125
Network Imaging Corporation 325
Orbital Sciences Corporation 325
PHP Healthcare 325
Potomac Electric Power Company 125
Primark Corporation 325
Shoppers Food Warehouse Corp. 176

Smithsonian Institution 126
Student Loan Marketing Association 126
United States Postal Service 126
The University of Maryland System 176
USAir Group, Inc. 326
Washington Gas Light Co. 126
Washington Homes, Inc. 176
The Washington Post Company 126
Woodward & Lothrop, Incorporated 126
The Wyatt Company 126

Waterbury, CT
Colonial Data Technologies Corporation 116
Uniroyal Chemical Company, Inc. 121
Webster Financial Corporation 122

Wausau, WI
Consolidated Papers, Inc. 332
Northland Cranberries, Inc. 335
Sentry Insurance, A Mutual Company 336
Wausau Paper Mills Co. 337

West Palm Beach, FL
American Media, Inc. 127
BE Aerospace, Inc. 127
Boca Research Inc. 128
Diversified Communications Industries, Ltd. 129
FPL Group, Inc. 129
Integracare Inc. 130
Levitz Furniture Inc. 131
Office Depot, Inc. 131
Oxbow Corporation 131
Quick & Reilly Group, Inc. 132
Rexall Sundown, Inc. 132
Safeskin Corporation 133
Sensormatic Electronics Corporation 133
Todhunter International, Inc. 134
TPI Enterprises, Inc. 134
W. R. Grace & Co. 134

Wheeling, WV
Weirton Steel Corporation 331
WesBanco, Inc. 331

Wichita, KS
The Coleman Company, Inc. 166
Fourth Financial Corporation 166
Koch Industries, Inc. 166
Lone Star Steakhouse & Saloon, Inc. 166

Williamsport, PA
American Recreation Company Holdings, Inc. 233

Wilmington, NC
Welcome Home, Inc. 258

Worcester, MA
Allmerica Financial 177
Allmerica Property & Casualty Companies, Inc. 177
Alpha-Beta Technology, Inc. 177
Paul Revere Corporation 185

York, PA
Bon-Ton Stores, Inc. 280
Dentsply International Inc. 282
York International Corporation 289

Youngstown, OH
Commercial Intertech Corporation 262
DeBartolo Realty Corporation 262
Edward J. DeBartolo Corporation 263
Phar-Mor Inc. 268

Nonmetro Area
Adelphia Communications Corporation 278
American Freightways Corporation 79
Ameristar Casinos Inc. 218
Arctco, Inc. 197
BB&T Financial Corporation 255
Ben & Jerry's Homemade, Inc. 321
Blair Corporation 280
The Buckle, Inc. 216

414   HOOVER'S MASTERLIST OF AMERICA'S TOP 2,500 EMPLOYERS

INDEX OF COMPANIES BY METROPOLITAN AREA

C&S Wholesale Grocers Inc. 321
Dakotah, Inc. 293
Dollar General Corporation 168
Frontier Insurance Group, Inc. 240
Fund American Enterprises Holdings, Inc. 321
Great Lakes Aviation Ltd. 164
Hancock Fabrics, Inc. 206
Horizon Bancorp Inc. 331
JLG Industries, Inc. 284
Kimball International, Inc. 162
K-Va-T Food Stores, Inc. 324
Kysor Industrial Corporation 192
Magna Bancorp, Inc. 206
Mesa Air Group 231
O'Sullivan Corporation 325
PC Connection 220
Perdue Farms Incorporated 175
Sanderson Farms, Inc. 207
Schwan's Sales Enterprises, Inc. 204
Semitool, Inc. 215
SERVISTAR Corp. 287
Softdesk, Inc. 220
Taylor Corporation 205
Trans Financial Bancorp, Inc. 169
Winnebago Industries, Inc. 165

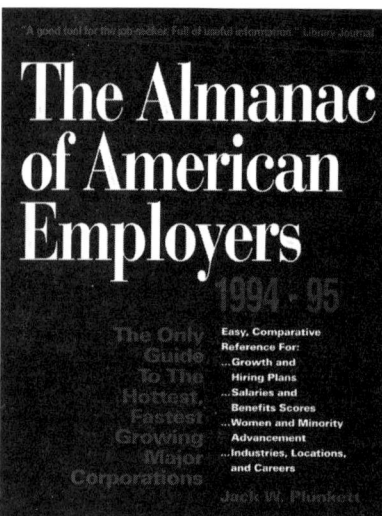

FIND OUT WHO'S HIRING NOW AND WHAT THEY'RE PLANNING FOR THE FUTURE.

"A good tool for the job seeker. Full of useful information."
— *Library Journal*

Whether you're looking for your first job or switching careers, *The Almanac of American Employers 1994–95* will give you valuable insight into the hottest US corporations with potential for future growth.

This information-packed guide is much more than an employer phone book. You'll find the kind of company information you need to get ahead in the competitive job market. Each company listing includes:

✔ Complete company name, headquarters address, phone and fax numbers, and key contacts, including top officers, human resources directors, and college recruiters

✔ A salaries/benefits rating

✔ Business descriptions

✔ Sales, profits, and estimated growth rates

✔ Benefits offered

✔ Office locations by region

✔ Key brands and divisions

✔ Recommendations for type of employment

✔ Growth plans/special features

✔ An overview of the corporate culture

Order your copy for only $109.95 and start planning your future today!

TO ORDER OR FOR A FREE CATALOG, CALL 800-486-8666
TO SEE OUR CATALOG ON THE INTERNET, GO TO
http:// www.hoovers.com or gopher:// gopher.hoovers.com

 The Reference Press, Inc., 6448 Highway 290 E., Suite E–104, Austin, Texas 78723
512-454-7778 • Fax 512-454-9401

The Resource For Career Practitioners

CAREER SAVVY

THE CAREER RESOURCES & MEDIA UP-DATE NEWSLETTER

NUMEROUS BENEFITS!

- Keep pace with new releases of books, catalogs, software, diskettes, CDs, Videos, etc.
- Learn income generating and cost savings ideas.
- Gain endless ways to: Attract clients, gain visibility, supplement your program, shorten client time, improve program quality, etc.
- Save reading and research hours while maintaining your professionalism at state-of-the-art level.

SUBSCRIBE TODAY!

Subscription Price: 12 monthly issues for just $24

Comprised of two 11 x 17 pages per month.

DEVELOPING EXECUTIVES, INC.
32780 Grand River Avenue
Farmington, MI 48336-3263
✆ 810 . 615 . 1811

New Books from JIST Works, Inc.
Specializing in Job Search Books for the '90s

America's 50 Fastest Growing Jobs, 3rd Edition
The Authoritative Information Source
By JIST Editorial Staff

This revision of a best-selling career book contains detailed job descriptions for the 50 fastest-growing occupations, and is based on the latest information from the U.S. Department of Labor. Also includes information about related occupations, a job search section, and growth projections by industry and for the self-employed.

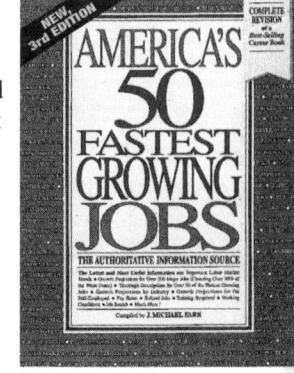

> ISBN 1-56370-199-5
> 8.5 x 11, Paper, 288 pp.
> Order Code T1-J1995   **$14.95**

Using the Internet in Your Job Search
By Fred E. Jandt and Mary B. Nemnich

This is the definitive, "hands-on" guide for job seekers with access to the Internet. This informative book explains how to:

- Connect to the Internet
- Find job listings and research potential employers on the Internet
- Use news groups to get leads
- Create electronic resumes and capture attention in the first screen
- and more!

> ISBN 1-56370-173-1
> 7.5 x 9.25, Paper, 240 pp.
> Order Code T1-J1731   **$16.95**

Using WordPerfect in Your Job Search
By David F. Noble

This unique computer book shows readers how to use the power of WordPerfect to create best-quality resumes, cover letters, and other important job search documents. Provides detailed, step-by-step instructions on how to create various types of resumes. Covers different versions of WordPerfect from 5.0 for DOS to 6.1 for Windows.

> ISBN 1-56370-177-4
> 7.5 x 9.25, Paper, 480 pp.
> Order Code T1-J1774   **$19.95**

These and other JIST books are available at fine bookstores or call JIST at 1-800-648-5478.

Get the books that get the jobs...

THE WALL STREET JOURNAL.
NATIONAL BUSINESS EMPLOYMENT WEEKLY
INTERVIEWING
Effective Techniques to Help You Answer Tough Questions and Make a Great Impression
SPECIAL BONUS:
A free issue of the National Business Employment Weekly, plus a 4-week free trial offer of The Wall Street Journal... An $18.95 newsstand value!

THE WALL STREET JOURNAL.
NATIONAL BUSINESS EMPLOYMENT WEEKLY
RESUMES
Real Sample Resumes and Proven Advice From Successful Job Hunters and Career Counselors
SPECIAL BONUS:
A free issue of the National Business Employment Weekly, plus a 4-week free trial offer of The Wall Street Journal... An $18.95 newsstand value!

THE WALL STREET JOURNAL.
NATIONAL BUSINESS EMPLOYMENT WEEKLY
NETWORKING
Insiders' Strategies for Tapping the Hidden Market Where Most Jobs Are Found
SPECIAL BONUS:
A free issue of the National Business Employment Weekly, plus a 4-week free trial offer of The Wall Street Journal... An $18.95 newsstand value!

THE WALL STREET JOURNAL.
NATIONAL BUSINESS EMPLOYMENT WEEKLY
Over 50,000 copies sold
JOBS RATED ALMANAC
Ranks 250 jobs by more than a dozen vital factors, including salary, stress, benefits and more
THIRD EDITION
LES KRANTZ

THE WALL STREET JOURNAL.
NATIONAL BUSINESS EMPLOYMENT WEEKLY
COVER LETTERS
Real sample cover letters that will help you get the job you want!
SPECIAL BONUS:
A free issue of the National Business Employment Weekly, plus a 4-week free trial offer of The Wall Street Journal... An $18.95 newsstand value!

From America's Career Authority

Available at your local bookstore

WILEY
Publishers Since 1807

HISPANIC
M A G A Z I N E

IN EVERY ISSUE:
- Business
- Career
- Cars
- Computers
- Travel
- Money
- Agenda
- Health
- La Buena Vida
- Music & Book Reviews
- Hispanic Calendar

SPECIAL FEATURES INCLUDE:
- Hispanic on Campus
- Top 100 Companies for Hispanics
- Hispanic Heritage Month
- Scholarships for Hispanics
- Accomplishments of Latinas
- Hispanic Entrepreneurs

HISPANIC is a monthly magazine for and about Hispanics, written in English. Each issue of Hispanic features upbeat, informative articles about Hispanics from Los Angeles to New York, from San Antonio to Miami.

Celebrate the rich and diverse Hispanic culture and keep up with notable Hispanics who are achievers in business, politics, arts, sports, entertainment, and other areas.

HISPANIC is a must for home or office, for schools, colleges, libraries, and community centers. To order your subscription, call toll free at 1-800-251-2688 or complete this form and return to: HISPANIC, P.O. Box 396 Mount Morris, IL 61054-7547

HISPANIC
M A G A Z I N E

☐ **$18 FOR 12 MONTHS!**
☐ **$30 FOR 24 MONTHS!**

Name: _____

Address: _____

City: _____

State: _____ Zip _____

Telephone: _____

Form of Payment:
(please complete all necessary info)

☐ Check   ☐ Money Order   ☐ Visa/MC

Visa/MC#: _____

Exp. Date: _____

Signature: _____

(All orders must be signed. Please allow 4–6 weeks for delivery!)

ARPI95

Get Your Career on Track

High Technology Careers Magazine is the first place experienced engineering, computer, DP/MIS, and technical professionals look for the latest information on today's changing job market. Editorial content includes featured articles on topics such as future trends, emerging technologies, and career advancement. Each issue details hundreds of job opportunities for design, software, telecommunications and hardware engineers as well as for programmers, analysts, and marketing professionals. Published six times per year. - **Subscription $29/Int'l $39.**

Future Outlook '95, published by High Technology Careers Magazine, is an annual employment guide targeting the hottest high-tech regions in the country. This publication also features employment opportunities and exciting articles on future global trends. Employment guide listings include: Northern California's hottest 500 employers, Texas' hottest 500 employers, Rocky Mountain region's hottest 350 employers, and Arizona's hottest 200 employers. **Published annually $14.95.**

To order a subscription to High Technology Careers or a copy of Future Outlook '95, call (408) 970-8800.

High Technology Careers Magazine,
4701 Patrick Henry Dr. #1901, Santa Clara, CA 95054
408/970-8800 or FAX 408/980-5103

"Net Money *is a superb guide to online business and finance!*"
—Hoover's Handbook of American Business

Don't miss out on time-saving and money-making opportunities! *Net Money* is the first and only guide to the personal finance revolution on the Information Highway. Learn how to file your taxes online. How to buy and sell from your home PC—stocks, bonds, futures, mutuals. How to download the latest in free software—mortgage calculators, desktop organizers, checkbook managers, budget makers, quote trackers, stock watchers, and business planners. And how to get access to thousands of dollars of information for free. *Net Money*, by the authors of the bestselling *Net Guide*, will help you make your PC into a fully loaded personal finance tool. *Net Money* takes you step by step through getting hooked up, joining the right services, and finding what you're looking for: organizing tips, company reports, stock quotes, investor clubs, government info, tax help, job posts, and business boards.

Net Money's smart and comprehensive listings make finding online personal finance resources easy.

Is there really a "personal finance revolution" going on? The way we do our banking, pay our bills, get loans, buy a house, find a job, and invest our money is changing rapidly. The possibilities of the networked world, "the Information Highway," are altering the way we think about and deal with our financial lives as profoundly as the introduction of consumer banking, mass credit cards, and mutual funds. With the vast resources of the Net—all described in *Net Money*—the information, speed, and convenience previously available to only a few are now available to all of us. Yes, it's a revolution.

Discover the Internet. YPN—Your Personal Network, the Internet service from the creators of *Net Money*, will take you onto the Information Highway and to the motherlode of free information resources. No prudent financial planner or canny investor should be without access to this remarkable new information medium.

Call 1-800-NET-1133 and get 15 FREE hours of Internet access. Or email info@ypn.com

RANDOM HOUSE
ELECTRONIC PUBLISHING
A Michael Wolff Book

In bookstores everywhere.
Or call 1-800-NET-1333 to order *Net Money* and get 15 FREE hours of Internet access on YPN—Your Personal Network!

Access valuable information on 8,000 prospective employers with

 **HOOVER'S COMPANY PROFILES:** Browse through in-depth profiles of 1,200 of the largest, most influential, and fastest-growing public and private companies in the US and around the world. Includes valuable information on major US firms from **Abbott** to **Zenith**, global giants from **Bertelsmann** to **Yamaha**, and today's hot-growth enterprises from **Boston Beer** to **Xircom**. Profiles feature operations overviews, company strategies, histories, up to 10 years of key financial and stock data, lists of products and key competitors, top executives' names, headquarters addresses, and phone and fax numbers.

 **MASTERLIST CAPSULES:** Access valuable information for all of the largest public and private companies in the US, plus over 200 major global firms. Select from more than 7,700 company entries from **AAON** to **Zynaxis**. Entries include headquarters addresses, phone and fax numbers, key officers, industry designations, stock symbols, sales-growth and current-year sales figures, employment data, and fiscal year-end dates.

INDUSTRY PROFILES: From drugs to computer software, from fiber optics to aerospace, this database provides fascinating facts about 200 key US industries. Contains five-year industry projections, descriptions of domestic and international markets, information on environmental conditions affecting US industry, plus more than 450 tables covering industry size measured by sales, employment, production, market share, and international trade patterns.

 **BUSINESS REFERENCE PRODUCTS:** The Reference Press, Inc., of Austin, Texas, is a leading publisher and distributor of reasonably priced business information in both print and electronic media. See our catalog on America Online, eWorld, and on the Internet at: Hoover's Online (http://www.hoovers.com or gopher://gopher.hoovers.com), Pathfinder (http://pathfinder.com/twep/Warner_Books), and Online Bookstore (http//marketplace.com/obs/obshome.html).

AVAILABLE ON:

http://www.hoovers.com
gopher://gopher.hoovers.com
800-486-8666

AMERICA ONLINE
keyword: hoovers
800-827-6364
preferred customer
number 11596

CompuServe
go: hoovers
800-848-8199

shortcut: hoovers
800-775-4556

farcast
info@farcast.com

http://www.infoseek.com

http://pathfinder.com/
twep/Warner_Books

http://www.quote.com

FOR MORE INFORMATION CONTACT THE REFERENCE PRESS AT:
e-mail: refpress6@aol.com

HOOVER'S DIGITAL BUSINESS INFORMATION
FROM THE REFERENCE PRESS

HOOVER'S COMPANY AND INDUSTRY DATABASE ON CD-ROM WITH 3 QUARTERLY UPDATES • $399.95

Get over 1,500 in-depth company profiles and nearly 200 detailed industry profiles with the Hoover's CD. This intuitive, no-nonsense CD-ROM is loaded with valuable business information that will make your business research tasks quick and easy. Hoover's CD includes all company profiles in *Hoover's Handbook of World Business*, *Hoover's Handbook of American Business*, *Hoover's Handbook of Emerging Companies*, and *Hoover's Guide to Private Companies*, plus many company profiles not available in print format. In addition, it includes over 200 industry profiles from the *U.S. Industrial Outlook 1994*. Available with annual update for only $249.95. **Call 800-486-8666 for a free demo CD-ROM.**

HOOVER'S ELECTRONIC MASTERLIST OF MAJOR U.S. COMPANIES • $199.95 1/2 OFF!

Hoover's MasterList of Major U.S. Companies 1994–1995 is now available in an easy-to-use software program for Macintosh and PC Windows users. Developed in Claris's Filemaker Pro, the program combines a simple intuitive interface (no user manual required) with a powerful, yet flexible, search engine. This versatile tool contains information on over 8,000 companies and over 15,000 CEOs and CFOs. In addition to search, sort, and retrieval features, the software includes a built-in mailing label and letter capability. The license permits use of the data for creating letters and labels for personal use only (not for resale). A version of the product that includes quarterly updates (the original plus 3 updates) is available for only $299.95. A data-only version is available for DOS users in an ASCII-delimited format which requires users to import the data into their own database, contact management, or spreadsheet programs.

TEXAS AND BAY AREA REGIONAL BUSINESS LISTS ON DISK
$49.95 EACH

Both the top 500 companies in Texas and the top 500 companies in the San Francisco Bay Area are available in easy-to-use Macintosh or Windows software programs. In addition to search, sort, and retrieval features, the software includes a built-in mailing label capability. A separate file is included on each disk with the names and addresses of the area's largest public-sector employers, key employers headquartered outside the areas, top media companies, and the most influential accounting firms, banks, and law firms with offices in the areas.

HOOVER'S MULTIMEDIA BUSINESS 500
$49.95

This CD-ROM contains the entire contents of *Hoover's Handbook of American Business 1995*. Search by company, key word, region, or industry. Access competitive information by using the hot spot to jump to numerous competitors. See and hear 30 minutes of multimedia video clips from over 75 top corporations. Cut and paste information into your own word processing documents. Click on the Prodigy link to log in and get the latest news and stock quotes for the companies profiled. CD-ROM drive and Windows required for use.

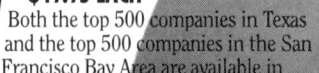

To place an order or for more information about our electronic products, contact Tom Linehan at 800-486-8666, fax 512-454-9401, or send e-mail to refpress6@aol.com

Get the Edge You Need for Your Next Interview Without Cutting Into Your Pocketbook

Hoover's Handbooks give you vital background information for 1,000 major companies

HOOVER'S HANDBOOK OF AMERICAN BUSINESS 1995

The more you know about your prospective employer's history and financial background, the more effective and impressive you will be in your interview. This information-packed book profiles 500 of the largest and most influential enterprises in America, which employ millions of people. It features company histories and strategies, up to 10 years of key financial and employment data, lists of products and key competitors, names of key officers, addresses, and phone and fax numbers.

[mu]st-have secret weapon for anyone looking to land a job at one of the [be]st firms in America.
[$3]5 hardcover; ISBN 1-878753-65-7; 1,275 pp.
[$6]5 CD-ROM (requires Windows)

Order ALL THREE for
only $99.95
A 15% Savings!

Company profiles also available in electronic format — call for details.

FOR A FREE CATALOG OR TO ORDER CALL 800-486-8666

TO SEE OUR CATALOG ON THE INTERNET, GO TO
http://www.hoovers.com or
gopher://gopher.hoovers.com

[HOO]VER'S HANDBOOK OF EMERGING [COM]PANIES 1995

[If you] want to know who's hiring right now, look [fur]ther. We've profiled 250 of the fastest-[grow]ing US companies, which are creating thou[sand]s of new jobs annually. Company [profil]es include overviews and strategies, up to [yea]rs of key financial and stock data, lists of [prod]ucts and key competitors, names of key [office]rs, addresses, and phone and fax numbers.
[Thes]e companies are the ones to watch!
[$2]5 hardcover; ISBN 1-878753-51-7; 406 pp.

HOOVER'S HANDBOOK OF WORLD BUSINESS 1995–1996

You may think **Columbia Pictures, Pillsbury,** and **Shell Oil** are US companies, but they aren't. If you're looking for a job, you need to be aware of these foreign giants and know where to locate them in the US and around the world. This invaluable resource profiles 227 non–US-based companies that employ thousands of Americans in the US and abroad. If you're interested in a career with an international firm, this book is for you.
[$3]5 hardcover; ISBN 1-878753-44-4; 608 pp.

The Reference Press, Inc.,
6448 Highway 290 E.,
Suite E–104
Austin, Texas 78723
512-454-7778
Fax 512-454-9401
refpress6@aol.com

THIS BOOK INCLUDES:
FREE WINDOWS SOFTWARE!

Every edition of *Hoover's MasterList of America's Top 2,500 Employers* includes FREE software loaded with FileMaker Pro an easy-to-use Windows program. This powerful program allows you to quickly :

✓ Search through 2,500 of America's key employers by state and industry

✓ Access the company capsules found in this book, which include headquarters, addresses, phone and fax numbers, names of top hiring executives, number of employees, **number of jobs added in the last year**, and industry descriptions

✓ Create mailing lists and cover letters

✓ Export data to other software programs

Buy your copy of *Hoover's MasterList of America's Top 2,500 Employers* and start using your FREE Windows software today Before you know it, you'll be contacting key hiring executives from such major US corporations as **AT&T**, **Wal-Mart**, **America Online**, and **Starbucks**.

INSTALLATION INSTRUCTIONS

1. Start Microsoft Windows
2. Insert Disk 1 in Drive A
3. From the Program Manager, select File Menu and choose RUN
4. Type "a:\setup" and press ENTER

Read the file "Readme.txt" for further information

Note: This program uses a runtime version of Claris Corp.'s Filmaker Pro database software. **If Filemaker Pro is already installed on your com you must follow the instructions in the file "readme.txt" in order for this program to run.**

Hoover's MasterList of America's Top 2,500 Employers
LICENSE AGREEMENT AND LIMITED WARRANTY

By using this software and the data contained in it (the "Software"), you are agreeing to be bound by the following agreement. This legal document is an agreement between you and The Reference Press, Inc. (RPI). RPI is willing to license the Software to you only on the condition that you accept all their terms contained in this license agreement. If you do not agree with these terms and conditions, RPI is unwilling to license the Software to you, and you should not use the Software. Promptly return the unused disks and all accompanying items to RPI for a full refund of any sums you have paid.

1. **GRANT OF LICENSE:** In consideration of your payment of the license fee and your agreement to abide by the terms and conditions of this Agreement, RPI grants to you a nonexclusive right to use and display the copy of the Software program on a single computer at a single location so long as you comply with the terms of this Agreement.

2. **OWNERSHIP OF SOFTWARE:** You own only the disks on which the Software is recorded. RPI and its licensors retain the right, title, and ownership to the Software recorded on the original disk and all subsequent copies of the Software, regardless of the form of media on which the original or other copies may exist. The license is not a sale of the original software or any copy to you.

3. **COPY RESTRICTIONS:** This Software and the accompanying printed materials are copyrighted by RPI and its licensors. You may not copy the Software, except when you make a single copy of the Software for backup or archival purposes only. You will be held legally responsible for any copying or copyright infringement which is caused or encouraged by your failure to abide by the terms of this restriction. Each usage of the Software by you or by parties obtaining the Software from you contrary to the terms of this license will subject you to a minimum fee of $500 per use to be paid by you to RPI plus statutory damages of up to $100,000 per use.

4. **USE RESTRICTIONS:** You may not network the Software or otherwise use it on more than one computer or computer terminal at the same time. You may physically transfer the Software from one computer to another, provided that the Software is used on only one at a time. You may not distribute or reprint copies of the Software, or any portion thereof, in electronic or print format to others. This Software may be used for your personal use only. You may not create lists or labels for resale or reprinting or use by third parties. You may not reverse, engineer, disassemble, decompile, modify, adapt, translate, or create derivative works based on the Software without the prior written consent of RPI.

5. **TERMINATION:** This license is effective until terminated. All provisions of Agreement as to warranties, limitation of liability, remedies or damages, and ership rights shall survive termination.

6. **LIMITED WARRANTY AND DISCLAIMER OF WARRANTY:** RPI warrants Software, when properly used in accordance with the documentation, will op substantial conformity with the description of Software set forth in the docu RPI does not warrant that the Software will meet your requirements or that tion of the Software will be uninterrupted or error-free. RPI DISCLAIMS AL WARRANTIES, EXPRESSED OR IMPLIED, INCLUDING WITHOUT LIMITAT IMPLIED WARRANTIES OR MERCHANTABILITY AND FITNESS FOR A PAR PURPOSE, EXCEPT FOR THE EXPRESS WARRANTY SET FORTH ABOVE. NOT WARRANT, GUARANTEE, OR MAKE ANY REPRESENTATION REGARD USE OF THE RESULTS OR THE USE OF THE SOFTWARE IN TERMS OF IT RECTNESS, ACCURACY, RELIABILITY, CURRENTNESS, OR OTHERWISE.

IN NO EVENT SHALL RPI OR ITS EMPLOYEES, AGENTS, SUPPLIERS, LIC OR CONTRACTORS BE LIABLE FOR ANY INCIDENTAL, INDIRECT, SPECIA CONSEQUENTIAL DAMAGES ARISING OUT OF OR IN CONNECTION WITH LICENSE GRANTED UNDER THIS AGREEMENT INCLUDING, WITHOUT L TION, LOSS OF USE, LOSS OF DATA, LOSS OF PROPERTY, OR CLAIMS OF PARTIES, EVEN IF RPI OR AN AUTHORIZED REPRESENTATIVE OF RPI HA ADVISED OF THE POSSIBILITY OF SUCH DAMAGES. IN NO EVENT SHAL ITY OF RPI FOR DAMAGES WITH RESPECT TO THE SOFTWARE EXCEED AMOUNTS ACTUALLY PAID BY YOU, IF ANY, FOR THE SOFTWARE.

7. **ACKNOWLEDGMENT:** You acknowledge that you have read this Agreemen stand it, and agree to be bound by its terms and conditions. You also agree t Agreement is the complete and exclusive statement of the agreement betwee RPI and supersedes all proposals or prior agreements, oral or written, and an communications between you and RPI or any representative of RPI relating ject matter of this Agreement.

8. **MISCELLANEOUS:** This Agreement shall be construed in accordance with the United States of America and the State of Texas.